Criminal Gods and Demon Devotees

Criminal Gods and Demon Devotees

Essays on the Guardians of Popular Hinduism

Alf Hiltebeitel, Editor

State University of New York Press

Published by
State University of New York Press, Albany

Printed in the United States of America

For information, address State University of New York
Press, State University Plaza, Albany, N.Y., 12246

Library of Congress Cataloging-in-Publication Data

Criminal gods and demon devotees: essays on the guardians of popular
Hinduism/edited by Alf Hiltebeitel.
p. cm.
Bibliography: p.
Includes index.
ISBN 0-88706-981-9. ISBN 0-88706-982-7 (pbk.)
1. Gods, Hindu. 2. Hindu cults. I. Hiltebeitel, Alf.
BL1216.2.C75 1989
294.5′216—dc19 88-24960
CIP

10 9 8 7 6 5 4 3 2 1

Contents

Plates

Note on Transliteration

The individual authors of this volume have generally determined the degree to which they adopted the precise scholarly conventions for the Indian languages they cited, or used Anglicized forms instead. The editor has, however, sought to bring about a basic consistency in Sanskrit and Tamil citations (for reasons of economy, the subscripted macron has been normally dropped from the Tamil consonants usually printed ḻ, ṟ, and ṉ). There has also been some regularization of Hindi, Marathi, and Telugu terms used in more than one article.

Preface

This collection of essays takes its inception from the editor's proposal to the Conference on Religion in South India (CRSI) in Spring 1984 that its next annual meeting be held on the theme that survives as the lead title of this book. The CRSI deserves the thanks of all involved for accepting and sponsoring the resultant program, and I would like to thank in particular Harry M. Buck and Paul B. Courtright, who in that year passed the CRSI chairmanship from the one to the other, for their help in encouraging and organizing the meeting. Held at the George Washington University from 7-9 August 1985, that productive conference featured the initial working drafts of the majority of these essays—those by Biardeau, Shulman, Narayana Rao, Erndl, Coccari, Stanley, Hiltebeitel, Hudson, and Waghorne—as well as memorable discussions catalyzed by the meeting's two designated discussants, Wendy Doniger O'Flaherty and Glenn Yocum. In addition, Sontheimer's essay comes to this book as the descendant of a paper he would have presented at that conference had he not been unable to attend it. And Masilamani-Meyer's essay arrives as a follow-up to inquiries about the conference.

Beyond the 1985 CRSI, the book has also had a chance to ripen and grow through two more conferences. At the November 1985 annual meeting of the American Academy of Religion at Anaheim, California, the panel organized by David Knipe on "Dialogues with the Disgruntled Dead" featured not only the first draft of his essay in this volume, but a chance for Coccari and Hiltebeitel to review their initial papers in relation to additional material. And the November 1986 Annual South Asia Conference at the University of Wisconsin, Madison, featured three panels on transgressive sacrality originally spearheaded by Sunthar Visuvalingam and chaired by Hiltebeitel, at which initial drafts of both Sunthar and Elizabeth-Chalier Visuvalingam's papers were read along with reworkings by Narayana Rao and Hiltebeitel of their initial papers, and commentary by Knipe and discussion with Coccari, Erndl, and Stanley. Finally, Lorenzen's essay comes as a spinoff of the Madison conference as a paper originally solicited for it by Sunthar Visuvalingam. Further unity to the book has thus been enhanced by the fact that all the essayists have taken stock of the discussion of transgressive sacrality, either at the Madison conference or through correspondence or conversations with the Visuvalingams, or with each other, with some having reflected on it in their papers.

Introduction

Alf Hiltebeitel

It is no doubt best to begin with some preliminary and minimal definitions. "Criminal gods"—if we can take the term *criminal* metaphorically, and extend it beyond societies with legal systems that give the term a technical application—are perhaps a worldwide phenomenon: gods who violate the sacred codes and boundaries by which other gods, and humans, would seek to live. What is specific to the "criminal gods" of Hinduism is the specifically Indian codes they violate—societal, sexual, theological, culinary, sacrificial—and the ways they violate them. "Demon Devotees," on the other hand, are perhaps uniquely Indian (though not necessarily uniquely Hindu), for their mythologies are shaped by a theology of *bhakti*, or devotion, in which the gods repeatedly convert their demon adversaries—sometimes by defeating them, but more often by killing them (implying the principle of reincarnation)—into their devotees. Because demons are also violators of sacred codes and boundaries, and because criminals can be regenerated too, there is bound to be overlap between these two types. The terms are not employed in this volume to fix these types, or even further to define them, but to draw our contributors into a common discussion of the problematics that surround such figures in the Hindu tradition. These problematics are best introduced by some discussion of the various papers.

Given the South Indian focus of the initial Conference on Religion in South India at which most of these papers were first read, and the resultantly large number focused on Tamilnadu, the essays are ordered to begin in Tamilnadu and return to it after a sort of counterclockwise tour of the subcontinent. This *apradakṣiṇa* or reverse ritual circumambulation is perhaps fittingly inauspicious for our "criminal" and "demonic" subjects, but its real purpose is to enable a certain order in the movement from paper to paper. It should also be noted that there is no pretension to covering the whole subcontinent by this progression. A selective bibliography can be consulted for further readings in some of the areas omitted, most notably Bengal, Central India, Karnataka, and Kerala.[1]

Madeleine Biardeau's "Brahmans and Meat-Eating Gods" opens the book for the same reason that it was the keynote paper at the 1985 CRSI conference. It is Biardeau whose work on the minor carnivorous gods who guard local goddesses, and whose myths frequently tell how they became those goddesses' devotees, has opened a number of major pathways into the interpretation of such figures. Her essay shares something of her own discovery of their significance. To Biardeau, they are not to be understood as isolated and outwardly deformed expressions of a popular, folk, or Dravidian religion that has somehow remained at its heart unviolated by the various forms of India's high or great tradition (that is, via Sanskritization, Brahmanization, Puranicization, et cetera). The view derived from such turn-of-the-century works as those of Oppert, Whitehead, and Elmore that the goal of research is to isolate the original non-acculturated component in such figures is implicitly rejected. Nor does Biardeau start from the premise that they are expressions of an alternate cultural dynamic, a strain of folk counter-culture within yet in some opposition to the larger whole (an approach that has some currency today among folklorists). Rather, Biardeau argues that such figures are best understood, in terms of her essay in this volume, in relation to the "whole of Hinduism," the inherent dynamics—social, theological, and historical—that sustain the unity of the Hindu tradition itself in both "its superior and inferior forms." To begin with, this means interpreting the mythical and cultic roles of these meat-eating gods in their rapport with Brahmanical values as seen, first of all, through the parts played by Brahmans in the same myths and cults. More than this, Biardeau attempts to demonstrate that the rapport between Brahmans and meat-eating gods is in certain cases worked out through mythic and ritual symbols that derive ultimately from the concrete apparatus of Vedic ritual: in this essay, most notably in connection with the *Aśvamedha* or Vedic Horse Sacrifice, and more generally in relation to the Vedic sacrificial post, the *yūpa*. The ultimately Vedic themes do not, however, descend directy into these folk cults, but through the medium of a bhakti rereading of the Vedic revelation which these popular cults carry forward, much transformed but with the traces of the transformations still discernible, from the initial bhakti mythologies of the epics and Purāṇas. Thus the rationale behind Biardeau's discussion of crushing goat heads in relation to themes of the *Mahābhārata*, and of Kāttavarāyan in relation to the classical figure of Kārtavīrya Arjuna.

Biardeau's brief discussion of Kāttavarāyan serves to introduce the focal figure of the two following essays by David Shulman and Eveline Masilamani-Meyer. As a cluster, these three opening essays provide the first extensive scholarly investigation of the remarkable folk corpus that surrounds this figure, who serves admirably to launch discussion of many facets of the Criminal God and Demon Devotee problematic. Indeed, in certain respects Kāttavarāyan provides the perfect starting point, because he more than any other single figure discussed in this book seems to *combine* traits of the criminal (as M. Arunachalam called him)[2] god with those of the demon devotee (as argued by Biardeau, who sees him as the demon Kārtavīrya converted). In all, the first three essays introduce Kāttavarāyan through three variants of his temple ritual (two in Biardeau's discussion, one in Masilamani-Meyer's) and through both local oral (Biardeau) and literary versions of his mythology (two by Shulman, three by Masilamani-Meyer, with a major one in common).

The text which both Shulman and Masilamani-Meyer discuss in common is the most widely circulated published chapbook version of Kāttavarāyan's story, the *Kāttavarāyacuvāmi Katai* (henceforth *Katai*). Masilamani-Meyer has in fact completed a translation of this text, and is preparing it for publication. Shulman also discusses another chapbook version of the story in the form of a drama, and Masilamani-Meyer two versions from palm leaf manuscripts.

From Shulman's essay, which takes the *Katai* as its main text, one can become familiar with Kāttavarāyan through this vulgate edition. Shulman provides a rich account of its version of his myth and a penetrating discussion of its major themes: the ambiguities of guarding and protecting; Kāttavarāyan's concealed affinities and identities with Brahman, king, and Untouchable; his mockery of Brahmans; his use of magic to conquer other magicians; the sexual tensions implied in his relations with his multiple fathers, mothers, and wives; the specific ambiguities of his obsession, as a seeming Untouchable, with the Brahman girl Āriyamālai that results in something of an abduction, a rape, and an unconsummatable marriage, and his ultimate destiny on the sacrificial stake; the ardency of his wives' lamentation; his double ambiance as boundary marker and boundary transgressor, encompasser and encompassed. As Shulman notes,

Kāttavarāyan shares much of this dossier with other "criminal" heroes. But Shulman observes that this text, in contrast to the drama, also shows Kāttavarāyan with unique traits besides: his Trickster-like transformability, his "permanent transience," his last trick being his mastery over his own impalement. He is the lone and alienated hero, severed from his divine parents Śiva and the goddess, their reunion requiring his ordeal. And his voluntary self-victimization elicits a kind of cathartic bhakti, exemplified by the lamentations of his wives as he dies—but doesn't really die—on the stake. And further in this vein, because the text works out its bhakti themes primarily in relation to Kāttavarāyan (whom it elevates, in effect, to an identity with Śiva's more Brahmanically recognized son Murukan), Shulman argues that Kāttavarāyan, at least in this text, "is not an exemplar of bhakti directed toward a higher deity."

In large measure, Masilamani-Meyer's essay confirms Shulman's sense for the uniqueness of the *Katai*'s portrayal of Kāttavarāyan, and also, by comparing it further with the two palm leaf versions, offers an interpretation of the cultural and religious dynamics behind his changing face. The most striking contrast is in the bhakti structures of the two texts. The primary palm leaf version repeatedly highlights Kāttavarāyan's devotion to his mother, the goddess: throughout his career he makes continuous pūjā offerings to her (be it noted that he also goes at least this far in the *Katai*), and sets up her temples. He has no identity with Murukan, and rather than being a god throughout his career who will play his last trump on the stake, his divinity comes about as an apotheosis through his *true* death and rebirth on the stake. And rather than separating him from Śiva and the goddess as the focus of a bhakti devoted to himself alone, his ordeal brings his cult into a rapport with that of these higher deities (his mother the goddess, his father Śiva, and in fact the whole Trimūrti), who through his death agree to accept offerings from his devotees, with he himself, their impure guard and soldier, as intermediary. Further in the same vein, the palm leaf versions clarify the links between Kāttavarāyan's mythology and the cult of the Seven Virgins. And finally, Kāttavarāyan is presented as a god whom all castes may worship, with no special anti-Brahman slant evident in his tricks such as there is, in a quite outspoken form, in the *Katai*. Masilamani-Meyer interprets these contrasts against the background of changing social conditions, and leaves a quite haunting sense of what is being lost and gained in the process. In terms of the distinctions between oral, palm leaf, and printed versions, it is clear that as an example of the latter, although the *Katai* has been able to take on a literary life of its own, it is also the most detached from the cult.

Velcheru Narayana Rao and David Knipe's papers follow the Coromandal coast up to Andhra Pradesh. Yet along with their pairing as discussions of Telugu popular culture, each essay also clusters significantly with those that bracket this Andhra pair. Narayana Rao's Kāṭamarāju has certain similarities with Kāttavarāyan which I will discuss in a moment. And with Knipe's and Elizabeth-Chalier Visuvalingam's papers, we meet in Vīrabhadra and Bhairava the two wrathful forms of Śiva from the pan-Indian Sanskritic tradition whom regional popular cults and mythologies so often connect, in various ways and guises, with our criminal gods and demon devotees. Indeed, each author takes up ways in which the Sanskritic mythologies of these gods take root in regional folk cults that virtually overlap with other popular traditions of these types.

One of my not-so-hidden agendas in bringing together essays on Kāttavarāyan and Kāṭamarāju for this book, and the initial conference that set it in motion, has been to raise the possibility that the two figures might be related. Because none of our authors have taken up this issue, either to pursue the possibility or rule it out, a few words are in order. At this point, a genetic connection between the two mythologies seems unlikely but still tantalizing in its possibilities. A major reason to discard the whole issue is that to pursue the apparent similarity in names, one would have to explain the difference in the "t's": dental in Kāttavarāyan, retroflex in Kāṭamarāju. This does not seem possible, and moreover, each name finds an easy etymology that incorporates these differences: Kāttavarāyan from *kā*, "to guard or protect" (see Shulman's discussion), and Kāṭamarāju from *kāḍu*, "forest" (see Narayana Rao). Yet as Shulman points out, the forest is Kāttavarāyan's "natural domain," and he has several epithets that mean "the lord who guards the wilderness." And conversely, Narayana Rao brings out Kāṭamarāju's protective-guardian aspect in a most provocative manner (reminiscent of Kṛṣṇa in the *Mahābhārata*), linking it with the extreme readiness of cowherd-warrior-kings to offer refuge to those who seek their protection (*śaraṇāgata rakṣaṇa*). This brings up a second point where the two mythologies seem to be far apart, for whereas the whole Kāṭamarāju cycle revolves around Golla-Yādava cowherds, with Kāṭamarāju as this community's chief divine hero, the story of Kāttavarāyan has next to nothing to do with cowherds. But again, the little that it has is intriguing. At least in the *Katai*, Kāttavarāyan is linked with cowherds through his cross cousin (i.e., legitimate) marriage with his *Kōnār* (herder) junior wife Karuppalaki. Could he be her cross-cousin without being in some undeclared sense a Kōnār himself? More than this, as Shulman notes, there is a recurrent incorporation into Kāttavarāyan's mythology of traits from that arch cowherd-"trickster" (or better cattleherder-*Kṣatriya*-"trickster") Kṛṣṇa. The Kāṭamarāju story, on the other hand, leaves no doubt about its hero's affinities with Kṛṣṇa: at one point, Kāṭamarāju proves that he is Kṛṣṇa himself (though as Narayana Rao points out, he also has links with Śiva). Narayana Rao thus shows that Kāṭamarāju's ambiguities and trickeries must be interpreted in a specific socio-mythical context, one that seems remote from Kāttavarāyan. But it is worth noting that Kāttavarāyan's "permanent transience" remains a fitting description of the fort-rejecting pastoralist ambience exalted for and by Kāṭamarāju.

Leaving genetic links between these two mythologies aside, a few words may be offered on further thematic links—ritual as well as mythic—between Kāṭamarāju and other figures dealt with in this book. I restrict myself to the scene that opens Narayana Rao's discussion, in which the seven year old Kāṭamarāju confronts the goddess Gaṅga when he goes to the battlefield at midnight to look for his father's corpse. The warfield here is not only the venue in which he meets Gaṅga, but also Pōturāju, the younger brother and guardian not only of Gaṅga but of numerous other Andhra village goddesses. We will meet Pōturāju again in this book under the Tamil form Pōttu Rāja as a guardian of the goddess Draupadī (see Hiltebeitel's article). Now in the Telugu story, Gaṅga demands non-vegetarian food from Kāṭamarāju for herself and Pōturāju: a sheep (or goat) tall as a palm tree and rice high as a mountain. This is Pōturāju's common fare in Telugu myths. More than this, it is also, in a Draupadī cult myth, the food that Pōttu Rāja under the name Pōrmannan demands for himself from Kṛṣṇa before he will serve the goddess Draupadī on the battlefield of the Mahābhārata war.[3] Because Kāṭamarāju reveals himself to be a multiform of Kṛṣṇa, we thus have similar configurations. In each case, over-seeing the battlefield requires non-vegetarian food, but with different accents. In the Tamil story, Pōrmannan is the newcomer-guardian to whom Kṛṣṇa supplies such fare so that Pōrmannan will be the goddess's battlefield guardian, and also, implicitly, so that the vegetarian Draupadī won't have to eat meat herself. In the Telugu story, Pōturāju, already in the goddess's service, objects only to extending that service to the warfield. Here the newcomer—who as the Kṛṣṇa figure is more than the goddess's guardian, though he seems to take on that role as well—supplies the food so that Gaṅga and Pōturāju, both meat-eaters, will watch over the battlefield on behalf of the

Gollas. Moreover, the appearance which Gaṅga presents to Kāṭamarāju on the battlefield is one that holds certain reminders of the story of Kāttavarāyan. Gaṅga tests Kāṭamarāju's resolve, and seeks to terrify him, by appearing with spears projecting from her head, on which numerous elephants and other corpses are impaled. Here again the hero's tricks involve a confrontation with the goddess and a variation on the impalement stake. Once Gaṅga has transformed herself from this horrendous form into a twelve year old girl and been tricked into bowing to Kāṭamarāju, Kāṭamarāju is faced with a prospect that is ultimately little more attractive than impalement. This dangerous girl wants to marry him. The double implication in this sequence that impalement equals marriage, and further a return to the mother, is not to be missed here any more than in the Kāttavarāyan story (see S. Visuvalingam in this volume). What is different, and striking, is that Kāṭamarāju uses his cleverness to avoid these pitfalls whereas Kāttavarāyan is ineluctably drawn toward them.[4] The result in one case is an ambiguous marriage that is not a real marriage, and in the other a non-marriage that is all too real.

Like Narayana Rao's paper, Knipe's takes us to a figure who, although he bears affinities with others discussed in this volume, also requires us to look at such affinities from an oblique angle. The Vīrabhadra cult of coastal Andhra (East Godavari District), which Knipe seems virtually to have (in scholarly terms) discovered one noisy fall night in 1980, links this wrathful projection of Śiva with the outrage of the disgruntled dead: the prematurely and deviant dead, and especially children, excluded from ancestral rites for deceased Fathers (and wives). Initially known through their possession of family members who remain alive, such undeparted spirits are known as *vīrabhadras* (with girls sometimes called *vīrakanyakās*), and are commemorated in the remarkable *liṅga*-shaped "ash-fruit" icons that grow through the attentions they receive in their cult. The central event of the cult takes the form of nocturnal processions, most notably at Mahāśivarātri, in which the ash-fruits are taken out, possession by the raging vīrabhadras is invited, and Vīrabhadra's own dance of destruction may be impersonated. It is to be noted that except for such deceased and living personifications, Vīrabhadra is not (or at least does not seem to be) a focus of iconic representation in the cult (the giant processional icon in plate 12 is of Śiva). The cult's main temple in Rajahmundry houses ash-fruit vīrabhadras, but no Vīrabhadra icon as such. So we do not see him, as we often do elsewhere, in a typical temple guardian role.[5] Yet guardian and protector functions are hardly absent. As their leader and prototype, Vīrabhadra protects the "children of rage," who are themselves incipient gods and goddesses. Among the officiants in his processions are current-day stand-ins for the Vīramuṣṭi, a name traditionally belonging to a caste that is reputed in earlier periods to have performed the tasks of guarding temples, monasteries, processional icons, and those who wear the *liṅgam*.[6] But most intriguing in this regard are some implications of Knipe's insights into the correspondence between Vīrabhadra's leadership of these nighttime processions and the Sanskritic mythologies of Vīrabhadra and the destruction of Dakṣa's sacrifice. If with Bhairava (and many other guardian gods), we see a multiform of Śiva at the margins of the temple protecting the deity within, and the principle of sacrifice which the temple and deity incarnate, then with Vīrabhadra we see something quite different. Rather than the guardian turned outward to protect, Vīrabhadra is the guardian turned inward to destroy. Still, he protects the sacrifice by destroying and then restoring the sacrifice that has, in effect, gone wrong: in the myth, the sacrifice of Dakṣa that results in the ultimate perversion, the sacrifice of the goddess herself, Śiva's wife Satī; and in the Andhra cult, the Vedic funerary rituals that reduce the disgruntled dead to leftovers, yet leave remainders which, as Knipe so nicely shows, become the growing icons that are themselves multiforms of the ritual apparatus that rejects them.

Chalier Visuvalingam's paper takes us not only from Vīrabhadra to Bhairava, but into a cluster of four papers that share with hers either a common concern with Bhairava (in the case of Lorenzen and Erndl), or with traditions of Vārāṇasī-Banaras (as with Coccari). Further, with the exception of Lorenzen's paper, which deals with newly discovered data that are primarily, but not exclusively, South Indian, the main focus of this cluster marks a tour through the North.

Although the chief focus of Chalier Visuvalingam's extensive fieldwork on Bhairava—at least to the point of writing—has been Nepal and Vārāṇasī, the paper takes as its point of departure Bhairava's more pan-Indian Sanskritic and Brahmanical dimensions: his purāṇic origin myth as the severer of the fifth head of Brahmā. Chalier Visuvalingam argues that the myth of this ultimate crime, Brahmanicide, situates Bhairava between a "social point of view which must necessarily condemn [him] to be an outcaste heretic criminal and the esoteric valorization of transgressive sacrality that exalts" his supremacy. In relation to what both the Visuvalingams call the dialectic of transgressive sacrality, the essay pursues Bhairava, and the elusive fifth head of Brahmā that clings to him so tenaciously, through a vast tapestry of prefigurations, transformations, multiforms, and analogues, from the center of Hinduism to its peripheries. As with Biardeau (and others in this volume), Chalier Visuvalingam seeks to relate the phenomena under study to the whole of Hinduism, from roots in the Vedic revelation (again, including the sacrificial stake and its multiforms) through epic and popular expressions, and also, with far greater emphasis than Biardeau, in Tantric and tribal manifestations as well. The heuristic, however, is different, for it is claimed of the dialectic of transgressive sacrality that it "encompasses" the "bhakti universe" which Biardeau places at the nerve center of such transformations, and that in effect it requires its "deconstruction." Be that as it may, at the core of Chalier Visuvalingam's interpretation of Bhairava are the royal implications of his Brahmanicide. These are traced in their symbolic background (linked in myth to the figure of Indra, the Vedic god of war and Kṣatriya king par excellence) to the initiatory scenario of the hypothetically reconstructed figure of the pre-classical Vedic royal *dīkṣita* (a king consecrated to be the patron of a sacrifice), who in the transgressive notations of his embryogonic death-and-rebirth is assimilated to a Brahman as both Brahman-slayer and Brahman-victim. And on the level of Hinduism as observed, the transgressive complex surrounding Bhairava is explored in relation to "the problem of the Mahābrāhmaṇa," whom Chalier Visuvalingam treats as a "dialectical figure" in relation to others, but who in himself is the Brahman funerary priest who impersonates the deceased in the rituals that enact the latter's death-and-rebirth, devours his or her sins, is both pure and impure, executioner and victim, and assimilated symbolically to a royal Untouchable. One important feature of this essay in relation to others in this volume is thus its exploration of the theme of initiatic death-and-rebirth in relation to the transformation from criminal/demon to god/devotee. The initiatory scenario is a tacit theme in the mythologies and cults of such figures as Kāttavarāyan and Pōtu Rāju-Pōrmannan (see Hiltebeitel and S. Visuvalingam in this volume). In the embryogonic death of Bhairava, the "royal" Brahmanicide, at Vārāṇasī, it takes on an explicit centrality.

Chalier Visuvalingam's essay introduces a group of ascetics from the late classical through medieval periods of Hinduism called Kāpālikas who took the Brahmanicide Śiva—or Śiva in his Brahmanicide form as Bhairava—as their divine model: like Śiva-Bhairava, they undertook a Great Penance of bearing a skull begging bowl (the skull, *kapāla*, being ideally or at least symbolically that of a Brahman, and linked mythically with the fifth head of Brahmā) along with a skull-topped staff (*khaṭvāṅga*). It is David Lorenzen who wrote the pioneer work on the Kāpālikas, and Lorenzen follows Chalier Visuvalingam's study with an updating of his earlier discussion of this sect in the light of previously unnoticed and new data. The recent discovery of Śaivite tantric texts describing Kāpālika worship and observances and newly found inscriptional evidence of donations to and from Kāpālika ascetics together confirm the actual organizational and institutional existence of the sect, which until recently remained uncertain. Lorenzen remarks on evidence from one early (sixth century) inscription from Karnataka that the Kāpālikas would have included Brahmans versatile in Vedic literature and rituals, in particular the Vedic Soma sacrifice, which may itself have provided one level of meaning to the apparently esoteric Kāpālika doctrine called *Somasiddhānta*. Also intriguing is the new inscriptional evidence from eleventh century Andhra that along with the six insignia (*mudrā*) that adorned the Kāpālika's person, he would hold not only the skull bowl and staff but the hourglass shaped *ḍamaruga* (Sanskrit *ḍamaru*) drum, the barrel shaped *mṛdaṅga* drum, and apparently some kind of trumpet. As Lorenzen says, musical instruments are often associated with Śaivite ascetics. More than this, the ḍamaru is borne by the *dancing* Śiva and is used in popular Hinduism in possession rituals, whereas the Kāpālika's khaṭvāṅga is also linked with ecstatic behavior and is said to dance on its own.[7] This group of *five* instruments might be recalled in connection with the discussion in my article of the myths that connect Pōtu Rāju-Pōrmannan with five ritual instruments—linked again with possession and the dance—in the South Indian Draupadī cult.

Also briefly introduced by Chalier Visuvalingam is the subject of Kathleen Erndl's essay: a cult of Jammu District, Kashmir, in which Bhairava (Bhairõ) is linked with the goddess Vaiṣṇo Devī. The fundamental opposition between the vegetarian (vaiṣṇava) goddess and the meat-eating, wine-drinking, and lustful Bhairõ is played out at a number of levels that find analogues in other articles in this volume. Like Pōrmannan, Bhairõ moves back and forth indiscriminately in his cravings for meat and sex. Like Kāttavarāyan, he becomes sexually obsessed with one of the Seven Virgins in the form of a Brahman girl (who this time is also the goddess herself, and the eldest of the seven rather than the youngest). As with myths about the goddess and the Buffalo Demon (see Hiltebeitel, this volume), the goddess lures him sexually to his doom: first through her Embryo-Womb Cave in which as the Brahman girl-goddess she has gone to hide from him to gestate in a form of her own womb-sanctum, and then into another cave from which she finally emerges in her fierce form as Caṇḍī to kill him. His killing results in his transformation into her guardian, his severed head rolling to the valley below while his body remains as a boulder to stand guard outside the cave. As Erndl indicates, Bhairava the beheader becomes Bhairava the beheaded, and moreover, as a guardian, he is further transformed into Bhairava the Child (Bāl Bhairõ), disarming him of his menacing sexuality and inverting the situation in which he had coveted the child goddess. One is reminded of the seven year old Kāṭamarāju faced with the prospect of marrying the goddess Gaṅga (see Narayana Rao in this volume). As elsewhere, it is also not just a matter of one guardian for Vaiṣṇo Devī but two, as Bhairõ is joined—after fighting him (compare Draupadī's two guardians, discussed herein by Hiltebeitel)—by a vaiṣṇava-vegetarian form of the monkey god Hanumān named Langūr Vīr. There are also two exemplary devotees: the meat-eating Bhairõ and the vegetarian Brahman Śrīdhar.

With Diane Coccari's essay, we return to Vārāṇasī. In the city which Bhairava guards and polices, overseeing the initiatory punishment in the experience of death that can transform death—even for sinners—into immediate liberation, we look at those who have, as it were, shared his terrain yet died without altogether claiming this ultimate benefit: the deified dead who linger in Vārāṇasī to receive a cult. We thus return to a terrain opened up for us by Knipe, moving once again from ultimately Brahmanical forms to popular or folk forms, and from the essentially mythic to the esentially human. For as a category, the deified dead are viewed as sharing a real human past, "an untimely, heroic, sacrificial or otherwise extraordinary" death, and a continued presence thereafter in a shrine, where as wakeful presences they may exercise their localized powers. Coccari shows both the underlying continuities within this broad category as well as the features that distinguish some of the most prominent types: yogins or ascetics with their *samādhis,* the tomb-stones that mark their initiatory deaths; female figures, including Satīs or widows who join their husbands on the funeral pyre; *Brahms,* the spirits of Brahmans, who may linger precisely to avenge their own Brahmanicides; Muslim deities, particularly those connected with the remarkably fluid cult of the Panchon Pir or Five Saints; and the "heroes" (*bīr*) from various low-to-middle caste groups, most notably those of the cattle-herding Ahir. As Coccari notes, the deified dead share a common ambiance. Yogins and Birs may overlap (as indeed yogins and heroes overlap in the *Mahābhārata*). Coccari's subjects have their affinities with many others in this volume. As throughout, one meets variations on the interaction between Muslim and Hindu deities, between iconic and aniconic representations, the theme of transfiguration into more benign and protective presences, and certain Birs linked with sorcery and exorcism and rituals of quieting and appeasement. And with regard to the Ahirs and the remarkable story of Bachau Bir, what is the link between transience and permanence that Shulman and Narayana Rao observe in connection with the figures of Kāttavarāyan and Kāṭamarāju, and which seems to find such persistent expression among cattle-herders, with their widespread cults of hero stones and their folk epic mythologies of opposition to kings and dominant landed castes?[8]

With the papers of Stanley and Sontheimer, we move from the north of India to the west and south, to the venue of the cult of Khaṇḍobā. Both authors have written extensively on Khaṇḍobā elsewhere. And it is primarily from their work that Khaṇḍobā stands now in rather clear profile, especially as he is worshipped in Maharashtra as an *avatar* of Śiva, preeminent *kṣetrapāla*, and *kuladevatā* to lineages within numerous castes, both high and low. Let us add that under the name Mārtaṇḍ Bhairav, and with attendant dog, Khaṇḍobā is also a form of Bhairava. In this volume Stanley retains his focus on the Khaṇḍobā cult in Maharashtra, but addresses not so much Khaṇḍobā himself as his demon adversary-devotees and non-vegetarian guardians. And Sontheimer extends his research from the Khaṇḍobā of Maharashtra to the overlapping cults of the related, and in some ways identical gods Mallanna in Andhra Pradesh and Mailāra in Karnataka.

Stanley's paper follows nicely from Coccari's. One moves from the "wakeful presences" of the deified dead to the "especially watchful places" (*jāgṛt kṣetras*) where Khaṇḍobā has his primary residences. Moreover, Stanley also emphasizes the similarities between exorcism rites that localize the power of ghosts and render that power either harmful or benign and the Khaṇḍobā cult myths which split the destinies of Khaṇḍobā's two demon victims in similar fashion: one, Malla, the god's incorrigible enemy whose wickedness can only be neutralized by trickery; the other, Maṇi, whose capitulation transforms him into a demon devotee. Further oppositions in the myths and cultic treatment of these two demons tally with distinctions noted elsewhere in this volume. Malla is the great magician, Maṇi the army general. Each receives three dying boons, Maṇi honorably, Malla dishonorably, with the result that Khaṇḍobā must trick Malla at each point. One should not miss the analogies between Malla's three boons and the three demands of Pōrmannan: each is tricked—one by Khaṇḍobā-Śiva, the other by Kṛṣṇa—into receiving inferior things, with the last of the three in each case involving the monstrous offering of goat. And in this vein, it is in relation to these two demons that the Khaṇḍobā cult works out its shaded distinctions between vegetarian and non-vegetarian offerings. Where Khaṇḍobā is offered only vegetarian food (that is, especially at his wakeful places), goats may be offered to Maṇi, or to the combined demon Maṇimal, or to an additional servant, Hegaḍī Pradhān, who then passes the meat on to the demons. Thus Malla receives the goat only indirectly or not at all, despite the fact that in the myth it is he whom Khaṇḍobā tricks into receiving the goat offering in a "cannibalistic" form as the last of his three dying boons. Especially interesting also in view of other essays in this volume is Hegaḍī Pradhān. Where this Minister brother-in-law is the brother of Khaṇḍobā's junior wife (and wife of lower status) Bānū, the Dhangar shepherd woman who is herself an incarnation of the goddess Gaṅgā, one once again comes across the elements of a recurring complex, reminding us of Kāttavarāyan's ties to the herder girl Karuppalaki, the Gollas' worship of Gaṅgā in the Kāṭamarāju story, and—as again with Bānū—the mythologies of herders' cleverness. And Hegaḍī Pradhān's brother-in-law status may further remind us of the affinities between Viṣṇu (whom he incarnates in oral, not written, versions of the Khaṇḍobā myth, and who figures frequently in South Indian mythologies as brother-in-law of Śiva), Kṛṣṇa (Viṣṇu's cowherd incarnation par excellence), and Pōtu Rāju (who as the younger brother to numerous goddesses becomes the brother-in-law guardian of their husbands as well—if and when, like Draupadī, they have them).

Sontheimer then takes us to the heart of his concern for this volume by the device of returning repeatedly to the notation MMKh for Mallanna/Mailāra/Khaṇḍobā. Although retaining a plural usage verbally ("MMKh transgress," "MMKh resemble," etc.), he shows that these three gods—from Andhra, Karnataka, and Maharashtra, respectively—have intersecting and overlapping cults and images, to the point of being multiforms of one "folk deity of the Deccan." Sontheimer begins and ends his essay with an emphasis on folk religion as an ongoing component within Hinduism, traceable back to folk strains, principally centered on Rudra, within the Vedic tradition itself. He does not, however, seem to want to reconstruct an original autonomy for this folk component or emphasize its counter-cultural character so much as underscore its self-conscious interactive character: the ways in which it intersects with other components, other hierarchical models, both Hindu and non-Hindu, of the Indian tradition. Folk gods like Khaṇḍobā, and their cults, thus retain Vedic traits not because of a bhakti rereading of the Vedic revelation, but because this folk strain has Vedic roots. And although the hierarchy of this folk religion is oriented around *tapas* and bhakti, there are differences, he argues, between folk bhakti and classical bhakti. It is instructive, considering how many of the same elements come under consideration (particularly in their discussions in this volume of continuities linking the Vedic horse sacrifice with popular folk cults), to compare the methods and insights of Sontheimer and Biardeau on these points. Sontheimer's paper also provides rich reflecting images on themes raised by numerous others in this volume: on the limits of applying Sanskritic models like the kṣetrapāla, Brahmanicide, and demon devotee to folk deities; on bandit kings, and rising kings as emerging icons (cf. Waghorne); on the Muslim components of Hindu folk cults (cf. Coccari and Hiltebeitel); on pastoral elements (cf. Narayana Rao); and on the affinities between ancestors, ghosts, clan deities, and heroes (cf. Coccari).

Having thus circled back from Maharashtra through the Deccan cult(s) of MMKh, the three closing papers return us to Tamilnadu. My own paper closes the cycle on specific figures who fall, however roughly, under the rubrics of our title theme, whereas Hudson's and Waghorne's papers extend the theme into related areas: Hudson into the violent acts of devotion of the Tamil Śaivite Nāyanārs, and Waghorne into the royal history and mythology of the Kaḷḷar kings of the former Tamil princely state of Pudukkottai.

My paper takes as its primary issue a theme that recurs in a number of this volume's papers: the rapport between two guardians in one cult. It is argued that in at least this one case, the categories of "demon devotee" and "criminal god" can be applied oppositionally, with further distinctions again worked out between vegetarian and non-vegetarian offerings, symbolic and real sacrifices, army marshalship and magic, iconic and aniconic forms, mobile and fixed forms, peripherality and centrality. Moreover, with the cult in question being that of Draupadī, the heroine of the *Mahābhārata* as South Indian goddess, one has the special opportunity to see how this bhakti folk cult works out these oppositions in parallel folk epic mythologies in both regional and classical forms. Finally, the rapport between Draupadī's two guardians is further examined on the level of their cult, iconography, and positions in Draupadī temples in relation to structures of the Vedic sacrifice as it has been transformed through the medium of bhakti Hinduism.

In extending the investigation into a discussion of saints, Hudson's essay provides an entrée into the larger question of the pertinence of our title theme to the interpretation of wider aspects of Hinduism. Sensitive to the inappropriateness of referring to saints as "criminal," Hudson uses that term sparingly, prefering the terms "violent," "fierce," and "fanatical" to describe the "cutting" acts of devotion that typify a goodly number—twenty-four of the proverbial sixty-three—of the Tamil Śaivite saints, the Nāyanārs. And indeed, one must be careful, as always, not to homogenize our subjects. As far as continuities go, one should appreciate that Hudson's contribution to the overall issue is both methodological and thematic. On the methodological side, over against the usual tide that presumes a great divide between the "restrained" classical bhakti of the epics and unrestrained emotive bhakti of sectarian traditions like that of the Nāyanārs, he stresses a double imbrication of epic themes and prototypes from the *Mahābhārata* into the Nāyanār hagiography of violent devotion. And he is alert to Vedic continuities as well, particularly in connection with the performance of violent acts before the liṅgam, for which there is precedent in earlier South Indian evidence that actual sacrifices were made before the liṅgam as a seeming multiform—to draw the discussion further—of the Vedic sacrificial stake. As to thematic continuities, one cannot miss in the stories of the Nāyanārs' fierce expressions of their love (*anpu*) of Śiva an alternate articulation of many of the themes that characterize the "criminal god" and "demon devotee": the sacrificial themes just mentioned, guardian functions, pure and impure offerings, Brahmanicide, and collectively the full range of caste identities. But the discontinuities are also marked, and easily perceived through Hudson's rich discussion of the theological ideosyncracies of the Tamil Śaivite concept of anpu. Let us just note here the contrast between the Kāpālikas, for whom Śiva-Bhairava is a kind of ultimate and cosmic archetype after whom one models oneself by carrying a skull bowl and experientially affirming the bliss of his union with the goddess (see Lorenzen in this volume), and the Nāyanār whose violent acts are stirred up in living conflict situations by Śiva's own anpu for his devotees, so that they entangle the Nāyanār with his fierce Lord, present either in the liṅgam or in others of his devotee-slaves, in astonishingly intense and intimate forms of violent love. Moreover, the sin of Brahmanicide, though still thematically present in the Nāyanār stories, recedes from its ultimacy. The ultimate sin is no longer Brahmanicide but Śiva-cide, the sin of killing one of Śiva's slaves or wounding his liṅgam, sins that are atoned for not by any skull-bearing penance to Vārāṇasī but, as in the story of Caṇḍēśvara

Nāyanār who kills his Brahman father, by the nullification of the sin through the anpu—shared with the ultimately unslayable but forever self-offering Śiva himself—that the sin itself intensifies. Despite its different theological emphasis, however, the story of Caṇḍēśvara Nāyanar provides an almost certain instance of a hagiographic legend constructed whole cloth out of mythic and ritual themes: themes, moreover, that are recurrent throughout this book. Caṇḍēśvara is none other than a humanized-sanctified version of Śiva's guardian deity, Caṇḍa, and his myth explains how as a saint he takes on not only Caṇḍa's name but that god's mythic and ritual functions: the status of "commander-in-chief and leader of all Śiva's servants," and the charge of receiving the remnants of the offerings from Śiva's worship at a position to the northeast of Śiva's temples.[9]

Waghorne's paper then takes up the dynastic history and mythology of the Kaḷḷar royal house, the Toṇṭaimāns, of Pudukkottai, relating our overall theme to the dynamics of historical interaction between this hinterland kingdom, its neighboring larger kingdoms, and ultimately the British. To reverse the order of her discussion to its sequential chronology, in the founding legends of the royal line, the first kings play out the typical inversion of their Kaḷḷar caste prerogative as robbers or plunderers who may be enlisted as guardians against other robbers like themselves: the pattern that led to the British dubbing the Kaḷḷars a "criminal caste." The initial stories—leading up to the establishment of independent Toṇṭaimān rule in Pudukkottai in 1689—show the Toṇṭaimān heroes taming wild animals and quelling rebellions in contexts that result in their becoming the protectors, guardians, or allies of the larger and more established neighboring kings of Ramnad, Madurai, and Trichinopoly, who invest them with a rich panoply of royal insignia called Biruthus (Tamil *pirutu*). Second, the cycle of stories about Vijaya Raghunātha Rāya, who ruled Pudukkottai from 1730 to 1769, concentrates on the absolution of this king's sins through his encounters with a Brahman ascetic, who instructs him to institute worship of Śiva in the palace and arrange for the annual performance of Dasarā, the royal festival to the goddess. It it notable that this ceremony is regarded as an expiatory rite for the king's sins, a reminder that this was also a function of the chief Vedic royal sacrifice, the Aśvamedha or horse sacrifice, which Dasarā, with its buffalo sacrifices, would seem to have replaced (see further Biardeau's discussion in this volume of village instances where these two rites have been fused together). One may also tie in this image of the sinful king theoretically with E. Chalier Visuvalingam's discussion of the royal Mahābrāhmaṇa: Vijaya Raghunātha is innocent of Brahmanicide, but in certain versions of their first meeting he inadvertantly wounds the Brahman sage before the latter instructs him. Finally, 1882 marks the assumption by Rāja Rāmacandra Toṇṭaimān of the title Brihadambal Das, "Servant of the goddess Brihadambal," a title in which Waghorne sees the fulfillment of a kind of emergent royal icon which, with its low caste robber foundations, royal Biruthus, sins, identities with other castes, and servant status to the goddess, bears—in its cumulative form—a resemblence to the converted demon devotee.

Finally, Sunthar Visuvalingam examines these essays from the standpoint of the dialectics of transgressive sacrality, looking particularly at the embryogonic symbolism of the royal dīkṣita as evidence not only for Vedic-folk continuities, but as a means to interpret both Vedic and folk themes, and arguing that this dialectic has been generalized within Hinduism as a whole, beyond the encompassment of bhakti. Here as elsewhere, astute readers will find it no more difficult to recognize the different methodological strains among our authors than the common threads that unify their subjects.

NOTES

1. On Bengal, see in the selected biblography the works cited by Sarkar 1986, Ostor 1980; on central India, see Babb 1975; on Karnataka, see Srinivas 1965; Prabhu 1972; Claus 1973, 1978; on Kerala, see Kurup 1973, Ayrookuzhiel 1983, Tarabout 1986.

2. See M. Arunachalam, *Ballad Poetry: Peeps into Tamil Literature* (Tiruchitrambalam: Gandhi Vidyalayam, 1976), 187-89.

3. See Hiltebeitel in this volume and further discussion, including that of other Telugu Pōturāju-goddess myths on this theme, in Hiltebeitel, *The Cult of Draupadī*, I. *Mythologies, From Gingee to Kurukṣetra* (Chicago: University of Chicago Press, 1988), 345-79.

4. Compare, however, Kāṭamarāju's "relentless duty to lead" others to their deaths in battle, another reminder of the *Mahābhārata* mythology of Kṛṣṇa and the Draupadī cult mythology of Kṛṣṇa and Pōrmannan.

5. Eveline Meyer, *Aṅkāḷaparamēcuvari: A Goddess of Tamilnadu, Her Myths and Cult* (Wiesbaden: Franz Steiner Verlag, 1986), 81, 83; Hiltebeitel, *Cult of Draupadī*, 41, 52, 372-73.

6. See Edgar Thurston, *Castes and Tribes of Southern India* (Delhi: Cosmo Publications, 1975), vol. 7, 407, 410-11.

7. See David N. Lorenzen, *The Kāpālikas and Kālāmukhas: Two Lost Śaivite Sects* (Berkeley and Los Angeles: University of California Press, 1972), 56, 63.

8. On hero stones, see the articles of Sontheimer and Murty cited in the Selective Bibliography in Günther D. Sontheimer and S. Settar, eds., *Memorial Stones. A Study of their Origin, Significance, and Variety* (Dharwad and Heidelberg, 1982); on herders in connection with folk epics, see Velcheru Narayana Rao, "Epics and Ideologies: Six Telugu Folk Epics," in Stuart H. Blackburn and A. K. Ramanujan, eds., *Another Harmony. New Essays on the Folklore of India* (Berkeley: University of California Press, 1986), 141, 144, 151-56; Gene H. Roghair, *The Epic of Palnāḍu. A Study and Translation of Palnāṭi Vīrula Katha* (Oxford: Clarendon Press, 1982), 28, 30, 102, 163, 214-15; Hiltebeitel, *Cult of Draupadī*, 32-35, 220-21, 226, 355, 399, 418; and Narayana Rao in this volume.

9. See the discussion in Erik Af Edholm, "Caṇḍa and the Sacrificial Remnants. A Contribution to Indian Gastrotheology," *Indologica Taurinensia* 12 (1984), 76-77. See further Hiltebeitel in this volume.

1

Brahmans and Meat-Eating Gods

Madeleine Biardeau

From the beginning of my Indological studies, I have been quite convinced that Hindu society was much less divided ideologically, that the top and the bottom were not so utterly alien to each other, than was usually contended, particularly among anthropologists. Being myself of classical philosophical training, I could not imagine how to convince others, including anthropologists, of this belief, and I was prepared to say that, after all, it was a philosophical matter that should not be debated in scholarly circles, because everyone had his own opinion beforehand. I now think, however, the Hindu gods have been with me, and even more so the Hindu goddess.

It was years ago, when I started studying the goddess both through texts and through fieldwork in South India, that my attention was drawn to a series of minor carnivorous gods who were all guardians and devotees of the goddess. Actually, although the texts taught me one side of the situation, fieldwork brought me another type of data which by and by started to make sense through my classical background. The more or less poor and local goddess temples I visited contained some lesser known deities who had the common property of being subordinate to the goddess. Quite by chance, I started in coastal Andhra and noticed in front of the so-called *grāmadevatā*, or village goddess temples one of these minor gods called Pōtu Rāju. By now I have published a few small articles about him, and especially about his usual shape as a wooden stake and its similarity to the Vedic sacrificial stake, the yūpa.[1] I have since been interested in following this plastic motif of the post under different versions in different parts of South India, and I am preparing a book on the whole subject.[2]

For the present I want to select two of these versions, but not mainly from the viewpoint of the post, which in our present cases can no longer be so easily compared to the yūpa, but from the angle of myth and ritual, which also introduces a number of classical references. The two versions are found in Māriyamman temples, one in the lower Kāverī basin mainly among temples on the north bank of the delta area, and the other in Kongunad. It is mainly the posts and rituals that differentiate the two, but these elements are both connected with mythic differences as well. Everywhere my visits to the temples were quite brief, and I never attended the festivals personally.

I shall discuss only two examples of the first category, which have in common at first sight an impalement stake in front of the temple. Māriyamman's shrine is always considered to be in the center of the village. Usually the local landlord caste is that of the Vanniyar, or exceptionally the Kaḷḷar.

The Valattūr temple (Papanasam Taluk, Thanjavur District) is a Māriyamman temple, as usual facing east. It is trying to revive its traditions. The Kaḷḷar are the dominant caste. The festival takes place in the month of Cittirai (April-May). The Kaḷḷar informants, including the headman of the village, explain that Vaiṣṇava and Smārta Brahmans live on the northern side of the temple, as do the Ācāri; all the Kaḷḷar live on the southern side. One Vēḷāḷar family provides Māriyamman with a priest. In front of the temple are a *balipīṭham*[3] and an impalement stake that served originally to impale Kāttavarāyan, that demon king who stole a Brahman woman. But Kāttavarāyan's friend, Cinnān, helped him out of the difficulty. A Ceṭṭi—that is, one of those rich merchants who used formerly to be attacked and robbed of their goods by the Kaḷḷar—passed by the *kaḻumaram* (a high hook-swinging post and not the low one now there) and asked what it was. Cinnān advised him to climb it and see for himself. So the Ceṭṭi did, and Cinnān quickly impaled him. Soon after, some eagles—*kaḻaku*—came and plucked out his eyes. Since then the Ceṭṭi has been worshipped on the kalumaram as Kaluvuṭaiyan: the Master of the impalement stake.

We can bypass most of the ritual, but must note some characteristic details. Inside the temple *maṇḍapam* are several painted wooden statues of Kāttavarāyan with his two wives, Kaluvuṭaiyan, Cinnān, and Karuppucāmi. There is a festival to the god Aiyanār that is celebrated at the same time as Māriyamman's in Cittirai. Some he-goats are offered both on Māriyamman's side and on Aiyanār's side, but in each case they are offered to the subordinate demon guardians, so that the distinction between the vegetarian Māriyamman and Aiyanār and the meat-eating demons is well marked. One or two days after the conclusion of the seventeen-day festival, there comes the day of "human sacrifice." This takes the form of *kāvaṭi* offerings, which are of three types: *alaku-kāvaṭi,* in which long needles (*alaku*) are stuck under the skin of those who stand under the vow; *pāl-kāvaṭi,* in which a stick is carried on the shoulder with a pot of milk at each end; and *tēr-kāvaṭi,* in which a tiny *tēr* or *rath* (a war chariot) is drawn by a rope and a hook fixed under the skin of the offerer's back. These offerings are brought to the goddess at the end of a rather long walk. Kaḷḷar are non-vegetarian people. But they show all respect to the vegetarian diet of Māriyamman and Aiyanār, who are the protectors of their village. The "tortures" for which they take vows are of a rather mild type and do not seem to upset the goddess, though the needles and hooks are removed as soon as the votary arrives at the temple.

One more thing: Kāttavarāyan seems to have some special link with the Kaḷḷar, because the latter spare him even though usually the impalement stake is meant for him as the one who stole a Brahman woman. The Kaḷḷar, although formerly a "criminal caste," regard themselves as Kṣatriyas, because there are Kaḷḷar kings. Kāttavarāyan is also a Kṣatriya, if we remember that he is the same as Arjuna Kārtavīrya, the oppressive king who stole the cow of the Brahman Jamadagni, whose wife Reṇukā is herself identical with Māriyamman. But this is not the only place where Kāttavarāyan is spared: it would be difficult to assume that he is forever sitting on the impalement stake and at the same time permanently staying with the goddess as her guardian and devotee. But the Tamil stories about Kāttavarāyan are very far from the epic and Purāṇic ones. One feature remains, though: he is still a warrior, and the cow turns into a Brahman woman in order to retain the classical pattern of distorted relations between Brahmans and Kṣatriyas.

In this Valattūr temple, Kāttavarāyan remains the first of Māriyamman's bodyguards, but Karuppu is the second. He has his own processional image made of painted wood. No element of the local myth refers to him, whereas Kāttavarāyan has his own followers and devotees. The presence of Karuppucāmi, however, as lower than Kāttavarāyan seems generalized throughout the area. The Māriyamman temple of Tirunanriyūr (Sirkali Taluk, Thanjavur District) is no exception to this rule. Though Māriyamman is still considered to occupy the center of the village, seven villages take part in her Cittirai festival, which lasts for thirteen days. The whole area is inhabited almost exclusively by Paṭaiyāṭcis (or Vanniyars). Māriyamman has a

Paṭaiyāṭci *cāmiyāṭi*, a man who is possessed by Kāttavarāyan.[4] In front of the temple, but on the other side of the modern road, there is a kalumaram, an impalement stake, that has one remarkable feature: its base is a kind of pyramid with five steps, which might be an unconscious symbol of the five Vedic sacrificial fires. In the inner maṇḍapam of the temple, there are two processional images of Kāttavarāyan and Karuppucāmi in the form of painted wooden statues. Kāttavarāyan is on horseback and accompanied by his two wives, one on each side. He is regarded as Māriyamman's son, and during each night of the annual festival, the main Paṭaiyāṭci priest sings Kāttavarāyan's story in a long and popular version that takes us far away from the classical story of Arjuna Kārtavīrya. On the seventh night, the marriage of Kāttavarāyan and the Brahman girl Āriyamālai is sung: a Brahman priest is called to celebrate the marriage, because Kṛṣṇa, Kāttavarāyan's maternal uncle, had promised him to act as his *purohita* for his wedding. The Brahman who comes is considered to be Kṛṣṇa himself. Māriyamman, regarded as Kṛṣṇa's sister, is called Śakti. Her link with Jamadagni and Paraśurāma has been completely forgotten, whereas she seems to have some antagonistic link with the local Śiva. Tirunanriyūr has a famous Śiva temple that was formerly sung of by the Nayanmārs. On the eighth night, some Paṭaiyāṭcis dress as Kāḷi (= Sanskrit Kālī), and gather around the kalumaram. Kāttavarāyan is to be punished with impalement by Śiva for marrying a Brahman girl. A *śūla*, a sharp metal pointed weapon,[5] is brought near the kalumaram, and the priest, singing the punishment of Kāttavarāyan, impales a sour lime on it, the sour lime being a substitute for Kāttavarāyan. Actually, according to the myth, the śūla can act as an impalement stake as long as it possesses its own vital principle—*uyir*—within itself. Otherwise it is dead and cannot have any effect. Śakti, Kāttavarāyan's mother, has advised her son to cut the kalumaram and change its place a little bit. That is why during the ritual the mobile śūla is slightly removed from the axis of the temple that connects Māriyamman inside and the kalumaram outside. In this way, and in the shape of an impaled lime, Kāttavarāyan preserves his life forever and will remain in front of Māriyamman. Śiva is angry and punishes Śakti to be reborn on earth as Māriyamman. The rebirth of Pārvatī as Reṇukā is also one of the late Purāṇic versions of Reṇukā's story (cf. *Sahyādrikhaṇḍa, Reṇukāmāhātmya*, Bombay 1877). Karuppu is just the goddess's other bodyguard, but he does not play any part in the local myth. Karuppu is still outside his own main area of worship and is inferior to Kāttavarāyan, but his status will continue to be low even when Kāttavarāyan disappears.

On the tenth day of the festival the tēr procession takes place, although the temple seems too poor to maintain a real tēr. A small statue of Māriyamman is carried on a bullock cart, but the procession follows the same chariot route as Śiva's procession. The same day, when the procession is over, the people under vows either take part in a firewalking ceremony, or have long needles stuck under their skin, or do both together. These are the only forms of violence in Māriyamman's worship, because he-goats that have been sacrificed on the first day are offered to the limit goddesses only. Nonetheless, a Brahman came to celebrate Kāttavarāyan's wedding. This shows a subtle understanding of Kṛṣṇa's significance as Viṣṇu's *avatāra* and brother of Śakti, who can take some liberty with Śāstraic rules: in this case blessing Kāttavarāyan's crime. His interference is rare in such a local type of goddess festival, but may be made possible through Śiva's importance and the transformation of Māriyamman into Śakti. Kāttavarāyan's crime is always the same and opposes pure to impure castes, vegetarian to meat-eating ones. But the goddess definitely needs him, in spite of her own purity and his impurity and reckless behaviour, or rather because of this reckless behaviour and his subsequent sacrifice. Through him only will she be able to protect the place without involving herself directly in the activities of bloodshed. In this particular local context, the whole of Hinduism is present in its superior and inferior forms. This will become even clearer when Karuppu's real status is brought to the fore. This takes us to the second version of Māriyamman's worship in Kongunad.

In an area of Kongunad north of Dhārāpuram (Periyar District), the connected festivals of Māriyamman in the center and Kāḷi on the outer limit of the locality are of a very rich and complex symbolism. In this same area, and particularly around Dhārāpuram, many goddess temples are identified with sites of the *Mahābhārata*, all of them, as far as I could see, linked exclusively with scenes of the *Virāṭaparvan*. I will describe only one such place, Civanmalai, where Māriyamman and Vīra-Kāḷiyamman are about one hundred yards apart, in an empty space, although they retain their traditional location at the center and on the limit of the village. Māriyamman's temple opens to the east, Kāḷi's as usual to the north. Māriyamman, two-armed, sits holding a sword and skull. Vīrakāḷi has four arms with the usual weapons, but she sits with her right leg raised on the seat, the left one hanging down, and her foot resting on the head of a Rākṣasa. Both festivals of sixteen days each start every year in Paṅkuni (March-April), and with only one day's difference between them. The same *paṇṭāram* priest acts in both festivals, and the same village headman.

We shall concentrate only on the main days of the festival. For Vīrakāḷi, these are days thirteen through sixteen, during which the processional image of the goddess goes around the whole village. The fifteenth day, however, is the most important. Early in the morning the caste women of four villages, including Civanmalai, bring lamps made of dough—*māviḷakku.* At noon they cook a *poṅkal*[6] in the temple courtyard. These elements of the ritual are very common. But in the evening something specific to this area takes place: a mare is brought by the headman, who has hired it. It stops just in front of the goddess. The paṇṭāram washes its feet and puts a poṭṭu mark on its forehead. He offers a pūjā both to Vīrakāḷi and the mare and sprinkles the latter with the pūjā water. There is a very tense silence while people wait for the mare to shake its head, and the music stops playing. When it does shake its head, the mare is then taken in procession by the headman, accompanied by one of the *pūcāri*s, who carries a tray with the ornaments of the Vīrakāḷi *mūlavar,* that is, the only movable parts of the main fixed image (*mūlavar*) in the shrine. First they go to a tank, where a he-buffalo is waiting. This buffalo has been bought by all the participants, or else is offered by some individual. The buffalo is bathed and a poṭṭu put on its forehead. The procession goes on: the mare with the headman, the buffalo led by the usual paṇṭāram of the temple and the other paṇṭāram carrying the goddess's ornaments. They go to the house of a Brahman, who has Vīrakāḷi as his *iṣṭadevatā.*[7] The Brahman performs a pūjā to the tray and puts some clothing and jewelry for the goddess upon it. He feeds the buffalo. Again the procession starts in the north-east direction and stops at an unmarked place where the pūcāri "calls all the goddesses." This rite is called *ammai alaittal.* Then the procession goes back to the temple and arrives at the same time as the *utsavamūrti* (processional image). The mare is sent back to its master, having completed its part. The buffalo is brought near a ditch that has been dug out just in front of the goddess. The headman must be present when the buffalo is sprinkled with pūjā water, shakes its head, and is beheaded by the paṇṭāram. Both head and body are pushed into the ditch and covered with earth. The paṇṭāram slaughterer, being in a trance, falls unconscious. He is brought back to consciousness with some water. Then the pongal that had been cooked in the morning is offered to the goddess with coconuts and bananas, the whole being returned to the offerers later. This whole rite—that is, the buffalo sacrifice—is called *tiruppu* and explained as *māṭu-tirupputal,* "the bringing back of the cows." This is a well-known episode of the *Virāṭaparvan* of the *Mahābhārata*, in which Arjuna brings home the cattle of Virāṭa which had been stolen by the Kauravas.

All this requires some decoding, beginning with the ritual connected with the mare and the "calling of the goddesses." The presence of a female animal is very rare in such rituals, and a mare was quite unexpected. At the start, it has its feet washed. Then it is worshipped on a par with Vīrakāḷi and sprinkled with water. Then there is complete silence when the animal is expected to shake its head. When it does so, this is considered a good omen, although usually this is the signal for the slaughter of the sacrificial animal. So on one side she is treated like the goddess and identified with her during the pūjā. But the foot wash and the sprinkling of the head can be seen as separate elements of a traditional horse sacrifice. Before it starts on its one year's wandering, the Vedic sacrificial horse has its feet washed. But the sprinkling of the head after the pūjā and the complete silence that accompanies it should be understood as a quite common sacrifical rite that takes place just before the beheading of the animal. So here the beginning of the horse sacrifice and the end, that is the sacrifice of the horse itself, are brought together, though they used to happen a year apart. But the sacrifice is not performed. It looks as if, as a mare, the goddess has been treated as a symbolic victim of a sacrifice that will actually take place later.

This reference to the horse sacrifice, unexpected as it is, allows an interpretation of the mysterious "calling of the goddesses"—*ammai* being the Tamil transcription of *ambā*, an early Sanskrit term of address for a woman, meaning "mother." We have to notice that both the mare, still in front of the temple, and the he-buffalo when it has been bathed at the tank, heve received a poṭṭu on their foreheads that is a sign of marriage. We remember that in the Aśvamedha, just after the death of the sacrifical horse, a symbolic copulation must take place between the horse and the main queen—the *mahiṣī*. At that time a voice calls ambā three times under slightly different forms: ambā, *ambikā*, *ambālikā* or *ambalī*. Here the mare stands for the *mahiṣī*, but in the meantime the sacrificial horse has been turned into a *mahiṣa*, a buffalo.

Along the same lines, we can interpret the visit to the Brahman as a remote reference to the horse sacrifice. When the horse starts on its one year's wandering, instructions are given to the young warriors who accompany it. If a Brahman says he does not know the Aśvamedha, his house should be plundered. He is not worthy of his Brahmanhood. There may have been very early Brahmans who shunned that type of sacrifice, which was so much like a war during its most important phases. Here, on the contrary, the Brahman invites the goddess as being his iṣṭadevatā, gives her presents and feeds the buffalo. In ancient terms, the Brahman accepts the horse's master as his king. Lastly, one more feature must be noticed: the paṇṭāram's fit of unconsciousness after the beheading of the buffalo. The paṇṭāram is possessed by the goddess, and his fit is a reminder of the sufferings an Aśvamedha brings to the earth or the kingdom that the goddess symbolizes. And even more clearly, the paṇṭāram's fit is a reproduction of Reṇukā's temporary loss of consciousness when she is beheaded. Reṇukā is a victim, or better, she is *the* victim. That is the reason why, at the beginning of this ritual, the mare is to act as the victim: when she shakes her head, she is supposed to agree with the expected suffering of sacrifice. That is further why she takes part in the procession, first alone, and then accompanied by the buffalo. The long procession is to be understood as the one year's roaming of the sacrificial horse.[8]

During this same time, Māriyamman's festival is going on with the same structure as Vīrakāḷi's, but one day later. Right from the beginning and for twelve days, a regular worship goes on in the temple, but every night Mādāri leather workers come to beat their drums and other men dance in front of the shrine. On the twelfth day (on which the *utsavamūrti* of Vīrakāḷi is brought down from the Subrahmaṇya temple in order to start the processions on the thirteenth day), Kavuṇṭars go and cut a branch of *pāccamaram*, that is, of a tree with milky sap. The branch must end in the shape of a three-pronged fork. They immerse this *kampam* (post) in the temple tank till night. In the evening the utsavamūrti of Māriyamman is brought down from the Subrahmaṇya temple. The ritual now underway will continue through part of the night. The paṇṭāram prepares a clay pot—kumbha—on a copper tray. He goes to the tank, takes his bath, and fills the kumbha with water. At the same time, the village headman takes the wooden kampam out of the water. The three objects are put on the bank of the tank and a *gurukkaḷ* of the Śiva temple blesses them and gives the pūcāri a *yajñopavīta*, or sacred thread. The same pūcāri also puts a *cāṭṭai* on his shoulder, that is, a kind of whip made of rope and having one end thicker than the other. A new pūcāri comes and carries the kampam, whereas the first one carries the kumbha full of water and decorated with mango leaves and a coconut on the top. All the way from the tank to the temple, men and women come and pour water on the two men's feet. The kumbha is put down close to the balipīṭham whereas the kampam is held upright by its side. After a pūjā to Māriyamman, the village headman digs out a hole right in the axis between Māriyamman's *mūlavar* and Tūṇaicāmi, a permanent stone post outside the temple. He kills a ram, puts its head in the hole for a while, and takes it out. This ram will be given to the Mādāris. Then the wooden forked stake is lodged into this hole. The main pūcāri puts the kumbha in the fork and ties it fast with palmyra leaf fibres. Māriyamman is given a dīpārādhanā, "an offering of light." During the next three days (thirteenth through sixteenth), the kumbha will remain tied on the stake and Māriyamman will receive a daily pūjā.

On the fifteenth day women bring *māviḷakku* (flour lamps) on a tray with coconut, bananas, and camphor. They come from outside in a procession and put their lighted māviḷakku lamps in a double row from the goddess to the post and give some dough and the rest of the offerings to the pūcāri. The village headman brings a ram in front of the balipīṭham as a clear offering to the goddess. The pūcāri sprinkles water on the animal and burns some camphor in front of it. Then everybody hushes up till the animal shakes its head. As soon as it does, it is beheaded by the village headman. As offered to the goddess it will ultimately be given to the pūcāri. No part of the victim is directly presented to the goddess nor given in a cooked meal. At noon, the women return to the temple and prepare pongal. A small quantity is offered to the goddess through the pūcāri, who will eat it. The rest they take back home.

In the afternoon, men and women who are under a vow take a bath in the *teppakkuḷam* (the Śiva temple tank for the floating of rafts with icons on them during festival time). From there they form a procession towards the temple while each dances and carries a fire-pot (*pūcaṭṭi*) with fire in it. The pūcaṭṭi used here is smaller than the one used only by the pūcāris in other places. It is carried with both hands outstretched. In front of these fire-bearers other men, in Māriyamman's garb, take the lead and dance without any pot. As soon as they enter the temple, the fire-pots are put down in front of the goddess. They will be left there and removed much later by the priest. Soon after this the utsava-mūrti of the goddess goes in procession around the village. Then the local cesspool cleaner goes around to inform the village people that they have to bring water to the kampam. They very soon turn up with the pots of water. The village headman brings a third ram, and after the usual ritual of sprinkling, silence, and the shaking of the animal's head, he slaughters it. Then the pūcāri breaks the ties of the kumbha atop the post and brings it to the mūlavar's feet, showing great respect. With the whip on his shoulder and one of the goddess's garlands around his neck, he goes into a trance and uproots the kampam. During all this, the people pour out their pots of water on the kampam and the pūcāri. The latter puts the ram's head in the hole and crushes it with the kampam. He fills up the hole with mud. The cesspool cleaner will get the body of the ram. Then the pūcāri, still in a trance and with the help of his assistants, the village headman, and the Mādāris, carries the kampam once around the temple, and then to the teppakkuḷam. There the kampam is immersed for good in the water.

In order to interpret this ritual, it must be connected with the parallel one to Vīrakāḷi. One may examine Brenda Beck's study of a similar Māriyamman festival of Kannapuram, and find it more interesting for its alternaton of a fire-pot and a water kumbha on the wooden post.[9] I also collected one such version, but associated with a Kāḷi festival that did not include either a mare or a buffalo. But the final interpretation we give here to the whole will not be essentially different from the one I would have given of the other version collected in Cennimalai, just a few miles away from Civanmalai. The benefit I found in the version selected for this paper was the complete dissociation of water and fire: water is brought to the kampam and the priests who take care of it, but at that time there is no burning fire. So this seemingly clear opposition disappears.

The fifteenth day on which the stake is removed and water profusely poured out is the day following the buffalo's sacrifice (fifteenth day, but one day earlier, at the Vīrakāḷi temple). Because we have discovered some reminiscences of the horse sacrifice, we had better start with this here as well. The forked stake also seems to be a heritage of the horse sacrifice. It is found east of the twenty-one sacrificial posts, just behind the central one and in the axis of the fire altar, and it is used quite at the end of the Aśvamedha, even after the avabhṛtha, the closing bath. It is called *viśāla yūpa* (cf. *Āpastamba Śrauta Sūtra* 10.22.23.1; *Baudhāyana Śrauta Sūtra* 15.37), and it receives the three last victims: a he-goat to Agni, a he-goat to Indra and Agni, and a he-goat to the Aśvins, perhaps in the absence of the *yajamāna*. This yūpa was made of wood with milky sap. Each victim is tied to one each of its three terminal prongs. The one we have here in front of the Māriyamman temple is not a mere yūpa like the Vedic one. Rather it is identified with the victim, like the Pōta Rāju in Andhra and Kāttavarāyan in the Thanjavur area. Water is connected with its arrival procession to the temple as well as with its uprooting and return procession to the teppakkuḷam. On its way to the temple on the twelfth evening it is accompanied by the kumbha which will remain tightly fastened to it for three days. The kumbha clearly stands for the goddess and is carried by her priest. The other paṇṭāram stands aside, because he has not been given any yajñopavīta nor any protective thread. One more weapon of the main pūcāri each time he has to carry the post is the whip, which we find in many situations where it symbolizes the rope to tie the sacrificial animal to the Vedic yūpa. In other versions of this ritual, like Beck's Kannapuram Māriyamman festival, a marriage is suggested between the post and the kumbha. Here there is no other sign of marriage than the placing and tying of the kumbha on the forked post. The goddess would thus seem compelled to stay on top of it for three days, the suggestion being that this marriage is forced upon the unwilling goddess, and the yajñopavīta given to the paṇṭāram to make him a Brahman priest temporarily to perform that mock marriage. It tallies quite closely with the widespread story of Karnataka, in which the goddess is a Brahman girl whose parents marry her by mistake to a low caste buffalo meat-eating boy. As a result she will be reborn as a goddess and the buffalo will be her attendant. In Beck's study and in a neighboring Māriyamman temple, a small stone stands permanently in that hole where the post is to be planted for three days, and is dug out every year and put aside. In each place this is a Karuppu. Karuppu's liking for water also helps identify him with the Buffalo Demon Mahiṣāsura. He has not given up his function as yūpa, because all three rams have been offered at the foot of this post, including the middle one clearly offered to the goddess.

One more detail should also be noticed. At the time of planting the wooden post, the village headman kills a ram and puts its head for a while in the hole where the post will be planted. Three days later, the pūcāri, in a trance, removes the post and puts the head of the third ram killed by the village headman into the hole. He crushes this head at the bottom of the hole before filling the hole with mud. The act of crushing in itself might have a meaning. The horse sacrifice is included in three days of Soma sacrifice, for which a plant is crushed and its juice extracted, and in which animals are also killed. In the *Mahābhārata* the clearest transformation of this rite on the battlefield is the death of Abhimanyu, whose head is crushed with a mace by Duḥśāsana's son. Abhimanyu, son of Arjuna and nephew of Kṛṣṇa, was the heir to the throne of the Soma dynasty and is the incarnation of Soma the Moon, or of Somavarcas, Moonlight. This horrible crushing seems to point to Abhimanyu as the Soma victim. The same thing might have happened to Duryodhana, after the breaking of his thighs, had Yudhiṣṭhira not stopped Bhīma when the latter was about to crush Duryodhana's head with his foot. Duryodhana also considered himself the heir of the Somavaṃśa. So in this crushing of the ram's head, there may be a forgotten trace of the Soma ritual in which the horse sacrifice was inserted.

Finally, we must notice one more thing about Māriyamman. She permanently wears a *tāli* and so is considered as a married woman. But very few people are willing to give more information about her husband. The gurukkaḷ of the neighboring Śiva temple was the only one to assert that Māriyamman was the same as Reṇukā, wife of the *muni* Jamadagni. During the three days she is sitting on the post she is considered as the wife of Mahiṣāsura. The rest of the year she is more or less consciously the wedded wife of the Brahman Jamadagni rather than his widow. But the ritual helps us to understand why. In the Thanjavur district, the prototype for her suitor Kāttavarāyan is Arjuna Kārtavīrya, the oppressive king of the classical myth, a king of certain marshy regions with Māhiṣmati (Rich in buffaloes) as his capital. But Kāttavarāyan was punished by impalement. Here, according to the local myth of Māriyamman, she was the victim of Mahiṣāsura or Karuppu. But nobody compels people to consider her a widow for the rest of the year. She may still be the wife of a living husband. Right from the *Mahābhārata* onwards, she has been the wife of Jamadagni, this unusually wrathful Brahman husband. One day he had her beheaded for a minor fault. Her son Paraśurāma did the beheading, but got his mother soon revived by his father. This is like an announcement of Arjuna Kārtavīrya's harassment and of the great slaughter of Kṣatriyas by Paraśurāma. The princess-goddess is the symbol of a kingdom and of the whole earth provided she has married the right king, that is, a good Kṣatriya respectful of Brahmans. The fire-pots, it seems to me, are clear symbols of the Brahman husband, that "all-devouring fire" (*Jamadagni*) impersonated by several epic figures, most notably the Brahman of the Khāṇḍava forest, a form taken by Agni himself as the fire that seeks to burn everything on earth, as in one of Kārtavīrya's stories. That is what the ritual has to say. Māriyamman-Reṇukā is harrassed by two suitors, her legitimate but Brahman husband, and either Kārtavīrya, demonic king of a marshy and unhealthy place, or Mahiṣāsura, who could be given the same definition. In both situations she is anything but the happy queen of a happy kingdom. That is why she has to be alone as a warrior goddess in her temple, but with the help of subordinate warriors.

We thus arrive at two conclusions, or two answers to two different questions. One concerns the demons turned into devotees. The demons are not a portion of the world's inhabitants that must be exterminated to the last. The world cannot live without them even if they stand on the impure side of society. They are needed, just as, for instance, the cesspool cleaner is needed. But they must behave themselves, and respect the world-dharma and their own dharma. In the case of Reṇukā, the situation is even more complex because as a princess she married a Brahman hermit who could not allow her to act as a princess. A Brahman king is a catastrophe, although if he acts as a Brahman, he is necessary to the world. As a princess, Reṇukā could also not marry a low caste man, for this again would violate the dharma. But a princess, because of what she symbolizes in the world, is always a temptation to all men from the top to the bottom of society, although only a dharmic king is allowed to marry her. It is not by chance that the deep link between lower and higher castes, pure and impure, is evinced by the goddess's worship. She obviously does not like meat, though princes are meat-eaters; in this way pure people may accept her, but because of her princely status, she needs help from impure, meat-eating castes, who are impersonated by the demons she has fought victoriously. In this way also, the impure side of society admits its subordination to the pure side.

As to our second point, it is not so surprising to unearth some scraps, almost beyond recognition, of the Vedic horse sacrifice, particularly in an area where the *Mahābhārata* seems to be so much alive even nowadays. The *Mahābhārata*, which concerns itself so deeply with the fight for dharma and provides the first known versions of the story of Reṇukā, Jamadagni, and Rāma Jāmadagnya, has also made great use of the horse sacrifice motif. Rāma Jāmadagnya himself performed an Aśvamedha after killing all the Kṣatriyas, but his Brahmanhood did not allow him to rule over the earth. He gave the whole earth to other Brahmans who were not able to rule either. Then too, the epic war itself makes use of distorted episodes of the horse sacrifice in order to bring about a complete destruction of the Kṣatriyas. The princess Draupadī, no warrior herself because she has husbands to fight, is given as the cause of this destruction. At the end, the victorious Pāṇḍavas, unable to complete this horse sacrifice on the level of the war, are left with no other choice than to perform another Aśvamedha, this time supposedly a ritual one although it looks rather far from the pattern of the sūtras. When a horse sacrifice has been interrupted by the death of the horse, a new horse should be selected at once and another Aśvamedha started.

It seems that it is very difficult to cut Hinduism into two irreconcilable parts. On the contrary, a local goddess cult says one must look to the whole.

NOTES

1. See especially Madeleine Biardeau, "L'arbre *śamī* et le buffle sacrificiel," in Biardeau, ed., *Autour de la déesse hindoue, Puruṣārtha* 5 (1981), 215-243.

2. Madeleine Biardeau, *Histoire de poteaux: variations védiques autour de la Déesse* (Paris: Bulletin de L'École Française d'Extrême Orient, forthcoming).

3. The conventional "offering pedestal," or "altar," that is usually set outside the entrance to a temple.

4. The cāmiyāṭi is the man who "dances the god (or the goddess)." He is not often of the same caste as the priest, who anyway ranks higher than he. As a rule he is associated with the animal sacrifice of a festival.

5. The śūla is usually Śiva's weapon, mostly when it is three-pronged (triśūla). The use here of this mobile śūla as an impalement stake, nearby the usual kalumaram, may not be totally explained by Śiva's presence: it has a classical model in the *Mahābhārata* (Citraśāla Press Edition 16.1.30; Poona Critical Edition 15.2.19). There Kṛṣṇa threatens his people with this same punishment on the śūla if they disobey his orders. The epic as well knows of Śiva as Śūlin, the "holder of the śūla weapon." Nowadays, the kalumaram itself it often called śūla.

6. Rice cooked in milk in an open mud pot over an open fire until it boils over, an auspicious sign of plentifulness.

7. This means that the Brahman is a devotee of Vīrakāḷi by personal choice.

8. This type of cult is found in a small area which includes Kannapuram, whose Māriyamman festival has been studied by Brenda Beck (see below, n. 9). It was at Perundurai (Periyar District, Erode Taluk) in the Cellaṇṭi Amman temple, on January 29, 1987, the day of Tai *amāvasyā*, that I by chance attended an oracular ritual of an unusual type. It would not be easily understood outside this area. A Vēḷāḷar Kavuṇṭar, a well-known cattle merchant of the place, had brought a small mare inside the temple and, after a *pradakṣiṇa*, placed her quite close to the shrine door and facing it. The animal was pure white all over. Her owner held her with a rope adorned with some flowers. The paṇṭāram priest came out and put a garland on the mare's neck. After a small pūjā, the merchant asked a question for which an answer was expected from the goddess through the mare. The priest poured out some water on the four hoofs of the animal, then on its back at two or three spots. The mare shook her head without too much energy. But that was not what the interested witnesses expected from her. After shaking off the water drops and after a few minutes of tense silence, the mare was supposed to quiver all over her body, obviously because of the remaining coolness of the water. But the movement did not seem to be initiated by the animal. It was to appear all of a sudden, and *that* was to be the answer to the merchant's anxious question (in fact this confusion between shaking and quivering often shows in the descriptions of animal sacrifices: I have attended ram and goat sacrifices where it was the quivering

that was expected, and not so easy to get as the shaking). That day it happened that the goddess-mare was not very cooperative and there was even some bargaining between her and the devotee: if I cannot achieve this within one year, shall we make it two years? I personally saw the mare quiver without any doubt, but it was not considered sufficient. Then the owner, obviously cross with the goddess, decided to repeat the whole process: pūjā, water pouring and silent expectation of the answer (plus the unavoidable *dakṣiṇā*, no doubt). Once more the result was not considered satisfactory, but the merchant stopped after three trials, anxious and tense as he was. Notwithstanding the ill will of the goddess on that auspicious day, a friend of the owner was eager to benefit from the same oracle and began with prostrating himself in front of the goddess's *mūrti* (icon) in order to establish a link. The mare was standing by his side. But the owner kept the rope in his hands, as if to assert his privileged relationship with the goddess-mare through the pūcāri. Every Friday the mare may hold the same role in the temple.

In this example, the mare is said to be possessed by the goddess. She is her medium, and that capacity of hers is active in the context of an elementary ritual that reproduces a sacrificial process having its source in the Aśvamedha. The Kāḷi festival has greatly helped in bringing this link to light.

9. See Brenda E. F. Beck, "The Goddess and the Demon: A Local South Indian Festival in its Wider Context," in Madeleine Biardeau, ed., *Autour de la déesse hindoue, Puruṣārtha* 5 (1981), 83-136.

2

Outcaste, Guardian, and Trickster: Notes on the Myth of Kāttavarāyan

David Dean Shulman

Ho incontrato il divino
in forme e modi
che ho sottratto al demonico
senza sentirme ladro.
—*Eugenio Montale*

In the rogues' gallery of popular divine or semi-divine heroes who figure so prominently in the village cults of southern India, the outrageous, protean figure of Kāttavarāyan occupies a place of enviable eminence. His cult, originally centered, it would seem, in Tiruccirāppaḷḷi District, extends through Tañcāvūr and South Arcot (although he is also known further south). His myth is recorded in what is perhaps the longest and most lurid of all such accounts of popular divinities, the *Kāttavarāya Cuvāmi Katai*,[1] as well as in other popular sources such as the the *Kāttavarāyan Caṇṭai ennum Kāttamuttu Nāṭakam*.[2] Underlying these printed sources there seems to be (or to have been) an original oral epic, or perhaps a series of epic-like ballads, similar to those recently recorded and discussed by Brenda Beck and Gene Roghair.[3] At times one senses the presence of this primary, oral text behind the shared phrasing, formulae, and themes in the two works just mentioned, which diverge sharply in their presentations of the plot and its development. Moreover, the printed text of the *Kāttavarāya Cuvāmi Katai* is often elliptical and obscure—perhaps as the result of the process of transferring an oral original to a written medium.[4] Clearly, we must look for oral versions of the Kāttavarāyan story, and any interpretations offered solely on the basis of the inadequate printed materials can only be tentative. We eagerly await the results of Eveline Masilamani-Meyer's current research on Kāttavarāyan as well as her complete translation of the text of the *katai*.

The following remarks are based in the main on the *Kāttavarāya Cuvāmi Katai*, although I shall cite material from the *Nāṭakam* as well. Even in its present, problematic state, the *Katai* is an extraordinarily rich text susceptible to analysis on many levels and from many points of view. Each of the major divisions of the text merits a detailed study, and the work as a whole needs to be seen in relation to similar ballads of this genre such as the *Maturaivīracuvāmi Katai* and the *Cuṭalaimāṭa-cuvāmi Kātai* and *vilpāṭṭus*.[5] There are important historical issues raised by the text and relating to the development of the Kāttavarāyan cult: for example, the persistent identification of the hero with Murukan. Certain of these issues will be touched upon here, but I shall concentrate more on the overall organization of the Kāttavarāyan myth and its semantics within the context of Tamil village religion. How are we to understand the role of this rather unpalatable deity whose cruel, violent pranks comprise the main substance of his myth?[6] Let us begin by briefly reviewing the complicated circumstances of Kāttavarāyan's birth (or rather births) as described in the frame-story with which the text opens.

A brief note, first, on the organization and external features of the text. After the invocations (to Vināyaka and Sarasvatī), the conventional apology for faulty learning and mistakes in Tamil (*avaiya-ṭakkam*), and the introductory frame-narration (pp. 5-41), the text is divided into 13 cantos (*vanam*). Each vanam begins with at least one invocation, in which we often find significant epithets of the ballad's hero inserted into an appeal to Vināyaka (to help the poet sing his story). The text defines itself as a *katai*, but its affinities lie with the metrical *mālai* compositions, most of which seem to date, at least in their present form, to the 18th and 19th centuries in Tamil Nadu.[7] The language of the text is heavily formulaic and tends toward the colloquial; late Urdu loan-words, misspellings, and various dialect features abound.

A. The Frame: Rakṣā, Rebirth, and a Father's Curse

The story opens with a test: Pārvatī doubted Śiva's claim that he gave sustenance (*paṭiyaḷakka*) each day to all living beings. She locked an ant in a casket; and when she opened the box the following day, she found the ant grasping tiny grains of paddy with its mouth. Now she was afraid and rushed to Śiva to ask for a means of atoning for her doubt. He sent her to create a luxurious flower garden on the bank of the Ganges near Kāśī. But who was there to guard the garden? Pārvatī rejected Śiva's first suggestions: "Gaṇapati will not do it, and Velan (Murukan) has become a whoremonger (*kūttikkaḷḷan*)." So Śiva created a child and sent him to guard his mother's garden.[8]

One day the Seven Maidens (*kannimār*) came from Kailāsa to bathe in the Ganges. They entered the garden and picked its flowers; then, leaving their clothes on the river bank, they went to bathe. The boy-guardian, incensed at the theft of his garden's flowers, hid the dress of the youngest girl. When the loss was discovered, the six other *kannimār* hastened back to Kailāsa to complain to Śiva, who came down at once, riding his bull together with Pārvatī. They found the boy standing in a *carakkonrai* tree. Asked to explain his theft of the girl's dress, he boldly declared, "I took the girl's flower-garment (*pūvāṭai*) because of *their* theft of the flowers!" But Śiva cursed him and called him an Untouchable. Now Pārvatī intervened and, looking at him with love, gave him a boon—he would not die in the burning-ground (*vekācuṭa-laiyile cākā varam*, p. 10). Śiva was now even angrier, and he cursed Pārvatī to lose her place in the left half of his body; she would become a demoness (*pēy, iruci, picācu, alakai*, all mentioned here). Terrified, Pārvatī asked when the curse would end; the god promised that it would end, and that she would be reunited with him, when the child was impaled on a stake (*kaḻu*). With this, Śiva departed for Kailāsa.

Mother and son were now left to confront one another. "Because of you I have been cursed," said Pārvatī; "and when will it end?—when you have been born four times and come seeking me."[9] She then bestowed on him the gift of knowing his former births and a host of Yama's demon-servants (*pūtakaṇam*). The child went north, to the shrine of Oṭṭapiḷḷaiyār, to be born (pp. 6-9).[10]

Before we follow him in his first births, let us note the outstanding themes of this introduction (the first half of the frame-story). It is surely striking that this myth of the guardian-gatekeeper of the goddess—as we find Kāttavarāyan in Tañcāvūr shrines of Māriyamman—opens with a double example of the theme of guarding or protecting (*rakṣā*). The initial, activating impulse in the story is Pārvatī's unsettling doubt about Śiva's ability to provide a universal protection and sustenance; the entire epic tale of earthly births, violation, and grisly sacrifice unfolds from this first moment of skepticism. The second stage, still firmly located in the divine sphere (the goddess's garden on the way to Kāśī), again calls up the theme of guarding: we meet our hero for the first time, born precisely to fill this function, because neither of his brothers is felt to be capable of doing so. (Incidentally, this is one of the few points in the text where a distinction is drawn between Kāttavarāyan and Murukan; elsewhere they are simply identified). As we shall see, the text is largely concerned with defining and discussing this very theme, i.e., with the nature and function of the guardian-gatekeeper, or of the boundary-zone that he constitutes around the central goddess. As the *Nāṭakam* explicitly states (16), one finds here an explantion for the hero's name: although Madeleine Biardeau has astutely noted a link between Kāttavarāyan and the epic-purāṇic figure of Kārtavīrya-Arjuna (and this link does exist openly in the fifth canto of our text, as we shall see), there seems no reason to doubt the tradition's own etymology of the hero's title—from *kā*, "to preserve, shelter, watch, guard, ward off, rescue, wait for."[11] Kāttavarāyan would then be the "guardian-king." Indeed, many other epithets applied to him in the text seem to be clearly built around participial forms of the same form (thus Kāttamunicāmi, p. 50; Vanaṅkāttacāmi, p. 49; Kāttavanār, *passim;* cf. Kāttān as a local deity name in Tamil Nadu).

But this guardian's fate is, from the beginning, problematic and laden with injustice. Following his duty and, we may add, the mythic precedent associated with Kṛṣṇa, he attempts a reprisal against the girl who has stolen flowers from the garden. The result is his father's unyielding and, it would seem, exaggerated curse. The always tenuous balance in Śiva's nuclear family is, as often, demolished, and events quickly escalate to the point of a seemingly incurable asymmetry and disharmony: although the conditions for a future restoration are, as usual, stated almost at once, the gravity of the situation is apparent in the violence prescribed for its redress. Pārvatī, seeking to mitigate the effects of Śiva's intervention, is exiled from the god's androgynous embrace; only the sacrifice of her son can heal the rift. The god disappears, having shattered not only his own wholeness but also, it would seem, that of the world: a dynamic imbalance and lack of symmetry now propel the leading figures through their transformations—the goddess turns to a violent asceticism, the son to an endless series of pranks, attacks, and other excesses. The story proper can begin.

It is very striking that the disturbance in the divine realm, indeed, in the normal composition of the deity himself, results from an act perceived in human terms as obviously unjust, that is, Śiva's unwarranted punishment of the guardian for acting out his natural role. The *Nāṭakam* chooses to emphasize precisely this perspective on the origin of Kāttavarāyan's checkered career; as the hero heads north toward his new birthplace, immediately after Śiva's curse and his dialogue with his mother, he sings a song:

> Because I guarded the garden,
> this curse came to me.
> Now I must put on a grand show
> in this earthly world.
> I will display my magic tricks
> and ruin the Brahman's family. . . .
> My magic will flourish,
> my names will be known
> through all the eight points of the compass.
> I will ruin round-eyed women
> with my power.
> If anyone challenges me
> I will play my tricks—
> and I shall serve women
> with love.[12]

Kāttavarāyan's magical pranks are clearly directed toward an antinomian goal, the destruction of the Brahman's family and of the "round-eyed" women he desires; both elements, the hero's anti-Brahmanism and his obsession with ravishing beautiful women, are persistent features of Kāttavarāyan's myth. At the same time, there is a note of service—not, perhaps, entirely ironic. And the whole identity now brazenly assumed by the child god and hero is explained in terms of the curse that sought him out and that seemingly inspires his angry, exhibitionistic drives. If Kāttavarāyan is, as we shall see, a kind of South Indian Trickster, the narrator still finds it necessary to reveal the logic that underlines this role. What is more, this logic seems very close to the basic theme of a tragic injustice—very often a premature death—that pervades many Tamil village myths of apotheosis and thus explains the origin of local deities.[13]

The double-edged role of the guardian; a dynamic imbalance and destabilization in the relations between Śiva, his wife, and their son; and the notion of an original injustice leading to dramatic and, perhaps, tragic effects—we can follow these threads through the length of the Kāttavarāyan story. But let us return, for the moment, to the frame story, which now shifts to the geographical heartland of Kāttavarāyan's myth, the villages of Puttūrakam or Putturaṅkam[14] and Ōmantūr in Trichy District.

Kāttavarāyan took the form of a lime floating on the water of the river beside Oṭṭapiḷḷaiyār's shrine in Puttūrakam. A Brahman girl who came to draw water ate the fruit and became ten months pregnant; as she was about to throw herself into the water, the child fell from her womb. She abandoned him in sorrow, and a Paraiya woman found him and took him home; but when her hut caught on fire from the baby's crying, the child had to be taken back to the Piḷḷaiyār shrine and left there. This was Kāttavarāyan's first earthly birth. He was next born from the womb of a deer that came to graze beside Kāḷi's shrine; the low-caste Valaiyan Civapputaiyān, servant to King Āriyappūrājan, adopted the baby and brought him up to the age of five. At that point Kāttavarāyan, already aware of his true identity, announced to his distressed and loving father that he was going to seek his mother. Carrying an ox-goad (*tārrukkōl*), he wandered in the direction of Ōmantūr, where the goddess Kāmākṣī was standing in penance under an enormous banyan tree on the bank of the Kampā River.[15] Tormented by hunger, he struck down a bird from the tree, which cried out to Kāmākṣī as it fell; the goddess now opened her third eye, in her forehead, and reduced her new-found son to ash. He became, first, a branch growing out of the ash, and then an infant in her arms.[16]

Kāmākṣī, wondering how she could bring up this child, fashioned a swing for him from the branches of the banyan. But the Seven Maidens from Kolli Mountain (*kollimalaikanniyarkaḷ*) came there and took the child from his all-too-willing mother. They instructed him in magic (*intirajālam, mantirajālam*), taught him how to go from one body to another and similar skills. Once again, at the age of five Kāttavarāyan insisted on returning to his "true" mother. He worshiped her with flowers—this formulaic scene will now recur at each of their subsequent meetings—and she blessed him, kissed him, warned him of her eye's terrible power, and prophesied: "You will ravage the virgins of this realm (*maṇṭalattu kannikaḷ*) in this Kali Age" (*Katai*, p. 24).

Kāmākṣī's prophecy is not, of course, an idle speculation; it may be said to define our hero's major interest. Meanwhile, the specific focus of his future activity has already come into being: Āriyappūrājan, hearing of the child "born" to his servant Civapputaiyān, sent his Brahman temple-priest (*kurukkaḷ*) to perform acts of worship and tapas in order to attain a child. The priest, Appāpaṭṭan, worshiped Śiva, Viṣṇu (Śrīraṅganāyaka), and Brahmā, and these gods gave him a lime, impregnated with the life of the youngest of the Seven Maidens, to feed to his wife, Annattuḷaciyammāḷ. She gave birth to a beautiful daughter, Āriyamālai. The astrologers foretold that she would be captured by the lord (*tēvan*) when she reached the age of sixteen, so Āriyappūrājan built twenty-one fortresses around her, to be guarded by thousands of watchmen under the command of Civapputaiyān.[17] The Brahman girl herself, enclosed within the rich pleasure gardens inside the walls, was renowned for her beauty and, in particular, for her remarkable hair (*kūntal*), which was divided into no less than sixty-three plaits, each like golden thread; a thousand servants were required simply to lift up this mass of hair.[18]

The major dramatis personae have now put in their first appearances, with one exception—Toṭṭiyattuccinnān, Kāttavarāyan's bosom companion and alter ego. Cinnān is a Toṭṭiyān magician from Kerala, always the land of black magic in Tamil folklore; conquered in the course of a magic contest by Kāttavarāyan, with the help of the shepherd-girl Karuppalaki who later becomes one of Kāttavarāyan's brides,[19] Cinnān accompanies Kāttavarāyan on most of his escapades. He is there when our hero falls in love, inevitably, with Āriyamālai: the two friends find her bathing in rivers of turmeric; Kāttavarāyan takes the form of a fish in order to see her and is then trapped in the endless strands of her hair. Cinnān, in the form of a Garuḍa, disentangles him and saves him (pp. 33-36). But the hero's emotional entanglement with the Brahman girl is already complete and now forms the major theme of the entire poem. The initial image of Kāttavarāyan as a fish trapped in Āriyamālai's hair suggests the subsequent unfolding of the plot: the story revolves around the forbidden connection between the high-caste Āriyamālai and the Untouchable hero (in this respect Kāttavarāyan is identified with his foster-father, Civapputaiyān, the Valaiyan-Talaiyāri; and the unclean associations of the fisherman—one of the Valaiyan occupations—are surely germane to the image selected here). Note, too, that the girl's very name resonates with the purity of the Ārya Brahmans and their culture; born to a kurukkaḷ—not, incidentally, on a par with the Smārtas[20]—she is also described as the daughter of a thousand *vaidika* Brahmans. Moreover, she is in effect adopted by the king, who has an equally high-sounding title, Āriyappūrājan.[21] Kāttavarāyan will persistently challenge the Brahmans and their royal protector, and humiliate them, in his relentless pursuit of Āriyamālai.

B. Sexual Politics and the Antinomian Hero

His problems begin, however, closer to home. Throughout the text, Kāttavarāyan has to argue and plead with his mother, Kāmākṣī, who seeks to divert his attention from Āriyamālai and thus save him from the sacrificial death that she sees as the inevitable outcome of his infatuation with her. It is important to remember that Kāmākṣī has, in effect, a vested interest in her son's eventual impalement, for the conditions of *her* curse make that event the prerequisite for her return to her husband Śiva. Nevertheless, she continually warns Kāttavarāyan *not* to pursue the Brahman girl because of the terrible danger involved. There is an interesting ambivalence here which may also be reflected in the internal relationships of this triad, which seem often to incorporate a dynamic of simultaneous repulsion and attraction. The prototypical conversation on this subject between the reluctant mother and her ardent son occurs at the very end of the frame-story, after Kāttavarāyan has seen Āriyamālai for the first time and declared his passion for her to his mother. He asks Kāmākṣī's permission to capture the girl; but the goddess replies, "She is the daughter of a Brahman (*ayan makaḷ*), from the highest *jāti;* you are the son of a Śaiva mendicant (*āṇṭi*).[22] Brahmanicide will overcome you, evil (*pāpam*) and disgrace will be yours, evil *karma* will come to you. Don't take this *pattini*—more a pattini than your mother—for your wife." But Kāttavarāyan has already stated his preference: "Only dead logs (*kaṭṭai*—also funeral logs, or a stake!) are with you; thought and life (*karutt'ellām . . . jīvan ellām*) are with Mālai." Kāmākṣī now launches into a detailed description of the forts and gardens that surround Āriyamālai; he has no hope of penetrating this vast armed camp. Then, to make things entirely explicit: "With this girl an impaling-stake (kalumaram) was born. The stake is growing by itself, untouched by the carpenter's chisel. . . . Why be burnt dry on a stake? Why should you writhe and die on the fisherman's hook (*tūṇṭil*)?[23] Must I be abused by everyone who sees you impaled, who will identify you as 'Kāmākṣī's son'? Forget the very name of Mālai, my son." But Kāttavarāyan is beyond persuading: "Let the impaling-stake come, let the fish-hook come—it is enough if the girl (*kanni*) comes to me. I am ready to suffer punishment and pain, for I am tormented by this endless lust for the woman" (pp. 37-41).

Usually these conversations end with Kāmākṣī's setting her son a trial—to draw a picture of Āriyamālai; to bring Kāmākṣī a piece of silk cloth from her braid, her pearl necklace, and her ring; to ruin the purity of the Brahmans in the village; to destroy the tapas of the Seven Maidens, etc. Each of these trials forms the subject of one of the subsections of the text; and in each case, of course, Kāttavarāyan is successful and therefore returns to press his demand for Kāmākṣī's blessing in his dubious romance. To the very end, she is reluctant to sanction his attack on the Brahman girl, although on another level she seems increasingly aware of, and unable to challenge any longer, the fact of his approaching impalement. Death on the stake is Kāttavarāyan's appointed fate (*viti*) or head-writing (*talaiviti*), as Kāmākṣī clearly recognizes and eventually states (see p. 175). This is the theme of ambivalence noted earlier: we should observe that several of the trials that Kāmākṣī sets her son are also seductive, in that they require contact with Āriyamālai (as well as with Kāmākṣī) and thus serve to feed the fire that is to consume our hero. Kāttavarāyan receives a contradictory message of encouragement and discouragement from his mother. This confusing double message is then reflected in one of the most striking elements in the entire narrative, that is, the complete lack of resolution in the tensions of the sexual triad at the heart of the tale.

Let us briefly plot these tensions as they unfold in the narrative. Kāttavarāyan wants Āriyamālai and is prepared to sacrifice everything to attain her, but to the end he defers to his mother's authority and seeks her permission; although he becomes impatient with Kāmākṣī, even has her bound in ropes and humiliated (pp. 160-62), and eventually decides to steal Āriyamālai on his own initiative, *without* his mother's consent, no sooner has he done so than he brings his stolen bride to Kāmākṣī, worships his mother's feet with the usual offering of flowers, and once again seeks her blessing (p. 174). Kāttavarāyan may be prepared to mount the stake, but he is clearly *not* able or willing to choose between his mother and his bride. The tension here remains constant. On the other hand, it is important to notice that the two female figures are *not* conflated (as they seem to be to some extent in the Tamil *sthalapurāṇa* literature and, according to Gananath Obeyesekere's analysis, in the Pattini mythology[24]); rather, wife and mother seem to functioin here as two opposed poles between which the indecisive hero unsuccessfully oscillates. Indeed, the basic opposition reproduces itself with reference to much larger sets of female characters, whose relations with Kāttavarāyan can be clearly mapped out. Like Murukan, with whom he is identified, Kāttavarāyan has multiple mothers. Aside from Kāmākṣī, there is the Brahman girl who first gives him birth (and subsequently disappears from the story completely); the Paraiya woman who adopts him (also lost to the story thereafter); a separate goddess Kāḷi, or more specifically Vallatu Māṅkāḷiyamman, to whom Kāmākṣī sends him (as having a greater power than hers, p. 125) and who attacks him, eventually swallows him, emits him again as a young child, and then instructs him in having a properly decorated stake prepared (pp. 126-31); and, finally, the Seven Maidens of Kollimalai, who adopt him and teach him magic and who continue to play an important part in his adventures thereafter. This last group provides a close tie to the Murukan mythology[25] as well as the one figure who seems partly to bridge the opposition mentioned earlier—that of the youngest Maiden (*iḷaiya kanni*, parallel to the seventh and always anomalous Kṛttikā) who actually falls in love with Kāttavarāyan. The story, told in the tenth canto, may be briefly summarized:

> Kāmākṣī sent Kāttavarāyan to destroy the tapas of the Seven Maidens, who had been standing on one leg, with their eyes closed, eating only the wind, for twelve years on the top of Kolli Mountain. Cinnān refused, at first, to help him, but he did make Kāttavarāyan a lute with which he sang to the women: "It is for me," he sang, "that you have been torturing yourselves for so long." The youngest Maiden recognized the truth of this satement and announced that the god had at last come for them from Kailāsa. The Seven Maidens came down from their mountain, but Kāttavarāyan fled from them, taking many forms—a tortoise, a goat, an ant, an ear-ring, a mouse. They also transformed themselves in order to chase him. Waiting for him to emerge from a hiding-place, they climbed coconut trees and ate the fruit. Kāttavarāyan sent Cinnān, disguised as a watchman, to catch them and bring them before Kāttavarāyan in his disguise as Civapputaiyān (his father). He sentenced them to be tied to a tree and beaten for having taken the garden's fruit.
>
> Taking the form of a colorful parrot, "Raṅkaiyan," he spoke to the Maidens, sat in the hand of the youngest, and was embraced and kissed by her. They went to bathe in the ocean of milk, and he promised to guard their clothes—but no sooner were they in the ocean than he stole their sarees from them. . . .[26] Burning with anger, they chased him to curse him, but he ran quickly to Kāmākṣī without daring to look back at them. She transformed him into a baby rocking in a swing made from branches of the banyan. When the Maidens arrived there and demanded to see Kāttavarāyan, she opened her third eye and turned them into seven stones (pp. 142-59).

This summary hardly does justice to the colorful metamorphoses and playful ironies of the text, but we may at least notice the repetition of the garden sequence from the frame story—with the innovation here of the hero's complete emancipation from any external control, including that of his father Śiva. His revenge could hardly be more complete. Once again he steals the Maidens' clothes (this time not only those of the youngest) in a patent imitation of the Kṛṣṇa myth, but this time they have no recourse; they end up in the form in which they are often worshiped in the villages, as seven stones. Kāttavarāyan achieves this result by becoming an infant beside his mother Kāmākṣī—a common enough solution to unbearable sexual tension in South Indian myth and folklore.[27] Here the tension seems to arise from the erotic role that Kāttavarāyan plays with relation to the responsive seventh Maiden, who admits her love for him and even unwittingly embraces him, although she clearly remains in some sense one of his mothers (and we should recall that she is also partly identified with Āriyamālai, born from a lime impregnated with the seventh Maiden's life-force). All in all, this complex linkage—mother and lover, chaste but voluptuous ascetic maiden—is unacceptable and even dangerous, as we learn not only from the episode's conclusion but also from the motif, commonly applied to the kannimār in village traditions, of the forbidden vision (thus the hero does not dare look back at them).[28] There is simply no room for the ambiguous eroticism here to find release; rather, it is quite literally petrified and thus defused, to the prankster-hero's great relief. We may also note the signal irony, a conventional one, involved in the young girl's recognition of Kāttavarāyan as her lover—for he is, indeed, the god for whom they have been yearning throughout the years of penance, even if he appears in an unanticipated and, in this case, thoroughly frustrating guise.[29]

Balancing this rather heavy load of maternal attention—Kāmākṣī, Kāḷi, and the Seven kannis—are three categories of wives. The central figure, as we have seen, is the forbidden Brahman girl, Āriyamālai—as "untouchable" by him as he is in *her* eyes. (Kāmākṣī several times pointedly refers to her as "untouchable fire.") Then there are two Ceṭṭi (merchant class) girls, Ukantalaki, whom Kāttavarāyan kidnaps in Canto 6, and Annamuttu, whose story is missing from our text but who appears prominently with the other wives in the impalement scene at the end.[30] Working our way down the social scale, we now arrive at Kāttavarāyan's cross cousin, hence his predetermined wife, Karuppalaki—the shepherd girl who saves his life at the beginning, during his contest with Cinnān and the latter's father in Kerala. Karuppalaki plays against Kāttavarāyan in a *malyuttam*, a contest involving goats, then cocks, then quail; she wins twice but loses the third trial, chases him into the temple where he is hiding, and, when he appears to her as Murukan, begs him to marry her. She, too, appears on the scene of the impalement together with the Seven Karuppans. She is seen as the daughter of Perumāḷ-Viṣṇu (hence the cross cousin tie, for Kāttavarāyan is the son of Viṣṇu's sister Kāmākṣī), and her father is apparently linked with the Tamil folk deity Karuppan or Karuppaṇṇacuvāmi (see pp. 117-22).[31] In addition to these major figures there are two excluded women whom Kāttavarāyan toys with and defeats—the washerwoman Vaṇṇāravalli (Vaṇṇaranalli in the *Nāṭakam*) and a demonic queen, Campaṅkitāci (pp. 97-100). Both die at our hero's hands, the former after a rather brutal trick (and after arrangements for her marriage to Kāttavarāyan are under way), the latter after a game of dice (another area in which Kāttavarāyan excels).

Having outlined this luxuriant series of women who attract the attentions of our hero, we may wonder about the relative paucity of male figures in the story. The only truly prominent and positive male is Kāttavarāyan's magician-companion, Cinnān the Toṭṭiyān. We should recall that the hero's troubles all begin with his father's vindictive curse, and that his second father, Civapputaiyān—note that there is a least a doubling here, although it fails to match the multiplicity of mothers—functions as Kāttavarāyan's outstanding opponent, the guardian of Āriyamālai (and as such the object of the hero's attacks and cruel practical jokes). We might thus describe the plot as a struggle in which the low caste hero, aided by his low caste friend and alter ego, is pitted against his father (or fathers) in his love for a high caste, hence unattainable woman—a love condemned by his divine mother and leading inexorably toward tragedy. Given these basic conditions of the plot, and despite the violence and cruelty described throughout, especially in Kāttavarāyan's relations with women, we might sense in this hero a peculiar brand of innocence. His doomed struggle, after all, is ultimately (and unfairly) derived from the initial fracture in Śiva's wholeness of being, a fracture which precedes Kāttavarāyan's birth and which produces the tortuous ambiguities of his guardian's role. With the deck stacked against him, as it were, Kāttavarāyan becomes a kind of wild card, an unpredictable joker obsessed with overcoming his low position, hostile to the oppressive world of social limits but unable finally to escape its compulsions. He is saturated with ambivalence—powerfully attracted to the various female figures but also repelled by them; never able to resolve their conflicting claims upon him; driven upward toward the untouchable Brahman girl (who, as we shall see, continues to elude him) even as he continues to give vent to his fundamental anti-Brahmanical (or anti-hierarchical) feelings. The underlying theme is one of alienation—of man from woman, son from mother, son from malevolent father—an alienation which proceeds from and reflects the initial act of self-division within the godhead (Pārvatī's doubt, separation and exile from Śiva's androgynous wholeness) and which results in the son's inability to integrate another being, especially a high female being, into his life.[32] Although he has, as we shall see, certain striking elements of personal autonomy, Kāttavarāyan remains, in another sense, trapped in an antithetical mode.

How does this story, reduced here to its barest skeleton, compare with those of other Tamil "criminal" heroes? Clearly, a major element is the recurring theme of violation, the attack upon conventional order (especially high-caste order with its boundaries). The central symbol of violation, a symbol which Kāttavarāyan shares with Maturaivīran among others,[33] is the ultimate *mesalliance* for which he strives—Untouchable male with Brahman female. Other acts of violation accompany this central dramatic theme. To mention only one more example, there is Kāttavarāyan's brilliant humiliation of the thousand Brahman villagers: one night he brings a thousand Paraiya men to sleep beside the Brahman wives, whose husbands are simultaneously transported, still asleep, to the beds of Paraiya women; when the couples wake in the morning, they discover the trick only by the fact that each of the spouses suddenly addresses the other in the wrong dialect! To complete the hapless Brahmans' pollution, Kāttavarāyan impersonates their revered *guru* (Kācikkurukkaḷ) and leads them in a crude travesty of a Brahman *homa* ritual, using the urine of demons as sacred water and producing new sacred threads for them from a buffalo's hide (all this, incidentally, at Kāmākṣī's instigation—pp. 132-42). It would be all too easy to interpret this and similar parts of the story as no more than violent anti-Brahman satire (which is, indeed, present in the telling); but this is a temptation to be resisted if we wish to arrive at a deeper understanding of the work. What can be said is that Kāttavarāyan's assault upon order forms part of the standard dossier of the South Indian low caste hero. To the essential antinomianism we may add other features mentioned earlier—the multiple birth (frequently a descent from heaven in ambiguous circumstances); the mixed ancestry (Brahman-Untouchable, or royal-Untouchable);[34] the specific interest in ravishing a virgin, usually a high caste woman or women; the association with magic and, perhaps, the social and geographical marginality with which magic is connected; the existence of a low caste helper or companion;[35] the tragic flavor, linked to a violent, sacrificial death undergone by the hero; and the hero's position on the boundary as a guardian or gatekeeper, with the ambivalence inherent to that role. Taken together, these items present a rough profile of a prevalent type, although individual heroes may develop one of the themes to an extreme (thus Cuṭalaimāṭan, for example, extends the practice of antinomian violation to the point of indiscriminate destruction and slaughter). Still, the list does not suffice. In the case of Kāttavarāyan, at least, we have to examine a further essential trait, already mentioned earlier—that of his Trickster-like transformability and transformative power.

C. On Binding, Loosing, and the Gambler's Tricks

At first glance it would seem that Kāttavarāyan meets the three conditions—"desecration, violence, and miscegenation"—that A. K. Ramanujan has noted as leading to "the eruption of demonic divinity.[36] Certainly, as a divinity our hero is indeed close to the demonic pēy worshiped in Tamil villages, although we must also draw in certain lines of distinction.[37] But the catastrophic progression of the typical local-goddess myth in South India—in which a village woman undergoes first a violent desecration and then an equally violent apotheosis which threatens the village—is altered in the present case. Here we have no proper apotheosis. Kāttavarāyan is divine from the very beginning (and persistently identified with Murukan). In addition, he is set off from the pattern of apotheosis by his constant playfulness which, however cruel his games, adds a new dimension to the career of the low caste rebel-hero.

Let us admit at once that Kāttavarāyan is not the cosmogonic or culture-creating Trickster of North American Indian myths.[38] Nor is he a heroic Prometheus whose acts of violation ultimately benefit mankind.[39] If we need a parallel, Hermes is perhaps closer than most. In any case, Kāttavarāyan definitely shares the "funny irregularity," the comic breaking of rules (specifically linked to a low social position) that Grottanelli sees as the Trickster's central quality.[40] I follow Hastrup and Ovesen in their attempt to distinguish the Trickster from the closely related culture hero:

> The diacritical feature of the trickster as opposed to the culture hero is that of his intrinsic ambiguity. He is both human and animal, man and woman, good and bad. The trickster *is* a tricky one, whereas the culture hero completes a trick. . . . The culture hero moves from the other world to this world with a strong personal integrity while the trickster stands with one leg in each world, integrating their aspects into one person. It is a permanent transience as opposed to the transitive permanence of the culture hero.[41]

"Permanent transience" nicely characterizes Kāttavarāyan's restless motion, which finds expression in a long series of disguises and metamorphoses as he plays his pranks. He also has the Trickster's characteristic craftiness and cunning as well as his transformative skills, which operate both on others and on himself. We have already noted his association with magic and seen his propensity for assuming animal forms; and we need not be surprised to find him masquerading as as woman:

> Kāttavarāyan pleaded with his mother to give him permission to capture Āriyamālai; she sent him to ask his uncle—perhaps *he* could help. So Kāttavarāyan went looking for Perumāḷ in Dvārakā. Cinnān took the form of a wandering Kuḷḷavanṭutātan-dancer, and Kāttavarāyan became a dancing-girl, the daughter of Kāttavīryan (= Kārtavīrya). At first Perumāḷ hid from them, but when he heard of the amazing beauty of Kāttavīryan's daughter, he sent for her and pleaded for her hand in marriage; tortured by desire, he promised to give her whatever she asked. As he rushed to embrace her, she announced that she was observing a vow (*nōnpu*). He brought her a garland that never faded, the traditional gift of clothes for the bride (*kūrai*), and the *tāli* marriage-necklace. "What else do you want?" he asked, and the young lady announced: "That you unite with me at once." He closed his eyes and raised his arms, and at that moment Kāttavarāyan thought of Cinnān, who brought him a rope with which to bind Perumāḷ. Taking his own form, Kāttavarāyan now appeared before the bound Perumāḷ and demanded a boon—the boon of decorating Āriyamālai with a (wedding) garland. His uncle, ashamed, agreed and said, "Not knowing your magic, I tried to unite with you (*un māyam ariyāmal unnai maruva vanten*);" and he asked that no-one ever be told how Kāttavarāyan had bound him in this way (pp. 100-105).

This canto continues with another escapade in which Kāttavarāyan, imitating Śiva this time, appears as an old man selling bangles to Kāmākṣī, the Seven Maidens, and, finally, Āriyamālai;[42] at length he succeeds in fastening the tāli around Āriyamālai's neck, while she is asleep (pp. 105-112).

The episode, a fairly typical example of our hero's tricks, provides a noteworthy link with the important figure of Kārtavīrya—another ambiguous guardian-thief who has been studied carefully by Madeleine Biardeau.[43] Kārtavīrya turns up here in the somewhat surprising form of his supposed daughter, and the text plays happily on the obvious similarity in names (see p. 102 line 35). In fact, this technical similarity also points to deeper affinities, although the text fails to develop this theme. Its major focus in this section is on the motif of binding the god, which is one of the central, recurring motifs of the entire text and a particularly expressive indication of Kāttavarāyan's Trickster-nature. Binding and loosing is, in a sense, the very essence of his story. He is himself doubly-bound—to the world and human birth, through his father's curse, and, as we have seen, to the inaccessible Āriyamālai, through his driving passion—but each time his opponents manage to bind him physically, he easily escapes. In the present instance he humiliates his uncle and leaves him tied and ashamed in an apparent caricature of the pervasive Tamil bhakti theme of binding the god with (human) love: thus Sahadeva binds Kṛṣṇa with mental ropes in Villiputtūrār's Tamil *Mahābhārata*.[44] In the bhakti usage, the god allows himself to be captured and tied down in a paradoxical act of self-limitation and in recognition of the bhakta's superior gift of devotion; in our poem, Perumāḷ is the hapless victim of his nephew's cunning prank. Kāttavarāyan has little difficulty in binding others, including, in the end, Āriyamālai herself. He revels in demonstrating his superiority in precisely this area:

> Kāttavarāyan was angry at his mother Kāmākṣī for stubbornly refusing him permission to capture Āriyamālai. Dressed as a conjurer (*añcanakkāran*), he incited the Brahmans, who were looking for Āriyamālai, against Kāmākṣī: that old woman performing tapas under the banyan tree could show them where the girl was hidden. The Brahmans grabbed Kāmākṣī by her matted hair and dragged her away, despite her screams. Now Kāttavarāyan appeared and said, "I am the one who stole Āriyamālai; tie me up." They bound him and took him before the king, who ordered him shackled hand and foot and locked inside an iron box with soldiers guarding it night and day under the command of Civapputaiyān.

Inside the box, Kāttavarāyan thought, "I have been caught because of my own foolish chatter." He called upon Mūtēvi to help him and threatened to crack his skull if the goddess did not come. Mūtēvi appeared, riding her ass. She put the guards around the box to sleep and released Kāttavarāyan. He shackled the sleeping Āriyappūrājan and locked him in the box in his place, and he cut off both sides of Civappuṭaiyān's mustache.

The Brahmans could not find the king until at length, after sunrise, Civappuṭaiyān awoke and opened the box. The king emerged, crying, "I have suffered my fate (viti)—I tied up that thief, but then *he* tied me! He is very clever; no-one can catch him. If we try to catch him, he catches us. If he comes to call Āriyamālai, we must not ask why." (pp. 160-65)

Although Kāttavarāyan seems to require the help of the inauspicious Mūtēvi, with whom he is in any case naturally associated, in fact his escape from his bonds is wholly predictable—as is his binding of his opponents. The episode is a fairly close repetition of an earlier one in the story (in Canto 1, pp. 64-66), where Kāttavarāyan is locked inside a Piḷḷaiyār shrine on Āriyappūrājan's orders, only to be released by Cinnān, whom he binds in his stead. There, too, Mūtēvi arrives to put the hundreds of thousands of guards to sleep so that our hero can make off with the royal elephant. Notice, how, in the episode summarized above, Kāttavarāyan's escape from his bonds inspires a moment of *anagnorisis* in the king. At this point it finally dawns on Āriyappūrājan that there is more to Kāttavarāyan's escapades than he had known, and that the elusiuve scoundrel has a real power and claim on the Brahman girl. The king suddenly realizes that Kāttavarāyan cannot be stopped or thwarted and this truth is brought home to him through a perception of what we might call the existential dimension of Kāttavarāyan's binding and loosing and being bound.

If the gift of slithering out of bonds belongs, along with the love for disguise, animal identities, and sexual metamorphosis, among the salient traits of the Trickster, so does Kāttavarāyan's passion for dice. Like Śiva, he is a gambler who almost invariably wins by cheating. His favorite game is *cokkaṭṭān* (which deserves a study in its own right); this is the game he plays (having taken the form of a marvellous parrot) with Āriyamālai, from whom he wins a pearl necklace, a ring, a thread from her saree and a strand of her hair (Canto 2, pp. 77-78), and, at a later point in the story, with the evil queen Campaṅkitāci (Canto 4, pp. 97-100). The skilled Trickster-gambler, specializing in cokkaṭṭān, seems to be a Tamil folk-type. We find him again in the most unusual of the *Matanakāmarājankatai* tales as the Brahman gambler who defeats Perumāḷ-Viṣṇu in his temple, robs the god of his wife, Lakṣmī, marries the heavenly *apsaras* Rambhā, and eventually triumphs by his wits over the god of death himself.[45] The Śaiva overtones of Kāttavarāyan's gambling are clear, although at no point does the text hint at any cosmic-chronological side to his playing. Rather, these games are part of his generalized penchant for trickiness and cunning.

D. On Being Impaled: Catharsis and the Bhakti of Mourning

There are Tricksters who are trapped by their own tricks, who become victims of their own illusions—but Kāttavarāyan is not one of them.[46] His tragedy takes another form. On one level, he appears to retain, to the very end, an autonomy in will and action that contrasts powerfully with the roles of other characters, especially Āriyamālai, the king, Kāmākṣī, and Śiva. *They* turn out to be subject to viti and also, in some sense, dependent upon our hero's choices, whereas *he* plays at viti, at once accepting and defeating it. On the other hand, this paradoxical triumph has a somewhat Pyrrhic quality, because it leaves the hero all too close to his beginnings, a low caste embodiment of divinity unhappily removed from the divine source identified with the originally androgynous Śiva. The Trickster's autonomy is tempered here by certain existential conditions surrounding his birth, his ruling passions, and his prospects for evolution and escape. Nowhere are these tensions more clear than in the climactic episode of the poem, which describes Kāttavarāyan's ultimate trick, enacted, inevitably, upon the stake:

> Kāttavarāyan came at last to take Āriyamālai (who had been hidden in Komutalavaṅku). He called to her: "Daughter of Appāpaṭṭar and Annatuḷaci, I am the Paraiya servant of your father; I am going to your father, come now with me." She followed him, a Brahman girl walking with an Untouchable; when a peasant from Acalūr saw them thus and asked her what it meant, she said, "This is the evil *vinai* that Śiva gave me; it is the fate written on my forehead." Leaving the girl with his mother Kāmākṣī, Kāttavarāyan took the form of Ārumukam and revealed himself in Puttūrakam. As he was worshiped there by all, he announced to the king, Āriyappūrājan: "I am the king who took Āriyamālai; you can see her tomorrow at the impaling stake. Perform the worship of the stake (*kaḻu-vaṭipūcai*)." Āriyappūrājan folded his hands in worship: "We are pleased,

O Ṣaṇmukha, that you are the one who took away our daughter—it is our good fortune that this happened."

Kāttavarāyan returned to Kāmākṣī, who once again warned him not to touch the Brahman girl; yet she recognized that he would die on the stake. He told her he was determined to experience his viti and asked that she give him the boon of embracing Āriyamālai; Kāmākṣī gave him sacred ash.

The following day Kāttavarāyan assumed his royal guise and sat in state at the base of the stake (kalumaram) as the pūjā was carried out at the order of Āriyappūrājan—offerings of goats, cocks, pigs, opium, ganj, liquor, millet-meal, etc. were brought to the stake. Cinnān brought Āriyamālai and the two Ceṭṭi girls, Annamuttu and Ukantalaki; all three were placed in special boxes (*kūṇṭu*) that had been prepared for them on the stake—Āriyamālai to the left, Annamuttu to the right, and Ukantalaki in the rear. Seven carpenters had, at Kāttavarāyan's instructions, installed secret devices in the wooden contraption of the stake; they mounted the steps together with him. The Seven Maidens came at Kāttavarāyan's call; he begged them to save him from sorrow. . . .[47]

Now his father's curse bore fruit. Kāttavarāyan impaled himself on the stake, to the cries of lamentation from everyone there. The three women, observing his great beauty, fainted and fell, crying, "What *tapas* have we done to merit this union with him?" Now Śiva in Kailāsa knew what was happening on earth; he was determined to overcome this unruly child (*maṭṭukk' aṭaṅkāta matam aṭakka vēṇṭum,* p. 188), despite his mother's boon that he would not die in the burning-ground. Śiva sent Kuṇḍodara in the form of a bee to bore a hole through the stake, but Cinnān forestalled the danger and bound Kuṇḍodara; Nandin rescued him from his bonds.

Kāmākṣī learned from messengers that her son had been impaled and, leaving Ammaiyappakārāḷan[48] to guard the site of her tapas under the banyan tree, she rushed to the stake. She wept and lamented: "My son, my son, this is the fruit of viti, the fruit of Śiva's curse. Did I not tell you that the stake was growing as you sought to touch Āriyamālai? You are dying, you are suffering, my beloved son." She was joined in her lamentations by the others—the thousand Brahmans, the kings and ministers, Annatuḷaciyammāḷ, Civapputaiyān the Valaiyan, the two Ceṭṭi girls, the Seven Maidens, and Āriyamālai herself (blaming herself: "It is all because of me; my mind cannot bear this suffering.") Ukantalaki cried out: "O my guru, Vel-Murukan, you are undergoing this terrible sorrow (*tunpam*) because of us."

Viṣṇu rushed to Śiva to plead with him: "Your son is suffering, and you pay no heed. My sister will weep, and the earth cannot bear her tears." But Śiva remained unmoved: the unruly son was ruined through his egoistic nature (*āṇavam*). Kuṇḍodara, Nandīśvara, and Nārada joined Viṣṇu in his desperate plea: Pārvatī was suffering terribly; the god must come. At last Śiva's heart felt compassion. With the 33 crores of gods, including Vināyaka and Velavar, he came to Tirucirāppaḷḷi, to the kingdom of Āriyappūrājan, to the stake set up in Pāccūrucālai. Now it was his turn to plead with his son. Unable to witness Pārvatī's sorrow, aware of his son's pain, he called to him, "O Paraiyan, Paraiyan, have mercy, come." Kāttavarāyan, revived by hot water and buttermilk, came down from the stake.

Karuppalaki the shepherd girl appeared together with the Seven Karuppar. Śiva ordered the marriage *pantal* to be built. The wedding ceremonies lasted for three days; Āriyamālai, Ukantalaki, Annamuttu, and Karuppalaki all received the wedding tālis from Kāttavarāyan. But after the wedding, Śiva called his son and said, "Live together with three wives; forget your desire for Āriyamālai." Then Śiva returned with Pārvatī to Kailāsa; Perumāḷ went home to Dvārakā; Brahmā and Sarasvatī went to Satyaloka; Velavar and his wives went to Tiruttaṇikai. Kāttavarāyan took his four wives to Tirucirāppaḷḷi and remained there with the two Ceṭṭi girls and Karuppalaki; Āriyamālai lived in the forest. (Cantos 12-13, pp. 167-200)

So, because this is the end of our text, the decisive act of hypogamous miscegenation is averted after all, even though the horrendous Brahman-Untouchable marriage does take place. This unexpected conclusion—which, we must note, is quite different from that of the *Nāṭakam*, where the marriage to Āriyamālai is celebrated without any suggestion that the happy couple will again be separated—has to be addressed in any attempt to interpret the poem as a whole. I see it as reflecting an unresolved tension embedded in this low caste hero's role. We will return to this question later. For now let us examine the central theme of this episode, the impalement. Has a sacrifice actually taken place, or not—and if so, under what conditions or necessity? Irony and ambiguity inform the passage. On the one hand, it is clear that Kāttavarāyan has to go through with this self-impalement. There is never really any doubt that he will come (literally) to this point: his entire career revolves around the twin facts of his lust for Āriyamālai and the punishment that, as his mother constantly reminds him, accompanies that lust. The whole conclusion seems overdetermined—by fate (viti), his father's curse, and the fact that only through Kāttavarāyan's impalement can the initial violation of balance and symmetry be healed, and the goddess restored to her place within Śiva's body. The sacrifice can hardly be avoided. On the other hand, there is a strong voluntaristic coloring to the event. Kāttavarāyan *chooses* to be impaled—he wants to experience (*anupavikka*) his viti—and he thereby demonstrates again the certain freedom that he brings to bear *against* viti and the curse. His dramatic submission becomes a form of mastery, and his impalement becomes his final trick. Like the Trickster he is, he manages to survive, to defeat fate and death, and even to witness Śiva himself begging at his feet. Unlike Maturaivīran, for example, who needs the grace of Mīnākṣī to survive mutilation, Kāttavarāyan manages alone.[49] He offers no devotion, in effect recognizes no deity as superior to himself. His own divinity is no doubt related to his supreme readiness to undergo this sacrifice, but it is equally to be seen in his ability to emerge from the violent sacrificial arena still intact.

But this victory cuts both ways. Kāttavarāyan's characteristic escape from death entails an equally characteristic element of loss, a continuation and, perhaps, the culmination of the theme of primary victimization that attaches to our hero from the beginning of his story. The stake is predestined for him. He somehow, cunningly, extricates himself from the natural result of this fate, by partially living it out; but at the same time the redemptive side of the sacrifice also eludes him. Śiva's curse was unfair, an injustice remedied, at least in part, by the great god's descent to Tiruccirāppaḷḷi to plead with his unfortunate son, whose sufferings he can no longer bear. But if we recall the initial conditions of the curse, it appears that Kāttavarāyan's death on the stake was meant to complete a process of division and devolution within the divinity, or in his relations with the world: the exile of the goddess from Śiva's body and her lonely tapas on earth express this tear in the wholeness of reality and reflect a basic sense of painful loss. The moment of sacrifice was to reverse this process so that a reversion to oneness—the androgyne reconstituted—could take place. In fact, something of this desirable conclusion is achieved: the goddess returns to heaven with Śiva after Kāttavarāyan's multiple wedding. But something of the division also remains. The stubborn and troublesome hero is still with us, in Tiruccirāppaḷḷi, a piece of divinity left over from the curse and its consequences, hungry for offerings, and still cut off from his desired high caste wife. He has refused the fate of reabsorption that was planned for him and even vanquished Śiva, so to speak. The balance has now shifted away from the remote realm of Kailāsa toward a still problematic hero enshrined on earth. This shift, preserved in the poem's conclusion, is a matter of considerable importance.

Kāttavarāyan is *not* an exemplar of bhakti directed toward a higher deity. On the other hand, he does elicit a kind of devotion toward himself, of a type quite distinct from other forms of bhakti. This is *not* the bhakti of separation (*viraha*) recently analyzed by F. Hardy in a brilliant study, nor is it related to the intellectual bhakti that Hardy sees, e.g., in the *Gītā*.[50] One could, perhaps, call it cathartic, in the Aristotelean sense of arousing and transforming—perhaps also purging—the tragic emotions of *eleos* and *phobos*. Its outstanding symptom is not ecstasy (the painful delights of viraha) but mourning or lamentation—*pulampal*, to use the term that pervades the description of the impalement scene. This type of devotion requires a victim for its lachrymose display of emotion, even if the victim subsequently recovers—as seems to be the usual case. Ritualized mourning for this divine victim seems here to be accompanied by a fascination with death, with violence leading to death, and with the notion of (tragic) fate.[51] The type is surprisingly widespread in myth and ritual on the level of village religion in South India: Obeyesekere has described an instance (and argued for a link with the *mater dolorosa* of Mediterranean religions) in the Pattini cult in Sri Lanka.[52] We find it in the bow song tradition,[53] in the Tamil folk genre of *oppāri*,[54] and in assocation with the gruesome events described in many South Indian folk compositions. Kāttavarāyan illuminates the cathartic pattern, no doubt a problematic one in the eyes of more heavily Brahmanical traditions and of the predominant Tamil viraha tradition linked to the great temples: and we note that even a popular text such as the *Kāttamuttu Nāṭakam* completely eliminates this aspect of the story, proceeding to Kāttavarāyan's wedding without even hinting at the gory scene at the stake.

E. Encompassed, Encompassing, Unencompassable?

This last development of the story in the *Nāṭakam* is intriguing. Can we discover its logic? We seem to be observing part of a wider pattern. Although I have not sought to present here anything like a systematic comparison of the two Kāttavarāyan texts I have cited, the *Katai* and the *Nāṭakam*, the surprising disparity of their conclusions calls for comment and may even point the way to a more general interpretation of the story. In one text, the *Katai*, we find a climactic series—the impalement, the cathartic bhakti that accompanies it, and, in the end, the unconsummated marriage with Āriyamālai. The *Nāṭakam* offers the reverse on all three counts—no stake, no catharsis, and no apparent difficulty over the marriage.[55] Both series apparently have their own integrity. It would be especially helpful at this point to be able to compare other, oral versions of the myth. But we may at least speculate on the possible meanings of the two patterns we have before us: why should the impalement, which, after all, produces the resolution of the story and leads immediately to the multiple wedding, be linked to Āriyamālai's ultimate escape from her Untouchable husband's embrace?

We might imagine that the *Nāṭakam* has attempted to Sanskritize or "purāṇicize" its folk material by eliminating the violent scene on the stake. This does not, however, answer our question. In fact, something rather different seems to have happened here. Far from achieving purāṇic respectability, the hero of the *Nāṭakam* remains a low caste black magician and Trickster who, as such, marries the forbidden Brahman girl. Indeed, she is no longer truly forbidden—this, as we have seen, is one of the major dividing lines between the *Nāṭakam* and the *Katai*. The former text seems to have no qualms about Kāttavarāyan's demonstrated superiority over the standard village hierarchy as exemplified by the pure Āriyamālai. Not so the much longer and more detailed version of the *Katai*, which seems to describe a much more ambiguous and complex relationship between the Untouchable hero and his society. There Kāttavarāyan is an embattled figure at odds with hierarchical norms, over which he achieves recurrent but always temporary or partial victories (by humiliating the Brahmans, outwitting the king, carrying off and even marrying women of higher castes than his), and which retain a certain degree of power over him to the very end. One is tempted to see in this particular Trickster's revolt the not uncommon theme of violation and boundary transgressions which serve ultimately to reinforce the violated norm. Thus, for all his apparent autonomy and trickiness, Kāttavarāyan eventually must acquiesce in the final loss of Āriyamālai to the forest, where she remains as inaccessible to him as she was initially, although she now wears his tāli wedding chain.

There is a further irony here. The forest is, in fact, Kāttavarāyan's natural domain, as many of his epithets remind us: he is *vanaṅ kātta cāmi* (p. 49) or *curaṅ kāttār cuvāmi* (p. 132) or *āraṇiyan tān kātta āṇṭavanār* (p. 167), all meaning "the lord who guards the wilderness." The forest here refers to the wild, uncultivated area beyond (and seen as surrounding) the village. This unsettled and unsettling *kāṭu* (*araṇya, vana* —recall that the major divisions of the *Katai* are called vanam) finds a proper representative *within* the settled village (*nāṭu*) in the ambiguous figure of the guardian at the gate of the goddess's shrine. This, we recall, is how we meet Kāttavarāyan throughout Tiruccirāppaḷḷi and Tañcāvūr Districts; and it is this same role as guardian that first defines our hero in the two texts we have studied. In a sense, then, Āriyamālai ends by entering *his* sphere at the same time he himself seems to become stabilized with his other wives in the town (Tiruccirāppaḷḷi). They pass each other on their separate ways in the course of their development. This, too, requires explanation: how are we to understand this final reversal in the Brahman girl's status, her envelopment by the wilderness, even as the wilderness-figure of her husband appears to emerge from this domain and to achieve a new fixity of place?

Perhaps the underlying conceptual issues here are related precisely to the primary, most basic role of our hero as a guardian deity situated between forest and village, outside the shrine of the goddess (Māriyamman; Kāmākṣī of our myth). Kāttavarāyan demarcates this boundary. He brings something of the forest into the village to which he is also paradoxically bound. But what is the actual nature of this boundary, and, for that matter, of the intimate tie between this guardian and the figure of the deity within? Certain complexities of the latter relationship have already become evident through Kāttavarāyan's behavior vis-à-vis his mother, Kāmākṣī (although his relations with Āriyamālai are equally relevant to this question). In the *Katai*, at least, the linkage seems to be a rather frustrating one rooted in the initial fracture in Śiva's being, which immediately produces the guardian's role. More generally, we can perhaps isolate three major patterns which determine this relationship, and the role of the boundary, in different texts and contexts. Two of them are present in the materials we have summarized here.

One pattern seems clearly to require the subordination of the guardian-gatekeeper to another divinity, usually that of the shrine he guards. Cuṭalaimāṭan's defeat by Murukan is a case in point.[56] This may well be the predominant pattern in cults such as Kāttavarāyan's, which also reflect in their organization a division of labor, usually sacrificial labor, so that the pure deity within the shrine can avoid contamination by the necessarily violent acts carried out by his or her servants. The essential notion here is one of encompassment and hierarchy. As is usual in India, it is the inner being (the deity in the shrine, like the divine principle within the body) that is primary, more encompassing, and higher than the surrounding "outer" forms. So in this case the boundary with its gatekeepers is ultimately subordinated to and, in fact, subsumed by the divinity that it appears to surround and contain. To some extent, the outer zone appears as a limited emanation, replete with violent division, of the more subtle (*sūkṣma*), less differentiated entity within. The relation between the two spheres is worked out in many of the village goddess myths, where the goddess descends—at the beginning of her festival—from a cooler, more detached mode of being into a worldly mode marked by heat, sexual arousal, anger, exterior manifestation (e.g., in the form of small-pox) and, in mythic terms, an ambiguous connection to a dangerous demon.[57] The festival helps move the goddess through this descent and back up and away, so that at the end of the cycle she is again cool, remote, and, perhaps, linked in a pacific, non-erotic marriage to her proper (non-demonic) spouse.[58] The same progression could be described in terms of the hidden "inner" deity's emerging outward in a temporary and sometimes dangerous sortie to the boundary with its male guardian figures. And the furthest point reached by the goddess in this devolution will undoubtedly be marked by a sacrifice, in one form or another, to be followed by the switch in consorts (demon replaced by the pacific Śiva) and a retreat to the original inner, and more encompassing state. Not surprisingly, we find Untouchables playing a key ritual role, apparently representing the demonic male figure of the myth, in the festival enactment of these events.[59] But a central element here is the lower figures' complete subservience and ontological dependence upon the higher (or that of the outer on the inner ones). Violent carnivores stationed at the edge of the shrine serve the vegetarian non-combatants within.[60] Moreover, the logic of this relation limits the direction of movement: as with the Sinhalese cosmology studied by Kapferer, it is the higher level that moves toward the lower, and back; "given that deities conceived as high in the rank order subsume lower orders in their being, it follows that these same deities can manifest themselves at those various levels which they subsume."[61] This is, or appears to be, a securely hierarchical system organized on consistent principles.

But it fails to explain Kāttavarāyan. If we follow the myth as we find it in both our texts, our Untouchable hero defies this type of relation. As we saw earlier, Kāttavarāyan is an unpredictable joker who cannot be subsumed. Rather, he consistently mocks and toys with the limited world of normative hierarchy that he finds in the village; and in one of the texts, the *Nāṭakam*, he achieves a clear-cut victory expressed in his marriage to Āriyamālai. In other words, in the latter case it appears that it is the outer boundary zone, with its wilderness associations, that is seen as primary, in some sense superior, and definitely more encompassing than the surrounded core. The lowest embraces all that is above it: the Untouchable Kāttavarāyan can incorporate and simultaneously transcend the whole of the social order, even as the forest absorbs all limited forms back into its wholeness. The comparison with the goddess festivals and their myths is instructive. Whereas the goddess eventually retreats back into her shrine, Kāttavarāyan remains on earth, married to a range of women representative of a wide social spectrum. Moreover, in *his* story, at least, the goddess is relatively helpless beside him. Kāttavarāyan achieves his final position through a rebellious ascent from Untouchability to a recognized power and cult, an ascent characterized by the constant violation of norms and limits; both the drive toward antinomian violation and the trickster's transformations that accompany it point to the primacy of the wilderness over the limited village order. There is, then, a hierarchy implicit in this view, but it is hardly the one we are accustomed to imagining. Here it is precisely the lowest, most outer sphere that is most dynamic, rich with generative potential, and capable of containing other powers and forms. The stress here is on movement and transformation, on a process which we may call *upward encompassment*—the lower expanding to incorporate and ultimately to dominate any initially higher (but actually less autonomous and viable) forms of being.

Something of this pattern is also clearly present in the *Katai*, both in this text's presentation of Kāttavarāyan's outrageous escapades, with the persistent suggestion of the hero's remarkable autonomy vis-à-vis the village norms, and in its depiction of Āriyamālai's fate—the Brahman girl finally swallowed up and encompassed by the forest, the realm closest to the Untouchable hero. But the overall picture is more complex. For one thing, the conclusion just noted—Āriyamālai in the forest—is susceptible to a rather different interpretation. For the Brahman has his own innate connection with the forest, or with the pure, undifferentiated potential which it may represent. In other words, the apparent opposition we have been exploring—high and low, inner and outer—may, under other circumstances, turn out to conceal a latent and even necessary affinity. At some point the two extremes may well coincide. Put somewhat differently, and schematically, we could envisage the relation between the two poles, exemplified here by the goddess and her trickster-guardian, as two concentric circles—the goddess safely within the first, the enveloping forest with its male gatekeeper-guardians as the second. The subtlety and refinement of the inner mode, embodying the farthest reaches of *saṃskāra*, can be set against the pure potentiality and somewhat menacing formlessness of the outer wilderness. But in fact either circle can encompass and absorb the other. Everything depends on where one stands and from what context or angle he is looking. What might appear as rigidly fixed in place at either the apex or the base of a hierarchical scale turns out to possess a high degree of fluidity and indeterminacy. In such a system, even the rebellious tricks of an Untouchable hero may well lose something of their sting.

Yet Kāttavarāyan continues to elude us. If we take the conclusion of the *Katai* seriously, neither of the two patterns we have outlined seems to fit. He is neither subsumed by the higher deities—in fact, he humiliates them by his suffering and forces Śiva to beg at his feet, thereby effectively altering the original, unjust curse—nor does he subsume them in his own being, as we see from his continued separation from Śiva and Pārvatī, in his earthly shrine, and from his final loss of Āriyamālai. Even if the joker cannot himself be subsumed, he is unable to subsume the others. He has, it is true, evolved and moved—away from the forest, into the more stable, domestic mode in the town. But this move only freezes and preserves the basic state of fragmentation, imbalance, and alienation that plagues Kāttavarāyan from birth. He is now truly at home nowhere, neither in forest nor village; unable finally to sever the bonds of hierarchy (his rebellion in fact reinforces them), he remains remote from Kailāsa with its promise of wholeness, still embroiled in antithesis, married to low and middle-range females while the higher females he desires are out of reach (Āriyamālai in the forest, Kāmākṣī in her shrine).[62] Even the restorative (if terrible) sacrifice has been denied him, so that his exile is rendered permanent. Initially a creature of the border, an ambiguous guardian, he remains there, prevented from moving either inwards or outwards toward one of the two related poles. All he retains from his violent and colorful career is his alienation. Is the articulation of this vision connected to the experience of the cathartic bhakti appropriate to this text, and to the social milieu which produced it? Is the logical link between the impalement and the unconsummated marriage the double-edged nature of the former, which then leads directly and inevitably to the latter?

This particular conclusion sets off Kāttavarāyan from a series of related figures in the world of South Indian village myth and legend. We have a basis for establishing a differential typology in which various antinomian heroes—the village demons (pēy), the purāṇic *asuras*, bandits such as Maturaivīran and Papaḍu, the crippled thief-hero of the *noṇṭināṭakam*, even, to an extent, the problematic local kings—can be clearly distinguished. This is not the place to develop these distinctions in detail. But perhaps the most striking contrast is actually elsewhere—between Kāttavarāyan, as we see him in his *Katai*, and the god with whom he is repeatedly identified by this text, Śiva's son Murukan.[63] One could, of course, speculate, in the absence of evidence, about the history of this linkage between a Tamil folk deity and the highly popular Murukan; and there are tantalizing questions of possible historical survivals in the Kāttavarāyan cult: does Kāttavarāyan's relation with Kāmākṣī conserve something of Murukan's association with Korravai?[64] Are the Seven Maidens of Kollimalai related in any way to the famous image of the goddess on this mountain (*kollippāvai*), which took the life of anyone who beheld it?[65] But none of this helps us to understand the poem as we have it or to perceive the burden of its hero's identification with this god. The *locus classicus* of the Tamil Murukan mythology is Kacciyappacivācāriyar's *Kantapurāṇam;* and one can easily see certain parallels between this text's version of the myth and the Kāttavarāyan materials. We have already mentioned the theme of the god's multiple mothers, and, of course, the link with Śiva. But there is also the striking theme of the god's multiple marriages. Don Handelman has recently argued, in a subtle study, that Murukan's marriages to Teyvayānai and Vaḷḷi help to stabilize a deity who has risen, in the course of fighting his asura enemies, from an initial situation of incomplete and undifferentiated integration to one of a higher-order, universal encompassment and holism. The double marriage allows the deity to move downwards again, toward the world in its properly hierarchical order, and to be reconstituted in it in part by the two very different brides he has chosen.[66] This description seems beautifully suited to the purāṇic milieu in which Kacciyappacivācāriyar worked. Kāttavarāyan belongs to a different milieu entirely and to a social background relatively remote from the great Brahmanical temples and their myths. The difference is reflected in our hero's career, with its unilateral direction—the ascent focused on the women he marries—and especially in the final, unhappy outcome of his story. Murukan marries the lowly Vaḷḷi, a crucial descent which marks the limit of his evolution into the world and which dramatizes his accessibility to his lowly devotees; the Untouchable Kāttavarāyan marries above himself in a desperate effort to transcend his situation and as a result of an abortive sacrifice which fails to heal the rift within the godhead. In both cases the marriage stabilizes a process of transformation and effects a change within the deity. But whereas Murukan's marriages incorporate and integrate the social extremes within the god's unfolding wholeness, Kāttavarāyan fails to reach the upper limit which has held him in thrall throughout his career. Āriyamālai recedes into the distance, and he remains stuck in his enduring state of fragmentation. This result—by no means the only interesting inversion by the *Kāttavarāyan Katai* of themes from the Murukan mythology—allows us to characterize our text as a kind of anti-*purāṇa* securely rooted in the social and cultural world of the lower castes. In this case as in others, the contrast is based on specific thematic and semantic transformations between texts which express the variation in context. Whereas the purāṇa is interested largely in working out the relations between the god's diverse roles and parts, and between him and the world, and in stabilizing and ordering the process of his devolution from high/inner being to lower, outer forms, the folk tradition sticks to its antitheses—exemplified here by the angry and playful victim-hero, at once hostile and bound to hierarchical norms, held in place between forest and temple, whose mode of willed self-sacrifice releases forces of empathy and cathartic identification that can overpower, at least momentarily, even the Brahmans and their great gods.

NOTES

1. Or *Kāttuvarāyan** (as on the cover of my edition)—but the correct form is probably Kāttavarāyan; see below. Like the majority of Tamil folk epic narratives, this one is falsely ascribed to the famous poet Pukalēntippulavar. I have used the Ār. Ji. Pati Company edition (Madras: Vakīsvari Accakam, 1974). An apparently identical version of the text has been published in Madras by Irattina Nāyakar and Sons.

2. Ascribed to Cāmikkaṇṇu Kaṇṭar (a Vanniyan from Mēṭṭuppāḷaiyam) (Madras: Irattina Nāyakar and Sons, n.d.). This text was kindly made available to me by Alf Hiltebeitel. Other versions of the story, which diverge considerably from the *Katai*, are the *Kāttavarāyan Kataippāṭal* (Madurai, 1971), and the texts mentioned briefly by A. Ciṅkāravēlu Mutaliyār, *Apitāna Cintāmaṇi* (New Delhi: Asian Educational Services, 1981), 405. See also Masilamani-Meyer in this volume.

3. Brenda E. F. Beck, *The Three Twins: The Telling of a South Indian Folk Epic* (Bloomington: Indiana University Press, 1982); Gene H. Roghair, *The Epic of Palnāḍu* (Oxford: Clarendon Press, 1982).

4. We cannot say when this occurred, or from what medium (oral dictation, palm leaves, paper) the printed edition was prepared. On the printing history

of the Tamil ballad, see M. Arunachalam, *Peeps into Tamil Literature: Ballad Poetry* (Tiruchitrambalam: Gandhi Vidyalayam, 1976), 73-81; Beck, *Three Twins,* 109-110.

5. On Maturaivīran, see D. Shulman, *The King and the Clown in South Indian Myth and Poetry* (Princeton: Princeton University Press, 1985), 355-66; on Cuṭalaimāṭan, see Marie-Louise Reiniche, *Les Dieux et les hommes. Étude des cultes d'un village du Tirunelveli, Inde du Sud* (Paris: Mouton, 1979), 202-17.

6. Arunachalam, *Ballad Poetry,* p. 189, faced with this same question, declares: "Ballad poetry would certainly have been better off without this story."

7. The use of the term ballad for these works is imprecise; in effect, the majority of the mālai and katai would be classed as folk epic. For a survey of this literature, see Arunachalam, *Ballad Poetry,* passim.

8. In the *Nāṭakam,* Aiyanār is also suggested by Śiva and rejected by Pārvatī. Then Śivasubrahmaṇya who dwells on Kollimalai decides he must help his mother and takes the form of a baby beside her as she performs tapas; at the age of twelve he becomes her guardian, with the name Kāttavarāyan.

9. It is not clear if four is meant as a precise figure or simply as "several," as is common in coloquial Tamil.

10. In the *Nāṭakam* (p. 27) he *asks* to be born in response to his mother's suffering because of Śiva's curse.

11. Thomas Burrow and Murray B. Emeneau, *Dravidian Etymological Dictionary* (London: Oxford University Press, 1961), entry number 1192.

12. *Kāttamuttu Nāṭakam,* p. 28. The last line is ambiguous: *mātarai* could refer to the women (plural) mentioned earlier, or to the Woman—i.e., the goddess.

13. See discussion in Shulman, *The King and the Clown,* 361-62.

14. The former is used by the *Katai,* the latter by the *Nāṭakam.*

15. The association with Kāmākṣī of the Kāmakkōṭṭam and the Kampai River at Kāñcipuram is evident.

16. Does this complete the "four" prescribed births? The text is elliptical and rather obscure at this point.

17. At a later point (pp. 63-64), the text specifies 700,000 guards (including Muslim *tulukkar*), 1000 Brahmans on elephants, 30 great kings, 300 ministers, 50 other kings, 1000 *tātiyar,* etc. Civappuṭaiyān's salary for this post is 1000 *pon* (19).

18. See pp. 19, 170. I refrain from developing here the links with Draupadī's hair; see A. Hiltebeitel, "Draupadī's Hair," in Madeleine Biardeau, ed., *Autour de la déesse hindoue, Puruṣārtha* 5 (1981), 179-211.

19. She in fact saves his life when Cinnān's father is on the verge of overcoming him. This entire episode is a major focus of the *Nāṭakam.*

20. See A. Appadurai, "The Puzzling Status of Brahman Temple Priests in Hindu India," *South Asian Anthropologist* (1983), 43-52.

21. This pattern recalls the story of Cuntaramūrttināyanār, by caste an Āticaiva who is adopted and brought up by a king, Naraciṅkamunaiyar: *Periya Purāṇam* 151.

22. Ironically—referring to Śiva himself?

23. Note, again, the imagery of the fisherman.

24. See my *Tamil Temple Myths* (Princeton: Princeton University Press, 1980); Gananath Obeyesekere, *The Cult of the Goddess Pattini* (Chicago: University of Chicago Press, 1984), 427-482.

25. On Murukan and the Kṛttikās, see Shulman, *Tamil Temple Myths*, 243-52.

26. I omit a further series of humiliations that Kāttavarāyan inflicts on the Maidens.

27. For examples, see my *Tamil Temple Myths*, 151-55, 288.

28. Cf. H. Whitehead, *The Village Gods of South India* (2nd. ed., Calcutta: Association Press, 1921), 26. Note that both here and in the frame story it is the youngest kanni who is the pivotal figure. It is also, perhaps, of importance that Kāttavarāyan impersonates his Untouchable father in order to punish the Seven Maidens.

29. As in the instances of Pārvatī's tapas for Śiva and Vaḷḷi's *kaḷavu*-union (union through "stealing" her) with Murukan (but with the opposite result).

30. The *Apitāna Cintāmaṇi* (see n. 2), loc. cit., citing a *Kāttavarāya Nāṭakam*, calls this figure Ukantāyi. The *Kāttamuttu Nāṭakam* knows her as Ocanti, one of Kāttavarāyan's *three* wives according to this text (the other two being Karuppalaki and Āriyamālai).

31. On the Karuppans, see Reiniche, *Les Dieux et les hommes*, 126 and 199 (noting a relation between Karuppu and Śāstā). Our text spells the name consistently as Kaṟuppaḻaki.

32. I am grateful to Don Handelman for comments on this point (and on this section as a whole).

33. E.g., Nāṭāncāmi: Stuart H. Blackburn, "Death and Deification: Folk Cults in Hinduism," *History of Religions* 24 (1985), 261. The marriage of a Brahman woman to an Untouchable male is one of the outstanding motifs of the village goddess myths throughout South India; see Brenda E. F. Beck, "The Goddess and the Demon: A Local South Indian Festival in its Wider Context," in Madeleine Biardeau, ed., *Autour de la déesse hindoue* (see n. 18), 95-96, citing in n. 17 a large body of literature on this motif. Muttuppattan reverses the marriage (Brahman male, Untouchable female): Reiniche, *Les dieux et les hommes*, 200-201.

34. Blackburn, "The Folk Hero and Class Interests in Tamil Heroic Ballads," *Asian Folklore Studies* 37 (1978), 131-49, argues that the high caste component in the hero's background is a result of purāṇicization.

35. Kannamma in Palnāḍu (Roghair, *Epic of Palnāḍu*, 347); Cāmpukā in Beck's Koṅku epic (*Three Twins*, 132-33).

36. A. K. Ramanujan, "The Relevance of Folklore," in press.

37. See the fine discussion by Reiniche, *Les Dieux et les hommes*, 185-217.

38. See Mac Linscott Ricketts, "The North American Indian Trickster," *History of Religions* 5 (1966), 327-50.

39. Klaus-Peter Koepping, "Absurdity and Hidden Truth: Cunning Intelligence and Grotesque Body Images as Manifestations of the Trickster," *History of Religions* 24 (1985), 204-207.

40. Cristiano Grottanelli, "Tricksters, Scapegoats, Champions, Saviors," *History of Religions* 23 (1983), 120.

41. K. Hastrup and J. Ovesen, "The Joker's Cycle," *Journal of the Anthropological Society of Oxford* 7 (1976), 13.

42. As in a Tamil version of the Dāruvana myth: *Tiruviḷaiyāṭarpurāṇam* 32. This episode is missing from the *Nāṭakam*, which picks up the story with Āriyamālai's transformation into a stone as she bathes in the river—the direct prelude, in that text, to her marriage to Kāttavarāyan.

43. Biardeau, "The Story of Arjuna Kārtavīrya Without Reconstruction," *Purāṇa* 12 (1970), 286-303; cf. her "Brāhmaṇes combattantes dans un mythe du sud de l'Inde," *Adyar Library Bulletin* 31-32 (1967-68), 519-30, and her further discussion in this volume.

44. Villiputtūrār *Pāratam* 5.4.33-40.

45. *Matanakāmarājankatai* (Madras, 1975), 159-69 (*cūtan katai*). Cf. *Kathāsaritsāgara* 18.2.187-99. K. Zvelibil, "A Contribution to the Study of Tamil Folklore: *Matanakāmarājankatai* and *Mayilirāvaṇankatai*," manuscript, 1985, p. 9, sees the Matanakāma story of the gambler as "an audacious and irreverent parody on bhakti legends."

46. See Bruce Kapferer, *A Celebration of Demons: Exorcism and the Aesthetics of Healing in Sri Lanka* (Bloomington: Indiana University Press, 1983), 111-12, 124-28. Cf. Don Handelman, "The Ritual Clown: Attributes and Affinities," *Anthropos* 75 (1981), 333: "The trickster is a creator, but is itself radically transformed by its own creations."

47. Two episodes are introduced at this point: the younger sister of the seven Karuppans spills a pot of curd, is beaten by her *māmi* (Kāḷi?), and utters a curse, which appears to have the effect of overdetermining Śiva's still operative curse (that Kāttavarāyan die upon the stake); then a Kanniṭaiyar mounts the stake, longing for the three women (184-85, 187). Both episodes require further elucidation, perhaps in the light of oral versions of the story.

48. A guardian-servant provided earlier by Kāttavarāyan (24-25).

49. *Maturaivīracuvāmi Katai* (Madras, 1972), 58-63, summarized in my *The King and the Clown*, 358-59.

50. Friedhelm Hardy, *Viraha-Bhakti: The Early History of Kṛṣṇa Devotion in South India* (Delhi: Oxford University Press, 1983).

51. See Blackburn, "Death and Deification," 272, on the power of the deified

dead: "They are as powerful as death itself, perhaps because they have met it in its rawest form; in other words, the deified dead have become the violence they have experienced. That force, driven inside them at death, then becomes a source that worshippers can call on to counteract other elemental forces of disease, disaster, and even death."

52. Obeyesekere, *Pattini*, 265-70 (note that my use of the term "cathartic" differs from his: see 381-82). For the classic Tamil parallel, see *Cilappatikāram* 18-19.

53. Blackburn, "Death and Deification"; idem, "Oral Performance: Narrative and Ritual in a Tamil Folk Tradition," *Journal of American Folklore* 94 (1981), 207-27. Pulampal-mourning may also be linked with cultic possession (total identification with the victim); cf. *kattiseva* in the Palnāḍu *vīrotsavamu:* Roghair, *Epic of Palnāḍu*, p. 28.

54. See, for example, *Irati Pulampal* of Citamparam Nārāyaṇa Piḷḷai (Madras, 1927), a mourning-song sung to the dead Kāma after his destruction by Śiva.

55. Although there is a pulampal scene earlier in the text, at the time of Kāttavarāyan's trial by magic in Kerala (52-56).

56. Reiniche, *Les Dieux et les hommes*, 206-207.

57. Richard Brubaker, "The Ambivalent Mistress: A Study of South Indian Village Goddesses and their Religious Meaning," Ph.D. dissertation, University of Chicago, 1978; cf. C. J. Fuller and Penny Logan, "The Navarātri Festival in Madurai," *Bulletin of the School of Oriental and African Studies* 48 (1985), 79-105, for a somewhat similar process occurring within a major Brahmanical shrine.

58. Fuller and Logan, "Navarātri Festival," 90-93.

59. Beck, "The Goddess and the Demon," 123-26.

60. See the classic exposition of this pattern by L. Dumont, "A Structural Definition of a Folk Deity of Tamil Nad: Aiyanar, the Lord," *Contributions to Indian Sociology* 3 (1959), 75-87. One should also note, however, that the "high," inner figures are necessarily drawn—perhaps for existential reasons—to the lower, outer ones; the goddess festivals elaborate this theme.

61. Kapferer, *Celebration of Demons*, 124.

62. I am again indebted to Don Handelman for this formulation.

63. If we follow the *Nāṭakam*, we are dealing with a specific, localized form of Murukan, i.e., Śivasubrahmaṇya from Kollimalai.

64. See *Tirumurukārruppaṭai* 258.

65. See *Kuruntokai* 89 and 100, with U. Vē. Cāminātaiyar's notes.

66. Don Handelman, "Myths of Murukan: Asymmetry and Hierarchy in a South-Indian Purāṇic Cosmology," in press.

3

The Changing Face of Kāttavarāyan

Eveline Masilamani-Meyer

A look at the basic story of Kāttavarāyan tells us that this god is a criminal.[1] His crime: the abduction of a Brahman maiden. His punishment: death at the "stake."[2] One version of the story seems to confirm that Kāttavarāyan has a character attributable to a criminal. Another version of the story, however, shows us an altogether different Kāttavarāyan; one who, far from fitting the description of a criminal, could rank as a model hero.

It is the disparity of character which Kāttavarāyan displays in different versions of his story that I wish to present and analyze in this paper. The comparison is meant to show how a god changes and to provide some explanations as to why he changes.

The changes in Kāttavarāyan's character can best be illustrated by a comparison of his changing relationship with the other persons figuring in the story. In the first part of this paper I deal with Kāttavarāyan's relationship towards his superiors: his parents, both divine and earthly, the king, and the Brahmans. In the second part, Kāttavarāyan's relationship with his women, the seven maidens, is explored.

In his relationship with others, Kāttavarāyan frequently makes use of his divine power and magic and of his gift to take on various forms and disguises. This aspect is discussed in part three. The fourth part deals with Kāttavarāyan's death, his apotheosis and the symbolism of the stake. This is followed by some observations regarding the basic story of Kāttavarāyan and the reasons which could have led to the changes in the narrative and the character of Kāttavarāyan.

In the last part I touch briefly upon the temples and present cult of Kāttavarāyan.

The three versions of the Kāttavarāyan story which are used in our comparison are:

1. *Kāttavarāyacuvāmi ammānai*, written on palm leaves.[3] This version is indicated henceforth by *Ammānai*.
2. *Kāttavanār cuvāmi ēcal.*[4] References to this version are marked *Ēcal*.
3. *Kāttavarāyacuvāmi katai*, published by B. Irattina Nāyakar and Sons, Madras, 1980.[5] References to this version shall be marked *Katai*.

Of the three versions, the *Ammānai* is the most coherent and the longest. It may well be the earliest version because it gives the fullest account of the story, does not show the discrepancies we find in the *Katai* and follows more faithfully the patterns of the existing cult of Kāttavarāyan. The temples mentioned in the *Ammānai* as having been established for Kāmākṣī and Kāttavarāyan are among the oldest and most important centres where Kāttavarāyan is worshipped.

In the *Katai* the narrative becomes more complex, the style less pure. As opposed to the other two versions, the *Katai* abounds in colloquial expressions and words borrowed from Telugu and Urdu (often incomprehensible even to the native Tamil speaker).

The *Ēcal* is an abridged and somewhat altered form of the *Ammānai*. I make use of it only where it significantly deviates from the *Ammānai*.

A. Kāttavarāyan's Relationship with His Superiors

His Divine Parents

Both the *Ammānai* and the *Katai* begin with a sin of Pārvatī. To test if Śiva truly feeds all the living beings, she hides an ant in a box. As punishment for her mistrust, Śiva orders her to create a flower garden.[6] Kāttavarāyan is to be the watchman of this garden. In the *Ammānai* Kāttavarāyan is born from a deer created in Śiva's mind. The *Ēcal* has Śiva and Pārvatī play in their form as deer with the result that Kāttavarāyan is born from their union. In the *Katai* Śiva simply creates Kāttavarāyan, and Kāttavarāyan's birth from a deer happens later.

As son of Śiva and Pārvatī, Kāttavarāyan guards the flower garden until the seven maidens (*kannimārkaḷ*) come to bathe in a nearby pond or river. They pick flowers and fruits for the worship of Śiva. Kāttavarāyan, who sees this, steals the clothes of the youngest maiden. The other six maidens report this to Śiva who then pronounces the following curse (*Ammānai*): Kāttavarāyan shall be born on earth as a son of Brahmans, spend some time in the house of a low caste weaver (*paraiyan*), later grow up in another house where he will get a name, and finally, because of a woman, die on the stake. The seven maidens will also be born on earth. Īśvarī then pleads with Śiva, and he adds to the curse the boon that Kāttavarāyan and the seven maidens will become deities.

In the *Ēcal* Īśvarī does not intervene. Śiva, along with his curse, grants Kāttavarāyan the boon to become a god.

In the *Katai* Śiva's curse is curt: "Be a Brahman, a Pariah, a fisherman, one on the stake!" But the goddess interferes and alters the curse to the effect that Kāttavarāyan shall not die. Thereupon she herself is cursed by Śiva. He orders her to leave his left side and to go (to earth) like an evil spirit. This curse will be lifted when Kāttavarāyan is on the stake.

Śiva's curse, and how it is pronounced, is already an indication of Kāttavarāyan's further relationship with his divine parents. Śiva is the ultimate source of power, without whose grace Kāttavarāyan cannot be saved. In both the *Ammānai* and the *Katai* Śiva tests his son's determination to die on the stake, but in the latter version the test is akin to a punishment meted out to Kāttavarāyan for his pride (see below). This pride is reflected, for instance, in the manner in which Kāttavarāyan introduces himself to the various people he meets. In the *Katai*, no matter what form he is in, Kāttavarāyan identifies himself as the son of Śiva, although thinly disguised, and not as the son of a Pariah. This has the effect that it places our hero on a higher plane but lowers Śiva.[7]

As a contrast, in the *Ammānai* Kāttavarāyan simply relates his story: his birth, Śiva's curse, and subsequent boon. Kāttavarāyan's somewhat closer relationship with Śiva in the *Ammānai* is also made clear by the fact that Śiva feeds him milk when he cries, abandoned in the forest by his Brahman parents. Incidentally, through his father's milk Kāttavarāyan receives the gift of knowing his previous birth(s). This gift he receives from his mother, the goddess, in the *Katai*.

Kāttavarāyan is the devout child of Kāmākṣī in both the *Ammānai* and the *Katai*. In the *Ēcal* the goddess's role is minimal. However, whereas the *Ammānai* consistently shows Kāttavarāyan in the role of a devotee towards a goddess (who is also his mother), we find that in the *Katai* Kāttavarāyan's role as child of the mother (-goddess) is emphasized. Not surprisingly Kāttavarāyan (in the *Katai*) is at one point burnt by Kāmākṣī and later falls into her hands as a child. Again, in order to save her son from the anger of the seven maidens, Kāmākṣī turns Kāttavarāyan into a child. In this version Kāmākṣī plays the true role of a mother. She worries about him, tries to deter him from his intention to abduct the Brahman girl Āriyamālai; she even gets irritated by his constant nagging for her permission in this endeavor.[8] She gives Kāttavarāyan various tests to take his thoughts off the Brahman girl and she tries various times to make him agree to a proper marriage with his cross-cousin (the daughter of Viṣṇu). The tension between mother and son seems to mount and at one point, towards the end of the story, Kāttavarāyan has the old lady beaten up by the Brahmans.[9] Kāttavarāyan says it is to break her pride because she keeps refusing him the permission to abduct Āriyamālai.

Śiva's curses place the goddess and Kāttavarāyan at par: both have to be on earth, both have to atone for their sin. Kāmākṣī does this by means of tapas, Kāttavarāyan by fulfilling his fate (curse).

In the *Ammānai* Kāmākṣī remains aloof, enthroned as goddess and wife of Śiva (Ēkāmparar). It is Kāttavarāyan's steadfast devotion to Kāmākṣī that causes her to respond to him, to even follow him to the various places where he establishes temples for her after his deification.

The fierce counterpart to the relatively benign Kāmākṣī in the *Ammānai* and the *Katai* is Kāḷi. Like Kāmākṣī, Kāttavarāyan considers her his mother (*tāy*). It is again in the *Katai* that Kāḷi's motherhood, coupled with a sense of antagonism towards her son, is more in evidence. Kāttavarāyan visits Kāḷi to obtain from her the boon which Kāmākṣī refuses to grant him: the abduction of the Brahman girl. Kāḷi tends the tree which will be the stake on which Kāttavarāyan has to die. Before the tree is cut, Kāttavarāyan proves his skill by catching the weapons Kāḷi whirls at him. He is finally swallowed by her. Kāḷi, however, cannot bear the kicks of Kāttavarāyan inside her belly and by means of a magic ointment (*añcanam*) she discovers who he is, releases him, and carries him in her arms as a child. Kāḷi finally grants Kāttavarāyan the permission to abduct Āriyamālai, but not without warning him a last time that he will have to suffer for it on the stake.

Kāttavarāyan's meeting with Kāḷi occurs early in the *Ammānai*. Here he visits Kāḷi for a different reason. After he has killed the birds in Kāḷi's forest,[10] conquered an assortment of demons and Asuras (muni) sent by Kāḷi, Kāḷi realizes that no mere mortal has come to call on her. She receives him, and after listening to his story, she grants him his wish and bestows on him her musical instrument (kiṇṇāram),[11] her drum, her magic sword, various powerful spells and mantras (*mantiram tantiram*), and the art to change his form.[12]

In brief, a mother-son relationship between Kāttavarāyan and the goddesses (especially Kāmākṣī) is more evident in the *Katai*. This relationship is not without tension, a sign that perhaps Kāttavarāyan experiences the motherly bond as too constricting. The *Ammāṉai* sees Kāttavarāyan in the role of a respectful devotee of Kāmākṣī, and Kāmākṣī as a benevolent goddess who intercedes with Śiva on behalf of her devotee. Neither Kāmākṣī nor Kāḷi play an active role in Kāttavarāyan's adventures and his abduction of Āriyamālai, but they do provide him with the necessary power or weapons (e.g., Kāḷi's sword). Here it is not Kāḷi who guards the tree for the stake, but Māci Periyaṇṇacāmi, the god who rules the Māci hill, the place where the particular tree used for the stake, grows.[13]

His Earthly Parents

Kāttavarāyan's closeness to the goddess(es) in the *Katai* compensates for the minimal relationship he has with his earthly mothers. The sequence of Kāttavarāyan's births in the *Katai* is as follows: an unknown Brahman woman swallows him in the form of a lime, gives birth to him and abandons him. He is found by an equally unknown Pariah woman and again abandoned. Then, seeing a female deer (Civapputaiyān's deer), Kāttavarāyan places himself on a blade of grass. The deer swallows him, and Kāttavarāyan is born again. A Pariah man finds him. He hands the child over to the same Civapputaiyān, a fisherman. In his house Kāttavarāyan grows up. For an explanation of this rather confusing sequence we have to turn to the *Ammāṉai*. Here Kāttavarāyan is born as a boon to two named Brahmans, Anantanārāyaṇan and his wife Maṅkammāḷ of Kalattūr. The astrologers predict Kāttavarāyan's unfortunate destiny. He is abandoned in a forest where Śiva and Pārvatī tend to him. A Pariah woman finds the child but is told the true identity of Kāttavarāyan in a dream. Knowing she would sin in raising a Brahman child, she brings him to Cēppilaiyān (the *Ammāṉai*'s counterpart to Civapputaiyān) and his wife Caṅkapiḷḷai, who raise him. Clearly two events which are separated in the *Ammāṉai*, Kāttavarāyan's first birth from a deer (mentioned above) and his being looked after by Śiva and Pārvatī in the forest, have converged in the *Katai*. Moreover, with the deer birth coming third in the *Katai* (rather than earlier, as in the *Ammāṉai*) as part of the story that leads to Kāttavarāyan's adoption by Civapputaiyān, the basic three part sequence required by Śiva's curse—Brahman-Pariah-fisherman—is replicated in the *Katai* treatment of that third episode. Kāttavarāyan's birth from Civapputaiyān's deer corresponds to another high caste birth, and the episode then introduces another Pariah to bring him to Civappuṭaiyān so as to complete the sequence.

Although Civappuṭaiyān (*Katai*) is of low caste, he is nevertheless the king's chief watchman. Fate wills it that he is responsible for the protection and security of Āriyamālai, and this makes him the enemy of his own son, Kāttavarāyan. Thus in one episode Kāttavarāyan disfigures his father by cutting off his moustache (certainly the greatest indignity that could happen to a policeman or a watchman). Except once, when Kāttavarāyan leaves his father's place to find his real mother, Kāmākṣī, there is no love lost between father and son.

This is not so in the *Katai*. Cēppilaiyān's role as father of Kāttavarāyan contains some tragic moments. Cēppilaiyān here is also chief watchman of the kingdom, but he has nothing to do with Āriyamālai's safety. Still, because of his position he has to follow the king's order and arrest Kāttavarāyan, who has to stand trial for the abduction of Āriyamālai. Cēppilaiyān fulfills the order with a heavy heart. His wife is equally distressed at the news of Āriyamālai's abduction by her son. She laments and cries. She is the one who warns Kāttavarāyan that his beauty would lead to tragedy, that he should avoid the high caste streets; and while Kāttavarāyan journeys to Kāḷi, she is thoroughly distressed and sends her husband to find her missing son. Even Kāttavarāyan's Brahman parents show some sentiments towards their son: they rejoice when his identity is revealed to them.

A very large part of the *Ēcal* describes how Cēppilaiyān tours the country in search of Kāttavarāyan. The king is adamant to have the sinner (Kāttavarāyan) produced before him and he threatens Cēppilaiyān that failure to find his son would lead to Cēpilaiyān's own death at the stake.

The King

In its treatment of the relationship betwen Kāttavarāyan and the king, the *Katai* stands in sharp contrast to the other versions. In the *Katai* the king (Āriyappūrājan) is portrayed as a sort of godfather to Āriyamālai. It is the king who exhorts the Brahmans to ask the gods for a child boon, it is he who bestows wealth on Āriyamālai, it is he who has a strong fortification built for her, and it is he who appoints Civappuṭaiyān as her guard. Needless to say, he is no friend of anyone who tries to abduct his adopted daughter. Twice he arrests our hero, but Kāttavarāyan escapes each time (with a little bit of help from Mūdevī who puts the king, soldiers, and guards into a deep sleep).[14] Once Kāttavarāyan imprisons the king in the very box in which the king had enclosed him. Kāttavarāyan also denigrates the king when, disguised as the king himself, he deliberately delivers a false judgment, having disposed of the evidence in favour of the accused washerwoman Valli, and then decrees a cruel and unjust punishment. Only at the very end are Kāttavarāyan and the king reconciled. The king invites him and his three wives to stay in Tiruccirāppaḷḷi.

In the *Ammāṉai* the king (Āriyappan) shows a very friendly disposition towards Kāttavarāyan. He assigns him the job of chief watchman over his kingdom. When the Brahmans accuse Kāttavarāyan before the king and demand that he be punished for Āriyamālai's abduction, the king is reluctant to believe them. It is only when the Brahmans threaten to kill themselves that the king orders Kāttavarāyan to be arrested. Throughout the story Kāttavarāyan shows the king due respect. The same is true in the *Ēcal* where, however, Kāttavarāyan is not in the employ of the king. Both the *Ammāṉai* and the *Ēcal* depict the king as a just ruler. In the *Ēcal* all events center around the king, and Kāttavarāyan's story unfolds at the king's court in an altercation between the accused, Kāttavarāyan, and the victim, Āriyamālai.

Kāttavarāyan's mockery of the king in the *Katai* can be read as a sign of Kāttavarāyan's self-importance and arrogance: being a god, he can scoff at earthly laws, he is not bound by human moral codes, and no matter how strong the fetters that are placed on him, he cannot be subdued. He truly is king, as his name, Kāttavarāyan (guard-king) implies. It is perhaps significant that this name is much more frequent in the *Katai* than the *Ammāṉai*, where he is most of the time called Kāttavan, the name given to him by Cēppilaiyāṉ. Kāttavarāyan's superiority over earthly bonds, however, is also evident in the *Ammāṉai*. He reduces the chains on his arms to powder, and it is only because he agrees to it that Kāttavarāyan can be brought before the king in chains. Here Kāttavarāyan's superiority, however, does not lead him to insult the king.

The Brahmans

The greatest deviation of the *Katai* from the *Ammāṉai* is in the way in which Kāttavarāyan's relationship to the Brahmans is treated. Nowhere is Kāttavarāyan's evil nature more forcefully exhibited than in his deliberate humiliation and defilement of the Brahmans.

A small indication of Kāttavarāyan's deviation from his otherwise correct behaviour towards the Brahmans is found already in the *Ammāṉai*. When the Brahmans lament over the fact that they have been defiled by the Pariah's abduction of Āriyamālai, Kāttavarāyan, disguised as a Brahman,[15] counsels them to cut off and throw away their hair locks (*kuṭumi*) and sacred threads (marks of their Brahmanhood). This would redeem them from their affliction. When the Brahmans follow his advice, Kāttavarāyan smiles. He quickly hides his smile when the Brahmans look at him. Kāttavarāyan obviously enjoys his joke, but one feels that he did not play it with vicious intentions.

In the *Ēcal*, Āriyamālai, during her wordy duel with Kāttavarāyan, accuses him of having beaten her father. Kāttavarāyan admits that he grabbed her father (the Brahman) by his hair lock and beat him, but he had reason to do so: he had caught her father stealing the god Rāma's belt. Apart from these instances there is nothing to indicate a disrespect towards the Brahmans, and even the quoted incident in the *Ammānai* does not necessarily signify a prejudice against them. Kāttavarāyan also plays his jokes on the soldiers.

In the *Katai*, Kāttavarāyan's first ridicule of the Brahmans takes place early in the story. Āriyamālai's servants, punished by her for not delivering Kāttavarāyan's love letter to her, seek help from the Brahmans.[16] It being night, the Brahmans take the servants to be evil spirits and pelt them with stones. When they recognize the servants and hear their story, they rush to the tree in which Kāttavarāyan is sitting and throw stones at him. Kāttavarāyan causes the stones to stick to the leaves of the tree. The Brahmans then attempt to pull Kāttavarāyan from the tree, with the result that in the end the 1000 Brahmans hang in the tree, each one holding onto the legs of another. Kāttavarāyan releases them from their plight. They fall down. Nearby a mule stands ready at Kāttavarāyan's command. One Brahman (Āriyamālai's father, Appāpaṭṭar) holds onto the mule's tail and is about to strike it to chase it away when he becomes stuck to it. Another Brahman rushes there to help and also gets stuck. One Brahman after another rushes to help until all the 1000 Brahmans and their wives are stuck in a row to the mule and are dragged through the streets of the Agrahāra.

One could perhaps justify Kāttavarāyan's action by seeing it as a punishment for the Brahmans' transgression of *ahiṃsā*. Nevertheless, it would seem highly exaggerated, as indeed are all Kāttavarāyan's punishments. Even if we could accept this episode as a practical joke played on the Brahmans in order to teach them a lesson, one cannot excuse the manner in which Kāttavarāyan pollutes their purity.[17] It is noteworthy that Kāttavarāyan receives the order to defile the Brahmans from Kāmākṣī, but how he does it is left to him, and even the goddess later complains that her son has taken the matter too far. Kāttavarāyan commands his servants, Yama's demons (a gift from his mother, Kāmākṣī), to make each Brahman male sleep beside a Pariah female and vice-versa. As if this were not enough, he later poses as a Kācikkurukkaḷ and tells the Brahmans that their sin will be expiated if they throw their hair locks (kuṭumi), sacred threads, *pañcāṅkams* and turbans into the homa fire.[18] After the Brahmans have done all this, Kāttavarāyan gives them, among other things, demon's urine instead of sacred water to drink and fashions new sacred threads and turbans for them out of cowhide. Then he tells them to bathe. When they are in the water, the leather swells up and begins to smell. It is only at this point that the Brahmans realize that they have been tricked.

These anti-Brahman episodes are apparently later additions to the Kāttavarāyan story.[19] They are still now in the repertoire of the professional singers. They are, however, usually not sung anymore.[20] What strikes us is that the Brahmans are depicted as very gullible and unobservant people who seem to follow their caste rules mechanically and stolidly, who are so engrossed in their *ācāra* that they cannot make room for exceptions, nor see the god when he stands in front of them. Of all the personae of the play we should expect the Brahmans to be the ones who would recognize a god. Although they realize that Kāttavarāyan has tricked them, they do not ask themselves who the trickster could be. Their only concern is to have proper punishment meted out to the man who abducted their daughter. Kāttavarāyan's ill-treatment of the Brahmans is made worse by the fact that they are his potential in-laws (all of them, because Āriyamālai is always described as daughter of the 1000 Brahmans) and, after all, in the *Katai* it is Kāttavarāyan's desire for Āriyamālai which is the moving force of the plot and not his wish to become a god.

B. Kāttavarāyan's Relationship With His Women

Āriyamālai

Kāttavarāyan succeeds in all three versions to take Āriyamālai captive. One would suppose that the abduction and Kāttavarāyan's relationship with Āriyamālai are of sufficient importance to deserve detailed descriptions. Strangely enough, the *Katai* mentions the abduction only in passing: Kāttavarāyan, in the form of Īśvara, tells his demons to settle Āriyamālai at Kōmutalaippār.[21] The next we hear of her is when Kāttavarāyan disguises himself as a Pariah (a Veṭṭiyān whose profession it usually is to dig graves and attend to the burning corpses). He tells Āriyamālai that her father (Appāpaṭṭar) is dying and that he will bring her home. On the way Āriyamālai wearies, and Kāttavarāyan says to her with arrogance (āṇavam): "You eat ghee and rice (every day), but you cannot walk (a short distance)."[22] Then he leaves her. A farmer asks her why she is walking with a Pariah. She replies that it is her fate (or bad *karman*) given to her previously by the three-eyed one. (This is one of the references which identify Āriyamālai with the youngest maiden, cursed by Śiva to be born on earth.) Kāttavarāyan then brings Āriyamālai to Kāmākṣī's place without the latter's knowledge.

We see Āriyamālai again at the end as one of the three women who are on the stake with Kāttavarāyan. When Kāttavarāyan has fulfilled his fate and has left the stake alive, he gets married to Āriyamālai, Ukantalaki, Annamuttu, and Karuppalaki. In the end, however, he gives in to Śiva's counsel: he forgets Āriyamālai and lives with his other three wives in Tiruccirāppaḷḷi. It is a rather disappointing end to what began as an intense love story. Kāttavarāyan first falls in love with Āriyamālai when he breathes the fragrance of the water she bathed in. To get a look at her, he changes himself into a fish and gets entangled in one of her locks. Kāttavarāyan has various other encounters with Āriyamālai. Usually he is disguised (e.g., as bangle seller) or he takes on another form (e.g., that of a parrot). These episodes, replete with erotic imagery, serve to depict the passion of the two lovers, but a true face-to-face meeting is avoided in the story. In this same version, Āriyamālai's actual identity as the youngest of the maidens (the one whose clothes he stole in the flower garden) is only briefly stated, and Kāttavarāyan does not seem to be aware of Āriyamālai's identity.[23]

Whereas in the *Katai* Kāttavarāyan's main goal is the possession of Āriyamālai (he says he does not care if he has to die on the stake, but at least he wants to have Āriyamālai), in the *Ammāṉai* the abduction of Āriyamālai is only a necessary step on the way to Kāttavarāyan's apotheosis, his main aim. In the *Ammāṉai* he literally enchants Āriyamālai with a spell. When she follows him, Kāttavarāyan attempts to dissuade her. He makes it clear to her that he is a Pariah, but this has no effect on her. We are not told whether this is because she is truly in love with him (her first sight of Kāttavarāyan, before she is enchanted by his spell, makes her swoon), or because of the spell. Kāttavarāyan settles Āriyamālai in Kōmutalaippār and marries her there with all the gods as witnesses. In the *Katai* Kāttavarāyan marries Āriyamālai before he abducts her. He tricks her, and after she wakes from her enchantment, she is less than pleased and decides to drown herself. Kāttavarāyan then turns her into a stone, from which state a pūjā releases her.

In the *Ammānai* Kāttavarāyan also insists throughout that he is inferior to Āriyamālai. In an idyllic scene we see Kāttavarāyan bringing fruits to Āriyamālai and exhorting her to eat first. She refuses as the wife should eat after her husband has eaten, but Kāttavarāyan uses the argument that he is a Pariah and she a Brahman, and therefore she should eat first. Shortly before Kāttavarāyan decides it is time for him to mount the stake, he reveals his true identity to Āriyamālai. He also tells her that she and the other six maidens will become goddesses. Furthermore, right from the beginning of the story, Kāttavarāyan is aware that Āriyamālai is the youngest maiden, the indirect cause of Śiva's curse. When brought to trial, Kāttavarāyan explains to the king and the Brahmans that he has committed no crime: he did not abduct Āriyamālai, on the contrary, it was she who followed him, despite the fact that he tried to dissuade her explaining to her that he is a Pariah (Kāttavarāyan conveniently forgets to mention that he placed her under a spell). Finally Kāttavarāyan discloses his Brahman birth. King and Brahmans rejoice and urge Kāttavarāyan to bring Āriyamālai back and to live happily with her. Kāttavarāyan, however, explains that his fate is different.

In the *Ēcal* Kāttavarāyan and Āriyamālai are depicted as opponents. Brought before the king they accuse each other, Āriyamālai insisting that Kāttavarāyan used various tricks and spells on her to abduct her, whereas Kāttavarāyan maintains that Āriyamālai fell in love with him and followed him when she saw his beauty. Perhaps the scene is nothing but a quarrel between lovers. In any case in this version Āriyamālai turns out to be the perfect match for Kāttavarāyan: she is his cross-cousin (i.e., Kāttavarāyan's mother's brother's daughter). This version also makes it clear that Āriyamālai is the youngest of the maidens.

The Seven Maidens

In both the *Ammānai* and the *Ēcal* we are told that the seven maidens have to be born on earth due to Śiva's curse. The *Ēcal* makes only the briefest mention of their names, places of birth, and the circumstances under which Kāttavarāyan meets them. The *Ammānai,* however, describes these meetings in detail. In the *Ammānai* all the maidens are in some way of help to Kāttavarāyan, and most of them feed him. I list the maidens in the order they appear in this version.

1. Cavutāyi born in Kaḷattūr. Kāttavarāyan first asks her for curds and buttermilk. He is in the disguise of a soldier. Then he kills the cock which she has raised and dedicated to her family deity Muttukkaruppan. As a gypsy, Kāttavarāyan revives the bird and advises everyone to worship Kāttavan and to name their children Kāttavarāyan, Kāttāyi, and Parimaḷarāyan (i.e., after him).
2. Karuppāyi from Kaccinakar. Kāttavarāyan as an old Brahman asks her for milk and curds.
3. Pūvāyi from Pāccūr. Kāttavarāyan eats chicken curry and drinks liquor at her shop. Pūvāyi later promises the soldiers to help them arrest Kāttavarāyan, and when he comes to her shop a second time, she serves him a curry meal and liquor in which she has mixed some drug so that Kāttavarāyan faints.
4. Nalli from Puttūr or Piccāṇṭārkōvil (Puttūr, Āriyamālai's birth place, lies next to Piccāṇṭārkōvil). Nalli is Āriyamālai's washerwoman. She hands Āriyamālai's clothes to Kāttavarāyan so that he can place a spell in them.
5. Ōntāyi from Vairiceṭṭippāḷaiyam, born into a merchant family. She is abducted by Kāttavarāyan and brought to Kōmutalaippār to be a helper and friend to Āriyamālai.
6. Nallataṅkāḷ from Mānpiṭimaṅkaḷam. She is a shepherd girl who climbs up the stake to quench Kāttavarāyan's thirst with buttermilk.

These episodes and their sequence are reminiscent of a pūjā. Kāttavarāyan is mainly a family or clan deity and he still receives the offerings of meat and liquor. Curds, milk and buttermilk are known to be cooling substances. These are often offered to devotees who perform (or have performed) particularly difficult vows (sacrifices) such as walking over hot coals.

In the *Katai* we are faced with a great confusion regarding the seven maidens. All the maidens just mentioned play a part in the *Katai*, but they are never equated with the original seven whose encounter with Kāttavarāyan in the flower garden leads to Śiva's curse. Their identity, however, becomes clear upon a comparison with the *Ammānai*. Campaṅkitāci is a great gambling lady. Kāttavarāyan defeats her in the game with the help of Cinnān who steals her magic bone. Kāttavarāyan releases the unfortunate kings who had lost the game, and then he kills the lady. Clearly Campaṅki corresponds to Cavutāyi, which gives her the only reason to be in the story. Similarly we are never told who Pūpi is. Kāttavarāyan gets thoroughly drunk at her shop and thus can easily be bound by the king's soldiers. Pūpi again is no other than the maiden Puvāyi of the *Ammānai*. The other maidens in the *Katai* are Valli, the washerwoman; Ukantalaki, corresponding to Ōntāyi; Karuppalaki, corresponding to Karuppāyi; Nallataṅkāḷ; and one extra, Annamuttu, who appears mysteriously towards the end of the story and becomes one of Kāttavarāyan's wives. Neither the *Ammānai* nor the *Ēcal* can offer an explanation for Annamuttu.

The *Katai* tells us of two sets of maidens: the first are the maidens from the Kolli hills. They are the ones who raise Kāttavarāyan and teach him the art of magic. The second set of maidens resembles the original set in the flower garden. The youngest of these maidens recognizes Kāttavarāyan as the god they have been doing tapas for. They pursue him, but he eludes them by taking various forms. In the end Kāmākṣī curses the maidens to become stones in order to save Kāttavarāyan from their anger. These maidens are perhaps a projection of the seven maidens of the Paccai hills in the *Ammānai*. In that text, on his way to see Kāmākṣī, Kāttavarāyan passes these hills and steals some fruits in the maidens' garden. Enraged, they set fire to the mountain. When Kāttavarāyan tells them who he is, they are pleased and wish to accompany him to Kāmākṣī. He tells them that this is not necessary and that he will bring Kāmākṣī to them, a promise he keeps.

In the *Katai* Kāttavarāyan's relationship with the *true* maidens—i.e., the ones who correspond to the *Ammānai*—is very ambiguous. He kills two of them, Valli and Campaṅkitāci. He marries three: Āriyamālai, Karuppalaki, and Ukantalaki. He helps one, Nallataṅkāḷ. The treatment of Nallataṅkāḷ is consistent in both the *Katai* and the *Ammānai*. Nallataṅkāḷ becomes the innocent victim of her family's wrath, perhaps a reflection of her "true" story.[24] In the *Ammānai* the family scolds her because she returns with a pot full of rice, gift of Kāttavarāyan, instead of the money she should have gained selling the buttermilk. In the *Katai* Nallataṅkāḷ inadvertently breaks the pot of buttermilk when she trips at the sight of the troups and crowds that have assembled to watch Kāttavarāyan die on the stake. When Nallataṅkāḷ gets beaten by her mother-in-law and her husband(s), Kāttavarāyan intervenes.[25] Kāttavarāyan's intervention on her behalf only becomes clear in connection with the *Ammānai* where it is she who offers Kāttavarāyan buttermilk when he is on the stake.

Whereas in the *Ammānai* Kāttavarāyan marries only Āriyamālai, in the *Katai* he has three wives (if we include Annamuttu, four). According to the *Katai*, Karuppalaki is Viṣṇu's (Perumāḷ's) daughter, i.e., she is Kāttavarāyan's cross-cousin and therefore his legitimate bride. Iconographically Kāttavarāyan is often depicted with two women: Āriyamālai, on his right, and Ōntāyi (Ukantalaki), on his left (see plates 1 to 3). One may wonder why it is the Ceṭṭi girl Ōntāyi rather than Karuppāyi (Karuppalaki) who is given this pride of place. One could argue that Kāttavarāyan's iconography was modelled on that of Murukan (with whom he is identified in the *Katai*) or Maturai Vīran. Of the two wives of these gods one is of high caste, and the other stems from a tribal, or low caste, origin.[26] With Āriyamālai already taking the position of the high caste wife, Karuppalaki (being his legitimate wife) is necessarily eliminated. Ōntāyi belongs to the merchant caste. She comes from Vairiceṭṭippāḷaiyam, a place named after Vairiceṭṭi whom Kāttavarāyan subdues. Vairiceṭṭi has found a place in the Kāmākṣī temple of this village (see below), and one can conjecture that Ōntāyi's place beside Kāttavarāyan has a historical reason, one connected with this Ceṭṭi family's previous influence in the area. As the case may be, we can see in the iconographic representation of the two wives an attempt at assimilating Kāttavarāyan with other, more famous deities such as Murukan, Aiyanār, and Maturai Vīran.

Summarizing Kāttavarāyan's relationship with superiors and women, we notice in the *Katai* a trend in Kāttavarāyan to free himself from various bonds: his low caste, his earthly parents, his dependence on the gods above him, and his responsibility towards his wife. He attains a certain independence which makes him bold enough to mock the very ideals and ethical codes which, in the *Ammānai*, he is part of and helps to maintain. Kāttavarāyan exhibits strains of cruelty in the *Katai* which seem to contradict his status as a god and which, together with his arrogance, make him akin to the demons.

C. Kāttavarāyan's Disguises and Use of Magic

In all three versions Kāttavarāyan knows the art of magic and of changing his shape. In all three versions again he takes the form of persons of various castes, from the Pariah weaver (*Ammānai*) and the washerman to the king and the Brahman. In the *Ēcal* and the *Katai* he also takes the forms of animals: frog (*Ēcal*), parrot, fish, etc. (*Katai*). The disguises serve him often to trick someone or to get himself out of difficult situations. For the same purposes Kāttavarāyan uses his magic. One of the first journeys of Kāttavarāyan in the *Katai* is to Kerala (famous for its magicians) where he meets Cinnān, the Toṭṭiyan. Kāttavarāyan takes the disguise of a snake charmer, a profession held

1. Kāttavarāyan temple, Vāttalai (Kōmutalaippār). On the right of Kāttavarāyan is Āriyamālai, on his left is Ōntāyi. The *koṇṭai* (hair tied into a knot) worn on the left side of the head was a fashion introduced by the Nāyaks. Photo by Eveline Masilamani-Meyer.

2. Kāmākṣī temple, Kūttūr. The statues of Kāttavarāyan, Āriyamālai and Ōntāyi are new. Facing the offering tray below Kāttavarāyan is the head of the merchant Vairiceṭṭi. The Kāmākṣī temple and its various shrines were recently renovated. Photo by Eveline Masilamani-Meyer.

3. Kāmākṣī temple, Vairiceṭṭippāḷaiyam. Kāttavarāyan, Āriyamālai and Ōntāyi. Below Kāttavarāyan's feet is the head of Vairiceṭṭi with a Vaiṣṇava *nāmam* mark. Photo by Eveline Masilamani-Meyer.

by Toṭṭiyans, who were also known to be sorcerers.[27] Perhaps an identification between Kāttavarāyan and Cinnān is intended here. Kāttavarāyan agrees to a competition in magic with Cinnān and loses. Cinnān later becomes Kāttavarāyan's friend and helper, Kāttavarāyan's own magic abilities thus being supplemented by Cinnān's superior magic power. Yet all this magic is of no use when it comes to the abduction of Āriyamālai. Cinnān refuses in the end to help Kāttavarāyan, seeing the abduction as a vain endeavor, but Kāttavarāyan is not perturbed. He praises his own skill and prowess and tells Cinnān more or less to go to hell.

As in Kāttavarāyan's behaviour with people, we notice a tendency towards evil in his use of magic in the *Katai*. Whereas in the *Ammānai* a negative magic act is usually offset by a positive one (the killing of a person is followed by a revival), in the *Katai* the negative prevails (e.g., the Brahman episodes, or the case of Valli who, together with her daughter, gets tricked several times and killed in the end).

Furthermore, one has to make a distinction between the magic power which all gods possess and the magic powers of the human sorcerer. This distinction is clearly made in the *Ammānai*. To start off with, Kāttavarāyan exhibits his magic power even before Kāḷi bestows on him her magic sword, mantras, etc. He places a spell on the birds in Kāḷi's abode and he singlehandedly subdues Kāḷi's armies of demons and evil spirits. More important, however, is that Kāttavarāyan as god (i.e., after his apotheosis) fights against two magicians. Cinnān, the Toṭṭiyan, has bound Māmatura Kāḷi with a spell, and she has to serve him (*ēval ceyya*). Kāttavarāyan challenges Cinnan, and after he has revealed his superior power, cuts off Cinnān's head. Incidentally, this is the only place in the *Ammānai* where we hear of Cinnān. Another sorcerer, Vairiceṭṭi, pleads for mercy after Kāttavarāyan has destroyed his witchcraft (*pilli*). Kāttavarāyan grants him the boon to become a deity called Ceṭṭiperumāḷ and to receive pūjā in Kāmākṣī's temple. Vairiceṭṭi's shrine is in the compound of the Kāmākṣī temple. Vairiceṭṭi has a *nāmam* on his forehead to mark his Vaiṣṇava affiliation. Meanwhile, Kāttavarāyan, who also has a shrine in this temple, is depicted with the same Vairiceṭṭi's head under his feet. According to the priest, Kāttavarāyan beheaded Vairiceṭṭi (see plate 3).

In the *Katai*, Kāttavarāyan learns all his magic while he grows up under the care of the seven maidens. Apart from having the sorcerer Cinnān as his helper, Kāttavarāyan makes ample use of his servants, Yama's demons (*pūtam*), whom he transforms according to his needs and who, more often than not, do "the dirty work" for him. In the

Katai we see in Kāttavarāyan's use of magic again a shift in values from a higher to a lower order.

D. The Stake (kaḻu), Sacrifice and Apotheosis

In all three versions Kāttavarāyan is aware that he cannot escape his fate: to suffer on the stake to atone for his sin (*pāvam tīra*). We have already mentioned that Kāttavarāyan's attention is shifted from a wish to become a god (*Ammāṉai*) to a desire to obtain Āriyamālai (*Katai*). In the *Katai* the scene of the stake is described with much pathos. Kāttavarāyan, pierced at various parts of his body by nails and hooks, languishes on the stake, while there is great wailing and lamentation among the spectators.[28] On each side and behind Kāttavarāyan are the three women: Āriyamālai, Ukantalaki and Annamuttu. We must imagine them standing on a platform, as each of the ladies is said to be in a box or nest (kūṇṭu). Even the gods feel pity and Viṣṇu, on behalf of his sister and all the gods, appeals to Śiva. If Kāmākṣī's tears fall on the earth, a great disaster will happen, he tells Śiva. Śiva gets angry and replies that Kāttavarāyan is a disobedient child and that he (Śiva) will not be moved to pity. It takes some convincing and the sight of his suffering son to make Śiva tell Kāttavarāyan finally to come down from the stake (*iraṅkaṭā!*) and to live. Kāttavarāyan descends, a great celebration follows, and Kāttavarāyan goes to live in Tiruccirāppaḷḷi with his wives—whether as god or man is left open (he receives a fort and various other earthly goods as dowry).

In the *Ammāṉai* Kāttavarāyan mounts the stake alone. He praises his parents (the gods) and blesses all the people. He calls the seven maidens (including Āriyamālai). They come to the bottom of the stake where they leave their bodies (*uṭal viṭa*, i.e., die) and join Kāttavarāyan. Kāmākṣī bestows on Kāttavarāyan his form as god (*teyva corūpam*). He shall receive the first pūjā in the sanctum of the Trimūrti (*mūvaruṭa cannitiyil mutalppūcai yunnatu tāṉ*).[29]

In the *Ēcal* Kāttavarāyan's suffering is described, but at the same time his being on the stake is said to be his play (*viḷaiyāṭal*). After Kāttavarāyan has blessed everyone, he dies like a child in a crib.[30]

The stake or stake tree (kaḻu, kaḻumaram) is a 60 foot long square pole of hard wood (ebony or teak). It is not pointed at the top. According to informants, it was not used for impaling people—which would in any case seem impossible at such a height—rather, the person who was to die was placed on a small platform close to the top of the pole and there tied and fastened with hooks. He was then left to die without food and water. Still today a number of temples own such stakes. They are used during the festival (see below). At the bottom the stake or pole is planted into a platform. Pointing skywards, this stake tree is a powerful symbol of Kāttavarāyan's deification, his ascension back into the sphere of the gods.

In the *Ammānai* the stake is used by Kāttavarāyan for yet another purpose. Kāttavarāyan journeys to Kāmākṣī's place. There, beyond many forests, in the middle of a flower garden, Kāttavarāyan does tapas by standing on a copper needle which is on top of a copper pot which in turn is on top of a 60 foot pole (kampam). The purpose of this severe tapas is to get a boon from his parents. Śiva, to test Kāttavarāyan, sends out one of his demons disguised as a Brahman. The Brahman tells Kāttavarāyan that he also had done tapas on a needle, etc., like Kāttavarāyan, only he had done it standing on his *head.* Śiva and Pārvatī, however, had not appeared to him, so he had given it up. Why should he (Kāttavarāyan) persist? He will have no chance at all. "Come down," he advises Kāttavarāyan. But Kāttavarāyan persists. The Brahman's taunts do not affect him, his faith cannot be shaken. Kāttavarāyan then lists a number of people who received boons from Śiva.

Kāttavarāyan not only displays faith, but also a strong will-power and self-assurance bordering on pride. He is prepared to put Śiva and Kāmākṣī to a test: he threatens to cut off his head with Kāḷi's magic sword, unless Śiva and Kāmākṣī grant him the following boons: to abduct Āriyamālai, to mount the stake, to become a god on earth (as guard of the Trimūrti), and, in addition, the boon that Śiva and Kāmākṣī will follow him and receive pūjā. When they refuse him the last part of the boon (to follow him), he again threatens to cut off his head. Śiva and Kāmākṣī finally have to agree to prevent a sin (*pāvam*).[31]

In the *Katai* this episode is divided. Just before Kāttavarāyan mounts the stake (after he has revealed himself to the king and others as god—Murukan), he begs Kāmākṣī again for the boon to abduct Āriyamālai. When his mother refuses, Kāttavarāyan plants a sword on the ground and threatens to throw himself on it. (Kāmākṣī never openly agrees, but because Kāttavarāyan does not commit suicide, we can surmise that he takes her silence to mean a positive answer). When Kāttavarāyan is on the stake, Śiva sends Kuṇṭōtaran, in the form of a beetle, to drill through the stake until it falls onto the ground.[32] As a reason Śiva says: "We have to subdue (bring down) his (Kāttavarāyan's) arrogance (*matam aṭakka*) to the point where he cannot bear it anymore." But Cinnān intervenes, ties up Kuṇṭōtaran and saves Kāttavarāyan's glory. The stake in the *Katai* becomes an instrument of punishment: Kāttavarāyan does not care if he dies, but he must have Āriyamālai, and it also becomes an instrument to prove Kāttavarāyan's independence. Śiva calls him a disobedient child. Kāttavarāyan's recalcitrance provokes Śiva, but Kāttavarāyan wins in the end.

Kāttavarāyan's suffering on the stake is a sacrifice. In the *Katai* the sacrifice is for selfish purposes—to gain Āriyamālai; Kāttavarāyan has already revealed himself as god, and his apotheosis does not depend on his death on the stake. In the *Ammānai* the sacrifice—a true sacrifice (Kāttavarāyan dies and is reborn)—transcends any selfish reasons: Kāttavarāyan wishes to become a god. But more than that, by his tapas and sacrifice he has persuaded his parents to follow him. Śiva and Kāmākṣī will therefore be established on earth and accept the offerings of the devotees. In other words, through the intermediation of Kāttavarāyan Śiva and Pārvatī have become directly accessible to the people on earth. The stake then becomes a symbol of sacrifice, rebirth, and transcendence, a means of access to the deities (through tapas); but on a more mundane level it also stands for the established order which forbids intercaste marriage.

E. Kāttavarāyan as God on Earth

Kāttavarāyan's birth to Brahman parents turns his sin into a superficial pretext for his true reason on earth: to become a god on *earth.* In the *Katai* Kāmākṣī shares Kāttavarāyan's fate. Śiva expels her from his left side, from heaven. He curses her to be a demon, an evil spirit, in other words, to become a goddess on earth, dangerous as an evil spirit. It is a characteristic feature of folk deities that they live on earth and are not, like Śiva, for example, enthroned permanently in heaven. Although these deities are established on earth, we have to understand that their access to heaven is not barred; on the contrary, they seem to shuttle between these two worlds or live in both worlds, a feat which the avatāra concept accommodates.[33] Why this urgency that the deity should be on earth? The deity has to be accessible to his devotee, receive his pūjā offerings, grant him his wishes. The deity takes possession of the devotee, speaks to or through him, etc. There may be another reason, one which is made explicit in the story of Aṅkāḷamman: Śiva curses this goddess to live on earth *and* to enjoy the fruits of all the offences or sins (pāvam) committed by humans.[34] Here, then, the deity's karman is clearly linked with that of the devotees. The deity has to interact with the worshippers and thereby becomes tainted or polluted. The sins or pollutions with which the deity (on earth) is charged are again removed by the deity's own suffering. This suffering can take the form of a death and rebirth or the form of severe tapas.[35]

The same idea that deity and devotee are not independent units but part of a larger system which places them in relation to each other is also expressed in the story of Kāttavarāyan. In the *Katai* Kāmākṣī's presence on earth can only be terminated when her son has fulfilled his fate, has mounted the stake, and we have seen that in the *Ammānai* Kāttavarāyan forces his parents to accord him his wish by threatening to cut off his head—an act by which he would charge them with guilt (*paḻi pōṭa*) and cause a sin.

Surely the purpose behind a marriage between a Pariah and a Brahman has a much deeper meaning than simply anti-caste sentiments. The marriage between a Pariah male and a Brahman female is the greatest transgression against caste rules. Offspring from such a union are classed among the lowest beings. The very gravity of the offense (compare Śiva's Brahmanicide) places Kāttavarāyan amongst the most despicable of men and makes him a criminal deserving a cruel death. But Kāttavarāyan, being born to Brahman parents, is in fact innocent, and his suffering at the stake becomes a sacrifice rather than a punishment. In other words, if Kāttavarāyan has to be born on earth as a god, he first has to die, and his death has to be *violent*. It is well-known that humans who die a violent, sudden, often unjust death, are later deified.[36] Śiva's curse, which involves the Pariah Kāttavarāyan with a Brahman woman, could therefore be a pretext to subject Kāttavarāyan to a violent death, to make him the innocent sacrificial victim. Still, the violence of Kāttavarāyan's death alone does not seem a satisfactory answer for the Pariah-Brahman marriage, a theme which underlies a number of myths or tales.[37]

The marriage of a Pariah god with a Brahman woman or of a Brahman goddess with a Pariah man, a god's double parentage (one set of parents being of high caste, the other of low caste, e.g., Kāttavarāyan, Maturai Vīran), and the theme of the split body (e.g., the story of Reṇukā) seem to be various expressions of the paradox that the deity in question is both a Pariah and a Brahman. A similar statement is perhaps made when a god is given two wives (one of high and one of low caste) or when a goddess has two lovers-husbands, one being a demon, the other Śiva.[38] The god on earth has to be both transcendent, free, beyond duality and conflict, untouched by creation and destruction, birth and death, and at the same time be immanent, undergoing birth and death himself. This double aspect makes the god a perfect mediator between the devotee, caught in the world of conflict, on the one hand, and the transcendent on the other.

Reṇukā's story is very apt. She is one of Brahmā's daughters and wife of a sage.[39] When she realizes that she has the body of an Untouchable, she does not return to her husband (probably in heaven) but remains as Māriyamman on earth, where she brings disease and death but also cures and rebirth.[40] Although she is involved in the violence and impure activities on earth, a part of her, symbolized by her Brahman head, remains in the realm of the transcendent, the pure. The head, we could say then, connects the goddess with the world of Śiva, whereas the rest of her body links her with the devotees on earth.

Although the deity (on earth) is both caught in the world of conflict and beyond it, we have to see him or her as part of a hierarchic system. Depending on the deity's place in the hierarchy, he or she is closer or further removed from the transcendent plane. In other words, the wholly transcendent (deity) is immanent in all, but not affected by anything, whereas the least transcendent (deity) is the most involved in and affected by the conflict.

Throughout the *Ammāṉai* Kāttavarāyan keeps repeating his life story. He states that he is born to Brahman parents, found by a Pariah and brought up by Cēppilaiyāṉ. The listener then is constantly aware of Kāttavarāyan's parentage. In the *Katai*, as we have already mentioned, our hero prefers to identify himself simply as a son of Śiva. Seen in the light of what we have said earlier, we could perhaps interpret Kāttavarāyan's marriage to at least two low caste women in the *Katai* as a compensation for his disregard of his low parentage. We could further explain Kāttavarāyan's change of character in the *Katai* as an attempt to take him (the god) out of the social and divine hierarchy (of the *Ammāṉai*) and then to place him back into it, but a step higher, closer to Śiva, as is shown in the following diagram:

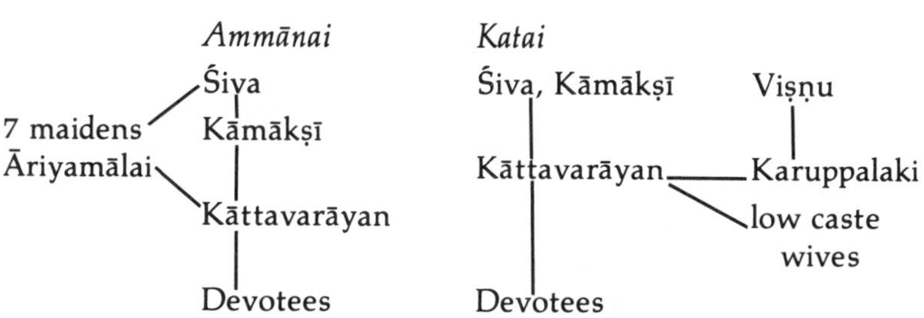

In the *Ammānai* Kāttavarāyan retains a close relationship with Kāmākṣī. He establishes temples for her and stays with her, receiving meat and liquor offerings from the devotees. As her "impure" guard, Kāttavarāyan holds a mediating position between her and the devotees. Kāmākṣī, in turn, stands in a mediating position between Kāttavarāyan and Śiva. In the *Katai* Śiva and Kāmākṣī return to heaven. Kāttavarāyan remains on earth alone, with his wives. In the *Katai* Kāttavarāyan has already been moved up to a level where he transcends opposites. He has lost, so to speak, his Pariah body. He can make fun of the Brahmans because he is a Super-Brahman, above caste hierarchy. But Kāttavarāyan has to remain on earth, and to compensate for the loss of his low caste body, he marries not Āriyamālai, but two women of low caste. At the same time, however, he secures his place in the hierarchy of the gods by marrying Karuppalaki, Viṣṇu's daughter, thus compensating for the loss of his relationship with Āriyamālai.

F. The Changing Face of Kāttavarāyan

Before we try to assess what could have brought about the change in Kāttavarāyan's face, let us list the main characteristics of our hero in the *Ammānai* and the *Katai*.

The *Ammānai* portrays Kāttavarāyan as a model hero: he fights heroic battles, he subdues dangerous (evil) enemies, he shows prowess, strength of willpower. He has devotion towards his divine parents and respect for his earthly parents and the king. He moves in and out of various castes (by means of his disguises and through his connection with the seven maidens).[41] Although some resentment towards Brahmans (as made explicit by Kāttavarāyan's mockery of them) cannot de denied in this version, it is of small importance to the whole story. In the *Ammānai*, on the whole, Kāttavarāyan shows himself as a god who favors all castes and whom all castes should or may accept. In the *Ammānai* Kāttavarāyan is a god, but he is also human (much more so than in the *Katai*). His humanness, his admission that he is a "fallen" god, a god who has to atone for his sin by being born on earth and whose fate it is to sin again, facilitates his devotees' identification with him.

Kāttavarāyan, as depicted in the *Katai*, mocks the social order (Brahman, king, low caste) and the divine hierarchy (e.g., when he makes his father, Śiva, a washerman, or when, as a dancing girl, he causes Viṣṇu to fall in love with him). He is a criminal (kills women), is filled with pride, is at times cowardly and mean and at other times brave and compassionate. He identifies himself with Viṣṇu (as Raṅkar—the colored one), and he claims as his true form that of Murukan. His main preoccupation is with women, but he also derides his own erotic leanings (his favorite form is that of a decrepit old man, and as such he once pleads with Cinnān, holding his own nose, to take him away quickly from the dangerous smell of women). Although Kāttavarāyan worships his mother Kāmākṣī faithfully every time he visits her to nag her about Āriyamālai, he is no model devotee, nor can his behaviour be a model *for* the devotees.

Kāttavarāyan's change from the innocent victim who is sacrificed at the stake to become a god on earth, accessible to his devotees (*Ammānai*), to an arrogant and sometimes mean prankster who turns the social conventions upside-down, cannot easily be explained.

Does the *Katai* reflect a decay of the social order and belief system, and is it possible that the *Katai*, by making the listener aware of the confusion, exhorts him to set things right? Kāttavarāyan's frustration at not receiving Kāmākṣī's permission to abduct Āriyamālai (—"Mother, how many times do I have to ask you for this boon?"—) was greatly exaggerated by the professional singers of the story.[42] Have the gods become indifferent to our needs, are they just playing with us instead of helping us? Even in the *Ammānai* Kāttavarāyan voices his discontent when he asks why he should feel guilty for something the gods indulge in as well (—"Did not Kṛṣṇa steal the clothes of the *gōpīs*," etc.—).[43]

If the story of Kāttavarāyan is to instill in the listener any noble sentiments and cause him to reflect on the eternal problem of life and death, the *Ammānai* seems more appropriate an instrument than the *Katai*. The *Ammānai* and the *Ēcal* are meant to be sung at the time of the festival. Those singers who themselves are devotees of Kāttavarāyan generally know the story as it is narrated in the *Ammānai* or the *Ēcal*.[44] As opposed to the *Katai*, the *Ammānai* is marked by a seriousness of tone. Its narrative is cohesive and clear. The *Katai* differs from the *Ammānai* not only in its comic scenes. It exhibits inconsistencies and it is replete with repetitions and often unnecessary details. We also see a greater use of erotic and stereotype imagery.[45] These signs point to the itinerant professional singer whose foremost interest it is to prolong his performance and to entertain his audience; a singer whose main concern is not to evoke feelings of devotion in the audience, but to enchant the listeners. The *Katai* sometimes reads like a scenario for a Tamil film, and it is not surprising that the Tamil film "Kāttavarāyan" is based on the story of the *Katai*.

Kāttavarāyan's change of character can be seen in relation to an increase of his popularity and a spread of his cult. There is a trend in the *Katai* to take Kāttavarāyan out of his parochial surroundings and to assimilate him or bring him into relation with more popular and known characters. Giants or Asuras of various names with whom Kāttavarāyan fights in the *Ammānai*, Periyaṇṇacāmi, and the magician Vairiceṭṭi are some of the figures who disappear in the *Katai*. Instead, Viṣṇu and Murukan enter the picture.[46]

The *Katai* disengages Kāttavarāyan from the limited geography of his cultic centres and transposes him into a more mythological realm. In the *Katai* Kāttavarāyan gains a certain independence, and this process is connected with a shift of values. Devotion and surrender (*Ammānai*) yield to self-confidence and detachment. Mockery, parody,[47] imagination, but also a certain clumsy rudeness are the means by which Kāttavarāyan hopes to appeal to the masses and propagate his fame. Kāttavarāyan's spread beyond the Tiruccirāppaḷḷi district proves that he was not entirely unsuccessful, but his position in the temple hierarchy shows that he has not been able to escape his role as guard and child of his much greater mother.

G. Kāttavarāyan in the Cult

We can only touch shortly upon the cult of Kāttavarāyan.[48] The story of Kāttavarāyan takes place in a relatively small area stretching from Tiruccirāppaḷḷi in a northern direction up to the two hilly ranges called Kollimalai (on the Nāmakkal side) and Paccaimalai (on the Perampalūr side). Puttūr (Āriyamālai's birth place) and Pāccūr (where Kāttavarāyan mounts the stake) are both close to Nocciyam which lies on the road following the Kāvēri westwards leading from Tiruccirāppaḷḷi to Āmūr. Kōmutalaippār (i.e., Vāttalai—where Kāttavarāyan settles Āriyamālai) lies on the same road approximately ten kilometers west of Nocciyam. Vairiceṭṭippāḷaiyam (from where Kāttavarāyan abducts the Ceṭṭi girl Ōntāyi to bring her to Āriyamālai) lies at the eastern foot of the Kolli hills.

With the exception of the temple in Vāttalai, I have not come across a temple dedicated to Kāttavarāyan alone. Usually he is a subdeity (*parivāratēvatai*) in a goddess temple: in the Tiruccirāppaḷḷi area mainly in temples for Kāmākṣī, in Tañcāvūr and west thereof in Māriyamman temples. In the South Arcot district we find Kāttavarāyan also in Aṅkāḷamman temples. The temple in Vāttalai was recently constructed. It faces a maṇḍapa at the tip of a small peninsula jutting into the Aiyāru (a branch of the Kāvēri). The maṇḍapa marks the place where Kāttavarāyan brought Āriyamālai (i.e., Kōmutalaippār).[49] The original Kāttavarāyan temple in Vāttalai, established 93 years ago, no longer exists.[50] There is now a separate temple to Kāttavarāyan and another temple in which we find Cinnān, Vināyakar, Kāmākṣī, Periyaṇṇacāmi, Āriyamālai, Kāttavarāyan, Ōntāyi, and Maturai Vīran. This is the only temple in which I have seen Cinnān. Apart from Kāttavarāyan, one often finds in Kāmākṣī temples the following *parivāra* deities: Māci Periyaṇṇacāmi,[51] Maturai Vīran, Ceṅkamāmuni (an Asura Kāttavarāyan fights on his way to Kāmākṣī's place—*Ammānai*), Vairavar (Bhairava), and some form of Karuppan. Kāttavarāyan is usually depicted with a kiṇṇāram in his hand. Āriyamālai and Ōntāyi stand on each side of him.

How old is the cult of Kāttavarāyan? Kāmākṣī was worshipped in Kūttūr as far back as 1310. This temple was established by Cōliya Vēḷāḷars, and a branch of the same family erected the temple in Vairiceṭṭippāḷaiyam. Both temples contain Kāttavarāyan and both temples are mentioned in the *Ammānai*. Most temple priests and singers of the story I spoke to thought that the events of Kāttavarāyan took place around 600 years ago.[52]

The two main castes who worship Kāttavarāyan as *kulateyvam* in the Tiruccirāppaḷḷi area are the Vēḷāḷar and Muttirājā. They are also the priests in the Kāmākṣī temples. Many families still celebrate the main festival for Kāttavarāyan, called "mounting the stake" (*kaluvērral*). In Pāccūr the festival took place in 1986 (in the month of Paṅkuni)[53] after a lapse of 20 years, a lapse due to family quarrels. A person of the family (they are Śaiva Vēḷāḷars) dresses up as Kāttavarāyan (see plate 4). He comes first to the Kāmākṣī temple, which lies in the middle of the fields. There Kāttavarāyan is tied with flower ropes and then brought to nearby Pāccūr, where he mounts the stake (see plate 5)—a 60 foot pole on top of which a small square hut has been set up (brightly lit with neon lamps). There Kāttavarāyan sits in a state of minor (?) possession.[54] One man, representing Nallataṅkāḷ, brings buttermilk up to Kāttavarāyan. An Ācāri (Smith) climbs up with a hook. He does not insert the hook in Kāttavarāyan's neck. (It used to be the practice to insert a golden hook in the person's neck). Towards dawn Kāttavarāyan descends the stake again and throws flower garlands as *prasāda* into the crowd. Some singers were present at this festival, but only very small portions of the story were sung. Obviously the festival has been curtailed to a large extent. Informants say that

4. Pāccūr. Mr. M. Katirvēl dressed as Kāttavarāyan before ascending the "stake" at the Kaluvērral festival in 1986. In his left hand he holds a silver kiṇṇāram. Photo by Rollo Masilamani.

5. Pāccūr. The kalumaram stored alongside the house of the Śaiva Vēḷāḷar family. The actor impersonating Kāttavarāyan has to ascend this 60 foot high "stake" during the festival. Photo by Eveline Masilamani-Meyer.

walking on sandals studded with nails used to be a feature of the festival. Furthermore, Kāttavarāyan used to be bound with heavy chains (see plate 6).

The ceremony performed for Kāttavarāyan in the Nellukkaṭai Māriyamman temple of Nākappaṭṭinam is still called *ceṭil utsavam* (hook-*utsava*), but instead of hooking Kāttavarāyan up on his back and raising him in the air, he stands in a square frame, which is pulled up and swirled around. The idea that the kalu, however, is a symbol for rebirth is still being transmitted. Every time Kāttavarāyan makes one round in the air, he hold a child in his arms. The parents believe that this will guarantee a long and healthy life to the child. It is also on this day that sick people are brought to the temple on a bier (like dead bodies) and "revived" by the goddes Māriyamman.

Traditionally the kaluvērral is the only festival celebrated for Kāttavarāyan. Since recently, however, a wedding festival for Kāttavarāyan takes place in Vāttalai also. There, as in a number of other temples, the kaluvērral is also celebrated, despite the protest of some devotees who believe that it should only take place in Pāccūr. What is truly unfortunate is the fact that the Kāttavarāyan story is no longer sung during the festival. The reason can partly be ascribed to the triumph of cinema songs and loudspeakers, but mainly to the great expenditure involved in the festival. Nowadays a kaluvērral festival lasts from one to three days, as opposed to the twelve or more days it would take to recite the *Ammānai*. The result is that the old professional singers use their palm leaf manuscripts as fire wood to cook their meagre portions of rice.

NOTES

1. The research on Kāttavarāyan and my work on a translation of the *Kāttavarāyacuvāmi Katai* has been made possible by a senior research fellowship from Tamil University, Tañcāvūr. I am very grateful to the Tamil University for having given me the opportunity to work on such a project. I also thank Dr. S. Rajaram, Tamil University, for his help in the translation of the *Katai*. An earlier draft of this paper was read by A. Hiltebeitel and S. Visuvalingam. I wish to thank both of them for their valuable comments.

2. "Stake," Tamil kaḻu. Although the stake has the connotation of an impaling stake, the kalu here is not used for impalement; see below.

3. The *Ammānai* consists of approximately 500 *olas*. It is in possession of Mr. Ramu Pantaram and was made available to me through Mr. Subrahmaniya Vattiyar of Vayalūr, to whom I am very grateful for his help. I also thank

6. Kāmākṣī temple, Kōppu. Chains and handcuffs with which Kāttavarāyan's impersonator used to be tied during the festival. Walking on sandals studded with nails was practised by the priest of this village up to two generations ago. Photo by Eveline Masilamani-Meyer.

Mr. G. Jothi and Mr. V. Bharathi for copying the palm leaf manuscript. To Mr. Jothi I am also grateful for accompanying me on my field trips in the Tiruccirāppaḷḷi area.

4. Copied from a palm leaf manscript in possession of Dr. M. Masilamani, teacher, Ayilāppēṭṭai, Kōppu. I am grateful to Dr. Masilamani for letting me make a xerox copy of the *Ēcal*. Large parts of this version can be found in *Kāttavarāyan Kataippāṭal*, edited by Na. Vanamamalai, Maturai Palkalaikkalakam, 1971.

5. David Shulman's article in this volume is based mainly on this version. His insightful analysis of the text anticipates some of my own conclusions, and a number of points he makes can be supported by my comparison of the texts.

6. *Nantavanam*, a garden with flowers meant to be used for worship. For a more detailed description of the content of the *Katai*, see Shulman in this volume. The ant story is also made the reason for which Aṅkāḷamman has to become involved with human beings. See Eveline Meyer, *Aṅkāḷaparamēcuvari: A Goddess of Tamilnadu, Her Myths and Cult* (Wiesbaden: Steiner Verlag, 1986), 9 ff., 66.

7. When Kāttavarāyan is disguised as a snake charmer (*jōki*) he says: "I am the son of Ēkāmparajōki." Disguised as a washerman he calls himself Kāttavaṇṇān, son of Ēkāmparavaṇṇān.

8. She gets irritated to the point where she simply burns Kōmutalaippār (see n. 21), to which Kāttavarāyan had brought Ukantalaki with her permission.

9. She is truly old. Her age is the reason she cites for her inability to raise her child, Kāttavarāyan, and for handing him over to the seven maidens who become his foster mothers.

10. In the *Katai* Kāttavarāyan kills the birds in Kāmākṣī's abode and thus gets her attention.

11. *Kiṇṇāram*, a kind of *vīnai* consisting of three to five gourds, attached to a bridge with three strings.

12. In the *Katai* Kāttavarāyan receives the latter from the seven maidens, his foster mothers.

13. Mācimalai belongs to the Kollimalai mountain range. Kāḷi's abode (*kāḷivanam*), although in the Kolli Hills, is not located on Mācimalai. The tree is either ebony (*āccā*) or teak (*tēkku*).

14. Mūdevī is the elder sister of Lakṣmī and is generally a goddess of ill luck.

15. More exactly, as a Brahman versed in the pañcāṅkam (an almanac embracing lunar days or phases of the moon, solar days or weeks, periods of the asterisms, the *yōkams* and *karaṇas*).

16. Āriyamālai's servants, instead of delivering Kāttavarāyan's love letter to their mistress, read and burn it. For this treachery they are blinded (!), and on their way they fall into a pit filled with cowdung and water prepared by Cinnān at Kāttavarāyan's instigation. They receive their eyesight back, but are then punished by Āriyamālai, who hears of their treachery through Kātta-

varāyan's song. Āriyamālai makes them shave their heads, place red and black dots on their faces and ride on donkeys. To be driven through the village on an ass was a punishment meted out to adulterers. See Edgar Thurston, *Ethnographic Notes in Southern India* (Delhi: Cosmo Publications, 1975), 45.

17. In the chapter "Vētiyarkaḷai ācāraṅkulaitta vanam."

18. Kurukkaḷ—an officiating Brahman priest in Śiva temples.

19. According to Mr. Subrahmaniya Vattiyar, Valayūr, the ribald parts of the Kāttavarāyan story were first introduced in the Tiruccirāppaḷḷi area some twenty years ago, in Uraiyūr.

20. Information from Mr. R. Kacinatan, Nakalūr, who sang the whole story on tape for me. He followed fairly closely the *Katai* version. When I asked him about these Brahman episodes, he sang one, a rather delightful one, which is not in the *Katai*: Kāttavarāyan (disguised, of course) sells fish powder to the Brahman ladies, telling them that it is some spice and that they should cook it with the rice, but be sure not to uncover the pot before the rice is ready to be eaten. When the Brahman men eat this meal, they praise it as the best meal they have eaten in their thirty years of married life.

21. Kōmutalaippār—"riverbank of the big crocodiles." See below, part G.

22. Āṇavam—one of the *mala* (stains) in Śaiva Siddhānta.

23. After a big pūjā to the gods, the lord of Śrīraṅka, Viṣṇu, turns the youngest of the maidens into a lime, which he gives to the Brahman woman, Annatuḷaci, to eat. She becomes pregnant and gives birth to Āriyamālai. We have seen above that Kāttavarāyan's birth happened the same way. The lime has a variety of ritual significances, one of them being fertility. Priests will give sacred limes to women who wish to get pregnant.

24. For a short synopsis of her story see Stuart H. Blackburn, "Death and Deification: Folk Cults in Hinduism," *History of Religions*, 24 (1985), 260.

25. She is said to be wife (*tēvi*) of seven Karuppan.

26. We find this pattern also in Maharashtra, where Khaṇḍobā's second wife, Bāṇāī, is of tribal origin. See Günther D. Sontheimer, *Birobā, Mhaskobā und Khaṇḍobā: Ursprung, Geschichte und Umwelt von Pastoralen Gottheiten in Mahārāṣṭra* (Wiesbaden: Steiner Verlag, 1976), 21, 61ff, and Sontheimer and Stanley in this volume.

27. See Edgar Thurston, *Castes and Tribes of Southern India* (Madras: Government Press, 1909), 186, 196-97.

28. It is difficult to determine exactly how the punishment was administered. According to the *Katai*, Kāttavarāyan was hanging on a hook and nails pierced his body.

29. The reference that Kāttavarāyan will be a guard or soldier (*cēvakan*) for the Trimūrti (Mummūrtiyar) occurs several times. No further explanation is offered.

30. According to Dr. V. Venugopal, Maturai Kamaraj University, the pun-

ishment was to place the criminal into a basket or box and hang him thus on top of a large pole for several days.

31. Perhaps we can see in Kāttavarāyan's tapas on top of the pole a correspondence to Arjuna's tapas in the Draupadī cult. Arjuna performs his tapas on top of a high pole in order to get the *pāśupata* weapon from Śiva. Information from A. Hiltebeitel.

32. As the Brahman doing tapas standing on his head in the *Ammānai,* the image of the beetle here also suggests a mockery of Kāttavarāyan's tapas—the small beetle causing the stake to fall on which Kāttavarāyan is heroically dying.

33. See Brenda E. F. Beck, "The Goddess and the Demon, a Local South Indian Festival and its Wider Context," in Madeleine Biardeau, ed., *Autour de la déesse hindoue, Puruṣārtha* 5 (1981), 92, and Meyer, *Aṅkāḷaparamēcuvari,* 48 ff.

34. Meyer, *op. cit.,* 11.

35. We see this clearly in the cult of Aṅkāḷamman where the goddess becomes once a year the sacrificial victim (see Meyer, *op. cit.,* 105 ff.), and in the cult of Kāttavarāyan where once a year Kāttavarāyan has to mount the stake. Kāmākṣī and Aṅkāḷamman are engaged in tapas while they are on earth.

36. See Blackburn who discusses this aspect in his "Death and Deification" (n. 24).

37. See Beck, "The Goddess and the Demon," 95, 96, and Blackburn, "Death and Deification," 261. The story of Nāṭān Cāmi, cited by Blackburn, is especially relevant because it contains a number of parallels to the Kāttavarāyan story. Like Kāttavarāyan, Nāṭān Cāmi possesses magical powers.

38. See Beck, "The Goddess and the Demon," 83 ff. A Brahman-Pariah combination in the god could be folk religion's answer to what Heesterman calls the "insoluble dilemma" of Hindu tradition, the incompatibility of the "turbulent order of conflict and the static order of transcendence." J. C. Heesterman, *The Inner Conflict of Tradition, Essays in Indian Ritual, Kingship, and Society* (Delhi: Oxford University Press, 1985), 2, 7, 9.

39. See Beck, "The Goddess and the Demon," 126.

40. See Meyer, *Aṅkāḷaparamēcuvari,* 16, 17.

41. The castes are: merchants, washermen, spinners, weavers, carpenters, smiths, shepherds and Brahmans.

42. Mr. R. Kacinatan, Nākalūr and Mr. S. Nakarajan, Varuttiyūr. See note 20.

43. "Did not Śiva hide a girl on his head? Did Indra's body not become covered with *yonis* because of his desire for Ahalyā? Did not Kōvalan's whole tragedy happen because he fell in love with (another) woman?"

44. In the Tiruccirāppaḷḷi area almost all families connected with Kāttavarāyan are in possession of a shorter or longer version of the Kāttavarāyan story (written on palm leaves).

45. Here are a few examples. Unnecessary details: the enumeration of all

the fishes which the king creates along with a river and parks for Āriyamālai; the list of jewelry with which he adorns her. Erotics: In the section *Vaṇṇāravalli Vanam*, Kāttavarāyan draws a picture of Āriyamālai on her sari. He begins at her head, and when he draws her thighs he simply faints. When Āriyamālai sees the drawing, she is surprised to find a mole drawn on one thigh. Inspecting her thighs, she discovers the mole. Stereotypes: Places or fortresses so high that no fly can enter; numbers: 7, 10, 21 (walls or fortifications); women who walk like swans; old man aged 90 and 10, aged 400 and 10 (for the last, compare Meyer, *Aṅkāḷaparamēcuvari*, 27, 28).

46. With these enter also some obscure persons such as Annamuttu and Ammaiyappan, A Vēḷāḷar boy without arms and legs, rescued by Kāttavarāyan, healed by Kāmākṣī and given the task to guard Kāmākṣī during her tapas.

47. Kāttavarāyan's mocking comment on Āriyamālai's ghee-soaked rice meals (*Katai*) parodies his devout offering of fruits to Āriyamālai in the *Ammāṉai*. Kāttavarāyan's command over and frequent use of Yama's demons (*Katai*) is a caricature of Śiva's use of *his* demon in the *Ammāṉai*. Kāttavarāyan's humiliation of Kāmākṣī (when he has her beaten up) makes a mockery of his devotion in the *Ammāṉai*.

48. I hope to be doing a detailed study of Kāttavarāyan's cult in the near future.

49. There used to be—and according to some people there still are—crocodiles in the river.

50. It was established by Mr. Parimaṇam Mutturājā, munsif of Kōppu. He was the grandfather of Dr. Masilamani's wife; see note 4.

51. He is an interesting god who deserves a full study. He lives on Mācimalai (Kolli hills), rides a tiger, receives animal sacrifices, and is identified with Viṣṇu.

52. At present I cannot say how far back the cult actually goes, but I hope that my further research on Kāttavarāyan will furnish such answers.

53. March-April, 1986.

54. Because a person in possession often loses control over his body, it would seem quite dangerous for "Kāttavarāyan" to be possessed while sitting on the 60 foot pole.

4

Tricking the Goddess: Cowherd Kāṭamarāju and Goddess Gaṅga in the Telugu Folk Epic

Velcheru Narayana Rao

The Gŏllas, a cowherding community of Andhra Pradesh, sing a long narrative with many lays, generally known as *Kāṭamarāju Katha*. During my field work in Andhra Pradesh in 1986,[1] I collected two versions of this epic, sung respectively by Gŏlla and Mādiga singers.[2] One version of this narrative, edited from a number of palm leaf manuscripts, is published by Tangirala Venkata Subba Rao.[3] In this paper I focus on the main hero of the epic, Kāṭamarāju, and his relationship with goddess Gaṅga. Later in the paper I suggest connections between the nature of their hero, Kāṭamarāju, their deity Gaṅga, and the Gŏlla caste self-image. First, a summary of the narrative of Kāṭamarāju and Gaṅga's first meeting.[4]

A. Tricking the Goddess

Kāṭamarāju is the third-generation hero of this epic story. His father Pĕddirāju dies in a battle with Vāliketuvarāju. Kāṭamarāju, a seven-year old boy at that time, goes to the battlefield to get his father's dead body. The battlefield is being protected by goddess Gaṅga and her brother Pōturāju. Gaṅga sends Pōturāju to check on who is invading her territory. Pōturāju asks her why he should have to watch over dead bodies: "If I take care of a village or a city, at least I will have food." Gaṅga says that as long as the Gōllas have salt and water, she will see to it that they give Pōturāju a sheep (or goat: *pōtu*) tall as a palm tree and rice as high as a mountain. Pōturāju then appears before Kāṭamarāju in his fierce form. He stops Kāṭamarāju and wants to know who he is and why he has entered the battlefield without fear in the dead of night. Kāṭamarāju, supported by Someśvara (Śiva), stands bravely and answers him. He lifts his sword and attempts to cut off Pōturāju's head for his insolence in questioning him. Pōturāju loses courage and runs back to his sister crying for help. All the Bhūtas (spirits) in Pōturāju's army run away in fear. Gaṅga consoles Pōturāju and prepares herself to meet with Kāṭamarāju. She creates an illusion around her and grows to be as tall as the sky. She projects twelve spears out of her head and impales an elephant on each spear. Over the elephants she stacks twelve corpses. She has twelve lamps for each corpse. She holds weapons in all her twelve hands. With jingling bells on her feet and burning coals on her head, a *kinnĕra*, a stringed instrument, on her shoulder, she comes making huge strides. She yells like thunder. Fire rises from the sky and sparks of fire fall on the earth. Biting her teeth fiercely, standing tall like a palm tree, she rains burning coals on the earth. Kāṭamarāju sees her and quickly pulls his sword. Someśvara pats Kāṭamarāju on the back and advises him that the deity is Kāṭamarāju's family deity and that he should speak to her with courage. Kāṭamarāju speaks fiercely, brandishing his sword. He says, "Do not come near, demon, I will break you into six pieces with one stroke." Gaṅga puffs her cheeks, rains more fire and asks him, "Who are you, human, why do you have to come at this hour to the battlefield?" Kāṭamarāju is furious for being asked this and insists on knowing who she is. Gaṅga warns him that even gods, including Indra, fear to enter the battlefield at that time of night. She demands that Kāṭamarāju identify himself. Kāṭamarāju defies her. Amazed at the boy's defiance and not knowing what to do to coerce him to obey her she softens her attitude towards him and says, "Don't you know who I am? Why don't you tell me your name, Blue-colored One?"

Addressing Kāṭamarāju with this name shifts his identity to a Kṛṣṇa image and introduces erotic connotations into the encounter. Now Gaṅga starts playing word-games and says that her name is Gourd with Tangles. Kāṭamarāju answers this riddle-like identification with a similar riddle: his name is The Sharp Sickle Which Cuts the Tangled Gourd. Gaṅga then says her name is The Lightning From a Frightening Cloud. Kāṭamarāju retorts that his name is Thunderbolt from the Lightning. The riddling continues. Gaṅga says her name is The Fate of Time. Kāṭamarāju says his name is Lord of Time. Gaṅga says her name is Bride of Battle. Kāṭamarāju says, if that is so, he is Bridegroom of Battle who would step on her foot and tie the marriage band.

Not having succeeded in the verbal encounter either, Gaṅga changes her posture. The marriage relationship hinted in the last exchange suggests further possibilities. She identifies herself as the deity of the Gŏllas, the primal power sitting on Śiva's head. Satisfied with this straightforward answer Kāṭamarāju identifies himself; he is the grandson of Valurāju and the son of Pĕddirāju, and his name is Kāṭamarāju. Gaṅga giggles and appears before him as young girl of twelve. She offers him protection. She was the one who saved the corpses from rotting, and guarded the battlefield so that even a male bee did not enter. As soon as he identified himself, she saved Kāṭamarāju from destruction. "Therefore," says Gaṅga, "lift your hands and bow to me, the deity of your family." Kāṭamarāju refuses to bow and says, "I am seven years old, and have never learned to bow to any one yet." Gaṅga laughs at him and to teach him how to bow, she lifts both of her hands and says, "This is how you bow." Kāṭamarāju laughs victoriously and says, "Gaṅga bowed to me first and I bowed in return."

Insulted by Kāṭamarāju's trick, Gaṅga says that if he is that smart, they should marry each other. Marriage is the means through which the deity desires to subdue Kāṭamarāju. Kāṭamarāju is angry at her words. He is grieving over his father's death. It is not right to ask him to marry her at that time. Gaṅga asks for food in return for her services of watching the battlefield. She asks for a sheep as tall as a palm and a heap of rice as high as a mountain. This she wants as long as time lasts and the Sun, Moon, and the stars endure. Although this food is also for her, she asks for it because she had already promised to get it for Pōturāju.

Kāṭamarāju asks in turn that Gaṅga show him his father's corpse and make it come to life and talk to him. She should help him avenge his father's death. If she does this, he will give her animal sacrifices and even human sacrifices. Also, if she is born in a particular family, that of the Marlas, he will marry her, too. Gaṅga is not sure Kāṭamarāju will keep his word and asks him, "Can I trust your word?" Kāṭamarāju assures her that she can. Gaṅga is pleased.

But Gaṅga's relationship with Kāṭamarāju does not go well even after this promise. Apparently Kāṭamarāju is not eager to keep his promise. When Kāṭamarāju intends to go with his huge herd to the south, where grass is plentiful for his herd to feed on, Gaṅga appears again. She stops his herd from moving further. She makes the Pāleru, a river in Nellore area where Kāṭamarāju's herd is resting, rise in flood. The cows are unable to cross the river. Kāṭamarāju is angered at Gaṅga's action. He refuses to feed her and worship her. She insists that he do so, or she will not let the cows go any further. She sprinkles magical rice on the cows and the cows get confused and scatter. Kāṭamarāju still refuses to worship her. He will not bow to a female deity. Gaṅga vows to make Kāṭamarāju worship her. Kāṭamarāju says that only women worship a female deity but men do not. He accuses her of playing games like a harlot. Gaṅga reminds Kāṭamarāju of the incident at the battlefield, the incident which happened when Kāṭamarāju was a seven-year old. Kāṭamarāju has made a promise to feed her. Has he forgotten that promise? Does he have no honor? A long argument ensues and Gaṅga brags about her superior powers and her association with Kāṭamarāju's family and clan. Polurāju, Kāṭamarāju's uncle, appears in Kāṭamarāju's dream and advises him to worship Gaṅga. Kāṭamarāju finally agrees. Receiving her proper worship, Gaṅga blesses Kāṭamarāju to move safely to the south and take revenge against the enemy kings.

The story of the strained relationship between Gaṅga and Kāṭamarāju does not end here. Gaṅga is born into the Marla family and asks her family members to arrange for her marriage with Kāṭamarāju. Kāṭamarāju has been preparing for his final battle with his enemies. Relatives on the bride's side and the bridegroom's side arrange for the wedding. Kāṭamarāju recalls his argument with the deity Gaṅga in the battlefield. He is unhappy that the women of his family are getting ready for his marriage with Gaṅga. This ruins the success he has had in the battlefield when he fought with Pōturāju and won his argument with Gaṅga. But he does not say anything against the women. He thinks that there must be a deeper reason for the events to happen this way and he quietly agrees to the marriage. Just as Kāṭamarāju is ready to pour the sacred rice on her head (a ritual event constituting the principal act of marriage),[5] the bride of the Marla family shows Kāṭamarāju her real form with twelve hands. Kāṭamarāju sees her and immediately realizes the bride is none other than the deity Gaṅga who has argued with him in the battlefield in the middle of the night. He thinks of her as his mother, the great goddess. He conceives of the thread on his wrist (*kaṅkaṇa*) as a band signifying a vow to kill his enemies rather than as a band for his marriage vows, and pours the rice on her head as an act of worship rather than as a ritual act of marrying. He makes an announcement that he is not going to untie the band on his wrist until he has defeated his enemies. The marriage is thus concluded.

The question remains whether this is a marriage or not. The singers of the epic say that Kāṭamarāju and Gaṅga never lived together. Subba Rao reports that singers he has talked to even claim that Gaṅga and Kāṭamarāju are never married.[6]

The conflict between Gaṅga and Kāṭamarāju extends to several male heroes of the epic, who represent Kāṭamarāju. One such hero is Yĕrrayya, Kāṭamarāju's associate. In the printed version of the epic, there is an incident where Yĕrrayya has an encounter with Gaṅga, more or less on the same lines as Kāṭamarāju has with the deity. In another incident Gaṅga makes an attempt to see Kāṭamarāju, but Basava, Śiva's mount, comes in the way and prevents Gaṅga from going to him.

On the other hand, Gaṅga seems to get along well with all the women in the epic, especially Pāpanūka, Kāṭamarāju's sister. Now Pāpanūka is born under a bad star, and it is told that if she gets married, she will ruin her husband's family. No one wants to marry her and take her into their family as a daughter-in-law. Attempts to marry her and bring the husband to stay in the bride's family as resident son-in-law do not succeed. The astrologers then suggest that a single-pillar mansion be built away from town and Pāpanūka be placed in that mansion. Accordingly, the mansion is built and Pāpanūka is brought there in her sleep. Gaṅga, however, appears before her and tells her the misfortune that is in store for her. While talking to Pāpanūka, Gaṅga tells her how her own life is unfortunate too: she is married to Kāṭamarāju but she has never had a chance to see him since the wedding.

B. The Births of Kāṭamarāju and Gaṅga

The ambiguous relationship of Gaṅga and Kāṭamarāju has deeper roots in their very births. To discuss the nature of these deities, we shall examine the stories of these births, first that of Kāṭamarāju and then that of Gaṅga.

The birth of Kāṭamarāju involves several Śiva-like deities. Pĕddamma, Kāṭamarāju's mother, is advised to worship Basava, Śiva's mount or vehicle. Her equals, the other daughters-in-law of the family, have been performing rituals to Basava seeking sons. But Basava rejects Pĕddamma's offerings. Distressed at this rejection, she invites a group of *jaṅgamas* and offers them food but they refuse to eat at her house because she does not have children. This makes her even more unhappy. Someśvara of Kaḷyāṇ appears in Pĕddamma's dream and tells her that if she goes to Kaḷyāṇ he will give her children. Her husband Pĕddirāju, however, does not want to go. He does not believe in Pĕddamma's words and laughs at her for believing in dreams. He does not want to leave his country, relatives, and brothers. Not having children does not bother him because he is happy treating his brother's children as his own. On one occasion, however, Pĕddirāju wants to hear a recitation of the *Basavapurāṇa*, and the Brahmans tell him that people without children should not listen to the *Basavapurāṇa*.

Meanwhile, Someśvara of Kaḷyāṇ decides to get Pĕddirāju to move to Kaḷyāṇ for begetting children. He sends Kāmadhenu, the wish-giving cow, to go to Pampādri, where Pĕddirāju lives. He sprinkles magic ashes on the cow which makes her pregnant. The pregnant cow goes to Pampādri and delivers a calf in Pĕddirāju's house. The calf laughs at her mother for delivering and pulling the straw of Pĕddirāju's house, knowing that he has no children. Pĕddirāju is sleeping at that time. He sees all this in his dream. In his dream he also hears the cow explaining to her calf that she did this to make Pĕddirāju go to Kaḷyāṇ. Pĕddirāju wakes up and relates his dream to his elders and asks them to interpret the dream to him. They say that the deity of Kaḷyāṇ has wanted to give him children. Therefore he should go to Kaḷyāṇ. Pĕddirāju decides to go and divides up his herds and cash among his brothers and sister. Pĕddirāju's sister, Kŏmarakka, chooses the heaviest of the cash boxes for her share. It turns out that the box contains the image of the goddess Durga. The brothers give her a large box of cash for expenses to worship the deity. Pĕddirāju then goes to Kaḷyāṇ. There, he and his wife see a group of young boys grazing cattle. The boys are worshipping a deity. Pĕddirāju finds that the deity is Kātakoṭeśvaruḍu. He also learns that they are worshipping the deity so their cattle might be "fruitful." He asks them if the deity will give children to him. They answer that he will get a son if he worships the deity. Pĕddirāju and Pĕddamma worship the deity and make a vow that if they should have a son, they will name him after the deity. As they fall prostrate before the deity, the deity gives Pĕddamma an unripe fruit and a ripe fruit. The deity explains in her dream that the unripe fruit is Kāṭamarāju, and the ripe fruit is Pāpanūka, a daughter.

That is how Kāṭamarāju and his sister Pāpanūka are born, as a result of Śiva's boon. But throughout the epic, the singers describe Kāṭamarāju as an avatar of Kṛṣṇa. They refer to him as the dark person and the herders trace his lineage from the Yadu of the *Mahābhārata*. Kāṭamarāju even sits on the seat of Kṛṣṇa—the one that Kṛṣṇa got from Indra and upon which only Kṛṣṇa may sit. Kāṭamarāju sits on the seat to prove that he is Kṛṣṇa himself.

As to Gaṅga's birth, it is also connected to Kṛṣṇa. The well known *Bhāgavatapurāṇa* story about Kṛṣṇa's birth is repeated in the epic. A voice from the sky predicts that Kaṃsa will be killed by his sister Devaki's eighth male child. A furious Kaṃsa imprisons the pregnant Devaki and her husband to make sure that he finds the child as soon as he is born so that he can kill him. Kṛṣṇa is born in the middle of night. As soon as he is born he tells his father to take him immediately to a cowherds' village across the Yamuna river to Yaśoda, who has just then given birth to a girl, and bring Yaśoda's girl-child to Devaki. This child, Yogamāya, is then presented to Kaṃsa, who comes the next morning ready to kill Kṛṣṇa. Kaṃsa is frustrated at the child not being the boy he has expected it to be, and throws her up in the sky to fall on his sword. Instead of falling down on the sword, Yogamāya flies into the sky, uttering a warning to Kaṃsa that the child who would kill him is growing up elsewhere.

This Yogamāya, the epic narrates, is born as Gaṅga. So from the background angle of these prior identities, Kāṭamarāju and Gaṅga, as Kṛṣṇa and Yogamāya, are brother and sister.

C. Tricking the Enemy

Kāṭamarāju's trickery is addressed not only toward the goddess but toward a king. Kāṭamarāju has a huge herd of cattle. As the singers describe it, it covers an area of six *āmaḍas* if it is together and twelve *āmaḍas* if it is scattered. Such a herd, the pride of the Yādava family, suffers from lack of fodder. It is predicted that if he moved south, to Nellore, there would be enough grass for his cattle.

The relationship between the king of Nellore and Kāṭamarāju is riddled with ambiguities. The agreement between them is apparently simple and straightforward; in return for all the male calves, the king will let Kāṭamarāju graze on the king's lands. The actual words of the contract read: "All the grass that is born out of the water is yours, and all the male calves born from the cows are ours." Kāṭamarāju's trick stems from an ingenious interpretation of these words. He grazes his cattle on the rice crop because it is also a kind of grass which grows from the water.

This leads to serious conflicts with king Nallasiddhi, resulting in a disastrous battle. The actual sequence of events which leads to the battle is not easy to reconstruct nor is it easy to determine who is at fault. In a manner similar to that of the *Mahābhārata* story, where complex motivations and conflicting principles make it difficult to determine who is right and who is wrong, the story of Kāṭamarāju also does not allow for easy categories of good and bad. Kāṭamarāju, however, does have a very strong determination to push the events towards the battle. He relentlessly tries by all the means possible to make the battle inevitable.

Nallasiddhi, the king of Nellore, is from the Coda family, the very same Coda family to which Kāṭamarāju's uncle's killer belonged. Kāṭamarāju takes this as an opportunity to avenge the death of his uncle. He describes to his associates how he killed all the persons against whom he had vowed revenge:

> I clobbered the killer of my great grandfather
>
> Killed the killer of my grandfather
>
> Tore up the killer of Simhādrirāju
>
> Uprooted the killer of Pĕddirāju
>
> Supressed the killer of Yĕranūkarāju
>
> Chopped up the killer of Nalanūkarāju[7]

Having avenged the deaths of all these ancestors, Kāṭamarāju exhorts his followers that now the time has come to avenge the death of Polurāju.

> The time to avenge Polurāju's death has come,
>
> and we should not go from here.
>
> Dispute has arisen between Siddhirāju and us,
>
> we cannot settle for peace with him.[8]

He thus exhorts his followers to avenge the death of his uncle. He even has a plan to precipitate conflict. He will pay all the rent for grazing on his land to the king and then will say: "We gave you all the money according to the contract. The contract says that all the grass born out of water belongs to us. You too are born out of water (along with grass). So, we bought you too. You are our property." Kāṭamarāju discusses this plan with the men of his community. He tells them that after declaring that he owns the king he will reveal the old grievance they hold against him and will force a battle. Then they will kill the king in the battle. Meanwhile, he instructs his men to take the cattle and graze them freely on the crops.

The singers of the epic claim that Kāṭamarāju was in the right. But they also insist that Kāṭamarāju advised his men to graze the cattle in the rice fields only as a retaliation to an attack by the local Boya hunters. The hunters were instigated by king Nallasiddhi's second wife Kundamādevi (his mistress according to one version) to kill Kāṭamarāju's cows. Subba Rao reports that some singers have told him that Kāṭamarāju himself kills Kundamādevi's pet parrot, because his cows were being annoyed by the bird's chirping noises.[9] Kundamādevi then retaliates by encouraging the Boyas to kill Kāṭamarāju's cows.

In any case, Kāṭamarāju's intentions of avenging his ancestor's deaths—*paga*—makes this motive the central theme of the epic. Although revenge is a common motive in the martial epics of North India—for example, a major theme of the *Ālhā* epic is the young Banāphars' revenge of the deaths of their fathers[10]—this is an unusual theme in South Indian epics.

D. Epics of Landed Castes and Epics of Trading Castes

Most of the prominently studied epics of South India are related to battle over territory, often a fight between cousins for control over land. Examples are the Palnāḍu epic from Andhra Pradesh and the Brothers story from Tamilnadu. These epics are claimed as their 'own' stories by the traditional land-owning "right hand" castes like Velamas, Reḍḍis, and Kammas in the case of the Palnāḍu epic, and Vēḷāḷars in the case of the Brothers epic. In these epics, male heroes dominate the story, with the role of the wives very much under control. Male heroes' relationships with sister or mother characters are stronger and considered more sacred in these epics than those with wives, who are always under check. Brenda E. F. Beck and I have shown that these epics reflect the ideology of the landowning castes. Men of these castes are proud, reflecting a macho spirit of willingness to fight and a determination to keep their honor untarnished. Beck says:

> The heroes belong to a dominant landed community, the Kongu Kavuṇṭars. The story describes how these Kavuṇṭars came to control much of the land in this local area and helps to justify their prominent political, economic, and demographic position today. It also reflects the fact that the local identity of this group is closely intertwined with images of the Kongu area as a whole. The Kongu (Veḷāḷar) Kavuṇṭars are a non-Brahman community who proudly eat goat, sheep, and chicken meat (although they do not eat beef). The men are proud of their militaristic personalities, as well as of their agricultural skills. In sum, they are proud to be non-Brahmans. Much of the flavor of this local story stems from the central role of this caste in the account.[11]

Another set of epics which I discussed relate to the left-hand castes. These epics are woman-centered and the female hero of these epics dies not in a battle, but by self-immolation. Men in these epics are largely passive. The conflict is centered around the issue of protecting caste integrity and elevating caste status. Threat comes in the form of an alien, aggressive power against which the female hero fights. Epics which fall into this category are *Sanyāsamma Katha*, *Kāmamma Katha* and *Kanyaka Ammavāri Katha*, all of which belong to the left-hand castes.[12]

While discussing these epics, I included *Kāṭamarāju* in the martial epic category, but I was unsure of that categorization. In a footnote I indicated:

> Despite the neat typology suggested here, *Kāṭamarāju Katha* appears to be anomalous, not quite fully "martial." Gollas are probably a trading caste who have adopted a landowning martial ideology . . .[13]

E. Epic of Ambiguities

The events of the epic bring out the ambiguous nature of the Gŏllas. They are caught between two clearly delineated caste groups, the right-hand caste and the left-hand castes. Heroic prowess propels them towards the right-hand group, a status they can acquire only through death on the battlefield. Their hero Kāṭamarāju has a relentless duty to lead them to this status. But at the same time, Gŏllas do not seem to want right-hand caste status. The ambiguous nature of the caste permeates all the events of the epic. Most importantly it is reflected in the very relationship Kāṭamarāju has with his caste deity, Gaṅga. As indicated above, Kāṭamarāju is both Śiva as well as Kṛṣṇa. As Śiva he is the ultimate destroyer. As Kṛṣṇa, he is the ultimate trickster. His dual identities also define the problems in his relationship with Gaṅga. As Śiva, Kāṭamarāju is Gaṅga's husband. One of Gaṅga's problems that is confirmed in many myths, both in Telugu and Tamil, is to get Śiva's attention exclusively for herself. She is Śiva's second wife, constantly competing with her senior co-wife, Pārvati. Śiva has the difficult job of maintaining harmony between his two wives and constantly fails to achieve it. Gaṅga herself is a slippery goddess. Her watery nature apparently makes her unstable. Kāṭamarāju attempts to control her, defy her superior claims, and subdue her so that she remains docile. As is indicated earlier, Kāṭamarāju's objection to bowing to her is clearly that she is a woman and as a man he wants to be superior to her. He tells Gaṅga to go to the women of his family who worship her. When their family divided their ancestral property, it was the woman Kŏmarakka who chose the goddess. She was even given extra money to pay for the expenses. So that is where Gaṅga should go to receive worship. Kāṭamarāju wants to keep his male status uncompromised by rejecting all the little female deities.

But there is another problem inherent in Kāṭamarāju's identity. As Kṛṣṇa, he is Gaṅga's brother because she was Yogamāya in her previous birth. And as a Viṣṇu figure, Gaṅga is his daughter. Gaṅga was born out of Viṣṇu's foot. Either way, it would be incestuous to be married to her. So the trickster in Kāṭamarāju tries to avoid the problem by postponing the promise of marriage to a later birth. The conflicting identities of a husband and father are inherently impossible to maintain in one unit. In addition, the problem of a dominant wife is no comfort either. It should be noted that Gaṅga is older than Kāṭamarāju; even when she appears as a young lady on the battlefield she is twelve whereas Kāṭamarāju is only seven. Locked in this situation Kāṭamarāju's strategies inevitably result in trickery.

Kāṭamarāju's relationship with King Nallasiddhi is also riddled with conflicting motivations. He needs Nallasiddhi's lands to graze his cattle, but he also needs to kill Nallasiddhi to avenge his uncle's death. Inasmuch as Kāṭamarāju needs the grass to graze his cattle, he needs the protection of the king who controls the land. But inseparable from this need is also Kāṭamarāju's desire to kill him. The dilemma is clear. Just as his relationship with Gaṅga is riddled with ambiguities, so also is his relationship with the king.

Kāṭamarāju is the king of the forest. His name, and his origin from Kāṭreḍu, the king of the kāḍu, forest, relates him to the wild areas. He is constantly moving from forest to forest, taking his huge cattle herd with him. His nature inherently opposes him to the stable, city-oriented kings. Like his ancestors, Kāṭamarāju, too, fights with ruling kings. Although there is an evident desire among the Yādavas for a status equal to that of kings, their leader Kāṭamarāju never seems to have interest in settling to rule a kingdom. One incident prior to the final battle with king Nallasiddhi makes this point clear.

Kāṭamarāju worries over the battle strategy. He remembers that all his forefathers were defeated in battle because they did not have the strategic advantage of fighting from a protected fort. He regrets not having a fort for himself. He is out in the open, exposed to the enemy who could attack at any time. He discusses this with his brother-in-law Padmarāghavuḍu, and asks him to build a fort for him. But

Padmarāghavuḍu advises him against a fort. He says, "Heroes who want to die in the battle do not need a fort. Forts are for timid people who want survive the battle. Your real forts are the cattle, and the Yādava warriors." Kāṭamarāju accepts this advice.

If Kāṭamarāju's nature sets him in conflict with kings, he is not particularly favorable to hunters either. Hunters worship Kāṭreḍu, the deity whose aspect Kāṭamarāju shares.[14] As mentioned earlier, the Boya hunters kill Kāṭamarāju's cows and the conflict between Gŏllas and Boya hunters in the epic indicates that Kāṭamarāju is not in harmony with the forest either.

Also, Kāṭamarāju is under a curse to live like a *saṃnyāsin*, childless and without family. The curse is given to his father by a group of saṃnyāsins, whose hermitage he had destroyed by mistake.

The picture that emerges of Kāṭamarāju is that he represents a bundle of opposites: married but a saṃnyāsin, lord of the forest but opposed to the hunters and wild animals, king but unwilling to rule a settled kingdom, warrior but successful through trickery, Śiva but also Kṛṣṇa.

If Kāṭamarāju represents ambiguous and trickster-like traits, Gaṅga does so too. She personifies *māya*, illusion, defying any possibility to grasp her real nature. With her unstable personality, she is described as "One who has feet on her chest." Very much like the Gŏllas, who want land to graze their cattle on but yet do not care for the land as a possession, Gaṅga, too, wants land to flow on, but does not want to live on it in any settled place. She is constantly moving. There is an element of trickery in Gaṅga's nature too. She has tricked Kaṃsa in her previous life. A story related about Gaṅga in Telugu folklore tells how in an effort to frustrate her co-wife Pārvati, she hides water, making it impossible for Pārvati to take a bath after her menstruation. She is also accused of being unstable. One of the many abuses that Yĕrrayya hurls against Gaṅga is that

> she married one, carried another and
> sat on the head of yet another.[15]

Reference here is to Gaṅga's marriage to Śantanu in the *Mahābhārata* story.[16] Gaṅga lives with Śantanu on the condition that he does not object to anything she does. Gaṅga then drowns, one after another, the seven children born to her by Śantanu. When Bhīṣma is born, Śantanu, who is unable to bear the thought of drowning this child, too, objects and Gaṅga promptly leaves him.

F. Gŏllas in a Tricky Life

The self-image of the Gŏllas in the epic is unmistakably clear: they think of themselves as Kṣatriyas. Male characters of the epic have their names ending in *rāja*, king, and the women have *devi*, indicating nobility and purity. Men constantly stand for values of bravery and willingness to die on the battlefield[17] fulfilling their *kṣātra dharma*, whereas women invariably resort to dying on the funeral pyre of their husbands to insure their status as *vīra patnis*, heroic wives. Similarly, the epic has repeated instances where the Gŏlla kings show extreme readiness to offer protection to anyone who is in distress, fighting and risking their own lives for them. This quality fulfills an important prescription for Kṣatriyas, that of śaraṇāgata rakṣaṇa, saving those who seek refuge. Closely connected with this quality is also the duty of a Kṣatriya to punish evil-doers and protect the virtuous. Details would be cumbersome to summarize, but every battle which the ancestors of Kāṭamarāju engage in is due to their eagerness to offer shelter and protection to refugees fleeing from an oppressive king.[18] Despite these demonstrations of valued Kṣatriya qualities, however, recognition of their status as Kṣatriyas remains a question. The self-image of the Gŏllas as rājas or Kṣatriyas notwithstanding, the epic heroes' attitude to the land is itself ambiguous. The Gŏllas want land, not to rule over, but purely to use for grazing. Their interest in land is rather functional and to that extent ambiguous. They want the land yet they do not want it. They want control over the land to use it, but do not really care who owns it. They do not want to own the land because they have no interest in fighting to protect it. Their heroism, therefore, does not consist in dying for the land, but in winning access to it by one means or another, including trickery and cunning. Their heroism, however, has another dimension, revenge, that is not found in the landed-caste epics. The epic repeatedly mentions the theme of avenging the death of their ancestors. Kāṭamarāju's interest, often hidden from the surface, is to avenge the death of his father. These ambiguities are reflected in the symbols Gŏllas use to represent themselves as a caste in the epic. They identify themselves with the Yādavas and trace their dynasty to Yadu of the *Mahābhārata*. The Yādavas of that great epic are themselves of an uncertain status, not being fully recognized as Kṣatriyas, as is the case with their leader, the god Kṛṣṇa. In the epic, the caste is referred to as Yādavas, but their enemy king Nallasiddhi and his associates regularly refer to them as Gŏllas.

In the Telugu sociological structure of right-and left-hand divisions among castes, the Yādavas do not clearly belong to either division. In pre-modern Andhra, Gŏllas were known as carriers of cash. Also, cattle are a form of money in an agrarian society. The Telugu word *sŏmmulu* is used both for golden jewelry, another form of money, as well as cattle. In its singular form, *sŏmmu* means "cash."[19] Dealings in cash and trade of cattle would put Gŏllas in the category of left-hand castes. In fact, Thurston reports that they belong to the left-hand caste division.[20] But their relationship with land brings them close to the right-hand castes. Fluidity of cash on the one hand and the solidity of land on the other pull this caste in two opposing directions creating a tension and a constantly tricky existence.

Women in Andhra, as in most parts of India, wear one end of their saree as a sash (called *paiṭa* in Telugu) over their shoulder. There is an interesting cultural symbolism in the style of wearing this paiṭa. Women of right-hand caste groups wear their paiṭa over the left shoulder and women of left-hand caste groups wear their paiṭa over their right shoulder. Gŏlla women wear it both ways: depending on the occasion. An aphorism popular in their caste says: right sash for caste use and left sash for going out.[21] Ethnographic information on Gŏllas is far from adequate to make definitive statements about their rituals, beliefs, and social styles, but bits and pieces of evidence from reported research and my interviews with persons of Gŏlla caste indicate their unwillingness to be classified into one or the other division.

The nature of their epic hero Kāṭamarāju, and their caste goddess Gaṅga, encapsulate the ambiguities and tensions of this caste. Both as individual deities as well as a couple with internal tensions between them, Kāṭamarāju and Gaṅga symbolize the ambiguous existence of the Gŏllas. The epic singers always begin their epic performance with a prayer to Gaṅga. In the rituals related to the epic, Gaṅga is the chief deity to whom all the offerings are made. In Enūtala, in the Nallamala hills of Nellore district in Andhra Pradesh, there are images of Kāṭamarāju and Gaṅga. Annually, in the summer Gŏllas perform a festival ritual to both the deities. And a big tree stands there separating the images of Gaṅga and Kāṭamarāju, blocking each from seeing the other.

NOTES

1. Research for this paper was made possible by grants from the Graduate School, University of Wisconsin-Madison and from the National Endowment

for the Humanities, Washington, D. C. My thanks are due to them and to David Shulman and Alf Hiltebeitel, who have read earlier versions of this paper and suggested many improvements.

2. Mādigas are an Untouchable community belonging to the left-hand division. They are the traditional priests of Gŏllas, and also sing the epic at weddings, funerals, and at the annual rituals related to the epic. In addition, Gŏllas themselves sing the epic. Both groups claim authority to sing the epic. I suspect some tensions between the two groups of singers, although there is no significant variation in the versions each group sings.

3. Tangirala Venkata Subba Rao, *Kāṭamarāju Kathalu*, 2 volumes (Hyderabad: Andhra Pradesh Sahitya Akademi, 1986, 1978).

4. Oral versions of the epic lack some important segments. The version I got of the arguments between Gaṅga and Kāṭamarāju is not complete. Also I do not have the birth of Kāṭamarāju in the oral version I collected. I therefore used the version of Subba Rao for the summaries given here of those incidents. For a short summary with other variations, cf. Wilbur Theodore Elmore, *Dravidian Gods in Modern Hinduism: A Study of the Local and Village Deities of Southern India* (Lincoln: University of Nebraska, 1915), 100-104.

5. Telugu marriages conventionally include a tying of tāḷi, the marriage band, as the ritual event signifying marriage. Here in the epic, however, there is no mention of tāḷi. The pouring of rice on each other's head by the bride and the bridegroom is included in all marriages. In this story the event has a more important significance than usual, in that it takes the place of tāḷi-tying.

6. Subba Rao, *Kāṭamarāju Kathalu*, vol. 1. pp. cxxxxii-iii.

7. Ibid., vol. 1. 95.

8. Ibid., vol. 1. 95.

9. Ibid., vol. 1. cxii.

10. William Waterfield and George Grierson, trans. and ed., *The Lay of Alha* (London: Oxford University Press, 1923), 57-143.

11. Brenda E. F. Beck, *The Three Twins: The Telling of a South Indian Folk Epic* (Bloomington: Indiana University Press, 1982), 25; cf. Velcheru Narayana Rao, "Epics and Ideologies: Six Telugu Folk Epics," in Stuart Blackburn and A. K. Ramanujan, eds., *Another Harmony: New Essays on the Folklore of India* (Berkeley: University of California Press, 1986), 134-49.

12. Narayana Rao, "Epics and Ideologies," 136-40, 144-47, 156-61.

13. Ibid., 147, n. 8.

14. Several literary texts in Telugu describe worship of Kāṭreḍu by hunters. Allasani Pĕddanna (sixteenth century) describes hunters who participated in the royal hunt cooking the game they had hunted and offering the food to Kāṭreḍu; *Manucaritramu* 4-60, as also Ponnekanti Telagnarya in his *Yayāti-caritramu*, 2-3. In Nellore and Chittur Districts of Andhra Pradesh farmers offer worship to Kāṭamarāju on the fourth day, the day of the cattle, of Sankrānti,

the harvest festival.

15. Subba Rao, vol. 2. 621.

16. J. A. B. van Buitenen, trans. and ed., *The Mahābhārata*, I. *The Book of Beginning* (Chicago: University of Chicago Press, 1973), 216-20.

17. In the landed caste epics men die on the battlefield. It is a requirement to the status of the hero that he die fighting to protect the land. In the Palnāḍu epic, the hero who has this status is the young Bālacandruḍu. In the Kāṭamarāju epic, most men die fighting, but not on the battlefield. They die from the wounds received in the battle, but after the battle. The oldest hero of the epic is Āvula Valurāju. He fights with Kalabhūta Gangurāju, the king of Khaṇḍĕmoṇḍĕmula-koṭa. He kills his enemy in the battle, but he himself dies later, due to the wounds received in the fight. His wife Vallamma commits *sati* and dies on her husband's funeral pyre. Valurāju's eldest son Simhādrirāju similarly dies fighting with Sindhubhaḷḷānirāju the king of Śrīkūrmamaṁ, again from wounds sustained in the battle. His wife Simhādrisīta dies on the funeral pyre of her husband. The pattern continues with Yĕranūkarāju, the third son of Valurāju, who fights with Yĕrrabhūpati. A significant exception to this pattern is the death of Pĕddirāju, Kāṭamarāju's father, who dies on the battlefield.

18. In the landed caste epics, the heroes die fighting against a faction of their extended family because of disputes regarding inheritance. The major issue in these epics is the rulership of the land. In the Palnāḍu epic, the dispute is between the cousins. Similarly in the Elder Brothers epic, the battle is between clansmen. Enemies in these epics have the same status. But in Kāṭamarāju, the fight is not over who should rule the land, but over an injustice done by a ruling king to someone or other who seeks the protection of the Yādava heroes. Yādavas fight for the cause of the people whom they offer to protect. Valurāju fights with the king of Khaṇḍĕmoṇḍĕmulakoṭa because some Brahmans who were in the service of the king seek Valurāju's protection. They were the king's accountants, and they embezzled some of the king's money. When the king was going to punish them for their crime, they asked for six months to make up for the loss of money, and escaped from the kingdom and sought Valurāju's protection. Valurāju offered them refuge, which resulted in a battle with the king. Simhādrirāju's fight with Sindhubaḷḷānirāju of Śrīkūrmam also is caused by a similar incident. Sindhubhaḷḷānirāju accused some Śrīvaiṣṇavas of thievery and tortured them. The Śrīvaiṣṇavas sought refuge with Simhādrirāju, who offered them protection and fought with Sindhubhaḷḷānirāju. In all these instances the kings with whom the Yādavas fought have a recognized status as ruling kings. Thus in the Kāṭamarāju epic the enmity is between the Yādavas and kings of a higher status.

19. One of the threats that Gaṅga makes against Kāṭamarāju is that without worshipping her, he cannot earn enough money to pay the grazing rent on land. If he agrees to worship her, she offers him "crores" of money.

20. Edgar Thurston and K. Rangachari, *Castes and Tribes of Southern India*, 7 vols. (Madras: Government Press, 1909), vol. 2, 285-96.

21. The image of Gaṅga in all the temples where Gŏllas worship her has her paiṭa on the right shoulder.

5

Night of the Growing Dead: A Cult of Vīrabhadra in Coastal Andhra

David M. Knipe

It is of the utmost importance to traditional Hindus that those who have lived and died remain contented in whatever guises of afterlife they exist. The singular fact that undergirds this importance is *saṃsāra*, transmigration, a cosmic process that dispassionately synchronizes afterlife with prelife. From late Vedic texts down to the modern ritual compendia in daily use for *śrāddha* rites, a recurrent phrase addressed to the ancestors is "Be satisfied," that is, be pleased and contented with all that we are providing, in the work of these rituals, for your physical and emotional needs. This attentiveness to the bodily and affective requirements of the dead, if more systematic than most, is nevertheless one that is shared with almost all traditional cultures, and is remarkable only to those in the modern world who forget their ancestors and believe the dead to be out of touch with life. Hinduism maintains an extraordinarily rich set of traditions concerning the livelihood of ancestors, not only in its great schedules of rituals but also in myth, folklore, iconography, drama, and dance. Some basic notions have been active for two to three millenia; others are untraceable but possibly a great deal older. These traditions display simultaneously a unique South Asian homogeneity, immediately recognizable, and a vivid overlay of local and regional expressions. Only a few of the latter have been objects of ethnographic study.

A concern found throughout the Hindu world, and again one shared with most traditional cultures, is anxiety over the fate of one who has died the *untimely death* (Sanskrit: *akāla mṛtyu* or *akāla māraṇa*). This phrase is accepted into most of the vernaculars of South Asia, *untimely* covering all those bad, unnatural, out-of-order deaths that are premature due to accidents, diseases, snake-bites, suicides, or other fates. It is applied in particular ways to cases of the deaths of infants, children, those who do not attain the marriage vows. In agricultural metaphor, often employed in human/plant/food homologies connected with death and rebirth, the untimely death may be considered insufficient ripening, or worse, something akin to crop failure, unseasonable killing. The subject of this essay is a regional cult that addresses the problem of deviant death, of Death that has worked perversely to frustrate the normal stream of personal birth and death and rebirth, and the orderly progression, generation to generation, of family lineages. When individuals die before they have attained the householder stage, that is, married and raising children who can attend to them ritually after death, they are cosmically stranded from the point of view of transmigration. Their persons excluded from ritual progressions and their lineages devastated, their dilemmas may leave no recourse but rage and malevolent behavior. If their premature deaths were violent ones, such rage may be compounded to the point of uncontrollability. They are among the most dangerous and poignant of the disgruntled dead, no one's "Fathers," for they never had the chance to become ancestors.

This essay, a preliminary report on a complex, eclectic, and frequently elusive set of traditions, is focused on a medium-sized town in the coastal zone of Andhra Pradesh, the town of Rajahmundry in East Godavari District, located on the left bank of the Godavari at the point where the great river splits into deltoid streams for its final forty miles to the Bay of Bengal. Fieldwork for this study was accomplished from September through December 1980, in January 1985, and from October 1987 through January 1988. Incidentally, this tradition, undiscussed in the scant ethnography of coastal Andhra, was not initially targeted for study, but surfaced in the form of nocturnal noise so demanding that another, quieter project was temporarily displaced.[1]

A. Procession, Possession, and Renewal

The riveting explosion of drums that shatters the midnights of Śivarātri, or such lunar months as Kārttika, Māgha, and Vaiśākha, can be heard from a distance of two miles. Those who know the staccato cadences distinguish beats that encourage states of trance and possession from those that rescue the possessed, pulling them down just in time and saving them from the prolonged terrifying embodiment of spirits who are both divine and demonic. For the drums belong to the ritual apparatus of *Vīrabhadruḍi sambaram*, the nocturnal procession of Vīrabhadra that is at once a defiant dance of death, a boisterous overnight pilgrimage, and a solemn celebration of renewal by a wider family that includes deceased children among its vital and active members.

The focus of these volatile minipilgrimages is upon the disgruntled dead, those who died in infancy or childhood only a few months back, or as much as sixty, seventy, or more years ago. They are centers of attention precisely because their presences are known to their parents and other family members, frequently from the days immediately following burial. In their demonstrable and often forceful continuity with the living, such presences call for two responses within the traditions of the cult in this particular town: first, routine food, the lighting of lamps, and other offerings in the form of pūjās either at a home shrine or in collective worship performed by a pūjārī in a Snake-anthill temple located at the south end of town and, second, annual regeneration via the long night's procession from the home or Snake-anthill temple westward across town to the Godavari River that forms the precise limit of human habitation. Let us consider details of the procession and the ritualists before turning to the home shrine, the temple traditions, and the mythic/folkloric backdrop to the tradition.

Vīrabhadruḍi sambaram, as it is known in Telugu, may be performed either on the great "night" of Śiva, Mahāśivarātri, the fourteenth of the dark or waning half of the lunar month of Māgha, which is celebrated in Rajahmundry for two successive nights, or at night throughout certain lunar months, Kārttika (October-November), Māgha (January-February), and Vaiśākha (April-May) being favored. As in other death traditions such as the pan-Indian Pitṛpakṣa, the fortnight of the Fathers (ancestors), the normally inauspicious waning lunar period is appropriate, and the night time is in keeping with otherworldly intercourse. The procession may be occasioned, however, by a forthcoming auspicious event in the family, particularly a marriage, or some milestone such as a new house or new job, or a vow or long pilgrimage to be fulfilled, and thus becomes a ritual means of including the deceased in occurrences of good fortune. A darker meaning may underscore the clangorous procession as well, the hope that it will for the time being "satisfy" the deceased, forestalling malevolence that might spoil the party, perhaps even the family destiny.

The procession has an order and a cast of characters. In the 1980s we are most probably witnessing the tail end of a longtime tradition, with substitutions in the lineup, absences of certain specialists, vague or missing associations between myths, symbols, and performances, and virtually no self-recognition by the ritualists or laity of how this tradition relates to rituals and performances elsewhere in Hinduism. What survives, however, is dramatically instructive, not only for our knowledge of regional Hinduism, but also of human responses to the universal tragedy of child death.

At the head of the procession are two (sometimes more) *prabhā*s in the form of red cloth banners stretched kitelike across bamboo frames about nine feet high, each carried upright like a sail by a man from the Kāpu (Cultivator) or Sāli (Weaver) castes. According to ritualists involved in *Vīrabhadruḍi sambaram* these prabhās add wholeness and beauty to the procession. Then come the musicians (*bhajantrī*), usually Barbers, but here in the local tradition Potters (Kummāris). They have special training on the drums, which appear in three sizes (the *vīraṇam*, *ḍōlu*, and *tassa*), all slung on ropes around the neck. The vīraṇam is rubbed intensely with a curved stick to produce a weird sound more tuba-like than percussive; when combined with the other drums the effect is overwhelming.[2] Wooden nine-holed flutes with reeds (*śahnai*) are also played, always by Muslims. All the musicians form a moving half-circle enclosing one or more representatives of ritualist groups such as *vīrakumāras*, *vīramuṣṭis*, and *jaṅgamas*, and these in turn precede the family group. The vīrakumāra, a "young male hero (vīra)," is dressed in brilliant red, sometimes olive green, the favorite colors of Śiva according to the ritualists, and he wears silver ankle bells, sometimes epaulettes. He may blow a conch-shell (*śaṅkha*), ring a bell (*ghaṇṭā*), carry a silver trident (triśūla) in his right hand or sometimes clenched cross-wise in his teeth as he gyrates, hands and arms arched together over his head in the swaying motions of a cobra. Some carry in the right hand a small *vajra*-like club. One Sāli man of 25 who makes his living producing cigars in a tobacco shop has danced as a vīrakumāra since he was nine, continuing the role performed by his father before him. Vīramuṣṭis, another category of processional dancers, are locally regarded as a Śūdra caste group of mendicants or beggars associated in exchanges with designated other castes, including the Kōmaṭis (Traders) of the twice-born castes. They are known for certain entertainment or ritual performances, and may be descendants of medieval groups who acted as temple guardians. But they are not currently represented in Rajahmundry, and other jātis have taken their roles, becoming "vīramuṣṭis" not by birth in a caste but by virtue of their specific style of dance. For example, another caste whose occupation is weaving, the Devangams, may become "vīramuṣṭis" for the purposes of the nocturnal procession. Popular etymology seems to play a role here, since *muṣṭi* indicates a "clenched fist" and the dancer who stamps his feet and clenches his fists is displaying the emotion of anger. The Jangams (jaṅgamas) are another Andhra Śūdra caste with longtime links to twice-born merchant groups, serving them in ritual performances. At one time, like the Vīramuṣṭis, they were evidently more closely involved in the processions, but now the Weavers or other jātis may in their absence substitute for them as well.[3]

After the prabhā-carriers, musicians, and various dancers comes the largest group in each segment of a procession, namely the family members who have engaged all the ritualists, usually by arrangements with the pūjārī of the Snake-anthill temple. The family may be a dozen persons or several scores in number, proceeding under canopies, one or another member (usually a brother or sister of the deceased) carrying atop his or her head the wooden, brass, or woven-straw tray from the home shrine, all of them surrounded not only by the cacaphony of thunderous drums, shrill flutes, shouts and stomping feet, but also clouds of smoke from *sāmbrāṇi* crystals burning in iron braziers or clay pots, a scented blue smoke intended, like specific cadences of the drums, both to create and alleviate a climate for momentous encounters with the world of spirits (see plate 7). And all along the streets and lanes of the town the arrival of that climate is announced by sudden violent seizures, possessions of the marchers, and even unsuspecting bystanders, by the spirits of children recently or long ago departed from the living family group (see plate 8).

As is the case elsewhere in South Asia from Tibet and Nepal to Sri Lanka, states of possession in coastal Andhra are frequent occurrences, regarded as serious occasions of communication with the worlds of the supernatural. In the *Vīrabhadruḍi sambaram* possessions are by those who have suffered untimely deaths before they could become ritually completed humans by means of childhood, educational, and marital life-cycle rites. Therefore possessions are outbursts from an incurably liminal realm. Rather than shrink from such chilling and dangerous contacts, marchers willingly risk their bodies as vehicles for the spirits, becoming agents who transmit to the family the immediate states of mind and wishes of their stranded kin. Although some men do become possessed, it appears to be largely the women in the family, and most frequently younger mothers in their twenties and

7. An extended family procession, one of many hundreds during the nights of Kārttika month, reaches the river after sunup. A ritualist with epaulettes on his fancy vest and noisy anklets of silver dances before them. Photo by David Knipe.

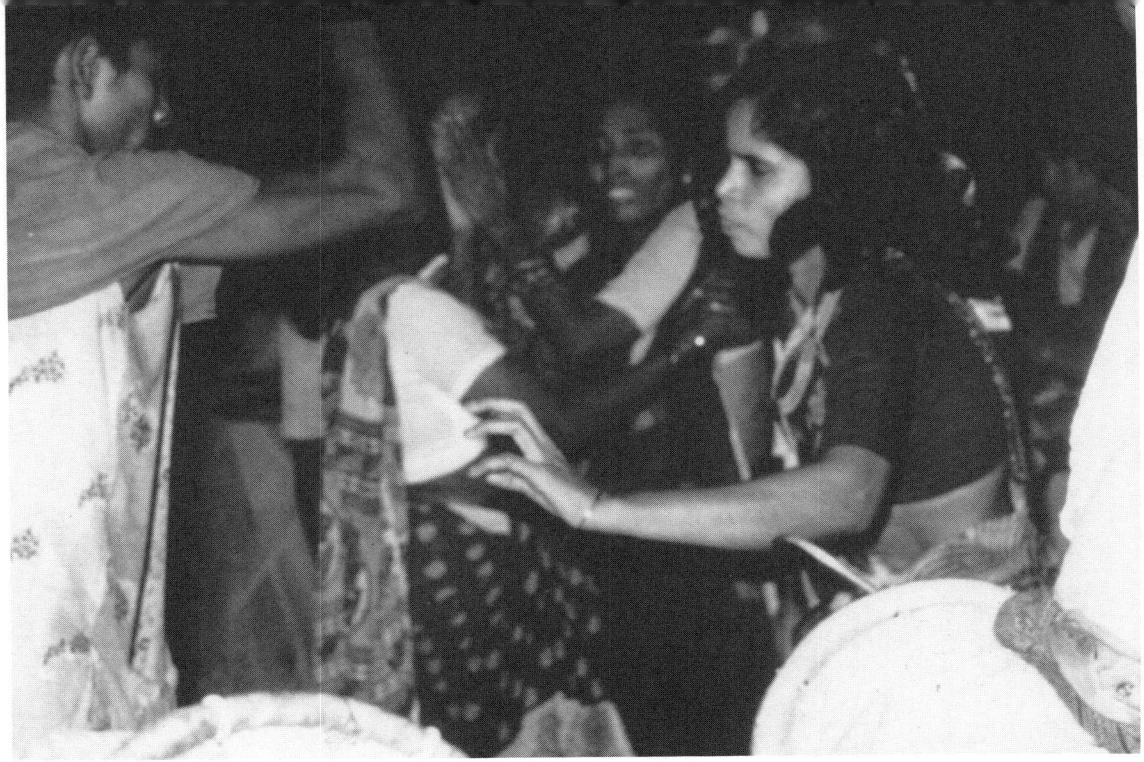

8. Two women whirling and about to fall to the ground in states of possession by deceased children's spirits during the nocturnl procession to the river. A "Vīramuṣṭi" stomps his dance at left, while a third woman claps her hands to the explosive beat of drums. Photo by David Knipe.

thirties, who sway or whirl, slowly at first, then quickly before they abandon the march and fall screaming to the ground. As they cry to Vīrabhadra "Save me, rescue me!" the circle of ritualists tightens about the writhing person, the incense pot is brought closer, and the eerie cadences of the drums and shouts of specialists turn to techniques of deliverance and consolation.

Those possessed are known to be undergoing a perilous ascent while they are out of self-control, and therefore they must be brought down, the safely completed descent being the salient charge of ritualists. Sometimes neither the incense nor the several extricating drum beats are successful in the rescue and a fresh lime must be torn in one hand, its juice poured on the head of the possessed one, and the halves thrown away in opposite directions. Coconut juice or water are available as alternatives for such *śāntikarma.* Frequently people who hear or observe processions going by their houses at three or four o'clock in the morning become possessed, and often, to prevent such spontaneity, susceptible persons are restrained and kept back from windows and doors. Such incidental, unanticipated possessions may be by spirits of one's deceased child kin, or even by other spirits, a woman, for example, being possessed suddenly by her husband's deceased former wife.

The last possessions occur at the riverside, at the special *ghat* (Telugu: *revu*) at which all processions conclude, and when these have ended in descent, and all of the wild (*raudra*) activity is over, the scene changes to one of calm and solemn pūjā. Family members bathe in the darkness of the river and the ash-fruits (vibhūti-paṇḍus) representing the deceased child, usually three in number, are taken from the head-borne tray and washed in the river, dried, provided with yellow turmeric powder and three vermilion stripes, then installed back on the tray for a complete schedule of offerings, including lamps, incense, halved coconuts, bananas, rice grains, flowers, cotton threads, and coins. Every member of the family presents herself or himself in *namaskāra* before this tranquil and opulent minishrine, after which the tray with its regenerated ash-fruits is hoisted again onto a brotherly or sisterly head for the composed and uneventful return journey (see plate 9). The routine rituals have once again established control.

An additional ritual of the *teppa* (float) is performed by many of the women at the riverside. It has two forms, which may be done separately, or as a sequence at once, *maila* (ritual pollution) being an annual ceremony for the removal of impurity, for which a pith float is set on the river, and *polla* (flower) for the celebration of an auspicious occasion, for which a sled-like arrangement covered with colorful

9. Another family returns from the riverside renewal of the home shrine's three ash-fruits, which are now covered with offerings of turmeric, red powder, coconut halves, bananas, mango leaves, incense, lamps, threads, rice grains, and other items. A ritualist accompanies at right. Photo by David Knipe.

papers is the teppa (see plate 10). Both forms of teppa contain burning ghee-lamps that present a warming scene to the families on the shore as they drift into the night on the dark currents of the Godavari.

Procedures at the riverbank may be under the direction of a vīrakumāra, vīramuṣṭi, or jaṅgam, or entirely without professional guidance. Although the majority of caste groups in attendance are non-Brahman, in correspondence with the predominant Śūdra-varṇa population of the town, and although local Brahman ritualists (*karmakāṇḍis*) describe *Vīrabhadruḍi sambaram* as a "non-Brahman event," Brahman families do take part in the process and individuals can be observed in states of possession or restraint from possession. From the numbers of participants it would appear that virtually the entire town, including the Scheduled castes or Harijans (Mālas and Mādigas), can become involved in these performances. In Kārttika and Mārgaśīrṣa 1980 there were from a dozen to twenty processions involving several hundreds of people each night, and during the two nights of Śivarātri 1985 crowds of several thousands were continuous.

B. Ash-Fruits, the Home Shrine, and the Snake-Anthill

The spirits of deceased children who possess one or another family member are represented iconically throughout the procession, as they are while installed in the temple or the home shrines, by the ash-fruits borne on the heads of marchers. These vibhūti-paṇḍus (Sanskrit/Telugu *vibhūti*, the "ashes" of cowdung sacred in particular to Śiva, and the combined mystical powers of Śiva, and Telugu *paṇḍu*, "fruit"), are usually three in number, as noted earlier, borne on a single-framed tray as a portable shrine in the procession. One of them comes from the Snake-anthill temple collection, whereas two more are purchased from the Potters. As a triad they move not in the ordinary sense of human motion, but by a process of interior struggle, combativeness, even warfare. We will return to this notion of the children of rage in parts three and four of this essay.

The vibhūti-paṇḍus are made of cowdung ash mixed with acacia gum and pressed by the Potters into molded cones with rounded tops. According to the Potters they are created in three sizes, small, medium, and large, named after measures of rice. Those that are carried are usually five to seven inches high, and this size predominates in the huge collection stacked in the Snake-anthill temple's interior shrine. But since these ash-fruits are said to "grow" as they are worshipped and renewed annually at the river, many of those installed in home

10. A young mother places a decorated "flower" float (*teppa*) with burning oil lamp on the Godavari River at the end of her Kārttika procession. It is for her infant son who died two years previously and frequently possesses her. Usually she performs the annual procession in Māgha month, but this night it was to include him in the auspicious occasion of entering new living quarters. Photo by David Knipe.

shrines and in the temple are larger, as much as two feet in height and almost as much in diameter at the base. Their growth, of course, is vivid testimony to the living, active, ripening presence of these individuals who are in but not of this world.

To cite an example, a young mother of three children lost her youngest, a boy eighteen months old, in 1978. He possessed her the day after his death. She recognized him as "a vīrabhadra," began his worship on a regular basis, and has performed pūjās for him ever since, unassisted by any priest or specialist. She does these every day and not just on the requisite Mondays and Saturdays. Usually it is in the month of Māgha that she performs the procession from her apartment in the center of town to the river. Because of the propitious occasion of moving to this new apartment in 1980, however, the procession was done in Kārttika. By 1985 she had performed the *Vīrabhadruḍi sambaram* seven times. In the home shrine—a yellow, blue, and white miniature temple of wood six feet high, elaborately decorated, and occupying a sizeable portion of the limited living space—the single vibhūti-paṇḍu, about ten inches high, is encircled by a silver serpent coil with five heads. When I was invited to see it, after an unannounced arrival at 9 p.m., it was covered with garlands of fresh flowers and surrounded by a dozen bananas, a cup with spoon, plates of cooked food, two lamps, and a number of other ritual items. She admits to being possessed frequently by this son, as recently as one month prior to my visit, and unconnected to the *Vīrabhadruḍi sambaram*. She has two other children, a son and a daughter, ten and five years of age in 1985.

A second example is a tragic case that occurred in a Potter family in 1976 when two brothers, five and three years old, died the same day from accidentally drinking insecticide. Their parents both died within the next year, of grief according to relatives. Pūjās to them as vīrabhadras fell to the responsibility of their uncle, their father's younger brother, who does the *Vīrabhadruḍi sambaram* annually in the company of the wider family and relatives. But like many other families that have lost children, this one does not undertake daily pūjās for them within the dwelling (although they have on their wall a garlanded photo of the two boys side by side in cradles readied for burial). Instead, vibhūti-paṇḍus representing the two boys are placed in the nearby Snake-anthill temple (see plate 11) where they are worshipped on a daily basis, along with hundreds of others, by the pūjāri, an elderly Kāpu man, or one of his six students.

This particular snake-anthill (Telugu *pāmu*, "snake," *puṭṭa*, "anthill," i.e., the mound made by termites, which are known in South Asia as

11. Interior shrine of the Snake-Anthill temple where devotees have stacked up hundreds of ash-fruits (*vibhūti-paṇḍus*) for collective pūjās. Note their replication of the natural white-ant (termite) turret at center, against which are leaning two carved wooden statues representing deceased female children as goddesses. Photo by David Knipe.

white ants) may be regarded as the center of the cult of Vīrabhadra in Rajahmundry. Throughout South Asia termite mounds are appreciated as sacred channels connecting the three worlds, their netherworld tunnels continuing up through this world into castle-like structures with turrets, self-arisen hierophanies silently stretching skyward, each a natural *axis mundi.* Termites are known to tunnel far into the earth, as deep as forty meters to locate water and bring it to the surface.[4] Their above-ground structures can be two meters high, so it is not surprising that their invisibly growing mounds are significant in popular cults of the dead.[5] The fact that anthills are universally regarded as residences of *nāga*s (serpents), more specifically cobras, is an additional reinforcement of this connection with chthonic realms, death, and rebirth.

Like all important snake-anthills, this one has its story. This locale in Tadithota at the south end of town was once a garden with an anthill inhabited by two cobras who returned to it no matter how many times snake-handlers tried to remove them. The snake-anthill became a shrine (*guḍi*) "about two hundred years ago." The current pūjārī, a 67-year-old Kāpu, remembers a simple hut around it when he was a boy growing up in the Vīrabhadra cult traditions associated with the shrine. Eventually it became the two-room edifice with blue-pillared, roofed porch that exists today. For many decades the pūjārī who preceded him was possessed here by the spirit of his deceased infant sister, who announced that it was she who would remain here in the form of the serpents. And indeed, although seldom seen, the cobras still are here, because they eat offerings regularly set out for them. A 17-year-old granddaughter of the former pūjārī (who died in 1981 "at the venerable age of 120"), is occasionally possessed, and indications are that the spirit is determining a successor "host." Because he does not become possessed, the current pūjārī is not a candidate for this additional responsibility.

The temple now consists of two rooms, an anteroom intended for the worship of Veṅkateśvara, Lord of Tirupati, and an inner room built around the five-foot-high termite mound, actually incorporating it into the walls of its northeast corner. When eyes adjust to the light of a single oil lamp, hundreds of ash-fruits may be seen on a foot-high shelf that projects from three walls, and in this otherworldly scene a striking congruency of form becomes apparent: the common five-to-seven-inch ash-fruits used in the processions are identical in size, proportions, even texture, to the termite-created turrets of their ancient castle rising from the earth. Whatever other avenues the vibhūti-paṇḍu symbolism might pursue (and these are to be discussed in the fourth part of this essay), this particular homology is clear and unmistakable: the invisibly growing ash-fruit-children are respectfully laid among the invisibly growing anthill peaks, where channels of communication to the other world are as open as they are ancient.

Ash-fruits fashioned by the Potters are not the only symbols in this chamber of the growing dead. Rising out of the ash-fruits blended into the termite turrets is an arch of hammered brass, crowned by a wild lion-faced mask. The arch may display the rainbow that emerges, according to popular belief,[6] from an anthill, and the mask above it the lion-faced avatara of Śiva. Stacked in corners are dozens of natural conical stones, squat rounded shapes like giant concrete mushrooms. More prominent are the goddesses standing erect at the center of attention among the ash-fruits with encircling nāga-coils and guardian hoods. They are in two guises, one fashioned by the Potters into a female figure from molded cowdung ashes and acacia gum (like the ash-fruits), painted with features, bright red sari, green blouse, and jewelry, and provided with a raised stick in her clenched right fist. This type is single, just under six inches tall, and is situated with a burning oil lamp just south of the termite mound. The other goddess style is multiple and entirely different, each 16 inches tall, crudely carved of black wood, arms at her sides. Her tiny breasts are bare, and a slim girdle on her wide hips is the only clothing but for bangles and what appear to be epaulettes on her shoulders. Her brows are triply lined, providing her with a vaguely worried gaze. Although the ash-fruits are requisite for both male and female children, these Vīrakanyakā goddesses are optional representations for girls alone, positioned in either one of these two iconic forms in the home shrine or in the temple.

C. The God, the Goddess, and the Children of Rage

Vīrabhadruḍi sambaram is a ritual procession well named: Vīrabhadra is the terrific deity born from Śiva's rage, a personification of uncontrollable anger that burst from the forehead of the great god who would not tolerate two events: the performance of a great world-reaffirming sacrifice that deliberately excluded him, and then, because of this unbearable insult, the self-immolation of his mate Satī. This tragedy of discrimination and outsiderhood, of self-mortification and brutal revenge, is a powerful one told throughout India, for it is the theme of Dakṣa's sacrifice, one that has its basis in the ambiguities of exclusiveness in the Brahmanic rituals of Vedic Hinduism. It has particular connotations in those few parts of South India such as coastal Andhra where great Vedic soma sacrifices are still performed in ancient authenticity by a tiny minority of vaidika Brahmans in the midst of a vast population of non-twiceborn-caste Hindus.

Fiery power, ascetic frenzy, mobility on the wind, the garment of red are already in the late Ṛgveda (e.g., 10:136) associated with the outsider god, Rudra, the fierce resident of the mountain wilderness. Later Vedic texts stress his isolation from the prescribed shares of sacrifices, regarding him always with awe. The opening line of the *Śatarudriya* celebrates the wrath of Rudra (*Vājasaneyi-saṃhitā* 16.1; *Taittirīya-saṃhitā* 4.5.1, the latter being one of the most frequently recited texts of Andhra vaidika Brahmans). It is in several different *parvans* of the *Mahābhārata*, the first *kāṇḍa* of the *Rāmāyaṇa*, and numerous Purāṇas, however, that certain myths prefigured in the Brāhmaṇas elaborate details of this collision of two opposing energies, one creative, the other destructive, both of them hunting the elusive and mysterious essence of the sacrifice. The centerpiece is an aśvamedha, a horse sacrifice intended to reintegrate and renew the cosmos, with all the deities but Rudra-Śiva invited by Dakṣa to take a share. Arriving with his troops (*gaṇas*, successors of the Rudras or Maruts of Vedic Rudra), Śiva is possessed by wrath that emerges from his brow (or from an uprooted twist [*jaṭā*] of his matted hair) in the form of uncontrollable Vīrabhadra, a fireball of vengenance who proceeds to dismantle the sacrifice and one of its components, namely, the gods. Dakṣa (Prajāpati) is singled out for beheading, this sacrificer becoming the sacrifice who flees as a deer into the skies.

Another dimension of the attack on Dakṣa's sacrifice is expressed in a variant, the dual manifestation of vindictive power, masculine Vīrabhadra and feminine Bhadrakālī or Mahākālī. Kālī as avenging angel may be seen here as the dreadful aspect of the goddess, balancing the benevolent and loyal Satī (Pārvatī), wife of Śiva. For in the Purāṇic versions of the Dakṣa myth, Satī is Dakṣa's daughter; in response to the unconscionable insult by her father to her husband she establishes her own sacrificial fire of self-immolation and her death precipitates the awesome rampage of Śiva/Vīrabhadra/Kālī.[7]

Significant threads of the myth are too numerous to trace here, but a few highlights can be selected from a single text. The *Śiva-purāṇa* portrays the dramatic scene in two quite different versions, *Rudra-saṃhitā* 2 and *Vāyavīya-saṃhitā* 1.[8] In both of them Vīrabhadra, Bhadrakālī, and the gaṇas cooperate in the carnage until the earth is soaked with the blood of the gods, and in both there is eventual restoration of the sacrifice and the gods by the grace of supreme Śiva, who is then eulogized by all. But whereas the former variant has the characteristics of a procession of heroes, a war party on the march, the latter one depicts a riot, chaos overwhelming order, the gaṇas totally out of control as the destruction overflows beyond the target sacrifice and threatens even the sun. It is the difference between a decisive battle and *pralaya*, the destruction of the universe.[9]

Numerous details in the Sanskrit *Śiva-purāṇa* are mirrored in the textless Telugu *Vīrabhadruḍi sambaram*. Vīrabhadra carries (in addition to other weapons) a club, thunderbolt, and spear, and he wears noisy anklets and gold epaulettes. There are terrifying drums (five are named in one passage), horns, and conches as cacophonous background for those who march and dance, shout, laugh, and cry. These frenzied dancers are the gaṇas (as those possessed in *Vīrabhadruḍi sambaram* are known as *gaṇacārīs*). Vīrabhadra's presence is that of a lion, he roars like a lion, and his lion-faced cohorts are mounted on lions (prominently displayed on the arch over the snake-anthill is a brass lion-mask,[10] and the ritualists today speak of the possessions of marchers as "lion-like," even as those possessed, in their moments of terror, shout to the lion-faced Śarabha, conqueror of the man-lion avatara of Viṣṇu, Narasiṃha).[11] Finally, we may note that the splendor and lustrous power (prabhā) of Vīrabhadra, marching at the fore, increases even as that of the sacrifice is depleted. (The significance of the red banners carried as forerunners of today's processions has been forgotten; it is said simply that they add beauty and wholeness, and they have always been called prabhās).[12] Almost all of these details occur in the *Mahābhārata* in the several tellings of the Dakṣa-sacrifice-myth, although not all in the same parvan. If one were to look for a tighter focus, a "program text" for *Vīrabhadruḍi sambaram*, it might well be one or another version of the *Śiva-purāṇa*.

Regardless of textual support, it is clear that in this part of coastal Andhra the wrathful Vīrabhadra, antithesis of establishment sacrifice and its circulation of cosmic energies, is alive and well. He is one Vīrabhadra, Śiva's rage personified, and many *vīrabhadras*, all the children of rage who, even if they died after taking their mother's milk for a single day, are said to be, like Vīrabhadra, the children of Śiva. The dual manifestation of the Sanskrit texts is here in the cult as well: male children become Vīrabhadra, female children become Vīrakanyakā, who is, like Bhadrakālī, a heroine-goddess.[13] There seems to be no role in the current processions for the goddess, but as noted earlier, one of the two goddess types, the one of molded ashes, is positioned in the Snake-anthill temple as a militant guardian with raised stick in hand. She is reminiscent of Bhadrakālī (also known as Jayā; cf. *Mahābhārata* 9.61.9-11), Vīrabhadra's feminine counterpart in the Dakṣa myth according to the *Vāmana-purāṇa* (4.21ff.), stationed club in hand to guard the south and east, as Vīrabhadra guards north and west. In the Snake-anthill temple this alert and brightly painted goddess is indeed facing south.

As an illustration of this interaction of deities and spirits with the human world, and one further example of personal participation in the cult, there is an extraordinary individual in the town, a lorry mechanic who serves as the second generation recognizing a child who died 52 years ago at the age of five. This 52 (or 57)-year-old spirit is his older brother who died when he, the future lorry mechanic, was only a few months old. His mother established the home shrine and performed pūjās until some twenty-odd years ago when the lorry mechanic took over the routine, adding his own shrine beside that of his mother, and attending to both. The family is Golla (Shepherd); he is successful in his work, married, with two children. But some years ago he was arbitrarily possessed by this spirit of his elder brother who demanded more attention. This interfered with his work, so he contracted with the spirit: if pūjās were performed every day, the older brother agreed to possess him only on the two nights of Śivarātri. And so the lorry mechanic has become the most celebrated ritualist in the *Vīrabhadruḍi sambaram* (see plate 12), dancing ecstatically for hours, his matted locks flying, a silver trident clutched in his hands. The brother has been satisfied with the dance, and life has been successful for the family. Eventually, says the lorry mechanic, his own son may take over the pūjās for his deceased uncle.

In his own mind the lorry mechanic is three things when possessed by his brother and dancing on Śivarātri. He is his brother the vīrabhadra, the god Vīrabhadra, and transcendent Śiva. Not only is he participating in the march on the sacrifice but also performing Śiva's epic *tāṇḍava* dance of world-destruction. And he is well versed, thus aware that these dances are one and the same. The life he now leads is deliberately and increasingly Sanskritized. He considers himself an *upāsaka*, with *brahmajñāna* as his goal. He describes the vibhūti-paṇḍu as "a liṅga," as "Śiva" (whereas most seem to regard it as something vaguely separate and familial). The additional small vibhūti-paṇḍus in his increasingly elaborate pūjā-room (already a third of the family living quarters) are apparently tallies of his annual performance roles.

12. A lorry mechanic from the Shepherd caste dances for three nights on (*Mahā-*) *Śivarātri,* trident in hand and matted locks flying like Vīrabhadra-Śiva. He is possessed by the spirit of his elder brother who died 52 years ago. Photo courtesy of Chelluboyina Apparao.

His worldview is a process of conscious refining: he has adopted Sanskrit terminology, thought, goals, and divested his belief system and daily practice of many local customs and outlooks. He wears the sacred thread (although a Śūdra) and has taught about a dozen people; many, he says, are afraid of the rigorous discipline he demands. His daily pūjās include not only worship of the giant ash-fruit of his elder brother and the collective smaller ones, but also other rituals of great length and power, with Sanskrit mantras throughout, all from memory (see plate 13). Following two hours of worship he meditates for another hour before beginning his day's work. The intensity of his religious life has recently increased: although still of vigorous build, he fasts routinely; he and his wife observe *brahmacarya;* his matted locks remain uncut; a long while on the threshold, he appears now to be closer to the entouage of Śiva-Vīrabhadra-Bhadrakālī than the world of householders and ailing lorries.[14]

D. Some Interpretations

The cult that we are considering focuses upon the human tragedy of infant and child loss. How does it reply to this devastation, surely one of the darkest of imponderable events in the human experience? The structure of the response is multiform, including first and foremost detailed ritual activities, both emotion-charged and cathartic (the nocturnal procession), and routine methodic (the home or temple pūjās). Second, the response is empathic and consolatory: the deceased child is not erased but remains a part of the family, the household, and the major events of its life. An iconic presence assures continuous communication for as long as the family cares to remember and include the deceased. Third, some living family members may actually be initiated and empowered by this painful event. They become, by possessions in the processions, "something more," gaṇacārīs, part of Śiva-Vīrabhadra's closest entourage, part of the Army of God in the mythic context. They are conduits of messages from the spiritual world, momentary embodiments of the spirits *and* of the god; not only are they in contact with avataras such as Śarabha or Vīrabhadra, but in a sense they are temporary avataras themselves during these mini-pilgrimages in the halfworld between one day and the next, between home and the river-frontier. Fourth, the cult opens up the response to a wider focus and gains mythic charter by recourse to paradigms of sacred violence, rage employed by supernatural powers to redress wrongful actions. And here the cult perceives wrongful action in two

13. The same lorry mechanic in daily morning pūjās, largely in Sanskrit, including extensive worship of the ash-fruits representing his brother (at left rear, under the brass serpent hoods). Photo by David Knipe.

dimensions, the overt, immediate action, the death out of order that threatens the family, and the covert, hidden action, the Brahmanic exclusiveness that threatens the median-rank caste groups, the Śūdras. In its own eclectic way the cult is an answer to the age-old, locally apparent exclusion of non-Brahmans from the vaidika soma rituals, and the exclusion of Śūdras and others from the *antyeṣṭi*, śrāddha, and related death rituals of the privileged twice-born castes. Finally, the cult is not only a means of participating in uncontrollable divine/demonic rage, but also of limiting that power. It is, of course, the rituals, all of them, that keep the lid on, and provide a local manifestation of the restoration, eulogy, and subsequent harmony that conclude the nights of rage on the cosmic scale of the Purāṇas. The demons that disrupt and subvert the cultural order are organized, restrained, and replaced in the jurisdiction of rites and their results.[15]

Viewed from this widening perspective then, the cult is more than a statement about the death of a child: it is a review of Hindu eschatology.

There is space here to examine in detail only a single aspect of this energetic and symbol-rich confrontation with the enigma of child death. Let us observe more closely the iconic presence of the deceased. At the center of the Vīrabhadra cult—procession, temple, or home shrine—is the vibhūti-paṇḍu. It is a simple, dull gray item and a rich, colorful, multifaceted symbol. To the Shepherd lorry mechanic with his goal of brahmajñāna and his Sanskrit *mantras* and pūjās, the object is first of all a liṅga of Śiva and the presence of Mahādeva. To the young mother the object is first of all a vīrabhadra, one of the hundreds in the town, but unlike all the others in that it is her son of eighteen months/nine years. And in the context of the Snake-anthill temple, with its chthonic, womblike darkness dominated by the self-arisen mound of the anthill, and its forceful figures of goddesses shining in lamplight, multiple powers are manifest. Not least of them are the manifold, restful, temporarily satisfied dead. We are in the presence of something perhaps far older than the Rudra-Śiva and Śaivism known to us from textual traditions.

The Ash

The name of the icon is revealing: ash-fruit. In Vedic Hinduism ashes are what we all become; they are the remnants of the sacred fires of our lives.[16] There is the beautiful Vedic prayer in the *Vājasaneyi-saṃhitā* (40.15) declared by a dying person, "Now my breath is the immortal wind, my body is ashes (*bhasman*)." Ashes are the evidence of sacrifice, proof that a powerful transaction has been accomplished, and the material sign of purification, healing, renunciation, and transformation. Consistent with the notion of life as continuous sacrifice, ashes become in Hindu symbolism both remnants of old existence and seeds of new creation.[17] Ashes (bhasman) smeared on the erect phallus of Śiva are mentioned in the *Mahābhārata*,[18] and a primary manifestation of the god (and therefore of his renunciant devotee, the *yogin*) is a body smeared with the ashes of the dead. But another ash, that of cowdung in particular, became important to Vaiṣṇavas as well as Śaivas: *vibhūti*, literally, a manifestation of power, development, expansion, became a favored term. This literal meaning is an accurate definition of the ash-fruit. Myths trading on classical Sanskrit and Tamil homologies between ash and semen, blood, or bone were augmented by regional folkloric accounts of the revival of heroes from their ashes, particularly by bathing them in a sacred river. From the Brahmanic distribution of charred bone fragments into the river within a year after cremation, to the popular Purāṇic tale of the evil man who attained *mokṣa* because a crow accidentally dropped one of his bones in the Ganges, we find a context for the regenerated remnant, the ash-fruit, at the end of its annual pilgrimage, bathed in the Godavari River.

The ashes of cowdung pressed into vibhūti-paṇḍus or goddess figurines represent those who are not burned. They are the icons primarily of median ranks in this area of coastal Andhra—from Shepherds and Potters to Weavers—and for many of these groups burial is standard disposal of the dead. In the context of the Vīrabhadra cult, the icon may represent one who could not be burned even if the Brahmanic code were adopted. It is possible that the sacredness of cowdung ash is a deep-seated concept of pastoralists in South India in its own right, apart from the significance of the ashes of cremation. Archeological evidence of great mounds of cowdung ash in the southern Deccan (Karnataka) indicates that seminomadic pastoralists periodically conducted massive conflagrations over their cattle-corrals and stockade-like habitats, perhaps ritually in connection with seasonal migrations to new grazing areas, and with mythic/symbolic connotations of regeneration. This evidence of cowdung ash-mounds takes us to circa 3000 BCE.[19]

The Fruit

The other half of the name for the icon is the Telugu word for fruit, paṇḍu, and here again there is graphic interplay of classical and regional Hindu expressions. In this Andhra tradition the deceased is understood still to be growing, ripening as a result of offerings and familial attentions. In the perspective of classical tradition and the doctrines of saṃsāra and karma, the deceased is also, like ashes, the result (*phala*, "fruit") of action, the sum total of a life now sacrificed as final offering (antyeṣṭi). Furthermore, in the classical funerary and śrāddha (ancestral offering) traditions the deceased is represented in the context of the Fathers by three *piṇḍas*, and those three balls, representing both the presence of the Fathers and food offerings to them,[20] are sometimes described as three fruits, the *kapittha*, *āmalaka*, and inner coconut. These three graded sizes of rice-balls called "fruits" remind us that the Potters of Rajahmundry—not the Brahmans, who in theory disown this rite—create three sizes of ash-fruits named after the three measures for rice. The homophony Sanskrit piṇḍa/Telugu paṇḍu is perhaps not lost in popular etymology and perception. We recall that there should be three of the vibhūti-paṇḍus in procession (even though only one in the temple or home shrine): riverside pūjās to these three could be seen as one counterpart to Brahmanic *tripiṇḍi-śrāddha* ceremonies performed at this same ghat. In any event, the two icons, paṇḍu and piṇḍa, illuminate one another suggestively in their uniform/triform symbolism, and their connections with rice and fruit, both motifs of rebirth: "it/they" are simultaneously offering and recipient, a circular system-in-itself energized in Andhra in the liminality of an annual procession. The iconically declared ambiguity of "the fruit of ashes" is appropriate for those who do not recycle and have no issue, and at the same time consistent with normative Hinduism in which every*thing* is the result of an offering (an eating), about to be offered (eaten) by something new (eater). In this symbol the something new (eater) is the something old (eaten), perhaps yet another way of remarking the untimely dead as vividly enclosed by an idiom set apart.

Ash-fruits are molded from cowdung ash cemented by a mixture of gum from an acacia, a tree of the mimosa family. Here is an additional symbol of growth and perpetuation, for resin, in the context of both classical and popular belief, is not merely plant juice. It is the essence, life fluid, semen, seed of the tree, its virtuality contributed to this icon of the dead.

The Stone

We should note here that the ash-fruit has the immediate appearance of neither ash nor fruit but stone. It reminds us of the almost universal significance of stone in the history of religions, and of its specific employment in South Asia in connection with the symbolism of death and the endurance of the human spirit that overcomes death. The upright stone, wide at the base, pointed or rounded at the top, may indeed be one of the most archaic symbols of South Asia. Recent excavators of a terminal upper paleolithic site in Madhya Pradesh tentatively dated 9000-8000 BCE may have identified a shrine built by hunter-gatherers, a platform with a central triangular stone of unique design. Its concentrically triangular interior laminations are entirely familiar to local peoples—tribals, caste Hindus, and Muslims—whose current shrines represent goddesses by similar stones on similar platforms.[21]

If we were to look for models of the specific rounded cone that is the small stone-like ash-fruit employed in processions, we might turn also to Harappa, where excavations have revealed stones ranging from tiny ones to some more than two feet in height, roughly the same range as the ash-fruits. But we have no explanation of their meanings in prehistoric Harappa. It is the multitude of mounds and rounded conical stones, in eastern Uttar Pradesh and Bihar, for example, that speak from living cults of the deified dead; the *piṇḍ, stūp,* or *thūhā* is established on a raised platform to represent a powerful spirit such as that of a Brahman or hero who has suffered an untimely, often violent death. These are the *brahm* and bīr (from Sanskrit *vīra*) stones, respectively.[22] They can be the size of the largest of ash-fruits, or sometimes much bigger. Counterparts are known from many regional cults of the dead, for example, the collective ancestral stones of the Kannada-speaking Coorgs of Mysore, embedded in earthen platforms, and their bīra hero stones.[23] The astonishing variety of hero and memorial stones connected with cults of the dead in South Asia is now the subject of regional and integral studies.[24]

Even great architectural monuments ca be reduced to the scale of the ash-fruits. The relief sculptures of such ancient Buddhist sites as Amaravati on the Krishna River, only a hundred miles west of Rajahmundry, display stūpas in miniature with worshippers, usually female, bending over or before them in namaskāra. These second-century BCE reliefs of tiny stūpas are arresting for several reasons: their parabolic shapes, like many ash-fruits but unlike the classical Śiva-liṅgas either on the Amaravati reliefs themselves or in contemporary Śiva temples in Andhra; an uncanny resemblance of the stūpas decorated with three encircling garlands to the ash-fruits undergoing pūjās with their three encircling vermilion stripes; the appearance of the mini-stūpas either singly, or in triads, again like the ash-fruits; the prominence of women in their worship. It is well known that stūpas are Buddhist reliquaries perpetuating older cults of the dead, and also that in the history of Andhra religion there was considerable interplay between vaidika, Buddhist, Jaina, Śaiva, and other traditions of death and rebirth.

But more important for our topic is the widespread tradition in Hindu funerary customs of using a small triangular or round stone (*śila* or *aśman* in the Sanskrit *paddhati*s and many vernaculars) to strike three holes in a large water pot held on the left shoulder of the chief mourner, allowing nourishing water to flow on the pyre or grave. This (or another) small portable stone can then become an icon of the deceased in post-cremation/burial ceremonies during his perilous journey as spirit (*preta*) to the other world and eventual incorporation into the company of ancestors (*pitṛ*s). As such, it is the recipient of offerings, and food in particular, during the ten-day period of ritual reconstruction of a temporary body for the deceased. A wider complex of symbols and surrogates during this period of gestation and rebirth (which is also a symbolic year) includes not only the stone (which survives today mostly in the Deccan) but also a small, dripping water pot, a pipal tree, a piece of cloth from the deceased, and a ritualist stand-in who eats the food offerings intended to nourish the deceased during his journey. Here is perhaps one of the oldest living belief-systems in India, the dead represented by stones (and sometimes ritual specialists as backup surrogates) demanding food in order to remain in existence.

How do we recognize the archaism of this belief? We have noted the congruence of three factors in the Vīrabhadra cult of the dead: the deceased are represented by ash-fruits that are stone-like, they are satisfied if their kin attend to them with pūjās that include food offerings, and because of these offerings and attentions by the family they continue to grow. Stones believed to grow from the ground because they are bathed and fed by worshippers, particularly women, are known from all parts of India North and South.[25] But it is Elwin who reported from his years of research among the Muria tribals of the Bastar plateau in Madhya Pradesh the universal Muria belief that memorial stones for the buried dead, whether slender squared-off *menhirs* eight feet tall or small phallus-like ones only a foot high (shown in his plates 31 and 34)

> grow in size if the soul of the dead is satisfied with the arrangements that are made for him. . . . A very small stone is put for a baby and it is believed that it will grow gradually until it has reached the size it should have been placed for a man of twenty.[26]

Here we have the recognition of the child-spirit whose development continues in the midst of the living. Even the ancient megaliths of the region are explained as *very old* because no one could have set up such huge stones. The Muria bathe their memorial stones after setting them upright, place marks of oil and turmeric on them, then set food (including rice) before them, and sacrifice a cow or bullock, tying the tail to the menhir of the deceased.

Several significant pan-Indian concepts concerning the dead begin to fall into place when we recognize certain homologies. First, the central religious fact about cults of the dead in South Asia, classical or folk, is continued ritual offering of food and water. Of all ritual attentions to the dead, food, usually cooked food, and most frequently rice, is the necessary and most significant offering. This food as a lump or heap (like rice) can be, simultaneously, the offering and its destination, the deceased.

Second, conical or rounded stones, as well as small triangular ones, can represent the deceased (or the ancestors collectively) and receive the food and water offerings. Furthermore, these stones can be equated to the food-becoming-spirit, for example, the same word *piṇḍ* labeling both stone and offering in Hindi (above) and Marathi,[27] or the stone-like, piṇḍa-like Telugu fruit, paṇḍu, of the Vīrabhadra tradition.

Third, the powerful disgruntled dead, a category that must include those cheated of a full life span (*āyus*), such as Brahmans who met violent ends, heroes (vīras) both martial and spiritual, children who never completed the basic passage to marriage, all undergo deification and are commemorated in stone. Speaking theologically, this multi-faceted subcontinental cult of the dead is flexible enough to lend itself in the direction either of a goddess, with all of her natural connections to the earth, the earth-mound, the cave, and rebirth, or to the great male lord of the cremation and burial grounds, namely Śiva. In certain instances we can observe that historically the latter has taken over the former. Speaking lithically, the stones of the deceased or collective ancestors can be seen, over time, as similarly directed, the mound-like for the goddess,[28] the more phallic, vertical ones participating in the symbols of the god, whose liṅga is an independent statement of regeneration. Many stones are vague enough to be androgynous, and that too is contextual. Other stones, like the triangular one that penetrates the full water pot, may participate in the fruitful coincidence of opposites, as mirrors of the liṅga in the yoni, or the multiple turrets of the anthill. Sontheimer has in fact recognized the further extension of the above homologies in the Mhasvad temple text in which the object embedded in the chamber under the *garbhagṛha* is a round stone, the food offering, the embryo in the womb (all signified by Marathi *piṇḍ*), a head-offering (from a death by decapitation), and the mūrti in which the temple deity was originally manifest, therefore the Śiva-liṅga (Marathi *piṇḍī*).[29]

Fourth, the routine of ritual feeding advances the spirit into spiritual realms less vulnerable for the spirit and less dangerous for the living. In the classical Hindu funeral tradition the complex of stone, tree (or tripod) and water pot, cloth, and surrogate/priest is no longer necessary after the tenth day, and (where it has been retained) the cloth-wrapped stone is tossed into a river. Incongruously, however, from the point of view of the doctrine of saṃsāra, the deceased still continues to require routine offerings of food and water in tradtional śrāddhas. On the other hand, for the untimely dead such advancement into celestial realms and eventual rebirth is closed; they have been dealt out of the game and remain fixed in stone. Throughout South Asia this belief endows them with fearsome power.[30] What we discern in the expression of the growing stone is thus not the progress of the deceased but vivid testimony to a care and feeding that are inclusive and nutritive.

Fifth, certain ritual specialists may be involved in this process that leads either to stability and control for the untimely dead, or toward eventual rebirth for those who have received an allotted span. Among them are the debased or "ignorant" priest on one hand, and the guardian hero (vīra) on the other, two significant and elusive figures in the history of South Asian religions.[31] Parts of North India have retained the water-pot and the degraded priest as surrogate, but not the stone, although medieval digests, for example, the *Antyeṣṭipaddhati* of Nārāyaṇa Bhaṭṭa's *Prayogaratna*,[32] have roles for the śila or aśman. In Andhra, on the other hand, the water-pot, stone, cloth, and chief mourner are linked, and there are indications of homologies between the surrogate stone and the ritualist for some communities. The chief mourner wears the stone wrapped in a piece of the shroud from the deceased on his person for the ten days, takes it to a river or other water source each day, bathes, cooks food, and offers it with water to the stone.[33] My own observations include a small water pot dripping on the stone for ten days, the equivalent of the pot on the tree broken by the Mahābrāhmaṇa of North India at the end of this phase.

E. Conclusion

To return to the portable ash-fruits of the cult of Vīrabhadra and their loci in the temple, the home-shrine, and the annual pilgrimage to the river, we must recall attention to the center of the tradition, the snake-anthill. However significant ash, fruit, rice, tree, stone, earth, embryo, phallus, and other substances may be as "natural" models with symbolic impact, it is clear from their placement among the multiple turrets of the anthill that ash-fruits replicate these self-existent signs. Hinduism has a fascination for that which is self-arisen (*svayambhū*) and appears by itself (e.g., Telugu *veliyu*). Many (most) things can become divine, but what is self-manifest has unlimited power in the three worlds. The limitless liṅga, the axis mundi whose netherworld/upperworld tips can never be found, is present in the goddess, as the ash-fruit grows in the cave-womb-temple, and the female spirit lives in the resident cobras. The ambition is androgynous, conjunctive, all-encompassing. The vibhūti-paṇḍus share in ascension symbolism as dramatically as chthonic disclosures, particularly when lifted with exaggeration onto the heads of the marchers, some of whom later "ascend" in the states of possession and transformation, enthused with the vīrabhadra of the family, the Vīrabhadra of the cult, and the lion-faced Śarabha whose roles in this command performance of the raging spirits are to eliminate those established laws and sacrifices that have left them no share. Ahead of the marchers fly the prabhās, the red banners that are ethereal, celestial forms of the liṅga. Beside them are the drums of terror and the destruction of this world, but also the drums of their salvation and extraction from the night of the growing dead.

NOTES

1. My gratitude is extended to M. V. Krishnayya, Reader in the Philosophy Department at Andhra University, Waltair, for his assistance in this project. Raised in the outskirts of Rajahmundry and long familiar with the town, he contributes the energy, insight, and enthusiasm that make this continuing study possible. I also wish to thank my colleague, Velcheru Narayana Rao, as well as Charles Nuckolls and Phillip Wagoner for their comments. Interpretations (and misinterpretations) rest with the author.

2. A. E. Crawley, "Drums and Cymbals," *Encyclopedia of Religion and Ethics*, J. Hastings, ed. (New York, 1912), vol. 5, 91, noted that "the music of the drum is more closely connected with the foundations of aurally generated emotion than that of any other instrument. It is complete enough in itself to cover the whole range of human feeling. . . ."

3. Thurston's notes on the Vīramuṣṭis of Vishakhapatnam District at the turn of the century suggest coherence of several caste groups including the Vīramuṣṭis, Dēvāṅgas, Kōmaṭis, and Jaṅgams, all more or less participant in the Liṅgāyat (Vīraśaiva) tradition. See Edgar Thurston, *Castes and Tribes of Southern India*, 7 vols. (Madras 1909), vol. 7, 406-11. This coherence is only partly visible now in East Godavari District.

4. John C. Irwin, "The Sacred Anthill and the Cult of the Primordial Mound," *History of Religions* 21 (1982), 348.

5. David M. Knipe, "The Temple in Image and Reality," in Michael V. Fox, ed., *Temple and Society* (Winona Lake, Indiana 1987), plate 1.

6. David Shulman, "The Serpent and the Sacrifice: An Anthill Myth from Tiruvārūr," *History of Religions* 18 (1978), 114, identifies this anthill-born rainbow with Vedic myths of the bowstring that decapitates Viṣṇu, opposite number of Śiva as well as "the sacrifice," and he adroitly connects this motif with the Dakṣayajña, Dadhyañc, and other myths in Vedic and Tamil texts concerning the removal and subsequent restoration of the head of the sacrifice.

7. Locations of the myth of Dakṣa's sacrifice in the *Mahābhārata*, *Harivaṃśa*, and seven Purāṇas are cited in Alf Hiltebeitel, *The Ritual of Battle: Krishna in the Mahābhārata*, (Ithaca, N. Y. 1976), 314, n. 45. In addition to Hiltebeitel (idem, pp. 312-35) recent perceptive discussions, each with a different emphasis, include Diana L. Eck, "The Sacrifice of Dakṣa and the Śākta Pīṭhas," paper presented at the American Academy of Religion annual meeting, Atlanta, 1986; Wendy Doniger O'Flaherty, "Dionysus and Śiva: Parallel Patterns in Two Pairs of Myths," *History of Religions* 20 (1980), 96ff., and *Asceticism and Eroticism in the Mythology of Śiva* (London 1973), 128 ff.; Stella Kramrisch, *The Presence of Śiva* (Princeton 1981), 322 ff.; Shulman, "Serpent and the Sacrifice," 122 ff.; and J. Bruce Long, "Dakṣa: Divine Embodiment of Creative Skill," *History of Religions* 17 (1977), 29 ff.

8. Edited by Jvalaprasada Misra (Muradabad 1965); cf. ET ed. by J. L. Shastri, 4 vols. (Delhi 1969-70). Problems of the text of "the Śiva Purāṇa" are beyond the scope of this paper, but there are numerous Sanskrit editions available and no two appear to be identical in contents.

9. Hiltebeitel, *Ritual of Battle*, 312-35, identified numerous parallels between the night raid by Aśvatthāman, inspired by Śiva (in the *Sauptikaparvan* of the *Mahābhārata*), and the attack on Dakṣa's sacrifice. Among the most intriguing of these from the perspective of this essay is the theme of the apparent destruction of the lineage, with the deaths of the Draupadeyas, sons of the five Pāṇḍavas, at the hands of the "child-slaying" Aśvatthāman. Of interest also

is Hiltebeitel's subsequent discussion in "Śiva, the Goddess, and the Disguises of the Pāṇḍavas and Draupadī," *History of Religions* 20 (1980), 147-74, of the Draupadī cult enacting Tamil versions of the epic both as ritual and all-night performance in the so-called "street-dramas" (Tamil *terukkūttu*), the Vanniyars providing most of the actors. "They are *śūdras* who view themselves as *kṣatriyas*, as it were in a disguise forced upon them by history" (p. 169). Described in this article is another epic figure, Arjuna, disguised an an androgyne in Śiva's *ardhanārīśvara* mode, including the anklets and epaulettes that we have observed in the vīramuṣṭis, and behaving as a eunuch-transvestite.

10. The photograph of a Vīramuṣṭi published in Thurston, *Castes and Tribes*, vol. 7, 409, shows a middle-aged man with upraised sword in guardian pose wearing a studded headband, *rudrākṣa* beads, a warrior's embossed metal belt and, suspended from his belt below the waist, three brass masks, the center one over his abdominal-genital area showing a lion like that in the Snake-anthill temple today, and the two flanking it showing Śiva and the goddess.

11. The *śarabha rūpa* (monster-form) of Śiva, appears to be conflated with the bhairava rūpa (Vīrabhadra) in the Rajahmundry cult and its symbols, as indeed it is in the *Śiva-Purāṇa* (and in other texts; cf. Jan Gonda, *Viṣṇuism and Śivaism. A Comparison* [London 1970], 106f.). The *Śatarudra-saṃhitā* of the Purāṇa (11-12) accounts for the origin of the thousand-handed, lion-faced monster with wings and matted locks of hair who dispatches the man-lion, Narasiṃha, and removes both his head and hide for Śiva to wear from that moment on. As with the Dakṣa sacrifice myth elsewhere in this same Purāṇa there is direct single combat between avataras of Śiva and Viṣṇu, concurrent distinction between a battle and pralaya, subordination and co-option of the sacrifice via the decapitation of Viṣṇu and Śiva's self-investment with the body of the man-lion. This Śaiva conquest is all the more effective in that Narasiṃha is the Vaiṣṇava paradigm of rage, counterpart to Vīrabhadra. The *Śiva Purāṇa* reference to Śiva wearing the (lion) head of Narasiṃha raises an intriguing speculation: the lion mask (head) on the arch over the anthill, and the lion mask over the genitals of Thurston's Vīramuṣṭi (n. 10), may not be Śarabha after all, but Narasiṃha. A mid-thirteenth century inscription from Malkapurum (Guntur District) refers to Śiva temple and village guardian-warriors known as vīramuṣṭis and vīrabhadras. The latter (and possibly the former as well) protected their charges by acts of decapitation, castration, and disembowelment, evidently self-inflicted; see Philip B. Wagoner, "The Hero Stones of Andhra," unpublished manuscript, University of Wisconsin-Madison, 1984. These self-immolated vīras evidently remained at their posts, so to speak, in the form of memorial stones of great power, not unlike satī stones.

12. In other districts of Andhra, I am told, such prabhās can be thirty or more feet in height, drawn in processions on bullock carts and steadied with guy wires. Elizabeth-Chalier Visuvalingam, in her article in this volume, mentions the cosmogonic new year festival performance in Bhaktapur, Nepal, in which Bhairava is erected as liṅga, a cross-shaped pole bearing two long

cloth banners. Not only does this description match the two prabhās of the Rajahmundry tradition, but in Bhaktapur the two banners represent the two serpents from which the festival, Bisket Jātrā, is named. We recall that the Rajahmundry snake-anthill, where the banners are housed, is the residence of two serpents.

13. The folk epic of the virgin goddess Kanyakā, whose center is Penugonda in West Godavari District, across the river from Rajahmundry, is summarized and discussed by Velcheru Narayana Rao, "Epics and Ideologies: Six Telugu Folk Epics," in Stuart H. Blackburn and A. K. Ramanujan, eds., *Another Harmony. Essays on the Folklore of India* (Berkeley and Los Angeles 1986), 131 ff. In a caste intrigue, to protect her Kōmaṭi (trading caste) kin, she sacrifices herself in a fire-pit (like Satī). Further, in the secondary epic, as the oral Telugu *katha* was transformed into a written Sanskrit Purāṇa, Kanyakā was identified (again like Satī) with Pārvatī. Both versions revolve around the perpetuation of caste, *gotra*, and family lineages. Thurston, *Castes and Tribes*, vol. 7, p. 409 refers to Kanyakā as Vāsavākanyā and Kanyākamma; the last name is used in Rajahmundry for Vīrakanyakā as well.

14. In several respects the lorry mechanic has moved into a role similar to that of the god-dancer (cāmiyāṭi) of Tamilnadu, as described, among others, by Stephen Inglis, "Possession and Pottery: Serving the Divine in a South Indian Community," in Joanne Punzo Waghorne and Norman Cutler, eds., *Gods of Flesh/Gods of Stone. The Embodiment of Divinity in India* (Chambersburg, Pa. 1985), 89-102. Inglis' account of processions by the Vēḷār potters of Madurai District contains other points of interest: the Vēḷārs make clay images for the festivals, as the Rajahmundry potters make the ash fruits (the latter, however, are musicians, but are neither pūjārīs nor among the possessed, as are the Vēḷārs); in the procession a Vēḷār cāmiyāṭi carries on his head a box containing pūjā materials.

15. Cf. Bruce Kapferer, *A Celebration of Demons: Exorcism and the Aesthetics of Healing in Sri Lanka* (Bloomington, Indiana 1983), 104.

16. David M. Knipe, *In the Image of Fire* (Delhi 1975), 132-37.

17. Wendy Doniger O'Flaherty, "The Symbolism of Ashes in the Mythology of Śiva," *Purāṇa* 13 (1971), 28.

18. Ibid., 35.

19. Bridget and Raymond Allchin, *The Rise of Civilization in India and Pakistan* (Cambridge, England 1982), 122-25.

20. David M. Knipe, "Sapiṇḍikaraṇa: The Hindu Rite of Entry into Heaven," in Frank E. Reynolds and Earle H. Waugh, *Religious Encounters with Death: Insights from the History and Anthropology of Religions* (University Park and London 1977), 117 ff.

21. See J. M. Kenoyer, J. D. Clark, J. N. Pal, and G. R. Sharma, "An Upper Paleolithic Shrine in India?" *Antiquity* 57 (1983), 88-94. The site is Baghor I in Sidhi District. Acquired from an escarpment two or three kilometers from the

site, the stone is 15 cm. high, about the median height (six inches) of the standard processional vibhūti-paṇḍus. It is, however, the interior set of laminations, roughly half the height of the Baghor I stone, that most resemble the exterior contour of the man-made ash-fruits.

22. See Diane M. Coccari, "The Bir Babas of Banaras: An Analysis of a Folk Deity in North Indian Hinduism," Ph.D. Dissertation, University of Wisconsin-Madison, 1986, 29 ff., 149 ff., and plates; Jack M. Planalp, "Religious Life and Thought in a North Indian Village," Ph.D. Dissertation, Cornell University, 1956, 774 ff.

23. M. N. Srinivas, *Religion and Society Among the Coorgs of South India* (Bombay 1952), 160 ff.

24. E.g., Coccari, "Bir Babas"; Wagoner, "Hero Stones of Andhra"; S. Settar and Günther D. Sontheimer, eds., *Memorial Stones* (Dharwar-Delhi 1982); Romila Thapar, "Death and the Hero," in S. C. Humphreys and Helen King, *Mortality and Immortality: The Anthropology and Archaeology of Death* (London 1981); Eberhard Fischer and Haku Shah, Vetra ne khambha—*Memorials for the Dead* (Ahmedabad 1973); W. G. Archer, *Vertical Man. A Study in Primitive Indian Sculpture* (London 1947).

25. E.g., Planalp, "Religious Life and Thought," 779; K. Sanjiva Prabhu, *Special Study Report on Bhuta Cult in South Kanara District, Census of India*, 1971, Mysore Series 14, Miscellaneous (a) (Delhi 1977), 59, with thanks to Alf Hiltebeitel for the latter reference.

26. Verrier Elwin, *The Muria and their Ghotul* (London 1947), 141.

27. Günther D. Sontheimer, *Birobā, Mhaskobā und Khaṇḍobā: Ursprung, Geschichte und Umwelt von pastoralen Gottheiten in Mahārāṣṭra* (Wiesbaden 1976), 27f.

28. The *bhavānīs* of a village in eastern Uttar Pradesh described by Planalp, "Religious Life and Thought," pp. 757, 920, are the spirits of girls killed by *bhūts*, aborted fetuses, victims of infanticide or other unusual death, and can be represented inside the house by small mounds or altars of clay. Originally considered malevolent, they can be incorporated into the family as tutelary deities, benign and protective except when angered. Bhavānī is the benign consort of Śiva, equivalent to Pārvatī. Bhavānī as anthill goddess is depicted in the photo of the anthill temple of Periyapalayam, Tamilnadu (see Irwin, "Sacred Anthill," fig. 3; cf. fig. 1), striking confirmation of a feminine correspondence involving child spirit/goddess/anthill.

29. Sontheimer, *Birobā, Mhaskobā und Khaṇḍobā*, 26 ff.

30. See Stuart H. Blackburn, "Death and Deification: Folk Cults in Hinduism," *History of Religions* 24 (1985), 261 ff.

31. These two figures appear in discussions by other authors in this volume, and in particular the study by Elizabeth-Chalier Visuvalingam. The complicated relationships between Bhairava, Birobā (cf. Sontheimer, *Birobā, Mhaskobā und Khaṇḍobā*), Vīrabhadra, Pōtu Rāju, Jagannātha, and other deities, as well as themes of decapitation, self-sacrifice, and multiform goddesses and heroines,

will no doubt be subjects of continuing study. On the Mahābrāhmaṇa (Mahāpātra), see Jonathan Parry, "Ghosts, Greed and Sin: The Occupational Identity of the Benares Funeral Priests," *Man* (n.s.) 15 (1980), 88-111, and my own remarks ("Sapiṇḍikaraṇa," pp. 116 f.; "Stalking the Sacrifice," *Journal of Asian Studies* 45 [1986], 355-58), the latter in connection with the "ignorant Brahman," Fritz Staal's term for the *avidvān* in certain Vedic rituals. For the Mahābrāhmaṇa in action in Banaras, see "Death and Rebirth in Hinduism," Program 15 of my video series, Exploring Religion in South Asia (Madison 1975). A remarkable parallel to the Mahābrāhmaṇa's ritual role in Banaras, which reaches a climax in his seemingly insatiable demand for food, an entire year's supply, on the eleventh day after the death of the one for whom he is surrogate, occurs in A. C. Bouquet, "Beliefs and Practices of the Jalaris in the Matter of Life Beyond the Grave," *Numen* 7 (1960), 205. Bouquet witnessed in a village of Jālāris, fishers of coastal Andhra, a performance by one of "the dasullu" (the Dāsarulu, Māla [Harijan] Vaiṣṇava singers and performers; cf. Gene H. Roghair, *The Epic of Palnāḍu: A Study and Translation of the Palnāṭi Vīrula Katha* [London 1982], 35f.). This "necromancer," as Bouquet labeled him, spoke for the dead when a small stone was seen to move. The spirit demanded "all types of meat, onions, chillies, coconuts, bread, liquor, etc." and got "a pretty good haul."

32. Ed. by Vasudeva Sharma, 2d ed. (Bombay 1937).

33. J. E. Padfield, *The Hindu at Home* (Madras 1908), 201 ff.

6

Bhairava's Royal Brahmanicide: The Problem of the Mahābrāhmaṇa[1]

A post-structuralist hermeneutic of Hindu mythico-ritual discourse based on the phenomenology of Transgressive Sacrality*

Elizabeth-Chalier Visuvalingam

Bhairava, terrifying aspect of Śiva, is the god of transgression par excellence, for he appears only to cut off the fifth head of Brahmā, Brahmanicide being the most heinous crime in the Hindu tradition.[2] Yet Bhairava's example was ritually imitated by the gruesome Kāpālika ascetics, who still have their successors in the modern Aghoris and Nāths, who have greatly contributed to the spread of his cult.[3] To this day, there are isolated reports in the newspapers of human sacrifices being offered to such terrifying divinities as Bhairava and his female consort Bhairavī for the attainment of magical powers; and the undying force of the imagery surrounding them in the Hindu psyche is testified to by its vivid exploitation in contemporary cinema.[4] In Nepal, as in Bali, he is identified with the bloody epic hero Bhīmasena, whose acts of sacrificial slaughter are given a tantric interpretation, while his wife Draupadī is identified with Bhairavī, and their joint cult is very popular among the Newars.[5] Unlike most other Hindu divinities he enjoys a folk cult that extends to various tribal communities on the periphery of or even beyond the Hindu cultural universe, and has conversely been instrumental in the "Hinduization" of bloody tribal divinities.[6]

At the same time, in his eightfold manifestation he also presides,

* *For Sunthar*

either alone or paired as consort with the eight mother goddesses, over the spatio-ritual organization of sacred cities like Vārāṇasī. In this centre of Hindu culture, Bhairava reigns as the policeman-magistrate (kotwāl), to whom pilgrims swarming in from the furthest reaches of the subcontinent must necessarily pay obeisance.[7] In Nepal he is practically the national god of many festivals, so much so that Akāsh Bhairab has been adopted as the emblem of the Royal Nepali Airlines, and the spatio-ritual organization, although modelled on ancient Kāśī, is far better preserved in Bhaktapur.[8] He plays a central role during Dasain not only in the *Nava Durgā* dances, which dynamically reintegrate the socio-religious community in its spatial extension, particularly in Hindu Bhaktapur, but also in Buddhist Patan, where the *Aṣṭamātṛkā* dance is performed in more pacific fashion by young Śākya (Buddhist) boys.[9] Though historically a late divinity, he plays a central role in cosmogonic New Year festivals deriving from an archaic Vedic model, like the Indra-Jātrā of Kathmandu (see n. 94), and he appears as the axis mundi or primordial world-pillar in the Bisket Jātrā of Bhatkapur (see n. 92). In one such festival, the Nuwakot Bhairavī Rath Jātrā, he incarnates himself for the sake of the community and its renewal in the hereditary function of the *dhāmi*, through whom he participates in bloody rites culminating in oracles before the king's representative for the whole of Nepal (see n. 135). Not only was he worshipped by dynasties of kings and is himself attributed royal traits or identified with the Hindu king, but his very Brahmanicide is only a legacy of the king of gods, Indra's decapitation of his royal chaplain (purohita) Viśvarūpa (see nn. 66 and 132). In the Kathmandu festival of Pachali Bhairab, he incarnates himself in an impure low caste dancer once every twelve years to renew the power of the king's sword by ritually exchanging his own sword with the latter (see n. 96). His cult is officiated not only by the semi-Untouchable Kusle house-holders, the successors of the Kāpālikas,[10] but also by the Brahman Buddhist tantrics called Vajrācāryas, the priestly elite of the Buddhist half of the Newar caste society. He has even been adopted by the esoteric currents of Tibetan tantrism and his anthropomorphic images have iconographically and functionally much in common with the Buddhist Saṃvara, Mahākāla, and Yamāntaka (see nn. 136-7).

In Jain temples of Vārāṇasī, Ujjain and Rajasthan, he is sometimes simply called "guardian of territorial limits" (kṣetrapāla) or given a new name, Mānabhadra/Maṇibhadra. Most popular in Rajasthan is the Jaina Nakoda Bhairava who, by drawing Hindu and Jaina pilgrims from all over the state, overshadows even the principal shrine of Pārśvanātha.[11] Bhairava is the typical kṣetrapāla for the more socio-centrally located pure divinities like Viśvanātha in Kāśī,[12] and also functions as the doorkeeper (*dvārapāla*) at the temples of such divinities. Yet there is not only a constant "confusion," if not identification, between the pure central divinity and his impure peripheral bodyguard, but even the Vaiṣṇava Jagannātha of Puri reveals himself, in the Śākta interpretation of his *rājapurohitas*, to be still Bhairava when he unites with Bhairavī in the form of the *devadāsī*.[13] Although his public worship in the Indian temples is nowadays conducted in a purely innocuous Brahmanical mode, his major temple festival of Bhairavāṣṭamī is wholly derived from the Brahmanicide myth, all of whose symbolism is strikingly retained in his iconography.[14] His vehicle, the dog, with whom he is himself also identified, is the impurest creature of the Hindu bestiary (see n. 126).

The Jūnā or "Old" Regiment of the militant Dasanāmi Nāga Saṃnyāsins, supposedly organized by Śaṃkarācārya, is also called the Bhairava Akhāḍā and its tutelary deity, though presently Dattātreya, was originally Bhairava. Most of their Maḍhis or sub-units (*maṭha* = "monastery") are named after some "*-nāth*," like Aghor-, Sahaj-, Rudranāth and, as is also the case for the Kānphaṭās, the most important thing in the Jūnā Akhāḍā, some of whose Nāgas (the Gūdaḍs) also wear ear-rings, is the *dhuni* (continuous fire). Their evident links with the Nāths, from whom they are outwardly often indistinguishable, have prompted suggestions that these Dasanāmis were originally Kāpālikas converted by Śaṃkara.[15] The tendency to interpret such phenomena evolutionistically as pointing to Nātha origins, however justified, must be balanced by the observation that among the Dasanāmi Nāgas, "there are Siddhas, that is those that have attained supernatural powers, who are always designated Nāths."[16] As in the case of the relations between the Rudra-Pāśupatas and the Bhairava-Kāpālikas, also called Mahāpāśupatas, the historical perspective must itself be replaced within a structural approach to the pantheon and cult system (see nn. 61-2). Apart from the branch Akhāḍā in Haridwar with its central temple of Ānanda Bhairava, the principal headquarters, which is in Vārāṇasī, also houses one of the *aṣṭabhairavas*, the Ruru or "Dog" Bhairava at Hanumān Ghāṭ.[17]

Most significant of all, he has been adopted by the Kashmir Śaiva theoreticians, most of them Brahmans, as the supermost expression of the Divine, symbol of a reality more ultimate than even the Brahman of Śaṃkara. Abhinavagupta, the greatest among them, who has provided us the most synthetic perception we have of Brahmanical culture,[18] goes so far as to exultantly identify himself with this terrifying Brahmanicide, even tribal, Bhairava.[19] It is impossible to do justice to all these diverse and often apparently conflicting aspects of Bhairava within the limits of the present paper.[20] Instead I will concentrate on demonstrating, primarily through an analysis of his origin myth, the ideology of transgressive sacrality that forms the very essence of the conception of Bhairava.[21]

A. The Origin Myth of the Brahmanicide Bhairava

Brahmā and Viṣṇu were disputing with each other for the status of supreme God and appealed to the testimony of the four Vedas, which unanimously proclaimed Rudra-Śiva as the Ultimate Truth of the Universe. But the disputants were unable to accept that Rudra, endowed with so many revolting symbols of impurity and degradation, could be identical with the Absolute Reality of Brahman. Brahmā laughed scornfully: "How could the Brahman, free of all attachment, lustily sport with his wife in the company of his troops of deformed churn-goblins (*pramaṭha*)?" Rudra's supremacy, however, was finally reconfirmed by the esoteric sound-syllable, Omkāra, quintessence of the Veda and most condensed symbol of Brahman, who pointed out that Śiva's wife is not adventitious to her husband but, on the contrary, embodies his own blissful essence.[22] Just then an immense pillar of flame manifested itself in their midst, within which was recognized the towering figure of the three-eyed Rudra bearing his trident, serpents, and crescent moon. But the fifth head of Brahmā taunted him: "I know who you are, Rudra, whom I created from my forehead. Take refuge with me and I will protect you, my son!"

Overflowing with anger, Śiva created a blazing Bhairava in human form, addressing this Kālabhairava as "Lord of Time-Death" (*kāla*) for he shone like the god of Death: "You are called Bhairava because you are of terrifying features and are capable of supporting the universe. You are called Kāla-Bhairava, for even Time-Death is terrified of you."[23] He ordered him to chastise Brahmā, promising him in return eternal suzerainty over his city of Kāśī (Vārāṇasī), the cremation ground of the Hindu universe, where final emancipation is assured. In a trice, Bhairava ripped off Brahmā's guilty head with the nail of his left thumb. Seeing this, the terrified Viṣṇu eulogized Śiva and devotedly recited his sacred hymns, followed in this by the repentant Brahmā. Thereby they gained his protection by realizing and acknowledging the supreme reality of Śiva. The severed head immediately stuck to Bhairava's hand, where it remained in the form of the skull, destined to serve as his insatiable begging bowl.[24] Enjoining him to honour Viṣṇu and Brahmā, Śiva then directed Bhairava to roam the world in this beggarly condition to atone for the sin of Brahmanicide. "Show to the world the rite of expiation for removing the sin of Brahmanicide. Beg for alms by resorting to the penitential rite of the skull (*kapālavrata*)." Creating a maiden renowned as "Brahmanicide" (*brahmahatyā*), Śiva instructed her to relentlessly follow Bhairava everywhere until he reached the holy city of Kāśī to which she would have no access.

Observing the Kāpālika rite with skull in hand and pursued by the terrible Brahmahatyā, Bhairava sported freely, laughing, singing, and dancing with the pramaṭhas. Stealing more than the hearts of all women, even the chaste wives of the Seven Vedic Sages (*saptarṣi*) as he passed through the Daru forest, the erotic ascetic arrived at Viṣṇu's door to seek redemption only to find his entry barred by the guard, Viṣvaksena. Spearing the latter and heaving the corpse of this Brahman on his shoulder, he pressed before Viṣṇu with outstretched begging bowl. Viṣṇu split his forehead vein but the outflowing blood, the only suitable offering, could not fill the skull though it flowed for aeons. When Viṣṇu then tried to dissuade Brahmahatyā from tormenting Bhairava, the criminal observed that "beggars are not intoxicated by the alms they receive as (are others) by drinking the wine of worldly honor." Viṣṇu venerated him as the Supreme Being, untainted by sins like Brahmanicide, and acknowledged that his dependence and degradation were a mere fancy. Before leaving joyously to beg elsewhere, Bhairava reciprocated by recognizing Viṣṇu as his foremost disciple and acknowledged the latter's status as "grantor of boons to all the gods." On arriving at Kāśi, Brahmahatyā sank into the netherworld, and the holy ground on which the skull fell, freeing Bhairava from his Brahmanicide, came to be known as Kapālamocana. It was on the eighth day (*aṣṭamī*) in the dark (waning moon) half of the month of Mārgaśīrṣa that Lord Śiva manifested as Bhairava. Ever since, by performing ablution at Kapālamocana one is rid of even the worst sin of *brahmahatyā;* and whosoever fasts on this day (Bhairavāṣṭamī) in front of Kālabhairava (temple at Kāśī) and stays awake at night is freed from great sins (see Plate 14).

In the Tamil transposition of the sacred geography of Śaiva mythology, the fiery liṅga appeared in the temple city of Tiruvaṇṇāmalai to become the sacred red mountain of Aruṇācala, which ritually reverts to its original form during the Kārttika festival when a blazing fire is lit on its summit. The *Liṅgodbhavamūrti* is generally depicted on the

14. Kāla Bhairava temple, Vārāṇasī. Kāla Bhairava adorned for Śivarātri festival (*Śivarātri śṛṅgāra*), 16 February 1987. Photo courtesy of N. Gutschow.

western face of the external face of the sanctum of Tamil Śaiva temples, with the boar Viṣṇu attempting to fathom its depths and the swan Brahmā aspiring likewise in vain after its summit. In the *Kāñcimāhātmya*, Bhairava spears the demon Antaka ("Death"), who was besieging Kailāsa, and fixes his lance on the ground on arriving at Kāñci in order to remove Antaka. It formed a pit filled with water, Śūlatīrtha, where the ceremonies for ancestors are performed on new or full moon days. Bhairava lets Antaka perform ablutions at the Śiva-Gaṅgā tank before granting him salvation and Antaka disappears into the Antakeśa liṅga he had erected and adored. Bhairava likewise removes Viṣvaksena from his lance and returns him to Viṣṇu, before being appointed by Śiva as the guardian of Kāñci, distributing the blood of the skull to all his gaṇas.[25] The Tamil Bhairava is released from his skull at Tirukaṇṭiyūr, "holy site of the (head-) cutting," where the temple of "the Lord of Brahmā's decapitation" (*Brahmaśirakhaṇḍīśvara*), in which Brahmā and Sarasvatī are worshipped beside Śiva, refers to Śiva-Liṅgodbhavamūrti in this context as "Aṇṇāmalaiyār." The apparently later temple of "Viṣṇu as liberator of Śiva (-Kapālin) from his curse" (*Haraśāpavimocana-perumāl*), with its own Vaiṣṇava version of the Brahmanicide myth, claims that, having released Brahmā's greedy skull at Kapālapuṣkariṇī (lotus pond) behind the temple by enticing it with "blood" (i.e., turmeric mixed with lime) rice, Viṣṇu directed the kapāla to Kāśī where its insatiable hunger would be satisfied by offerings of *Nārāyaṇa-bali* (performed especially for those who die at an inauspicious moment, *pañcaka*).

The original Kāla Bhairava temple was located on the banks of the Kapālamocana Tīrtha itself, in the Omkāreśvara area north of Maidāgin, where Bhairava remained as the "Sin-Eater" (*Pāpabhakṣaṇa*) par excellence to devour the accumulated sins of devotees and pilgrims. If the pilgrims to Kāśī do not fear death there, this would be because their pilgrimage to the *Mahāśmaśāna* is conceived on the ritual model of Bhairava's own arrival at Kāśī for absolution from his terrible sin and his subsequent establishment there. The paradox of Bhairava's scapegoat function even after his "purification" can be explained as a "lawful irregularity" resulting from the two opposing valorizations, diachronically disjoined in the myth, of his transgressive essence; it matches the complementary paradox of the pure Kāśī-Viśvanātha himself being identified esoterically with the impure criminal Bhairava.

B. The "Supreme Penance" of the Criminal Kāpālika-Bhairava

Bhairava's twelve-year wandering as a beggar, bearing Brahmā's skull as public testimony to his crime and begging from the seven houses of the Seven Sages in the Daru forest, all of these and other traits, like his exclusion from settlements and inhabiting the cremation grounds, correspond exactly to the prescribed punishment for Brahmanicide in the Brahmanical law books. But whereas in Hindu society such Brahmanicides, even if themselves Brahmans, were treated as horrible outcastes and considered wholly degraded, Bhairava is exalted in the myth as the supreme divinity by Brahmā and Viṣṇu, the latter even recognizing that he remains untainted by the sin of Brahmanicide. Although the punishment of Bhairava corresponds perfectly to the norms of Brahmanical orthodoxy, his simultaneous exaltation corresponds rather to the doctrines and practices of the Kāpālika ascetics, who took the Brahmanical Bhairava for their divine archetype. Even when themselves not originally Brahmanicides, these Kāpālikas performed the Mahāvrata or *Great Penance* bearing the skull-bowl and skull-staff (khaṭvāṅga) of a Brahman in order to attain the blissful state of spiritual liberation and lordship (*aiśvarya*) that confers the eightfold magical powers.[26] Theirs was the "Doctrine of Soma" and, although the term is reinterpreted to suit the later sex-rites of the Tantras, it still retains the central Vedic reference to bodily sexual fluids and their spiritual transformation.[27] The Kāpālikas experienced the spiritual bliss of Bhairava in the felicity of sexual union induced and enhanced by the partaking of meat and wine.

Cast in the image of his sex partner (Bhairavī), the *maiden* Brahmahatyā appears in all her ambiguity, as both his supreme punishment and his sole means of beatification, and imposes a causal connection between the two opposed meanings. The obvious explanation is that the sense of honour and self-respect is the greatest obstacle to spiritual realization, so that the Kāpālika's social and moral degradation itself assures his complete surrender to his transcendental aim (Lorenzen, p. 77). But why Brahmanicide? Whereas Bhairava is presented in the myth as undertaking the kāpālika vow as punishment in order to expiate his Brahmanicide, the Kāpālikas in pursuit of their *supreme penance* have always been associated with human sacrifices (Lorenzen, pp. 85-7). Right from Vedic times, the theory of sacrifice presupposes that the consecrated victim should be defectless, pure and auspicious, and that with the ideal victim being a Brahman, Brahmanicide, or whatever it symbolizes, would itself be productive of great power. The purifications that the sacrificer had to undergo after the sacrifice moreover resembled the expiation of the criminal, and the dīkṣita was in fact equated to a Brahmanicide. But the sacrificial mechanisms revolved around the identification of the sacrificer, the victim and the divinity, and ultimately offered the sacrificer the means of sacrificing himself to the divinity, but through the mediation of the victim with whom he was symbolically identified.[28] The Kāpālikas' practice of sacrificing their own flesh and blood as oblations probably carries the notion of self-sacrifice to its logical conclusions.[29]

The Brahman in Hindu society conserves his Brahmanhood only through the observance of a multitude of interdictions intended to maintain and accumulate his ritual purity. Not only the other great sins (*mahāpātaka*) of incest, stealing a Brahman's gold, drinking wine and associating with such an offender, but any, even trivial transgression, voluntary or involuntary, of the norms of ritual purity is assimilated by the legal codes themselves to a "Brahmanicide." Thus the utilization of the left (impure) instead of the right (pure) hand during the ritual procedures of eating, dropping of hair or fingernails into one's food, splashing of saliva (Bhairava is sometimes described as "drooling-tongued" *lalajjihva*), intercourse with low caste women, and so on, are all productive of "Brahmanicide."[30] That the decapitation also symbolizes the reversal of Brahmanical purity and the disguised valorization of ritual impurity is confirmed by Bhairava's execution of this transgressive act par excellence with his *left* thumb-*nail*, a trivial detail otherwise unduly emphasized in the myth. If Bhairava could have been so widely adopted with all his Kāpālika attributes by other left hand currents of Tantrism like the Kaulas and later Nāths, who, however, did not imitate the Kāpālika model literally, this would be due to the wider application of the Brahmanicide image to their own transgressive exploitation of disgusting ritual impurities in order to attain Bhairava-Consciousness. Bhairava's beheading of Brahmā's fifth head is indeed symbolic of *all* manner of transgressions of the norms of classical Brahmanism and it is in this sense that it is "symbolical for the emergence of the Tantra-influenced period in Hinduism." (Goudriaan, *Hindu Tantrism*, p. 66; see n. 22).

From a sociologizing angle, it could be asserted that the five-headed Brahmā represents the fourfold Brahma-Veda with the central fifth head transcending the ritual plane to correspond to the Brahma-Absolute of the renunciate saṃnyāsins, still close to Brahmanical orthodoxy in their concern for purity and self-control. For according to one version of this mythical corpus, Brahmā grew his four heads because, filled with incestuous desire, he did not want to lose sight of his daughter as she performed a ritual circumambulation of him. Then, being ashamed, he sprouted the fifth head bearing the traits of an ascetic above the other four (Kramrisch, pp. 251-2; see n. 2). The opposition between this fifth head born of shame and the shameless Bhairava would then be the confrontation between two conceptions of the supreme divinity, two modes of renunciation, that of the orthodox Brahman saṃnyāsin and that of the transgressive Śaivite ascetic in his hedonistic exploitation of extreme impurities.[31] The correctness of this interpretation may be judged by the transposition of the mythical beheading, with no alteration in the basic structure but reinforced by philosophical debate, into the legendary accounts of the *advaitin* Śaṃkarācārya's (abortive) decapitation by the Kāpālika "Fierce" (Ugra-) Bhairava in the textual traditions of both the opposing currents of renunciation. In both cases, Śaṃkara's non-dualistic Vedāntic doctrines of the unreality of the world or of the superiority of inaction (non-performance of rites) is turned against its own author who, in a dilemma, is compelled to voluntarily offer his head to Ugra-Bhairava. In the tradition of Gorakhnāth, in many ways a deradicalized prolongation of the Kāpālika current, Ugra-Bhairava opposes Śaṃkara's non-dualism with his own Absolute that is "beyond both dualism and non-dualism" and finally manifests his true identity as the fierce god Bhairava to behead the detached propounder of the non-dual Brahman and his four disciples; and only then, on being revived, did *true detachment* arise in them (Lorenzen, pp. 31-38; see n. 3).

Using text-critical philological methods, the beheading myth has also been interpreted, on a sectarian basis and from an evolutionistic historical perspective, as reflecting the power-relation between the members of the Hindu trinity and showing how different versions in turn exalt the status of either Brahmā, Viṣṇu or Rudra, depending on the Vaiṣṇava or Śaiva character of the Purāṇa concerned (Stietencron, "Bhairava," pp. 865-6; see n. 2). What matters here, however, is that the basic structure of the episode has been retained in practically all the versions. If its intention could be reduced to a sectarian exaltation of an extra- or even anti-Brahmanical Bhairava or the deliberate devaluation of the Brahman, there would have been no sense in Śiva instructing Bhairava to strictly conform to the Brahmanical legal prescriptions for the expiation of Brahmanicide. The fact that Bhairava scrupulously performs it amounts to a full valorization of the Brahman (= Brahmā) as demanded by traditional Hindu society. At the same time, it could not have been intended to glorify Brahmā as such, for the latter clearly admits the supremacy of Bhairava, and even Viṣṇu lauds him as the Supreme Reality despite his outward appearance as a criminal beggar steeped in impurity. The real conflict is rather between the two opposing poles of the sacred, one of interdiction incarnated in the non-violent, chaste, truthful, pure, self-denying classical Brahman and the other of transgression represented by the savage, impure, hedonistic Kāpālika-Bhairava who beheads this Brahman or his divinity. The myth in its ambiguous essence reveals the ambivalent compromise between the social point of view which must necessarily condemn Bhairava to be an outcaste heretic criminal and the esoteric valorization of transgressive sacrality that exalts him as the supermost divinity, *both* precisely because he has performed the transgression par excellence in Brahmanical society. Although Bhairava had to publicly proclaim his crime for twelve long years before being absolved of Brahmanicide at the sacred city of Kāśī, he was rewarded with suzerainty over this socio-religious centre of Hinduism precisely because he had carried out the order to decapitate Brahmā's fifth head.[32]

C. The Apollonian Viṣṇu and the Dionysiac Bhairava: Bhakti and Initiatic Hierarchies

Although Viṣṇu, unlike Brahmā, is a supreme divinity of the cult of devotion (bhakti) and even of the saṃnyāsin, he still participates in and prolongs the pure, conservative pole of the sacrificial order, universalizing it in the very process of loosening its links with the material reality of the Brahmanical sacrifice as performed by the exclusive *Śrotriyas* specializing in its ritual technique. But unlike Viṣṇu and although also a supreme divinity of asceticism and bhakti, Rudra participates in and prolongs the highly impure, violent, and dangerous element that the sacrifice sought to productively manipulate within itself and that it assimilated to all that was destructive and menacing outside the sacrifice.[33] This contrast between the two gods of bhakti, in terms of their relative proximity and opposition to the pure sacrificial order (*dharma*) incarnated in the classical Brahman, is very well expressed in the *Kaṅkālamūrti* episode where it is the Brahman Viṣvaksena who stands at the threshold barring the transgressive Bhairava's access to the conservative Viṣṇu. It is by killing Viṣvaksena, by repeating his Brahmanicide, that Bhairava comes face to face with Viṣṇu, and it is evidently due to this peculiar circumstance of their encounter that the Apollonian Viṣṇu favours the Dionysiac Bhairava in a mode that is more tantric, more transgressive, than socially orthodox. For blood, like saliva and fingernails, is highly impure.[34] The unwarranted slaying of his faithful Brahman doorkeeper does not at all perturb Viṣṇu, who rather rewards Bhairava in like manner for his violent transgression. In the form of the Man-Lion Narasiṃha, especially popular with the esoteric Pāñcarātras, and also as the equally tantricized Boar Varāha, Viṣṇu does closely approach Bhairava in character, to the point of emerging like Bhairava from the sacrificial (stake-) pillar. The myth then reveals two different, but complementary, faces of the bhakti ideology incarnated in Viṣṇu: an orthodox face linked to Brahmanism and preoccupations with purity, and the other, secret, face turned towards the transgressive valorization of impurity symbolized by Bhairava.[35]

The same complicity seems to have existed between the Olympian Apollo and Dionysos, the god of transgression in ancient Greece. Not only did the impulsion vivifying the Dionysiac cults come from the Delphic Apollo, but Dionysos himself shared Delphi with Apollo to the point of sometimes appearing to be the real master of the sanctuary, it being claimed that he even preceded Apollo there. Similarly, Thebes has its own sanctuary of Dionysos *Cadmeios* and, although he presents himself as a stranger before his own natal city, the most powerful of the Theban gods is Dionysos, with Apollo, again his accomplice.[36] "Apollo wanted this close liaison with his mysterious brother, because their reigns, despite their abrupt opposition, are, however, in reality bound to each other by an eternal tie"; "the Apollonian world cannot exist without the other. That is why it has never refused it recognition" (author's trans.).[37] Whereas the royally munificent protector-god Viṣṇu radiates life and prosperity through the politico-religious order deriving from the union of the two highest castes (Biardeau, *L'Hindouisme*, p. 108; see n. 12), the obscure "popular" outcaste destroyer-god Bhairava remains like Dionysos close to the embryonic potentialities of savage nature and death (-in-life) in order to inspire the frenzy of possession that has earned him and his adepts the enduring epithet of "Mad" or *Unmatta* (-Bhairava).[38] As executioner-cum-victim, both Bhairava and Dionysos are identified with the phallic sacrificial post drenched in blood, and the embryogonic dimension of Bhairava's Brahmanicide is not without parallel notations in Dionysos' birth from his dead mother, reflected also in his cult.[39]

This comparative excursus merely points to the universality of this complementary opposition between the interdictory and transgressive poles of the sacred which is prior to and ultimately quite independent of the bhakti ideology. From the exoteric socio-religious point of view, Viṣṇu is superior to Bhairava, who is no more than the terrible policeman-god protecting the boundaries of the socio-religious community and, as doorkeeper, the access to its temples from hostile external forces. He preserves the socially central divinity, like Viśvanātha in Vārāṇasī, from any direct contact with impure elements which are nevertheless vital for the proper functioning of the social whole. The terrifying divinity of transgression can never become the object of public cult as such, and the only means for him to receive communal worship is by transforming himself into the equally terrifying protector-god for a more central pacific and benign divinity. Thus Kālabhairava's promised suzerainty over Kāśī has been translated in reality into his being the policeman-magistrate of Lord Viśvanātha. The myth achieves this "conversion" from criminal to kotwāl through Bhairava's purification at Kapālamocana tīrtha at Kāśī. But if the kotwāl nevertheless remains there as the scapegoat Sin-Eater par excellence, this is no doubt because even as the criminal Kāpālika, he had already transcended both good and evil and always remained untainted by them.[40] Yet the pure central Śiva-Viśvanātha of Kāśī has always been inwardly identified by his priestly vaidika custodians with the transgressive Bhairava of the impure marginal Kāpālika ascetics, so much so that until very recently he still received secret tantric worship every morning (*nitya-pūjā*) in the right hand (*dakṣiṇācāra*) mode with symbolic substitutes of the "five 'M's" (*pañcamakāras:* viz. meat, fish, wine, parched beans, and sexual intercourse), from the pūjārīs who used to smear themselves with ashes from the cremation ground. And human heads were sacrificed to him in the form of pumpkins at the sacrificial stake (*yūpastambha*) *within* the temple. During Kāla-Bhairava's birthday on Bhairavāṣṭamī, he also used to be secretly worshipped as the destructive Saṃhāra-Bhairava, and only on that day, seven different fruit and vegetable juices were mixed together (*saptarasa*) to constitute nectar (*amṛta* = Soma), with which the *śivaliṅga* was bathed before its distribution to devotees. Depending on availability watermelons, jackfruit or coconuts were used instead of pumpkins as substitutes for human heads. It is likely that in much earlier times real blood sacrifices were offered in the temple itself.[41]

This should hardly surprise us when, from the esoteric standpoint of transgressive sacrality, Viṣṇu himself recognizes Bhairava as the supreme divinity. Nevertheless, Bhairava himself is anxious to "keep up the appearances," to maintain the distinction between what can be described as the exoteric and esoteric hierarchies, for he recognizes Viṣṇu's supremacy in the socio-religious domain in exchange for the latter's recognition of his own metaphysical and initiatic supremacy. The collusion between the two corresponds perfectly to the oft-repeated dictum of the Bhairavāgamas that one should be a (Bhairava-worshipping) Kaula within, a Śaiva without, a Vaiṣṇava in the public assembly (*sabhā*), *and* an orthodox vaidika (Brahman) in everyday (ritual) life.[42]

D. The Transgressive Fifth Head of Brahmā and the Pāśupata Ultimate Weapon

The sociologizing approach not only cannot account for Viṣṇu's unorthodox reception of Bhairava but it also fails to do full justice to the symbolic signification of the fifth head of Brahmā himself. For the majority of versions characterize this fifth head with transgressive notations that we would rather expect to discover in the Kaula Bhairava. There it is the fifth head, as opposed to Brahmā's normal four, which proposed incest to his daughter, who indignantly cursed him to always speak contrarily or bray like a donkey, whereupon the fifth head always spoke evilly and coarsely. Or once when Śiva visited, Brahmā's four heads praised him, but the fifth made an evil sound provoking Śiva to cut it off. Because his four heads were incapable of lying, Brahmā had to sprout the fifth head in the form of a she-ass to utter the lie that he had reached the summit of the immeasurable liṅga. Elsewhere, it is generally gluttonous and characterized by loud malicious laughter.[43] All these traits are synonyms insofar as they signify transgression through parallel codes like the sexual, linguistic, animal, moral, alimentary, and aesthetic. Contrary, nonsensical or obscene speech and cacophonous sounds universally signify transgression,[44] and that other "Brahman par excellence" (*Mahābrāhmaṇa*), the obscene, gluttonous, laughing Vidūṣaka of the Sanskrit drama, also comically reveals his hidden transgressive function through such *disfiguring* speech, as his very name implies. The donkey, like the dog, represents the impure outcaste in Vedic symbolism as is evidenced in the ritual prescription for the Brahman-slayer to wear the skin of an ass (or dog).[45] And when associated with Brahmā or a Brahman, it can only signify transgression. The Vidūṣaka has a voice resembling that of a donkey and does not hesitate to swear lies by his sacred thread.[46] Although in the Head Cutting (*Śiraśchedaka*) Tantra, Brahmā's fifth head subsequently receives esoteric Tantric doctrines from his decapitator,[47] and the Vidūṣaka himself is depicted in open collaboration with the Kaula preceptor

Bhairavāvanda,[48] the "Case of the Severed Head"[49] was already a Vedic mystery, just as the Vidūṣaka himself has been derived from Vedic prototypes with the pre-classical initiate (dīkṣita) as prime model.[50]

All this converges to show that Brahmā's fifth head itself represents a crucial dimension of transgressive sacrality in the pre-classical Brahmanical sacrifice whose material reality was slowly eliminated from the classical reworkings of the same. Hence Brahmā's invariable portrayal with only four heads in classical iconography, and the occasional chaste purity of the mythical fifth head corresponding to the purificatory function of the classical consecration (*dīkṣā*) as a preparation for the sacrifice proper.[51] The transgressive fifth head, however, specifically expresses the values of the pre-classical dīkṣita who was charged with evil, impurity, and a dangerous sacrality during his regression into an embryonic deathly condition before he could be reborn as a Brahman. In his incoherent, abusive obscene speech and through many other such traits, the dīkṣita belonged to the same type as the impure militant, even criminal, Vrātya-ascetic, the Vedic predecessor of later "shamanizing" Śaiva ascetics like the Kāpālikas and (Mahā-) Pāśupatas, and it has been suggested that the human head beneath the fire altar is a legacy of this consecrated warrior.[52] Brahmā was originally the Vedic Prajāpati and his beheading by Bhairava is in fact the later Hindu version of Rudra piercing his victim Prajāpati as the latter, in the form of an antelope, was uniting incestuously with his own daughter. Prajāpati is equated with the sacrificer (victim, and the sacrifice) and the dīkṣita during his embryonic regression wears the black antelope skin conferring the *bráhman*. On being pierced, Prajāpati or his head became the constellation Mṛgaśiras, the Antelope's Head (Orion), and so too is Bhairava's appearance celebrated, in his temples, on the eighth day of the month of Mārgaśīrṣa, Head of the Antelope. The festival of *Bhairavāṣṭamī* probably corresponds to the celebration of the *Ekāṣṭaka* at a time and region when the year began with the first (*pratipada*) lunar day of the dark fortnight of Mārgaśīrṣa, also called *agrahāyana*, the "commencement of the year."[53] All these notations reinforce the thesis that Bhairava is in many ways the transposition of the transgressive (royal) dīkṣita.

The magical powers that the Kāpālika seeks to attain are themselves symbolized by the Pāśupata missile equated with the *Brahmaśiras*, or "Head of Brahmā," that his left hand bears in the form of the skull bowl to justify his and Śiva's appellation of Kapālin.[54] The implication is that such powers are unleashed by the violation of fundamental taboos symbolized here by (the decapitation of) Brahmā's fifth head.[55]

In the *Mahābhārata*, the only two heroes to wield this ultimate weapon, to be used only in the most extreme circumstances and never against human enemies, are Arjuna-Indra, the exemplary Hindu king, and Aśvatthāman, who got it from his father Droṇa-Bṛhaspati, the purohita (chaplain) of the gods on earth.[56] Preceptor to both the Pāṇḍava-Devas and their Kaurava-Asura cousins, Droṇa-Bṛhaspati belonged nevertheless, like his more powerful homologue Śukrācārya, to the demoniac camp, and yet remained inwardly partial to his favorite pupil, Arjuna, to whom he finally offered the victorious trophy of his Brahman head.[57] The magical power of transgressive rites features in the *Atharvaveda* in which the purohitas specialized, and these Brahmans are credited with the formulation and systematization of the emerging Tantric traditions, so much so that the *Atharvaveda* "was often claimed as the Vedic source of the Tantric tradition and thus the earliest Tantric text *'avant la lettre'*" (Goudriaan, p. 16; cf. p. 30; see n. 22). In one Purāṇic myth, the Aṅgirasas, already called *vairūpa* in Vedic times, are ridiculed for their deformity, and the likewise *virūpa* (deformed) Vidūṣaka is often caricatured as a purohita and pretends to magical powers.

Born of a fusion of Rudra, Anger, Lust, Death, and other terrible substances, Aśvatthāman is not only a Brahman, but is further the only and inseparable son of Droṇācārya, incarnation of Bṛhaspati who, even more than Brahmā, represents the values of the brahmán-priest and purohita. It is the death of "Aśvatthāman" (the elephant) that makes Droṇa's decapitation possible, and the terrestrial Rudra's final punishment for misusing the Brahmaśiras and his infanticide (*bhrūṇahatyā* = brahmahatyā) of the unborn Parikṣit is to wander eternally in a condition resembling that of the *bhikṣāṭana*-Bhairava. As soon as he is born, Aśvatthāman neighs like a horse and his very name (*Aśva-*) refers to the horse; and Brahmā's fifth head was also a horse's head, that which in the Vedic esotericism alone knew the secret of the hidden Agni and Soma.[58] Because it is the Brahman who wields this power by transgressing, under exceptional circumstances, the very taboos that have made him a Brahman, it is not surprising that Rudra, the transgressor, is always represented as the son of Brahmā, born of some impure aspect of the latter like his wrath (as Manyu) or blood (Kramrisch, pp. 114-5). Notwithstanding secondary sectarian elaborations, the hostility between the two, culminating in the sudden parricide, is expressive of the sudden rupture that transgression introduces into the mode of being of the Brahman. Moreover, in conformity with the religion of interdictions, it permits the presentation of the sacrificial beheading as a (mere) punishment for the primordial incest.[59]

The "sacrilegious" notations of Brahmā's fifth head may be multiplied by comparing it to other figures of transgression within Brahmanism itself, but my purpose here is to merely emphasize that the transgressive essence of Bhairava is in many ways bequeathed to him by the very head he decapitates. Otherwise, the glorification of Bhairava in mythological traditions that remain at heart Brahmanical and claim to amplify the Vedic doctrines will remain incomprehensible. Unlike the Śūdra Unmatta-Bhairava resolutely opposed to caste distinctions, the Kāpālikas (re-) converted by Śaṅkara appear to have been all Brahmans. Epigraphic evidence suggests the existence of Brahman Kāpālikas specializing in the *Atharvaveda*,[60] and it is such adepts who must have served as intermediaries between the Brahmanical sacrifical ideology on the one hand and low caste Kāpālikas having no access to Vedic texts and resorting entirely to the Bhairavāgamas on the other. Lorenzen (*Kāpālikas*, pp. 81-2, 189) has sharply differentiated the Supreme Penance of the Kāpālikas from that of the Pāśupatas, which conforms rather to the *Māhāvrata* of Patañjali's *Yogasūtra* ii.30-31, prescribing the unconditional practice of the five restraints (*yama*): non-violence (ahiṃsā), truthfulness (*satya*), non-theft (*asteya*), chastity (brahmacarya), and non-possessiveness (*aparigraha*) regardless of status, place, time, and occasion, virtures enjoined by later Pāśupata texts like the *Pañcārthabhāṣya* and the *Ratnaṭīkā*, and later cultivated assiduously by their monasticized successors, the Kālāmukhas, especially in the Deccan area.

But a problem remains. Not only is the Pāśupata weapon, in the form of the Brahmaśiras, identified by *Atharvaśiras Upaniṣad* 67 with the Pāśupata Vow with which the Vedic sages were imbued on Śiva-Bhairava's appearance in the Deodar forest, but there also exists the troubling category of the Mahāpāśupatas, who were alternatively identified with the Pāśupatas, Kāpālikas and especially the Kālāmukhas, and yet generally distinguished from all three categories.[61] The true significance of this confusing category lies not so much in its elusive historical determinations but rather in the abiguity of the term *Mahāvrata* and the (dialectical) continuity between the interdictory pole of the (nevertheless symbolically transgressive) Pāśupatas and the transgressive pole of the (nevertheless ascetic) Kāpālika yogins. This intrinsic ambivalence is revealed even in their monastic reorganization as Kālāmukhas, whose preceptors not only sometimes bore the name Kālabhairava but even dedicated temples to (Vīrabhadra, Kālī, and the Kāpālika-) Bhairava. Tondaimān of Kāñci brought to Tiruvorriyūr "from the banks of the Ganges 500 Brāhmaṇa Mahāvratins and dedicated several images of Kālī and Bhairava and one of Śiva in the form of a teacher of the Mahāvratins."[62] The Kālāmukhas were not only mostly erudite Brahman-*paṇḍitas* but also were often expert in *both* Pāśupata and Vedic traditions, so much so that their priest Honnaya is praised in the same verse as a Mahāvratin, Mahāpāśupata, *and* a Śrotriya. That a Kālāmukha inscription invokes Śiva-Lākulīśa as "the heart of Brahma shining as a stone on which is inscribed the *śāsana* of the Vedas which extol the abode of Viśvanātha" (p. 114), is hardly surprising when the *Pāśupatasūtra* is partly based on the (Kāṭhaka-) *Taittirīya Āraṇyaka* (p. 182, n. 48). Indeed, just before the Kāpālika is addressed as "Mahāpāśupata," the ridiculous Pāśupata of the *Mattavilāsa* is himself addressed, like the laughing Vidūṣaka, as "Mahābrāhmaṇa." Likewise, in Ānandarāyamakhin's *Vidyāpariṇayana* (IV, after v. 32) the Kāpālika Somasiddhānta defends his use of wine, meat, etc., prohibited in the (classical) Veda, by affirming "the doctrine of the authoritativeness of the Veda with compliance to the *Bhairavāgamas*" (Lorenzen, pp. 88-9).

Although Brahmā's ritual purity matches the extreme asceticism of Śiva (-Bhairava) and both are defined by an essential transgressive dimension, Brahmā expresses these values only within the context of the Brahmanical sacrifice and Vedic tradition whereas Rudra expresses them even independently of this context despite his intimate links with the violent, dangerous, transgressive pole of the Vedic sacrifice. It is on this background that the well known opposition, complementarity and identity of Brahmā and the five-headed Śiva should be analyzed (O'Flaherty, *Asceticism*, pp. 111-138; see n. 2). The Brahmāstra that Arjuna-Indra receives from the *brahmán* Droṇa-Bṛhaspati (purohita) is no diferent from the Pāśupatāstra he wins through the favour of the outcaste tribal Kirāta-Śiva; and if Arjuna bears this Brahmaśiras like the Untouchable Kāpālika, this is because Bhairava himself inherited his Brahmanicide from the Vedic Indra.

E. The Royal Dīkṣita: Arjuna's Penance and Indra's Brahmanicide

The exoteric image of the exemplary relation between the royal sacrificer (yajamāna) and his officiating purohita is mythically represented by the couple Indra-cum-Bṛhaspati/Brahmā, for it is only through the preliminary purification of the classical dīkṣā, amounting to a (temporary but) veritable Brahmanization, that any (non-Brahman including) warrior from the Kṣatriya caste could engage himself in the sacrifice proper.[63] Whereas the mere ferocious warrior Bhīma (-Bhairava) is hardly distinguishable from a Cāṇḍāla-executioner in his savage acts of sacrificial slaughter (*paśumāram*), and is in fact subtly identified with his victim, the demoniac Duryodhana, by the simultaneity of their births, the model-king Arjuna, although partaking in his elder brother Bhīma's physical force and military prowess (*bala*), is nevertheless imbued with ascetic self-denial (*indriyajaya*), yogic concentration (*ekāgratā*), and the whiteness of Brahmanical purity implied in his very name.[64] It is because this renunciatory dimension is integral to Hindu kingship that it is the Brahman-like Dharma-Yudhiṣṭhira, and not the Kṣatriya Arjuna, who is consecreted king by the *Mahābhārata* to perform its Rājasūya sacrifice. And if Bhīma distinguishes himself from Duryodhana by his subservience not only to his elder brother Dharma but also to his younger brother, this is because (the "crowned" *Kirīṭin-*) Arjuna synthesizes in himself the antithetical bráhman and *kṣatra* of his elder brothers and is himself, although the very incarnation of imperial Victory (*Jaya*), ever devoted to Dharma.[65]

But the transgressive universalization of the (pre-classical) royal dīkṣita, charged with the impurity of death, is expressed not only through his identification with Prajāpati as the sacrificial Year/Universe but also in the mytheme of Indra's decapitation of his demoniac purohita Viśvarūpa. Arjuna's father, the king of the gods, undergoes the embryonic "expiation" for his Brahmanicide within the stalk of the lotus-womb in an island pond, before he is discovered by the feminized Agni in the maternal waters. "Indra's contamination by evil (*anṛta, pāpman*) recalls the similar state of the sacrificer, who seeks to transfer this burden to his rival contender (as Indra transfers it to various carriers); both the year-long trial of the evil-laden god and the period of hiding in diminished form in the lotus pond must be linked to the gestation-like dīkṣā of the sacrificial cult. Indra becomes, in effect, the embryo carried in darkness, surrounded by impurity, awaiting a violent birth."[66] The inherent comic possibilities of royal transgression are especially exploited in the exemplary Arjuna's disguise as the "virile eunuch," Bṛhannaḍā, during the Pāṇḍavas' thirteenth embryonic year of exile in the Fish (-Womb) country Matsyadeśa of king Androgyne (Virāṭa). "In ritual terms, this year of hiding, like Indra's period of fearful concealment in the lotus pond, is a kind of dīkṣā—a moment of ritualized separation, 'regression' to an infantile (or, indeed, embryonic) state, and, at the end, an initiatory rebirth."[67] Just as this regression is often projected onto the mother figure, like the Gaṅgā or Vaiṣṇo-Devī, the androgynous fusion of the dīkṣita with the womb within is conversely also expressed by the maternity of the king himself. Thus, in the *Pañcavaradakṣetramāhātmya*, Indra disguises himself as a pregnant woman to approach his mother for final refuge and on being discovered is transformed into a leper, who in despair instead embraces his wife Paulomī. In the final analysis, the transgressive dīkṣā is but the internalized sacrificial process of the Brahmanized yajamāna giving royal birth to himself (see n. 87).

Arjuna, on receiving the dīkṣā from Yudhiṣṭhira, is endowed with a technique of *anamnesis* or "recollection" (*pratismṛti*), and his succeeding quest probably refers to an inward journey to a pre-natal condition before ascending to a supra-human condition. Like the Brahman Vrātyas consecrated to Rudra, he is armed not only with yoga and tapas but also with the real equipment of a warrior as if he were setting out on the sacrifice of battle, in which he is invariably preceded by Rudra. The Brahmanicidal Vedic homology between the outcaste (*niravasita*) Rudra and the royal Indra[68] underlies the epic identification of the initiated Arjuna with the impure Kirāta-Śiva insofar as they simultaneously pierce the demoniac transposition of the sacrificial boar (*yajña-varāha*). "Dumb" (Mūka) like the dīkṣita himself observing his vow of silence, the boar apparently substitutes for Arjuna himself as sacrificial victim, for the royal dīkṣita is immediately thereafter bodily crushed by the impure Kirāta into a deathly embryonic (piṇḍa) condition. It is paradoxically the defiling embrace of the tribal Rudra that renders Arjuna wholly auspicious and not only confers upon him the transgressive Brahmaśiras but also the access to heaven (*svarga*).

This is hardly surprising when it is this same transgressive dimension underlying the sacrificial order that prompts Yama-Dharmarāja to appear before Yudhiṣṭhira himself as a dog, Bhairava's own theriomorphic form, in order to ensure his entry to svarga. Indeed, it is only after he executes the symbolic Brahmanicide of his elder brother Dharma, followed by his own symbolic suicide through a megalomaniac self-exaltation recalling the universalization of the dīkṣā, that Arjuna actually kills his eldest brother Karṇa, the solar hero hidden in Varuṇic obscurity. Although Aśvatthāman-Rudra, lacking the yogic and Brahmanical accomplishments of Arjuna-Indra, is incapable of retrieving the destructive magical power of his Brahmaśiras, he has acquired his sorcerer's techniques only by virtue of his Brahman parentage, just as the present-day, often gruesome, magical practices on the folk and popular level still correspond, unknown to their own perpetrators, to the symbolic order, selfishly perverted, of the Brahmanical sacrifice. The social opposition between the central (divine) king and the marginal sorcerer lost in the petty possibilities of black magic should not obscure their mirror-like complementarity and the ultimate identity of self-abnegation and magical violence in the priestly first-function incarnated in the dual divinity Mitra-Varuṇa. The "Śivaized" Aśvatthāman's equine notations assume their full significance only in the light of the identification of the sacrificial horse of the Aśvamedha with (Agni-) Prajāpati, equated with the dīkṣita, who sprung as the Ṛgvedic Sun from king Varuṇa's embryonic waters.[69]

F. The Sin-Eating Bhairava: Death and Embryogony in Kāśī

It is because Bhairava incarnates the transgressive essence of the (royal) yajamāna guilty of murdering the sacrificial victim, that the *Skanda Purāṇa* (4.81.1-25) returns the compliment by making the Vṛtrahan-Indra himself expiate his Brahmanicide like a foul-smelling Kāpālika, before finally freeing himself at Kapālamocana by discharging the Evil Man in himself, in the form of a golden self-image, onto a reluctant Brahman. For this condescension, the degraded Mahābrāhmaṇa is not only, like the royal scapegoat Vidūṣaka, reviled by the citizens of Banaras for whom he still performs their rites, especially funerary rites, but also rendered Untouchable,[70] like the Sin-Eating (*Pāpabhakṣaṇa* Kāpālika-) Bhairava even after his supposed purification at Kapālamocana. This inner identity of the (Mahā-) Brāhmaṇa and the Untouchable finds its mythical parallel in the identical funerary notations of Bhairava at Kāñci and Brahmā's fifth head at Kāśī (*supra* n. 25). And just as the greedy purohita-like Vidūṣaka is constantly pampered with gifts of food (especially piṇḍa-like *modakas*), jewellery, clothes, and other valuables, the Mahābrāhmaṇas too, most of all the *Dom*-(Yama-) *Rāj* of today, heap their fortunes by virtue of their ritual function.[71]

Even on the sociological level, it is the Kusle-Jogī, successor of the Kāpālika, who plays the role of Mahābrāhmaṇa among the Newars of Nepal, not only by receiving the clothes of the dead at the *chvasa*, the ritual stone where the quarter's death-and-birth impurities are deposited, but also by receiving food offerings including meat, fish, etc., during the *nhaynamā*-rites on the seventh day after the death. The mythical justification is the decapitation of Brahmā's fifth head during the inauspicious pañcaka (*dhaniṣṭa nakṣatra*), the depositing of his clothes at the chvasa to be taken away by Gorakhnāth, who revives the lifeless Brahmā on the seventh day in the temple of Baṭuk Bhairava. The Newars still deposit a five headed Brahmā figure at the chvasa to neutralize the possibility of a chain reaction of five deaths due to the untimely death during the pañcaka. Thus the impure initiatic death of the Brahmanized dīkṣita finds its funerary transposition in the condensed ritual figure of the Banarasi Mahābrāhmaṇa who impersonates the dead man's ghost (preta) and is indeed consubstantial with the deceased, and this sacrificialization of natural death (-ritual) finds its mythical counterpart in Bhairava, through his conquest of Death, usurping the very throne of Yama in Kāśī, the cremation ground of the Hindu universe.[72]

The funerary application of the origin myth finds semi-independent expression in the sneering demon head of the Brahma-Rākṣasa (or -Piśāca), apparently a former *tīrtha*-purohita like the Piśāca of the *Kāśī-Khaṇḍa*, decapitated by Bhairava, and now regularly receiving tīrtha-śrāddha offered by pilgrims on their way to Gaya to fulfill their ritual obligations towards their ancestors (pitṛ), and also the tripiṇḍī-śrāddha for the calming and exorcism of evil spirits (preta, piśāca, bhūta, etc.). It is through such mechanisms exteriorizing the degraded Untouchable dimension of the Mahābrāhmaṇa that the Brahmā presiding over the pure domain of the classical Vedic sacrifice has been transformed into the lowly popular village Brahms, hardly distinguishable from the unhewn stone Bhairavas and the earthen-mound Bīrs.[73] Bhairava's frequent appellation as "Lord of Ghosts" (*Bhūtanātha*), no doubt owes a great deal to this universe of death and the manipulation of its shadowy denizens by low caste specialists like the Ojhas, who gather at Maṇikarṇikā during *Kāla-Rātri* (Diwali) to recharge their magical powers before the image of Baṭuka Bhairava. Like Dionysos, whose feet are licked by the watchdog Cerberus while returning from the kingdom of Hades, with whom he is identified by Heraclitus, Bhairava is the fullness of Death-in-life. Through his initiatic death, even the Pāśupata (and no doubt the Kāpālika) was assimilated to the laughing exuberance of a preta; and the Vrātya, like the dīkṣita, was already a dead man even in the midst of life.[74]

Lorenzen suggests that Bhairava's Brahmanicide origin myth is derived, at least in part, from the *Mahābhārata* story of the Rākṣasa head, decapitated by Rāma, sticking to the thigh of the sage Mahodara who was relieved of it only by bathing at the Auśanas tīrtha on the Sarasvatī River, which thereby came to be known as Kapālamocana, "probably identical with a tank of this name on the Sarsuti or Sarasvatī River ten miles southeast of Saudhara."[75] If the Kāpālikas came to Kāśī instead, this was because, by flowing north, Mother Gaṅgā herself strives here to return to her own source, and even now the sacred tank at Maṇikarṇikā beside the cremation-ghāṭ is believed to be nourished directly by the primordial waters of the Himalayan Gaumukh whence she emerges to sanctify the Hindu subcontinent. The uterine equivalence of the Hindu goddess Gaṅgā and the Vedic god Varuṇa is betrayed in mythico-ritual conjunctions like Varuṇa having performed penance with Gaṅgā-devī to be appointed lord of the waters and aquatic creatures at Kāñci (*Kaṅkāvarēccaram*).[76] The embryogonic fusion of dīkṣita with maternal womb permits the projection of traits like androgyny and regression on the mother symbol itself, as in the case of Vaiṣṇo-Devī having spent nine months in her own womb.

This ever-present embryogonic significance, lent to Kāśī by the reverse flow of the Gaṅgā, literally engulfs the sacred centre of Hinduism, when her flood waters likewise reverse the flow of her tributary, the Varuṇa, and its seasonal sub-tributary, the Matsyodarī, to encircle the entire city and its inhabitants in its womb, thereby transforming it into the primordial mound of archaic cosmogony. The Omkāra temple on its hillock on the banks of the former Kapālamocana at the heart of the sacred city was transformed by this primeval deluge into an island, just like its prototype, the Omkāra *jyotirliṅga* of Central India in the middle of the sacred Narmadā River. It was during this rare but exceedingly auspicious "Fish-Womb Conjunction" (*Matsyodarī-Yoga*), when the Gaṅgā itself is the Fish-Womb (-Lake), that the Brahmanicide Bhairava plunged into the amniotic waters of Kapālamocana originally situated at the confluence of the Matsyodarī and the backward-flowing Mother Gaṅgā. Hindu kings apparently continued to imitate the example of the Kāpālika-Bhairava right up until the final short-lived efflorescence of Vārāṇasī before the Muslim conquest, for a Gāhadvāla inscription records that in the twelfth century king Govindacandra bathed in the Gaṅgā at Kapālamocana in (during) the Fish-Womb (conjunction) and made a land-donation to a Brahman.[77]

But for his exceptional socio-political status, the Hindu king is no more than the sacrificer par excellence. And indeed the perpetual cremation of corpses at Maṇikarṇikā, the navel of Kāśī, reproduces the embryogonic implications of Bhairava's initiatic death, thereby transforming the "Great Cremation Ground" (*mahāśmaśāna*) into the cosmogonic centre transcending the spatio-temporal order of the Hindu sacrificial universe that ceaselessly (re-)emerges from its womb to (re-)dissolve in this microcosmic pralaya modelled on the fire sacrifice. Discus (*cakra*) and lotus pond (*puṣkariṇī*) are equivalent womb symbols, and the primordial Cakrapuṣkariṇī that Viṣṇu dug with his discus and filled with his sweat in the course of his cosmogonic austerities (tapas) is ultimately identical with the lotus pool behind the Viṣṇu temple at Tirukaṇṭiyūr where the *brahmakapāla* of the Tamil Bhairava fell. This embryogonic significance of the Cakrapuṣkariṇī, renamed Maṇikarṇikā when the nectarine (amṛta-) Soma concentrated in Śiva's ear-ring fell into it from his ear (-womb), is confirmed by the proximity of Viṣṇu's Foot (*pada*), the mysterious source of the Gaṅgā beyond even Gaumukh, receptacle of Viṣṇu-Trivikrama's renowned "third stride," where the most eminent corpses are burnt.[78] As a preta, the dead man, represented by the Mahābrāhmaṇa, returns to the womb, represented by a water pot hanging from a sacred *pipal* tree, and his new body is nourished with a daily *modaka*-like rice ball (piṇḍa) so that on the tenth day it is fully formed like a newborn baby, and it is ready to be transformed into an ancestor (pitṛ) on the eleventh day, when the Mahābrāhmaṇa is worshipped, fed, given gifts, and departs having smashed the water pot dwelling of the *pret*.[79] This embryogonization of death, not specific to cremation, is equally applicable to the Harappan funerary urns and burial elsewhere: "burial in the embryonic position is explained by the mystical interconnection between death, initiation, and return to the womb. In some cultures this close connection will finally bring about the assimilation of death to initiation—the dying man is regarded as undergoing an initiation."[80]

Even quite independently of the Kāpālika-Bhairava's entry into Kāśī within the fish-wombed Gaṅgā and his dip at Kapālamocana, Bhairava's begging from the Seven Sages in the Daru forest ritually imitated by the Brahmanicide Kāpālikas' begging from seven houses during their twelve-year wanderings as prescribed by the law-books, is already charged with the embryonic notations and impurity of the dīkṣā. It is akin to the twelve-year exile of the Pāṇdavas accompanied by the menstruating Draupadī, which culminates in their thirteenth year incognito as embryos in the Fish-Country of king Matsya (see n. 67). For the forest is already the "womb of Brahman" (*brahmayoni*) in the *Brāhmaṇas* and seven is the embryogonic number par excellence right from the Vedas, as exemplified especially by the seven-holed anthill substituted for the severed head of the *Agnicayana*, which in fact assimilates the decapitation to an embryonic regression.[81] The present-day Dārānagar was settled after the cutting-down of the Dāruvana within Kāśī near Vṛddhakāla and Haratīrath. This is why, even after having lost its paradisaical forest-hermitages, Kāśī still remains Ānandavana, "The Forest of (the) Bliss (of Brahman)"; and its seven concentric circles, corresponding to the seven yogic spinal centers, are guarded by fifty-six divinized icons of the *Mahābrāhmaṇa* appointed as eight Gaṇeśas to the cardinal points of each circle, serving again thereby as mediators between him and the eight traditional kṣetrapāla Bhairavas.[82]

Reflected also in the pilgrimage cult at Vaiṣṇo-Devī, the symbolic identity of the transgressive Bhairava in the womb of the Gaṅgā with the demon-devotee as sacrificial victim, is worked out in the founding myth of the Bisket Jātrā at Bhaktapur, where the Kāla Bhairava of Kāśī lost his head forever to Vaiṣṇavī appearing as Bhadrakālī. The bloody obstetrics of the dīkṣā is particularly evident in Andhra Pradesh where Aṅkammā dismembers the foetus of her homonym, the queen-mother Gaṅgā (Gaṅgammā), at the twelfth year of her pregnancy, and the sacrificial scenario finds its prolongations on the folk level in the Tamil cremation ground cult of the infanticide Aṅkāḷamman where Iruḷappan, the child-Śiva, is not only the dark-one like Kāla-Bhairava but is also identifiable with his royal father (Kāśī-) Vallāḷarājan.[83] Having torn open the belly of her alter ego, Aṅkāḷamman cradles "her" dismembered child, like the baby Dionysos-Lyknitès, in the womb of the winnowing fan. Killing his mother Semele by his very birth, the terrible Dionysos is likewise his own victim, not only driving the Maenads to devour the cubs of savage beasts, but himself lacerated as live bull (= Zagreus) in Crete. And in Tenedos he was sacrificially axed to death in the form of a newborn calf of a cow treated like a mother who had only just delivered. Dionysos was clearly identified with the sacred king when he united ritually with the queen Basilinna, in the name of the entire city, during the Athenian "death-festival" of the Anthesteries.[84]

Suvarṇakalā-Bhairava is worshipped beside Naṭarāja in the sanctum of the Cidambaram temple; more significantly, a daily secret *cakrapūjā* is performed towards noon for the *Ākāśa-liṅga* itself, where the divinity is first of all invoked with the appropriate *yantras* and mantras in the form of Ākāśa-Bhairava by the officiating dīkṣitas (cf. *supra* n. 13). Expressed through such symbolic equivalences as the embryonic intercalary thirteenth month containing within itself the ritual (Prajāpati-) Year as a totality, the universalization of the sacrificer through the dīkṣā has been displaced from Bhairava, charged with the impurity of death, to his purified alter ego Kāśī-Viśvanātha, the "Lord of the Universe," who remains the implacable indifferent witness to the violent scenario enacted by his surrogate; hardly unexpected when the reformed classical sacrifice has already concentrated the cosmic Prajāpati within the renunciate nature of the pure yajamāna who has conquered Death, but only symbolically.[85] At Puri, however, the divinized king, although still retaining his inner purity as in his ritual substitute of a young Brahman celibate (*Mudra Hasta*), remains "Lord of the Universe" (Jagannātha) only through the operations of death and rebirth performed upon him by impure "tribal" Śabara-priests, whose mythic ancestor won this prerogative by his sacrilegious killing of a bull at the instigation of the king's minister. This dīkṣā-like "Body-Renewal" (*Navakalevara*) of the royal Viṣṇu, already prefigured in his yearly "sickness" (*anavasara*) followed by the chariot-drive (*ratha-yātrā*) inaugurated by the king transformed into an Untouchable sweeper, is presided over by the Bhairava-like Narasiṃha, and occurs only during an intercalary month of Aṣāḍha. All this serves as sufficient preparation for the eventual revelation of the probably transgressive connotations of the mysterious *brahmapadārtha* that vivifies Jagannātha from within and is transferred by the blind-folded Śabaras in so uncanny an atmosphere.[86]

The royal character of the pure central divinity, even in the absence of a real king, is also seen at Tiruvaṇṇāmalai where once every year Śiva-Aṇṇāmalaiyār is informed of the death of the virtuous king Vallāḷa, and after a mourning ceremony is crowned son-successor to the childless king. A historical Ballāḷa stands in the Aṅkāḷamman myth behind the demoniac Vallāḷarājan, whose seven-walled palace, equated with the cremation ground at whose centre lies the pregnant queen-goddess, is but an image of Aṇṇāmalaiyār within the womb (*garbha-gṛha*) of the Tiruvaṇṇāmalai temple with its seven concentric enclosures. Moreover, at Kumbhakonam, where the Kāśī-Viśvanātha temple stands on the Mahāmagha lake formed from the amṛta spilled from Brahmā's primordial pot (-womb), and wherein the nine most sacred rivers of India led by the Gaṅgā mix their waters once every twelve years, Vallāḷarājan is even promoted to the king of Kāśī, embryogonic center of the Hindu sacrificial universe. Would this not be precisely because the dīkṣā underlies all legitimate kingship in India? It is in the polar axis formed by the epi-central Tiruvaṇṇāmalai temple-capital and the peripheral cremation ground of Mēl Malaiyanūr, substituted for the Mahāśmaśāna, that the pan-Indian Brahmanicide myth (*kapparai*) centred on Kāśī and the regional historically determined myth of Vallāḷarājan (pregnant cremation-figure) would have fused to provide the mythical background to the ritual complexities of the cult of Aṅkāḷamman. The kapparai received from the Kapālin is itself identified with Aṅkāḷamman who then "takes the *avatāram* of Brahmā and goes to the cremation-ground;" and the pregnant cremation-figure of the goddess-victim is itself identified with a Brahman woman. By donating the transgressive fifth head of Brahmā to the goddess before fusing with her as a child to form the primordial androgyne, (Śiva-) Kapālin indeed mediates between the blood-thirsty Aṅkāḷamman of the low caste Cempaṭavar fishermen and the purified Brahmanical milieu of Aṇṇāmalaiyār, the Tamil transposition of Viśvanātha as the fiery axis mundi that originally manifested itself at Kāśī.[87]

G. The Khaṭvāṅga-Bhairava: Executioner, Victim, and Sacrificial Stake

The immeasurable world pillar traversing and uniting the three cosmic levels of netherworld, earth, and heavens, from which Bhairava emerges to appropriate Brahmā's central head, is reduced to more handy ritual proportions in the cranial staff (khaṭvāṅga) which the Kāpālika wields as a weapon.[88] On the basis of the explicit textual evidence of Tibetan Buddhist tantras further elucidated by the oral traditions of their lamaistic practitioners, the khaṭvāṅga, surmounted successively by a fresh moist head, a half decomposed one, topped by a dry skull, and provided with a Brahmanical cord (yajñopavīta), has not only been identified with the world-tree, also called Amṛta and growing in the cremation ground, but the entire symbolic complex has been derived from esoteric psycho-physical, especially sexual, techniques centering on the production of the ambrosia of "supreme felicity" (*mahāsukha*), through a process of alternating ascent and descent within the *suṣumnā.* This ritual system, comprising other implements like the sacrificial dagger (*phur-bu = kīla*) and the alchemical fireplace-skull standing on three heads, refers back to the liberating murder by (a Buddhist divinity like Heruka assimilated to) Bhairava of the demonized, and still terrible, Rudra, but in a scenario that deliberately underlines the consubstantiality of divine killer and demoniac victim amidst the transgressive valorization of impurities (like excrement, etc.) converted into nectar.[89] Although philosophically elaborated in the light of specifically Buddhist tenets, the underlying techniques and formal symbolic system are clearly derived from the Hindu, and even Vedic, universe.

The theatrical irony achieved by Euripides in *The Bacchae* through the mirror-like symmetry of the masked Dionysos confronting the royal Pentheus, travestied as a Bacchant before falling from the tree top to be torn apart by the Maenads led by his own mother, reveals itself in the Corinthian ritual, where the bloody tree honoured as a divinity is carved into effigies of Dionysos, to be a veritable identity. Hardly had the tree bearing the "unequaled" (like Dionysos) Pentheus, whose glory should rise to heaven, straightened itself to aim upwards at the sky; no sooner had Dionysos himself disappeared letting his victim fall to his sacrificial fate, than from the earth a divine fire-ball streaked heavenward.[90] In the sixth Act of *Śākuntala*, the Vidūṣaka, violently twisted by Indra's charioteer in three places (*tribhaṅga*), like his own crooked staff (*kuṭilaka*), explicitly compares himself to the immolated sacrificial victim, and the kuṭilaka itself is a caricature of the Brahmanical staff *daṇḍakāṣṭha* (= *brahmadaṇḍa*), which is assimilated even in the Buddhist tantras to the tripartite axis mundi. Planted on the border of the sacrificial altar (*vedi*), precisely half-within and half-without, the yūpa represents the neutralization of the opposites (*coincidentia oppositorum*), especially evident in the conditions governing the bloody sacrifice performed by Narasiṃha on emerging from the (cosmic) pillar. This aspect is fused with its phallic dimension, evident in its later transposition as the śivaliṅga emerging from the yoni, especially in the impure phallic names of the three brothers of whom only the middle one Śunaḥśepa is designated as the Brahman sacrificial victim. Although no longer the site of the actual immolation in the purified classical ritual, the sacrificial stake, still expressive of the essential identity of the Vedic sacrificer and his divinized victim, is described in a Vedic hymn as stained with blood.[91]

During the cosmogonic New Year festival of Bisket Jātrā at Bhaktapur, Bhairava is erected as the liṅga in the form of the cross-shaped pole bearing two long cloth-banners representing the two slaughtered serpents from which the festival derives its name. The copulation between the pole and supporting mound of earth is also enacted in the ritual collision of the chariots of Ākāśa-Bhairava and Bhadra-Kālī, who comes specially to witness the erection of the liṅga and the death of the snakes. She is probably no different from the lusty but deadly princess of the founding legend from whose nostrils the snakes emerged every night to slay her lovers until an unknown prince slew them instead through his exceptional vigilance and even married her. On the last day of the year (Caitra *masant*), a buffalo is sacrificed at the *pīṭha* of Bhadra-Kālī and the Untouchables (Pore) bring its head up to the central Taumadhi square where the Ākāśa-Bhairava temple is situated and destroy it as soon as the New Year pole is erected. From there a "death-procession" consisting of a traditional bier carrying a pot (*bhājā-khaḥca*, the first term *'bhājā'* meaning not only "pot" but also the large "head" of a thin person), instead of a real corpse, returns to the liṅga late the same night. After being left beside the neighbouring Bhadra-

Kālī pīṭha, the bier is then brought back to Taumadhi, when the pole is pulled down on the evening of the first day of Baisākh. The bier, which was formerly used to collect from the palace the suitors killed by the twin snakes, comes in vain for the corpse of the victorious prince and returns instead with the substituted "pot-head" to the pīṭha beside the cremation ghāṭ. The erection of the liṅga, often associated with a snake (like Gaṇeśa's trunk or the Vidūṣaka's kuṭilaka), signifies above all the neutralization and annihilation of the opposing vital breaths (*prāṇa/apāna*) resulting in the raising of the serpentine *kuṇḍalinī* up the median channel (suṣumnā) in the very act of sexual (and even incestuous) intercourse. Like Mahākāla, the suṣumnā is said to devour Kāla (death) represented by the alternating lateral breaths; and in the Tibetan tantras Rudra "eats" or is "eaten" by his mother in the cremation ground beside the cosmic tree called *Amṛta* or *Khaṭvāṅga* and especially "Fornication," and ultimately attains deliverance to become Mahākāla.[92] The sacrificed buffalo ritually actualizes the initiatic death of not only the royal lover but also of Kāla-Bhairava who came from Kāśī out of curiosity to see the pole-festival, originally consecrated to Bhadra-Kālī alone, only to be discovered by the Tantric priests and to be decapitated before he could escape. Even now, a very secret, closely-guarded bundle accompanies Ākāsh-Bhairab as he goes to regularly unite with his demanding consort, and it is understood that its contents are linked to the severed head.

With the assimilation of the greenery at its extremity to fecundating semen eagerly sought by barren couples, the pole is no different from the imposing erect liṅga of the Unmatta-Bhairava at the Paśupatināth temple, which newly married couples touch reverentially in order to be assured of offspring. The sexual identity of the victim and executioner is clearer in the founding myth of the festival of Indreśvar Mahādev at Panauti where, pursued by the insatiable Bhadra-Kālī, Śiva plunged into the confluence of two rivers defining the site of the temple only to emerge, like the invisible median river, as the perpetually ithyphallic Unmatta-Bhairava to take her three times from behind. The phallic identity of the yūpa is especially evident in the buffalo sacrificed to Thampa (= Stambha) Bhairava, "just before the temple precincts of Indreśvar. The animal is destined for Unmatta Bhairava, but as this god is situated within the pure sacred precincts of Indreśvar, its throat is slit outside, before Thampa Bhairava conceived here to be his double."[93] At Paśupatināth, animal sacrifices are offered on particular occasions to Unmatta-Bhairava himself, within the precincts, and the pure central Śiva participates indirectly through a ritual cord linking him with Bhairava.

The royal character of the Bisket cosmogony becomes explicit in the Indra Jātrā of neighbouring Kathmandu where the liṅga is identified instead, as in the Vedic cosmogony, with the (*dhvaja*-emblem of the) king of the gods Indra, who rains on the Valley before the full moon of Bhādra (September).[94] As prescribed by the *Bṛhat-Saṃhitā* (chap. 43), the pole is dragged on the 8th day of the bright half of Bhādrapada into the capital and the festival begins with its erection on the 12th day. Like the dīkṣita bound in Varuṇa's noose, wooden statues of Indra bound in cords are placed, often in prison-like cages, at the foot of the pole(s), or, like a thief with outstretched arms on high scaffolds. The actual role of sacrificial victim is assumed rather by the Kirāta king Yālambara whose head, violenty chopped off by Kṛṣṇa before he could join the losing side in the Mahābhārata war, landed at Indra Chowk, where it is still worshipped as Ākāsh Bhairab, even after being reinstated as the official emblem of the Royal Nepali Airlines. The founding myth, however, suggests that it is Indra himself who undergoes the sacrificial death. For Indra's mother, having secured the release of her son from the Valley people who had bound him for stealing their *pārijāta* flowers, was leading back to heaven the dead of the previous year, when the chain of the procession broke and the souls fell into the lake Indra Daha. In the ritual, on the evening before the full moon a farmer costumed as a Dagini (*ḍākinī:* female demon) emerges from Maru Hiti, where Indra had been imprisoned, to lead a procession of women from households where death had occurred and search for the fallen souls, and hundreds of them subsequently make the eight mile pilgrimage to bathe on the dawn of the full moon in the Indra lake, believing that they are accompanied by Indra himself.

Although Indra's mother does not appear as such in the funeral procession, the royal Nepali mother goddess Taleju emerges in procession the same afternoon as the pre-pubertal virgin Kumārī, escorted by two boys representing Gaṇeśa and Bhairava. On the full moon evening, i.e., the second day of the procession, the Kumārī, after having paused before the black Ākāsh Bhairab at Indrachowk and the Sweto Bhairab at Hanuman Dhoka, (re-)legitimizes the king's rule for the following year by placing the sacred red *ṭīkā* mark on his forehead. More light is shed on its significance by the cruel slaughter of an enraged buffalo during the Sawo Bhaku demon dance within the old royal palace, where it is the blood of its decapitation by Ākāsh Bhairab (dancer), attended by Caṇḍī and Kumārī, that is used for the ṭīkā on the witnessing king. One would be justified in juxtaposing it to the offering of Kāla-Bhairava's alias, Kāśī-Viśvanātha's own head, during the Bisket-Jātrā to Bhadra-Kālī. The full moon marks the beginning of the dark half of Āśvina (of Bhādrapada in the *amānta* reckoning) when the most potent *Mahālaya-śrāddha* is performed for the departed ancestors (pitṛ), particularly when the Sun is in Kanyā (Virgo). The calendrical determinations clearly reveal the funerary rites to be a popular transposition of the royal dīkṣita's mortal regression into the virgin-womb of the mother (-goddess) to be reborn afresh for a New Year of legitimate sovereignty.[95]

The tension between the royal "Āryan" sacrificer and his impure alter ego finds festive dramatization in the ritual conflict between the incoming procession of Indra and the inhabitants who display their hereditary masks of Bhairava before their homes, like the famous Ākāsh Bhairab itself outside his temple at Indra Chowk, a scenario that is cast in the image of tribal Yālambara's legendary capture of the invading Āryan chief. But their ultimate identity is evident not only in the merger of the essentially black (Kāla-) Bhairava and white (Arjuna) Indra in the intermediate figure of the royal Sweto or White-Bhairab who reveals himself before the royal palace only during the Indra Jātrā, but also at the very end of the festival when a funeral-like procession drags the Indra-pole to be immersed in the sacred waters of the Bagmati river before being retrieved and hacked into splinters to feed the sacred flame at the nearby shrine of Pacali Bhairab beside the cremation ground. And once every twelve years, Pacali Bhairab, whose name has been derived from the Vedic Licchavi institution of the *pañcāli*, assumes the form of an impure Mālākār (gardener) to renew, through their exchange of swords, the King's waning power.[96] It certainly cannot be accidental that the cosmogonic marriage of Lāṭ-Bhairõ's pillar to the well at Kāśī coincides with Indra-Jātrā and is celebrated exactly on the full moon of Bhādra, which is most inauspicious for marriages for it signals the beginning of the death rituals of the pitṛ-pakṣa.[97]

Although nowadays identified with the Purāṇic Kapāli-Bhairava, originally located to the northwest of Vāsukīkuṇḍ in the present day Nāg-Kuān area, Lāṭ-Bhairõ is in fact the ancient Kula—no different from the Mahāśmaśāna-Stambha (pillar) where the original Kāla-Bhairava used to not only devour the sins of pilgrims but also administer the "punishment/suffering" of Bhairava (*bhairavī yātanā*), alone conferring final emancipation (mokṣa) even on the worst of sinners (see plates 15 and 16). The policeman-magistrate (Kotwāl) apparently presided over the public ritual execution of criminals in what probably

15. Lāṭ Bhairava pillar, Vārāṇasī. Lāṭ Bhairava (Bhairõ) adorned for Śivarātri, 26 February 1987. The top of the pillar rises above its decorated metal encasement, which shows Lāṭ Bhairõ's face. Photo courtesy of N. Gutschow.

16. Face of Lāṭ Bhairõ on encasement around the Lāṭ Bhairava pillar, Vārāṇasī. Śivarātri decoration. Photo courtesy of N. Gutschow.

was a significant cremation ground, which would account for the terrible character even of its metaphysical transposition.[98] But if the most virtuous of saints cannot aspire to that salvation which even and especially Brahmanicides are assured of in Kāśī, this is only because Bhairava as executioner-cum-victim is identical with the all-devouring Fire of Consciousness (also called *Kula*) that consumes all the impurity of sin, and because the sacrificial death was itself assimilated to its fiery ascent up the suṣumnā as the (mahā-) śmaśāna (pillar), now remaining as the Lāṭ-Bhairō. The perpetual cremation at Maṇikarṇikā, where three streams unite(d) to flow out as the Brahmanāla or Pitāmahasrotas into the milky way of the Gaṅgā, confirms that all death in Kāśī is (modelled on) the initiatic process whereby this flame of consciousness pierces through the sinciput at the "aperture of Brahmā" (*brahmarandhra*) to be freed forever.

Even the apparently alternative fate, reserved especially for those who sin in Kāśī itself before dying there, to be transformed into ghoulish Rudras (rudrapiśāca) before undergoing the rudrayātanā at the Mahāśmaśāna-stambha, conforms rigorously to the above model of initiatic death. The (mystic) decapitation of the Tibetan adept, corresponding to the *kapālakriyā* performed on the Banaras corpse, when the divine life-force escapes through the brahmarandhra, also corresponds to the murderous liberation of Rudra by a Bhairava-like (*Jigs-byed*) divinity who penetrates the demon at the base of the spine to flash like an arrow or comet through "the opening of the Door of Heaven." Rudra had already received the tantric initiation in his original incarnation as the master "Deliverance-Salvation/Black," whose name "alludes to his ambiguous nature: he will do evil, but will be finally delivered with the status of the god Mahākāla."[99] This salvation often occurs in the explicit context of copulation belonging to the same symbolic complex, which is not foreign to the Hindu cremation rites (see n. 115). Since the annual festival of the Kula-Stambha was already being celebrated, in order not to become a Rudrapiśāca, on the full moon of Bhādra, this must have in all probability already been in the form of a cosmogonic marriage, in which case the bridegroom must have come from his original temple on the western bank of Omkāreśvara. The figure of the Rudrapiśāca would itself appear to be a mythic projection of the ghostly (*pretavad*) Rudra-Pāśupatas who had their chief center at Omkāreśvara, where they had many *āśramas* and haunted the Aghoreśvara (or Śrīmukhi) cave. Since Bhairava functioned as Sin-Eater at both the Mahāśmaśāna-Stambha where as Kotwāl he executed the ultimate punishment, and also Kapālamocana where as Kapālin he was freed of the ultimate crime of Brahmanicide, it is perfectly logical that, in the wake of the Muslim occupation of Omkāreśvar, Kapālamocana has come to be (re-)identified with Lāṭ-Bhairõ tīrtha, where the Kapālin remains as executioner, victim, and pillar of the world.[100]

The variants on the Ghāzī Mīyā̃ story, retold by the Muslims around the area of the Lāṭ, seem to have grafted onto the martyred warrior many significant fragments of this archaic Hindu mythico-ritual universe of sacrificial death. A bridegroom discovered that he had been chosen to be the next victim, on the very day of his imminent marriage, at the problematic temple of Somnāth near the confluence of the Varaṇā with the Gaṅgā at Rājghāt, where human sacrifices were once regularly offered to the divinity. Responding to the hysterical condition of the victim's mother, Ghāzī Mīyā̃ bathed in the Gaṅgā and took his place, but the image started sinking as soon as he placed one foot across the threshold. The Muslim hero nevertheless managed to seize the head by its tuft and kick it, before dispersing the hair which grew as a type of grass wherever it fell. In a common variant, Ghāzī Mīyā̃ removed his own head to avoid seeing and being seduced by the hundreds of naked women sent by the king's astrologer in order to destroy the power of his purity and thereby render him an easy sacrificial victim. Nowadays, it is the Lāṭ which is popularly held to be sinking into the ground, and Kāla Bhairab was decapitated at the Bhaktapur cosmogony when he had almost completely disappeared into the earth on his underground escape route to Banaras.[101] Through that resilience and adaptability so characteristic of Hindu genius, Kāla-Bhairava still makes his annual pilgrimage as the royal bridegroom from his present-day temple to re-enact, in the middle of the Muslim Idgāh, his fateful marriage by crowning (*mukuṭ*) the Lāṭ-Bhairõ with his own head (see plate 17). The popular wisdom of colloquial (Hindi) language still refers to the cremation (ground) as the "place of the bride" (*dulhan kā sthān*) and as the "last marriage" (*ākhirī śādī*), and if the Newars can be so confident that the head of Kāla-Bhairava at Kāśī is not his real head, this is probably because he had already been regularly surrendering it to the Mahāśmaśāna-Stambha even before offering it to Bhadrakālī at Bhaktapur.

H. The "Tribalizing" Ekapāda-Bhairava and Anuttara in Trika Metaphysics

The Mhaskobā, worshipped by the pastorals and tribals of Maharashtra at such places as Javalī, Mhasvaḍ, Borban, Vīr, and, especially,

17. Lāṭ Bhairava at Vārāṇasī decorated with the head of Kāla Bhairava, with crown (*mukuṭa*), set atop the central pillar, for Lāṭ Bhairõ's marriage to the nearby well. Lāṭ Bhairõ's face on the outer encasement shows through the decoration. Photo by Elizabeth-Chalier Visuvalingam.

Sonārī, is identified by them as the Brahmanicide Kālabhairava of the Kāśī myth who settled down at these places to satisfy his devotees. And Birobā (Vīrabhadra) is not only identified with Kālabhairava but is also constantly called Kāśiliṅga-Birāppā. Precisely because of his transgressive essence and his wild, wandering character, Bhairava has been instrumental, through his heretic, outcaste, even criminal adepts, in the Hinduization of local pastoral and tribal divinities, who gradually came to be identified with one or the other of his varied forms. This has been clearly demonstrated for the Deccan region (Maharashtra, Karnataka, Andhra) in the exemplary case of Khaṇḍobā/Mārtaṇḍa-Bhairava. As a result, Bhairava has often two wives, the legal one coming from the settled agricultural or merchant upper caste culture, and the mistress, also the favorite, coming from the hunting or gathering tribal community and retaining all her savage associations.[102] The splitting of the essentially black (Kāla-) Bhairava into two opposing yet complementary forms, black and white, encountered iconographically in Rajasthan, Madhya Pradesh, and especially Nepal, and also in ritual, as in the Navadurgā-dance of Bhaktapur, probably also reflects the purification or *whitening* of Bhairava as he climbs up the ladder of caste society, just as Rudra had already been rendered auspicious in the form of Śiva. Where other divinities like Viṣṇu or especially the goddess have been able to play a similar Hinduizing role, it is only by assuming terrifying forms, like Narasiṃha, resembling Bhairava. The goddess takes a form approaching that of Bhairavī, consort of Bhairava, and the couple, being often confused in their sex, facilitate the transition even from an aboriginal goddess, like the wooden post Khambheśvarī or Stambheśvarī, to the purified male Śaiva cult. Conversely, in the mythology of the Dhangars, Śiva repeatedly assumes the form of a Gosavī, who, as the successor of the Kāpālikas and Nāths, must have "tribalized" Hinduism even while playing a Hinduizing role among the tribal Kolis, Gavlis, Kunbis, and other groups beyond the pale of Brahmanical culture. The deified Gosavī still worshipped by the Marāthās, Dhangars, Mālīs, etc., "is called Viśvanāth because he comes from Kāśī," and is indifferently named "Mhasvaḍ-Śīḍ, Kāla-bhairava, Bhairavnāth, Śrīsiddhanāth or Kāśiviśvanāth."[103]

Bearers of a transgressive sacrality that transcends the barriers which separate the caste society from the outcaste tribals with their blood-thirsty divinities, the adepts of Bhairava were in the ideal position to incorporate such deities into the Brahmanical symbolical universe by endowing them with traditional attributes and even to elevate them to the level of all-caste Hindu divinities[104] or even into the supreme position of pan-Indian gods of pilgrimage. Lord Jagannātha of Puri is believed to have evolved from an original tribal divinity, worshipped by the mythic Viśvāvasu, and the "tribal" Śabara priests, who even now officiate alongside the orthodox Brahmans, are alone charged with the ritual impurity of the fatal obstetrics they perform on the divinized king, himself then identified with the demonic *daitās*. Their transgressive *śabarī*-pūjā is supervised by the only Brahman, the Pati Mahāpātra, who also inserts the brahmapadārtha into Lord Jagannātha. Born of the union of the Āryan king Indradyumna's Brahman Vidyāpati with the tribal Viśvāvasu's daughter Lalitā, the Pati Mahāpātra, like the Mahābrāhmaṇa, incorporates in himself the opposing poles of the pure and the impure. In fact, the three main divinities actually become Gaṇeśa during the bathing festival that marks the onset of their "illness."[105]

In the earliest Orissan temples, the various forms of Śiva are invariably depicted with upraised (*ūrdhva-*) liṅga, and at one stage of his historical evolution Jagannātha was apparently identified with Bhairava, the form he still assumes to symbolically copulate with the devadāsī (= Bhairavī) during the evening ritual (see n. 13). It has been suggested that the ithyphallic single-footed Ekapāda Bhairava, whose images are so frequent in predominantly tribal Orissa, was easily able to assimilate, through his very iconography, tribal wooden post divinities accepting blood sacrifices.[106] But this Tantric divinity associated with the Yoginīs is himself derived from the Vedic Aja Ekapāda, a multiform of Agni who appears as the central pillar of the world and is juxtaposed to Ahir-Budhnya, "the Serpent of the Deep" (see n. 94). The inherent tension of the Vedic yūpa, standing ambivalently astride the sacrificial boundary,[107] could equally permit the pacific assimilation of bloody tribal posts *and* the exteriorization of its own sacrificial violence effaced in classical Brahmanism. It is probably because of Jagannātha's identity with the tribal Vedic sacrificial post that the wood (*dāru*) for Jagannātha's new body during the Navakalevara is cut down from a tree chosen through such transgressive criteria as the following: on a snake hole with creeping snakes, beside an anthill; near a cremation ground, Śiva temple, river, pond; surrounded by three mountains, on a crossing of three ways (= confluence of rivers).[108]

Even the tribal goddess represented by the primitive forest posts fits in well with the female Tantric identity of Jagannātha as Kālī; and the androgynous pillars on the fringes of the Hinduizing process correspond to the feminization of the (royal) dīkṣita as he regresses into the forest-womb. The wooden posts representing Pōtu Rāju, often identified with Bhairava in Andhra Pradesh, are made of the fiery wood of the female—indeed maternal—*śamī* tree. The inner tension would seen to have split the yūpa model so that the post is doubled into a peripheral Pōtu Rāju before the village goddess temple at the very limits of the agglomeration, and an identical isolated post, also of śamī, often at the very centre of the village under (the marriage of) a pipal (*aśvattha*) and *nīm* (substituting for the śamī) tree. The ritual identity of centre and periphery becomes evident only when Pōtu Rāju, identical with Mahiṣāsura, is brought from the marginal post as a buffalo to be sacrificed to the goddess beside the central pillar of the village world. Arjuna becomes a eunuch only after having placed his fiery weapons in the womb of the śamī tree on the cremation ground hillock identified with (the corpse of) their "dead mother."[109] The "tribalization" of Vedic embryogony through such womb-symbols as river, pond, snake hole, etc., is especially striking in Maharashtra where Mhasobā, Birobā and especially Khaṇḍobā as Mārtaṇḍa-Bhairava live as a snake within the anthill; their mother, who is identified with Gaṅgā-Sūryavantī, the place of the hidden Sun, where the Agni-Soma treasure is retained in the symbolic value of turmeric powder.[110]

Bhairava represents all that terrifies the caste Hindu by violating the fundamental socio-religious norms that govern his life, and thereby functions as the natural focus and melting pot for the assimilation of countless local and regional tribal divinities outside these norms, but none of whom—not even Pōtu Rāju who has played a similar role in South India—can claim the pan-Indian, even pan-South Asian, and indeed Brahmanical credentials of Bhairava. If the "Kashmir Śaiva" Brahman theoreticians have preferred Bhairava among all possible divinities to represent the absolute (*Anuttara*) more absolute than the Brahman of Śaṃkara, this is no doubt because his criminal and tribal associations correspond perfectly to the ritual violations of Kaula praxis through the exploitation of extreme impurity in order to accede to this absolute. Although the transgressive ideology itself is Vedic and certainly Brahmanical, the exoteric classical image of the Brahman as the pivot of the system of socio-religious interdictions centered on purity necessitated the assumption of the transgressive function by another divinity who would appear as outside this socio-cultural universe, as wholly "Other."[111] And when this current assumes an institutionalized form, as in Tantrism, that would admit even outcastes and tribals and must hence necessarily appeal to extra-Vedic authority, it is clear that the fifth head of Brahmā, who for all his transgressive notations still remains strictly a god of the Brahmans and even then hardly worshipped, could no longer serve this purpose. Despite the numerous popular, folk, tribal, and even non-Indian elements that have contributed to the genesis and development of Tantrism, one recognizes "within the tantric systems the same fundamental notions as in the rest of Hinduism: the structure, identicial in its elements, is entirely overturned through a different utilization" based on an esoteric reading reversing the accepted values of the tradition.[112]

Much of the symbolic universe of the Kāpālika-Bhairava has been retained, minus the actual imitation of the Brahmanicide penance itself, in the ritual praxis of the later Kaulas, many of them Brahman householders, who based their practices, like the Kāpālikas, on the Bhairavāgamas.[113] In terms of spiritual orientation, however, the difference between the two currents appears to be primarily one of degree, although that would have been sufficient to necessitate a considerable deradicalization of the actual practice of the cult. The Kāpālikas were extremists in the sense that, although courting sensual pleasures, they had renounced normal life in the world and pushed asceticism and degradation to its very limits. In contrast, the householder Kaulas, precisely because they continued to live in the world and participate in the values of the caste society, had to cultivate and elaborate a closed private rather than an ostentatious public mode of the ideology of transgression. Unlike the unbridled almost disincarnate eroticism of Bhairava and his Kāpālika followers, the sexual transgression of the Kaula householder is especially modelled on that of Brahmā's fifth head: incest. Abhinavagupta attributes his highest metaphysical realization to his initiation into the technique of the "Kula-sacrifice" (*kulayāga*), also called "Primordial Sacrifice" (*ādiyāga*), consisting primarily in the bliss of transgressive sexual union, reinforced by the exceptional consumption of meat, wine, and even more impure reproductive and disgusting substances, like menstrual blood. He specifically recommends the choice of mother, sister, daughter, etc., as sexual partner (*dūtī*) and as in the case of the Vidūṣaka, the projection of the goddess incarnated in the partner as "hunch-backed" (*kubjā*), lame or otherwise deformed, underlines through a geometric, ambulatory or visual code the transgressive character of the union. The aim is to establish oneself in the absolute Bliss of Bhairava-Consciousness through the exploitation of the latter's partial and conditioned manifestation in the joy of sexual union, which is, however, more total and self-absorbing than the other pleasures of ordinary life, especially as it involves the participation of all the five senses and the mind resulting in their unification.

All the incoming sensory impressions serve as food to kindle and fuel the sexual fire that blazes forth to serve as the vehicle for the expansion of the unsullied all-devouring Consciousness.[114]

Outside of this esoteric technique and its soteriological intention, such fundamental transgressions are unequivocally condemned. They presuppose the tantric physiology by attempting during sex to redirect the dispersed energies of ordinary consciousness and the laterally opposed vital airs to the base of the spine before channelling their flow upwards along the axial suṣumnā, expressed mythico-ritually by the meeting of three ways, confluence of three rivers, killing of two snakes, opening of the third eye and so on. Embryogonic notations are also not lacking, as in the invocation of Ānanda-Bhairav(ī) in the wine pot (which also explains the fertile fishlets placed in them by the Newars during their Bhairava festivals), and especially in the androgynization of the officiant through wearing female attire and ornaments just after his consumption of the female reproductive substance (kulāmṛta) from the Śrī-Pātra which thereby transgressively fills him with Brahman. For the *bhrūṇa* is an embryo before its sex can be determined. The funerary notations from ancestor worship also suggest the initiatic death in the very act of intercourse, as is underlined by the recommended performance of this cakrapūjā in the cremation ground and by the initial invocation of Kālī engaged in inverted sexual union astride the corpse (*śava* = Śiva) of Mahākāla-Bhairava, sexual union with the deceased being optionally prescribed for the wife in certain Brahmanical funerary texts.[115] The final picture that emerges is that of the deathly embryonic regression of the wholly sexualized consciousness to the base of the spine before its upward ascent towards final liberation. The blissful state of Bhairava-Anuttara thereby realized is an indescribable indeterminate fusion of the twin-state (*yāmala*) of the quiescent transcendent (*śānta*) and emergent immanent (*udita*) poles of the supreme consciousness. Those intent on final emancipation concentrate exclusively on the former dimension, whereas those seeking the lordship of creative (magical) powers and longevity particularly cultivate the latter aspect. This integral mode of conceiving the bio-sexual and metaphysico-spiritual dimensions of the "primordial sacrifice" has permitted the claim that a child born of such an experience (*yoginībhū*) would be endowed with the innate disposition and extraordinary aptitude for reclaiming it for himself (see n. 115).

The continuity between the trances due to possession by the lowly folk or tribal divinity accompanied by savagery and miraculous feats made possible by the enhanced regenerative capacity of the body, and the deliberate metaphysical identification with the awesome mystery of the absolute, also called "possession by Bhairava" (*bhairavāveśa*), within the context of the Kulayāga or even independently through purely gnostic exercises, reveals itself even in the Trika retention of terms meaning "trembling, swooning," etc., which derive from that primitive base. The union of the highest gnostic Brahmans with the lowest impurest castes, associated with such public rites of possession, within the closed circles of orgiastic transgression, renders problematic any purely evolutionistic explanation of the tension within the term *āveśa*, "possession." Except for the intermediate zone where the external determinations of the caste society have imposed the central image of Brahmanicide on Bhairava, the symbolic configurations at the tribal level continue to reflect the esoteric psycho-physical techniques that have conferred the highest metaphysical realization on Abhinavagupta at the summit of the Hindu universe.

Although initially distorted by a structuralizing gaze, Lévi-Strauss' Amerindian *Mythologiques*, on careful rereading, progressively reveal a shamanistic world composed of the same or similar naturalistic symbols of transgression, embryogony, nectarine honey (or maple syrup), all-devouring fire, the "symplegades" motif, ascent up the world tree through the door of heaven, etc., that could be restored to its true dimensions by a hermeneutic based on the phenomenology of transgressive sacrality. "This ecstatic experience is not in opposition to the general theory of Brahmanic sacrifice, just as the shaman's trance fits in perfectly into the cosmo-theological system of the Siberian and Altaic religions. . . . It remains to inquire if Indian religious life, as a whole and with all the symbolisms that it includes, is a creation—'degraded' in a measure, in order to become accessible to the profane—produced by a series of ecstatic experiences on the part of a few privileged persons, or if, on the contrary, the ecstatic experience of the latter is only the result of an effort toward 'interiorization' of certain cosmo-theological schemas that precede it. The problem is pregnant with consequences . . ."[116] More precisely, it would be premature to claim that the tribal symbolic order owes these common structures to a tribalizing Hindu Bhairava, when the latter could himself have been born from the fusion of numerous tribal "Bhairavas" with the symbolic projection of the Brahman(ized) dīkṣita. The social distancing between orthodox Brahman and outcaste is only the permanent fixation of the opposition between the pure and the impure, which in primitive societies and in pre-classical Brahmanism are defined rather in terms of alternation. In predominantly tribal and less thoroughly Brahmanized

Nepal, where, to my knowledge, the Brahmanicidal origin myth is hardly retold and the corresponding Bhairavāṣṭamī not celebrated, Bhairava comes as often from Lhasa as from Vārāṇasī; and through the transgressive mytheme of his own decapitation, he has been enthroned as national god, a public status he has yet to attain in Hindu India.

I. Mitra-Varuṇa and the Niravasita-Bhairava: The Royal Mahābrāhmaṇa

The dialectic of transgressive sacrality provides us with fresh insights into the complex structural transformation of the Vedic dualistic universe dominated by the opposition between the deva Indra and the asura (Mitra-)Varuṇa into the subsequent Hindu trinity of Brahmā, Viṣṇu, and Rudra, each of whom is in his own way a "god of the Totality."[117] The term *Asura,* used only in the singular in the earliest portions of the Rig Veda, seems to have originally referred to a "Lord" of peoples hostile to the Indra-worshipping Āryans[118] and probably characterizes this Lord as endowed, like the later brahmán, with *mana*-like magical power (māyā). Although Mitra-Varuṇa, the Asura(s) par excellence, and the chief of the Devas, Indra, stem from two different cultural worlds, and perhaps even two opposing civilizations, they already reveal in the Vedic religion a significant structural opposition which can be defined just as well in terms of priestly "first" versus warrior "second" function or as sacred versus profane kingship.[119] Mitra-Varuṇa is a dual divinity because it expresses the complementarity of the pure interdictory Mitraic and the impure transgressive Varuṇic poles of Vedic sacrality, also translated into the opposition between the upper and nether worlds of a dualistic cosmos.[120] This internal opposition is retained in the later Brahmā of the ritual texts, for he is primarily the mythical projection of the purohitas, the foremost among whom, the Vāsiṣṭhas, are explicit incarnations (*maitrā-varuṇi*) of Mitra-Varuṇa.

Nevertheless, the overlapping functions of Indra and the Indian (and Iranian) Mit(h)ra, who shows the greatest reluctance to strike at Vṛtra (and bears the *vazra* like Indra's vajra), requires that we replace the notion of a spatial structure defined by fixed terms with a dynamic dialectic that seeks to define each mythico-ritual entity in terms of the vectors that determine its transformations. Such a dialectic, already implicit in the pre-classical dīkṣā, may be described as an upward movement of purification of the profane (royal) sacrificer represented by

Indra, who accedes to the sacred (only) through the mediation of the Mitraic pole of Brahmā before his transgressive plunge as the dīkṣita into the impure womb of Varuṇa. That this entire dialectic can be internalized within a single personage is indicated by the identification of sacrifice as Prajāpati with both Brahmā (officiant) and yajamāna or sacrificer represented by Indra (Heesterman, IC, pp. 27, 33, 50, 94; see n. 49). The mythic interferences and the hybrid figures that correspond to them on the socio-religious level must be reduced to their ideological coordinates in order to arrive at their Hindu transformation.

Brahmā represents the isolative domain of the sacred within the late Vedic cultural universe (*madhya deśa*) as opposed to non-Vedic India, which it could absorb and assimilate only by expanding and reorientating its profane pole so as to counter the secularizing tendency on its geographical borders, such as gave rise to post-axial Buddhism with its separation of a revalorized profane kingship finding its apogee in the Mauryan empire and Aśoka on the one hand and the exaggerated religious renunciation of the monastic order on the other.[121] Thus the Vedic Mitra practically disappears and Varuṇa is relegated to a subsidiary position, but without losing his embryonic associations with the subterranean waters and the demonized Asuras even in the epic (Kuiper, VV, pp. 74-93). Brahmā, although omnipresent, recedes to the background along with the this-worldly mythico-ritual sacrality of the pre-classical Brahman. Instead, the gods of bhakti rise to prominence with Viṣṇu embodying the vector uniting the profane Kṣatriya with the pure pole of Brahmā to generate the religious image of the king as the protector and even pivot of the socio-religious order (dharma), and Rudra incarnating the vector linking him with the transgressive pole of Brahmā to generate the equally religious image of the king as the savage destroyer in the impurity of the hunt and the violence of battle.[122] This explains how the model of the profane Hindu king, Arjuna son of Indra, can nevertheless be alternatively identified with Viṣṇu-Kṛṣṇa and also with Rudra-Śiva.[123] But if instead of Arjuna, the *Mahābhārata* crowns as king the "Brahman" Yudhiṣṭhira, identified as Dharma with his impure Śūdra alter ego Vidura, born "equal to Mitra-Varuṇa" who ruled over the earlier Vedic *ṛta*, this is because Yudhiṣṭhira expresses most fully the hidden (transgressively) sacred dimension of Hindu kingship that still underlies its secularized prolongation. Any total picture of Hindu kingship must necessarily integrate the sacred kingship of Yudhiṣṭhira and the profane kingship of Arjuna-Dhanañjaya as the complementary poles of a single model.[124]

If the Brahmanical tradition has succeeded in retaining its specific symbolic universe and the continuity of its cultural identity even in the process of "colonizing" the subcontinent, this has, however, been achieved only at the cost of reducing the public image of the ideal Brahman to his primarily ritual (and not racial) purity so as to confer upon him the social preeminence of the world-renouncer, even while he continues his ritual traditions. This classical reform of the Vedic sacrifice is epitomized by the transformation of the transgressive pre-classical dīkṣā into a purification of the sacrificer conferring upon him the temporary status of a Brahman.[125] The Vedic-Brahmanical universe of values occupies primarily the top-right triangle of the oversimplified transformative diagram below:

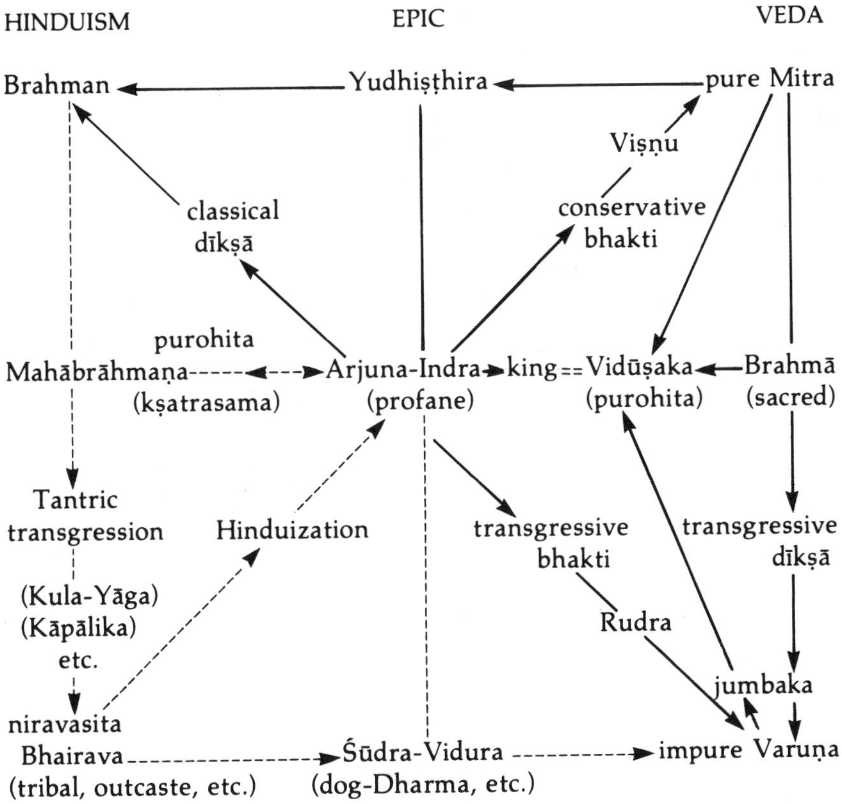

Transformation of Vedic "Dualism" into the Trinity of Hindu Bhakti

If we nevertheless find certain Hindu figurations like the *kṣatrasama* (= Kṣatriya) purohita beside the king, the impure sin-eating Mahābrāhmaṇa as representing the priestly Brahman, Dharma incarnated in the Śūdra Vidura, and the more problematic Brahmanicide and even tribal Bhairava, projected beyond the Brahman-Varuṇa axis onto the lower left triangle (where the vectors are represented by broken lines) enclosing the extra-Brahmanical universe, this is because these "lawful irregularities," although they each have their Vedic counterparts on the right half of the diagram, cannot be satisfactorily accounted for by the system of values of classical Brahmanism alone. That these disconcerting projections are not mere vestiges of the pre-classical system but serve a positive function is immediately evident in the key figure of the lowly kṣetrapāla extra-Vedic Bhairava, who has been exalted to occupy the transgressive position corresponding to that of Varuṇa in Vedic religion. That Bhairava should appear in the guise of Cāṇḍāla is natural in view of the latter's ritual functions of being excluded (niravasita) from the village, having dogs and donkeys for his wealth, wearing the garments of the dead and carrying corpses, and appropriating the belongings (clothes, ornaments, beds) of the criminals they execute, suggesting an identification (see nn. 97-8). The underworldly seat of Varuṇa's cosmo-ritual ṛta becomes the impure foundation of the socio-religious Dharma incarnated in the Śūdra Vidura and in Yudhiṣṭhira's dog before the latter reveals its transgressive dimension fully as Bhairava's theriomorphic form; and all these figures retain their essential identity with Yama, Dharma-Rāja, lord of Death.[126]

From a purely sociological standpoint, the Mahābrāhmaṇa as funerary priest is a category which is not pure enough to be ranked as a proper Brahman, and yet not so impure, like the Dom cast in the image of Yama-Rāja, as to cease being a Brahman. But I use the term Mahābrāhmaṇa here, still in accordance with Hindu usage, rather as a dialectical figure, extending to other personages like the purohita, Vidūṣaka, Pāśupata, and even the Brahman Kāpālika, who contains within himself the opposing extremes of the pure and the impure, Mitra-Varuṇa having become the transgressive conjunction of Brahman and outcaste. Rāmānuja condemns the Kāpālikas because they claimed that even a Śūdra could instantly become a Brahman by receiving the dīkṣā to ascetically undertake the Mahāvrata, and the Kusle descendants of the Kāpālikas play the role of Mahābrāhmaṇas among the Newars. Even the Dom-Rāja of Banaras claims descent from a *fallen* Brahman in an ancestral myth that simultaneously accounts for the origin of the Maṇikarṇikā tank. It is in this context of lawful irregularities generated by the suppressed affinity of Brahman and outcaste, that paradoxical sociological phenomena, inexplicable in terms of a purely linear non-cyclic hierarchy, like that of (only) the lowest outcastes (Cāṇḍāla) being contaminated by contact with Brahmans and not accepting food even from them, must ultimately be explained.[127]

The broken vectors reveal that, far from being symptomatic of the inner contradictions of the reformed classical system, its irregular projections serve as receptacles and tentacles governed by an implicit intentionality: assimilation of the non-Brahmanical universe without surrendering the continuity of Hindu identity with its roots in the Vedic Revelation. Thus we see two opposing yet complementary movements. On the one hand, there is the process of Hinduization or Sanskritization whereby tribal divinities are identified with Bhairava, who is himself whitened as he ascends the social hierarchy, just as entire groups of Śūdras and even tribals can acquire sufficient power and influence to receive Kṣatriya status, before receiving the purifying classical dīkṣā to become (temporary) Brahmans. And on the other hand the tantric Brahmans, like the Kāpālikas and Kaulas, descend through the dīkṣā to identify themselves, in the midst of egalitarian transgressive rituals, with Bhairava incarnated in the niravasita-Cāṇḍāla.

Also revealed in the diagram is that, from a socio-religious point of view, Hindu bhakti primarily serves the historically determined function of bridging the profane with the pure and impure poles of the sacred, which, however, survives independently of bhakti in the figure of the five-headed Brahmā whose fifth head is now borne by Bhairava. It is in this way that Viṣṇu and especially Rudra-Śiva, in whom the impure sacred can appear in the guise of the profane and vice versa,[128] could have played a crucial role in the process of Hinduization by countering, on the religious level, the Buddhist tendency to desacralize the world in favour of renunciation and transcendence alone. Although each of the Hindu trinity occupies only one face of the triangular Vedic structure, they are all equally entitled to be gods of the totality only by symbolically incorporating the opposing apex of the triangle and thereby revealing the dialectical movement of their interlocking identities. Thus Rudra finds his purified counterpart in the ascetic and auspicious Śiva, and Arjuna's very name "Bībhatsu" identifies him not only with the "Brahman" Ajātaśatru but also with the white foeless Mitra disgusted at the thought of doing violence to Vṛtra. Viṣṇu, like Arjuna, finds his black Varuṇic counterpart in the name Kṣṛṇa he assumes in the *Mahābhārata;* and Brahmā becomes profanized in the figure of the royal purohita projected as the martial Droṇa, or even the Brahmanized warrior Bhīṣma-Pitāmaha. The goddess, apparently eclipsed from this male-dominated scenario, participates as the tripled consort of the trinity and finds her centre of gravity at the womb-like Varuṇic pole as the menstruating Kṛṣṇā-Draupadī projected towards the effeminate long-haired Keśava as the auspicious Śrī-Lakṣmī. It is no doubt for this reason that she is identified in the Newar Bhīmsen temples with the blood-thirsty Bhairavī and placed between the vegetarian Arjuna and the bloody Bhīma-Bhairava (see n. 5).

Just as the passive sacred kingship of Dharmarāja is overshadowed by the active central role of Arjuna-Dhanañjaya intent on the conquest of the quarters (Jaya), it is the profanized public image of the Hindu king that occupies the mediating role in our diagram not only between the synchronic opposition of the pure and the impure but also diachronically between the Vedic heartland traced by the peripatetic sacrificial black antelope and the Hindu subcontinent with its imperial South East Asian expansion. His temporal power continues to participate in the legitimizing spiritual authority of the sacred only through the ritual bi-unity he forms with the royal purohita who always precedes him, just as the Kṣatriya Pārthasārathi (Kṛṣṇa) stands before Pārtha (Arjuna) as two Kṛṣṇas on the same chariot equipped for the sacrifice of battle.[129] Unlike his royal patron who is actively involved in the mundane preoccupations of his ephmeral realm, and although apparently on the same profane level as his indispensable but polluting partner, the Brahman purohita still remains primarily a specialist of the sacred, incorporating in himself the extreme tension between the pure Mitraic and the impure Varuṇic poles of Brahmā.

He appears problematic only because this deathly sin-eating pole has been systematically obscured in the classical image of the ideal Brahman. For the same reason, his symbolic counterpart in the deformed "Brahman par excellence" with his exaggerated (jumbaka) Varuṇic dimension now appears in the Sanskrit drama as the ridiculous extra-Vedic (*avaidika*) Vidūṣaka, with so many tantricized traits. Yet the Vidūṣaka, protected by Omkāra, is not only a Śrotriya through all his abundant Vedic symbolism. Even his sexuality reveals the triangular sacrificial dialectic: chastely warding off all the symbols of lust with his crooked stick on the one hand, and obscenely indulging in symbolic incest with the same upraised phallic kuṭilaka on the other, this "counsellor in the science of love" (*kāmatantrasaciva*) nevertheless furthers the royal hero's marriage with the heroine, herself incarnating the prosperity of the kingdom.[130] The (not only sexual) universalization offered to the king's profane individuality by the opposing poles of the sacred in the (brown-)monkey-like joking-companion (*narmasaciva*) is also reflected in the awesome multiform monkey-banner (*kapidhvaja*) of Arjuna's chariot, and finds its metaphysical expression in the terrifying "Universal Form" (*viśvarūpa*) assumed by Kṛṣṇa, himself elsewhere identified with the Vedic Vṛṣākapi or "Virile Monkey."

Although the twin gods of bhakti occupy and even encompass the two royal or profanizing faces of the sacrificial triangle, the dialectic of transgression is impossible without the vertical dimension of the sacred in Brahmā, in whom the opposing yet complementary poles of the pure and the impure are both separated and united. Indeed, not only does the dialectic of transgressive sacrality wholly encompass the universe of bhakti, it also finds independent and prior symbolic expression in the mytheme of Indra's Brahmanicide of his purohita Viśvarūpa.[131] If Bhairava later decapitates Brahmā with his left thumb-nail, he is only following the illustrious example of the ambidextrous royal Arjuna, who was not only guilty of Droṇa's Brahmanicide but also wielded, as Savyasācin, his infallible bow Gāṇḍīva with his unerring left hand. There has been hardly any need, until now, for an abstract Indian term corresponding to the complex concept of transgression when the Hindu vocabulary had already captured its dialectic in the vivid image of Indra's royal and Bhairava's criminal Brahmanicide, defining it with such mythico-ritual and even juridical precision. If it is Brahmā's inability to create that is responsible for his decapitation by the filial Śiva, this is only because the Brahmanical sacrifice is ultimately the process of winning life out of death. Although subordinated to the classical Brahman through his public image as the profane Indra, as the divine protector Viṣṇu and even perhaps as the ascetic yogin and destructive warrior Śiva-Rudra, the ambivalent Hindu king reasserts his independent magico-religious power as Lord of the Universe through his hidden tantric identity as the Brahmanicide Bhairava, but only because he thereby creatively incorporates in himself the dialectical Vedic figure of the universalizing royal Mahābrāhmaṇa.[132]

J. Bhairava Worship Today in North India and Nepal

Bhairava is no longer such a focus of transgressive practices as he was in the past, for his cult in India has been "Brahmanized," in the sense of purified, to such an extent that it nowadays differs little from the temple cult of any other orthodox Hindu divinity. This may be attributed to various socio-cultural transformations, especially the political domination of proselytizing and puritanizing Islam after the 12th century, followed by the socio-economic domination of the modern rationalizing mentality that has interrupted even the process of syncretic assimilation at the folk level reflected in the cult of Ghāzī Mīyā̃ (see n. 101) and the Five (Muslim) Saints (Pāñcõ Pīr) in the North, in such transgressive figures as Muttāl Rāvuttan, alias Muhammad Khān, in the southern Draupadī cult, and in Mallu Khān's sacrilegious "pilgrimage" to Mecca in the Central Indian cult of Mallanna.[133]

Although the Brahman priests offer meat, fish, and wine on behalf of their devotees to the divinity during special (*viśeṣa*) as opposed to "ordinary" (*sāmānya*) worship in the major "nuclear" temples, as in the Kālabhairava temples of Ujjain and Vārāṇasī, and connive at animal sacrifices performed by devotees sometimes in the compound, they do not offer blood sacrifices themselves (at least publicly) at these temples. Nevertheless, the dynamic head (*mahant*) of the Kamacchā Baṭuka-Bhairava temple (relatively recent, it is not included in the aṣṭabhairavas of Kāśī), next in popularity only to the Kāla-Bhairava temple, regularly offers goat sacrifices to the renowned goddess Vindhyāvāsinī at the Vindhyācal hills. She is guarded by Ānanda, Ruru, Siddhanātha and Kapāla Bhairavas to the east, north, west, and south, respectively, of the town, while Lāl Bhairava stands before the police station on the main road leading to her shrine. In all these temples, offerings of limes are presented as substitutes for human sacrifice. Within the compound of the goddess herself are images of Pañcagaṅgā, Kapāla, and Kāla-Bhairavas, and in April, 1986 I accompanied an all-male party led by the Mahant from Banaras in order to celebrate his restoration of the temple of Bhūta-Bhairava in the monkey-infested jungle behind the Kālī temple frequented by Ojhas (spirit mediums) on the other side of Vindhyācal. The popular and influential Mahant has himself composed a "Hymn to Baṭuka-Bhairava" (*stotram* in Sanskrit), and is actively involved in the celebration of Bhairavāṣṭamī and "Lāṭ kā Vivāḥ" (marriage) and other festivals at the Kālabhairava and Lāṭ-Bhairõ temples. Indeed, such is his activity that it is now rather Baṭuka Bhairava who plays the role of the traditional Krodhana Bhairava rather neglected in the nearby temple of the goddess Kāmākhya, whose own Mahant from the Nirvāṇī Akhāḍā is quite ailing. Baṭuka is in fact the *sāttvika* double of the less imposing but original Ādi (Krodhana-)Bhairava in a separate room of his temple, who still receives essentially *tāmasika* pūjā every evening on the model of the pañcamakāra performed by one of the most fervent, blissfully intoxicated (unmatta), disciples with fish, wine, meat, *puris* (mudrā) and *vadas* symbolizing *mithuna*. Although the Mahant himself performed the goat sacrifice for Bhūtanātha Bhairava in the forest, the party of revelers was subsequently offered two different modes of feasting (*bhoj*): vegetarian and non-vegetarian. Sometimes accompanied by a devotee seeking the fulfillment of particular desires (*kāmya*-pūjā), he still performs solitary worship in the cremation ground of the Hariścandra ghāṭ on the Gaṅgā by pouring wine on the śiva-liṅga, etc.

The founding story, retold by him, tells of an ascetic guru named something like Baṭuk or Śiva-Rām Puri who, having quarrelled with his disciple at Allahabad, decided to settle here at Kamacchā with his image of Krodha Bhairava in order to continue his *sādhana*. There his renown grew to the point of attracting the attention of the childless Balvant Singh. The royal embryogonic dimension is thus retained in the king of Banaras receiving a blessed fruit from the sādhu to beget his successor Rājā Chet Singh, and rewarding his new-found preceptor with land and properties. When the envious disciple came to rejoin his guru, the latter shed his mortal coils in a fit of anger and his *samādhi* is supposed to be beneath the shrine of the present "Original-Angry-Bhairava." The disciple, having assumed ownership of the properties, later rediscovered through a dream the image of Baṭuka Bhairava, which was excavated with the help of king Balavant Singh in the compound of the present temple built by the king in 1733 to commemorate the birth of his son. The present lineage of Mahants, descended from that rebellious disciple, found peace only after having observed a rigorous sādhanā for seven generations before Krodhana Bhairava, who is still worshipped as (the union of?) Ānanda Bhairava and Bhairavī. The mythical version of the goddess Caṇḍī having discovered Baṭuka-Bhairava as a child (*baṭu*) at the bottom of a lake during the universal dissolution (pralaya) and adopting him with compassion, which the Mahant attributes to the *Mārkaṇḍeya Purāṇa*, probably reflects the initiatory scenario of the baby Kṛṣṇa swallowing the eternal youth Mārkaṇḍeya during the pralaya.[134] Baṭuka is indeed considered the child of Sahasracaṇḍī, whose image is found within his sanctum.

The resilience of the cult, even quite independently of fixed institutionalized frameworks of transmission, may be judged from the example of an adept of Vikrānta-Bhairava at Ujjain. Living in a modern city environment and employed in the Vikram University, he has succeeded in attracting devotees from all walks of life, including university lecturers, government officials, journalists who make it their duty to report on its evolution, etc. Although originally an exclusive goddess-worshipper before establishing himself with his family at Ujjain, he had then visions of Bhairava and was directed by the goddess to meditate on Vikrānta-Bhairava. On the banks of backward flowing Kṣiprā, he kept nightlong vigils in the cremation ground beside the ruined and derelict temple of Vikrānta-Bhairava on the ancient city-pilgrimage route (*pañcakrośī*) around the outskirts of the city, whose sacred geography is modelled on that of Kāśī. Thereby he has acquired spiritual powers (*siddhi*) which permit him to exercise his clairvoyance *gratis* every morning for the general public that flocks to him. A regular weekly cult has now spontaneously revived at this temple, not far from the major temple of Kāla Bhairava once patronized by the Mahārājas, and his devotees gather there, despite its great distance, in the late evening for worship in a rather "neo-Vedic" mode with *havan*, etc. What is most interesting is that he has received no regular initiation into the worship of Bhairava, and has instructed himself into the appropriate ritual utterances (mantra), gestures (*nyāsa*), mystic diagrams (yantra), procedures (paddhati), etc., only after having received his vocation through visions. However, although it is his assiduous psycho-physical discipline (sādhana) that has reanimated the cult, the transgressive element is, as far as I can tell, completely effaced.

But the original character of Bhairava worship may be appreciated much better by balancing this picture with his various roles in Nepal, where he has always enjoyed Hindu royal patronage, first under the Licchavis like the famous Aṃśuvarman, then under the Newar Mallas, and now under the Gorkha Shāhs, patrons of the syncretizing Nāth cult. During the Bhairavī Rath Jātrā festival,[135] the dhāmī of Nuwakot is possessed by, or rather becomes, Bhairava, and his wife likewise incarnates Bhairavī who has an important temple there and is said to have conferred the Nepal Valley upon her devotee, the Gorkha conqueror Prithvī Nārāyan Shāh, creator of modern Nepal. The entire Newar community, with tribals from distant parts and the onlooking Gorkha people, participates in this Hindu festival, officiated over especially by Brahman Buddhist priests who now come all the way from Kathmandu. It climaxes in the sacrifice, especially when the "Sindūr Procession" reaches Devī-Ghāṭ on the confluence of the Taḍhi and the Triśūlī-Gaṅgā, of numerous goats and buffaloes, from whose gushing throats the dhāmī as Bhairava gulps down the fresh blood, just like the Bhairava dancer during the "Nine Goddess" (Navadurgā) dances of Bhaktapur. Then, before the shrine of Jālpa Devī at the confluence and in secret before the representative of the king of Nepal, he proclaims oracles for the entire kingdom which are then communicated to the king. Once in twelve years the dhāmī visits the king at Kathmandu in order to receive a new set of ritual attire and insignia. Pacali Bhairab himself is often represented in myth as a king with impure traits, sometimes from Vārāṇasī or Lhasa, who had the habit of frequenting the cremation ground beside the Bāgmatī (-Gaṅgā) before becoming petrified there after wrapping himself in a funeral mat (see n. 96). At Bhaktapur it is the used funeral mat of the highest Brahman, the rājapurohita, that serves as the canvas for painting the ritual mask of Ākāsh Bhairab that is affixed on the outer wall of his temple to receive public worship (see n. 132).

The Buddhist Mahākāla used to fly, it is said, between Kāśī and Lhasa, but was immobilized in mid-air by a powerful Tibetan Lama and forced to settle down at the edge of the Tuṇḍikhel royal parade ground. "In his role as defender and guardian, Mahākāla is one of the chief protectors of all the other Valley gods, a task he shares with Śaṅkaṭa Bhairava of Te-bahal, Kathmandu. In the Kathmandu Valley, representations of Mahākāla rarely conform to his textual description, and often incorporate aspects that are rightly those of other divinities: Saṃvara, Hevajra, and Heruka, emanations of Akṣobhya. Conceptually related to Bhairava, from whom he probably derives, the Buddhist deity is teamed with Bhairava in practice, shares some aspects of his iconography, and the name Mahākāla, one of Bhairava's epithets. Like Bhairava, too, Nepalis conceive of Mahākāla as a pīṭha *devatā*, the temple of the Tuṇḍikhel Mahākāla, Kathmandu, for example, representing his pīṭha, which is paired with a companion *deochem* inside the town. Thus it is often difficult, if not impossible, to distinguish the two deities. Iconographically, even the famous Kāla Bhairava of the Kathmandu Darbar Square conforms as much to Saṃvara as to Bhairava."[136] The spontaneity with which Tibetan pilgrims make it a point to venerate this Kāla Bhairab at Hanumān Dhoka is no doubt due to this identification. It is significant that the Newar Vajrācāryas, for whom Bhairava is to all appearance not the kuladevatā, are nevertheless custodians of his secrets and sometimes even central officiants at his public cult for the Hindu community.[137] Particularly venerated within the Gelugpa sect, the Vajra-Bhairava mentioned in an inscription of Śivadeva II is another name of the fierce Yamāntaka, and the history of his lineage worship is found in the Tibetan text entitled "Jam-Doyangs Bzhao-Pai Rdorje," where the revelation is attributed to Mahāsiddha Lalitavajra of Uddyāna. The Kāśī-Lhasa axis so constant in the Newar ethnography of Bhairava is probably to be explained by Tibetan Buddhism having played, after his original adoption from Hindu India, a preponderant role in the spread of his cult in Nepal.

Also known as Adālata (Court) Bhairava, the towering black solitary image of Kāla Bhairab before the palace gate at Hanumān Dhoka was the chief witness before whom government servants were annually sworn into office, a function that corresponds perfectly to his now practically defunct role of policeman-magistrate of Kāśī. Litigants and accused criminals also swore while touching Bhairava's foot, and he who bore false witness vomited and died on the spot. As late as the nineteenth century he was the occasional recipient of human sacrifices, such as (Mitra-) Varuṇa had earlier demanded in order to paradoxically maintain the awesome ṛta hidden firmly within the heart of the Vedic socio-cosmic order.[138] Although much of the symbolism surrounding Bhairava is no longer understood even by his most ardent devotees and the cult itself is being rapidly effaced, one has only to replace these symbols in their original context to recognize the transgressive mode of sacrality that inspires them. And although this symbolic constellation, an integral part of the galaxy of criminal gods and demon devotees, is typically and in many of its elements exclusively Indian, it is the vehicle of a dialectic of transgression that flourishes under different modalities in archaic and primitive religions and is not wholly absent in the other world religions. Increasingly claimed to be both historically and principally *the* original sacred, this ideology assumes in India the form of the terrifying Bhairava to pose awkward questions that we modernists, as ethical and rational humanists, would have no doubt preferred to leave unanswered, had not the secular counter-sciences of anthropology, psychoanalysis, and linguistics converged in the ever-widening and deepening archaeology of contemporary *scientia* to insistently proclaim with Michel Foucault the inevitable and imminent dissolution of an already shrunken Man.

NOTES

1. This greatly expanded revised version of my paper "Adepts of the god Bhairava in the Hindu tradition," presented to the Assembly of the World's Religions, 15-21 November 1985 (New York), will appear with further revisions in Sunthar and Elizabeth Visuvalingam, *Transgressive Sacrality in the Hindu Tradition*, Transgressive Sacrality Series vol. 1 (Cambridge, Mass.: Rudra Press). I am grateful to Harvey Paul Alper for having presented this version to the pilot conference on "Transgressive Sacrality in the Hindu Tradition," 15th Annual Conference on South-Asia, University of Wisconsin-Madison, 8 November 1986. I thank my husband, Sunthar Visuvalingam, for having provided the

basic interpretative framework for my materials on the Bhairava cult and for allowing me to use his unpublished materials on the Vidūṣaka. Thanks are also due to Hélène Brunner-Lachaux and F. B. J. Kuiper for detailed criticisms of this and earlier versions of the paper, and to Alf Hiltebeitel for his patient editing.

2. See P. V. Kane, *History of Dharmaśāstra,* 2nd ed., Govt. Oriental Series (Poona: Bhandarkar Oriental Research Institute, 1973), IV.10-31; 87-96 (expiations); II (1974), 147-151. The numerous versions of this Brahmaśiraś-chedaka myth from the Purāṇas can be found assembled and partly analyzed in the following five works: H. von Stietencron, "Bhairava," *Zeitschrift der Deutschen Morgenländischen Gesellschaft* (= ZDMG), Supplementa I, Part 3 (1969), 863-71; W. D. O'Flaherty, *Asceticism and Eroticism in the Mythology of Śiva* (1973; rpt. Delhi: Oxford Univ. Press, 1975), 123-7, and *The Origins of Evil in Hindu Mythology* (Delhi: Motilal Banarsidass, 1976), 277-86; S. Kramrisch, *The Presence of Śiva* (Delhi: Oxford University Press, 1981), 250-300; E. Meyer, *Aṅkāḷaparamēcuvari: A Goddess of Tamilnadu, Her Myths and Cult,* Beiträge zur Südasienforschung, Südasien Institut, Heidelberg University, vol. 107 (Wiesbaden: Franz Steiner Verlag, 1986), esp. 36-8, 158-215 (kapparai = Brahmā's head).

3. See D. Lorenzen, *The Kāpālikas and Kālāmukhas: Two Lost Śaivite Sects* (Delhi: Thomson Press, 1972); J. P. Parry, "Sacrificial Death and the Necrophagous Ascetic," in *Death and the Regeneration of Life,* ed. M. Bloch and J. Parry (Cambridge Univ. Press, 1982), 74-110 and "The Aghori Ascetics of Benares" in *Indian Religion,* ed. R. Burghart and A. Cantlie (London: Curzon Press, & N. York: St. Martin's Press, 1985), 51-78; G. W. Briggs, *Gorakhnāth and the Kānphaṭā Yogīs* (1938; rpt. Motilal Banarsidass, 1982), 218-27, 159-61; G. Unbescheid, *Kānphaṭā: Untersuchungen zu Kult, Mythologie und Geschichte Śivaitischer Tantriker in Nepal,* Beiträge zur Südasienforschung, Südasien Institut, Heidelberg University, vol. 63 (Wiesbaden: Franz Steiner Verlag, 1980).

4. In the Hindi film "Bhairavī of the Netherworld," (*Pātāla-Bhairavī*), which played all over Northern India around 1985, the tantric adept seeks magical powers through human sacrifice to the goddess. The manner in which the unwitting hero-apprentice tricks the would-be Nepali executioner into himself becoming the victim corresponds exactly to one of the founding legends of the Nava Durgā cult of Bhaktapur, itself associated with human sacrifice, recorded by G. Toffin, *Société et Religion chez les Néwars du Népal* (Paris: Centre National de la Récherche Scientifique, 1984), 468-69. Although the message of the film is modern and recommends the rejection of such dangerous powers, the scenario is the stereotyped traditional one.

5. M. Anderson, *Festivals of Nepal* (London: Allen & Unwin, 1971), 235; Bhīma-sena's twelve-yearly visit to Lhasa in the form of a Newar farmer, is linked with their embryonic thirteenth year of exile (p. 238). The impure aspects of the menstruating Kṛṣṇā are very well described in A. Hiltebeitel, "Draupadī's Hair," *Autour de la Déesse Hindoue,* ed. M. Biardeau, *Puruṣārtha* 5, 179-214.

6. G. D. Sontheimer, *Birobā, Mhaskobā und Khaṇḍobā: Ursprung, Geschichte und*

Umwelt von Pastoralen Gottheiten in Mahārāṣṭra, Schriftenreihe der Südasien-Institut der Universitatät Heidelberg, vol. 21 (Wiesbaden: Franz Steiner Verlag, 1976); G. S. Nepali, *The Newars: An Ethno-Sociological Study of a Himalayan Community* (Bombay: United Asia Publ., 1959), 298-305.

7. Kubernath Sukul, *Vārāṇasī-Vaibhav* (Patnā: Bihār Rāṣṭrabhāṣā Pariṣad, 1977), 102-7 (in Hindi); D. L. Eck, *Banaras: City of Light* (London: Routledge & Kegan Paul, 1983), 189-201; E. Visuvalingam, "Bhairava: Kotwāl of Vārāṇasī," in *Vārāṇasī Through the Ages*, ed. T. P. Verma et al., Bhāratīya Itihāsa Saṅkalan Samiti Publ., no. 4 (Vārāṇasī: BISS, 1986), 241-60.

8. See N. Gutschow, *Stadtraum und Ritual der newarischen Städte im Kathmandu Tal: Eine architekturanthropologische Untersuchung* (Stuttgart: Kohlhammer, 1982), 50-53; M. Slusser, *Nepal Mandala: A Cultural Study of the Kathmandu Valley* (Princeton: Princeton Univ. Press, 1982), vol. I, 328, 345-6; Toffin, *Société et Religion*, 441-2, 458-66; J. F. Vézies, *Les Fêtes Magiques du Nepal* (Paris: Cesare Rancillo, 1981), 26-7. For Maharashtra, see Sontheimer, *Birobā*, 97, 192. For Airlines emblem, see Vézies, 70, 162; Anderson, *Festivals*, 151.

9. For Bhaktapur, see Gutschow, 63, 96-102; Slusser, 347-8; for Patan, see Anderson, 145; Vézies, 65-66.

10. J. K. Locke, *Karuṇamaya: The Cult of Avalokiteśvara/Matsyendranātha in the Valley of Nepal* (Kathmandu: Centre of Nepal and Asian Studies, Tribhuvan Univ., 1980), 427-36. Although patronized chiefly by the farmer (Jyapu) caste, the regular officiants at the Bāgh Bhairab temple of Kīrtipur (Nepali, *Newars*, 301-2, linking it to the Baghoba or Vaghdeo of Maharashtra) and the original Pachali Bhairab at Pharping (my fieldwork in Sept.-Oct. 85) are Kusles. For the problematic relation, between the Kusles and the Kānphaṭās, see Unbescheid, *Kānphaṭā*, 130-51.

11. There are Jaina tantric texts, like the *Bhairavapadmāvatīkalpa* (1047 A.D.) of Malliṣena (Mysore), dealing with transgressive Bhairava-type rituals of black magic, which need to be reconciled with the exaggerated role of ascetic self-denial and non-violence in Jaina orthodoxy. With Mahānātha for her Bhairava, the Hindu Pūrṇeśvarī also received Jaina worship and the ritual founding of her pīṭha is described in the *Śrīpadmāvatīpūjana*, a Śākta treatise.

12. "The god of the great temple of pilgrimage is—whatever be his name and his myth—the pure god, withdrawn into himself, the god of ultimate salvation. His most "terrible" forms are besides considered at the limit to be not proper for the cult, because dangerous even for the devotees. They are relegated to the most inaccessible sites, surrounded with all kinds of taboos, pacified with appropriate offerings. . . . In short, even though the god is the master of the universe of which the temple is the centre, he does not have *hic et nunc* a direct function of protector. This is delegated to an inferior god, Bhairava being the protector of territory—kṣetrapāla—in his classic form. The principal sanctuary does not pretend to represent the god in his supreme form—*contradictio in terminis*—but suggests to the maximum his renunciate nature as the

final reason of the world"; M. Biardeau, *L'Hindouisme: Anthropologie d'une Civilization* (Paris: Flammarion, 1981), 149 (author's translation).

13. F. A. Marglin, *Wives of the God-King: The Rituals of the Devadāsīs of Puri* (Delhi: Oxford University Press, 1985), 197. While reporting on the secret Kaula (Bhairava-) cakrapūjā being performed in the Jagannātha temple, Marglin (p. 218) refers to the rumors of a secret underground chamber located beneath the inner sanctum, pointing out parallels of cakrapūjās being performed below the sanctum elsewhere (p. 328, n. 4); there is one, now in disuse, in the Banaras Aghori ashram. During our pilgrimage (June 1985) to Badrīnāth, the Rāwal himself confirmed that there was a "*bhairavī-cakra*" beneath the main image, and J. C. Galey informs me (oral communication, Feb. 1986) that formerly the king used to ride to battle wearing the arm-band of Bhairava supposedly kept beneath the image of Badrīnāth. Such facts only serve to reinforce my earlier solution to the riddle "Bhairava: Policeman, Criminal or Supreme Divinity of Transgression?" (Kotwāl, 257-9) that Bhairava is indeed the ultimate form of Viśvanāth. This article aims to demonstrate this from the perspective of transgressive sacrificial embryogony.

14. There are three basic iconographic representations of Bhairava which derive from this myth. As Brahmaśiraśchedaka he grasps by its hair the severed head whose dripping blood is greedily lapped up by his dog. As Kaṅkālamūrti he is shown spearing a man or already bearing the latter's corpse (or skeleton) on his shoulder. In both cases, he is either naked or wearing a tiger or elephant skin, a garland of human skulls, snakes around his neck and arms, and is grotesque with dark-skin and monstrous fangs. Third, as the milder Bhikṣāṭanamūrti he roams begging for alms (from the wives of the Seven Sages in the Daru forest).

15. G. S. Ghurye, *Indian Sadhus*, 2nd ed. (Bombay: Popular Prakashan, 1964), 103ff; Lorenzen, *Kāpālikas*, 46; S. Sinha and B. Saraswati, *Ascetics of Kashi: An Anthropological Exploration* (Varanasi: N. K. Bose Memorial Foundation, 1978), 93; Swami Sadānanda Giri, *Society and Sannyāsin: A History of the Dasanāmi Sannyāsins* (Rishikesh: Sadānanda Giri, 1976), 21 (for list of *maḍhis*). See Briggs, *Gorakhnāth*, 10-11, for Gūdara, "the Aughar sect of Śaivites founded by a Dasnāmi by the name of Brahmagiri, through the favour of Gorakhnāth, who is said to have invested the ascetic with his ear-rings" (cf. also Ghurye, 107). The spear emblem of the Mahānirvāṇi Akhāḍā is known as Bhairavaprakāśa (Ghurye, 105; Giri, 27) and, according to Briggs, the Dasanāmis, who were "special devotees of Bhairava" (p. 12, n. 4), also wore the *hāl mataṅgā* cord of the Kānphaṭā Yogis. Bhairava is indicated by a black dot and line (respectively, between and below two curved red horizontal lines indicating Hanumān), in the ṭīkā of a Dasanāmi (loc. cit.)

16. Ghurye, *Indian Sadhus*, 108. According to one of the informants of Sinha and Saraswati, *Ascetics*, 93-4, "there are sixty-four Maḍhis among the Shaiva Saṃnyāsis of which the Dasanāmis have fifty-two Maḍhis and the Nāthpanthis have twelve, Bārahpanthi as they [the Nāths] call themselves. It is

interesting that on the samādhi of Bhartṛhari, located in the fort of Chunar, the Nāthpanthis and the ascetics of Joona Akhara officiate by turn as priest and Mahanta. From the list of the Mahantas of the samādhi, it transpires that in the line of Munnanāth, Kaṅgalināth, Jakhanāth, and Tulsīnāth—all Nāthpanthis—came Kamalānanda Bhārati and Jagadānanda Giri—the Dasanāmi. At present, a disciple of Jagadānanda Giri is acting as the priest of the samādhi while a disciple of Sandhyānāth stays there and gets a share of the collections. All these point to a tradition that brings the Nāgas closer to the Nāthpanthi Yogis."

17. E. Visuvalingam, "Kotwāl," 247 (see n. 7). Among the other Bhairavas of Haridwar, the Kāla Bhairava temple just before the Bilvakeśvara Mahādeva, although still officiated by a (female) Nāth, has fallen into the possession of the Ānanda Akhāḍā. The Kāla-Bhairava shrine (facing a Baṭuka Bhairava shrine), within the Paśupatināth Mahādeva temple now belonging to the Nirañjanī Akhāḍā, was (re-?)installed by a problematic Śravannāth, and the Nirañjanī Akhāḍā is itself located further downstream on the Śravannāth Ghāṭ.

18. *Abhinavagupta and the Synthesis of Indian Culture*, ed. S. Visuvalingam, Kashmir Shaiva Series (Cambridge, Mass.: Rudra Press, forthcoming). For a preliminary discussion, see especially his paper presented to the national seminar (Srinagar, 20-24 September 1986) on "The Significance and Future of Kashmir Shaivism," appearing in the same volume.

19. "O Death (= Time)! do not cast thy gaze most terrible with anger on me; (for) steadfast in the service of Śaṃkara and ever meditating on him, I am the terrifying power of Bhairava!" *Bhairavāṣṭaka*, v. 4. Cf. L. Silburn, *Hymnes de Abhinavagupta* (Paris: Institut de Civilization Indienne, 1970), 48, 50, 53. Also S. Kramrisch, *Presence*, 281-87.

20. See n. 2. The variations bear on a number of points like the father-son relationship between Brahmā and Rudra, presence or absence of Viṣṇu, direct decapitation by Rudra or indirectly through Bhairava, the ascetic or transgresive connotation of Brahmā's fifth head, and so on. In one version, the beheading episode is preceded by that of the emergence of the cosmic liṅga. I give below only an abridged and simplified rerendering of the *Kūrmapurāṇa* version.

21. See S. Visuvalingam in this volume. I thank the Government of India, first the Ministry of Education and Culture, then the University Grants Commission, for having consistently supported this research, which I am presently continuing with the Romain Rolland fellowship from the French Government. I also thank Niels Gutschow, Corneille Jest, Charles Malamoud, André Padoux, and Gérard Toffin for their interest in my work.

22. Despite its general associations with ritual purity, the formless Omkāra, who assumes (human) form to laughingly reconfirm the eternal sexual biunity (mithuna) or twin (yāmala) nature of Śiva, is itself already identified as a Mithuna (sexed couple) in *Chāndogya Upaniṣad* (I.1.6). The conceptions of mithuna

and yāmala are indissociable in tantric doctrine and practice as attested to particularly by the *Yāmala* group of Tantras, subdivided into *Brahma-*, *Rudra-*, *Jayadratha-* and other Yāmalas. "Internal evidence suggests that the Yāmalas were produced by circles which developed a tendency towards Śāktism. P. Ch. Bagchi—perhaps exaggeratedly—credits the authors of the Yāmalas—by tradition they were the eight Bhairavas, manifestations of Śiva—with some important new developments, among which are the Śākta orientation and the rendering accessible of their sādhanā to non-Brahmans"; see T. Goudriaan, *Hindu Tantrism*, Handbuch der Orientalistik, Zweite Ableitung, vol. 4, 2 (Leiden: E. J. Brill, 1979), 22; cf. 11.

23. For the oppositional identity of Yama and Kāla-Bhairava, expressing that between (the ritualization of) natural and (the lived experience of) initiatic death, see my "Kotwāl," 253-56, and Stein, n. 89 *infra*. Yamāntaka is likewise identical with Yama; Stein, *Dictionnaires des Mythologies* (offprint; Paris: Flammarion, 1981), 5. In fact, originally Yama himself seems to have had an initiatory function as in the Naciketas legend, which he would have retained in his later role of Dharmarāja.

24. J. Deppert, *Rudra's Geburt: Systematische Untersuchungen zum Inzest in der Mythologie der Brāhmanas*, Beiträge zur Südasien-Forschung, Südasien-Institut, Heidelberg University, vol. 28 (Wiesbaden: Franz Steiner Verlag, 1977), p. 129, n. 1, rightly links the stuck-fast head of Brahmā to the "rolling head" of the Vedic Namuci, decapitated by Indra, and underlines the parallelisms with the Amerindian mythology treated by Lévi-Strauss, where the all-devouring, polluting head is again sometimes transformed into the moon (Soma). It would be interesting to attempt to reinterpret Lévi-Strauss' "transformation" in the light of this analysis of the (transgressive) significance of the *Brahmaśiras* (see nn. 27 and 116 below). For Viṣvaksena, see Deppert, 283-84.

25. The incessant resounding of the dancing Bhairava's anklet bells can still be heard at a certain spot in Kāñci. See R. Dessigane, P. Z. Pattabiramin and J. Filliozat, *Les Légendes Çivaites de Kāñcipuram: Analyse de textes et iconographie*, Publications d'IFI no. 27 (Pondicherry: Institut Français d'Indologie, 1964), items no. 40 and no. 49, p. 44, no. 65 (p. 95).

26. Lorenzen, *Kāpālikas*, 74-81, 92-95; Stietencron, "Bhairava," 867; O'Flaherty, *Origins of Evil*, 285; (see nn. 3 and 2).

27. Lorenzen, *Kāpālikas*, 82-3, 90-2. See W. D. O'Flaherty, *Sexual Metaphors and Animal Symbols in Indian Mythology* (1980, rpt. Delhi: Motilal Banarsidass, 1981), 17-61 on sexual fluids. A reanalysis of the mythico-ritual complex centred on honey in South America and on its equivalent maple-syrup in North America in the light of the psycho-physical techniques employed for the "alchemical" production of "nectar" (amṛta) in the Tibetan traditions interpreted by R. A. Stein will no doubt reveal a universal "Soma-doctrine" exploiting radical impurities like menstrual blood (see nn. 24 and 116). See C. Lévi-Strauss, *Mythologiques II: Du Miel aux Cendres* (Paris: Plon, 1967) and *Introduction to a Science of Mythology III: The Origin of Table Manners* (New York: Harper & Row, 1979), 412-22.

28. See S. Visuvalingam's section B. in this volume. Also J. Parry, "Death and Cosmogony in Kashi," *Contributions to Indian Sociology*, 15, Nos. 1 and 2 (1981), 361; "Sacrificial Death," pp. 80 and 102, n. 14; see n. 3 *supra*.

29. Lorenzen, *Kāpālikas*, 17, 76-87; cf., Briggs, 108-9.

30. For the mahāpātakas, see Kane, *History of Dharmaśāstra*, IV, 10-31, and II, 757ff. for food pollution.

31. Biardeau, in M. Biardeau and C. Malamoud, *Le Sacrifice dans l'Inde Ancienne*, Bibliothèque de l'École des Hautes Études, Sciences Réligieuse, vol. LXXIX (Paris: Presses Universitaires de France, 1976), 100-2.

32. Cf. E. Visuvalingam, "Kotwāl," 257. For this equivocal logic of polarized values proper to myth but which is necessarily reduced and fragmented in their translation or development into sectarian and especially rationalizing philosophical thought, see J.-P. Vernant, *Myth and Society in Ancient Greece* (Sussex: Harvester Press; New Jersey: Humanities Press, 1980), chaps. 7 and 9, and especially 239-40.

33. The best analysis of the complex structural relation between Brahmā, Viṣṇu, and Rudra in terms of the Brahmanical sacrifice is found in Biardeau, *Le Sacrifice*, 89-106; *L'Hindouisme*, 107-8; and *Dictionnaire des Mythologies* (Flammarion: offprint, no date) on "Viṣṇu/Śiva: Dieux suprêmes de la *bhakti* hindoue" (134-8).

34. For the universally fundamental character of the blood-taboo, see L. Makarius, *Le Sacré et la Violation des Interdits* (Paris: Payot, 1974), 22 and *passim*.

35. The non-dualistic Śaivism of Kashmir has borrowed and inherited many elements like its cosmological schemas from earlier Pāñcarātra schools prevalent in that region. Cf. A. Eschmann, "Varāha and Narasiṃha" and "Narasiṃha's Relation to Śaivism and Tribal Cults" in *Cult of Jagannātha*, 101-6, also 175 (see n. 86 *infra*).

36. Walter F. Otto, *Dionysos: Le Mythe et le Culte* (Paris: Mercure de France, 1969), 211-17; Marcel Detienne, *Dionysos mis à Mort* (Paris: Gallimard, 1977), 204, and *Dionysos à Ciel Ouvert* (Paris: Hachette, 1986), 31-3, 98. Cf. also the problem of the Dionysiac Hyacinth, whose tomb lay beneath the statue of Apollo at Amyklai; Agamemnon's sacrifice to Dionysos in the sanctuary of Apollo; Delphos, eponym of Delphi, born from the union of Apollo with Thyia who first served Dionysos and gave her name to the Thyiades who led their furious dances on Parnassus for both Dionysos and Apollo (Otto, *loc. cit.*). See also W. Burkert, *Homo Necans: The Anthropology of Ancient Greek Sacrificial Ritual and Myth* (Berkeley: Univ. of California Press, 1983), 123ff. The extent to which Dionysos can be (re-)interpreted in the light of the dialetic of transgressive sacrality and the symbolic configuration it has assumed around the figure of Śiva-Bhairava (see Detienne, 1986, p. 7) may be judged from S. Visuvalingam's Section A. in this volume.

37. Otto, *Dionysos*, 217, 151. In the *Bacchantes* of Euripides, Tiresias, the hoary Bacchant, belongs to Apollo, the other great god of Thebes, and alone among those close to Pentheus, he will be spared the animosity of Dionysos: "without

outraging Phoibos, he honours Bromios, the Great God (*Megas Theos*)" (Detienne, 1986, 46). "Finally theological speculation even identified them" (Otto, 212; cf. also Detienne, 1986, 92).

38. For the two poles, pathological and divine, of the Greek *mania* and its Dionysiac character, see Vernant in J.-P. Vernant and P. Vidal-Naquet, *Mythe et Tragédie II* [henceforth MT II], (Paris: La Découverte, 1986), 18, 40 (wine), 241 (Rohde), 245, 260-7; criticized by Detienne, 1986, p. 108, n. 79; cf. also Otto, *Dionysos*, 101, 132-6; and Burkert, *Homo Necans*, p. 184, n. 25. Like Dionysos, Bhairava is even identified with the wine that flows freely in the tantric orgies; see Otto, 107-8, and ch. 12; Detienne, 1986, 45-66. It is the thread of transgressive sacrality that holds together the semantic fluctuations of the term *unmatta* meaning "drunk," "mad," even "foolish" and especially "ecstatically joyful." For the reductionist rationalism underlying the procedures of exclusion that finally made possible the modern endeavor to "capture" folly by clinically objectivizing its abnormal manifestations, see Michel Foucault, *Madness and Civilization: a History of Insanity in the Age of Reason*, 2nd ed. (London: Tavistock, 1971). For the confrontation of psychoanalysis and "enigmatic folly," see *Transgressive Sacrality in the Hindu Tradition* (see n. 1).

39. See Otto, *Dionysos*, chaps. 3 and 16, for the intimate links of Semele (and Aphrodite) with the consort of Dionysos, Ariadne, who also dies during pregnancy and lies at Argos in the underground sanctuary of the "Cretan" Dionysos (190-7; Detienne, 1986, p. 105, n. 45). Ariadne has also affinities with the humid element and the ocean, from which Aphrodite was born.

40. E. Visuvalingam, "Kotwāl" (see n. 7), 254; and 255-6 for bhairavī-yātanā; 257-60 for "purification," which may be understood rather as the re-inscription of transgression in a sacralizing symbolic order. See also Eck, *Banaras*, 324-44. Cf. O'Flaherty, *Origins of Evil*, 167, on Indra; see n. 2.

41. These secret traditions are being divulged only because the traditional pūjāris, who have recently been dispossessed of their rights in the Viśvanātha temple, now feel freer to speak about them, especially as they also fear that these rites have been discontinued.

42. For the variations of this formula, but based on the same principle of ascending interdictions and descending transgressions, see Kane, *History of Dharmaśāstra* (see n. 2) V, pt. 2, p. 1076, n. 1744. For an informed discussion, see Abhinavagupta, *Tantrāloka* IV.24, 247-53 (with commentary). The Kāpālika's Brahmanhood is suggested by the legal exception that a Brahman (alone) may kill a Brahman.

43. Kramrisch, 264; O'Flaherty, *Asceticism*, 126; Meyer, *Aṅkāḷaparamēcuvari*, 166-7, 36 (on malicious laughter); 37, 161-5 (on greed); see n. 2.

44. Makarius, *Le Sacré*, 282, 287 (see n. 34). Cf. the various instances classified in Dayak under *djeadjea* "acts contrary to nature" in R. Caillois, *L'Homme et le Sacré*, 2nd ed. (Paris: Gallimard, 1950), 100-1, and in C. Lévi-Strauss, *Les Structures Élémentaires de la Parenté* (1967; rpt. Paris: Mouton, 1971), 567-8. For the symbolic

equivalence of noisemaking, eclipses, incest, unruliness, and polychromy, see Lévi-Strauss, *The Raw and the Cooked: Introduction to a Science of Mythology* I (1970; rpt. Harmondsworth: Penguin, 1986), 312 and *passim*.

45. Lorenzen, *Kāpālikas*, 75; Deppert, 102-3.

46. See G. K. Bhat, *The Vidūṣaka* (Ahmedabad: The New Order Book Co., 1959), 51, 258, for the donkey-voiced Vaikhānasa of the *Kaumudīmahotsava;* 127, 247, for Vasantaka's blasphemous lying in the *Ratnāvalī*. The most learned Śrotriyas of the Veda were barred by the legal codes from giving witness at trials. For Dionysos' links with the ass, see Otto, *Dionysos*, 179; see n. 36.

47. Information and photocopy of relevant pages of manuscript by courtesy of Dr. G. J. S. (Alexis) Sanderson, Oxford.

48. In Rājaśekhara's *Karpūramañjarī* where Kapiñjala, serving as "court-jester" (Bhat, *Vidūṣaka*, 135), finally officiates as the priest in the king's wedding brought about by the grace of Bhairavānanda.

49. By J. C. Heesterman, *The Inner Conflict of Tradition: Essays in Indian Ritual, Kingship and Society* [henceforth IC] (Chicago: University of Chicago Press, 1985), 45-58, on the central human head of the *Agnicayana*.

50. Sunthar Visuvalingam, "Abhinavagupta's Conception of Humour: Its Resonances in Sanskrit Drama, Poetry, Hindu Mytholgy and Spiritual Praxis," Diss. Banaras Hindu University (1983).

51. See G. U. Thite, "Significances of the *Dīkṣā*," *Annals of the Bhandarkar Oriental Research Institute* 51 (1971), 163-73, for the "Brahmanization" (of even the Kṣatriya Indra) through the dīkṣā (169) as "purification" (171-2). See esp. *infra* n. 125. In Deppert, *Rudra's Geburt* (see n. 24), pp. lvi, 56, 82, 90, the contradiction between the apparent purification and the (symbolic) incest has led to the false assumption that the latter mahāpātaka represents the symbolic exaggeration of Brahmanical ritual purity, unfortunately undermining the basic argument of this otherwise most original and stimulating book.

52. J. C. Heesterman, "Vrātya and Sacrifice," *Indo-Iranian Journal*, 6 (1962), 1-37; and also his paper on "The Notion of Anthropophagy in Vedic Ritual," presented to the pilot conference on "Transgressive Sacrality in the Hindu Tradition"; also IC, 40, 86, 92, 227 n. 46 (see nn. 1 and 49). The problem of the warrior-Brahman pointing to vrātya-circles (ibid., 3, 106) is retained in the aggressively militant (*ātatāyin*) Brahman who seems to point to Kāpālika-type circles, and the *Dharmaśāstras* are obsessed by the question whether slaying such a Brahman, who has otherwise no place in their official system of values, constitutes a Brahmanicide requiring expiation (p. 162). Cf. Kane, *History of Dharmaśāstra* (see n. 2), II, 148-151; III (1973), 517-8; IV, 19, where the possibility of the ātatāyin being full of tapas and expert in Vedic lore is raised.

53. In this case, it would have also been connected with Indra's pole (dhvaja) festival celebrated around the New Year; F. B. J. Kuiper, *Varuṇa and Vidūsaka: On the Origin of the Sanskrit Drama* [henceforth VV] (Amsterdam: North Holland Publishing Co., 1979), 134-7, 30. Kramrisch, *Presence*, 250-1, 294-5; Deppert,

Rudra's Geburt, 3-6, 81-93, 265-284 (myths 1-4, 10); see nn. 2 and 24. The term *Aṣṭakā* indicates originally the eighth lunar day of the dark half of the month, and later especially of the months of Mārgaśīrṣa, Pauṣa, and Māgha, as a time particularly appropriate for the performance of funerary rites (śrāddha). Because the year began in ancient times on the full moon of Māgha, its eighth, considered even younger than the beginning of the year and marked by the first and most important festival, was called *Ekāṣṭaka*, the wife of the Year, when those undertaking the *Samvatsarasattra* should undergo the dīkṣā; Kane, *History of Dharmaśāstra* (see n. 2) IV, 353-6, n. 805; V. 1, 660. In *Atharvaveda* III, 10, *Ekāṣṭaka*, the day of Indra's birth (v. 12), is sung not only as the mother of Indra and Soma but also as the daughter of Prajāpati (v. 13), apparently replacing the Uṣas of the Vedic New Year (Deppert, *Rudra's Geburt*, 190).

54. Lorenzen, *Kāpālikas* (see n. 3), 2, 13, 27, 41, 54-5 *Mattavilāsa*, 60 *Prabodhacandrodaya*, esp. 80-1.

55. Kramrisch, *Presence*, 257-9; Makarius, *Le Sacré* (for transgressive magic).

56. See G. Dumézil, *Mythe et Épopée I: L'Idéologie des trois fonctions dans les épopées des peuples indo-eruopéens* (Paris: Gallimard, 1968), 191-203, 213-20, 253 [henceforth ME I); M. Biardeau, "Études de Mythologie Hindoue [henceforth EMH]: Bhakti et Avatāra," part IV, vol. LXIII (1976), p. 124 n. 1, p. 212 n. 2; and part V, vol. LXV (1978), 121-5, 151-5 for its equivalence to the *Pāśupatāstra* obtained by Arjuna from Rudra, both parts in *Bulletin de l'École Française d'Extrême Orient* (Paris); Kramrisch, *Presence*, 257-9.

57. Although it is Dhṛṣṭadyumna who actually decapitates Droṇa, the Kāñcī myth makes Arjuna absolve himself of the Brahmanicide at its Kapālamocana-like Caruvatīrtha, just as Aśvatthāman does for his foeticide (Dessigane et al., *Légendes Çivaite*, 62; see n. 25). It is through Śukra's Brahmanicide, identified with his consumption of wine and "hair" (=kaca), that Bṛhaspati's son Kaca wins the secret of immortality in the stomach-womb of the demoniac purohita.

58. Kramrisch, *Presence*, 262; O'Flaherty, *Sexual Metaphors*, 213-32.

59. As major transgressions (mahāpātaka), Brahmanicide and incest must be equated rather than opposed, as by Deppert (*supra* n. 51). Although from the orthodox psychoanalytic point of view, the parricide is the means to incest, transgressive sacrality even goes to the point of identifying the decapitation itself with incest as in the case of Paraśurāma's matricide replacing his Brahman mother Reṇukā's head with that of an Untouchable woman. In the sacrificial ideology, it is the Brahman officiant himself who assumes the maternal role of giving (re-) birth to the sacrificer (Heesterman).

60. Lorenzen, *Kāpālikas*, 28; 42, 48 (Śaṃkara); P. Jash, *History of Śaivism* (Calcutta: Roy and Chaudhury, 1974), 65-6. For their links with Vedic Soma sacrifice, see Lorenzen and S. Visuvalingam in this volume.

61. Lorenzen, *Kāpālikas*, 9, 12, 18-19, 107, 151, 173. For the Pāśupata-vow, see Kramrisch, *Presence*, 257-9, 290-1.

62. Lorenzen, *Kāpālikas*, 167; see 155-6, 158, 164, cf. 67; for the Vedic affilia-

tion of Pāśupatas, see 103, 105, 114, 131, 142-3, 149, 151 (Honnaya), 156, 161-4. Bhagwan Deshmukh's lecture on epigraphic evidence of Kālāmukha activity in the Marathwada region of Maharashtra, cited in *Times of India* (13th Jan., 1985), mentions two such ascetics supervising the construction of temples dedicated to Śiva in the form of Vīrabhadra and Kālabhairava. Dakṣa's beheading by the former is a multiform of Bhairava's decapitation of Brahmā. Yamunācārya's and Rāmānuja's confusion of the two sects in order to discredit the Kālāmukhas (Lorenzen, 4-6) probably also reflects their perception of this continuity.

63. Heesterman, IC, p. 27; "Vrātya," p. 15.

64. Biardeau, EMH IV, 231-6 (Bhīma); EMH V, 116, 121-4 (Arjuna). For the "Brahmanization" of the ideal Kauṭilyan king through his basic qualification of "victory over the senses" which would have no doubt sublimated his petty self-interest into a dharmic imperialism (*vijigīṣā*), see Heesterman, IC, 131-2.

65. Biardeau EMH IV, 237-8. For Yudhiṣṭhira, see Dumézil, ME I, 152-4; Biardeau, EMH IV, 231 (birth from Dharma); EMH V, 88, 94-119, for a systematic contrast between Yudhiṣṭhira's and Arjuna's respective claims to the status of ideal king, that is nevertheless heavily weighted in favour of Arjuna's royal bhakti. Hence see n. 124.

66. David D. Shulman, *The King and the Clown in South Indian Myth and Poetry* (Princeton: Princeton University Press, 1985), 226; see 218-235. For the identification of dīkṣita and victim in the Aśvamedha, see S. Visuvalingam's section B in this volume.

67. Shulman, ibid., 256-75, where, however, only the "chastity" of Bṛhannaḍā has been underlined. See esp. Biardeau, EMH IV, 207-8; V, 187-200 (see n. 56); Hiltebeitel, "Śiva, the Goddess, and the Disguises of the Pāṇḍavas and Draupadī," *History of Religions* 20 (1980), 147-74, where the androgynized Arjuna actually identifies himself with the royalty of the impure "Brahman" Yudhiṣṭhira. See nn. 87 and 109.

68. Deppert, 80, 153-5; see Heesterman IC, 126 (Vrātya); Biardeau, EMH V, 148-60 (Arjuna); see nn. 24, 49, and 56. For Arjuna's "suicidal Brahmanicide," see Hiltebeitel, "Two Kṛṣṇas," 24; see n. 129.

69. See Eggeling, *Śatapatha Brāhmaṇa*, vol. 5, xviii-xxiv; and Dumézil, ME I (see n. 56), 192, 213-20, 250, for Aśvatthāman. See Hiltebeitel's contribution to this volume for a telling example of the retention of sacrificial notations even in the magical transgression of a deviant "Muslim" figure Muttāl Rāvattan.

70. O'Flaherty, *Origins of Evil*, 160-1. Niels Gutschow informs me that the only (ritual) clowns known to him in Bhaktapur are the manhandled Mūpātras, apparently Newar for Mahāpātras (= Mahābrāhmaṇas), who are normally farmers hired to play the scapegoat role.

71. J. Parry, "Ghosts, Greed and Sin: The Occupational Identity of the Benares Funeral Priests," *Man* (N.S.) 15 (1980), 88-111. For the Vidūṣaka being pampered with gifts, see Bhat, *Vidūṣaka*, 59-61; food and modakas even soaked in wine, 67-73; parody of Brahman, 223 and *passim*. For the theoretical inclusion

of the Dom, who is otherwise excluded from the empirical category of Mahābrāhmaṇa, see Veena Das, *Structure and Cognition: Aspects of Hindu Caste and Ritual*, 2nd ed. (Delhi: Oxford Univ. Press, 1982), 148-9.

72. Parry, "Ghosts," 91-6: "The Funeral Priests as 'ghosts'." Cārāyaṇa, the Vidūṣaka in the *Viddhaśālabhañjikā*, actually dons the (leftover) clothes and ornaments of the king himself; see Bhat, *Vidūṣaka* (see n. 46), 265. Cf. Eck, *Banaras* (see n. 7) 24, 193, 325, 344; and n. 23 *supra*. For dīkṣā as "mystical death," see Thite, "Significances of *Dīkṣā*," 170-1; for embryonic death, see Heesterman, "Vrātya," 30-1, n. 86; for Kusle, see Unbescheid, *Kānphaṭā*, 139-41.

73. See Coccari in this volume, and idem, "The Bīr Babas: An Analysis of a Folk-Deity in North Indian Hinduism," Ph.D. Diss. Univ. of Wisconsin-Madison, 1986; also Meyer, *Aṅkāḷaparamēcuvari* (see n. 2), for the Tuluva Brahmeru-Bhūta (p. 165) and other Brahms (180-2) like the Jaina Brahmadeva and the Nāga-Brahma (see esp. p. 182, n. 4). Although there is no Brahmā corresponding to the kapparai in the cult of Aṅkāḷamman, the Mahābrāhmaṇa Vināyaka plays a greedy role at the cremation ground in the Brahmanicide myth (36-7) and in the ritual. The Vidūṣaka in the *Adbhutadarpaṇa* is a marrow, fat, and meat-devouring Brahmarākṣasa called, like Gaṇeśa, Mahodara.

74. Heesterman, "Vrātya," 10, 30; Thite, "*Dīkṣā*," 171; Otto, *Dionysos*, 121-4.

75. *Kāpālikas*, p. 79, n. 29. The *Mahābhārata* myth not only serves as the missing link between the earlier and later forms of the Brahmanicide penance, between Sarasvatī and Gaṅgā, but also reveals the executioner and victim to be only the two poles of the single Mahābrāhmaṇa.

76. Dessigane et al., *Légendes Śivaites*, 63. Although on the Gaṅgā bank, the inlet is on the opposite side of Maṇikarṇikā tank and the incoming water tastes differently from Gaṅgā water, as I was able to confirm myself during Maṇikarṇikā-Devī's festival on 12-13th May, 1986, for which the tank was emptied for cleaning.

77. See Lorenzen, *Kāpālikas*, 30; Eck, *Banaras*, 112-20; Sukul, *Vārāṇasī-Vaibhav*, 50. J. Irwin, "The Sacred Anthill and the Cult of the Primordial Mound," *History of Religions* 21 (1982), 339-60. It is possible to identify the primordial mound not only with the bisexual embryo but also with the world-egg (*brahmāṇḍa*) as the ovum before its fixation on the uterine wall; see F. B. J. Kuiper, "Cosmogony and Conception: A Query," *Ancient Indian Cosmogony* [henceforth AIC], ed. J. Irwin (Delhi: Vikas, 1983), 90-137. Omkāra also embodies the unstructured (*anirukta*) ritual speech imitated by the dīkṣita's stammering.

78. Eck, *Banaras*, 238-51; J. Parry, "Death and Cosmogony in Kashi," *Contributions to Indian Sociology*, 15 (1981), 337-9, 351, 357. For Viṣṇu's foot, which invariably recurs at Hari-kī-Paurī (Haridwar) and other tīrthas on the Gaṅgā, see Kuiper, AIC, 41-55: "The Three Strides of Viṣṇu."

79. Parry, "Ghosts," 94; see n. 71. Also idem, "Death and Digestion: the symbolism of food and eating in north Indian mortuary rites," *Man* (NS), 20 (1985), 612-30, for the piṇḍa as fusion of male and female reproductive sub-

stances (*kuṇḍagolaka*), etc.

80. See Eliade, *Rites and Symbols of Initiation: The Mysteries of Birth and Rebirth* (1958; rpt. New York: Harper Torchbooks, 1965); also his *Myths, Dreams and Mysteries: The Encounter Between Contemporary Faiths and Archaic Reality* (1960; rpt. Glasgow: Collins, 1968), esp. chaps. 7-8. For the embryonic significance of the Harappan urns, see D. D. Kosambi, *Myth and Reality* (Bombay: Popular Prakashan, 1982), 67-81.

81. Heesterman, IC (see n. 49), 54-5, 218 n. 61; David D. Shulman, *Tamil Temple Myths: Sacrifice and Divine Marriage in the South Indian Śaiva Tradition* (New Jersey: Princeton Univ. Press, 1980), 110-131, 243-67. For the wilderness as the "womb of kingship" see Heesterman, IC, 6, 118, 126, 142, 144, and 233, n. 61.

82. Sukul, *Vārāṇasī-Vaibhav*, 55; Eck, *Banaras*, 29-31, 182-8; Parry, "Death and Cosmogony," 341; E. Visuvalingam, "Kotwāl," 247-9 (see nn. 7 and 78).

83. Meyer, *Aṅkāḷaparamēcuvari* (see n. 2), 191 (Gaṅgammā); 82, 139, 189, 196 (Iruḷappan); 185, 196 (Kāśī-Vallāḷarājan); 83, 144 (Kāśi-Viśvanātha as consort of Aṅkāḷamman). This (re-)interpretation of the goddess cult of the cremation ground is based on S. Visuvalingam's review in *Transgressive Sacrality* (see n. 1). For Vaiṣṇo-Devī, see S. Visuvalingam on Erndl's contribution in this volume.

84. Otto, *Dionysos*, 60, 71-3, 78, 90-2, 108-24, 134-5, 138-44, 152, esp. 189, 200-3; Burkert, *Homo Necans*, 125, 213, 232f; Detienne, *Dionysos à Ciel Ouvert*, 61-2; see n. 36. For the official and civic character of the Athenian integration of the transgressive Dionysos, see J.-P. Vernant, *Annuaire du Collège de France* (Paris, 1983-84), 476-7.

85. Heesterman, IC, 26-44, 91, 94, 102, 104, etc.

86. G. C. Tripathi, "Navakalevara: The Unique Ceremony of the 'birth' and 'death' of the 'Lord of the World'," in *The Cult of Jagannātha and the Regional Tradition of Orissa*, ed. A. Eschmann, H. Kulke and G. C. Tripathi (Delhi: Manohar, 1978), 260. See Marglin, *Wives*, 265, where the oldest Śabara, who transfers it, is expected to die within the year; and da Silva, *Pouvoir* (see n. 103).

87. Meyer, *Aṅkāḷaparamēcuvari*, 37; cf. 165; 192-3, 179-80, for the problematic relation between the "Śaiva" king and the "Śākta" Cempaṭavars. M. L. Reiniche, "Le temple dans la localité: Quatre examples au Tamilnad," *L'Espace du Temple: Espaces, Itinéraires, Médiations, Purṣārtha* 8 (Paris: EHESS, 1985), 107, 110 (Aṇṇāmalaiyār); 102 (Kumbhakonam); 106 (Liṅgodbhava at Tiruvaṇṇāmalai). Brahmā himself is the classic figure of the "pregnant male," comparable to the young Greek who had to imitate labor pains, with appropriate cries and gestures, of a pregnant woman during certain sacrifices dedicated to Dionysos (Otto, *Dionysos*, 195). For Dionysos himself was not only the "effeminate stranger" (Euripides) whom Ino was asked to rear as a girl, but was also sometimes called "androgyne" (Otto, p. 185). His cousin-victim Pentheus is travestied in the feminine attire of his Bacchant-devotee before being torn apart and it is the same actor who plays the role of his mother-devourer Agavé (Vernant, *Mythe*

et Tragédie, vol. 2, 251-2, 255-6); cf. Shulman, *Tamil Temple Myths*, 294-316.

88. E. Visuvalingam, "Bhairava's cudgel or Lāṭ Bhairava" (1986), 250-3 (see n. 7). For its relation to the world-tree, the number 7, and tripartition, see M. Eliade, *Shamanism: Archaic Techniques of Ecstasy*, Bollingen Series LXXVI (New Jersey: Princeton Univ. Press, 1964), 259-287, 403-6 (yūpa as cosmic tree, Buddha's seven strides).

89. Rolf A. Stein, *L'Annuaire du Collège de France* (Paris), 1971-72, 499-510; 1972-73, 463-70; 1973-74, 508-17; 1974-75, 488-95; 1975-76, 531-6; 1976-77, 607-15. According to him (1974-75, 490), the primitive form, alone retained in Sino-Japanese tantrism, of Bhairava's khaṭvāṅga, "seems to have been a club formed of a skull fitted onto a long bone. It resembles the *yamadaṇḍa*, Yama's staff." I thank Prof. Stein for his offprints.

90. Vernant, MT II, 251-54; Detienne, *Dionysos à Ciel Ouvert*, 42; cf. Burkert, *Homo Necans*, 177, 198 n. 14.

91. Biardeau, *Dictionnaire*, 89-90, 109-13; Stein, *Annuaires*, 1972-73, 469; 1974-75, 491; see nn. 33 and 89. Also S. Visuvalingam's section B. in this volume. Nevertheless, Hiltebeitel's paper in this volume suggests that anthropomorphized posts like Pōttu Rāju, and even the Muslim Muttāl Rāvuttan, still conserve not only the symbolic values but also the bloody function of the Vedic yūpa.

92. Stein, *Annuaires*, 1971-2, 504-7; 1972-3, 470; 1974-5, 489; Briggs, *Gorakhnāth*, 308; Anderson, *Festivals*, 41-6; Vézies, *Fêtes*, 23-4; Gutschow, *Stadtraum*, 81-96. Details of the funerary procession were supplied by courtesy of Niels Gutschow, who made a special study of it on 13th April 1987, after our personal discussion of death symbolism in the Newar New Year festivals.

93. Author's translation of Toffin, *Les Néwars*, 512; cf. 516, 250.

94. References to Nepal, *Néwars*, 359-69; Anderson, *Festivals*, 127-37; Slusser, *Nepal Mandala*, 268-9; and Gutschow, *Stadtraum*, 138-46, 58-63, are completed below by my own fieldwork at Kathmandu from 25th Sept. (beginning of Indra Jātrā), until 28th Oct. 85, facilitated by a grant from the C.N.R.S. "équipes de recherche" 299 and 249. For its derivation from the New Year festival of Vedic cosmogony, the role of Asura-Varuṇa, and the later role of the *jarjara* (= dhvaja) in the preliminaries of the Sanskrit drama, see Kuiper, VV, *supra* n. 53. According to the *Bṛhat Samhitā*, the pole should preferably be from an Arjuna tree, and another staff should also be raised as Indra's mother. Another Gṛhya Sūtra prescribes the Indrayajña with oblations to Indrāṇī, Aja Ekapāda, Ahirbudhnya, etc. to be performed on the full moon day itself of Bhādrapada (see Ekapāda-Bhairava, n. 106 below). Kane, *History of Dharmaśāstra*, II, 824-6, derives from the Indramaha the annual raising of a bamboo staff in the Deccan and other places on the first day of Caitra, which corresponds to the Bhaktapur Bisket Jātrā where the pole is identified with Bhairava (= Kāśī-Viśvanāth) instead.

95. See Shulman, *Tamil Temple Myths* (see n. 81), 138-92, 223-43; and esp.

S. Visuvalingam's review article "Are *Tamil Temple Myths* really Tamil?" presented to the VIth World Tamil Conference, Kuala Lumpur, 15-19th November 1987. See Kane, *History of Dharmaśāstra* IV, 530-2 for Mahālayaśrāddha.

96. Anderson, *Festivals*, 156-63; Slusser, *Nepal Mandala*, 47-8, 235, 238-9; Gutschow, *Stadtraum*, 135-8. I was unable to study the exchange of swords in October 1987, as the grants to study the festival season were released only in 1988. With the rapid erosion of traditional structures there is no guarantee that the ritual will still wait to be studied after twelve years.

97. E. Visuvalingam, "Kotwāl," 252. For the equation of the fallen Indrapole with the victimized dīkṣita, see S. Visuvalingam's treatment of the Brahman Cārudatta condemned as an Untouchable to be executed by Cāṇḍālas as an offering to the goddess at the stake in Act 10 of the *Mṛcchakaṭikā* in *Transgressive Sacrality* (see n. 1).

98. Sukul, *Vārāṇasī*, 205-6 (on Kapāli-Bhairava), 103-5, 247-8; *Kṛtyakalpataru* 54 and *Kāśīkhaṇḍa* 33.114-5 cited by Sukul on 260-1; 105, 121. Sukul (p. 121) had suggested a separate Kula Stambha supposedly erected by Aśoka only because he recognized the wholly Hindu character of the Mahāśmaśāna Stambha.

99. Stein *Annuaires* (see n. 89), 1971-72, 504; 1972-73, 464-5; 1973-74, 509-11; 1975-76, 535-6; 1976-77, 609. For *Rudrapiśāca*, see Eck, *Banaras*, 339; Sukul, 37-8; see n. 7. For *Brahmanāla*, see Sukul, 51-2; Parry, "Death and Cosmogony," 343 and n. 8; see n. 28. Researchers into *Near Death Experiences* (NDE), especially those who have undergone it themselves, should not have much difficulty, despite the Indian cultural context, in recognizing the inner coherence of this mythico-ritual universe.

100. Sukul, 71-2, 119, 121 (citing *Kāśīkhaṇḍa* 100.99), 150-2, 250, 347-8; E. Visuvalingam, "Kotwāl," 252, 255.

101. Anderson, *Festivals*, 43; see n. 5. Mary Searle Chatterjee kindly shared with us her summary of the two versions, now included in her as yet unpublished paper on "Religious Division and the Mythology of the Past." Chatterjee added that she had seen a painting for sale in Britain of human sacrifice being offered at a "Somnāth temple" (label) in Benares. Ghāzī Mīyā's annual wedding with Zohra Bibi, celebrated on the first Sunday of Jyeṣṭhā (May-June) by the Muslims of Adampura, also appears to have been an unconsummated tragic union. For the victim as bridegroom, see esp. S. Visuvalingam on *Mṛcchakaṭikā* Act X; see n. 97.

102. Sontheimer, *Birobā*, 29-30, 200-2, 252 (Mhaskobā); 46, 48, 184, 196 (Birobā), 61-3, 240-1 (two wives). See also his "Some Incidents in the History of the God Khaṇḍobā," *Asie du Sud: Traditions et Changements*, Proceedings of the VIth European Conference on Modern South Asian Studies, 8-13 July 1978 (Paris: C.N.R.S., 1978); "The Mallāri/Khaṇḍobā Myth as Reflected in Folk Art and Ritual," *Anthropos* 79 (1984), 155-170. See also Shulman, *Tamil Temple Myths*, 267-94 for Vedic antecedents.

103. Sontheimer 1976, 29, 31, 95-97, 243; R. N. Nandi, *Religious Institutions and Cults in the Deccan* (Delhi: Motilal Banarsidass, 1973), 114ff. on "The Beginnings of Tantric Cults," esp. 121-2: "Stambheśvarī"; cf. Eschmann, "Hinduization of Tribal Deities in Orissa: The Śākta and Śaiva Typology," in Eschmann et al. ed., *The Cult of Jagannātha*, 79-97; Goudriaan, *Hindu Tantrism*, 37; and Nepali, *The Newars*, 298-305, for the "aboriginal origin" of the Nepali Bhairavas. For a cogent critique of such genetic approaches seeking to explain Hindu divinities like Jagannātha or Bhairava (purely) in terms of their evolution from non-Brahmanical, even pre-Āryan, substratums, see J. C. Gomes da Silva, *Pouvoir et Hierarchie* (Bruxelles: Unversité Libre de Bruxelles, in press).

104. Sontheimer, *Birobā*, 29, 31, 95-7, 243 (Gosavī); 176-9, 284.

105. Marglin, *Wives*, 273; 243-7: daitās' consanguinity with the king; their representing Jagannātha, 256, 261, 276-9; king as sweeper: 241, 254, 258; obscenities and dissolution of caste boundaries including the Brahman/daitā opposition during the car festival, 275; Pati Mahāpātra: 250-1, 264-75; Gaṇeśa: 249, 271.

106. H. von Stietencron, "The Śaiva Component in the Early Evolution of Jagannātha," 119-23; and A. Eschmann, H. Kulke, G. C. Tripathi, "The Formation of the Jagannātha Triad," 174-5, 189, both in Eschmann et al., *Cult of Jagannātha* (see n. 86); also 104-5.

107. C. Malamoud, "Village et forêt dans l'idéologie de l'Inde brāhmaṇique," in *Archives Européennes de Sociologie*, XVII (1976), 3-20, esp. p. 10, n. 36.

108. Tripathi, "Navakalevara," 236-8. There is also the inexplicable procedure of drawing the inverted figure of a man on the tree followed by the sacrifice of an "animal" in the form of a white gourd, before the Jagannātha-tree is actually cut down (247-9). Interestingly, the lama explains the inverted khaṭvāṅga suspended just over the kapāla recipient of the alchemical fire-place by the practice, unattested in the texts, of the adept being (mystically) decapitated while upside-down (Stein, *Annuaire*, 1976, 534-6). See nn. 86 and 89. But compare S. Visuvalingam's treatment of the motif of the inverted tree in the Kāttavarāyan narrative in this volume.

109. See Biardeau, "L'arbre *śamī* et le buffle sacrificiel," *Autour de la déesse Hindoue*, 215-43. For the maternity of the androgynized dīkṣita, see nn. 67 and 87.

110. Sontheimer, *Birobā*, 249, 252, 183-6, 204f.; Marglin, *Wives*, 327 n. 1, 264 (for Jagannātha as Kālī); see nn. 6 and 13. The stone pillars representing the goddesses Pītabalī and Khambheśvarī, along the Orissan trunk road, are dubbed liṅgas, and the rock-goddess is encircled by a "*śakti*" to become a svayambhū liṅga as at the Bhairava-temple at Purāṇacuttack; Eschmann, *Cult of Jagannātha*, 95-6 (see n. 86).

111. For a similar explanation of the supposedly "foreign" origin of the Greek Dionysos in terms of his transgressive otherness institutionalized through the controlled trance, the officialized thiase, the festive *komos*, the theatre, etc. at

the very heart of Greek civilization, see Vernant, in Vernant and Vidal-Naquet, MT II, 246, 251, 255, 257, 259, 269; the transgressive dimension is underlined especially at p. 105 by V.-Naquet, and by Detienne, *Dionysos mis á Mort*, 7-8 (see nn. 38 and 36).

112. Author's trans. of Biardeau, *L'Hindouisme*, 162, cf. 164; cf. Goudriaan, *Hindu Tantrism*, 17, 32, 36-7; see nn. 12 and 22.

113. Lorenzen, *Kāpālikas*, 49; see n. 3. For the Kaula "deradicalization" of Kāpālika ideology, and the role of the esoteric Krama school, see Alexis Sanderson, "Purity and power among the Brahmans of Kashmir," in *The Category of the Person: Anthropology, Philosophy, History*, M. Carrithers, S. Collins and S. Lukes, eds. (Cambridge: Cambridge Univ. Press, 1986), 190-216; "Maṇḍala and Āgamic Identity in the Trika of Kashmir," in *Mantras et Diagrammes Rituels dans l'Hindouisme* (Paris: Editions du CNRS, 1986), 169-214.

114. Abhinavagupta, *Tantrāloka*, Kashmir Series of Texts and Studies no. LVII (Bombay: 1936), vol. 11, chap. 29.10 (transgression); 11-13 (wine); 83-9 (comm.), 142-9 (mantric power due to neutralization of opposing vital airs in the median channel); 96ff. (*dūtīyāga*); 97-8 (transgressive definition of *brahmacārin*); 101-3 (transgression of caste, incest); 104-15 (sexualization of consciousness); 115-28 (yāmala *śāntodita* state); 128-9 (kuṇḍagolaka); 129-142 (*vīryavikṣobha*); 156-61 (*bhairavāṣṭakapadam*); 162-3 (yoginībhū); 181-5 (internalized cremation through the all-devouring Kāla-Fire of the universal dissolution); 138-9 (*piśācāveśa*, demoniac possession when a higher state of consciousness is blocked at a lower level instead of vice-versa). This description of the Kulayāga has been "conflated" with the practices of the Puri *rājagurus* (Marglin, *Wives*, 217-42; see n. 13), and from my manuscript of the *Unmattākhyakramapaddhati*, analyzed in my Ph.D. Diss. (Paris, 1981). See also K. C. Pandey, *Abhinavagupta: An Historical and Philosophical Study*, 2nd ed. (Varanasi: Chowkhamba, 1963), 607-23; and Abhinavagupta, *Parātriṃśikāvivaraṇa*, KS no. XVIII (Bombay: 1918), 45-51. The yāmala state can be usefully compared to the sexually differentiated roles of Mitra and Varuṇa when this dual divinity mythically unites with the divinized courtesan Urvaśī in the Purāṇas.

115. Parry, "Sacrificial Death," 81; Marglin, *Wives*, 224-5, 237; 224, 239-40 (kulāmṛta); 218, 233-4 (cremation ground).

116. Eliade, *Shamanism*, 411, 414; see also 421-7 for "Shamanism among the Aboriginal Tribes of India," particularly the Śavaras. For Lévi-Strauss, see nn. 27, 24, and 44. See Heesterman, IC, 35, for the pure/impure alternation in the sacrifice; see n. 49.

117. Kuiper, VV, 35-7, 75-6, 102-6, 166-8, 193; AIC, 48-9; see nn. 53 and 77. For some of the fundamental issues involved in this problematic transformation, see Biardeau's review of VV in *Indo-Iranian Journal* (1981), 293-300.

118. W. E. Hale, *Asura in Early Vedic Religion* (Delhi: Motilal Banarsidass, 1986), who is, however, unable to explain *Ṛgveda* X.124 from his purely evolutionistic perspective (86-92), whereas Kuiper, VV, 13-42, has provided a coherent

interpretation of this "transfer of sovereignty" to Indra in terms of his mythical dialectic. It would be sound methodological procedure to provisionally separate the significance of Varuṇa from the evolution of the Asuras before reintegrating the Asura Varuṇa of the Ṛgveda; contrast Kuiper, VV, 5-13.

119. Deppert, *Rudra's Geburt* (see n. 24), 85-6, 134-44 (sacral kingship of the pre-Āryan Middle-Eastern type), 233-5. Cf. Kuiper, VV, 24-6 for Varuṇa's kṣatra.

120. See G. Dumézil, *Les dieux souverains des Indo-Européens*, 2nd ed. (Paris: Gallimard, 1977), 55-85, and especially his *Mitra-Varuṇa*, 2nd ed. (Paris: Gallimard, 1948); Kuiper, AIC, 9-22; VV, 45-6, 59-60 (see nn. 77 and 53). Dumézil's and Kuiper's positions had remained irreconcilable because the former had come to perceive Mitra-Varuṇa primarily in sociologizing terms as the priestly summit of the trifunctional hierarchy whereas the latter continued to relegate Mitra to the under-world simply because he shares the Asurahood of his twin Varuṇa, despite the recognized difficulties of Mitra's partiality for the upper-world and the mythic interferences with Indra; cf. Kuiper, "Remarks on the Avestan Hymn to Mithra," *Indo-Iranian Journal* (1961-2), 36-60; esp. 46-53, 57-9; "Some Observations on Dumézil's Theory," *Numen*, 8 (1961), 34-45. A transgressively dialectical approach would equate Varuṇa, as the under-worldly pole of Dumézil's Mitraic first function, with the demoniac tribal Bhairava intruding from the embryogonic chaos beyond the Vedic universe; cf. Gomes da Silva's paper on "Hierarchy and Transgression" (see n. 1). Along with S. Visuvalingam, I thank Prof. Kuiper and the late Prof. Dumézil for having so much sympathetically encouraged our efforts to synthesize their respective insights into the basic structures of Vedic religion.

121. Heesterman, IC, 95f., 228 n. 1. For the socio-economic transformations and the technological innovations that determined the emergence and conditioned the growth of early Buddhism from its Magadhan cradle, see D. D. Kosambi, *The Culture and Civilisation of Ancient India in Historical Outline* (Delhi: Vikas, 1970), where the rise to prominence of the merchant classes and the expansion of commercial circuits should be especially emphasized.

122. This necessarily modifies L. Dumont's thesis of the total secularization of kingship in Hindu India; cf. Biardeau, *supra* nn. 33, 64 and 68; and esp. Hiltebeitel, "Towards a Coherent Study of Hinduism," *Religious Studies Review*, 9 (1983), 206-11.

123. For the identification of the royal kirīṭin Arjuna with the avatāra-Kṛṣṇa in the ṛṣi-couple Nara/Nārāyaṇa, see Biardeau, EMH V, 89-94, 177; for Arjuna's Rudraic dimension, neglected by her, see Hiltebeitel, "Śiva," 151-60; see nn. 56 and 67. Born from the anger of Kṛṣṇa-Nārāyaṇa, it is Rudra himself who precedes Arjuna into the battlefield and is really responsible for the carnage; see J. Scheuer, *Śiva dans le Mahābhārata*, Bibliothèque de l'École des Hautes Études, Science Réligieuses, vol. LXXXIV (Paris: PUF, 1982), 279-91; also 222, 228, 241-2 and *passim*.

124. Dharma forms a bi-unity with Arjuna no less than Kṛṣṇa does, which

also explains the peculiar joking relationship between Kṛṣṇa and Yudhiṣṭhira, such as when they flatter each other with the credit for Bhīṣma's fall. Kuiper, "Some Observations," 42-4, rightly deduced that Yudhiṣṭhira as the incarnation of Dharma (= *ṛta*) must represent Mitra-Varuṇa, but had difficulty reconciling the underworldly Varuṇa with the passive sacral purity of the upperworldly Pāṇḍava. Biardeau, "Contributions à l'étude du mythe-cadre du *Mahābhārata*," *Bulletin de l'École Française d'Extrême Orient*, 55 (1969), 97-105, seeks to reconcile Dumézil's Mitra and Kuiper's Varuṇa within a totalizing Hindu perspective by seeing in Dharma the prolongation, profoundly transformed by the renunciation ideal, of the socio-cosmic order of the Vedic ṛta. Cf. *supra* nn. 65 and 67. Nevertheless, Kuiper had already suggested the typological equation of the Śūdra-Vidura with the epic Varuṇa and ambivalent purohita-figures like Uśanā Kāvya, and Viśvarūpa (VV, 93-101), which would imply that Yudhiṣṭhira himself is a (royal) Mahābrāhmaṇa.

125. Heesterman IC, 27, 92; cf. 4, 43-4, 155, 200, 232, n. 32, 154, 208, n. 12; see esp. n. 51 *supra*.

126. See Kuiper, VV, 67-74: "Varuṇa as a Demoniacal Figure and as the God of Death," for his links with his successor Yama-Dharmarāja associated with the Fathers (pitṛ); 60-6: for the close association with Death and the Fathers of the virūpa-Aṅgirasas, who are later the repository of the magical practices of the *Atharvaveda*. Instead of seeing in the dog Dharma that accompanies Yudhiṣṭhira to heaven the transgressive dimension of the Brahmanized Dharmarāja, Biardeau's Hindu bhakti is obliged to purify Yama's dog, and all the other impure symbols invested in "The Royalty of Yudhiṣṭhira," of the pollution of Death; EMH V, 109-10. See *Manu* X.51-6; cf. Deppert, *Rudra's Geburt*, 59-62 (on Cāṇḍāla); D. White's paper on "Dogs, Dice and Death," delivered at the Transgressive Sacrality conference (see nn. 24 and 1); and Sontheimer in this volume.

127. Cf. Gomes da Silva, *Pouvoir et Hierarchie;* I thank the author for sending the typescript of his Lévi-Straussian critique of (the prolongations of) Durkheimian sociologism (in Louis Dumont's anthropology of Indian civilization). For Rāmānuja, see Lorenzen, *Kāpālikas*, 6.

128. See Biardeau, *Le Sacrifice*, 99, n. 2, 25 n. 1; Shulman, *The King and the Clown*, 247-8.

129. See A. Hiltebeitel, "The Two Kṛṣṇas in One Chariot: Upaniṣadic Imagery and Epic Mythology," *History of Religions* 24 (1984), 1-26, where he points out that on occasion Arjuna/Kṛṣṇa are compared to Indra/Varuṇa or Śiva/Brahmā on the single chariot of Brahman. They are again identified as the doubled Kṛṣṇa while helping Agni in the sexualized sacrifice of consuming the Khāṇḍava forest. See Heesterman, IC, 151, for the early function of the purohita as charioteer for the king and Kṛṣṇa's role in this context; 79, 151 (king as Brahman); 37-8, 42 for the polluting king/purohita relation (esp. contrast p. 155).

130. See M.-C. Porcher, "La Princesse et le Royaume: sur la représentation

de la royauté dans le *Daśakumāracarita* de Dandin," *Journal Asiatique*, 273 (1985), 183-206. Like the northern *ḍombikā* (dance), the southern *ulā* could also be seen as an expression of this universalizing dialectic rather than as a sexual contradiction, as in Shulman, *King and Clown*, 312-24. The brahmacarya of the "chaste" Hanumān in the *Rāmāyaṇa* is interpreted in folk variants rather as an exaggerated virility matching that of Vṛṣākapi.

131. O'Flaherty, *Asceticism* (see n. 2), 104-11, 146-64; see n. 66. For the deconstruction of (Tamil) bhakti through the dialectic of transgressive sacrality, see S. Visuvalingam's section D. in this volume.

132. See G. Toffin, "Les Aspects Religieux de la Royauté au Népal," *Archives de Sciences Sociales des Religions* 48/1 (1979), 53-82; "Dieux souverains et rois dévots dans l'ancienne royauté de la vallée du Népal," *L'Homme* 26 (1986), 71-95, esp. p. 84, n. 19 raising the problem of Bhairava, and Sontheimer *Birobā*, 192, 250. For Brahmā's inability to create, see O'Flaherty, *Origins of Evil*, 284 (see n. 2). Cf. Shulman, *Tamil Temple Myths* (see n. 81), p. 90ff. and especially S. Visuvalingam's section B. in this volume.

133. See S. Visuvalingam's treatment of the contributions of Coccari, Hiltebeitel and Sontheimer in this volume.

134. G. J. Held, *Mahābhārata: An Ethnological Study* (London: Kegan Paul, Trench, Trubner & Co., 1953), 182-85. The link with Kāla-Bhairava on the one hand and the angry Guru on the other, is perhaps to be found in Śiva, who emerges as the furious Mṛtyuñjaya/Kālakāla from the liṅga to slay Yama when the latter tries to forcibly claim Mārkaṇḍeya, destined for Death at the (perennial) age of sixteen. All fieldwork in Banaras was carried out with the indispensable help of Om Prakash Sharma. I also thank all the numerous devotees of Bhairava in India and Nepal for allowing me to participate freely in their cult and aiding me to understand it better.

135. Vézies, *Les Fêtes*, 72-5. I had the good fortune to witness this festival in April 1985, with a grant accorded by the C.N.R.S. "équipe" 249, and to interview all the participants, above all the dhāmī himself. For Aṃśuvarman, see Slusser, *Nepal Mandala*, 337.

136. Slusser, *Nepal Mandala*, 291-2, 237; p. 239, n. 101 for Vajra-Bhairava. During my fieldwork in July 1985 in Ladakh, the lamas often described terrifying figures like Yamāntaka in the *gonpas* as "Bhairava," who is already called "destroyer of Yama" (= Yamāri) in his Purāṇic origin-myth.

137. It was Aśakāji Vajrācārya, the teacher of the Aṣṭamātṛkā dances to the Śākya boys at Patan, who also gave me the details of the eight cremation grounds haunted by the aṣṭabhairava of the Valley. According to him, some Vajrācāryas still worship Bhairava at these sites in order to obtain various siddhis.

138. *Ṛgveda* V.62.1: *ṛtena ṛtam apihitam dhruvam vām. . . .* See Nepali, *Newars*, 300; Slusser, *Nepal Mandala*, 237. See S. Visuvalingam's treatment of judicial terror in "Psychoanalysis, Criminal Law and Sacrificial *Dharma*," in *Transgressive Sacrality*; see n. 1.

7

New Data on the Kāpālikas

David N. Lorenzen

The early Indian "ascetics" known as the Kāpālikas can be regarded as archetypal in at least two senses. In the first place, to their opponents, whose writings until very recently have been our principal source of information on Kāpālika beliefs and practices, the Kāpālikas represent the archetype, or stereotype, of an immoral and heretical ascetic. In Sanskrit literature, Kāpālika characters mock Vedic doctrines while they either prepare a human sacrifice or drink and carouse with comely female disciples. In the second place, however, some of these sources suggest that the Kāpālikas in fact ritually modeled their lives on a divine archetype, on the god Śiva-Kapālin who must endure a lengthy penance to atone for the sin of having cut off one of the five heads of Brahmā. This symbolic reenactment of Śiva's Great Vow (*mahāvrata*) earns the Kāpālikas their title of Mahāvratins.

This doubly archetypal character of the Kāpālikas, or at least of their literary portraits in the writings of their opponents, has made them apt objects of scholarly analysis from a variety of structuralist, symbolicist, and archetypicist points of view. Examples can be found in my *The Kāpālikas and Kālāmukhas*, in Wendy O'Flaherty's discussion of the Śiva-Kapālin myth in her *Origins of Evil in Hindu Mythology*, and in Elizabeth-Chalier Visuvalingam's article in this volume and in her "Bhairava: Kotwāl of Vārāṇasī."[1]

The most exciting recent discovery relevant to the Kāpālikas is Alexis Sanderson's identification of a corpus of unpublished Śaivite tantric texts which describe Kāpālika worship and observances. The most important of these texts is the *Jayadrathayāmala*, manuscripts of which are preserved in the national archives of Nepal and have been photographed by the Nepal-German manuscript preservation project.

Sanderson has yet to publish a full descriptive analysis of this material, but some preliminary discussion of it is available in his recently and soon to be published writings.[2]

Most so-far published source material relevant to the Kāpālikas found in Indian literature and epigraphy has been discussed in my *The Kāpālikas and Kālāmukhas*. The most important literary omission is the story of Ciruttoṇḍa contained in the Tamil *Periya Purāṇam*, a text of the twelfth century.[3] This legend relates how a Bhairava ascetic came to the house of the devotee Ciruttoṇḍa and demanded to be fed the flesh of Ciruttoṇḍa's son. The father dutifully killed his son and had his wife cook the flesh. When the meal was served the ascetic revealed himself to be the god Śiva and returned the son to life. Although the text does not specifically call the ascetic a Kāpālika, his character is obviously congruent with the Kāpālika archetype.

Another important, although brief, previously unnoticed reference to the Kāpālikas is found in the well-known Nāth-sampradāya text, Svātmārāma's *Haṭha-yoga-pradīpikā*.[4] Svātmārāma claims to describe the Amarolī mudrā "according to the *khaṇḍa* doctrine of the Kāpālikas." The Amarolī mudrā is a variant of the better known Vajrolī mudrā, a sexual yogic exercise in which the adepts reabsorb the fluid released during intercourse.

A few other previously unnoticed references to the Kāpālikas in published Sanskrit sources have been identified and discussed by Minoru Hara and A. C. Barthakuria.[5] Unfortunately, none of them adds much of significance to our understanding of Kāpālika beliefs and practices.

Recently Nāgendra Nāth Upādhyāy of Banaras Hindu University has published a monograph in Hindi on *Bauddha Kāpālik sādhanā aur sāhitya* in which he discusses the beliefs and practices of what he claims to be a tradition of Buddhist Kāpālikas.[6] He has in fact produced a useful study of Buddhist tantricism, some early schools of which do seem to have been strongly influenced by the Kāpālikas. It seems clear, however, that the original Kāpālikas were Śaivites and not Buddhists. Apart from Kṛṣṇācāryapāda's well-known and probably metaphorical references to himself as a Kāpālin in his *caryāpadas*,[7] references which in any case come from a tradition as much associated with the Nāths as with the Buddhists, Upādhyāy has not offered, in my opinion, sufficient evidence to justify specifically calling the tantric Buddhists of his study Kāpālikas. On the other hand, Alexis Sanderson, who has been working with unpublished manuscripts of the Buddhist *yoginītantra* tradition, claims that this tradition should be considered to be "a variant of the Śaiva Kāpālika."[8]

Until Sanderson's identification of the corpus of Kāpālika texts preserved in Nepal, I held a small but lingering doubt about whether an organized Kāpālika sect in fact ever existed. It is now clear that this skepticism was largely unjustified. Nonetheless, even this Kāpālika literature will not be sufficient to adequately locate the Kāpālika sect in historical time and space. For this, epigraphical evidence is absolutely essential. Unfortunately, very little such evidence has so far come to light. Up until now only two inscriptions have been identified which clearly record donations to persons who are likely to have been Kāpālika ascetics.[9] Both are from western India. A copper plate grant found in Igatpuri, Nasik District, registers a donation of a village to finance the "Guggula-pūjā" at a temple of the god Kāpāleśvara. The donees were the Mahāvratin ascetics who lived at the temple. The donor was the early Cālukya king Nāgavardhana who lived about the middle of the seventh century A.D. A second copper plate grant, found near Tilakwādā in Baroda District, registers a grant made in A.D. 1047 to "the muni named Dinakara, a Mahāvratadhara who was like the Kapālin, Śaṃkara, in bodily form." The donor was a vassal or official of the Paramāra king Bhoja.

In recent years two other epigraphs have been edited and published which can be identified as grants from and to Kāpālika ascetics, although the editors of the inscriptions have not made this identification. The more important inscription was found at Kolanupaka, ancient Koḷḷipāke, in Nalgonda District of Andhra Pradesh.[10] It is written in highly Sanskritized Kannada prose and is dated in Śaka year 973 (A.D. 1050) during the reign of the Cālukya (of Kalyāṇa) king Trailokyamalla (Someśvara I). It records the donation of some land to Caṇḍamayya, a servant of Gaṅgamarāja, by a Brahman (*vipra*) named Somi-bhaṭṭāraka. This Somi-bhaṭṭāraka is said to be the chief (*sthānādhipati*) of the temple of Śaṃkareśvara (= Śiva) in Koḷḷipāke.

The inscription gives us the first word portrait of a Kāpālika ascetic from a source sympathetic to these ascetics. After a few words whose joint sense is not totally clear, the inscription refers to Somi-bhaṭṭāraka as "devoted to the meaning of the Somasiddhānta issued from the lotus mouth (? of Śiva)." He is said to be "sprinkled with ashes; adorned with the six insignia (mudrā); and holding a khaṭvāṅga club, a skull (kapāla), *ḍamaruga* and *mṛdaṅga* drums, and a *kāhala* (? = trumpet)." Next he is called a "bee (buzzing round) the lotus feet of the glorious (god) Śrīnātha." Finally he is said to be a "Mahāvratin, an ocean of generosity and a treasury of truth and asceticism."[11]

The most interesting aspects of this description of Somi-bhaṭṭāraka are the mention of his devotion to the doctrine of Somasiddhānta and the mention of the six insignia, the khaṭvāṅga club and the skull. Somasiddhānta can be better discussed after reviewing the contents of the second new Kāpālika inscription. The mention of the six insignia, the skull, and the khaṭvāṅga club provides an important and surprising confirmation of the statements about the Kāpālikas made by Yāmunācārya and his disciple Rāmānuja, both contemporaries of Somi-bhaṭṭāraka. In his *Āgamaprāmāṇya* Yāmunācārya claims that the Kāpālikas assert that:[12]

> The fruit of liberation (*apavarga*) is attained through knowledge of the six insignia (*mudrikā-ṣaṭka*) and through wearing them, not through the understanding of *brahman*. He who knows the essence of the six insignia, who is proficient in the highest mudrā, and who meditates on the Self as seated in the vulva (*bhagāsana-stha*) attains nirvāṇa. (The Kāpālikas) define the six insignia as the *karṇikā* (earring), the *rucaka* (necklace), the *kuṇḍala* (earring), the *śikhāmaṇi* (crest-jewel), ashes (*bhasma*), and the sacred thread (yajñopavīta). The skull (kapāla) and the khaṭvāṅga are declared to be the secondary insignia (*upamudrā*). If the body is marked with these (various insignia) one is not born again here (on earth).

In Somi-bhaṭṭāraka's inscription the reading of the term *six insignia* (*ṣaṇmudrā*) is not completely clear, but a comparison with Yāmunācārya's text confirms the reading, particularly since the skull and khaṭvāṅga in both appear immediately afterwards. The ḍamaru and other drums and musical instruments are frequently associated with Śaivite ascetics, but do not seem to have been special insignia of the Kāpālikas. Ashes are, of course, worn by nearly all Śaivite ascetics.

A detailed discussion of the six insignia and the two secondary insignia is found in my *Kāpālikas and Kālāmukhas* and need not be repeated here. The significance of the *Mahāvratin*, which the inscription applies to Somi-bhaṭṭāraka, is likewise discussed at length in the same monograph.[13] I would only note here that I do not agree with Minoru Hara's suggestion that "the adjective *mahat* in the *mahā-vrata* may have had a pejorative connotation" as in the case of the term Mahā-brāhmaṇa.[14] It is clear from this inscription and from many other sources that the Kāpālikas themselves called themselves Mahāvratins. It is unlikely that they would have done so if the term was pejorative.

In the second new inscription, it is the donee who appears to belong to the Kāpālikas, although the identification is considerably more problematic in this case. The inscription was found in Bangalore District.[15] It is written in Sanskrit and Kannada and has been dated in about the sixth century A.D. The donor was the "Pṛthivī-Koṃkaṇi-mahādhirāja" named Durvinīta. In his fourth regnal year Durvinīta gave the village of Peṇṇa-ūr as a *brahmadeya* to "Kāpāliśarman, who belonged to the Kutsagotra, the Taittirīyacaraṇa, and the Prāvacana-kalpa; who was a resident of Upakoṭṭa; whose rites were characterized by sacrifices with Soma; and who was the son of Agniśarman."[16]

The name Kāpāli-śarman makes it fairly likely that the donee was a Kāpālika. We have noted that Somi-bhaṭṭāraka was called a vipra, *i.e.*, a Brahman. Kāpāli-śarma is not merely a Brahman, he is a learned Brahman evidently well-versed in Vedic literature and rituals. His association with Soma sacrifices is particularly noteworthy since it suggests some relation between such sacrifices and the Somasiddhānta of Somi-bhaṭṭāraka.

What was this doctrine called Somasiddhānta?[17] In the lists of four (or more) Śaivite sects frequently found in Sanskrit sources the term *Soma, Sauma* or *Saumya* sometimes appears in place of Kāpālika. Kṣīra-svāmin's commentary on the *Amarakośa* equates Kāpālins, Mahāvratins, Somasiddhāntins, and Tāntrikas. In Kṛṣṇamiśra's *Prabodhacandrodaya* and Ānandarāya's *Vidyāpariṇayana* the Kāpālika characters are both called *Somasiddhānta.* Several commentaries on Kṛṣṇamiśra's *Prabodha-candrodaya* derive the term *soma* from *sa-Umā* or *Umayā sahitaḥ, i.e.* "he who is with Umā" or the god Śiva as the lover of Umā-Pārvatī. This folk etymology obviously agrees well with the sexual symbolism characteristic of tantric Hinduism, but Kāpāli-śarman's association with Soma sacrifices or rites suggests the possibility of a more orthodox, Vedic background to the term. Vinodacandra Śrīvāstav has criticized me for identifying Somasiddhānta as the doctrine of the Kāpālikas alone, suggesting that *Somasiddhānta* and *Nyāyasiddhānta* may have been equivalent terms.[18] This equation would make it possible to connect the philosophical affiliation of the Kāpālikas with that of the Kālāmukhas, who are known to have been mostly Naiyāyikas, but the evidence which Śrīvāstav cites to support his hypothesis is clearly insufficient. In virtually all cases the term *Somasiddhānta* refers to the doctrine of the Kāpālikas or, in one or two references, other tantric ascetics. Until further evidence is discovered, there is little reason to connect Somasiddhānta with Nyāya or any other known philosophical school.

The image of the Kāpālika ascetic in Indian literature is an interesting and valid topic of study independent of its possible correspondence or non-correspondence with historical reality. Nonetheless, the attempt to reconstruct this historical reality is obviously an endeavor of equal or greater interest. The recent identification of a corpus of Kāpālika texts preserved in Nepal promises to revolutionize our understanding of actual Kāpālika beliefs and practices. A better understanding of the historical evolution, distribution, and strength of the Kāpālikas also requires the identification and analysis of whatever epigraphical material exists relevant to these ascetics. The inscriptions of Somibhaṭṭāraka and Kāpāli-śarman add important historical data to what is already known about the Kāpālikas.

NOTES

1. D. Lorenzen, *The Kāpālikas and Kālāmukhas* (Berkeley: University of California Press, 1972); W. O'Flaherty, *The Origins of Evil in Hindu Mythology* (Berkeley: University of California Press, 1976); E.-C. Visuvalingam, "Bhairav: Kotwāl of Vārāṇasī," in V. P. Verma (ed.), *Vārāṇasī Through the Ages* (Varanasi: Bharatiya Itihas Sankalan Samiti, 1986), 241-60. See also H. von Stietencron, "Bhairava," *Zeitschrift der Deutschen Morgenländischen Gesellschaft*, Supplementa I, Teil 3 (1969), 863-71; S. Kramrisch, *The Presence of Śiva* (Princeton: Princeton University Press, 1981); S. Gupta, D. J. Hoens, and T. Goudriaan, *Hindu Tantrism* (Leiden: E. J. Brill, 1979); and J. Parry, "Sacrificial death and the necrophagous ascetic," in M. Bloch and J. Parry (eds.), *Death and the Regeneration of Life* (Cambridge: Cambridge University Press, 1982), 74-110.

2. Alexis Sanderson, "Purity and Power among the Brahmans of Kashmir," in M. Carrithers *et al.* (eds.), *The Category of the Person* (Cambridge: Cambridge University Press, 1985), 190-216; "Maṇḍala and Āgamic Identity in the Trika of Kashmir," in *Mantras et diagrammes rituels dans l'hindouisme* (Paris: Éditions du Centre National de la Récherche Scientifique, 1986), 169-207; review of two *āgama* texts edited by N. R. Bhatt in *Bulletin of the School of Oriental and African Studies*, 48 (1985), 564-68; entries on "Krama Śaivism," "Śaivism in Kashmir," and "Trika Śaivism," in M. Eliade, ed.-in-chief, *Encyclopedia of Religion* (New York: Macmillan, 1987), vol. 13, 14-17; and "Śaivism and the Tantric Traditions," in Stuart Sutherland (ed.), *The World's Religions* (London: Coom Helm Press, forthcoming). Sanderson kindly supplied me with this information and copies of most of the material. Two other probable Kāpālika manuscripts—*Kāpālikamatavyasthā* and *Somasiddhānta*—are listed in G. Kavirāj's catalogue, *Tāntrik sāhitya* (Lucknow: Hindi Samiti, 1972).

3. See M. A. Dorai Rangaswaṃy, *The Religion and Philosophy of Tevaram*, 4 vols. in 2 (Madras: University of Madras, 1958-59), 1018; and Yogi Suddhananda

Bharathi, *The Grand Epic of Saivism* (Madras: South India Saiva Siddhanta Works Publishing Society, 1970), 168-75. See also Hudson in this volume.

4. Svatmārāma, *Hathayogapradīpikā* (Madras: The Adyar Library, 1972), verse 3.96.

5. M. Hara, Review of *The Kāpālikas and Kālāmukhas*, by D. Lorenzen, *Indo-Iranian Journal*, 17 (1975), 253-61; A. C. Barthakuria, *The Kapalikas: a Critical Study of the Religion, Philosophy and Literature of a Tantric Sect* (Calcutta: Sanskrit Pustak, 1984).

6. N. N. Upādhyāy, *Bauddha Kāpālik sādhanā aur sāhitya* (Allahabad: Smṛiti Prakaśan, 1983).

7. See Lorenzen, *Kāpālikas and Kālāmukhas*, 69-71; and P. Kvaerne, *An Anthology of Buddhist Tantric Songs* (2nd ed.; Bankok: White Orchid Press, 1986), 37, 113-22, 150-55.

8. Letter to me dated 16 January 1987.

9. See Lorenzen, *Kāpālikas and Kālāmukhas*, 27-28.

10. P. V. Parabrahma Sastry, *Select Epigraphs of Andhra Pradesh* (Hyderabad: Government of Andhra Pradesh, 1965), 7-10.

11. *mukha-kamaḷa-vinirggata-Sōmasiddhāntābhiprāya-parāyaṇaṃ [*bha]smōddhūḷita-ṣa[*ṇmu]ḍrā[* = drā]ḷaṃkrita-khaṭvāṃga-kapāḷa-ḍamaruga-mṛdaṃga-kāhaḷaṃ śrī-Śrīnātha-pāda-paṃkaja-bhramara-mahāvrati-dānāṃburāsi-satya-tapō-nidhi-. . . .* The starred additions and correction are my own as is the translation.

12. Yāmunācārya, *Āgama-prāmāṇya*, ed. J. A. B. van Buitenen (Madras: Ramanuja Research Society, 1971), p. 43, lines 7-16. The translation is mine. Rāmānuja repeats the same verses minus the first and last. See Lorenzen, *Kāpālikas and Kālāmukhas*, 1-4.

13. See Lorenzen, *Kāpālikas and Kālāmukhas*, 2-7, 73-82.

14. Hara, Review, p. 257, n.

15. K. V. Ramesh, *Inscriptions of the Western Gangas* (Delhi: ICHR and Agam Prakashan, 1984), 70-74 (no. 19).

16. *Kutsagotrāya Taittirīyacaraṇāya Prāvacanakalpāya Upakoṭṭanivāsine Someneṣṭaviśiṣṭakarmmaṇaḥ Agniśarmmaṇaḥputrāya Kāpāliśarmmaṇe. . . .* My translation differs from that of Ramesh who renders the phrase *Someneṣṭa-viśiṣṭa-karmmaṇaḥ* as "whose religious rites were rendered special by his performance of those rites with *sōma.*" Ramesh notes, however, that an earlier edition of the inscription in the *Mysore Archaeological Reports* reads *someneṣṭi-* rather than *someneṣṭa-*. Even granting that Ramesh's reading is orthographically correct, it makes better sense if the text is amended to the reading given in the earlier edition.

17. See Lorenzen, *Kāpālikas and Kālāmukhas*, 82-83.

18. V. Śrīvāstav, "Kāpālik evaṃ Kālāmukh: ek aitihāsik samīkṣā," *Journal of The Bihar Puravid Parishad* 3 (1979), 155-78. Śrīvāstav fails to cite the most interesting piece of evidence in favor of his hypothesis. G. Tucci has suggested that the term *na ya xiu mo* found in Chinese translations of Harivarman's lost

Sanskrit work *Tattvasiddhiśāstra* is equivalent to *Nyāyasauma* or *Nyāyasaumya*, which may be equivalent to Somasiddhānta. See G. Tucci, "Animadversiones Indicae," *Journal of the Royal Asiatic Society of Bengal*, n.s. 26 (1930), 125-60 (n.b. pp. 129-30). Śrīvāstav further speculates (p. 174) that Soma may be the name of the human author of the Somasiddhānta. This is a plausible suggestion but is not supported by any concrete evidence.

8

Rapist or Bodyguard, Demon or Devotee? Images of Bhairo in the Mythology and Cult of Vaiṣṇo Devī

Kathleen M. Erndl

Vaiṣṇo Devī is a popular goddess worshipped in a mountain cave shrine near Katra, District Jammu in northwestern India. She resides there in the form of three piṇḍīs (rock outcroppings) representing the Śākta trinity, Mahālakṣmī, Mahākālī, and Mahāsarasvatī. Vaiṣṇo Devī is said to be the only shrine in India in which all three forms of the goddess are present in svayambhū (self-born) form. She is considered to be the eldest of a group of goddesses, called the "Seven Sisters," who are collectively worshipped as aspects of the pan-Indian Mahādevī (great goddess) who slew the buffalo demon Mahiṣāsura. Hindus worship these goddesses primarily for material considerations such as fertility, wealth, and happiness. They do not see these material desires as contradicting the ultimately saving power of the goddess' grace, for the cult of the goddess is world-affirming and non-dualistic. Neither do they see these desires as contradicting the flavor of bhakti (devotion) which thoroughly permeates the cult. Rather than seeing the goddess' favors as being simply transactional, they see them as her way of showing love to her devotees.

At the shrines of all the Seven Sisters, the question of animal sacrifice is an ambiguous one. Priests and devotees recognize that animal sacrifice is traditional in goddess worship and that the goddess is fierce and bloodthirsty as well as benevolent and protective. Yet the practice of animal sacrifice is rapidly dying out, being replaced by Vaiṣṇava-type vegetarian offerings. The Vaiṣṇava practice of vegetarianism has influenced worship at the shrines of all of the Seven Sisters, but nowhere has the influence been so strong as at the shrine of Vaiṣṇo Devī. The name Vaiṣṇo itself comes from *vaiṣṇava* or its feminine form *vaiṣṇavī*, meaning literally pertaining to or a follower of the god Viṣṇu. In the northwest of India, these terms commonly have the extended meaning of vegetarian. Thus, Vaiṣṇo Devī is the vegetarian goddess. She accepts no animal sacrifice and does not even permit pilgrims to wear leather shoes while making the twelve kilometer hike up the mountain to her cave temple. The theme of vegetarianism crops up again and again in the myths of Vaiṣṇo Devī and her sisters, with the figure of Bhairo playing a pivotal role.

As the title of this paper indicates, Bhairo is an ambiguous character. On the one hand, he represents all that is opposed to Vaiṣṇava ideals of propriety: he is a *tāntric*,[1] a meat eater, a wine drinker, and a lascivious womanizer. On the other hand, he is the ideal devotee whom the virgin goddess Vaiṣṇo Devī rewards by granting two boons, mokṣa (liberation) and the homage of pilgrims. One is tempted to posit the explanation that the Vaiṣṇo Devī cult is an amalgam of at least two separate strands, a Vaiṣṇava strand in which vegetarianism, chastity, and themes from the *Rāmāyaṇa* are dominant and a Tāntric or Śākta strand in which animal sacrifice, sexual union, and the theme of the goddess slaying the buffalo demon are dominant. According to this interpretation, the figure of Bhairo could be seen as a remnant or vestige of an earlier tantric substratum which was later supplanted by a dominant Vaiṣṇava ideology and practice. As tempting as this explanation may be, I am not entirely satisfied with it, because the underlying structure of the Vaiṣṇo Devī myth presents itself as a unity with bhakti emerging as the major theme. I will demonstrate this point with a close look at the story of Vaiṣṇo Devī and Bhairo.

Oral and written sources for the myths of Vaiṣṇo Devī are reasonably homogeneous. The written sources consist of popular bazaar pamphlets in colloquial Hindi which pilgrims buy and read as part of the pilgrimage experience. Most of these popular pamphlets start out by telling the story of the great goddess as it appears in the second and third episodes of the Sanskrit text *Devī Māhātmyam*, that is, of her creation through the combined powers of the gods and her killing of the demons Mahiṣāsura, Śumbha and Niśumbha. The inclusion of these mythic episodes clearly identifies Vaiṣṇo Devī as an aspect of the pan-Indian great goddess.

The story more immediately relevant to the cult of Vaiṣṇo Devī concerns her birth and establishment in the sacred geography of Trikūṭ mountain. The first episode, detailing her birth and apotheosis, takes place in the Treta Yuga, connecting Vaiṣṇo Devī with Viṣṇu and the *Rāmāyaṇa*. The second episode, detailing the founding and discovery of the shrine, occurs in the present Kali Yuga, connecting Vaiṣṇo Devī with Bhairo and the Nāth sect of yogis.

The following is an abridgement of the story taken from a popular pamphlet in Hindi.[2]

From time to time Mahāśakti takes on different forms to destroy evildoers and protect devotees. At different times this Mahāśakti who was born of the accumulated brilliance (*tej*) of the gods has taken on the forms of Mahākālī, Mahālakṣmī and Mahāsarasvatī, the symbols of *raj*, *tam*, and *sattvik* qualities.[3]

In the Treta Yuga, when Rāvaṇa and the other demons worked their evil, the three Mahāśaktis, in order to protect the dharma, pooled their powers and produced a śakti in the form of a beautiful divine maiden (*kanyā*). They sent her to take birth in South India as the daughter of one Ratnasāgara. She was given the name Trikūṭā. Later she became known as Vaiṣṇavī or Vaiṣṇo, because she had been produced as a part (*aṃśa*) of Viṣṇu.[4]

At a very young age, the goddess Trikūṭā had already distinguished herself with supernatural (*alaukika*) powers and was attracting holy men and devotees from far away who came seeking her darśan. After some time, Trikūṭā with her father's permission went to the oceanside to perform austerities while meditating on Lord Rāma and waiting for him. After Sītā had been abducted by Rāvaṇa, Rāma passed her way with his army of monkeys and saw the divine maiden seated in a deep trance (samādhi). She told him that she was performing austerities in order to obtain him as her husband. Rāma replied that he had made a vow to remain faithful to only one wife, Sītā, in this incarnation. But Trikūṭā would not change her mind. Finally, Rāma promised that he would return later and marry her if she would recognize him. While returning to Ayodhyā from Laṅkā, Rāma appeared before her in the guise of an old man, but she did not recognize him. Rāma consoled her by promising that in the Kali Yuga when he would incarnate as Kalki, she would be his consort. In the meantime, she should go to a cave on Trikūṭ mountain in North India where the three Mahāśaktis live and perform austerities there. Sending Hanumān and the other monkeys to be her sentries, he told her that she would become famous as Vaiṣṇo Devī.

In this way, it is believed that the goddess became established in her cave. With the passing of the ages, the Mother showed her divine play (līlā), and other stories arose. In the Kali Yuga the following story has become well known:

> About 700 years ago, in Hansali village near Katra there lived a Brahman named Śrīdhar who was a great devotee of the Mother. One day he was performing a kanyā pūjā (worship of small girls as manifestations of the goddess) in order to obtain a son. When Śrīdhar began to feed the girls, Vaiṣṇo Devī, in the form of a divine maiden, appeared among them. She ordered him to host a grand feast for his village and the surrounding area the following day. He knew that she must be some kind of śakti, so he went from village to village inviting people to the feast. On the road he met a group of mendicants led by Gorakhnāth and invited them as well. Gorakhnāth issued a challenge that Śrīdhar would never be able to satisfy him, his disciple Bhaironāth, and his 360 other disciples, as even Indra himself had been unable to satisfy them.
>
> The next day when the guests began to arrive, Śrīdhar was worried that he would not be able to feed them all, but they all managed to fit into his tiny hut and the divine maiden began to serve everyone food. When she started to serve Bhaironāth, he objected to the vegetarian fare, demanding to be served meat and wine. The maiden replied that this is a Brahman's house and that one should accept whatever is offered in a vaiṣṇava feast. Bhairo became angry and tried to grab her, but she was able to read the evil desires in his mind and disappeared.
>
> Bhairo set out in search of her, stopping at stations along the way [each of which is now a feature of the pilgrimage route]. The first place was Darśanī Darvāzā where one catches the first glimpse of Trikūṭ mountain. Farther along the route, the goddess struck a rock with her arrow (*bāṇ*) in order to produce water for her thirsty companion Langūr Vīr [a form of Hanumān]. This stream is now known as the Bān Gaṅgā. At a place farther up the mountain, the goddess looked back to see if Bhairo was still following her. Because her footprints are still there, the place is called Caraṇ Padukā. After some time, she came upon a small cave and climbed inside. Just as a child remains in its mothers's womb for nine months, so did the maiden remain in the cave for nine months performing austerities. Bhairo also arrived there and inquired from a nearby mendicant if he had seen a maiden. The mendicant said, "The one whom you consider to be an ordinary woman is actually the Mahāśakti and Ādikumārī (primeval virgin)." But Bhairo ignored him and entered the cave. The Mother used her trident to make an opening and emerge from the

other end of the cave. This cave is now called Garbh-jūn (Sanskrit—*Garbhayoni*), and the place is called Ādikumārī.

Bhairo continued to follow her even though she kept telling him to go back. Mahāmāyā (Great Illusion) was capable of doing whatever she wanted, but Bhairo's desire was also true! Finally, the goddess entered a beautiful cave on Trikūṭ mountain, posting Langūr Vīr at the door as a guard. Bhairo attacked and almost killed him. At that point, Śakti took on the form of Caṇḍī [a fierce form of the goddess] and cut off his head. The head fell into the valley below, while the body remained at the entrance to the cave where it can be seen today as a large boulder. As his head was severed, Bhairo yelled out, 'O Ādi Śakti (Primeval Energy), O Generous Mother, I am not sorry to meet death, because it is at the hands of the Mother who created the world. O Māteśvarī (Mother-Lord), forgive me. I was not familiar with this form of yours. Ma, if you don't forgive me, then the coming age will view me as a sinner and castigate my name. A mother can never be a bad mother.[5] Hearing these words again and again, the gracious Mother gave him the boon that after worshipping her, people would also worship him, and he would also attain mokṣa (liberation). If people worshipped at his shrine, their wishes would be fulfilled. A temple was built where Bhairo's head fell, and pilgrims stop there today on their way back from Vaiṣṇo Devī's temple.

In another version of the story,[6] a multiform of Bhaironāth appears as Bhairo Bali or Bhairav Bali, an evil king who tortured followers of the Vaiṣṇava tradition. The episode occurs also in the Kali Yuga but before and in addition to the episode with Bhaironāth. The king Bhairo Bali controlled a kingdom from the Satluj to the Jhelum Rivers in the Panjab. One day Vaiṣṇo Devī held a feast. Bhairo Bali saw her and wanted to marry her, but she refused, so he chased her up the mountain. On the way, the goddess liberated many places from the rule of the evil king and established goddesses there. In this version, the story continues in the same way summarized above, repeating the section on Bhaironāth.

After Vaiṣṇo Devī's beheading of Bhaironāth, the story continues:

Meanwhile, the devotee Śrīdhar who had hosted the feast was so upset when the divine maiden disappeared so precipitously that he stopped eating and drinking. To show him her grace, the Mother appeared before him and showed him her cave dwelling, taking him through the whole pilgrimage route. Upon awaking, Śrīdhar searched for the cave he had seen in his dream. He eventually found it and received there a face-to-face vision (*sākṣāt darśan*) of the Mother. She gave him a boon of four sons and instructed him to continue worshipping her. Thus, Śrīdhar is credited with the propagation of Vaiṣṇo Devī worship, and the present day temple priests trace their descent from him.

Pilgrims who worship Vaiṣṇo Devī at Trikūṭ mountain today trace the steps which the goddess took in her flight from Bhaironāth, including the literal crawl through the womb-cave at Ādi Kumārī. Thus, they are symbolically re-enacting Bhairo's pursuit of Vaiṣṇo Devī. Bhairo at his shrine is called Bhairo Bābā. He is known to possess people occasionally, usually men, just as Vaiṣṇo Devī possesses women. While worshipped by some pilgrims for favors, he is clearly subordinate to Vaiṣṇo Devī.[7] It used to be considered necessary for pilgrims to stop at Bhairo's shrine to pay homage to him after worshipping Vaiṣṇo Devī as she decreed in the charter myth, but in recent times this practice has decreased. Now a new path built by the Dharmārth Trust bypasses the Bhairo temple entirely. If one wants to visit it, one must make a special effort. But the myth of Bhairo with its tantric overtones is still well-known, despite the attempts of some religious leaders and pamphleteers to downplay Bhairo's disrespectful behavior and present him as a simple Nāth or Yogī who was an ordinary devotee of Vaiṣṇo Devī.

As mentioned above, Vaiṣṇo Devī is worshipped in her cave shrine in the form of three lumps of stone called piṇḍīs, said to represent Mahālakṣmī, Mahākālī, and Mahāsarasvatī. The middle piṇḍī, Mahālakṣmī, is also called Vaiṣṇo Devī.[8] In popular bazaar lithographs, she is portrayed as having eight arms and as being seated on a lion or tiger. She holds in her arms a discus, club, and conch—emblems of Viṣṇu—and a trident, sword, and bow and arrow—emblems of Śiva. She holds a lotus in one of the remaining arms and displays the "fear-not" gesture (abhaya mudrā) in the other. She is flanked on the right by the Vaiṣṇava monkey god Hanumān, or Langūr Vīr. On the left is Bhairo in the form of Bāl (child) Bhairo, white in color with four arms holding a severed head, drum, chowrie, and sword and accompanied by a white dog. This seems to be a gentle or tamed version of the Bhairo found in the Vaiṣṇo Devī myth and of the Bhairava who is a fierce form of Śiva described in the Purāṇas and found as a folk deity all over India. This iconographic depiction of Vaiṣṇo Devī has become standard for most of the other goddesses (such as the Seven Sisters) in the Panjab Hills who are manifested in their temples in the aniconic piṇḍī form. It could be called the generic Śerāṅvālī (Lion Rider or Lion Woman) poster iconography (see plate 18).

18. Popular calendar print of Vaiṣṇo Devī flanked by Hanumān and Bhairo against the background of a schematic map depicting important stopping places on her pilgrimage route. At the top are Brahmā, Viṣṇu and Śiva tossing flowers. Photo by Kathleen Erndl.

Who is this Bhairo who accompanies Vaiṣṇo Devī as a bodyguard? The figure of Bhairo or Bhairava appears in several places in Purāṇic mythology, usually as a fierce form of Śiva and with some connection to themes of decapitation or dismemberment. The locus classicus is in the myth of Bhairava's decapitation of Brahmā in the *Skanda Purāṇa*.[9] The story states that because of Brahmā's disrespect, Śiva takes on the form of Bhairava and cuts off one of Brahmā's five heads, leaving him with the now customary four. The skull sticks to Bhairava's hand as evidence of his Brahmanicide. The severed head in the hand of Bhairo found in the Vaiṣṇo Devī iconography clearly identifies Bhairo with this Purāṇic Bhairava, and Bhairo's own decapitation at the hands of Vaiṣṇo Devī can be interpreted as a mythic reversal.

Most relevant to the goddess cycle of mythology is Bhairava's appearance in the story of Satī and the creation of the śākta pīṭhas (seats of power), a story which developed out of the ancient myth of the destruction of Dakṣa's sacrifice.[10] The Śākta version most commonly told in connection with the Vaiṣṇo Devī cycle can be summed up as follows:

> Satī, the wife of Śiva, was a daughter of Dakṣa. One day Dakṣa held a sacrifice to which neither Satī nor Śiva was invited. Satī died of sorrow (or threw herself into the fire) because of the slight. When Śiva heard of Satī's death, he and his attendants destroyed Dakṣa's sacrifice. Śiva became inconsolable, carrying Satī's body on his head, wandering over the earth doing the dance of destruction. The gods became anxious. According to one version, Brahmā, Viṣṇu, and Śani (Saturn) entered the corpse by yoga and dismembered it bit by bit. According to another version, Viṣṇu alone cut up the body with his discus. The places where the parts of Satī's body fell became pīṭhas, resorts of the goddess, each of which houses a different manifestation of the goddess along with a different form of Bhairava.

According to various schemes, there are four, seven, eight, forty-two, fifty-one or one-hundred and eight of these pīṭhas. Sources vary as to which part of Satī fell in which place, with texts reflecting regional biases. According to popular belief connected with the northwest cult of the goddess, her tongue fell at Jvālā Mukhī, breast at Kangrā Devī, eyes at Nainā Devī, forehead at Mansā Devī, feet at Cintpurṇī, and arms at Vaiṣṇo Devī. Thus, Bhairo can be loosely identified with Śiva who manifests himself as the subsidiary consort-guardian Bhairava at goddess shrines.

Bhairo is depicted in the Vaiṣṇo Devī myth and in some popular religious art as a member of the Nāth order of sādhus. The Nāths, recognizable by their characteristic bored ears and large earrings, are an unorthodox group of Śaivite mendicants who are found in fairly large numbers in the Panjab area. They have a close connection with the goddess cult in the area and even have rights to part of the temple of Jvālā Mukhī, a sister to Vaiṣṇo Devī. As Elizabeth Visuvalingam points out in her article in this volume, the Nāths have long been associated with Bhairava, seeing him as the epitome of the ideal of transgressive sacrality. In connection with the Vaiṣṇo Devī cult, the Nāths represent a Śaivite or tantric, as opposed to Vaiṣṇavite, style of religious practice.

It is clear that Vaiṣṇo Devī is identified at least on one level with Durgā, the killer of Mahiṣāsura. This identification is made explicit in the popular pamphlets which tell the *Devī Māhātmyam* myths and then call Vaiṣṇo Devī an avatār or incarnation of the same goddess. One particular pamphlet has arranged the various stories into an ingenious cosmogonic scheme, "The Lion-rider in the Four Ages."[11] In the Satya Yuga, the three episodes of the *Devī Māhātmyam* (the killing of the Madhu-Kaiṭabha, Mahiṣāsura, and Śumbha-Niśumbha) occurred; in the Tretā Yuga, the part of the Vaiṣṇo Devī story that deals with Rāma. In the Dvāpara Yuga, there was no avatār, but the goddess gave power to Arjuna to fight the *Mahābhārata* war, and the Pāṇḍavas performed their horse sacrifice.[12] In the Kali Yuga there were the stories of Śrīdhar and Bhairo, Dhyānū Bhagat, Tārārāṇī, and others.

It is not unreasonable to see Bhairo as a multiform of Mahiṣāsura, the buffalo demon, particularly when one remembers that Bhairo is a form of Śiva and that Śiva is often identified (particularly, as David Shulman points out,[13] in South Indian sources) with the buffalo demon who is killed by his bride. In some versions of the Mahiṣāsura story, the demon attains liberation through decapitation at the hands of the goddess just as Bhairo does at the hands Vaiṣṇo Devī. The bhakti interpretation would be that Bhairo chased her up the mountain out of devotion, however misplaced, and further proved his devotion through decapitation, the ultimate self-sacrifice.

The theme of decapitation appears in several other myths of the Vaiṣṇo Devī and Śerāṅvālī cycle. The offering of coconuts at goddess temples is explained by a charter myth in which the devotee Dhyānū Bhagat cuts off his own head and offers it to the goddess who promises that henceforth she will accept coconut offerings instead. In another story, the devotee Tārārāṇī, who is accused by her husband of impurity for eating meat at a sweeper's *jagrātā* (all night worship of the goddess), forces her husband to decapitate and eat his horse and son to satisfy the goddess. Their heads, like Dhyānū's, are subsequently restored by the goddess. The priests at the goddess temples tell about having witnessed devotees' tongues grow back after they cut them out and offered them to the goddess.

The *Rāmāyaṇa* connection adds another rich dimension to the Vaiṣṇo Devī myth, resulting in some rather startling reversals. In the *Rāmāyaṇa*, it is Rāma who undergoes tests to win Sītā. In the Vaiṣṇo Devī story, it is Vaiṣṇo Devī who performs austerities in order to win Rāma, but ultimately loses him for failing to pass a test. In the *Rāmāyaṇa*, it is Sītā's *pativrata* (vow to remain faithful to one husband) which is emphasized. In the Vaiṣṇo Devī story, it is Rāma's *patnīvrata* (vow to remain faithful to one wife) which is emphasized. In the *Rāmāyaṇa*, Rāvaṇa abducts a helpless Sītā. In the Vaiṣṇo Devī story, Bhairo attempts but does not succeed in raping the independent and powerful Vaiṣṇo Devī. In the *Rāmāyaṇa*, Rāma kills Rāvaṇa in order to regain Sītā. In the Vaiṣṇo Devī story, Vaiṣṇo Devī kills Bhairo without any help and makes it clear that she has gone through the whole chase scene as a way of displaying her līlā, divine play, as the great Śakti who is the queen of illusion. The scene of Vaiṣṇo Devī "becoming Caṇḍī" and slaying Bhairo is reminiscent not only of Durgā killing the buffalo demon but of Sītā in tantric versions of the *Rāmāyaṇa* (such as the *Adhyātma Rāmāyaṇa*) taking the form of Kālī and killing Rāvaṇa herself. From this point of view, the events in the Vaiṣṇo Devī story mirror those in the *Rāmāyaṇa*, and Bhairo can be seen as a multiform of Rāvaṇa, the Vaiṣṇava embodiment of transgressive sacrality par excellence. But Rāvaṇa himself can be seen as a multiform of the buffalo demon, as Alf Hiltebeitel suggests.[14]

At an explicit level in the Vaiṣṇo Devī story, there is an obvious tension between tantric (or Śaiva/Śākta) values and Vaiṣṇava values. Tantric values are represented by Bhairo who can be seen as the vīra or hero who seeks union with the goddess through meat, wine, and sex. Vaiṣṇava values are represented by Śrīdhar, the Brahman who performs traditional pūjās and makes vegetarian offerings. However, the two are reconciled through the theology of bhakti. Bhairo and Śrīdhar can be seen simply as two different types of devotees. Bhairo takes a transgressive approach and attains mokṣa at the moment of the most extreme self-sacrifice. But the more moderate Śrīdhar is not neglected either; he receives the full darśan of the goddess and is granted the boon of sons. Bhairo and Śrīdhar are two sides of the same coin. The goddess graciously accepts both types of devotion.

NOTES

1. For the purposes of this paper, *tantra* is a religious practice or method which advocates reversals of accepted societal norms, transgressive sacrality par excellence. A *tantric* is a person who subscribes to such practices.

2. *Śrī Vaiṣṇo Devī Darśana aura Nau Deviyoṅ kī Kathā* (Haridvāra: Harabhajana Siṅgha eṇḍa Sansa, n.d.) is the primary source I am using, mentioning other versions when relevant. The text given here is my own abridged translation which sticks closely to the colloquial and interpretative tone of the original.

3. These are the Hindi equivalents of the three Sanskrit *guṇas* (qualities), rajas, tamas and sattva which are active, inert, and pure, respectively. Here the three major aspects of the goddess (Mahāśakti, the "Great Energy") are being identified with the three guṇas in the same way that the male deities Brahmā, Śiva, and Viṣṇu often are.

4. This last sentence appears to be a *non sequitur*, as we have just been told that the Trikūṭā was produced through the combined powers of the three great Śaktis. The composite nature of the myth is evident here.

5. This is a vernacular allusion to the famous verse in the *Saundaryalaharī*, traditionally attributed to Śaṃkara, which says, "A son may be a bad son, but a mother can never be a bad mother."

6. Recounted in Bālakṛṣṇa Śarmā, *saṅgrahakartā* (compiler), *Mātā Vaiṣṇo Devī* (Kaṭrā: Bhavānī Pustaka Mahala, n.d.). A similar portrayal of Bhairo is found in a low budget feature length film on Vaiṣṇo Devī. The use of the name Bali is suggestive of the antagonist in the story of the Dwarf incarnation of Viṣṇu and may be used in some versions of the Vaiṣṇo Devī story to strengthen Vaiṣṇava associations.

7. Georgana Foster ("The Shrine of Vaiṣṇo Devī: Some Comparative Aspects of Iconography and Mythology," unpublished manuscript, 1983) has suggested that the new road was purposely built by the Dharmārth Trust in order to downplay the Tāntric or Śaivite elements of the cult which Bhairo suggests.

8. It may be significant that Vaiṣṇo Devī is identified with Mahālakṣmī, the form of the goddess who in the second episode of the *Devī Māhātmyam* killed the buffalo demon, Mahiṣāsura.

9. *Kāśī Khaṇḍa*, 15-16. This story is discussed by Diana L. Eck in *Banaras: City of Light* (London: Routledge and Kegan Paul, 1983), 107-108 and 189-195 *passim*. Further discussion is found in E.-C. Visuvalingam's article in this volume.

10. For an extensive discussion of the development of this myth, see D. C.

Sircar, *The Śākta Pīṭhas* (Delhi: Motilal Banarsidass, second rev. ed., 1973). The versions mentioned in this paper are found in *Devī Bhāgavata Purāṇa* 7.30 and *Kālikā Purāṇa* 16.18, respectively.

11. *Cāra Yugoṅ meṅ Śerāṅvālī* (Haridvāra: Harabhajana Siṅgha eṇḍa Sansa, n.d.).

12. This episode figures in the story of Tārārāṇī, an exemplary female devotee of the goddess.

13. "The Murderous Bride: Tamil Versions of the Myth of Devī and the Buffalo Demon," *History of Religions* 16,2 (1976), 120-147.

14. "Rāma and Gilgamesh: The Sacrifices of the Water Buffalo and the Bull of Heaven," *History of Religions* 19,3 (1980), 187-223.

9

The Bir Babas of Banaras and the Deified Dead

Diane M. Coccari

Worship of the "deified dead" is common in the North Indian city of Banaras and the surrounding region.[1] Among the most prominent classes identified by Hindus are Birs (bīr); Brahms (brahm); Pirs (*pīr*), Shahids (*śahīd*) and other "Muslim Deities" (*musalmānī devatā*); memorialized gurus, ascetics or yogis ("Babas:" *bābā*); and local goddesses (*satī māī, caurā māī, saiyarī māī*, etc.). These stand out among other miscellaneous varieties of ghosts or spirits (bhūt-pret: here a compound which does not distinguish the two elements) as being "deities" (devatā) to their worshipers, a status often initiated by the establishment of a shrine and the onset of regular worship. There is some justification for viewing the deified dead as an analytical category: tradition holds that they share a human past; an untimely, heroic, sacrificial or otherwise extraordinary end to life; a continued presence at the site of the shrine; and a localized and particularized power to effect or influence certain exigencies in the lives of worshippers. Nonetheless, significant distinctions are made by believers among the various types of dead, and these deities share many characteristics and functions with other local and regional gods of less certain origin. As space does not permit a thorough treatment of all the above-named classes of deities, an overview of these figures followed by a more detailed description of those called Bir or Bir Baba (Bir = Sanskrit vīra or "hero") will permit us to both contextualize a particular group and explore it at greater length. With the help of oral accounts and a folk song about a contemporary Bir, I will demonstrate something of the timeless and ongoing process of "deification" of a human hero and the nature of worship of these deities.

A. The Deified Dead: Some Examples

Ascetics' Tombs

Banaras contains many small neighborhood shrines which are said to be the samādhis (tombs) of beloved ascetics or guru figures. Although these are attended, worshiped, and petitioned much like other local shrines of the deified dead, the presence at the shrine of the ascetic has less to do with untimely death (akāl mṛtyu) than certain popularly held ideas about the spiritual exercises of the yogi. The range of usage of the term samādhi helps convey something of the perception of the presence of an entombed ascetic. For instance, it happens on occasion that a particular yogi will announce his intention to "take samādhi" (samādhi *lenā*) for a specified number of days in a carefully prepared, airless tomb, as did one "Pilot Baba" in Banaras in December of 1981. The adept then theoretically utilizes his yogic skill to drastically retard bodily functions, obviating the need for sustenance and air for the duration of the entombment. The body will appear cold and lifeless, yet the germ of life remains in the highest cakra at the top of the skull. During this time the individual may be seen at other locations, as he is able to move about freely and perform other miracles in this condition. This is a dramatic example of the yogic meditation which eventually leads to the attainment of samādhi, in this case the ultimate goal or stage of spiritual attainment after which the being of the yogi is permanently transmuted or transformed. Sometimes an ageing adept will state his intention to "take samādhi" to signal his departure from this life in his present body: he wills his death/release/immortality by this culminating yogic act. An ascetic buried in his samādhi/tomb is therefore understood to be present either as an immortal body or as a liberated, disembodied consciousness hovering about the shrine. Deceased sectarian guru figures, in particular, are addressed, attended, and worshiped as though they are living and still capable of intercession in the lives and spiritual progress of their followers. The memorialized yogi is viewed as a wakeful presence in much the same way as the other deified figures mentioned here, characterized by an imminence and responsiveness to human needs and concerns. The figure of the Bir—to be discussed below—is sometimes conflated with the entombed ascetic, a natural development in view of the existence in the tradition of warrior ascetics, yogis who become physically powerful as a result of ascetic observances, and heroes whose physical might implies disciplined spiritual attainment, or who are assumed to have saintly characters. There are even Bir Babas in Banaras (named Jog or Jogi Bir) who are said to be yogis who met with violent and untimely ends, another conflation of the two traditions.

Female Figures

There are numerous village and neighborhood goddesses in the Banaras area who clearly emerge from this process of honoring or placating the human dead with shrine and ritual attention. The Satis and related goddesses (Chaura Mai, etc.) are the most obvious examples, but so too are the more ambivalent Maris and Bhavanis, ghosts generated from the untimely death of pre-pubescent (even unborn) female children.

Those with whom I spoke made it clear that the Sati's heroic act of self-sacrifice is not viewed as an untimely death in the normal sense: it is the optimal course that a wife follow her husband—without whom she is incomplete—into the next world, culminating her life of faithfulness and service. It is even said that the Sati may ignite the funeral pyre by the energy of her own *sat*—"truthfulness" or "virtue," the accumulated essence of her extraordinary and life-long devotion. That the Sati is worshiped as a goddess even before her death testifies to the power and auspiciousness engendered by her wifely discipline and awe-inspiring courage. Although in theory she joins her husband in his fate, the very power of the event establishes the Sati as an earthly goddess; she is believed to be present at her shrine and able to bestow blessings upon petitioners. The general attitude toward Satis is one of honor and reverence, and the goddesses are depicted with corresponding benevolence.[2]

This is not true of the Mari (*marī*) or Bhavani (bhavānī). A greater effort is required to mollify these spirits and, if need be, transform and redirect their jealous anger into support for the living. Planalp discusses the process whereby malevolent Bhavanis are transformed by enshrinement and worship into the family goddesses of low caste, village Hindus.[3] The intrinsic ambivalence of the female ghost/goddess permits easy identification with the disease-goddess cycle and other ambivalent goddess types.

Brahms

Small shrines to deities called Brahms or Brahm Babas are found in many Banaras neighborhoods and are scattered throughout the countryside. In the broadest sense, a Brahm is a ghost or deified ghost of a member of the Brahman caste.[4] Equal to the spiritual stature of the living Brahman, the Brahm ranks high among other ghosts. In some cases Brahm shrines are established by Brahmans to "quiet" the spirit of a family member who tenaciously asserts his presence after death and fails to accept other forms of pacification. The Brahm is honored as an ancestor, is called upon to bless his kin, and may become in time the Brahm Baba of a wider and more diverse population. In other cases a shrine is established with the intention of inflicting ill upon those who have wronged the deceased figure or have had a hand in his demise. Not only is it most serious to be involved in the death of a Brahman because of the sin (*pāp*) that results, but a Brahman may inflict his ghost like a powerful curse upon an enemy, resulting in a virulent form of posthumous retribution. This particular form of protest is available to a Brahman who feels himself wronged yet is powerless to seek justice by other means, and is likely to occur in a confrontation with a wielder of temporal authority upon whom a Brahman is in some sense dependent. The theme of Brahman-Kṣatriya (Thakur) interdependence/animosity occurs quite frequently in this regard, as the Thakur is often the dominant or landowning caste in this area of North India. It occurs in the stories told about Harasu Brahm, the reigning deity at a regional pilgrimage site in nearby Bihar which draws large numbers of Banarasis for exorcism, fertility, and wish fulfillment. Banaras' own premier Brahm Baba site is Pisach Mochan Temple, an account of which may be found in the *Kāśī Khaṇḍa* of the *Skanda Purāṇa*.[5] In contrast with oral versions of the Pisach Mochan story which provide the mandate for the Brahm Baba's role in the liberation of disgruntled spirits, the Puranic version tends to divest the figure of the brahma piśāca or brahma rākṣasa of its authority as an embodied deity in favor of a parable of sorts on the subject of sin, karma, and salvation.

Muslim Deities

"Muslim Deities" are incorporated into the pantheons of many low caste and rural Hindus. In the last century it was common for an individual to declare himself a *Panchpiriya*—a worshiper of the Panchon Pir (*pā̃ñcõ pīr*) or Five (Muslim) Saints—when asked to give his religious affiliation. The model for the aggregate of five being based, most likely, upon the Shiite quintet of Muhammad, Fatimah, Ali, Hasan, and Husain symbolized by the hand carried in Muharram processions, the expansion of the cult saw the progressive incorporation of local figures. In the Panjab, where the Indian version of the cult seems to have originated, the list of Panchon Pir consisted of prominent Sufi (mainly

Chisti) saints living in the 13th and 14th centuries;[6] as the cult spread to the south and east, there was a tendency for some of the saints to be replaced with historical or quasi-historical Islamic martial heroes—the religious warriors (*ġāzī*) or martyrs (śahīd) whose localized cults were already established in a given region. Further expansion of the Panchpiriya cult resulted in the progressive dilution of Islamic elements and the inclusion of purely local Hindu or "tribal" deities and deified dead, including Satis and other goddesses. The most prominent figure associated with the Panchon Pir in the Uttar Pradesh/Bihar/Bengal area is Ghazi Miya (ġāzī mīyā̃) said to be Salar Mas'ud, the nephew of Mahmud of Ghazni. Legend has it that the hero became a martyr at the young age of nineteen when he "led an expedition into Oudh and was killed in battle at Bahraich in A.D. 1034."[7] There is evidence in the late 13th and early 14th centuries of the great popularity of the legends of Salar Mas'ud, and the rapid growth of the cult centered at his tomb in Bahraich, in what is now Uttar Pradesh. The next several centuries witnessed the expansion of the institutions surrounding the tomb, the development of a hereditary priesthood, and the elaboration of cultic practices and oral traditions surrounding the hero. In the late 19th and early 20th centuries, eyewitness reports of Europeans portray the tomb of Ghazi Miya at Bahraich as a major pilgrimage center with an annual fair which drew 50,000 to 100,000 pilgrims—both Hindu and Muslim—from all over India. Replicas of the Bahraich tomb were to be found in other North Indian cities and towns, serving as localized centers of the cult.[8] In addition to the pilgrimage and tomb-centered worship which continues to this day, the Panchon Pir are worshiped in the homes of low caste Hindus as family deities. Writers have described the household shrines from the Panjab to Bengal as consisting of (1) a small, earthen mound topped by a spear, trident, or hand-shaped piece of iron, (2) five wooden pegs, or (3) replicas of Muslim graves or tombs. Daily, weekly, and annual worship is performed in the usual manner for household deities, often assisted by a Muslim Dafali, the hereditary priest of Ghazi Miya.[9] Although the influence of the Arya Samaj and corresponding Muslim fundamentalist movements have brought about a decline in the worship of Ghazi Miya, certain Hindu castes (most conspicuously the Doms in Banaras) continue to attend the local and Bahraich tombs and worship the quintet as family deities. Hindu attendance at the tombs of Muslim martyrs and saints—whether or not they are included in the Panchon Pir—remains a visible phenomenon. In Banaras, the tomb of Bahadur Sayyid or Shahid—said to be a martyr who later "revealed" himself (*jāhir ho jānā*) at his grave through the working of miracles—overflows with pilgrims on Thursday of each week. The water used to bathe the tomb is touted for its healing properties, and the saint is plied with written and silently expressed petitions for blessings and intercession. The courtyard is alive with possession activity; the predominantly low caste Hindu women resolve their struggles or destinies with possessing spirits under the authority of the resident saint or "Baba."

While in some senses the worship of Muslim deities by Hindus is specialized—as the use of Ghazi Miya by a Hindu Bhagat (oracular devotee of the goddess) to assist in the removal of Muslim ghosts (*jinn, śaitān*)—the household worship of Muslim deities, their position in many villages as guardians, and the general activity at tomb sites are analogous to that of the non-Islamic deified dead. In the role of Bhut Nath (or Jinn Nath: "Lord of Ghosts") in particular, the Pir/Shahid, Bir and Brahm are equally the sources of healing, wish fulfillment, and exorcism.

B. The Banaras Bir Babas

The most common representation of the Birs or Bir Babas[10] found on the periphery of Banaras' inner precincts and throughout surrounding villages is a primordial looking clay mound (piṇḍ, stūp, thūhā) set upon a raised platform (caurā, *cautarā, cabūtarā*). The practice of raising an earthen mound over the remains of the powerful and honored dead is an ancient one on the subcontinent, and was no doubt the tradition upon which the Buddhist *stūpa* was based. In the Banaras area, this clay mound is the generic form for the propitiatory *sthān*[11] of the untimely dead, seen also as a memorial to a respected individual or to an act of heroism or self-sacrifice. The shrines of Bir, Brahm, Mari, Bhavani, the Muslim martyrs and saints of the Panchon Pir, Satis, and the samādhis of Nath sadhus may be marked with this type of aniconic image (see plate 19). This rough clay shrine may be made more permanent with cement and whitewash, or replaced by other aniconic constructions in the shape of tall, rounded cones, posts, or four-sided pyramids with small niches set in one side. In Western Bihar—a region contiguous with the Varanasi District of Eastern Uttar Pradesh—Bir images are of carved wood or stone and have similarly evolved from a basic funerary marker, in this case a wooden post. As is true of aniconic images in general, there is a tendency to anthropomorphize the rough form over time. In the case of the mound or cone, a metal face of a "heroic" type with a large moustache is added to the featureless symbol;

19. The temple of Ahira Bir at Kolhua Vinayaka, Vārāṇasī. An example of a cone or mound-shaped image. Photo by Diane Coccari.

the top of a wooden post is carved into a head followed by the outlines of a rudimentary body. This latter process is illustrated by the striking Bir images studied by Archer in Bihar.[12]

Banaras' inner city neighborhoods contain a variety of Bir images. A sculptural fragment uncovered by construction or scooped up in nets from the Ganga may be established as a particular Bir by an individual inspired by a vision or dream of the forgotten figure. Numerous small, open-air shrines with empty niches may be identified as Birs, or sites marked only by sacred trees are known by the name of a Bir Baba. If anthropomorphic images are employed, they frequently take the form of militant looking ascetics, standing upright with top-knot, loin cloth, and water pot; a club or battle axe slung over one shoulder (see plate 20). These latter images are one answer to the Birs' original lack of anthropomorphic iconography, and similar images are employed in the small shrines to ascetics (Babas) and other deified dead, perhaps minus the weaponry. The found images, too, provide an easy solution to the Birs' human form; the appearance of the fragment may even determine the figure's name, as "Naked Hero" for an image of a Jain Tirthankara, or "Headless Hero" for a decapitated sculpture of the Buddha.

It is the lower to middle ranking rustic classes that make up the majority of the Birs' followers, but particular shrines may draw members of any caste or class, hopeful of a blessing, cure or resolution to an intractable problem.[13] Worshiped chiefly by neighbors of the shrines, the Birs are approached most frequently on Tuesdays and Sundays and during seasons of festival activity. It has become very popular of late to organize a *varsik srngar*, an "Annual Decoration" Ceremony in imitation of the ritual programming of the city's major temples. The small shrines are newly whitewashed, painted and decorated; *āratī* pūjā, all night performances of devotional and folk music, and even martial competitions among the city's various wrestling *akhāṛās* are financed by neighborhood donations. The neighborhood and village Birs that are the guardian deities or Dih Babas of particular domains are propitiated commensurate to this role. The Dih Baba (sometimes paired with a Sati or disease goddess) controls the ingress and egress of all supernatural forces and influences across village or neighborhood boundaries; his realm of authority extends to minor village deities, ghosts, other more vaguely defined magical energies, and—by extension—those humans who would wish to manipulate those beings and forces. Most individuals find occasion to approach the Dih Baba for permission or assistance within his realm of authority;

20. A painting of Daitra Bir Baba on the exterior wall of the deity's small temple in Chait Ganj, Vārāṇasī. An example of "militant ascetic" iconography. Photo by Diane Coccari.

exorcistic healers (*ojhā*) must cultivate a working relationship with their Dihs if they are to find success in their manipulations of the supernatural. Ojhas, in particular, introduce what we might call a "transgressive" element into the Bir cult: some engage in an eclectic blend of sorcery and tantric ritual (popularly called tantra-mantra), including blood sacrifice and offerings of liquor and cannabis, and it is through this "tantric procedure" (tantrik paddhati) that worship of the Bir is thought to yield the most immediate results.

To the devotee, the Birs are powerful local deities (devatā) who are "awake" (*jāgtā hai*) and attentive to human needs. Their power is derived from the violent, untimely, tragic or unjust nature of their deaths, while the character or inherent nature of the individual also has implications for the nature and vigor of the spirit. The jealous anger of these souls, directed at the living, may be "quieted" (*śānti karnā*) by the establishment of a shrine and ongoing ritual attention, and transmuted into a more benign and protective presence. Any low caste person may become a Bir, but certain castes have a propensity to remain active at the locations of their shrines, and are therefore more likely candidates for posthumous deification. Certain castes (Teli, Nat) are identified in people's minds with magic and the supernatural, and make particularly fearsome ghosts. Others, like members of the Ahir caste, are of a heroic substance which has implications for the vigor of their spirits. Many of the Banaras area Bir shrines are said to contain Ahir deities.

The Ahir have long maintained a tradition of caste heroism. Although many, especially urban, Ahirs have moved into other professions, the traditional occupation of this caste is cattle-keeping, herding and breeding, and providing the milk of their animals. Typical of pastoral groups and in keeping with cattle herding and the related activities of cattle raiding and protection, the Ahir cherish a view of themselves as brave fighters and leaders among a collection of allied castes with whom they are found in village settings. The Hindi oral epic *Lorikī*—understood by many Ahirs of Eastern Uttar Pradesh to be the oral history of their caste—eulogizes the heroism of their ancestor Lorik Yadav and provides historical proof of Ahir martial glory.[14] The Yadava Movement of this century, with its claim of Kṣatriya status for the Ahir, is also testimony to this heroic identity.[15] The tendency of the Ahir to establish memorials to their untimely dead and to worship these as caste heroes is no doubt part of this history and self-perception. Many of these shrines remain family, clan or caste deities, or guardians of cattle fertility, safety and health. Others become village guardian deities or attain the status of regional pilgrimage sites known for exorcism and wish fulfillment.

What follows is the story of one such Ahir Bir Baba. Oral accounts and a folk song about the hero's tragic death demonstrate the timeless process of heroic death and deification.

C. Bachau Bir: The Making of a Contemporary Bir Baba

The story of Bachau Bir is an excellent example of how people perceive the emergence of a deity known as Bir Baba, in this case through the martyrdom of a local hero. Bachau or Bachan Yadav was an historical individual who lived in a small village outside of Varanasi, who met a violent death at the hands of caste enemies. The estimates of informants and certain details of the story place the critical incidents of the tale during the 1920s. There is no doubt much truth to the accounts of his death, but more important than the determination of historical accuracy is an appreciation of the oral traditions surrounding this figure, now represented by a tall, conical image in a small roadside temple. Many people in the city know some version of Bachau's story, but it is told with particular vehemence by members of the Ahir caste. The existence of a *birahā* song, written by a local Ahir songwriter about the climactic events which resulted in Bachau's death, has no doubt contributed to the ability of informants to relate this portion of the story in such vivid detail.[16] The great-nephew of the hero tells other stories about his locally famous relative:[17]

> Bachau Yadav was an Ahir who was very brave and strong. He was a wrestler and carried a fighting staff (*daṇḍā*) so big that no one else could lift it. He had the strength and power of ten men. He was honorable, and would always deal with his enemies fairly. He would never fight anyone who was defenseless. If he saw that someone was in trouble, he would help them. His "liver" (*kalejā*) was bigger than anyone's; it weighed 14 *pau*.[18]
>
> When Bachau was a young man, he fought with a tiger. The tiger came out of the jungle to the east of Sir Govardhanpur, and chased Gokal Chaudhari, the village headman. The headman, out of fear, climbed a tree and began to shout for help. Everyone else ran away, but Bachau Yadav caught the tiger in his arms and began to beat it. He called to the other villagers, "Will you wait for the tiger to eat me before you will come?" So the village people came and started to beat the tiger. Bachau killed this tiger, and the authorities later gave him a reward.

Bachau had many enemies, especially among the Thakurs. He had a long-standing feud with Riddhi and Siddhi Singh—the two sons of Ambe Singh—and Babua Singh, who was a wrestler. He had also made an enemy of Gudari Mama, who was an associate of Bachau from a Yadav *jāti*. Gudari Mama killed his brother's wife for no reason, so Bachau had him "outcasted" (*samāj se nikāl diyā*). The headman, whom Bachau saved from the tiger, outcasted Gudari Mama on Bachau's word. This ended his eating, drinking, smoking the *hukkā*, etc., with the Yadavs. Gudari Mama did not accept this social punishment and agree to perform the appropriate expiation, but met with Bachau's Thakur enemies and schemed to take revenge upon him.

This account serves as a prelude to the birahā song about the hero. Bachau's enmity with the Thakurs was to come to a tragic end:

The Song of Bachau Bir[19]

My Rama O Ram

It happened right in Sir Karhiya, next to Hindu University,
where Malviji had some land.
This tale of mighty Bachau Bir, friends,
Listen to this story beyond compare, friends.

They say that Malviji had some land
where Kṣatriya Ambe Singh also had a claim.
Ambe Singh went there and took his stand.
Refusing to back off, Malviji stood his ground.

Malviji regarded Bachau as his younger brother.
He said, "Have the deed written in your name."
The surveyor would come to measure the land, friends.
Listen to this story beyond compare, friends.

There was an old feud between Bachau and Riddhi-Siddhi.
The Thakurs wanted to kill him by deception.
Leaving his axe at home, Bachau went out empty-handed.
His wife pleaded, "Take it! You are dealing with enemies!"
Bachau said, "Today I will go without a weapon."
"I too will take my place among gentlemen."

But the Thakur gang was powerful, friends.
Listen to this story beyond compare, friends.

> [SPOKEN] Bachau Bir's wife said to her husband, "Take your axe with you." He answered, "Very important people will come, so I will go empty-handed when the field is measured." But the Thakur gang was powerful, friends. People had already gathered . . .

The clouds spread across the sky.
The manly, tiger-like Bachau left his house.
The clouds spread across the sky.

The mighty Riddhi-Siddhi had an old feud with Bachau.
At every step Bachau thought, "The Thakur gang is powerful."
Going to the surveying of the field, his eyes grew red with rage.
Before him were eighteen men, their lances and spears sharpened.
Eighteen young Thakur men, brave and alert as tigers.
The tape was taken up. The measuring began. Young Bachau stood alone.

The clouds spread across the sky.
They began to taunt him in front of the official.
The clouds spread across the sky.

Babua Singh spoke sharply, "Don't miss this chance, men!"
"Block Bachau's way. Don't let him escape."
In this spirit Gudari Mama spoke.
The day was Monday. "Don't miss this chance, men!"

The official realized that there would be a fight.
He went up to Bachau and said,
"You are in great danger."
("Don't miss this chance men!")
"Get in my carriage and come away with me."
But Bachau said loudly, "Today I will see how tough the Thakurs are."

The clouds spread across the sky.
"I will break their skulls and beat them with my fists."
The clouds spread across the sky.

Taking up their weapons, the Thakur gang moved in.
Shouting a war cry, the men came out into the field.
Their staffs, knives and spears were flashing.
They challenged Bachau by twisting their moustaches.
"Today . . . in this field."
Giving this challenge, the Thakur gang moved in.
Steadily Bachau said, "Don't be so proud."
"I killed your father. You too may lose your life."
"Riddhi-Siddhi, don't be so proud. Your whole family may be destroyed."
"If my staff is to rain down blows, sparks will fly."
The Thakur gang moved in.
In the face of the assembled gang, Bachau Bir did not run.
Bachau asked the Thakurs for half an hour's time.

The clouds spread across the sky.
"Or allow me to have a staff," he asked the crowd in the field.
The clouds spread across the sky.

> [SPOKEN] From the time that they surrounded him, Bachau asked, "Please give me a staff." But they completely closed him in.

Babua's Thakur men did not hesitate.
Running toward him, every man leaped upon Bachau.
Staffs began to fly with a swishing sound.
Jhimmal Yadav broke away and began to run.
Grabbing his staff, it seemed like Bachau set it on fire.
He chased them five *bīghās*, beating them back.
He started to move in the direction of his house.
Ahead was a wire fence that surrounded the university.
Catching his foot, the man like a tiger fell.

[SPOKEN] Alone, fighting eighteen young men, he chased them five *bīghās*. He thought, "Now I can escape and run toward my house." Ahead was the university, and surrounding it was a barbed-wire fence. He caught his foot and fell.

Young Bachau fell like a fallen tree.
Sticks and knives again fell upon him.
As sticks and knives again fell upon him,
Out in front came Gudariya Mama.
He said, "If you leave this man alive,"
"If he lives, he will find us and kill us."
"If he lives, he will find us and kill us."
So he beat him with two staffs.

[SPOKEN] Gudari Mama, who was Bachau's own uncle, said, "If we let Bachau go and he lives, then the lives of eighteen men will not be spared. Finish him today. Gudari Mama beat him with two staffs.

When Bachau's body was carried to Bhelupur Police Station,
In the middle of the journey, Bachau attained the Heaven of Heroes.

The clouds spread across the sky.
The corpse was quickly taken for an autopsy.
The clouds spread across the sky.

Every Ahir went with the body, O didn't they?
Bachau Bir's heart weighed fourteen pounds.
He could drink the milk of one buffalo, and eat three pounds of food.
Listen, listen,
Tears started to flow and fall from many eyes, O didn't they?
One great fighter had left the Yadav family.
Yadav Guru Bihari was the first to praise the hero in song.
Pattu's songs are also famous, aren't they?

Hearing the news of Bachau's death, all of Banaras-Kashi
was sad.
The Judge gave the ruling, "Hang Riddhi-Siddhi!"

The clouds spread across the sky.
Yadav Ram Sakal speaks this with flowing eyes.
The clouds spread across the sky.

My Rama O Ram

The particulars of the construction of Bachau Yadav's shrine are unclear and further obscured by the hagiography that inspires the birahā song and other, especially Ahir, renderings of the tale. The song concludes that Bachau attained the "Heaven of Heroes" (bīr gati) immediately upon his death. Those who share this view are likely to refer to the shrine as a *yādgār* or "memorial" established to honor and remember the hero. At the same time, Bachau's great-nephew tells that the wife of Babua Singh—one of Bachau's enemies—began to light lamps at the place where Bachau died before any shrine was built, ostensibly to appease Bachau's angry spirit. The shrine itself was built by Bachau's family, who may have been similarly contacted by the spirit of their slain kinsman. Local people blame the more recent troubles that have visited Bachau's family—including the madness of a grandson—on their periodic neglect of the shrine. Thus Bachau is believed to have "bothered" (*tang karnā*) both friends and enemies after his death, necessitating acts of ritual propitiation, including the establishment of a sthān.

In Bachau's case, the elements of the bhūt-pret complex are clear: The young man's death was violent and unjust, the type of death an angry ghost is likely to avenge. Yet his Ahir eulogizers, themselves perpetuating a long tradition of Ahir heroism, choose to hyperbolize the strength (expressed in part by the size of his "heart/liver"), bravery and nobility of their hero, pronouncing bīr gati as the fate of their castemate. This particular blending of heroic themes and ideas about the behavior of ghosts is characteristic of the Bir phenomenon. Bachau's story illustrates the process whereby a living individual becomes a local deity: a tragic death, the ghost of the victim contacting the living through a vision, dream or possession, the building of a propitiatory shrine to house the spirit and provide a place of worship, the heroic hagiography. Critical to this process is the establishment of a shrine and the onset of worship. It is said that the activity of worshiping serves to increase a deity's power. As one informant put it, "Like the way in which we 'give respect' to our leaders and they become powerful, in that way the [Bir's] power increases from worship." If a Bir is discovered to be particularly "awake" and effective in "getting things done," he draws a wider circle of devotees, which further increases his power. The power engendered from a premature and violent death is channeled to constructive purposes. The ghost who might ravage the health and well-being of a family or village may be enlisted as its special protector. Yet intrinsic to the nature of the bhūt cum devatā is a continued ambivalence. The Bir may be angered by the neglect of his shrine, lash out for no apparent reason, or remain inexplicably silent.

Now, his great-nephew says, Bachau does not bother anyone. He is worshiped as a deity (*devatā ke rūp me pūjate hai*), and acts for the welfare of all. When people come to him with special desires, they are always fulfilled. The modest brick building that houses Bachau Bir's memorial faces the Banaras Hindu University wall where he is said to have fallen in flight from his enemies. The shrine is mainly attended by people from villages in the immediate area. Bachau Bir is not the Dih Baba or guardian deity of a village (an older Bir shrine serves this function), but is the special patron of certain castes, especially the Ahir. The Annual Decoration Ceremony at the small temple is held on the day of Govardhan Puja, another festival historically linked to the Cowherd caste.

NOTES

1. Research for this article was conducted from September 1980 to May 1982 under the auspices of the American Institute of Indian Studies. Most of the topics in the following discussion are covered in greater detail in my dissertation, "The Bir Babas of Banaras: An analysis of a Folk Deity in North Indian Hinduism," University of Wisconsin 1986.

2. Although I think that this attitude represents a large body of opinion regarding Satis, it must be noted that I spoke mainly with men about this subject. The total benevolence of the Sati is problematical: It would not surprise me to find an aura of ambivalence surrounding some of these figures, especially given the possibility of coercion.

3. Jack M. Planalp, "Religious Life and Values in a North Indian Village," Diss. Cornell University 1956, 576-9.

4. There are female Brahms, but most of the public shrines tend to be for

male figures. I have been told several stories of female Brahms bothering their husband's second wives, but these were "quieted" (śānti karnā) or "seated" (*biṭhāna*) at a temple of a powerful Brahm Baba.

5. The Sanskrit *piśācamocana* story is found in the *Kāśī Khaṇḍa* of the *Skanda Purāṇa*, part 54.

6. William Crooke, "Panchpiriya," *Encyclopaedia of Religion and Ethics* (1917), IX, 600-601. See also Crooke, *Religion and Folklore of Northern India* (London, 1926; rpt. Delhi: Chand & Co., 165-166; Richard Greeven, *The Heroes Five* (Allahabad: Pioneer Press, 1892); Kerrin G. V. Schwerin, "Saint Worship in Indian Islam: The Legend of the Martyr Salar Masud Ghazi," in *Ritual and Religion Among Muslims in India*, ed. Imtiaz Ahmad (Delhi: Manohar, 1981), 146-151; R. C. Temple, *Legends of the Panjab* (Patiala: Language Dept., 1962), I, 98-120.

7. Crooke, *Religion*, 160.

8. Schwerin, "Saint Worship," 146-151.

9. Little has been written about the Dafalis, the drummer-priests of Ghazi Miya. Crooke mentions that they are converted Mirasis, a low Hindu musician caste (note 14 in Schwerin, "Saint Worship," 154), but the period of their conversion and assumption of the priestly role is unknown. They are, in any case, the main bearers of the oral traditions regarding the life of Ghazi Miya and his retinue in the form of folk songs, some of which have been translated by Greeven in his *Heroes Five*. Planalp describes the worship of Ghazi Miya by a Dafali in a Teli household ("Religious Life," 768-770). See also E. Visuvalingam in this volume.

10. A vīra in Sanskrit is a "brave, eminent man, hero or chief," one who possesses vīryā, "manliness or manly vigour, valour, strength, power, energy, virility." Monier-Williams, *Sanskrit-English Dictionary* (New Delhi: Motilal Banarsidass, 1976), 1006. The term *bābā* is used as one of endearment and respect for male kin (a son, husband, father, paternal grandfather) or of deference for an ascetic or very old man. This use of *baba* to express closeness and respect is easily extended to a venerable male deity who has a personal relationship to the worshipper.

11. The Hindi *sthān* or Bhojpuri *asthān* derives from the Sanskrit *sthāna*, a "place, spot, locality, abode, dwelling, house, site": Monier Monier-Williams, *Sanskrit-English Dictionary* (Oxford, 1876; rpt. Delhi: Motilal Banarsidass, 1976), 1263. These may also be called *devasthān, bhūtasthān* or *bīrasthān*, depending upon the nature of the being felt to inhabit a site.

12. See W. G. Archer, *The Vertical Man: A Study in Primitive Sculpture* (London, 1947).

13. The castes recorded by this researcher included Ahir, Gaderiya, Kunbi, Kurmi, Kumhar, Mali, Pasi, Bhar, Rajbhar, Kol, Gond, Manjhi, Mallah, Khatik, Teli, Dhobi, Dom, Chamar, and Rai Das.

14. See Shyam Monohar Pandey, *The Hindi Oral Epic Loriki* (Allahabad, 1979) and *The Hindi Oral Epic Canainī* (Allahabad, 1982), and Arjundas Kesari, *Lorikāyan*

(Mirzapur: Lokruchi Prakashan, 1980) [in Hindi].

15. See M. S. A. Rao, *Social Movements and Social Transformations: A Study of Two Backward Classes Movements in India* (Delhi: Macmillan, 1979), and "Caste and the Indian Army," *The Economic Weekly* 16 (August 29, 1964), 1439-1443.

16. The term *birahā* is said to derive from the Sanskrit *viraha* meaning "separation." *Birahā* is a folk music genre originating with the Ahir caste. The older forms (*khaṛī birahā*)—some containing the puranic themes of Krishna and his separation from the Gopis—are remembered only by a handful of old men and are very rarely sung. Bihari Lal Yadav is said to have originated a newer form of birahā in the early 1900's. The birahā that is current today is a mixture of folk song genres and tunes from Hindi films. The songs cover a variety of moods and subjects: devotional, heroic, social, political, humorous, bawdy, and romantic.

17. From an interview with Makar Yadav, conducted by O. P. Sharma in November, 1982.

18. A *kalejā*, translated as both *liver* and *heart*, is understood as the organ in the body which is the seat of knowledge and power. If one eats the kalejā of an individual (as witches are purported to do), one may obtain these things from them. By reporting that Bacau's *liver* or *heart* weighed 14 pau (very big and heavy), the singer is praising his superhuman might.

19. "Bachau Bir" was written by Ram Sakal Yadav, son of Pattu Yadav, the foremost *celā* of Bihari Lal Yadav, the originator of modern birahā (see the song's signature lines). The song as recorded was sung by Hans Raj Yadav in Varanasi in 1982. I would like to thank Hank Heifetz, Dr. Ashok Kalrah and O. P. Sharma for their help with translation and transcription.

10

The Capitulation of Maṇi: A Conversion Myth in the Cult of Khaṇḍobā

John M. Stanley

Introduction

The cult of Khaṇḍobā[1] is a large, principally non-Brahman cult in the Western Deccan.[2] Members of virtually all castes in the region are numbered among its devotees, including a few Brahmans and even some Muslims, but it is dominated by the peasant castes (Marathas and Kunbis), local shepherds (Dhangars), fisher folk (Kolis), watchman and ex-criminal castes (Ramoshis), and several formerly *balutedār* castes (traditional village servants) including gardeners, tailors, leather workers, and the formerly untouchable Mahars and Mangs. Temples of this god are found from Nasik in the north to Hubli in the south and from the Konkan coast on the western edge of Maharashtra to the western edge of Andhra and north west edge of Karnataka. Hundreds of small temples are found in the villages in this area, nearly all with a charter myth tracing the god's first appearance in the village to one of the eleven "especially wakeful places" (jāgṛt kṣetras) of Khaṇḍobā.

The eleven jāgṛt kṣetras of Khaṇḍobā all claim to be the original place of Khaṇḍobā, the place where he came to earth to conquer two demons, Maṇi and Malla, who were threatening the earth (or in some stories, merely the local region) with some form of chaos. The dominant jāgṛt kṣetra in the northern part of the cult (and arguably throughout the whole of the Deccan) is Jejuri in Poona District of Maharashtra.[3]

The stories of the battle between Khaṇḍobā and the two demons are preserved in two forms: oral stories told both ritually and casually by Vāghyās[4] and other cult functionaries, and written accounts preserved in both Sanskrit and Marathi. The principal written version of the myth is the *Mallāri Māhātmya*. It exists in both Sanskrit and Marathi versions[5] and claims to be part of the *Brahmāṇḍa Purāṇa*. The *Jayādri Māhātmya* and *Mārtaṇḍ Vijay* are later than the *Mallāri Māhātmya* and tell much the same story, but include some of the additional details contained in the oral stories.

A. Khaṇḍobā's Victory over Maṇi and Malla

The Frame Story

One of the most interesting features of the *Mallāri Māhātmya* version of the Khaṇḍobā myth is the frame story in which it is set. The *Mallāri Māhātmya* begins and ends with a scene in Śiva's private quarters in the Jewel Hall on Mount Kailas. In the opening scene Pārvatī begs her Lord Śiva to tell her a very special secret, a particularly important secret that has two parts. First, she wants to know which of all the places in the world is Śiva's "favorite and most sacred place, the most wonderful of places where men can be granted all worldly desires, salvation, and eternal enjoyment." Secondly, she begs to know which particular avatār is Śiva's favorite avatār, through which he is most accessible to men. Śiva grants Pārvatī's request by telling her a story, the principal function of which, as we shall see, is to provide a charter myth for one particular place (Prempur) as the premier place in all the world for the granting of navas.[6]

The Story of the Avatar of Mārtaṇḍ Bhairav

The story that Śiva tells Pārvatī is this. Once, long ago, in the Kṛta age, the seven sons of Dharma established a beautiful and holy ashram on Mount Maṇical. There, accompanied by their wives and families, they practiced austere devotion and created a beautiful atmosphere where trees blossomed plentifully, where flowers were always in bloom and where there was no enmity or hostility. Even animals with natural hostilities played peacefully together, and those with a ferocious nature offered no threat to human beings. Indeed, everyone and everything was at peace.

Then a demon chief named Malla, accompanied by his younger

brother, Maṇi visited the ashram and began to perform terrible acts of destruction. They tore up the gardens that the ṛṣis had planted; they destroyed all of the flowers and pulled the trees out by the roots. They raped the ṛṣis' wives and murdered their children and threw the dead bodies into the wells, and they slaughtered and ate the ṛṣis' cows and elephants.

The ṛṣis were finally so troubled by the chaos the demons produced that they decided to go to the gods to ask for help. They went first to Indra, but he told them that he could do nothing to stop the demons because they had such great powers of devotion. They were able to perform tapas[7] for long periods of time at great intensity, thus producing large quantities of energy. Indeed, they had practiced this extreme devotion to Brahmā for many years, standing on a single toe and subsisting on smoke alone. So great was the energy they had generated that Brahmā was forced to grant them any boon they asked. They asked to be able to do whatever they wanted with impunity, to be able to plunder, rape, and pillage without any human, demon, or god being able to stop them or kill them. Brahmā granted this boon and so they were invincible. Indra could do nothing. The ṛṣis then proceeded to Vaikuṇṭha to ask Viṣṇu for help, but the answer was the same. Nothing could be done to stop the demons. Their devotion to Brahmā had been too powerful.

The ṛṣis then made the long journey to Mount Kailas and told their story to Śiva. Here the response was very different. Śiva reacted to the news of the demons' chaos-producing destruction with fearsome anger and made a vow of his own. He vowed that the destruction of the two demons was imminent. He rose from his throne in a rage, tore out by the roots a lock (jaṭā) of his matted hair, and threw it on the fire altar, instructing the terrified ṛṣis to anoint it with ghee. The smoke from the matted hair and burning ghee took the form of a monstrous and fierce spiritual power, a female monster, a vicious and terrible engine of destruction with fearful teeth and jaws and a loose, long tongue. She was named Mahāmārī (later to be known as Ghṛtamārī). She immediately made a vow to fight the demons to their destruction.[8]

Then the Lord Śiva, himself, declared his determination to take the avatār of Mārtaṇḍ Bhairav and descend to the earth to organize an army to defeat the terrible demons. Mārtaṇḍ Bhairav was a form of Śiva never seen before, a form in which "he would freely grant power and protection to men in return for even a small amount of devotion." His appearance was like that of the sun. His clothing was golden and flaming, his teeth like flashing rubies; and he was surrounded by barking dogs.[9] In this new form the Lord Śiva organized a large army to do battle against the two demons. The leader of his army was Skanda, whose own personal corps of soldiers was mounted on peacocks. Skanda's lieutenants, each leading a corps of soldiers, were Indra, Agni, Yama, Nairṛta, Varuṇa, Kubera, Brahmā, Viṣṇu, the sun, the moon, and Gaṇeśa, whose troops had elephant heads and rode mouse-faced horses. Śiva, himself, in his flaming form of Mārtaṇḍ Bhairav, was mounted on his usual vehicle, Nandī.[10]

The army of Malla was equally impressive. His corps of troops[11] was comprised of countless demon warriors mounted on elephants. Each battalion of demons was led by a fierce demon general. Maṇi, mounted on his white horse, was the leader of the whole army, the counterpart of Skanda, while Malla hovered as overseer of the whole battle, a kind of master magician general. After the initial battle resulted in a terrible slaughter of most of the demon army, Malla called on each of the demon generals to do individual battle with Khaṇḍobā's battalion leaders. One by one Malla's generals were defeated until only Maṇi was left.

The Capitulation of Maṇi

Enraged at the defeat of his generals, Maṇi charged directly at Khaṇḍobā to engage him in individual combat. A long and fierce battle followed in which Maṇi fought extremely well, surprising Khaṇḍobā with his magical ability to change shapes and assume different forms. Finally, still astride his white horse, having assumed the form of a horse-faced demon, neighing so fiercely that he agitated the whole world, Maṇi was worn down by Khaṇḍobā's superior strength and knocked from his horse by one of Khaṇḍobā's missiles. He fell, along with his white horse, into a water tank. From that day forward the tank was named *Maṇical* and it remains in that place to this day.[12]

Khaṇḍobā approached the fallen demon and placed his foot on the demon's head (in the posture of a conqueror), but just as the sole of his foot touched the conquered demon's head, Maṇi experienced a total change of heart. Indeed, he reached out to take hold of Khaṇḍobā's foot as it was approaching his head, placed the foot of the conquerer on his own head, and offered a great hymn of devotion to the victor so genuine that Khaṇḍobā was moved to offer him one final boon. Maṇi asked for three things: 1) that all the people of earth should have great wealth, good fortune, enjoyment, sons, horses, and elephants in this life and, after this life, liberation; 2) that Maṇi should, from that time forward, always reside in Khaṇḍobā's presence;[13] and 3) that Khaṇḍobā should accept Maṇi's horse as his vehicle (*vāhan*). Khaṇḍobā granted Maṇi's three-part boon immediately.[14]

Malla's Defeat and His Final Request

After Maṇi's defeat and wondrous reform, Malla was given an opportunity to similarly surrender. He refused, vowing to fight on to destroy gods, men, and animals "until the heavens are godless, society is without human beings, and the earth without even one last snake."[15] Then, issuing a loud war cry so fierce that, as far away as Mount Kailas, Pārvatī's crown fell from her head, Malla led what was left of his badly damaged army onto the battlefield. He was immediately engaged by Ghṛtamārī, the "terrible instrument of destruction" that Śiva had created from the lock of his matted hair. Ghṛtamārī began to devour Malla's elephants and chariots and horses and foot soldiers, chewing iron, bone, and tusks into ashes and dust with her terrible jaws. After all but Malla were devoured, she turned to face him in individual battle, but she was no match for his terrible strength and magical powers. One hundred arrows from Malla's magic bow were lodged in her head, twenty-seven in each breast, and another hundred through her neck and shoulders.

When Ghṛtamārī was near defeat, Khaṇḍobā, taking pity on her torture, came to her rescue and engaged Malla personally in one last terrible battle, which tested the full limits of the magical skills of both god and demon. Finally, Malla was knocked to the ground unconscious. Khaṇḍobā approached the supine demon, placed his foot on his head and was about to sever his head from his body when Malla also repented (or appeared to repent) and offered to Khaṇḍobā a hymn of seemingly unmitigated praise. Khaṇḍobā assumed that Malla was sincere in his praise and granted him one final boon. Malla asked for three things: 1) that his name should always be pronounced before that of his conqueror, 2) that his head should always be under Khaṇḍobā's foot or under the feet of his devotees, and 3) that he should be given as *naivedya* the bodies of ten thousand men.[16] Khaṇḍobā granted the first boon by taking the name Malhāri (killer of Malla) or, in the more Sanskritized versions, Mallāri (enemy of Malla); he granted the second by cutting off the demon's head and placing it under the threshold of his temple where it would always be under the feet of his devotees (see plate 21);[17] and he granted the third by giving Malla the head of a goat and saying: "You would ask to eat more men? You want the flesh of your own kind as naivedya? In this way you shall have it. You will forever have the head of a goat and receive naivedya of goats. Thus

21. The head of the demon Malla under the threshold of the Khaṇḍobā temple at Jejuri in Purandhar Taluk, Pune District, Maharashtra. Photo by John Stanley.

you will always be devouring your own kind, and thus is your final boon fulfilled."

The Closing of the Frame

After the final destruction of Malla, the ṛṣis all gathered to offer praise and devotion to Khaṇḍobā for their deliverance from the destructive demons. So great was their devotion that Khaṇḍobā offered them any one boon they would ask. They asked that he not leave them, but remain always there at that place where he had overcome the demons. Khaṇḍobā was very pleased with their devotion and granted their wish, and on the sixth lunar day of the bright fortnight of the month of Mārgaśīrṣa[18] he returned to that place with his śaktī, Mhāḷsā (an avatār of Pārvatī herself), in the form of a svayambhū lingam[19] and a svayambhū yoni.

Then all of the ṛṣis and all of their families and all of the Yakṣas and Nāgas and all of the men of the earth came to that place and offered devotion to the liṅgam and yoni. Khaṇḍobā and Mhāḷsā were so pleased by this devotion that they came out of the liṅgam and yoni and declared to the great array of gathered devotees that they would grant yet one more boon: From this time forth all who come to this place with devotion would receive "abundant cattle, sons, horses, happiness, treasure, territory, women, jewels, victory, success in disputes with opponents, glory, salvation, and protection." Khaṇḍobā added some suggestions of forms of worship that he considered especially pleasing to him,[20] and declared his special accessibility to people of low caste:

> Even if a person is of low caste, he is always dear to me. Whatever is to be given should be given to him and whatever is to be received, should be received from him. He deserves the same respect as I.[21]

Then the scene returns to Kailas where Śiva is telling Pārvatī the story that she had begged of him, thus fulfilling the boon and closing the frame:[22]

> So, Pārvatī, that is the place dearest to me, where, in the Kali age, I bestow favors on men. It is the only place of pilgrimage that grants both enjoyment and liberation from bondage. And we, O goddess, made it our residence out of compassion for men. Whatever object men may desire with strong feeling, it is obtained by them there. O beautiful goddess, because of your devotion I have spoken out of love, telling you this highest secret.

B. Myth Variants and Additional Stories

In telling the story of Khaṇḍobā's battle with the demons, I have, to this point, followed the basic outline of the *Mallāri Māhātmya.* For the most part the oral stories follow this outline, elaborating numerous details, but often they add entirely new stories to the central core of the myth.

Further Sanskritization of the Dramatis Personae

One of the most noticeable additions in the oral stories is the tendency to explain all of the elements of the story of the battle with the demons in terms of the Śaivite pantheon. Not only is Khaṇḍobā the avatār of Śiva and Mhāḷsā the avatār of Pārvatī, but Hegaḍī Pradhān, Khaṇḍobā's "minister," is explained as an avatār of Viṣṇu, and Bānū (or Bāṇāī), Khaṇḍobā's second wife (who is a Dhangar), is said to be an avatār of Gaṅgā. Moreover, Khaṇḍobā's faithful dog, who assists him in his battle against the demons,[23] is regarded as an avatār of Kṛṣṇa; Kṛṣṇa's flute is magically changed by Khaṇḍobā's *bhaṇḍār* into a beautiful girl who becomes the prototype of the Muraḷīs;[24] the *laṅgar,* the ritual chain traditionally carried around the neck by many of Khaṇḍobā's devotees and broken in certain rituals as a test of the devotee's faith, is regarded as an avatār of Śiva's snake (nāga); Maṇi is the avatār of Madhu and Malla of Kaiṭabha; and the horse, although still thought of as a gift of the conquered and reformed Maṇi, is also considered an avatār of Nandī.

One Demon or Two

In many of the myth variants preserved at small temples in Maharashtra, the Khaṇḍobā story is told with only one demon in the cast of characters. His name is Maṇimal and he rides a white horse. The story of this composite demon is substantially the same as the story in the two-demon version except that the boons and the requests of the two demons are conflated and compressed. It is usually Malla's final request (that he be given naivedya of his own kind) that is attributed to the composite demon; the horse (sometimes called "Maṇi") is given to Khaṇḍobā before the demon is killed by decapitation; there is no explicit chartering of the "Malhāri" name of Khaṇḍobā, and the demon is localized in a nearby shrine where goat naivedya is now offered. Where the story is told in this form, the emphasis seems to be on establishing the moral superiority of Khaṇḍobā over the demon and chartering a place in the cult where non-vegetarian naivedya can be offered. Some story tellers explain Maṇimal as a single horse and rider demon in two parts: Malla being the demon himself who makes the final request to be given goat naivedya and Maṇi being the horse he is riding.

New Warriors in the Battle: Mhāḷsā, Bānū, and the Dog

According to the structure of the written story, Mhāḷsā, Khaṇḍobā's first wife, does not make an appearance until after the demons are both conquered and Khaṇḍobā, as a boon to his devotees, agrees to return to Jejuri to remain forever. Bānū, Khaṇḍobā's second wife,[25] does not appear at all in the *Mallāri Māhātmya* and in the oral stories she appears only after Khaṇḍobā and Mhāḷsā have lived at Jejuri for some length of time. There is one very popular story in the cult, however, in which Mhāḷsā, Bānū, the dog, and the horse enter the scene much earlier and play a crucial role in the battle against the demons. One version of the story goes like this.[26]

When the Lord Śiva had declared that he would take the Khaṇḍobā avatār to fight the two troublesome demons, Pārvatī said that she wanted to come too: "You are always taking avatārs and leaving me here alone. This time I want to come along." Śiva says:

> OK, OK, after I conquer the two demons, we can settle there and live for a while. You can take the avatār of Mhāḷsā, the daughter of Timaśeṭ, the Lingayat grocer. After the battle is over and it is safe, I will come and marry you and bring you to my palace in Jejuri.

At this point Gaṅgā, who, from her place in Śiva's hair, had been witnessing the entire episode of the ṛṣis' visit and Śiva's reaction, speaks out with stern determination declaring that she wants to come along too.[27] Śiva responds: "OK, OK, You can take the avatār of a Dhangar (shepherdess) and I will come to your village and marry you, too, and bring you to the palace in Jejuri." Pārvatī then speaks: "That is all fine,[28] but why can't we come with you now. We could surely help in the battle." And Gaṅgā, still clinging bravely to the still shaking locks, adds, "Yes, we could help; we could help; you will need us; you will see."

Śiva, however, manfully refuses to accept their help in the battle, and, declaring that this is really man's work, he suddenly grabs hold of his snake, sprinkles some bhaṇḍār[29] on it which turns it into a laṅgar, wraps the laṅgar around his neck and charges off to assume the Khaṇḍobā avatār and do battle with the demons. Here the Vāghyā enacts the assumption of the flaming aura of the Khaṇḍobā avatār and the beginning of the fight with the demons. The Vāghyā makes it clear from his dramatization that he expects no trouble in conquering the demons without aid from anyone.

Very early in the battle, however, Maṇi is wounded and, because he is so young, the drops of his blood create more demons as soon as they touch the ground.[30] Khaṇḍobā valiantly tries to slay all of the demons that are springing up from the drops of Maṇi's blood. The Vāghyā acts out the impossible mission of killing the multiplying demons without spilling any more blood. Soon Khaṇḍobā realizes that he needs help and he sends for Pārvatī and Gaṅgā. The two goddesses immediately assume their respective avatārs and join the battle, catching the drops of blood from Maṇi's wounds and from those of all the other blood-generated demons before they fall to the ground.

At first they try to catch the blood in their mouths, but that, the Vāghyā indicates through gestures, is a futile attempt; then they use bowls shaped just like the *koṭmās*[31] of the Vāghyās and Muraḷīs, but even this is not enough. The Vāghyā at this point acts out the frustration of the two goddesses. They run back and forth shouting: "What to do? What to do?"[32] Fortunately, Khaṇḍobā's dog has come along with Bānū. He sees the problem and immediately begins catching the falling drops of blood in his mouth. The Vāghyā sings several verses describing the dog's prowess, each punctuated with the refrain: "This dog catches so much blood; so much blood!" After each refrain, the Vāghyā acts out the amazing efficiency of the blood-catching dog, and adds a special, extra hymn of praise for the dog of Khaṇḍobā who saves the day.[33] And, indeed, in this version this is precisely where the battle turns. When Maṇi sees that his blood is not regenerating demons, he begins to tire. Khaṇḍobā is able finally to wear him down and, catching him in a weakened position, throws a discus-like missile and knocks him unconscious.

Other variants of the battle story depict Bānū, Mhāḷsā, the dog, and the horse, all assisting Khaṇḍobā in the battle in diverse ways. In some Bānū uses her bow with its magic arrows. In some Mhāḷsā or (rarely) Bānū is mounted on the horse with Khaṇḍobā, fighting the demons with sword or spear. In several versions Khaṇḍobā's white horse plays an active role in the attack against the demons, sometimes holding their heads down on the ground while Khaṇḍobā approaches to apply a *coup de grace* (see plate 22).[34] There is one version of the story that is told, so far as I know, only in picture form (see plates 23 and 24).[35] It depicts Mhāḷsā mounted in front of Khaṇḍobā on the white horse, piercing the side of one of the demons with a spear,

22. Khaṇḍobā's horse holding the two demons' heads under its front hooves. A folk bronze from northern Karnataka. Photo by John Stanley.

23. Khaṇḍobā fighting the two demons with help from Mhāḷsā, the horse, and the thigh-biting dog. A popular oleograph. Photo by Alf Hiltebeitel.

24. A painted frieze of the same scene as plate 23 in a small Khaṇḍobā temple at Medankar Wadi in the village of Chakan, Khed Taluk, Pune District, Maharashtra. Photo by John Stanley.

while the horse strikes at his head with a foreleg and the dog joins the attack burying his teeth in the same demon's right thigh. The other demon is grabbing at the reins of the fighting horse and swinging a war club at Khaṇḍobā who is in the process of dismounting and attacking the demon with his sword.

C. Rituals Associated with Maṇi

Although most of the information about Maṇi comes in the form of myth, there are two important rituals in the Khaṇḍobā cult that are especially focussed on Maṇi.

Campāṣaṣṭhī

The sixth lunar day (*tithi*) of the bright fortnight of the month of Mārgaśīrṣa is known throughout the Khaṇḍobā cult as Campāṣaṣṭhī.[36] At most temples in the cult this is thought to be the day on which Śiva assumed the Khaṇḍobā avatār to do battle with the demons. In and around Jejuri, however, Campāṣaṣṭhī is remembered as the day on which Maṇi surrendered to Khaṇḍobā and made the gift of the horse. Some special rituals are performed for Maṇi. A long cue of bhaktas forms to do pūjā and ārati to Maṇi's image in the temple courtyard, the large stone image of Khaṇḍobā's horse is covered with yellow turmeric powder (bhaṇḍār), and goat sacrifices are made in front of the shrine of Hegaḍī Pradhān on the hillside below the Khaṇḍobā temple. Although pūjā is performed to the Maṇi image regularly at Jejuri, this is the only place in the cult and the only time in the ritual calendar of the cult in which special offerings are made to the former demon.

Naivedya: Who Eats What?

The second ritual in the cult associated with Maṇi is the acceptance of non-vegetarian naivedya.[37] While at all of the jāgṛt temples of Khaṇḍobā, as well as at many of the smaller ones, the cultic rituals within the temple precincts are strictly vegetarian, many of Khaṇḍobā's devotees consider him to be a meat-eater and require some way to offer him naivedya of goat flesh. Others who do not offer meat to Khaṇḍobā himself still make a point of offering meat to a demon or a demi-god associated with Khaṇḍobā. Hence at all Khaṇḍobā kṣetras, even the most vehemently vegetarian jāgṛt temples, there is some provision for the offering of meat. These meat offerings can follow three patterns: a) they may be offered to Khaṇḍobā himself *outside* the vegetarian temple precincts; b) they may be offered to Maṇi or Maṇimal (or to a messenger who will carry the naivedya to them) *outside* the temple precincts; or c) they may be offered to Khaṇḍobā himself *inside* the temple precincts. Meat offerings are never, to my knowledge, offered to any demon *inside* the temple itself.[38] At Jejuri, where pūjā is performed to and darśan taken of Maṇi within the temple courtyard (see plate 25), naivedya is offered to him halfway down the hill in front of an image of Hegaḍī Pradhān,[39] Khaṇḍobā's Dhangar brother-in-law (Bānū's brother). Hegaḍī Pradhān then sends the offering on to the demons.[40]

D. Discussion

The most obvious functions of the story of the capitulation of Maṇi are to reinforce the etiological charter of Prempur as the premier place of navas-granting, to support the claim of Jejuri to be that place, and to reinforce generally the institution of navas-granting. That is the central purpose of the *Mallāri Māhātmya* as is shown by the frame story and the second request of Maṇi which occurs at (or very near) the structural center of the written myth. It is Maṇi's second request that is repeated at the end of the frame story to close the frame. Indeed the whole point of Pārvatī's initial request and of Śiva's telling of the story is contained in the content of Maṇi's second capitulation request. Beyond this, however, there are several important themes to consider.

The Struggle Between Order and Chaos

The story of the defeat of Maṇi and Malla is essentially a story of the triumph of order over chaos. The two demons threatened the order of the ṛṣis' garden and ashram, not only with physical destruction, but with terrible forms of social and ritual disorder;[41] they achieved the power to do that effectively and with impunity through a form of devotional meditation in which they proved to a god the intensity of their devotion. Their misuse of the gift from the god threatens the order of the world itself. Only a special form of another god can set things right. When he sets things right, he does so in a way that establishes a special power at a special place for the granting of wishes from humans who offer devotion to him. Thus, the overcoming by Khaṇḍobā of the chaos-producing power of the demons establishes both a place and an institution where the continued overcoming of instances of chaos that threaten human existence can be accomplished.[42]

25. The image of Maṇi installed in the courtyard of the temple at Jejuri. Photo by John Stanley.

Degrees of Chaos-Producing Demonality

But the story also indicates that there is more involved in conquering chaos than would first appear. For one thing, according to one possible interpretation, it would seem that there are two degrees of chaos represented by the two different demons.[43] Throughout the written version of the story Malla is represented as the more thoroughly demonic of the two brothers. It is Malla who is identified as the demon king. Maṇi is but one of his many vassals. Even early in the story at the beginning of their destruction of order, Malla is decidedly the more demonic. While both brothers participate fully in the chaos-producing acts, Maṇi's actions are subordinate to Malla's. Moreover, Maṇi expresses serious reservations about some of the things they are doing. He tries to convince Malla that some of their actions are so evil that they should refrain from them "lest [their] evil be remembered forever." Malla responds, "How can we not do these acts? It is our nature."

Further, although both brothers are mentioned as objects of Śiva's anger following the ṛṣis' report of their actions, it is Malla who is singled out for the fiercest denunciation: "Malla has disturbed me just as a rat who is nearing its end breaks the box containing the dreadful serpent." And it is Malla to whom Śiva refers when he declares: "That great wretch, who has broken to pieces the beautiful cages of the swan-like god Rudra, is on the verge of death."

The starkest example of the different degrees of chaos represented in Maṇi and Malla, respectively, is seen in a comparison of their "last requests" after they are subdued by Śiva. Maṇi's genuine repentance allows for his reform and transformation into a demigod. His final wish always to be in the presence of Khaṇḍobā is genuinely offered and is accepted without irony. Indeed, it results in the establishment of a cult of Maṇi within the very precincts of Khaṇḍobā's temple.[44] His request that all humans may receive "treasure . . . etc" is genuinely consonant with the purpose of Khaṇḍobā in assuming the avatār. Finally, his wish that Khaṇḍobā accept his horse and Khaṇḍobā's acceptance of it show how totally Maṇi's intent has become one with the intent of the conquering god of order. Clearly, Maṇi's conversion is genuine.

Malla's apparent conversion in the conversion hymn attributed to him is just as clearly not genuine. When, as a result of it, he is offered three final requests, his intransigence, the enormity of his vows of destruction and, most of all, his final request for the bodies of humans as naivedya are in stark contrast to Maṇi's requests. Malla is unregenerately evil and so he must be killed—destroyed, not reformed. He is decapitated and his horned head is placed under the threshold of the temple (see plate 21) where the feet of Khaṇḍobā's bhaktas will defile it on the way to their darśan of their god.[45]

This interpretation is based on the *Mallāri Māhātmya* version of the myth and those oral variants which follow it. In many other oral stories, however, the two demons are not consistently distinguished, and may likewise be portrayed on a par iconographically, as in plate 22, where both demons' heads are trod under the horse's hooves, and at Dhamankeḷ, where Khaṇḍobā subdues each of them equally, holding their heads under his knees (see plate 26). Sometimes there is, as we have seen, one composite demon; sometimes the identities of the two are confused. Although it is an important motif in the written version of the myth, the distinction between regenerate and unregenerate evil is deemphasized or non-existent in many other oral stories.

The Necessity to Control a Conquered Demon's Power

Whether one demon or two, whether reformable or unregenerate, demonic power must be controlled as well as conquered. Two types of this control are represented by two separate motifs in the stories: a) the motif of the localization of the power of the conquered demons; and b) the blood motif.

Maṇi and Malla have generated a great deal of power and energy both, initially, through their devotion to Brahmā[46] and, subsequently, through violent and chaotic actions they performed as a result of that devotional power. The worldview in which the stories are written seems to assume that that power must be localized and controlled rather than merely destroyed or reformed. The same logic that governs other instances of the release of demonic power, such as the exorcism of a ghost, seems to be operative in the case of the conquering of these demons. The assumption in the case of ghost exorcism, both in the Khaṇḍobā cult and generally throughout the Deccan, is that the exorcised ghost's power must be localized. The purpose of the localization is normally control—to keep the ghost's power from possessing someone else. Iron nails are driven into trees, or some other ritual marker is created either at the point of the exorcism or at a point nearby where three roads intersect.[47] Sometimes, however, the power of an exorcised ghost is such that it can be not only controlled, but appropriated for help and assistance—reformed, in a sense, into a demigod. In the story of Maṇi and Malla it would seem we have a similar dynamic at work. Malla's power, if we accept the *Mallāri Māhātmya* version of the demons'

26. The central image in the Khaṇḍobā temple at Dhamankeḷ, Junnar Taluk, Pune District, Maharashtra. The three stone *piṇḍī*s in front of the Khaṇḍobā image are Khaṇḍobā (center), Mhāḷsā (left), and Bānū (right). The female figure to Khaṇḍobā's right is Mhāḷsā; the face peering over his left shoulder may be Bānū. The small figure with a sword toward the front and to Khaṇḍobā's right is Hegaḍī Pradhān, here identified as a Dhangar and avatār of Viṣṇu. Photo by John Stanley.

identification, is unregenerately demonic. It must be localized, but the localization is only for purposes of identification and control. Since the localized power will do no one any good, no cult is established to appropriate the power. Still, whatever residual energy may be left of Malla's demonic power must be kept under control. And so it is localized under the threshold of the Khaṇḍobā temple where it will be constantly under the feet of his devotees. The power of Maṇi, however, is another story. His power is reformed before it is localized and its localization is not merely for the purpose of control but for ritual appropriation. He becomes a new demigod, and the marker of his localization (the mūrti of Maṇi) is given a place of honor in the cultic precincts of Khaṇḍobā's most watchful (jāgṛt) temple. Pūjā to this mūrti is regularly offered and various other rituals for the appropriation of its power are routinized (see plate 27).

The blood-drop motif provides an even more interesting example of the need to contain the conquered power of a demon. So long as his blood is uncontained, Maṇi's power for the production of chaos is infinite, but once the regenerating power of the blood can be contained, he can be subdued, reformed, and localized. The stories giving both Mhāḷsā and Bānū the very important roles of "closing off of the infinite process"[48] of Maṇi's power add to their prestige in the cult. But most important of all in this respect is the role ascribed to Khaṇḍobā's dog. Dogs are normally considered unclean in Hindu thought, but they are special to Khaṇḍobā, and giving the dog a special role in the defeat of the demons both charters the special place that dogs have in the cult[49] and provides a mythic libretto for one of the very important cultic rituals of the Vāghyās, the imitation of the dog at a number of the established festivals in the cult.[50]

Naivedya

At several points in its development groups of meat eaters have been assimilated into the Khaṇḍobā cult. Some of these were Untouchable castes, such as Mahars and Mangs; some were nomads, such as Dhangars. As I have shown earlier, at virtually all Khaṇḍobā kṣetras there is some provision for offering meat, either to Khaṇḍobā, himself, or to one or both of the demons he conquers. At temples where most of the devotees are meat-eating, there is no problem, as it is assumed that Khaṇḍobā himself accepts meat naivedya and, therefore, goats are slaughtered and offered to Khaṇḍobā within the precincts of the temple itself. At most Khaṇḍobā temples, however, and certainly at all of those considered really jāgṛt, vegetarian naivedya is the only thinkable

27. Bhaktas taking darśan of Maṇi in the courtyard of the Jejuri Khaṇḍobā temple. Photo by John Stanley.

offering to the god.[51] At these temples especially one of the important functions of the story of Malla's last request is to charter the place of a meat-eating godling associated with Khaṇḍobā at a location nearby, but distinct from, a Khaṇḍobā temple precinct. Where this is the principal function of the story, it does not seem to matter whether the demon who gets the goat naivedya is Maṇi or Malla or the composite demon, Maṇimal. Where, as at Jejuri, the demon is so closely associated with Khaṇḍobā as to have his image permanently established in the temple precincts, the meat-eating aspect of the reformed demon is omitted or deemphasized.

E. Conclusion

The story of Khaṇḍobā descending to earth to destroy two troublesome demons is a local instance of a widely known Hindu myth. At the central core of one particular variant of that story, noteworthy both for its popularity and the high literary quality of its principal written version, is the account of the capitulation and conversion of one of the demons and the decapitation and disposal of the other. The converted demon's name is Maṇi. The story charters a temple in the city of Prempur on Mount Maṇical as the best and most effective place in all the world for the granting of navas to Khaṇḍobā's bhaktas. Different aspects of the myth are variously emphasized in the oral versions of the story, including the easy accessibility to Khaṇḍobā of all castes and groups, the chartering of various devotional rituals associated with the overcoming of chaos, the distinction (relatively non-invidious) between meat-eating and vegetarian followers of the god, and the establishment of an acceptable place and method for the offering of meat naivedya in the cult.

NOTES

1. *Khaṇḍobā* is by far the most popular name of this deity, although he is also known as Mhāḷsākānt and Khaṇḍerāv in Marathi, as Malhāri and Mailār (in both Marathi and Kannada), and as Mallanna (in Kannada and Telugu); see Sontheimer in this volume. In addition there are striking parallels to Jyotibā, Kedarnāth, Mhaskobā, Bhairobā, and Aiyappan (all horse riding non-Brahman deities), although he is not identified with them.

2. The research for this paper was made possible by grants from the American Institute of Indian Studies and Lawrence University.

3. Interestingly, Jejuri is the only temple to have an image of one of the demons within the Khaṇḍobā temple itself.

4. Vāghyās are special ritual functionaries in the cult having the responsibility of begging alms for the god and, along with Muraḷīs (their female counterparts), singing and dancing in his honor. The ritual functions at which Vāghyās and Muraḷīs sing (especially the all night songfests known as *jāgraṇs*) are the source of many of the stories in the cult.

5. The Marathi version by Siddhapal Kesasri is by far the most popular and has gained a special status in the cult. Most printed versions of the Khaṇḍobā story are based on this version. Günther Sontheimer is concerned to de-emphasize Khaṇḍobā's Sanskritic and Brahmanical associations. He rightly points out in his "Rudra and Khaṇḍobā: Continuity in Folk Religion," in M. Israel and N. K. Wagle, eds., *Religion and Society in Maharashtra: South Asian Studies Papers No. 1* (Toronto: Center for South Asian Studies, University of Toronto, Coach House Press, 1987, 1-31) that when told in the context of the folk religious narratives, the *Mallāri Māhātmya* myth is de-Brahmanized and made to fit the context of folk religion, but his claim that "the content of the Māhātmya is still hardly known to the majority of the devotees" does not correspond with my field observations. Indeed, I found both the content and the structure of the *Mallāri Māhātmya* (including the frame story) to be widely known and popular in the folk traditions I observed.

6. A *navas* is a vow made to Khaṇḍobā to perform some service or extraordinary feat for him as a sign of the intensity of one's devotion, in return for which he grants a request or boon. The requests, in contemporary cult practice, are usually simple and specific (e.g., good crops, male children, victory in a wrestling match, success in an upcoming business deal, etc.), although sometimes more general (e.g., happiness, success, long life, etc.). The vows are usually to perform some simple cultic ritual (e.g., to make a pilgrimage, sacrifice a goat, make pūjā a certain number of times, etc.). In the recent past more extreme vows [e.g., dedication of a child to the life-long service of Khaṇḍobā or vows to perform extraordinary feats of strength or endurance of pain (including hook-swinging and firewalking)] were common at all of the jāgṛt kṣetras of Khaṇḍobā. Rivalry grew up both within the Khaṇḍobā cult and with other cult centers about which temple was the best place for navas granting. See John M. Stanley, "Special Time, Special Power: The Fluidity of Power in a Popular Hindu Festival," *Journal of Asian Studies* 36 (1977), p. 31, n. 31. It is no accident that all the kṣetras that claim to be Prempur are known as places for navas-granting.

7. *Tapas* here is the devotional energy, usually conceived of as heat, created by especially intense devotional procedures.

8. In the *Mallāri Māhātmya* and in most of the oral stories Ghṛtamārī's anger and vow seem focused especially on Malla. See below.

9. This is the only mention of the dogs in the *Mallāri Māhātmya*, but dogs become increasingly important in the oral stories. See below.

10. It is especially noteworthy that in the *Mallāri Māhātmya* Nandī is not replaced by the horse until after the capitulation of Maṇi. The oral stories, however, have Khaṇḍobā mounted on a horse from the beginning of the battle —often with Mhāḷsā mounted behind him assisting in the combat. The name Mārtaṇḍ Bhairav is used consistently throughout the *Mallāri Māhātmya* from this point forward, but the oral stories nearly always use the name of Khaṇḍobā or one of his other vernacular names.

11. The later oral stories will number this army anywhere from two-hundred thousand to ten billion. The numbers are nearly always even.

12. Both in the written forms and the oral forms of the story, etiologies such as this abound.

13. In some of the versions this is taken to mean that his head should always be under Khaṇḍobā's foot. In Jejuri this is assumed to be the charter of the presence of the image of Maṇi in the temple courtyard.

14. This wish-granting story is actually a three-part charter myth. The granting of the first wish provides the charter of the special navas granting power of the Prempur temple on Mount Maṇical. Indeed the same formula will be used again in the close of the frame story. The granting of the second request charters the presence of Maṇi's image in the temple courtyard, and the granting of the third wish charters the horse as Khaṇḍobā's vehicle.

15. The fierceness of this vow is intended, as is the enormity of Malla's final request, as an indication of a deeper degree of demonality on the part of Malla. It is clear from this point on that Malla will remain unreformed and unreformable.

16. The last request does not appear in the *Mallāri Māhātmya*, but it is an important motif in most Vāghyās' renditions of the story. The number of humans that Malla asks for varies from five-hundred to ten million. Whatever the number, the point is that Malla is totally unrepentant and will keep devouring humans as long as he can.

17. This is told as an etiology of the carved stone heads of horned demons found on the thresholds of several Khaṇḍobā temples. In Jejuri such a head is said by my informants to be the head of Malla, although Günther Sontheimer reports being told it was the head of Dakṣa. See Günther D. Sontheimer, "The Mallāri/Khaṇḍobā Myth As Reflected in Folk Art and Ritual," *Anthropos* 79 (1984), p. 160, n. 15.

18. Campāṣaṣṭhī or Campā's sixth; see below at n 36. This day is also identified in the cult as the day on which Maṇi surrenders to Khaṇḍobā and gives him the horse.

19. The liṅgam is a common popular representation of Khaṇḍobā. Early in the cult, before heavy Sanskritization, these representations were called piṇḍī, and both male and female forms were the same—a rounded protrusion of stone that seemed to thrust itself out of the earth. After these representations of the god were identified as liṅgams of Śiva, a distinction was drawn in the cult

between created liṅgams and self-revealed ones. A svayambhū liṅgam is, thus, a self-revealed manifestation of Śiva. No human hands carved it. Śiva, himself, in this case in his form of Khaṇḍobā, thrust forth a manifestation of himself.

20. Thus chartering several of the cult's important festivals and rituals.

21. *Mallāri Māhātmya* XXI:11.

22. *Mallāri Māhātmya*: XXII:34-38. Not only is this frame an important part of the structure of the *Mallāri Māhātmya*, it is often employed by Vāghyās and other cultic story tellers in their telling, singing, or dramatizing individual episodes of the myth.

23. See plates 23 and 24.

24. Muraḷīs are the female counterparts of Vāghyās. They are dedicated as children to Khaṇḍobā and are considered his brides. See above, n. 5.

25. In the southern cult Bānū is not regarded as a proper wife of Khaṇḍobā, but a concubine. In fact the Bānū stories are for the most part a chartering of the gradual acceptance of Dhangars into the cult. They abound with motifs of rivalry between Bānū and Mhāḷsā and Bānū's clever perseverance in finally winning a full-fledged place in Khaṇḍobā's household.

26. In the following account I have tried to preserve the dramatic structure of the Vāghyā's account. It was a story that he had often sung in a more elaborate setting with other Vāghyās and Muraḷīs playing out the various roles. In this single narrative version he assumed several roles himself, acting them out with a great sense of timing and dramatic skill.

27. The Vāghyā acts out the great difficulty Gaṅgā has had holding on to Śiva's flying hair during his fiercest anger. She is fatigued and frightened by her ordeal, but speaks determinedly. Indeed this determination becomes a character trait of Bānū in all of the later stories in which she and Mhāḷsā are rivals.

28. In many other stories Pārvatī doesn't think it is fine at all. Indeed, the rivalry between Mhāḷsā and Bānū that is so important an element in most of the stories usually begins already in the frame story with rivalry between Pārvatī and Gaṅgā, but, in this version, Mhāḷsā and Bānū are virtually friends.

29. *Bhaṇḍār* (turmeric) is Khaṇḍobā's special ritual powder. It is used in many rituals in the cult and in many of the oral stories the sprinkling of it accounts for Khaṇḍobā's magic powers. In a strict sense mention of the bhaṇḍār is anachronistic at this point in the story since Śiva's powder is white ash.

30. In this version the Vāghyā makes clear that Malla's blood did not work in this same way. The explanation, confirmed later in an interview, was that Maṇi's blood had this power because he was the younger brother.

31. *Koṭmā* is the village Marathi word for *koṭambā*, the square-shaped brass or wooden begging bowl carried traditionally by Vāghyās and Muraḷīs in which they beg alms for Khaṇḍobā.

32. In one version, when Khaṇḍobā realizes there is too much blood for

Mhāḷsā and Bānū to catch it all in their koṭmās, he sprinkles bhaṇḍār on the two goddesses and changes them into swarms of ants in which form they suck up all of the spilled blood from the ground. This is one of several stories where stinging and biting insects provide aid to Khaṇḍobā or his devotees.

33. The Vāghyā especially enjoys this part of his story. He plays the role of the clever, dashing dog with gusto, running to and fro to catch the spattered drops of blood of many young demons, thus saving the day for Khaṇḍobā. Vāghyās believe that they are descended from Khaṇḍobā's dog. They have a special affinity for dogs and often play the roles of dogs in festivals. In some of the festivals, especially in the southern cult, they will spend the festival day on all fours, barking and growling their devotion to Khaṇḍobā. Vāghyās also have a special relationship with tigers. See John M. Stanley, "Nishkama and Sakama Bhakti: Pandharpur and Jejuri," in M. Israel and N. K. Wagle, eds., *Religion and Society in Maharashtra* (Toronto: Coach House Press, 1987), and Alf Hiltebeitel, "Animals and Humans in Hindu Mythology and Ritual: Some Popular Bhakti Examples," paper presented at the Association of Asian Studies Annual Meeting, Washington, D.C. 1984.

34. Several folk bronzes illustrate this moment in the story. See plate 22. Compare the folk bronze published in Sontheimer, "Mallāri/Khaṇḍobā Myth," Fig. 3.

35. Story tellers in the Khaṇḍobā cult do not regard this picture as authentic. I have shown this picture to many story tellers asking them to tell me the story of the picture only to receive a disparaging response: No, that is only a picture; Mhāḷsā was not even in the battle; or Mhāḷsā was, but the dog was not; or the dog was in the battle, but only to catch blood. Still, the picture remains the most popular depiction of the battle with the demons, indeed one of the most popular of all depictions of Khaṇḍobā in the cult. Reproductions of it are sold in temple towns all over Maharashtra, and in many small temples (e.g., Medankar Wadi, Chakan Taluk, Pune District; see plate 24) there is a reproduction of this picture in the temple itself. For many Khaṇḍobā bhaktas this depiction is the principal vehicle of the story of the battle, whatever the story tellers think about its accuracy. In some temples the self-wounding of a bhakta's thigh is mentioned along with hook swinging and the piercing of the foot between the ankle and the Achilles tendon as extreme rites of devotion (*bagaḍ*). When the thigh is wounded in this ritual, the blood is allowed to drip onto the piṇḍī and the ritual is referred to as "self-sacrifice."

36. Campā's sixth, so named after an especially devout Dhangar bhakta of Khaṇḍobā called Campā who could not afford to offer sweet cakes (*puraṇ polī*) as naivedya to her Lord, but offered instead some of her own cooked food, an onion and eggplant *roṭi* called *bharit roḍgā*. Puraṇ poḷī is generally identified as a Brahman offering. Bharit roḍgā is a rural dish associated especially with Dhangars. Khaṇḍobā's acceptance of the poorer offering charters his special approachability to Dhangars. Günther Sontheimer insists that the Campāṣaṣṭhī festival at Jejuri is part of the "Brahmanized" cult and therefore not to be taken

seriously. His argument is based on the association of the *ṣaṣṭhī* tithi with Skanda and the association of Skanda with Brahmans ("Rudra and Khaṇḍobā," n. 8). He is correct in his rejection of the mythological association of Khaṇḍobā with Skanda, but he overlooks other important non-Brahman and non-Skanda associations with the ṣaṣṭhī tithi—including the Campā legend and the idea clearly fixed in the cult that this was the day of Maṇi's capitulation.

37. Compare Madeleine Biardeau's treatment of vegetarian and meat-eating gods in this volume.

38. Pūjā and ārati are performed to Maṇi within the temple precincts at Jejuri, but non-vegetarian naivedya is never offered.

39. Hegaḍī means "brother-in-law." Pradhān means "minister." Hegaḍī Pradhān is the brother-in-law minister of Khaṇḍobā. There are two Hegaḍī Pradhāns in the Khaṇḍobā cult: one is a *vāṇī* (a Liṅgāyat merchant caste); he is the brother of Mhāḷsā. The other is a Dhangar; he is the brother of Bānubāī. At some temples there are shrines to both Hegaḍī Pradhāns, but usually there is only one. Even at temples where there is only one shrine, it is sometimes identified as the Dhangar Pradhān by some informants and the Liṅgāyat Pradhān by others. Both are, by some informants, said to be the avatār of Viṣṇu. At Jejuri it is the Dhangar minister who receives the naivedya and carries it to the demon.

40. There is considerable confusion about which demon gets the naivedya and precisely how it is taken to him. Some informants at this shrine claim the offering goes to Maṇi only. Some say it goes to both demons and some insist that it goes to the composite demon Maṇimal. The logic of the story would seem to require that Malla should receive at least some of the goat naivedya; otherwise the irony of Malla's being given the head of a goat doesn't work. Some bhaktas at this shrine insist that Malla was killed and cannot receive naivedya at all, but Maṇi receives it because of his genuine conversion and the gift of the horse.

41. E.g., the rape of the ṛṣis' wives and the throwing of the dead bodies into the wells.

42. For a treatment of navas-granting as an instance of overcoming chaos, see Stanley, "Special Time, Special Power" and "Nishkama and Sakama Bhakti."

43. The composite demon in many of the oral versions loses much of this distinction.

44. Identification of this mūrti is not unequivocal. In his "Mallāri/Khaṇḍobā Myth," pp. 158-59, Sontheimer identifies the mūrti as Malla, although he notes some confusion and points out that it is sometimes identified as "Maṇi, the Malla" or even Maṇi. In my experience informants consistently identified the image as Maṇi or occasionally as Maṇimal, but never as Malla nor "Maṇi, the Malla."

45. See above, n. 17.

46. In the oral stories the god to whom they do the initial devotion is usually

Śiva himself rather than Brahmā. Indeed, in the most popular depictions of the demons they are wearing Rudrākṣa beads indicative of bhaktas of Śiva.

47. See John M. Stanley, "Gods, Ghosts and Possession" in E. Zelliot and M. Bernsten, eds., *The Experience of Hinduism* (Albany: State University of New York Press, in press).

48. I am grateful for this insight to Wendy O'Flaherty's commentary to the original presentation of this paper.

49. Dogs have important ritual functions at all Khaṇḍobā festivals where they are ritually covered with bhaṇḍār and become an object from which a devotee can take Khaṇḍobā's darśan.

50. The Vāghyās canine rituals were well-known, not only in the Khaṇḍobā cult, but throughout the Deccan, as early as the seventeenth century. The Viṭhobā devotee and poet-saint Tukaram writes one of his most famous abhaṅghas in the persona of a Vāghyā, barking out his devotion to Khaṇḍobā. See Stanley, "Nishkama and Sakama Bhakti."

51. Some informants were especially vehement about this, striking the ground with a stick and spitting to emphasize the distastefulness of the idea that Khaṇḍobā would ever receive non-vegetarian naivedya. One informant, when told of temples where Khaṇḍobā did accept goat meat, was openly disgusted at the idea and insisted that if a god did eat meat at the temples I was telling him about, that god could not possibly be Khaṇḍobā.

11

Between Ghost and God: A Folk Deity of the Deccan

Günther D. Sontheimer

Abbreviations:
AV=*Atharva Veda*, *BŚS*=*Baudhāyana Śrautasūtra*, Ka.=Kannaḍa, *M.Māh.*=*Mallāri Māhātmya* (Skt.), Ma.=Marāṭhī, MMKh=Mallanna/Mailāra/Khaṇḍobā, *MV*=*Mārtaṇḍa Vijaya* (*Ma.*, 1821), Tel.=Telugu, *TB*=*Taittirīya Brāhmaṇa*, *TS*=*Taittirīya Saṃhitā*, *VS*=*Vājasaneyī Saṃhitā*.

A. Introduction: Spread and Antiquity

One of the most famous folk gods of Andhra Pradesh is Mallanna often identified with Mallikārjuna of Srisailam in the Kurnool district.[1] Srisailam, in the Nallamala Hills of the Eastern Ghats, was nearly inaccessible until recently. The ancient cult of Mallikārjuna also attracted pilgrims from Maharashtra from at least the twelfth century onwards. They called the god Sirigiri Mallaya, a name still used in Karnataka, Andhra, and Maharashtra.[2] Many religious currents have met in the cult of Mallikārjuna, especially those of Śaivite "sects," beginning from the Pāśupatas and Kāpālikas to the Liṅgāyats, and it also has its epic and purāṇic contacts.[3] As is so often the case with famous cults, forest tribals (Cẽñcūs) and/or pastoralists (Gollas) are said to have been the discoverers of Mallikārjuna. The immediate access to worshippers of all castes and religious affiliations is not only characteristic of Mallanna/Mallikārjuna but also of the god Mailāra of Karnataka, and Khaṇḍobā alias Mallāri/Malhāri/Mairāḷ of Maharashtra. Scholars usually compare these three deities, whose interregional identity is confirmed by itinerant devotees and medieval literature. The identification is explicit in border areas of the three adjoining states, e.g., in Pember/Prempur (Khanapur), near Bidar, at the border of Maharashtra and Karnataka. Here Mallanna is also known as Mailāra as well as Khaṇḍobā. Such is also the case at Warangal in the Telengana area of Andhra Pradesh, where Katta Mallanna is called Khaṇḍērāyā. A folk song from Malegaon, further north of Pember, in the Nanded district of Maharashtra, identifies Khaṇḍobā with Mallanna:

> On the stony heath of Malegaon
> surrounded by four bastions
> there Malhāri resides
> the god Mallanna . . .[4]

We are dealing here primarily with the folk deity Mallanna/Mailāra/Khaṇḍobā (MMKh) rather than with the sectarian or the purāṇic Śiva. Folk religion has its own identity and may not necessarily subordinate itself to the values of the Brahman. Moreover, other hierarchical models may exist beside that of the Brahman, as Richard Burghart has argued.[5] According to him, there is the Brahman, the ascetic, and the king, each claiming highest rank and godhood within their respective hierarchy. The hierarchies do not face each other as rigid structures, but interact. Elements of each heirarchy are incorporated into the other hierarchical model. The highest ranking person of the other hierarchy was assigned an honourable, but subordinated rank within the enlarged model. Similarly I would like to suggest that the cult of MMKh, though borrowing values from the other traditions, is expressive of an autonomous current, that is, folk religion, which interacts with other currents, but is not necessarily subordinated to them. Ecology certainly also plays a role. MMKh are mainly worshipped in dry or (now diminished) forested areas of the Deccan. The devotees belong to a wide range of groups which are known by different names in the three states, but follow the same traditional occupations. Prominent among them are the traditional agricultural, trading, pastoral nomadic, hunting, and predatory castes. Many of these castes had martial proclivities in the past. Devotees include Untouchable castes as well as Brahmans. In Maharashtra it is mainly Deśastha Brahmans who worship Khaṇḍobā as their family deity. This link with the Brahmans might tempt us to label MMKh as the usual Bhairava who is connected with Brahmanicide and the destruction of the yajña (as in the case of Dakṣa's sacrifice). But the link to the Brahmanical ritual-social order of the world, as formulated in terms of the *cāturvarṇya* system, is generally not emphasized. No doubt this is also a theme, but it is introduced by Brahmanical sources, like the Sanskrit *Mallāri Māhātmya* which I briefly deal with at the end of this essay. Considering the transgression of the sacred, social order, we come to learn that MMKh transgress more orders than that of the Brahmans, e.g., that of the Liṅgāyats and the Muslims. In short, the mythological, ritual, historical, social, and ecological context of the cult does not permit us to emphasize *a priori* the importance of the *varṇa* hierarchy, the Brahmanical value of ritual purity, or the Brahman's spiritual superiority (in Dumont's terms) over worldly power (*kṣatram*). Often MMKh resemble a bandit, or a rising, pre-imperial king rather than a pacified kṣetrapāla and protector of the cāturvarṇya system, of Brahmans and cows. They convert and accumulate their devotees from many groups by means of aggression, robbery, love marriage or marriage by capture (apparently in the inverted *pratiloma* order), feats of prowess, tricks, and miracles. They create their order of society not primarily by seeking sanction in the Brahmanical order and becoming a kṣetrapāla or a "demon devotee." Hierarchy is determined by bhakti (which does not necessarily correspond to the "classical" modes of bhakti) and tapas. From the point of view of sects and the Brahman's point of view the deity may be considered to be just a bhūta, or an inferior godling, that is, a *kṣudradevatā* or kṣetrapāla. But for the actual worshippers he is *central to their life and beliefs*, irrespective of how others choose to call their deity.

Folk religion seems to be singularly conservative and there are striking continuities between MMKh and their antecedent Rudra. Rudra was primarily a god of certain groups mentioned, e.g., in the *Śatarudrīya* of the *Taittirīya Saṃhitā*. Their culture was outside, though interconnected with that of the Vedic sacrificial priests who subordinated Rudra as Agni in the agnicayana ritual. For the latter he may have been a "demonic" intruder connected with impurity and death which had to be eliminated. Vedic passages reflect a god who is earthbound, "demonic," with magic powers, potentially ubiquitous in nature, yet very much bearing personal characteristics. These would usually suggest iconic worship, but if we take texts like the *Śatarudrīya* literally we must conclude that Rudra's followers viewed him as the "charismatic" living leader of their respective group. He is the mediator between the divine unmanifest, untamed elements of *nature*, which he incorporates and controls, and his followers who worship him. But the borders are fluid and all three partake of each other. The follower imitates his leader, the leader, in turn, imitates Rudra in dress and ritual. Here we find the early roots of bhakti, the root of which is *bhaj* = "to participate." Rudra is called *sthāpati* (*TS* 4.5.2.i.) which may refer to a chieftain or to the leader of the Vrātyas,[6] *mantrī* (*TS* 4.5.2.k)—the lord of the "spells"; *senānī* (*TS* 4.5.2.a)—the leader of the army; *vāṇij* (*TS* 4.5.2.k.)—the merchant; and *daivya bhiṣaj* (*TS* 4.5.f.)—the divine doctor. Rudra is connected with robbers and thieves, heroes and warriors, lords of horses, and dog keepers. Horses, dogs, and cattle are his animals, and he often manifests himself in these animals. He is a hunter with bow and arrow and is associated with forests and mountains. He is the lord of the fields, that is, a kṣetrapati (*TS* 4.5.2.g.) rather than a mere "protector" (kṣetrapāla). All these features survive and are reflected in the MMKh cult. For example, Mallanna is said to be "indistinguishable among bandits" (Tel. *dongallō dorakaḍu*) in Golla traditions[7] and Khaṇḍobā is reputed to be "close to thieves"[8] and is associated with ex-predatory communities like the Rāmośīs (Beraḍs). Most noteworthy are the special followers of Rudra, the Vrātyas, whose dress and rituals closely resemble the special devotees, the Voggus of Andhra, the Vāghyās of Maharashtra, and in particular the Vaggayyas of Karnataka. That the Vaggayyas actually envisage an *imitatio dei* is demonstrated in the Mailāra temple of Aduru in the Dharwar district. Here the typical long woolen black gown of a Vaggayya is displayed on the wall inside the shrine and it is said to be the gown of Mailāra. The imitation of the human leader who incorporated the divine and himself became Rudra, e.g., the Ekavrātya in his cosmogonic ritual (*AV* XV), seems to have been a common feature before manifestations of the divine in mūrtis became popular (but cp. *TS* 4.5.6.c: "to him of the amulet"). We need not view the later sects worshipping Śiva or Bhairava with their peculiar rituals of *imitatio dei* as the antecedents of the Voggus, etc., but would rather suggest direct continuity between the ancient Vrātyas and the present day Voggus, etc. Parallels of such impersonations of the deity also include the devotee of the early Murukan, the *vēlān* dancing in a frenzy until he became Vēlān, that is Murukan himself.[9] Similarly the *devṛṣī* ("shaman") in the Khaṇḍobā cult is possessed by the god in the form of the wind and virtually becomes Khaṇḍobā. The Svāmi at Mailar (Hadagalli Taluka, Ballari District) impersonates Mailāra in the form of a king. In the traditions of the Gollas Mallanna/Mallikārjuna may turn up as a Jaṅgama, a Liṅgāyat renouncer, a "walking liṅga," as it were, to test his bhaktas. And in the cult of Khaṇḍobā the god may turn into a Vāghyā for the same purpose.

B. Manifestations of the Folk Deity

The Living God on Earth, God as King and Other Appearances

For the devotee MMKh is a living powerful god (e.g., Ma. jāgṛt) who exists "here and now" on earth and is not confined to a purāṇic heaven. He is worshipped in a temple primarily in the form of a svayaṃbhū liṅga (Ma. *piṇḍa*) which has to be distinguished from the liṅga installed in the usual Śiva temple where the liṅga has to be enlivened by Brahmans in the ceremony of *prāṇapratiṣṭhā*. Accordingly the temple priests of Mallanna are not Brahmans, but Gollas (at Warangal Yerru Gollas) or Liṅgāyats, and in the case of Khaṇḍobā Guravs rather than Brahmans. In addition to the liṅga there are usually brass mūrtis of the gods. In the case of Mallanna the mūrtis are four feet high (e.g., in Komarelli, Jangaon Tk., Warangal Dt., in Warangal: Katha Mallanna, and Ailōni/Iloni/Inoli, near Warangal) and made of clay (see plates 28 and 29). Mailāra's mūrti at Mailar is also made from the clay of a termite mound. It is from this mound, filled with dreadful serpents, that the god is said to have appeared for the first time. Possession, firewalking, hook-swinging, and animal sacrifices are still practised and point to a folk deity *par excellence*. It is only in recent times that such customs recede, except in outlying areas. MMKh are worshiped by different groups as their leader, reflecting their respective occupations. But they are especially worshiped like a royal god, or like a god as a king, and as such the god of dynasties and would-be dynasties of kings. For instance Mallanna was the *kulasvāmī* of the Kākatīya (thirteenth century), Mailāra of a chief of Bhujanganagar (fourteenth century), Khaṇḍobā/Khaṇḍerāyā was the family deity of the Holkars and the Gaikwads (eighteenth century), and so on. It was especially in Karnataka and Maharashtra that the royal and martial aspects of the cult flourished. The temples of Khaṇḍobā often resemble fortresses, as, e.g., in Jejuri (Pune District) which is said to be his capital (Ma. *rājdhānī*; see plate 30). The brass mūrtis, often donated by kings, resemble kings. They reflect the historical period of the Vijayanagara empire and, in the case of Khaṇḍobā, they resemble, when dressed, a Maratha Sardār. The face of Mallanna is usually adorned by a Muslim beard. Representations on silver plaques used as house gods or as amulets and brass mūrtis show him seated on a horse accompanied by his wife or śakti. His weapons show the martial and sacrificial background of the cult: trident (triśūl)

28. Images of Mallanna, Golla Kētamma (left), and Balaji Māḍaladevi at Kommarelli, Jangaon Taluk, Warangal District, Andhra Pradesh. Contemporary lithograph. Photo by Günther Sontheimer.

29. Images of Mallanna and his wives in the temple of Ailōni, near Warangal. Contemporary lithograph. Photo by Günther Sontheimer.

30. The Khaṇḍobā temple on the Gaḍkoṭ ("Hill Fort") at Jejuri. The temple in the so-called Peshva style was recently renovated in the Tamil style. Photo by Günther Sontheimer.

and hourglass-shaped drum (ḍamaru), sword (*khaḍga*) and shield (Ma. *dhāḷ*) or a bowl (Skt. *pātra*, Ma. *paraḷ*).

MMKh are also treated like a king and act like a king. At Jejuri Khaṇḍobā is carried in a palanquin for a hunting expedition on Somvati Amāvāsyā, that is, on a no moon day falling on a Monday. The procession moves from the Gaḍkoṭ (Hill-Fort) to the river where the god takes a bath with his devotees after his hunt. The ritual is reminiscent of the aśvamedha: Khaṇḍobā's horse is led by a Muslim far ahead of the palanquin. The devotees (e.g., the Dhangar shepherds acting as hunters with spears) eagerly try to touch the hoofs or the head of the horse and walk with it. The "hunt" concludes with a common bath of the god and all the participants. At the end of the Vedic sacrifice the king takes a final bath (avabhṛtha). His followers join him and become free of sin.[10] In the old (nineteenth century) songs of the Vāghyās (bards of the god), the hunt to the river Karha is mentioned as well as Khaṇḍobā's circling the earth on a horse.[11] In the *VS* (23, 17-19) the sacrificial horse is identified with Agni, Vāyu, and Sūrya. According to the *Śatapatha-Brāhmaṇa* (13, 2, 7, 13-15) the mantra says that the victim will conquer the same realms as these deities. Agni, Vāyu, and Sūrya are forms of Rudra, the war god. Khaṇḍobā is similarly identified with fire, such as the indispensable torches (Ma. *divṭī*, Ka. *divaṭī*), or the flame that is worshipped on a platter. He is the sun as Mārtaṇḍa Bhairava, and in the form of turmeric powder (Ma. *bhaṇḍār*, Ka. *baṇḍāra*, Tel. *baṇḍāru*). MMKh's special day is Sunday. But he is also the wind (Ma. *vāreṃ*) who possesses devotees and makes them act like horses. Horse and dog are associated with Rudra as well as MMKh. Dogs (preferably black) are worshiped throughout the cult of MMKh. The elementary, undomesticated manifestation of the divine in the form of an as yet wild dog is still experienced by the Kois, who belong to the Gonds. They revere wild dogs even if they kill cattle.[12] A similar concession is made to Rudra, whose connection with the dog is close, as for instance in a passage from the *BŚS* (14.23; *TB* 2.4.1.6.): If a dog passes between the *garhapatya* and *āhavanīya* fire, impurity is removed by making a cow walk over it, and the sacrificer hands over his cattle to Rudra (who is Agni). Unlike those made over to Rudra (*TS* 2.1.7), cows are, of course, not sacrificed to MMKh, although sheep used to be sacrificed to him and were slaughtered by Khaṇḍobā, according to oral traditions, such as when he destroys the herd of sheep of Bāṇāī, his second wife. Mallanna's army consists of seven dogs, a number which may easily increase: King Mārtaṇḍa has 700 dogs, and sometimes they amount to seven crores (*yeḷkoṭi* = Tel., Ka., but the term is also very much used in the Khaṇḍobā cult). The horse or the dog may appear in the dream of the devotee and summon him to Jejuri. For those who are not worshippers of MMKh the dog may spell death and disaster. Khaṇḍobā may take the form of a dog and punish those who insult his bhaktas. But the god also grants freedom from the state of a wild animal and the present day Vāghyās, the special devotees of Khaṇḍobā, are examples of this: they were actually tigers, but gained their human form, or rather turned into the faithful dogs of the god by having the vision of the god.[13] The dog and also the humans impersonating it are epitomes of faithfulness and protection. The dog is useful to the hunter and the shepherd; hunting and protecting are characteristic activities of the king. Thus there are famous examples of Maratha kings and Sardārs which show much loyalty and affection between masters and their faithful dogs. In this light it may not sound so ridiculous that King Śāhū (1707-49) would dress and treat the dog that had saved him from a tiger as a Sardār,[14] or that Malhārrāo Holkar would not dine with the Peśvā unless his dog was admitted to the dining hall. He would rather eat with his dog outside on the verandah.[15] We should add that Śāhū as well as Holkar were devotees of Khaṇḍobā. The same reverence for dogs prevails in the Mallanna cult. When Mallanna and his brother Bayanna sleep during the night, the dogs keep watch (Tel. *kāvali*) for wolves, jackals, and tigers. When Mallanna distributes the milk of sheep, he makes twelve leaf cups: seven for the seven dogs, one for the goddess Pōśammā, one for Agni, one for Nāgasarpam, one for Bayanna, and one for himself. There may be a thirteenth cup for the wind god. It goes floating in the air and Mallanna tells Bayanna that the wind god is carrying away his cup.[16]

The Life-Increasing God

MMKh accept promises and fulfil wishes (Ma. *navas*, Ka. *harike*, Tel. *mokkubaḍi* = vow). Such wishes may be earthbound like victory in battle, children, rain, good harvest, cattle, recovery from illness, and good marriages. Especially fertility and marriage are important incidents. The marriage has to be sanctioned by the god and the couple has to present themselves to their kulasvāmi. In Warangal at the Katta Mallanna temple Yerra Gollas enact a ritual on an elaborate design on the floor on which the marriage of Kētamma, the first wife of Mallanna is performed. Newlyweds still wearing the marriage clothes (coloured yellow with turmeric), come to the Katta Mallanna temple, and perform the marriage of Mallanna with Kētamma as a fulfilment of their vow. After the marriage ritual Golla and Kuruva women dance on the design and some get possessed. In Pali (Satara District) Khaṇḍobā's marriage with Mhāḷsā, his first wife from the Liṅgāyat Vāṇī (merchant) community, is annually performed. Dense clouds of turmeric powder envelop the marriage procession. Turmeric powder is reputed not only to heal but also to cause fertility in marriages. It is also identified with the life-giving sun (= Sūrya [masc.]) who in oral traditions impregnates women. The custom of girls "married" to MMKh is especially emphasized (and nowadays disapproved) in the cult of Khaṇḍobā where they are called Muraḷīs. Along with the Vāghyās, the bards of Khaṇḍobā, the Muraḷīs perform dances at jāgraṇs, which are vigils in honour of Khaṇḍobā arranged by patron devotees of the god. These parties of devotees who sing and dance in honour of Khaṇḍobā may remind us of the *puṃścalī* ("harlot"), the Vrātya, and the *māgadha* or *sūta* (bard) who jointly wandered and must have performed and begged in the name of their god Rudra.[17]

The Desire for Nearness or Unity with the God

Not only is earthly life enriched and increased in the constant company of the god in thought or in ritual, but death promises nearness or even unity with the god. This even led to ritual suicide by heroes (vīras), as in the case of the Vīramuṣṭis mentioned in the *Krīḍābhirāmamu*, the Kañcavīras of Mailāra, and the Vīras of the Khaṇḍobā cult.[18] Unity or nearness may thus be rather violently achieved by special devotees (in the past), or comes with the normal death of those devotees who worship MMKh as their kulasvāmi. Numerous stone mūrtis and new as well as weathering inscriptions on steps, now more and more replaced by new steps and thus forgotten forever, commemorate heroes and/or ancestors in Jejuri. Similar to the ancestor cults of tribals like that of the Dhangars of Maharashtra or the Gonds, the ancestors are close to and eventually merge imperceptably with the clan deity in worship. But MMKh are not just deities of a single clan or caste, or group, but are lords of many clans and castes, as if of a confederacy. MMKh are the leaders of hosts, dead and alive, like Rudra. In accordance with the notion that the god is living here and now, it is not the distant Kailās on which the departed soul rests. A certain concession seems to be made to this folk god on earth in a Marathi ārati appended to the Sanskrit *Mallāri Māhātmya* when it is said:

> The mountain of the fortress of Jejuri is in the form of a *liṅg*.
> In the world of mortals this is the peak of another Kailās.

Jejuri *is* Kailās an old Vāghyā song confirms.[19] The same claim is made in Kommarelli in the case of Mallanna. Similarly the mountain of Shingnapur (Satara District) is said to be the seat of Śambhu or Mahādeva, who is rarely called *Śiva* except in a Sanskritic text or context; and Srisailam (Kurnool District) is the seat of Mallikārjuna. Mallikārjuna also serves as a kind of Śiva on earth, other than the distant purāṇic Śiva, perhaps reflecting the notion preeminent amongst tribals that gods live on the surrounding mountains. Ancestors in the Khaṇḍobā cult, and Khaṇḍobā himself, are also worshiped in the form of metal plaques which depict heroes (Ma. *vīras;* see plates 31-32). The worship of these plaques on Somavatī Amāvāsyā on the Karha river at Jejuri is accompanied by the songs and dances performed by the Muraḷīs and Vāghyās. A common meal is shared by ancestors and living descendants. The ancestors appear and possess their descendants. What happens to ascendants after three generations nobody knows. They certainly do not become *viśve devāḥ* according to the classical śrāddha ritual, which anyway, the *MV* maintains is not performed at Jejuri. Perhaps the lesser known Brahmanical "folk" antyeṣṭi rituals as dealt with by the 16th century Nārāyaṇabhaṭṭa explain the folk belief: here the deceased is transformed into Rudra by the ritual.[20]

Criteria for Ranking of Bhaktas

A blend of tapas and bhakti determines rank in the cult of MMKh, although there is no written explicit formulation for it. Translated into the notion of god as King, it is bravery (*śaurya*) and loyalty (bhakti). This reflects the historical relationship between king and loyal followers, e.g., in the Vijayanagara empire.[21] Feats of bravery are reflected (historically) in the self-mortifications of the various kinds of heroes (vīras) in the MMKh cult. The ritual of hook-swinging may have been performed mainly to pay off vows in order to get life-increasing wishes fulfilled, like fortunes or children (a wish which after all may ultimately express a desire for "immortality"), but the essential aim of bhakti is nearness or unity with god. A Vāghyā song typically expresses these aspirations:

> Give me the banner of success, o King Mālurāyā Mārtaṇḍa || But don't give me the sense of pride, [lest] people will laugh at you || This is all I beg from you || Protection and death signals your eternal, famous banner || 1 ||
> Don't give me so many riches, I request you || I don't want the distinction between man and man. How is it that you make one serve with a flywhisk and grant another a huge vessel of success || 2 ||

31. Metal mould used by goldsmiths for preparing plaques. Such plaques are used in house shrines in the cult of Khaṇḍobā, and also in the cult of Mallanna. They depict ancestors as warriors (*vīras*) and are used in ancestor worship (actual size 2½ × 2 inches). Photo by Günther Sontheimer.

32. A mould depicting Khaṇḍobā and his wife. At the bottom the usual dog is shown. Photo by Günther Sontheimer.

Just give me kith and kin, for having a family, for making my clan grow ||
Don't send me away and make me wander, my life remains with you ||
Your eternal, famous banner of success flutters || 3 ||
Keep, o keep your shadow over Śivajī Vāghyā || With the mercy of love, let me and my companion Rāmcandra sit beneath it. People will resort to your feet, o Lord, with the new sword in your hand || 4 ||[22]

The most faithful bhakta does not wish anything except the company, nearness or unity with the god. The god himself is (Ma.) *bhūkela* = "hungry for true bhaktas" (*MV* 5.12), or (Tel.) *bhaktavatsala* = "gracious to his bhaktas." Thus according to a legend it was a member of the "untouchable" Māṅg (Mātaṅga) caste who sacrificed his life for the foundation of the fortress in Jejuri. This is interpreted as an act of bhakti because by his sacrifice he wanted to persuade Śiva to stay forever on earth, that is in Jejuri (which Śiva did). The Māṅg became the guardian god of the temple having his shrine near the main gate of the outer temple wall. His name is Yeśvant Rāo and he became a *havildār* (officer of a fort). Today he is famous for healing bone fractures when vows are made to him. Thus it appears that the divine doctor, Rudra, alias Khaṇḍobā, has delegated some of the medicinal powers to Yeśvant Rāo and thus moved to a greater degree of purity, because traditionally doctors are ritually impure.[23] Similarly the existence and practice of values of faithfulness and bravery may elevate the devotee or hero while transfering something of his own lowliness to his god or lord. Yeśvant Rāo's legend reminds us of the Velugoṭi family to which the chiefs of Venkatagaon belonged. They first came into prominence during the reign of the Kākatīya king Gaṇapati who ruled at Warangal from 1198 to 1263 AD. The founder of the Rēcerla clan, of which the Velugoṭi family is an offshoot, was a farmer at the village Anumangallu, called Cevvi Reḍḍi.[24] The *Vēlugōṭivarivaṃśāvaḷi* contains variants of the story of Cevvi Reḍḍi.

According to one version, Cevvi Reḍḍi discovered by chance a *treasure trove*, to take possession of which he had to sacrifice his faithful Untouchable servant *Rēca*. The servant willingly offered himself as the victim. In pursuance of a promise Cevvi Reḍḍi changed the name of his *gotra* into Rēcerla in commemoration of his faithful servant who cheerfully faced death for his benefit.

According to another version, Cevvi Reḍḍi, while returning home from his field after dark, encounters a *vetāla*, a demon. Cevvi Reḍḍi bravely defends himself with a club; the demon, pleased with his bravery, confers upon him certain favours and vanishes. From then on

Cevvi Reḍḍi became popular as Bēṭāla Reḍḍi, whom King Gaṇapati invited to his court and granted favors including the government of a district. Finally he establishes a kingdom at Rēcerla.

The *Mallāri Māhātmya* explains the name of Mallāri in a similar way: Mārtaṇḍa Bhairava is pleased by the bravery of the defeated demon hero (vīra) Malla (*M.Mah.* 16.41) and on the request of Malla his name becomes part of Mārtaṇḍa's name. Mārtaṇḍa is now called Mallāri = "the enemy of Malla" (*M.Māh.* 17.36).

Devotion and tapas are also the elements in another prototype of a bhakta in the Khaṇḍobā cult. Local traditions in Jejuri tell of a bhakta who every day climbed up the path to the old Khaṇḍobā temple on the distant, high plateau (Karhe Pathar). He certainly did not go there for material wealth, but to be near his god. When the bhakta grew too old to make the arduous ascent, the god descended from the high, distant hill to the hill just above the town of Jejuri. On account of his devotion and self-sacrifice the devotee and his descendants were given the first rank amongst the *mānkaris* (Ma.), that is, those bhaktas entitled to ritual privileges in temple rituals. Thus the flagstaffs of the descendants of the devotee still have precedence over those of other bhaktas in processions.

C. The Followers of Mailāra, Mallanna, and Khaṇḍobā According to Ritual, Oral Literature, and History

The Vaggayyas and the Festival at Devaragudda and Mailar

Especially noteworthy are two great festivals which are celebrated in the cult of Mailāra: the Dasarā festival at Devaragudda (at Ranebennur near Harihar, Dharwad District) and the festival at Mailar (Hadagalli Taluka, Bellari District) in the month of Māgha (February/March). The latter lasts for eleven days beginning from Rathasaptamī day and ending two days after the full moon day. On both occasions the struggle is against the demons Maṇi and Malla. Some say in Devaragudda that Malla was killed in Devaragudda and Maṇi at Mailar, but in Mailar we are told that it was here that Maṇikāsura and Mallāsura were killed in battle. A mock battle against the demon is enacted in Mailar. The special followers of Mailāra, the Vaggayyas (see plates 33 and 34), who closely resemble the ancient Vrātyas, the followers of Rudra, play a prominent role in the ritual. They are also called Gorappas or Goravas and are mentioned in medieval Kannada inscriptions. Although most of the Vaggayyas are from the Kuruba shepherd

33. A Vaggayya or Gorappa from Karnataka in his black woollen overcoat that is beset with a zigzag pattern and has the typical fringes at the bottom. The indispensible begging bowl from which he eats like a dog at rituals is not visible. Photo by Günther Sontheimer.

34. A Vaggayya from southern Andhra/Karnataka with a bearskin cap and a necklace of cowrie shells. Photo by Günther Sontheimer.

community, there are also members of other communities, from the low Taḷvāra (sword) caste up to (allegedly) the Brahmans. But whereas the Kurubas are Vaggayyas for their whole life, most of the members of other communities observe the rites of a Vaggayya/Gorappa only on special occasions. Among the Taḷvāras, the eldest son should become a Gorappa after his father dies. He does not regularly wear the typical attire of a Gorappa. He is supposed to wear it on every full moon day, on Sundays, and during the (Ka.) jātrās. On these days he goes begging.

On the first day of the battle ritual a black flag is hoisted as a sign that war is declared against the demons. Milk is boiled and is allowed to spill as a good omen forecasting the victory of Mailāra. Again the Vedic Rudra comes to mind: it is milk which is boiled in the *pravargya* ritual in a vessel called *gharma*. The vessel is also called *mahāvīra* and Rudra is identified with it.[25] The next day group fighting is enacted which involves throwing sweets at each other. This is said to be a sign that war has begun. Whereas Maṇikāsura is defeated easily (it is not shown how), Mallāsura accepts defeat only on the eleventh day. Early in the morning before sunrise thousands of devotees, many of them temporary or lifelong Gorappas dressed in their long, black woollen gowns converge on a hillock outside Mailar. They are the army of Mailāra. The whole army of devotees, said to (mythically) consist of seven crores (Ka. *yeḷkoṭi*), moves towards the hill in complete silence. Many devotees carry brass torches which evokes the impression of a nocturnal wild hunt of Rudra. The god is represented by the Svāmi of the Devasthān (temple) who rides a white stallion and is accompanied by a bearer of a royal parasol. Besides there are mūrtis of Mailāra and his wife mounted on a wooden structure covered by cloth. When the top of the hill is reached the masks and the huge leather sandals of the god and his wife are quickly carried around a platform seven times accompanied by thick throngs of devotees who loudly scream "Yeḷkoṭi Mallāri Mārtaṇḍa."[26] *Yeḷkoṭ* may also refer to the seven crores of enemies defeated by Mailāra, but throughout the tradition of MMKh it is also suggested that enemies may become devotees of the god. Finally, the god has defeated and slain the demon: a cloth which has so far concealed the huge wooden mask of the demon is pulled away from under the feet of the deities. The day closes with the *karṇikotsava* (festival of prophecy). This ritual is more or less the same at Devaragudda. It takes place there during the Dasarā time and is performed on the ninth day.[27] In Mailar an old Kuruba who has fasted for eleven days (in Devaragudda on the ninth day) climbs a bow (Ka. *billa*) which is eighteen feet high. After climbing the bow to the top he is possessed by the god in the form of wind. He then utters prophecies for the coming year. He did not participate in the activities of the other Vaggayyas, but (as observed in Devaragudda) quietly sits under a Banyan tree in a grove until his appointed moment has come. At his side the huge bow is placed against the tree (see plate 35). The Vaggayya's attire and the rite he performs remind us of the Ekavrātya as described in *AV* XV who becomes Rudra and is described as having a red back and a black belly (*AV* XV.1.7.). The shoulders and back of the Vaggayya who becomes Mailāra are covered by a red cloth with the zig zag border characteristic of the dress of the Vaggayyas and imitative of a rugged fur; in front the black woollen gown in visible.

Another important ritual in Mailar and Devaragudda is the *pavāḍā*, a "heroic, magical feat."[28] In Mailar it is celebrated after the slaying of the demon, in Devaragudda on Dasarā day. It is performed by the so-called Kañcavīras, recruited especially from Kuruba Vaggayyas, and (in Devaragudda) also by Māḍigas. Their heroic feats reflect an aggressive loyalty towards their god. They wield weapons like iron prongs, swords or tridents, and pierce their calves with painted iron rods, or with an instrument resembling a pointed tent peg made of the wood of a palm tree. The most important incident of the ritual is carried out by a young unmarried Vaggayya preferably twelve years old. He is the first who has to perform the ritual of piercing the leg in front of the god. He then simultaneously passes two thorny twigs of the *babbuli* tree through the wound. After that he passes a long rope through the wound. One might wonder whether the rope in this act of bravery does not indicate the tie with which an initiate symbolically binds himself to the god. The whole ritual also has (self-) sacrificial undercurrents. Thus, it is said that once upon a time the god demanded human sacrifice. Some exquisitely carved medieval stone heads, apparently from mūrtis, are deposited behind the temple in Mailar where the pavāḍā is performed. They are said to be the heads of vīras who died in self-sacrifice. The term Kañcavīra (so far the etymology is unclear) is locally said to be a corrupt form of pañcavīras, that is, "five heroes" who voluntarily cut off their heads in front of the god. Curiously this story resembles the tradition of Mhaskobā in Maharashtra where the god demanded as a proof of faith the five immature children of the founder of the cult. The god obligingly turned the victims into lambs and the children were left unscathed. Dhangar shepherds of Maharashtra still offer a "row" (Ma. *dāvaṇ* $<$ Skt. *dāmanī*) of five sheep to Khaṇḍobā. There are persistent and pervasive suggestions that in the past young rams and humans could be alternate sacrificial victims.[29] The Kurubas

35. The oldest Kuruba who climbs an eighteen foot-high bow (on the right) during the Dasarā festival and in the process becomes "Mailāra." Devaragudda, Dharwad District, Karnataka. Photo by Günther Sontheimer.

are said to have gained their importance in Mailar because Mailāra slew the demon in the form of a Kuruba. A reflection of this may still be the substitute sacrifice of a lamb by Kurubas on the day of the battle. It is taken to the hill where the demon manifests itself in the form of a wooden mask, actually somewhere to the side of the hill.[30] Again we have the suggestion that the enemy of the god, the demon, becomes the follower (alive, or dead in the form of a bhūta), or we may say, the demon becomes a devotee. While considering the sacrificial connotations in the ritual connected with Mailāra we may start wondering whether the "sacrifice" of the Kuruba youth which takes place at the end of the battle, does not faintly echo an incident in the aśvamedha sacrifice. Both festivals, at Mailar and Devaragudda, have close connection with horse rituals and they resound with the cracks of the whips of Gorappas. They enact the galloping of horses and are possessed by the wind of the god. The Gorappas, who are also called Kudureyappas, are said to be the cavalry of the god, and the festivals are also called (Ka.) *kudureya habba* (the festival of the horse). It does not, therefore, seem too farfetched to refer to the Vedic *Vādhūlasūtra*, which says that at the end of the aśvamedha the immature, weeping son of a sūta (bard) is to slaughter the horse, whose head falls off in the process. The youth is to lose his own head if he does not know how to properly cut up the horse, as the latter has to be restored thereafter. Falk suggests that the youth has been selected by a game of dice in which the loser is called "dog." In younger texts the youth, as the dog, is no longer the scapegoat, but an actual dog is killed.[31] No actual aśvamedha, of course, or anything resembling it is practised in Mailar or Devaragudda, but we should keep in mind the importance of the horse in the Dasarā ritual which may have had its antecedent in the classical aśvamedha sacrifice. Horses in the Dasarā ritual were especially conspicuous at the spatially and historically close capital of the Vijayanagara empire.[32] Moreover, the young Kañcavīra who is the "dog" of Mailāra and who sacrifices himself to his god, the "Lord of the Horses" (Skt. *hayapati*, or *aśvapati*), tying himself to the god by passing a rope through his leg, strengthens the impression that the ritual has contacts with the Vedic Rudra. In the *Vādhūlasūtra* the young sūta is taught a song with which earth, ether, and wind are requested to heal the injuries of the horse, and heaven and the *nakṣatras* are involved to restore the form of the horse.[33] In the cult of MMKh it is a pinch of turmeric powder, the very substance of the sun, which heals the wounds of the victims with immediate effect.

The Expelled Son of the Kāpus/Reḍḍis

The Kāpus or Reḍḍis are the most important agriculturist caste of Andhra, equivalent to the Marathas of Maharashtra and the Gavḍās of Karnataka. In the traditions of Komarelli and Ailōni, Mallanna is said to have been born miraculously as the seventh and youngest son of Ādireḍḍi and Nīlamma, king and queen of Kollapuri Paṭṇam.[34] According to the myths told in these traditions, when these two treat Parameśvara with miserliness and forgetfulness, the god appears in the form of a Jaṅgama and turns the tide of their fortune. Their kingdom becomes ridden with drought and famine, and the cattle perish. Kollapuri Paṭṇam becomes a ghost city. Ādireḍḍi and Nīlamma leave Kollapuri with their six sons. They live in the wilderness, or rather in the outskirts of Kalyāṇapuri Paṭṇam. They are not allowed by the "liṅga-wearers," i.e., the Liṅgāyats, to enter the city. They live by selling firewood, work as laborers, and collect food in the forest for twelve years. During this period they pray to Śiva to rescue them from their plight. It is then that Śiva the bhaktavatsala turns up in the disguise of a Jaṅgama promising them a son who would be of great strength, illustrious, and bear the name Mallanna. Mallanna is born (Tel. *māyāmānuṣa vigrahadu*) and eventually restores his family to power and rules Kollapuri Paṭṇam. But the brothers or rather the six sisters-in-law turn against him and when the property is divided (land, cattle, and houses) Mallanna receives as his share uncultivable land, that is, hilly and forested areas, and bullocks not capable of drawing the plough. Mallanna clears the forest for cultivation by felling trees, digging up termite mounds (Tel. *puṭṭa*) and burning the undergrowth. While digging the termite mound he hits upon a golden nose ring. Once upon a time Pārvatī was presented a young sheep by Śiva which multiplied to the amount of one crore. Pārvatī kept her nose ring as a lock on the sheep. Satisfied with the bhakti of Mallanna, Pārvatī directs him to tend them for seven years and to take care to kindle the fire near the termite mound perpetually. In accordance with the command of Pārvatī, Mallanna makes a perpetual fire in a bowl-shaped brazier (Tel. *kumpaṭi*). He milks the sheep every day, boils the milk in the kumpaṭi, and worships the termite mound by pouring the boiled milk into it.

In the different versions of the story told by the Gollas, who are the traditional pastoralists of Andhra, certain motifs remain constant: the youngest brother who has to be satisfied with the wilderness as his share and is driven out, like Rudra, the youngest son of Brahmā, or the *kaniṣṭha* of the Vrātyas who becomes nirvasita and has to seek his fortune to establish himself. In the case of the Vrātya, cows had to be gained on an expedition as the basis for establishing his own household.[35] Throughout the oral traditions of Mallanna we hear about the adventurous efforts of Mallanna to win recognition and supremacy over his adversaries, like the kaniṣṭha Vrātya "who wants to come to the top."[36]

Another recurring feature of the oral tradition is the association of fire with the termite mound from which Mailāra/Mārtaṇḍa Bhairava (the "sun") also emerged in Mailar. When the fire—indispensible to boil the sheep milk, which is ambrosia (Tel. *amrutamu*)—near the mound is extinguished, Mallanna has to steal Agni from a Rākṣasa who holds captive the Brahman girl Ratnāṅgi. Slaying the demon he gains both, the fire and the girl. There is no mention in this version to this effect, but we may surmise that the Rākṣasa is a Brahmarākṣasa.[37] His skull (Tel. *netti, pucca, kapālamu*) serves as the bowl for gruel (Tel. *ambali toṭṭi*). The fire seems to be closely connected with the termite mound and the origin of Mārtaṇḍa Bhairava. In another legend Mallanna finds sheep and Bhairava in the form of a dog in the mound.[38] Oral traditions call him Bayanna, who is his brother and is found in the mound. He is a naked (cf. Nagna-Bhairava), rather stern character, particularly bent on protecting the purity of the sheep flock.[39] He is one-legged and may be compared with Ekapad Bhairava or *aja eka-pāda* who besides being one of the Māruts in the *Ṛgveda* and *AV*, is also identifiable with Rudra and Indra.

The Marriages of Mailāra, Mallanna, and Khaṇḍobā

Mallanna, although miraculously born as the son of Ādireḍḍi and Nīlamma, exists or moves outside of or between castes, and that is the seed and precondition of his eventual power and rise to a king of all. Much to the displeasure of his brothers and sisters-in-law he did not marry a girl from their caste. He marries Ratnāṅgi, a Brahman girl; he also married Pagiḍikāḷḷi Padmākṣi after miraculously performing several tests. Ultimately he has five wives, like Khaṇḍobā. But it is mostly two wives who are prominent in the cult of MMKh. One is closely connected with the Liṅgāyats. She is said to be a Vāṇī (Ma. grain merchant) and is variously called (in Tel.) Bhramarāṃba Mēdala, Māḍala, Mādaci, or (in Ka.) Māḷaci, Māḷavva, Gaṅgi Mālavva, or (in Ma.) Mhāḷsā. Thus Mallanna also takes the form of a merchant, and is often mentioned in connection with itinerant merchants, like the Perikes or the Gōne Kāpus (Tel. *gōne:* jute bag).[40] In Malegaon, the Khaṇḍobā center in the Nanded district, Khaṇḍobā is said to have manifested himself in a jute bag of a merchant caravan.[41] The god coming along with merchants in the form of a stone lodged in the hoof of pack oxen is a frequent motif in the oral traditions of the Dhangar shepherds. In this way Khaṇḍobā comes to marry Mhāḷsā, the daughter of Timma Śeṭ, a Liṅgāyat Vāṇī, at Pali in the Satara district. According to the Golla traditions a Kommarelli Mallanna comes riding on a horse to the Balijas in Sindhu Paṭṇam in the form of an itinerant bangle seller named Gājula Mali Seṭṭi. The Balijas have amassed their riches by cheating the traders and others who pass through their town. By his powers Mallanna outtricks the traders, acquires all their wealth and marries Balije Māḍalamma showing her his greatness (*mahimā*). She fails to recognize it in him when he turns into a leper. Thus again he moves out in search of a true, devoted wife and finds her in Golla Kētamma. She is the daughter of rich Gollas who own a big herd of sheep. They are courteous, truthful, and generous.[42] The god marrying a tribal woman is common all over the Deccan and goes back to the Caṅkam literature where it is the tribal Vaḷḷi who is the beloved of Murukan.[43] The "marriage" with the tribal woman often has elements of transgression and is an occasion to display the miraculous feats of the god. In the case of Bāṇāī, he herds nine lakhs of sheep all alone and even slaughters all of them, only to restore them to life with a pinch of turmeric powder.[44] Invariably the oral traditions about two wives, one coming from the merchant community (identified with Pārvatī on the Sanskritic level), and the other coming from the "forest" (often identified with the classical Gaṅgā), oscillate between the two poles of a love relationship (as between the early Murukan and Vaḷḷi) and bhakti and/or renunciation. In the old songs of the Vāghyās Khaṇḍobā is often blamed by Mhāḷsā for his infatuation towards the dirty Bāṇāī. The songs of the Vāghyās regarding Khaṇḍobā's wives are often ambiguous: they may be understood as erotic, but the listener may also interpret them in terms of bhakti. Khaṇḍobā, who may turn up as a Pathān on horseback, actually has five wives in Jejuri: Mhāḷsā, the Liṅgāyat; Bāṇāī, the Dhangar shepherdess; Phulāī Māḷin, from the gardener caste; Raṃbhāī Śimpin, the tailor woman; and Candāī Bhāgvāni, the Muslim woman. By his marriages he transgresses the normal social order, yet this transgression fuses together heterogenous groups with different social and ecological backgrounds. Notions of ritual purity and impurity tend to be obliterated in his cult. No wonder the cantankerous "first" wife, Mhāḷsā, coming from the vegetarian Liṅgāyat caste complains about Bāṇāī who has polluted the house, is uncouth and stinks, and should actually stay in the wilderness (Ma. *rān*) where she comes from.[45] Yet Mhāḷsā catches fish and Bānū (Bāṇāī) watches the fun (Ma. *tamāśā*). "Where is the Liṅgāyat in this?" Not only that, but

> Bānū and Mhāḷsā are of different castes
> For the god Mallārī they eat from the same plate
> The Bāṇāī of the Dhangars, the Mhāḷsā of the Vāṇīs
> How can she swallow (even) a morsel?[46]

In Devaragudda the episodes of the hunt and the love adventure of the god with Kurubattyavva, the shepherd girl, are enacted by the devotees after Dasarā. The god is taken to the river on horseback and is accompanied by one group equipped with whatever weapons there are in the temple. There are by agreement two parties. One is Mailāra's and the other is his father-in-law's. During the mock hunt—some people pretending to be tigers and others chasing them—Mailāra is understood to love the Kuruba girl. The news leaks out and reaches his first wife Gaṅgi Mālavva. Thus by the time the first party returns from the mock hunt they are not allowed to enter the temple by the Gorappas and Gorammas who are already in the temple. They enact the anger of Mailāra's first wife by evicting Mailāra as well as the hunters. After Mailāra's party confesses the mistake they are allowed inside.

The Encounter with Other Religions

The recognition of MMKh as Mallikārjuna, Sadāśiva, Tribhuvana and so on, although claimed by his followers, was not undisputed by certain other groups. Some Jains seem to have accepted Khaṇḍobā as their *tīrthaṅkara* Mallinātha, perhaps confusing him with Mallanātha = the "Lord of Malla" (*M.Māh.* 19.3), according to earliest inscriptional reference in Jejuri.[47] They also called the Mallikārjuna of Srisailam Mallinātha.[48] Maṇi, the demon, is mentioned in the context of earlier Jain *basadis* superseded by MMKh cults. The temple at Mailar is thus said to have been a Jain establishment. Actually it may have been Maṇibhadra, the tutelary deity of caravans, popular among Jains, who was worshiped amongst Jains, e.g., in Prempur near Bidar in Karnataka. The present-day temple is situated on a traditional trade route leading from the Godavari Valley, via Malegaon to Bidar. A Jain mūrti of a person in dhyāna posture shows the Jain affiliation. The mūrti is now relegated to a small shrine at the border of the kṣetra. The Brahmanical *Mallāri Māhātmya* which is connected with Prempur expressly refers to the place as "the capital of the enemy of Maṇi" (18.9: Maṇidviṣa) and not to Malla, or "Maṇi *and* Malla." In front of the temple a huge stone nāga (serpent) faces Khaṇḍobā in the temple and takes the position of the defeated demon who has turned into a bhakta. If it is true that Maṇibhadra and Maṇināga are identical this would further suggest a connection with the Jains. Maṇi, who is a great hero (vīra) in the *Mallāri Māhātmya*, may be one of the fifty-two vīras (*bāvan vīr*) mentioned in Jain sources.[49] The Jain author Brahmaśiva (c. 1150-60) of Karnataka classed Mailāra amongst the kṣudradevatās and claimed that he was a Jain warrior who died with obstinate valour in battle.

Reputed Vīraśaiva saints like Śaṅkaradāsimayya tried to prove that Mailāra was nobody else than a *demon* and that it was Śiva and not Mailāra who slew Malla.[50] Yet Liṅgāyats, especially the common folk, accepted MMKh and are often temple priests (as in Devaragudda). Or else they established temples, such as one in Odela (Karimnagar District) which was founded by a Balajiga.

Cakradhara, the "founder" of the Mahānubhāva sect predicted in the thirteenth century that the Viṣṇu and Śiva temples would decay and kṣetrapālas like *Mairāḷa* would become established in the Kaliyuga.[51] This prediction can actually be said to have been confirmed by historical facts if we think of the fall of the Yādava empire and the eventual decay of its ("Hemadpanti") temples. In the fourteenth century the *Krīḍābhirāmamu* praises the village deity Mailāra as the "great hunter," "ocean of kindness," "who makes an impossible task possible (such as catching an invisible deer)" and commends him "to the praise of noble people."[52] It may have been about the same time when the *Mallāri Māhātmya* established an "etymological" identification of Mailāra/Mallāri and Mairāḷa with Śambhu and Viṣṇu.[53]

Some Maharashtrian bhakti saints also tended to classify Khaṇḍobā as a kṣetrapāla or kṣudradevatā or simply a bhūta. Saint Rāmdās ranked him in one place of his work amongst the village deities or ghosts and in other places identified him with Rāma. He also called him Mallu Khān.[54]

According to the Golla Kathā of Hyderabad the confrontation between Mallanna and the Balijas (i.e., Liṅgāyats), the brothers of Māḍalamma, ends by Mallanna turning them into dogs and causing them to be reborn as Voggus. They behave like dogs (in rituals), get possessed by Mallanna and make predictions.[55] Mallanna or Khaṇḍobā is also called Rautrāy at Devara Hippargi near Bijapur. The temple clearly has Muslim antecedents. Rautrāy fights a Liṅgāyat Rākṣasa, called Dariyappa who lives in a maṭha. Instead of the usual Nandī in front of the temple at Devara Hippargi we find here the horse as *vāhana*.

MMKh's relationship, as we have indicated, also extends to the Muslims. Thus a Golla kathā tells us how Mallanna acquired turmeric powder (Tel. *pasupu baṇḍāru*) which he needed for his marriage with Bhramarāṃbā.[56] He has to fetch it from Mecca (*sic*) where he goes in the guise (avatāra) of a fakir. The inhabitants of Mecca are Śiva bhaktas. They wear a waist band (Tel. *mola dāram*), never drink liquor or eat meat (Tel. *māḍhu māṃsamu*). But he spoils their customs and traditions (Tel. *ācāra vyavahārālu*). Mallanna spends 12 years in Mecca as a servant. He makes the well go dry. The inhabitants of Mecca ask him if he knows any means of restoring the water to the well. He tells them that if they slaughter a black cow (Tel. *kaṛri āvu*) and eat it, the water in the well will be restored. He makes them cook *kanduru* (Tel. for a Biryani-like dish) with the meat of the black cow and causes them to smoke *gañja*. He then asks them to look into the well and they see water. They develop a great faith in Mallanna. When after twelve years the well is again filled with water, baṇḍāru (which may also mean *gold* and is the substitute for gold in the rituals of the MMKh cult) erupts near the well. The inhabitants of Mecca get engrossed by the sight of water and gold and, infatuated, they fall into a deep slumber (apparently caused by Mallanna). When they wake up Mallanna has disappeared with the baṇḍāru. They launch a hunt for Mallanna whom they call Malkhān. They almost catch up with him. At that moment Mallanna jumps into the Gaṅgā (a general name of a river) from which an outstretched arm emerges. The Turakas (Turks) wonder whose hand it could be and chop it off. Gaṅgā thus saves Mallanna with the hand. In return for this help Mallanna promises Gaṅgā that she would be known as Bipatma (Bibi + Padma) and worshiped every year. She would be taken in a procession on an elephant on the day of the *urus* of Pīrla Panduga.

Although the particular place of the celebration of Gaṅgā could not be ascertained and this tradition seems to be confusing, the general background becomes clear if we think of the historical symbiosis in the Deccan between Liṅgāyats and Muslims on the level of folk religion and in the realm of mysticism. Sufis and Liṅgāyats could identify to some extent on the level of mysticism. Rituals in which a jaṅgama turns up in a procession dressed as a Pīr are known from Bidar.[57] Mallanna and Khaṇḍobā were worshiped by Liṅgāyats *and* Muslims. In a Marathi inscription dated Śaka 1625 and Faslī 1113 (1703) the Śiva of the Liṅgāyats is identified with Mallukhān: *Śrī guruli(ṅ)ga ja(ṅ)gama vibhūta-rudrakṣa-bhuśena sadās(ś)ī(i)va s(ś)aṅkara s(ś)ambhu Mahādeva Mā(a)hārudra: Maluṣ(kh)ān.*[58] It is, however, Khaṇḍobā who is very often called Mallu Khān or Ajmat Khān and his affiliation with the Muslims is visible in the style of his temples (as in Jejuri or in Andur, Osmanabad District). He appears as a Paṭhān on horseback, one of his wives is Muslim, and the keeper of the god's horses and his kotvāl is a Muslim in Jejuri. In the *Mārtaṇḍa Vijaya* (24.30-31) Muslims are expressly said to be his bhaktas. A typical instance of this mutual appreciation is a special order issued by the Sultan of Bijapur, Ibrahim II in 1614, in which he assured the right of pilgrims to perform rituals to Khaṇḍerāo or Mallāri at Naldurg and the reinstatement of the annual jātrā.[59] It is only when attacked that Khaṇḍobā reacts violently. Thus the *Mārtaṇḍa Vijaya* (36.43) also mentions that Mārtaṇḍa Bhairava annihilated the Mlecchas, i.e., Muslims. At Prempur, near the capital of the Bidar Sultanate, the daityas Maṇi and Malla are said to have been Muslim kings. And in the *Jayādri Māhātmya* which pertains to Jejuri, the daityas are said to have been born in the "Yavanakula."[60] According to the local legend and songs of the Vāghyās, 900,000 hornets were sent by Khaṇḍobā through a hole in the wall of the fortress at Jejuri to drive away the army of Aurangzeb. The same story involving hornets is told by Gollas about Srisailam:[61] In this account, Chatrapati Śivājī, while fighting Aurangzeb, enters the forest of Srisailam. Feeling very thirsty he approaches Pārvatī and requests her to give him a bowl of milk (Tel. *pāla cambu*). Before Śivājī can empty the bowl Pārvatī manifests herself in innumerable lives (Tel. *janmālu*), or rather bhramaras (Tel. *tummeda:* hornets), attacks Aurangzeb, and uproots his army. When Śivājī sees the slain enemies, he addresses her: "From now on your name is not Pārvatī, you are Bhramarāṃbā." To this day one can hear the sound of hornets (Tel. *tummedala jhuṃkāramu*) in the wall behind Bhramarāṃbā.

On the whole we may draw the conclusion that, like the ancient Rudra, MMKh seemed to be acceptable to the common folk irrespective of caste and creed. The *Mārtaṇḍa Vijaya* (5.12; 24.30u.33) summarizes this in its own way: "Hungry" for devotees Mārtaṇḍa Bhairava does not know of jāti, varṇa, or kula (eminent family). Caṇḍālas and Mlecchas are welcome as bhaktas.

The Position of the Brahmans and the Mallāri Māhātmya

Seen from the viewpoint of folk religion, the position of the Brahmans in the cult of MMKh was not and is still not dominant. Nor was it *a priori* established according to orthodox-śāstric principles. Yet many Brahmans claimed them as their kulasvāmī. The Brahmans' principles and ideals tended to be incorporated and subordinated to folk religion. Sanganna, the son of Brahmans of the Viśvāmitra Gotra, is born at the same time as Mallanna according to the traditions of the

Gollas. He becomes Mallanna's companion, is equal to him, and is also called the disciple of Mallanna.[62] On the purāṇic level Viṣṇu is identified with the brother-in-law of Khaṇḍobā, who is on the folk level his minister (Heggaḍī Pradhān), the brother of Mhāḷsā and a Liṅgāyat (Śaivite) Vāṇī. Śrī Venkaṭeśvara of Tirupati in Andhra is also a brother-in-law of Mallanna. Mallanna, while testing the bhakti of his wife Balija Māḍalamma, keeps her in a fort on a mountain. He goes away and returns as a leper. She curses him, and wishes that he dies. Her duty is to fetch water to cure him, but Mallanna makes all the water disappear. Māḍalamma plans to go to Tirupati, to her brother Veṅkaṭeśvara (popularly known as Veṅkanna) to fetch water. Before she goes to him, Mallanna arrives at Tirupati and warns Veṅkaṭeśvara not to give her any water. Not to displease his sister, and rather scared of Mallanna, Veṅkaṭeśvara leaves Tirupati to avoid his sister. This episode shows Mallanna was still superior to Veṅkaṭeśvara.[63]

In Devaragudda the minister is actually represented as Viṣṇu with sword, mace, conch, and "book," but he is assigned a place outside the temple precincts. The *Mārtaṇḍa Vijaya* knows a story which shows the Brahmans were not only worshippers of Khaṇḍobā, but had to respect and accept certain basic incidents of the cults lest they would be confronted with evil consequences:

> A mischievous Brahman mocks at a Vāghyā and his chain (then) carried around the neck: "How can your Mallāri possibly break the worldly fetters (Ma. *bhavabandhana*)? If you bind it to your neck, and, calling his name, break it with one jerk, then I shall rest assured." To the dismay of the Brahman the Vāghyā breaks the chain with a single jerk calling upon Malhāri, "the liberator from worldly fetters" (Ma. *bhavamocaka*). The Brahman turns into a dog, bites people so that they take to their heels. His wife makes a vow to Mārtaṇḍa to perform a yātrā without footwear so that her husband may get freed of his affliction. His *ahaṃkār* vanishes and he becomes Malhāri's bhakta. (*MV* 34.54-70)

Versions of the myth of Mallāri probably precede the Sanskrit *Mallāri Māhātmya*. According to an inscription at the temple of Ailōni dated 1369 it is Arjuna with the help of Śiva who kills the demon Malla. Śiva is from then onwards called Mallikārjuna.[64] The *Mallāri Māhātmya*, considered to belong to the *Kṣetrakaṇḍa* of the *Brahmāṇḍapurāṇa*, purports to point out the authoritative, purāṇic grounds and to establish the Brahmanical credentials of the cult of Mailāra and Khaṇḍobā. The work is a masterpiece not only because of its beautiful, narrative style, but also for its skillful attempt at transforming a rather "rustic," "demonic," "impure," and "violent" cult. Śiva becomes an avatāra on the request of the seven Ṛṣis, or Brahmans (*dharmaputras*), as Indra and Viṣṇu are unable to defeat the demons. They became invincible on account of their tapas which had elicited a boon from Brahmā. As Mārtaṇḍa Bhairava, Śiva fights the demons Maṇi and Malla who raided the āśrama of the Ṛṣis, overthrew the yajña (and even urinated into the sacrificial fire), killed cows, and molested the women of the Brahmans. Thus everything that is sacred to the Brahmanical order is at stake, but the demons are defeated in a tremendous battle, a *raṇa-yajña*, or battle-sacrifice. After the defeat of the valorous demon kings, their *ahaṃkār* disappears and on their death they attain the god (*sannidhi* or *sayujyatā*, the term also used in the *M.Māh.* is *vilaya:* 17.42). We have attempted to show elsewhere that Maṇi and Malla, the demon kings, are an epitome of the rising king, the "robber king," and of communities not exactly belonging to the Brahmanical fold or paying respect to its orthodox-śāstric implications like yajña, varṇa etc.[65] The Brahmanical attitude to the "outlandish," impure manifestations, as exemplified by the Purāṇas and, in the particular case, in the *Mallāri Māhātmya*, was to incorporate or ignore some aspects of these cults and demonize others. Maṇi and Malla were said to belong to the Prahlāda kula.[66] That they made their followers worship their mūrtis is noted as especially aggravating and objectionable.[67] We may sense here perhaps an attitude which was opposed to the old notion that a king could be a god who stands at the top of his own spiritual, ritual, and social hierarchical model without overriding Brahmanical control. According to the *Mallāri Māhātmya*, the folk deity was split into the pure purāṇic Śiva and the demon who is impure until he is defeated and becomes the demon devotee, and a dvārapāla. He is now subordinated to a Śiva, who protects the yajña and dharma of the Brahmanical order. As Shulman has observed of the bandit king or pre-empire king: "His world is the ancient sacrificial universe which allows destruction its place before the splitting of Brahman and kingship in the interests of maintaining the Brahman's ideal uncontaminating sacrifice."[68] Historically, many Deśastha Brahmans were worshippers of Khaṇḍobā and seemed to be warriors rather than "ideal Brahmans." For instance, a Maratha general of the artillery, Panse, whose fort was called Malhārgaḍ, donated the huge sword to Khaṇḍobā in the eighteenth century.[69] The sword was given a mythical ancestry which was traced back to Aśvatthāman and his avenging sword.[70]

The splitting of the folk deity into the demon and Śiva seems to be also reflected in our view in the battle ritual at Mailar. At the end of the battle, the head of the demon, which is not to be seen before this moment, appears at the feet of the god, as if the god has shed his own asuric form.

The status of the folk deity is also slowly eroded by the texts. The *Mallāri Māhātmya* (18.14) still mentions amongst the offerings of the gods to Mallāri/Mairāḷa incense, lights, betel, and animals (*paśu*). The Marathi version by Siddhapāl Kesarī is also explicit and stresses that plates filled with meat, etc., are offerings to the god Mairāḷa (18.19). In the *Mallāri Māhātmya* the dying demon requests Malla that Śiva should fulfill the wishes of those bhaktas who worship him by *chedapātādi*, by "causing themselves to be cut, etc." This may refer to the hook-swinging rite nowadays only continuing in a mild form, or the self-mortification of the vīras (17.37). The Marathi translation of the *Mallāri Māhātmya* by Siddhapāl Kesarī, however, renders these customs disparagingly as *ugra* (violent, demonic) bhakti. The *Mārtaṇḍa Vijaya* (by Gangādhara, of 1821) goes even a step further and styles animal sacrifices and self-tortures as (demonic) *rākṣasī* bhakti (35.53).

In accordance with this evaluation of the modes of bhakti, worship was further restructured in the texts. For instance, possession (so essential in folk religion) by the god in the form of the wind has the still lower demonic appellation of piśācī bhakti. but *sāttvikī* bhakti, "true bhakti," is the feeding of a Brahman in the form of Mārtaṇḍa (*MV* 35.47, 55; 35.48, 61).

It was on a Sunday, on the sixth of the month of Mārgaśīrṣa (Campāṣaṣṭhī) that Mārtaṇḍa and his wife (śakti) Mārtaṇḍa Bhairavī manifested themselves at Prempur as svayaṃbhū liṅgas made of clay under a wishing tree, together with Maṇi who rides a horse (*M.Māh.* 18.3f.). He manifested himself on the request and for the protection (*rakṣārtham*) of the dharmaputras (*M.Māh.* 18.5f.). In the "city of Prempur" the god was made accessible to all varṇas and jātis through dhyāna (meditation) (*M.Māh.* 18.9); and he fulfills wishes: cattle, sons, horses, and a kingdom without enemies, full of horses and elephants, and women for kings (18.28f.) and, for Brahmans, recognition by the king, and victory in disputes against those who speak wrongly or pervertedly (18.30).

We must voice some caution as to the results and influence of the *Mallāri Māhātmya*. Its full contents are vaguely known by circles beyond the Brahmans. Most of the devotees apprehend that Śiva has become an avatār to kill the demons, "for the sake of the bhaktas," *not* specifically for Brahmans and their values. Numerous depictions show Khaṇḍobā with his wife Mhāḷsā killing the demons, but nowhere is it shown who the particular bhaktas were whom he rescued. The songs of the Vāghyās rarely refer to the story of the seven Ṛṣis or dharmaputras, which admittedly, may not have been the function of the songs.

D. Conclusions

Mallanna could shelter under the umbrella of the ancient cult of Mallikārjuna of Srisailam and thus obtain his legitimization as Śiva. Mallikārjuna, however, had and still has a cult which involves worship by people from various quarters, including tribals who have free access to the temple. It is not a monopoly of purāṇic mythology or of Brahmanical worship. Mailāra and Khaṇḍobā gained their Brahmanical credentials through the *Mallāri Māhātmya* (and other texts like the *Jayādri Māhātmya* and *Mārtaṇḍa Vijaya*) in which Śiva becomes an avatāra to defend the orthodox-śāstric Brahmanical order. It is, however, doubtful how far the *Māhātmya* has become an authoritative scripture for groups of devotees beyond the immediate addressees. Māhātmyas are not compulsory law which sanction the traditions of a particular cult once and for all and for all devotees. The acceptance of the tradition "codified" by Māhātmyas depends on the degree other groups of devotees are aware of its contents and are persuaded by it. This awareness may spread nowadays more easily and quickly with the increasing literacy and proliferation of printed temple pamphlets (which, however, mostly do *not* or only marginally refer to the Brahmanical features of the *Māhātmya*). Even if devotees know of the existence of the *Māhātmya*, and may or may not know of its contents, acceptance may just amount to lip-service. The focus is still on the folk-religious character of the cult which derives its innate values from its direct accessibility to a god who lives "here and now" and not in some distant purāṇic heaven. His worship is based on forms of bhakti and tapas which do not necessarily correspond to the codifications of the ninefold bhakti in "classical" bhakti texts. Bhakti and tapas can take violent forms and reflect the attitudes of the hero and ascetic. MMKh are folk cults, but they are more than local village deities (grāmadevatās) or caste gods who are normally said to be typical examples of folk religion and only to cater to practical, material wishes of the devotee. The closeness and company of the god, or god as king, in this life or afterlife is one of the ardent wishes of the devotee. In the Khaṇḍobā cult it is voiced by the desire expressed in the songs of the Vāghyās: let us go to Jejuri.[71] The wishes of the devotee are often expressed in simple words, not in classical terminology: I do not want anything. Just remember me and let me be near you. There is no reason to give me anything.

An unwritten principle of the cult is that the god tests the sattva, genuineness of his devotee. The bhakta has to recognize the god in his disguise which is only possible by shedding one's ahaṃkār. Thus the demon bragging about his riches and mocking at the obscure ascetic on his nandī is nearly doomed. It is his bravery that saves him in his death. Bāṇāī suffers the loss of her sheep until she recognizes the god in the old leper.

The position of god also resembles that of the nascent or robber king, or even the king at the imperial center, like Kṛṣṇadevarāyā of Vijayanagara. The robber king has no (or not yet an) axe to grind as regards varṇa and impurities. His followers are recruited from all groups without reference to caste and creed. The king at the center may have to pay attention to varṇa and śāstric dharma, but how far is a matter to be examined in each case. Notwithstanding the dharmic-śāstric order he will have to take an "ecumenical" or "secular" attitude towards other castes and religions, e.g., the Muslims. MMKh tend to have the same neutral attitude towards the hierarchy of caste and religion.

The openness to all communities and the earthboundness which is an essential ingredient of folk cults, but results in impurity, exposed the cult to moral censure from various quarters and other religious currents. That Khaṇḍobā as an avatāra of Śiva remains on earth is an anathema to the Purāṇas. Mostly Śiva is represented on earth by Bhairava, Vīrabhadra or some other partial manifestation who fulfils mundane, impure functions. Most of the devotees would emphasize that Khaṇḍobā is a full avatāra of Śiva/Śaṃkara and not the usual Bhairava. Śiva as Khaṇḍobā on earth also takes over many attributes and characteristics of the defeated demon, like royal insignia, weapons, and animals, e.g., the horse.

A cult of a god on earth which admits access to all communities and allows violent rituals to be performed besides animal sacrifices in his name (now offered to Bāṇāī or the demon), Muraḷīs (devadāsis) and so on, always evoked a mixed reaction in old Marathi literature. The quick metamorphosis from an ascetic beggar who rides an old bull and carries an ant-eaten club (khaṭvāṅga) to an illustrious king with rich clothes, and a horse with a saddle studded with jewels is "a touchy point not to be disclosed." This is the view of the poet Nirañjanamādhava (d. 1790) in a humorous praise song (stotra) dedicated to Khaṇḍobā.[72] Because Khaṇḍobā is reputed to be rather fierce and impetuous in his reaction to those who fail to observe their family duties towards him, and to cause the trouble and affliction characteristic of ghosts, he must be a ghost (bhūt). This is the argument of a Christian missionary apparently supported by a Kokaṇastha Brahman in a discussion with a Deśastha Brahman. The discussion took place around 1855.[73]

At the end of the nineteenth century a Maharashtrian Brahman on a pilgrimage through India reached Jejuri and remarked with some disdain:

> There the Pūjārīs are Guravs and many of the Śūdra caste, etc., come for darśan. Therefore Ragunātha could see that ritual purity and impurity were very little respected. After he had performed the yātrā according to family dharma he went to Moreśvar (Morgaon) to have darśan of Gaṇpati.[74]

Marathi proverbs and expressions emanating from sources outside the cult reflect that the cult could not be ignored, and yet tend to discredit it. The dramatic performance of rituals, the participation in the play (*kheḷ*) of the god, is an important ingredient of folk religion, and very much so in the cult of MMKh. The Marathi term *kheḷkhaṇḍobā* actually refers to the wind of the god possessing the devotee and tossing him around, but it is taken to mean "utter demolition," "devastation," or "destruction." Essentially, the MMKh cult remained then a cult that preserved the identity of Rudra between the classical-purāṇic Śiva who is worshiped in a Brahmanical temple in the form of a liṅga, and, on the other hand, the Śaivite sects such as Kāpālikas and Kālāmukhas, who became extinct, and their successors the Nāthas and Liṅgāyats, though admittedly, it incorporated and shared features of these two other important currents of Hinduism. In fact, we may say that the cult is a mirror of all currents of Hinduism, but it is *folk religion* that is emphasized.[75]

NOTES

1. This paper includes material which was collected during a stay in Maharashtra from August 1984 to April 1985. I am grateful to the German Research Association for financial support. M. L. K. Murty, Deccan College, Pune, has helped me in my field research in Andhra Pradesh and in transcribing and translating oral texts. I received the same help from Dr. Rajaram R. Hegde, Deccan College, Pune, in Karnataka. To both I am most grateful. Data tape-recorded and observed in the field are not specifically documented here. The

reader is referred to a previous article of mine (see n. 47) where further references will be found.

2. S. G. Tulpule, *Marāṭhī Vaṅgmayācā Itihās, khaṃḍa pahilā* (Puṇe, 1984), 41 ff.

3. N. Ramesan, *Temples and Legends of Andhra Pradesh* (Bombay, 1962), 12.

4. Tārā Parāñjpe, "sīmā pradeśātīl bhāvagaṃgā: stāngīte," *Paṃcadhārā* 14 (1981), 22.

5. Richard Burghart, "Hierarchical models of the Hindu social system," *Man* (N.S.) 13 (1978), 519-536.

6. *Pañcaviṃśa Brāhmaṇa* 24.18,2; *BŚS* 28.24; Harry Falk, *Bruderschaft und Würfelspiel* (Freiburg, 1986), 18.

7. *Golla Kathā I* (Hyderabad). Told by Voggu Mallesh, Ray Mallesh et al.

8. According to a story told by a Dhangar shepherd, N. K. Mane; the story is at least 137 years old, as it is referred to in the *Jñānoday*, a missionary journal. See G. N. Morje (ed.), *Jñānoday-Lekhan-Sār-Sūcī* (Bombay, 1986), 459: What was told by the Dhangar with humour and visible relish proves the depravity of the cult from the point of view of the *Jñānoday*.

9. A. K. Ramanujan, *Hymns for the Drowning* (Princeton, 1981), 115.

10. P. V. Kane, *History of Dharmaśāstra*, vol. II, pt. II (Poona, 1941), 1236.

11. Śrī Sadguru Bhāūmahārāja yāṃcyā saṃgrahāṃtīl, *Śrī Khaṃḍobācīṃ padeṃ* (publ. by V. D. Gokhale, Puṇe, 1951), *pada* 22 (*Somvatīpada*), *pada 19*.

12. Syed Siraj ul Hassan, *The Castes and Tribes of H.E.H. The Nizam's Dominions* (Bombay, 1921), 231.

13. Rā. Rā. Bāpurāv Khaṃḍerāv Khāḍe, *Śrīkṣetra Jejurī-māhātmya* (*Puṇe, 1924*), 51. This story is a *verbatim* translation of a passage in the (unpublished) Skt. *Jayādri-Māhātmya*.

14. *Maharashtra State Gazetteers, Satara District* (Rev. Edit., Bombay, 1963), 140, fn. 1.

15. Mukund Wamanrao Burway, *Life of Subhedar Malhar Rao Holkar* (Indore, 1930), 183.

16. *Golla Kathā I* (Hyderabad).

17. J. W. Hauer, *Der Vrātya* (Stuttgart, 1927), 149.

18. G. D. Sontheimer, "Dasarā at Devaraguḍḍa. Ritual and Play in the Cult of Mailāra/Khaṇḍobā," *South Asian Digest of Regional Writing*, 10 (1984), 1-20.

19. *Khaṃḍobācīṃ padeṃ, pada* 24.

20. I owe this reference to Klaus W. Müller who is working on the *antyeṣṭi-paddhati* of Nārāyaṇabhaṭṭa for his Ph.D.

21. Günther D. Sontheimer, "Folk Deities in the Vijayanagara Empire: Narasiṃha and Mallanna/Mailār," in A. L. Dallapiccola (ed.), *Vijayanagara—City and Empire* (Wiesbaden, 1985), 144 ff., 158. See Upendra Thakur, *The History of Suicide in India* (Delhi, 1963), 61 f. for the devotion between master and servant in the case of Kuvara Lakṣmaṇa, a general of the Hoysala King Vīra Ballāḷa II

(1173-1220), who committed suicide along with his wife and some of his soldiers. The relationship between lord and master, as in the case of MMKh and devotee, is indicated in the inscription: "Between servant and king there was no difference: the glory and the marks of royalty were equal in both." Kuvara Lakṣmaṇa and his wife became united with Garuḍa and Lakṣmī, respectively, suggesting that the Hoysala king was Viṣṇu. This fits well with the notion that for the "hero the king is god."

22. *Śrī Khaṃḍobācīṃ padeṃ*, 2.

23. Joachim Deppert, *Rudras Geburt. Systematische Untersuchungen zum Inzest in der Mythologie der Brāhmaṇas* (Wiesbaden, 1977), 96 f.

24. K. Venkata Ramanayya, *Vēlūgoṭivarivaṃśāvaḷi* (University of Madras, Madras, 1939), 2.

25. J. W. Hauer, *Der Vrātya*, 129 f. I could not see the ritual myself, but was told about it by Shri Guru Jayachandra Wodeyar Swamy, who also provided other information about the cult of Mailāra.

26. Sontheimer, "Dasarā . . . ," 12 and n. 40.

27. Sontheimer, "Dasarā . . . ," *passim*.

28. Sontheimer, "Dasarā . . . ," 13 ff.

29. Young boys often are the first to discover Khaṇḍobā or Mhaskobā or similar gods. They are priests in some temples in the Anantapur District. For the representation of heads of rams and humans alternating under the pādukas of Khaṇḍobā, see S. Settar and G. D. Sontheimer (eds.), *Memorial Stones* (Dharwad, N. Delhi, 1982), 272 f. (figures 21-23).

30. I am not sure whether the lamb is actually killed nowadays.

31. Falk, *Bruderschaft*, 160 ff., 162.

32. Sontheimer, "Folk Deities . . . ", 150 f.

33. Falk, *Bruderschaft*, 161.

34. Dharmapuri Venkatayya Pantulu, *Ailōni Mallanna Kathā*. (A Compilation from the Golla Kathā) (Warangal, 1964) 1 ff. (cited as Golla Kathā II); G. R. Varma, *Mailāra Dēva* (Varman Publications, Tadepalligude, 1973), 38.

35. *Golla Kathā I* and *II;* Falk, *Bruderschaft* . . . , 52; Deppert, *Rudra*, 94 ff., 108.

36. Falk, *Bruderschaft . . . , ibidem. Jaiminīya Brāhmaṇa* 2.227: agrakāma.

37. *Golla Kathā I.* According to this oral version it was just a rākṣasa, but the narrators are sometimes confused about the sex. It is also a rākṣasa according to the traditions at Komaravelli: Varma, *Mailāra Dēva*, 38. According to *Golla Kathā II*, however, it is a Brahmarākṣasī.

38. Varma, *Mailāra Dēva*, 30 ff.

39. *Golla Kathā I.*

40. Varma, *Mailāra Dēva*, 30 ff.

41. Sontheimer, *Birobā, Mhaskobā und Khaṇḍobā, Ursprung, Geschichte und Umwelt von pastoralen Gottheiten in Mahārāṣṭra* (Wiesbaden, 1976), 151; *Census of India 1961*,

vol. X, pt. VIII-B, *Fairs and Festivals of Maharashtra* (Bombay, 1969), 190 f.

42. *Golla Kathā II*, 19 ff.

43. The name of the village Kommarelli or Kommaravelli in Jangav Taluk, Warangal District, has been associated with Kumāra (Murukan, Skanda) and his wife Vaḷḷi. The three heads in front of the mūrti in the temple of Mallanna may be the three demons Cūr, Ciṅkamukan, and Tarakan whom Murukan killed (*Kāntapurāṇam, kāṇḍam* 2-4 by Kacciyappa Civācāriyar. See Kamil Veith Zvelebil, *Tamil Literature* [Wiesbaden 1974], 185 ff.).

44. Sontheimer, *Birobā*, 63 ff.

45. *Khaṇḍobācīṃ padeṃ, pad* 14.

46. Tārā Paranjpe, ". . . stāngīte . . .", 22.

47. G. D. Sontheimer, "Rudra and Khaṇḍobā: Continuity in Folk Religion," in Milton Israel and N. K. Wagle (eds.), *Religion and Society in Maharashtra*, University of Toronto, Center for South Asian Studies (Toronto, 1987), 1 ff., at 13 ff.

48. Sontheimer, "Rudra," ibid.

49. Vasudeva S. Agrawala, *Ancient Indian Folk Cults* (Varanasi, 1970), Appendix, Nr. 2 and 4.

50. Sontheimer, "Rudra," 14 f.

51. V. B. Kolte (ed.), *Līḷācaritra, Uttarārdha, līḷā* 436 (Muṃbaī, 1978).

52. Viṣṇukonda Vallabhārayadu, *Krīḍābhirāmamu*, v. 145 (Secundarabad: Andhra Pradesh Book Distribution, 1972).

53. *M.Māh.* 18.11-13: The syllable *ma* means Śambhu, the syllable *a* Viṣṇu; if these two [gods] are on earth, the word *mela* (ma + a + ila) comes into existence. He is an enemy (ārāti) to this mela. On account of this word analysis Mallāri's name has become Mailāra. The syllable *ra* and *la*, it is said, are homophones: from this Mairāla comes into existence.

In 18.10 we are told that the mūrtis of "Śambhu and Mārtaṇḍa Bhairavi are made of clay" (mahīmayī), but the traditions that Mailāra/Mallanna emerged from a termite mound are omitted.

54. Sontheimer, "Rudra," 19 ff.

55. *Golla Kathā I.*

56. *Golla Kathā I.*

57. H. K. Sherwani, *The Bahmanis of the Deccan* (Hyderabad, 1953), 195; Richard Maxwell Eaton, *Sufis of Bijapur 1300-1700* (Princeton University Press, Princeton, 1978), 250.

58. G. H. Khare, *Mahārāṣṭrācīṃ cār daivateṃ* (Pune, 1958), 150. *Epigraphia Indo-Moslemica 1921-22*, 20.

59. Eaton, *Sufis*, 99.

60. Khāḍe, *Jejurīmāhātmya*, 70.

61. Golla Kathā I.

62. *Golla Kathā II.*

63. According to traditions recorded from Gollas in Sultanabad (Karimnagar District).

64. D. C. Sircar (ed.), *Annual Report on Indian Epigraphy for 1957-58* (Delhi: Government of India Press, 1961), 8-9, 21. M. L. K. Murty and Günther D. Sontheimer, "Prehistoric Background to Pastoralism in the Southern Deccan in the Light of Oral Traditions and Cults of Some Pastoral Communities," *Anthropos* 75 (1980), 163-184, 168.

65. Sontheimer, "Rudra," 16 ff.

66. *M.Māh.* 14.14; *M.Māh.* (by Cintāmaṇi, in Ma., A.D. 1821) 1.23.

67. *M.Māh.* (by Cintāmaṇi) 1.97: they called themselves *īśvara*. Cp. *M.Māh.* 7.27 (by Vināyaka, in Ma., A.D. 1872!): they uprooted svayaṃbhū liṅgas, destroyed the mūrtīs of other gods, [and] caused their own mūrtīs to be worshiped.

68. David Dean Shulman, *The King and the Clown in South Indian Myth and Poetry* (Princeton, 1985), 344.

69. Keśav Raṅganāth Pānse, *Pānse gharāṇyācā itihās* (Puṇeṃ, 1929), 130.

70. Khāḍe, *Jejurīmāhātmya*, 72: Aśvatthāman promises to offer the heads of the five Pāṇḍavas to Duryodhana. After praising the gatekeeper at the camp of the Pāṇḍavas, that is Śiva/Tripurahara, he receives a sword from Śiva to kill the Pāṇḍavas. He enters the camp and beheads five youths who resemble the Pāṇḍavas (acc. to *MV* 35.23, Aśvatthāman mistakes them for the five Pāṇḍavas), offers the heads at the feet of Duryodhana and returns the sword to Śiva. This curious version again reminds us of the pañca vīras, and the davāṇ of the Dhangars, see *supra.*

71. *Khaṇḍobācīṃ padeṃ, pada* 21: *calā jāūṃ pāhūṃ jejurī . . . .* Whether a particular act of devotion, like bringing water from the river in kāvaṭis (a watervessel and the ritual) and bathing the god, has practical (*bhukti*) or transcendental (*mukti*) results, depends on whether it is practised with *sakāma* or *niṣkāma* according to the *MV* 22.34 ff. See also John M. Stanley, "Niṣkāma and Sakāma Bhakti: Pandharpur and Jejuri," in Milton Israel and N. K. Wagle (eds.), *Religion*, 52-67.

72. L. R. Pāṃgārkar (ed.), *Nirañjanamādhavāṃcā kavitāsaṃgraha*, pt. 1 (Poona, 1919), 64 ff., 66. See also Rāmdās, in Sontheimer, "Rudra," 19.

73. R. C. Dhere, *Khaṃḍobā* (Puṇeṃ, 1961), 117-119. Referring to Mare Micel, *Khaṃḍobācī goṣṭ* (Mumbai, 1855).

74. Gaṇeś Sadāśiv Śāstrī Lele, *Tīrthayātrā Prabaṃdha* (Pune, 2nd ed., 1964), 134.

75. Cp. G. D. Sontheimer, "Hinduism: The Five Components and Their Interaction," in G. D. Sontheimer and H. Kulke (eds.), *Hinduism Reconsidered* (in press).

12

Draupadī's Two Guardians: The Buffalo King and the Muslim Devotee

Alf Hiltebeitel

Draupadī is the chief heroine of the *Mahābhārata*, the Sanskrit epic which is thought to have been given its classical shape from about 500 B.C. to 400 A.D. She is born from a fire sacrifice as an incarnation of the goddess Śrī-Lakṣmī; marries the five Pāṇḍavas; is humiliated and abused after her eldest husband loses her as his last stake in the dice match with his Kaurava cousins; joins her husbands in exile; spurs them to avenge her in battle; joins them in their victorious coronation; shares their kingdom; and finally accompanies them on their final ascent toward heaven. Such, in brief, is her role in the classical epic. On the surface, it is a rather male-defined one, especially when one takes into account that most of the epic action is controlled by the Pāṇḍavas' ally Kṛṣṇa, incarnation of the god Viṣṇu. But Draupadī is also regarded as a goddess, with her own cult centered at the medieval capital of Gingee in northern Tamilnadu.[1] In this context, although it is recalled in her cult's folklore that she is an incarnation of Śrī, she is in many ways more a multiform of Durgā or Kālī, and she is further similar to many "lineage" and "village goddesses" of rural South India. In her cult, her epic roles are deepened and in certain ways transformed, so that the actions of the male heroes now largely revolve around her. But she is still very much the classical epic's heroine. In fact, her festivals are organized around a multi-levelled recreation of the *Mahābhārata*. Along with the local epic-related rituals of each village, town, or city temple that holds a festival for her, the cult has its itinerant specialist performers who are hired for each festival from outside the locality: the *pāratiyārs* or *pārata-piracaṅkis* (*Mahābhārata*-reciters) who narrate classical Tamil versions of the epic story, and the terukkūttu dramatists who enact its key episodes in nightlong dramas. It will be necessary to keep these different "performance levels" in mind as we address the subject of this essay: Draupadī's two guardians Pōttu Rāja and Muttāl Rāvuttan. The pāratiyārs, dramatists, and local ritualists often view these two heroes quite differently.

Neither Pōttu Rāja nor Muttāl Rāvuttan figures in the classical Sanskrit epic. Yet informants of these different types, all in their own ways, bring each of them into relation with both the *Mahābhārata* and the regional mythology of Gingee. Let me introduce these figures through this essay's title. Although Draupadī cult informants do not know it, Pōttu Rāja means the "Buffalo King."[2] As we shall see, his ritual links can be traced to the South Indian buffalo sacrifice, and his mythic associations to Mahiṣāsura, the "Buffalo Demon" who is the foe and victim of the goddess Durgā. One will thus not be misled to expect that the Draupadī cult will link him with scenes and symbols of sacrifice. Meanwhile, the name Muttāl Rāvuttan derives its second element from a term meaning a Muslim horseman or trooper, and is a common title for Muslims in certain districts of Tamilnadu.[3] Yet here again, the meaning of the name is much forgotten and often transformed. Nonetheless, with Muttāl Rāvuttan one is introduced to the incongruity of a Muslim guardian of a Hindu goddess who is herself the heroine of a pre-Muslim epic.[4] In his case, one should also expect to find him linked with symbols of sacrifice and violence, but with the further dimension that he handles them as an "outsider," as one whose position in the cult is that of the periphery, the realm of the "other."

A. Their Icons

The problematic of their relationship is most immediately tangible at the level of the icons which represent them materially at Draupadī temples. I begin with a generalized statement about what may be called the norm, and proceed to two revealing examples that are striking for certain exceptions.

The usual situation is for there to be two icons of Pōttu Rāja and one of Muttāl Rāvuttan.[5] Both deities will thus have fixed stone icons outside the temple, but only Pōttu Rāja will have a wooden or metal processional image (utsavavigraha) like those of Draupadī, the Pāṇḍavas, Kṛṣṇa, and sometimes other epic heroes and heroines. Pōttu Rāja's stone and processional images have a certain variety, but they are not essentially different from each other in their iconography. Whether sculpted in the round out of wood or of metal, or in relief on stone, he usually holds a sword or sacrificial knife in his upraised right hand, and either a severed human/demon head or the body of a subdued animal, usually the lion, in his left hand (see plate 36).

While Muttāl Rāvuttan has only fixed images, they are iconographically much more more varied. Many temples represent him "aniconally" or nonanthropomorphically by one or more stones: rectangular slabs, rounded lingam-like shapes, rough-hewn rocks which rise to a point, conical pointed stones that suggest an impalement stake, or even squared off posts surmounted by a tapered button. As we shall see, there are also Draupadī temples where the stake or post-like forms represent Pōttu Rāja. Sometimes Muttāl Rāvuttan's stone turns into his own saint's tomb: his dargāh (a Muslim term) or samādhi (a Hindu one). In one such case (at Avalurpēṭṭai, Tiruvannamalai Taluk, North Arcot) the typical rock slab is projected in outline from the samādhi's southern end; in another (at Kolar, Kolar Taluk, Karnataka) a miniature mosque is outlined around it. Sometimes, however, Muttāl Rāvuttan also has a full-flowered anthropomorphized iconography. Stone and color-painted plaster images, sometimes in the open air, sometimes in a maṇḍapa, show him seated in an easeful position with one knee (left or right) raised to hold an elbow, the other leg tucked beneath him or forward to overhang his dais; he has a paunch, mustache, turban, beard, and sword; and in some of the large maṇḍapas he has fez-wearing attendants who offer him bottled liquor or potted toddy (see plate 37). He is further attended by animals: most commonly by a "flying" horse, building upon his identity as a Muslim trooper, and in some cases also by dogs and a tiger or lion which sit at his feet, and a parrot which perches on his arm.[6]

Most of these iconic features will require further discussion in connection with these two heroes' myths and rituals, but for the moment I turn to a matter of high consistency and great importance that relates their iconographies directly together. No matter whether Muttāl Rāvuttan is a simple stone, the main figure in a maṇḍapa, or some combination of the two, he is regularly situated in one position: to the northeast of the inner sanctum, and in the ideal case directly to the north of the fixed stone icon of Pōttu Rāja. Meanwhile, this stone Pōttu Rāja is invariably set to face directly into the inner sanctum of the temple so that the icon is in the line of sight of Draupadī, the goddess, within.

36. *Pañcaloha* (five metal) processional image of Pōttu Rāja at the 1986 Draupadī festival in Mēlaccēri, Gingee Taluk, South Arcot, Tamilnadu. The icon rests on Draupadī's "chariot," which it has "led" in procession through the village to the point where the icons can now watch a nightlong Mahābhārata drama. Photo by Alf Hiltebeitel.

37. Muttāl Rāvuttan in his maṇḍapa at Vīrapāṇṭi, Tirukoyilur Taluk, South Arcot District, is represented both aniconically by the stone daubed with *kuṅkum* in the foreground (behind the offering tray with turmeric powder and a rupee note), and iconically with beard, paunch, emptied liquor bottle in right hand, and attendant with toddy pot to his right. Three large clay horses stand outside the maṇḍapa for him to ride. Photo by Alf Hiltebeitel.

Against this general pattern, let me now note how two temples significantly depart from these norms. The first is the temple at Mēlaccēri (Gingee Taluk, South Arcot), the village known also as "Old Gingee" (*paḻaiya ceñci*) where, as we shall see in the myths of Pōttu Rāja, Draupadī is said to have taken her second birth. Here, in an unusual, if not unique feature (as it is in my fieldwork), Muttāl Rāvuttan is worshipped in two forms. In one he receives vegetarian offerings, in the other non-vegetarian ones. The former are made to an image of Muttāl Rāvuttan as a horse-rider (a *rāvuttan*) sculpted in relief on a stone plaque that is set beside a similar slab portraying Pōttu Rāja, who also receives vegetarian offerings. These two slabs stand together in the position usually reserved for Pōttu Rāja: here under the entrance to a Pōttu Rāja maṇḍapa, so that Draupadī now looks out at *both* of her guardians from her inner sanctum rather than at Pōttu Rāja alone (see plate 38). As to the non-vegetarian offerings, these are made at Mēlaccēri to a typical "aniconic" Muttāl Rāvuttan in his customary position, out of the goddess's line of sight, to the northeast. What is most exceptional about the Mēlaccēri configuration is that Muttāl Rāvuttan should receive not only his customary non-vegetarian fare in his solitude, but vegetarian offerings beside Pōttu Rāja. The Mēlaccēri temple thus provides Muttāl Rāvuttan with a "purified" form to go along with his more commonly found impure one. Notably, the purified form is that of the human horseman, leaving the aniconic rock "detached" and to the side to receive the traditional impure offerings that normally befall him. One may suspect that Muttāl Rāvuttan has been purified in this exceptional way at Mēlaccēri because it is there, as we shall see, that Draupadī "converts" him to her service. Indeed, the configuration of the icons may at one point have reflected this Gingee mythology.

The second temple is at Kalahasti (Kalahasti Taluk, Chittoor District, Andhra Pradesh), where again one finds iconographical peculiarities that go deep into Draupadī cult mythology. The essentials were kindly assembled by the Kalahasti temple pūjārī, who placed the processional icon of Pōta Rāju (the Telugu form equivalent to Tamil Pōttu Rāja) on the platform of the fixed Pōta Rāju so that the two could be photographed together with Muttāl Rāvuttan (see plate 39). What is unusual here is the design of the stationary Pōttu Rāja. Coated with turmeric and daubed with red *kuṅkum*, it is clearly an example of the type of Pōtu Rāja found widely in Andhra Pradesh, where Pōta Rāju (Telugu spelling) is represented by, and is the name for, the sacrificial post that stands outside temples to village goddesses.[7] Similar post-represen-

38. Fixed stone images of Pōttu Rāja and Muttāl Rāvuttan face the inner sanctum of the Mēlaccēri Draupadī temple. Pōttu Rāja's distinguishable features include a curved knife in his upraised right hand, matted hair, and what looks to be a head dangling from his left hand. Muttāl Rāvuttan rides a horse and carries a club. Photo by Alf Hiltebeitel.

39. Pōta Rāju's wooden processional icon set on the platform of the post-shaped stationary Pōta Rāju, with "Muhammad Khan"'s tomb to the right. Kalahasti Draupadī temple, Kalahasti Taluk, Chittoor District, Andhra Pradesh. Photo by Alf Hiltebeitel.

tations of Pōttu Rāja are not unknown in the Draupadī temples of northern Tamilnadu,[8] but they are highly exceptional and strikingly different from the far more common iconic Pōttu Rājas in bas relief on stone slabs. So the Pōta Rāju post at Kalahasti can be identified as a transitional type. Draupadī is not a "village goddess" at Kalahasti, nor is she one in Tamilnadu. She is more a lineage goddess, linked with lineages within specific castes (mainly Vanniyars in Tamilnadu, Vanne Reddis at Kalahasti). This will help to explain certain major differences between Draupadī's Pōttu Rāja, and the Pōta Rāju of Andhra village goddesses: differences which will be observed when I discuss the place of our two heroes in Draupadī cult ritual. Moreover, Pōta Rāju's mythology at Kalahasti is a precise and easily recognized conflation of the mythology that connects him on the one hand with village goddesses in Andhra Pradesh and the mythology that connects him on the other with Draupadī in Tamilnadu. Although he does of course serve Draupadī in her temple, according to the pūjārī he is also the younger brother of the Seven Śaktis: "Poleramma, Ankālamma, etc.," a group in which the pūjārī did not, let us note, include Draupadī. This group goes more commonly in Andhra by the name of the "Seven Sisters," the village goddesses with whom Pōta Rāju is repeatedly connected in Andhra myth and ritual.[9] In the Draupadī cult within Tamilnadu, Pōttu Rāja has no sisters whatsoever, although we shall see that he does retain a "junior brother" status relative to Draupadī by his marriage to the Pāṇḍavas' younger sister Caṅkuvati, another Draupadī cult folk creation. Meanwhile, this same Kalahasti Pōta Rāju, a brahmacārin or celibate, became a "disciple" (*śiṣya*) of Dharma-Yudhiṣṭhira, Draupadī's eldest husband. Pōta Rāju's father, named Maharṣi, was the guru of the Kauravas, and had some sacred books of astrology with which he would be able to fix the date of the Mahābhārata war in a way that would favor the Kauravas. At the behest of Kṛṣṇa and Sahadeva, the youngest Pāṇḍava who is reputed in South Indian epic folklore to have been an astrologer himself, Pōta Rāju went and requested the books from his father, and when the latter refused to yield them, Pōta Rāju cut off his father's head. This is then the head which Pōta Rāju's processional icon still holds at Kalahasti. Meanwhile, where one expects to find Muttāl Rāvuttan in this Kalahasti configuration, one is not disappointed. But his name has been forgotten. Just north of the fixed Pōta Rāju post, and almost adjacent to it, is the samādhi or *ghori* (said to be a "Hindustani word" for a tomb) of Muhammad Khan. One is told that he was a Muslim devotee of Draupadī who died here, and had no connection with the Mahābhārata war. But he was also a "second disciple" of Dharma-Yudhiṣṭhira. These Telugu stories of Pōta Rāju and "Muttāl Rāvuttan" are all—even including the forgetting of the latter's name—fragments of the Draupadī cult's Tamil mythology, which we must now turn to more closely. For the moment I will just note two things. First, it is no accident that Pōta Rāju has a transitional mythology in Kalahasti. The Tamil Draupadī cult clearly marks a southern extension of Pōta Rāju's diffusion, which would seem to have its origin and center in Andhra Pradesh. And second, it is no accident that both Pōta Rāju and Muhammad Khan, alias Muttāl Rāvuttan, are "disciples of Dharma." For in the Draupadī cult, Dharma-Yudhiṣṭhira is the incarnation of Dharmarāja Yama, the god of death: death being the very function which our two guardians must each in his own way oversee for Draupadī the goddess.

B. Their Double Mythologies

Draupadī cult mythology sometimes links Pōttu Rāja and Muttāl Rāvuttan variously together, and sometimes treats them separately. I will apporach the links between them, however, from a structural perspective that is not made explicit in the myths themselves, but is implicit within the cult's mythology as a whole. This implicit structure is the mirror relation between Draupadī's Gingee mythology and her epic mythology, something already hinted at in the mythic fragments just cited. It is, in fact, precisely in the mythologies of Draupadī's two guardians that this mirroring structure is given its most fundamental articulation. Not surprisingly, the "folk cult" reveals this underlying structure through two "folk deities."

What this means is that Pōttu Rāja and Muttāl Rāvuttan each have both a Gingee mythology and an epic mythology, and that in each case the two mythologies replicate each other's most decisive features. To make this point as simply as possible, I must thus summarize four myths, keeping discussion of sources and variants to the bare essentials. I turn first to Pōttu Rāja, beginning with a sort of consensual summary of his mythology of Gingee.

> In ancient times there was a descendant of the Pāṇḍavas named king Cunītan, whose kingdom was being ravaged by a demon, usually named Acalamman or Acalammācuran. The demon was himself a descendent of the demon Baka, who was killed by Bhīma, the Pāṇḍava strong man, in the *Mahābhārata*. Acalāmman had vowed to destroy Cunītan and his kingdom in revenge, and had obtained a boon which made him virtually in-

vulnerable: with a hundred, or more rarely a thousand, heads, he could not be killed, for even if ninety-nine were cut off, the hundredth could not be severed. If it fell and touched the ground, the person who severed it would die.

In dire distress, king Cunītan learned from his advisors that only Draupadī—the supreme Śakti—could cut the demon's heads, and ordered the performance of a fire sacrifice to bring her—his ancestress—forth for a second birth. In most versions this second birth took place at Gingee, and more particularly at the Mēlaccēri Draupadī temple. And this is so either because King Cunītan had all along been the king of Gingee (the usual version), or because he had come to Gingee from the traditional North Indian epic capital of Hāstinapura to look for the ṛṣis who could perform his sacrifice. Moreover, the Mēlaccēri Draupadī temple abuts on a jungly mountainous terrain called the Mēlaccēri Forest (kāṭu), which either was all along, or became after Cunītan's migration to the south, the demon's base of operations.

When Draupadī rose from the fire, she agreed to protect Cunītan and their common lineage, but she was perplexed at what to do about the demon's last head. Then, however, she thought of Pōttu Rāja, and sent Cunītan to bring him to her. When Draupadī and Pōttu Rāja finally joined forces, they had a full complement of cultic implements and sacrificial weapons. These are variously enumerated, but most commonly include the *vīrapampai* (heroic *pampai* drum), *vīrakantakam* (heroic turmeric powder), *vīrakuntam* (heroic lance, also called *cūla* [Sanskrit śūla], trident, but usually with five tines), and *vīracāṭṭi* (heroic whip). These were either born with Draupadī when she rose from the fire, or they were originally the property of Pōttu Rāja, who brought them with him as he entered her service. They are both cultic implements, and the weapons used to kill the many-headed demon.

When Draupadī and Pōttu Rāja at last confronted Acalāmman, the demon taunted Draupadī with his invulnerability. But without saying anything Draupadī cut off all his heads, and Pōttu Rāja caught the last one, thus preventing it from touching the ground. After this Pōttu Rāja vowed that he would always hold the head in his left hand, thus protecting Draupadī, the Gingee kingdom, and all Draupadī temples beginning with the Mēlaccēri temple which King Cunītan would build on the spot of Draupadī's Gingee birth, or, according to others, the spot at which she disappeared immediately after killing the demon. Images of Pōttu Rāja perpetually holding a head in his hand thus show him fulfilling this mission.

In the Draupadī cult, and particularly at Draupadī festivals, Pōttu

Rāja's Gingee mythology is narrated primarily by the pāratiyārs. The terukkūttu dramatists know it, and the troupe I knew best, aware of my interest in such stories, even improvised a play to portray it. But it is not part of their festival repertoire of dramas. Now the pāratiyārs, professional reciters of classical Tamil versions of the *Mahābhārata* (most commonly the *Makāpāratam* of Villiputtūr Ālvār), embody a classical tradition of epic expertise. They are accorded a certain deference within the cult for their prestigious literary knowledge. Moreover, as individuals they are usually of at least equal and often higher caste rank (some being Aiyar Brahmans or Vēḷāḷars) than the main population of the cult (usually Vanniyars), from which the terukkūttu actors are usually drawn. In contrast to the classical and literary prestige of the pāratiyārs, the dramatists are viewed as presenting a popular and essentially non-literary or oral tradition.

It is important to insist that these distinctions between high and low, classical and popular, and text and oral are by no means absolute. Indeed, it is the large common ground in which they overlap, mutually influence, and mirror each other that is the main concern of this section. But they do have direct bearing on the two mythologies of Pōttu Rāja. One thing which the pāratiyārs clearly achieve in espousing the Cunītan cycle is a story that links Pōttu Rāja with Draupadī without bringing him directly into the classical epic story. This they know too well to allow such an intrusion, and several pāratiyārs spoke with disdain of the stories which do link Pōttu Rāja—and sometimes Muttāl Rāvuttan—with the epic's main action. In fact, two pāratiyārs were met who eliminated Gingee from the myth just discussed, and told instead that king Cunītan ruled and remained in North India, and that his sacrifice, and Draupadī and Pōttu Rāja's defeat of the demon, took place in the Himalayas. Indeed, one of these two pāratiyārs identified Cunītan's North Indian kingdom as Kauśambī, a detail which he seemed at the time to have pulled out of a hat, but which I was soon astonished to be able to trace to numerous Sanskrit Purāṇas, where one can learn that the Pāṇḍavas' descendants moved their capital to Kauśambī after the flooding of their prior capital of Hāstinapura, and that the Tamil name Cunītan derives from one of those very descendants, whose Sanskrit form is Sunītha. Such classical and antiquarian precision represents one pole toward which the pāratiyār versions may tend, a pole directly opposite the more popularly oriented mythology of the dramatists. For the dramatists show no restraint in involving Pōttu Rāja directly in the *Mahābhārata*'s main action, and most drama troupes include in their repertoires a play which does so. Turning now to Pōttu Rāja's epic mythology, it is this drama that supplies our main source. In these stories Pōttu Rāja is usually called Pōrmannan, "War King," a *nom de guerre* that defines the Mahābhārata war as the venue in which he will play his main "folk epic" role.

That the dramatists should be unrestrained in linking Pōttu Rāja with the *Mahābhārata* is not surprising, since they are hired at Draupadī festivals to present plays in a Mahābhārata cycle. More than this, however, it is the dramatists who negotiate the mythological middle ground between the classicism of the pāratiyārs and the popular, and in many cases ritually inspired, mythology of local Draupadī temples. One will thus also find the Pōrmannan story in local temple variants, especially outside the area frequented by today's drama troupes. The drama's short title is "Pōrmannan's Fight." There is a chapbook edition of the play[10] which, like other publications of terukkūttu dramas, was probably inspired by prior oral versions and palm leaf manuscripts. Actual performances basically keep to the story as one finds it in the chapbook, but with much improvisation, frequent departures, and variation from troupe to troupe. My summary will keep these factors in mind.

The play opens with the Pāṇḍavas at a place called Nūtanāpuri, the "New" or "Extraordinary City," seemingly a new name for the city in which they reside after their forest exile and period of concealment to await the outcome of the negotiations that will determine whether there will be a Mahābhārata war. Kṛṣṇa joins them there, and tells them that Draupadī cannot win the forthcoming eighteen day war unless she is supplied with five items: again variously named, but including, as above, the heroic whip, heroic pampai drum, heroic turmeric powder, heroic lance, and also the pūcāri's turmeric box (*paṇṭāra peṭṭi*). Note that while dramatists, like local temple pūcāris who sometimes know this story, prominently mention the paṇṭāra peṭṭi, the pāratiyārs did not: one of a number of indications that the dramas are closer to the ritual idioms of the temples. These five items, says Kṛṣṇa, now belong to Pōrmannan in Civānantapuri, "The City of the Bliss of Śiva." And he divulges how they can be obtained, setting in motion the elaborate scheme that unfolds for the rest of the play.

Pōrmannan is introduced doing a pūjā with the coveted articles. He is portrayed with "demonic" facial make-up (red coloring with white dots, large moustache) and gestures (protuding tongue, bulging eyes, bellowing sounds, menacing movements), which he comically displays before introducing himself, his city, and his genealogy. He mentions his patrilineal descent through four generations, all the names ending in the suffix *lingam*, his father variously called Śivalingam and Gurulingam. As to his city, it has seven forts, and because he keeps the five pūjā instruments, it is impenetrable. And anyone who enters his fort to take them will die.

Now Bhīma, at Kṛṣṇa's direction, approaches the city disguised as a woodseller. (Here, to explain what follows, Kṛṣṇa would seem to know a background myth that has not surfaced in any of the dramas: the city was created when Pārvatī once took up a piece of wood and drew its design. Śiva then decreed that as wood created it, so it would destroy it.)[11] When Pōrmannan calls Bhīma before him, he allows Bhīma to rest the logs against the outer fort wall. Represented by a curtain held by two actors, the wall drops to the ground. Pōrmannan is furious, and orders Bhīma imprisoned, which Bhīma allows as it is part of Kṛṣṇa's scheme.

Now Kṛṣṇa and Arjuna come to the rescue, each in woman's guise. Arjuna appears as a beautiful young woman of sixteen named Vijayāmpāḷ, a name which disguises one of his own names, Vijaya or "Victory," and openly evokes the goddess Durgā for whom Vijayā is a familiar epithet and Ampāḷ a term for woman, mother, or goddess. Meanwhile, Kṛṣṇa is a decrepit hundred year old crone or "grandmother" (pāṭṭi), claiming to be Vijayāmpāḷ's mother. When they reach Civānantapuri, they announce that they are the woodseller's mother and sister and mourn his loss. Pōrmannan orders them brought before him. Smitten with immediate lust for Vijayāmpāḷ, he fails to register the incongruity of their ages. Falling over the old woman, sticking his tongue in and out, he keeps up a mad chase until finally he says he wants to marry Vijayāmpāḷ and will do anything to have her. First the old lady says she will give him her daughter if she gets her son back, and Pōrmannan complies. And then the old lady, Kṛṣṇa, asks for the pūjā articles so she can perform a Śiva-pūjā. With considerable fanfare, as this is one of the play's central moments, Pōrmannan hands them over to Vijayāmpāḷ. The grandmother then says she must go outside the city to perform the rite, and over Pōrmannan's salacious protests, takes Vijayāmpāḷ with her on the promise that they will soon return for the wedding. Furthermore, catching Pōrmannan at his most lovelorn and dimwitted, the old lady now insists that he promise, according to the chapbook version, that if they do *not* return within about one-and-a-half hours, Pōrmannan will destroy his city, plough it to dust, make the earth even, and sow it with castor and cotton. Moreover, in the performed version of the troupe I knew best, a version known also at various local temples, she (Kṛṣṇa, the old lady) also makes Pōrmannan promise to cut off his father's head; for Pōrmannan's father, an ardent Śiva bhakta, would protest the release of the five implements and not allow his son to aid the Pāṇḍavas or come to the war. Only after Pōrmannan has met these conditions can he come searching for Vijayāmpāḷ. It is of course this fragment of the whole that we met above in a much transformed variant at Kalahasti, where Kṛṣṇa gets Pōttu Rāja (not Pōrmannan) to kill his father in order to secure for the Pāṇḍavas the knowledge of when to begin the Mahābhārata war.[12]

Kṛṣṇa and Arjuna now go back to Nūtanāpuri, shed their female guises, and rejoice with Draupadī and the other Pāṇḍavas in the weapons that will allow Draupadī to win the eighteen day war. Meanwhile, the abject Pōrmannan destroys his fort, sows castor and cotton, and in my primary troupe's version, kills his father. When he arrives at Nūtanāpuri, he dances and postures like an iconic Pōttu Rāja, holding an upraised sword in his right hand and a wadded ball of white cloth—his father's head—in his left. But he has of course the rude awakening that his bride-to-be is a man. Undaunted, he says that if he was promised a wife he must get one, and Kṛṣṇa tells the Pāṇḍavas to give him their younger sister Caṅkuvati. Let us note that this was the point at which one of the pūcāris (the Tindivanam Draupadī temple priest) who knew a version of this story paused to explain why Pōrmannan must continue to hold the head: Kṛṣṇa told him to keep holding it while the Mahābhārata war was in progress, and not to drop it lest it destroy the world if it touched the ground; thus he should not be hasty about marrying Caṅkuvati. But in the play Pōrmannan finally sets the "head" aside, and Caṅkuvati is sent for. Seeing her, Pōrmannan quickly redirects his affections. Kṛṣṇa then insists on one condition for the marriage: that Pōrmannan agree to serve as leader of the Pāṇḍavas' army in the eighteen day war. Here at last Pōrmannan insists on his own bargain in return. He will lead the Pāṇḍava army, but Kṛṣṇa must supply him with three things: a mound of poṅkal like a mountain, a flour-lamp like a hill, and a he-goat as tall as a palm tree. Kṛṣṇa supplies these with various tricks, ordering the poṅkal put on a mountain, the goat put on a palm tree, and the flour lamp put on a tamarind tree to make the objects as big as demanded. Indeed, in a second troupe's performed version which omits the episode of the father's head, Kṛṣṇa gives Pōrmannan a live cock "instead of the goat," and Pōrmannan bites its neck in half on the stage and then raises its severed head with his right hand while holding its carcass lowered in his left. Disappointed with all these substitutes, but reluctantly satisfied, Pōrmannan contents himself with Caṅkuvati, bringing the play and the story to a happy ending.

Now it is clear that the Gingee mythology of Pōttu Rāja and the epic mythology of Pōrmannan tell strikingly different stories. Indeed, in the first the primary action focuses on the protection of a kingdom, while the latter focuses on a kingdom's destruction. From this angle, both could be studied in relation to other stories of these two different types. But what is more striking is that despite the narrative differences, the two myths mirror each other's most decisive features. The following chart demonstrates this in brief compass. Keep in mind that where I summarize the *Mahābhārata,* I do so as it is known in Draupadī cult circles.

Pōttu Rāja at Gingee	*Pōrmannan in the* Mahābhārata
1. Marginal forest setting, between the kingdom of Gingee and the Mēlaccēri Forest.	1. Marginal forest setting, between forest exile and the war over the kingdom.
2. The weak, exiled king, a descendant of the Pāṇḍavas, cannot defeat a hundred-headed demon; only Draupadī can defeat him, with the aid of Pōttu Rāja.	2. The weak, exiled Pāṇḍavas cannot defeat the hundred Kauravas, demons incarnate (= a hundred heads); it will be Draupadī who will win the war and Pōrmannan who will lead the army.
3. The five ritual weapons used to defeat the demon are either born with Draupadī or brought by Pōttu Rāja.	3. The five ritual weapons that Draupadī needs to win the war are secured, through trickery, from Pōrmannan.
4. Pōttu Rāja must hold the demon's last, central head.	4. Pōrmannan is tricked not only into bringing the weapons, but his father's head.

There are other complementarities as well, but only one need detain us. While the Gingee myths retain the name Pōttu Rāja, with its unrecognized and apparently forgotten meaning of "Buffalo King" (see n. 2), the Pōrmannan myth has as its unmistakeable subtext the myth of the *mahiṣāsuramardana:* the "Killing of the Buffalo Demon" (Mahiṣāsura) by the goddess Durgā. For not only is Arjuna a Durgā multiform. He himself is Draupadī's surrogate on the mission to Pōrmannan's kingdom, a mission which reanimates one of the perennial themes in the mythology of the goddess and the Buffalo Demon: the goddess's seduction of the demon to draw him into battle. If, as Biardeau has so persuasively and insightfully argued, Pōttu Rāja is ultimately "identical with Mahiṣāsura, but with a Mahiṣāsura who has been converted"[13] by his death at Durgā's hands, one can see how both of his myths devolve from such a premise. Indeed, among guardian deities Pōttu Rāja is the perfect type of the "demon devotee." In the Gingee myth, he is the already converted demon, brought into the service of Draupadī as he is into the service of various Andhra village goddesses, one and all, like Draupadī, multiforms of Durgā. And as the "War King," we get a glimpse of him as a multiform of the Buffalo Demon himself, seduced by the goddess into engaging her in battle, and implicitly defeated in the yielding of his weapons. Yet Pōrmannan never fights the goddess. So far as his myth goes, his combative traits are first deflected against his kingdom and his father, and then, more in parallel with Pōttu Rāja's service to Draupadī at Gingee, channelled into his leadership of the Pāṇḍava army. Once defeated as Mahiṣa, he now helps the goddess combat other demons not unlike his former self.

Turning now to the mythology of Muttāl Rāvuttan, the situation is far more diffuse. At local temples, the little stones which usually represent him are often not, or are no longer, mythologized at all. Sometimes informants would look embarassed when asked about them, and then admit surprise if it came up that he was a Muslim. Sometimes they would know that he was a Muslim, but had no recollection of his name. Or, as at Kalahasti, a more generalized Muslim name would be supplied. And for some his Muslim identity had been eclipsed by a Hindu one, with rāvuttan replaced by rāja, making him a Hindu king, or in the case of the pāratiyār who linked king Cunītan with Kauśambī the claim that *raut* is a name for North Indian Brahmans! In fact, no other feature of Draupadī cult mythology is more fragmented and obscure. Unlike the mythology of Pōttu Rāja, of which something is known at virtually all levels of Draupadī cult involvement, myths of Muttāl Rāvuttan are told only by a scattered few.

Once again, however, the variants organize themselves into two groups: those which connect him with Gingee, and those which connect him with the *Mahābhārata*. My best sources on both were the two terukkūttu actors who led the troupe whose Pōrmannan holds his father's head. They observed that Muttāl Rāvuttan's Gingee myth was the least known, and to be found at only a few local temples, while his Mahābhārata story had only slightly wider circulation, primarily through a terukkūttu drama which they did indeed know, but had only been asked to perform once (that is, before I requested them to do it again). I have found nothing to contradict this comparative judgment about the two stories. Be it noted, however, that whereas Pōttu Rāja's

Gingee mythology is transmitted primarily from the repertoire of the pāratiyārs, Muttāl Rāvuttan's is to be found elsewhere. For while some pāratiyārs do link Muttāl Rāvuttan with the myths about King Cunītan and Pōttu Rāja, he is never more than the latter's tag-along in such accounts. Thus, in both North Indian and Gingee variants, he may be Pōttu Rāja's "friend," with both of them serving Cunītan as army leaders and ministers (*mantrins*, in the one case noted, a Brahman). But he is never given a role of his own in this myth, which is clearly first, foremost, and most essentially a myth about Pōttu Rāja. Moreover, other pāratiyārs who tell the Pōttu Rāja-Cunītan myth eschew Muttāl Rāvuttan entirely, saying that he has nothing to do with that story, and moreover that he "spoils" the *Mahābhārata* and is a mere popular fiction. The Gingee myth *distinctive* to Muttāl Rāvuttan thus has no place at this learned level. Let us now turn to the account which the two dramatists claimed to have heard so infrequently in the course of their visits to local Draupadī temples.

> Muttāl Rāvuttan was born in Gingee. One night he had a dream in which Draupadī-amman told him that she would give him whatever he desired if he would sacrifice a pregnant woman to her. Muttāl Rāvuttan had a pregnant younger sister named Pal Varicai (Row of Teeth). He readied her for sacrifice, but Draupadī stopped him, thinking: "She is a woman like me." She praised Muttāl Rāvuttan's dedication, however, and told him that she would still grant him a boon. Whatever he thought of would be done; but he must give up his religion and come serve at her residence (i.e., her temple): "Serving at my feet, you can live with me." Muttāl Rāvuttan thus gave up his religion and came to serve Draupadī. Henceforth it was agreed that she would receive pure offerings of milk, flowers, vegetables, and fruits. And he would receive live sacrifices (*uyiriṇaṅkaḷ paliyiṭutal;* i.e., blood sacrifices) such as cocks, goats, and even humans.

The ritual ambiance and local temple provenance of this story are unmistakable. It is clearly concerned with themes of sacrificial violence, and in particular with inversions of what normally acceptable sacrificial violence would entail. For Muttāl Rāvuttan agrees to sacrifice not only a woman (regular sacrificial victims are males), and not only his younger sister, but his pregnant younger sister. Nothing like this ever went on in the Gingee of King Cunītan and Pōttu Rāja. Clearly Muttāl Rāvuttan's myth and sacrificial propensities are of a different shading from those of his cohort. For light on this distinction, one must turn to some background ethnology.

If the mythology of Pōttu Rāja, alias Mahiṣāsura, reveals him as a perfect type of the "demon devotee," the Gingee mythology of Muttāl Rāvuttan finds its closest analogues in stories of the type which M. Arunachalam wrote about under the inspired heading of "ballads glorifying criminals."[14] His main examples are in fact Kāttavarāyan, Maturai Vīran, and Cuṭalai Māṭan. For present purposes, one may call this second type that of the "criminal god," although it is important to note that the two types need not always be distinct, as in the case of Kāttavarāyan who seems not only to have his "criminal" career but to be a converted form of the demon Kārtavīrya Arjuna.[15] The closest of these figures to Muttāl Rāvuttan, however, is Cuṭalai Māṭan, a "guardian" deity for various gods and goddesses popular in southern parts of Tamilnadu. Indeed, his myth sheds considerable light on some of the more baffling themes and missing connections in our all too brief myth of Muttāl Rāvuttan. Both are *mantiravātis* (Sanskrit *mantra-vādi*): that is, "mantra-speakers" or magicians, and in particular black magicians, a trait of Muttāl Rāvuttan's that my informants will make explicit in their version of his epic mythology. More than this, Cuṭalai Māṭan shares the telling trait of a predilection for sacrifices of pregnant females. In a contest with another mantravādi in Kerala, he seduces or rapes the opponent's daughter; makes her pregnant by a subterfuge; gets the adversary to offer him a pregnant goat, pregnant sow, and a young girl pregnant for the first time (apparently the same one he had made pregnant himself), and finally arranges for the opponent's own sacrifice by getting the king of the country to have him buried up to his neck and trampled by the royal elephants.[16] These Tamil myths linking mantravādis with the sacrifice of pregnant females surely reflect and derive from actual mantravādi practices of Kerala.[17] The cult of *oṭi*, "breaking the human body," called for an initiation in which the novice would mesmerize a pregnant woman into leaving her house at the dead of night, get her to lie down naked, extract the embryo from her womb into a gourd, cut it up, substitute another substance for it, consume flesh and liquor, and learn to prepare from "the sixth or seventh month's foetus of a primapara" a potent medicinal substance called *pilla thilam* or "baby oil" by mixing the liquid (thilam) with fine powder from a human skull.[18]

These mantravādi myths clearly portray "criminal gods" of an extreme type. Yet one should observe that both result in the termination of the odious sacrifices when the mantravādi is subdued. Cuṭalai Māṭan actually gets his adversary to perform the various sacrifices on his behalf, and then turns to a more ordinary "criminal" career before finally subordinating himself to the higher Hindu gods as a recipient of blood sacrifices.[19] And Muttāl Rāvuttan, after he has apparently been tested by Draupadī in the dream that nearly brings him to sacrifice his pregnant younger sister, is told not to perform this rite before he "converts" to Draupadī's service as the guardian who accepts animal "and human" offerings. He thus gives up his mantravādi ways and his Muslim religion, but at the same time retains such traits, turning his "meat-eating" religion and his magical gifts to the advantage of the "purer" Hindu deity whose grace now extends, in return, to include Muslims.

Turning now to Muttāl Rāvuttan's epic mythology, one may observe that his Gingee myth leaves many open questions. How is it that Muttāl Rāvuttan's younger sister, this "Row of Teeth," comes to be pregnant? One hears of no husband. And how is Muttāl Rāvuttan so easily subdued and converted by Draupadī-amman? In the Cuṭalai Māṭan myth the impregnation and the subjugation of the sacrificing mantravādi are accounted for, in effect, by Cuṭalai Māṭan himself. Does Draupadī have someone "similar" to subjugate Muttāl Rāvuttan and to impregnate his sister? Not quite. But she does have someone to subjugate him: Pōrmannan. And, rather than impregnate his sister, she has someone to marry his daughter: Pōrmannan's son Allimuttu. Muttāl Rāvuttan's main epic myth thus *sequentially* presupposes the epic myth of Pōttu Rāja under his alias Pōrmannan. But more than this, it is in such transformations as these that one can now see how Muttāl Rāvuttan's epic mythology (for it is more than just one myth) is still a complex refraction, purified of its most nefarious mantravādi elements, of his *own* Gingee myth, and not—the point to emphasize—of the Gingee myth of Pōttu Rāja.

The relation between Muttāl Rāvuttan and Pōrmannan is actually highlighted in the play's title: "The Marriage of Allimuttu and Mallikā, called the Pōrmannan-Muttāl Rāvuttan Combat" (*Allimuttu Mallikā Tirumaṇam ennum Pōrmannan-Muttālrāvuttan Caṇṭai*).[20] Indeed, the play begins where "Pōrmannan Caṇṭai" left off: Pōrmannan and Caṅkuvati are now parents, and their son Allimuttu has had time to grow up in the indefinite post-war period. The account follows a performance staged at my request by the troupe led by my two chief dramatist informants.

> First on stage, Muttāl Rāvuttan sings of himself boastfully as a great mantravādi, and tells that he has created his daughter Mallikā through the power of his mantras. Then Mallikā enters and boasts further of her father's powers before he sends her to a forest garden to gather flowers. Next Caṅkuvati is introduced, calling for her son

Allimuttu, and Allimuttu arrives to tell her that he is going to the forest to hunt. When he sees Mallikā, it is another antic romp of love at first sight followed by a comically abrupt proposal of marriage. Mallikā is receptive, but says her father won't allow her to marry anyone. Moreover, he is a Muslim and a great mantravādi, able to do whatever he wishes, and he has the boon that he cannot be defeated or killed by anyone born through a womb. Only if he is subdued (aṭakku) can they wed. Allimuttu, undaunted, tells her his maternal uncles, the Pāṇḍavas, will solve his problem. He goes to Dharma, and Dharma calls his brothers and Allimuttu together to subdue Muttāl Rāvuttan. But Muttāl Rāvuttan's mantras deprive them of all their strength, and he takes them off to prison. Once again, Kṛṣṇa comes to the rescue. He praises the Pāṇḍavas for challenging Muttāl Rāvuttan. But he says they can only be freed, and Muttāl Rāvuttan subdued, if Draupadī—born from fire rather than a womb—joins with Pōrmannan to defeat him. Draupadī then sends Pōrmannan to fight Muttāl Rāvuttan. But when he approaches, Muttāl Rāvuttan asks him, "Who is your mother?" Pōrmannan says his mother is "the uniquely chaste lady Draupadī" (*ekappattini turōpatai*), apparently confirming that his own birth is also non-uterine. He then adds that he bears the five cultic weapons that, in his own myths, had served him and Draupadī in their victories at Gingee and in the Mahābhārata war. Muttāl Rāvuttan recognizes immediately that his mantras are futile against such an arsenal, declares himself ready to be Pōrmannan's slave (*aṭimai*), and asks for refuge (*caraṇākati*) at Draupadī's feet. Draupadī accepts his submission and says he can henceforth sit at the north side of her residence or temple (*ālayam*), and be ready to fight for her at all times. And she tells him, in the closing scene, to let his daughter Mallikā marry Allimuttu.

Needless to say, the two terukkūttu plays share many themes and a common structure. But their mythical subtexts are remarkably different: in one case the myth of Durgā and the Buffalo Demon, in the other the lore of mantravādis. It is the latter which we must now pursue further in its varied epic guise.

Acutally this is not Muttāl Rāvuttan's only epic myth. Local informants at Draupadī temples also know a number of more fragmented stories that connect him with the *Mahābhārata*. Thus one claimed that he performed an eighteen day pūjā to help the Pāṇḍavas at Kurukṣetra; one that he and Pōttu Rāja were friends and both generals who fought there for the Pāṇḍavas (rather than for king Cunītan); several that he drove Pōttu Rāja's war chariot; and another, noted from Kalahasti, that he and Pōttu Rāja were Dharma's disciples. In fact, a connection with Dharma undergoes a revealing elaboration in a temple variant from Chinna Salem (Kallakuruchi Taluk, South Arcot), one which also seems to be a multiform of the terukkūttu story. In this account, Muttāl Rāvuttan was the Muslim field general of a Hindu king named Muttāla Mahārāja of the North Indian kingdom of Muttālappuram who came over to serve the Pāṇḍavas when the king married his daughter Muttālakkanni to Dharma. Muttāl Rāvuttan did this because he had always been devoted to Muttālakkanni, and wanted to serve her until his death. So he also served the Pāṇḍavas as the guardian of the northern gate of their palace. Here, instead of just one "Muttāla," there are three: the girl, the Muslim field general, and the Hindu king. Moreover, it would seem that Muttāl Rāvuttan's own mythology has been split: In one aspect, he is still the Muslim field general who comes to serve Draupadī and guard her northern gate; and in the other, he remains the father of the girl whose marriage into the Pāṇḍava family secures his "Muslim" service to Draupadī, but as the father he is now a Hindu king. One is reminded how his icons are often given a Hindu name. In the case of the Chinna Salem myth, the split solves the problem of how the Pāṇḍavas or their descendants could intermarry with Muslims: Allimuttu marries Muttāl Rāvuttan's Muslim daughter; Dharma marries Muttāla Mahārāja's Hindu daughter. And in the case of the icons, the occasional Hindu identity solves the incongruity of Draupadī having a Muslim guardian.

But most telling in terms of tracing the affinities between Muttāl Rāvuttan's Gingee and Mahābhārata myths are his various dealings with young girls. For once again, one finds him in another strange attachment of this type: this time his lifelong devotion to the Hindu princess Muttālakkanni. One may now note further that even in the terukkūttu drama, Muttāl Rāvuttan holds his daughter, whom he has created by his mantras, in a kind of magical enthrallment. All of these variants preserve and present different legacies of his mythology as a mantravādi. In the Gingee and terukkūttu myths, it is ultimately Draupadī who rescues the girl from her enthrallment. And in the Chinna Salem myth it is the girl's marriage to Dharma which attenuates it. Moreover, in either case, whether it be by Draupadī or Dharma, the freeing of the girl as the occasion of his dedication to the Pāṇḍavas implies Muttāl Rāvuttan's "conversion," since the other name for a Draupadī temple is a Dharmarāja temple. And whether it be as a result of his conversion at Gingee or his conversion within the *Mahābhārata*, one finds Muttāl Rāvuttan in the same iconic, mythic, and ritual position: accepting his submission "at Draupadī's feet," and beginning his service as the guardian of the northern gate of her residence-palace-temple. Let us now recall the relative position of Pōttu Rāja, and rethink our findings in relation to the ritual rapport between the two of them.

C. Their Ritual Roles: Hierarchy, Boundaries, Transgressions, and Sacrifice

The contrast between Pōttu Rāja and Muttāl Rāvuttan is rarely better expressed than in the positions which they assume vis à vis the goddess at the ends of their myths. Hierarchically, whereas Muttāl Rāvuttan accepts service at Draupadī's feet, Pōttu Rāja stands directly before her eyes. In one case they are head-to-foot, in the other eye-to-eye and thus head-to-head. Within the Indian symbolic lexicon these are clearly expressions of hierarchy. But they are also expressions of bhakti: the first a gesture of submission or taking refuge, the latter of viewing the deity or taking darśan. Furthermore, whereas Muttāl Rāvuttan guards the Draupadī temple's northern gate, Pōttu Rāja is posted before the entrance to her inner sanctum. Here one is dealing not so much with hierarchy (and verticality) as with horizontal spatial boundaries. Yet while their myths tell how both Pōttu Rāja and Muttāl Rāvuttan finally come to be *fixed* in these positions, they also build up to these conclusions by showing how each, before reaching his appointed station, begins as a transgressor of hierarchies and boundaries. This is most striking, in terms of hierarchy, in the caste-transgressing implications of their multiple caste affinities. Within the Draupadī cult Pōttu Rāja (or Pōrmannan) is usually regarded as either a Brahman (or brahmacārin, as at Kalahasti) or Kṣatriya, but his low status and servant roles clearly stem from the same set of associations that result in his being impersonated by Untouchables in parts of Karnataka, Andhra Pradesh, and Maharashtra.[21] And Muttāl Rāvuttan is sometimes a Brahman, sometimes a Hindu King of slightly changed name, and usually a non-caste Muslim. Muttāl Rāvuttan is also regarded as having transgressed spatial boundaries as a representative of the incursion of Islam from North into South India. Indeed, he is sometimes said to have been positioned at Draupadī's northern gate to guard against further Islamic penetration. More than this, nothing yet has been said about the major transgressive themes of their myths: for Pōttu Rāja, holding a severed head—in some versions his own father's—unto eternity; and for Muttāl Rāvuttan, holding young girls—in some cases his daughter or sister—in various forms of enthrallment, with varying implications of aborticide. The conclusion of this essay will examine such matters as these against the background of the further contrastive roles of these two guardians in the realm of Draupadī cult ritual.

I have already described the positions of their stationary icons, and the contrastive vegetarian and non-vegetarian types of offerings these usually receive (Mēlaccēri excepted). And I have further observed that of the two, only Pōttu Rāja has a mobile processional icon. Yet these matters are each far more complex than I have so far allowed. Pōttu Rāja figures at the center of virtually all Draupadī cult temple and festival activities, while Muttāl Rāvuttan is repeatedly relegated to zones of peripherality and obscurity. Thus one pāratiyār could scoff at icons and stories of Muttāl Rāvuttan, seeing them as irrelevant to the cult. Yet in his version of Pōttu Rāja's Gingee myth, he could have Draupadī show her gratitude for Pōttu Rāja's head-holding service by decreeing that he be the first recipient of all respect (*māriyatai*) and all pūjās within her temples and festivals, and close by saying that without Pōttu Rāja there is no festival. Indeed, from the beginning of a festival to its end, Pōttu Rāja's icons are omnipresent, and are treated as if they represented one of the festival's high dignitaries, though which one in particular it is impossible to say, since just as Pōttu Rāja transgresses caste boundaries, so one sees in the festival presences of his icons something of the Brahman, something of the temple trustees as festival patrons (in the role of yajamāna), something of the possessed pūcāri, and something of the demon in every devotee.

If one can state matters summarily, however, the division of ritual roles bears on an interpretation of sacrifice, one which is itself a double reinterpretation of the sacrificial themes of the *Mahābhārata* and of South Indian animal sacrifices of the type that in Andhra are offered to village goddesses and Pōta Rāju. Moreover, the division is not just between Pōttu Rāja and Muttāl Rāvuttan, but between the two of them and Draupadī, the goddess who *mythically* severs a demon's hundred heads and uses ritual weapons to win the Mahābhārata war. On the face of it, however, and in the view of informants, in terms of actual ritual the Draupadī cult involves no animal sacrifices. Draupadī in particular receives none herself, and Pōttu Rāja, at least as represented by his icons (one does find Pōrmannan in his dramas demanding goat meat and eating live rooster), is vegetarian. The primary ritual function of Pōttu Rāja's roving processional icon is thus to oversee *symbolic* sacrificial offerings—involving actors, icons, effigies, and possessions rather than real live oblations—that involve reenactments of the major killings in the *Mahābhārata* myth of the "sacrifice of battle." Meanwhile, without a processional icon, Muttāl Rāvuttan is predictably absent from such reenactments of the epic war. For as with his myths, so also in the rituals he is usually unrepresented at the epic war scenes, although one informant said he accompanies Pōttu Rāja's icon *invisibly*! Just as Draupadī can't see his stationary icon, we can't see his portable one.

But if Draupadī requires no *real* animal sacrifice *within* the time and space of her festival, she *allows* them—and, according to the myth of Muttāl Rāvuttan and his pregnant sister, actually arranges for them—on its temporo-spatial periphery, the place where Muttāl Rāvuttan is visibly fixed. Here one finds him represented most often by the little offering stones that are ultimately, and in some cases quite recognizably, multiforms of a sacrificial post. Meanwhile, the stationary icon of Pōttu Rāja that receives vegetarian offrings *usually* represents him in human form, and only rarely—as at Kalahasti (see n. 8)—in a multiform of the sacrificial stake which so widely represents him in Andhra. This is not to say that Draupadī's Pōttu Rāja entirely relinquishes his associations with the sacrificial stake. His stationary icon is normally placed in conjunction with the balipīṭham (offering stone) and temple flagstaff, and at some temples the base of the flagstaff bears his image. Although I cannot develop the point here, there are continuities between the sacrificial post and the flagstaff. Moreover, Pōttu Rāja-Pōrmannan's ritual weapons include the trident or pike, a portable multiform of the sacrificial stake, and the whip, a multiform of the rope that binds sacrificial victims to it.[22] But as far as their stationary icons go, he does in large part relinquish the sacrificial stake's explicit representation to Muttāl Rāvuttan, marking its movement from the center of a village goddess type cult to its periphery in the cult of Draupadī. For not only are non-vegetarian offerings made to Muttāl Rāvuttan's little stones outside the goddess's line of sight. They are made at *no regular* time in her festival: at various places only by private arrangement with the pūcāri during the festival, or at nonfestival times, or at a special ceremony after the festival is over.

Yet if the offerings to Muttāl Rāvuttan are set off and apart at Draupadī festivals, they are still part of Draupadī's cult. His most consistent offerings are liquor and goats, with these and most additional items—cocks, hens, meat curries, parched spicy Bengal gram ("a standard item in liquor shops, . . . said to prevent nausea produced by an excessive consumption of alcohol"),[23] marijuana, opium, chapattis, cigars, cheroots, cigarettes, and horse gram for his horse—being common fare for such "criminal" gods and heroes.[24] But in Muttāl Rāvuttan's case it is to be understood that certain of these things—

meat, chapattis, drugs, liquor, and perhaps Bengal gram—combine to caricature him as a Muslim. His iconography make this conclusion inescapable.

Invisibility, peripherality, irregularity, historical incongruity, and religious otherness: One might think that Muttāl Rāvuttan's position on the margins of the Draupadī cult derives from some supposed vagueness or slackness of folk Hinduism, or some inevitable concession to "popular" survivals of "Dravidian animal sacrifice." These, however, cannot be our conclusions. For the periphery to which Muttāl Rāvuttan is consigned is not without its precise ritual definitions. First of all, as Biardeau has observed, the northeast is "the habitual position of the kṣetrapāla," the "guardian of the field."[25] As kṣetrapāla of the Draupadī temple, Muttāl Rāvuttan is much like other deities of this designation, most notably—also with his dogs, tigers, horses, liquor, and drugs—the god Khaṇḍobā in Maharashtra.[26] But while the pan-Indian kṣetrapāla Bhairava may also have this same cluster of attributes, he has one that, in the Draupadī cult, is connected not with Muttāl Rāvuttan but with Pōttu Rāja: the head held in the hand. I will return to this point shortly. Moreover, the kṣetrapāla with his "habitual position" to the northeast shares this precise location with a related figure in Brahmanical temples. This is the nirmālyadevatā, the deity—often a lower form of the temple's main deity—who receives the "residue of offerings" (nirmālya) of the main deity, guards it from violation, and handles its impurity.[27] I have not found Muttāl Rāvuttan actually receiving Draupadī's nirmālya. But the offerings he does receive are in effect the nirmālya of the violent aspects of her mythology.

Surprisingly, such continuities as these are rooted not within some "folk religious" miasma but within the framework of the traditional Vedic sacrifice as it is conserved, yet transformed, through the medium of popular bhakti Hinduism. For the relative positions and functions of Muttāl Rāvuttan and Pōttu Rāja also have, of all things, a Vedic pedigree. In the Vedic animal sacrifice, the northeast is associated with the *śamitṛ*, the "appeaser" priest (from the root *śam-*, to appease, to pacify) who is responsible for killing the sacrificial animal by the allegedly "appeasing" and non-bloodletting means of suffocation or strangulation. It is to the northeast of the *mahāvedi*, the additional "great altar" required for animal sacrifices, that one finds the *śāmitra*, the *śamitṛ's* fire (and sometimes a shed) on which the śamitṛ cooks or roasts the limbs and other portions of the victim after cutting them: a process which must have included some handling of the victim's severed head, even if the texts are rather quiet on this point.[28] What is significant for our purposes is that the śamitṛ's fire is distinct from the sacrificial post (the yūpa), which is set at the eastern end of the mahāvedi. In this regard, the yūpa corresponds to the typical position occupied by the temple flagstaff, which, as noted earlier, is connected not with Muttāl Rāvuttan but Pōttu Rāja. With these overlapping ritual structures now before us, let us traverse them one last time while recalling the icons and mythologies of our two heroes and their goddess.

As Draupadī cult mythology itself should recommend, let us take our cue from the cult's bhakti framework, which encompasses and orients its sacrificial imagery. For present purposes, I would propose that Muttāl Rāvuttan and Draupadī represent two poles of a bhakti continuum. While Draupadī's appeal to Kṛṣṇa during her disrobing represents bhakti at its most sublime, her devotion is cointerpoised by numerous expressions of inferior bhakti, among which that of Muttāl Rāvuttan ranges toward the bottom. The important thing is that such inferior bhakti has itself two potentials: it can be transformed into higher bhakti, or it can take on perverse forms linked with drunkenness, black magic, and the crudest parodies of sacrifice such as the willingness to offer up a pregnant sister. It is a ritual function of Muttāl Rāvuttan, mantravādi and Muslim, to stand at the boundary between these possibilities. On the one hand, he is surrounded by animals that evoke violence, impurity, magic, and possession; his attendants ply him with liquor, his devotees with marijuana and opium. In Draupadī cult contexts, drunkenness and narcotics are thought of as inducing a kind of impure, or "polluted" possession, one which is essentially demonic and stands in opposition to higher forms of possession which become vehicles for bhakti. Yet Muttāl Rāvuttan does not simply indulge himself in such pastimes. To be sure, he partakes of what he is offered. But he is said to neutralize the offerings' dangerous effects so that when they are returned to the offerer as *prasādam*, they have lost their heating or intoxicating qualities. One must thus understand that when liquor, drugs, and various hot foods are offered to the little stones that represent him, he detoxifies them so that the offerers (or sometimes the pūcāri) can consume them *unaffected*. Like other "criminal gods" and "demon devotees" who are "converted" to the worship of the goddess, he thus retains facets of his "former" character, but places them at the service of higher expressions of bhakti. His myths, rites, and icons thus represent him in a variety of trespassive modes, while they also fix the boundary situations through which his cult enables Draupadī's devotees to neutralize their dangers through worshipping him.

If Muttāl Rāvuttan's service is to neutralize outside dangers, Pōttu Rāja's can in part be characterized as neutralizing dangers from within. This he does by forever holding the head that would destroy the goddess, the kingdom of Gingee, or the world itself if it fell. Let us recall in this connection that the pan-Indian prototype of the head-holding guardian deity is Bhairava, who holds the head of Brahmā as a result of having committed the ultimate violatory act of a divine Brahmanicide that is also a patricide, for Brahmā is father of the gods. Although this is not the place to demonstrate it, there are reasons to suspect that Pōttu Rāja's icons derive this feature, at least in part, from the iconography of Bhairava. And his myths also evoke, and indeed divide, the same violatory themes. For in one case the hundred-headed demon, whose last head he holds, has the traits of a Brahmarākṣasa, a Brahman who claims the royal function through defying a weak king. And in the other, he carries the head of his own father. Let us note here further that Pōttu Rāja's head-holding, like that of Bhairava, is bound up with myths and rituals of possession, and that the various ritual weapons he comes to share with Draupadī include means both to induce possession (the whip, the trident) and to neutralize it (the whip, turmeric powder). All this sounds remarkably like Muttāl Rāvuttan. But Pōttu Rāja's possession is normally not tinged with drunkenness or drugs.[29] Rather, in terms of myth, it is rooted in themes of sacrifice turned toward bhakti: in one aspect recalling the transformation of his buffalo animality into service to the goddess, and in another the link between the severed head of Brahmā and the madness of Bhairava that is prelude to the experience of liberation or divine union. But it is especially the icons that clarify such distinctions. For if one recalls the Vedic model that keeps our two heroes in their intimate rapport, one sees the very opposite of the situation one might expect. In effect, Muttāl Rāvuttan and Pōttu Rāja have made a trade. Out at the northeast periphery where the kṣetrapāla Bhairava would normally hold the head of Brahmā, and where the śamitṛ would dismember the sacrificial animal and thus have to handle the "head of the sacrifice,"[30] one finds Muttāl Rāvuttan represented by multiforms of the sacrificial stake which one might normally expect to find at the end of the central eastern axis of the mahāvedi or, *mutatis mutandis,* of a village goddess temple. And at the eastern end of this central axis, where one might expect to find the stake itself, one finds Pōttu Rāja, the erstwhile stake of Andhra, holding the sacrificial head instead. The post and the "head of the sacrifice" have thus reversed their positions. A complete discussion of this reversal would have to take into account the Draupadī cult's treatment of other "primary elements of the sacrifice" as well: most notably the body of the victim and the sacrificial fire. But for the moment it is enough to observe that the reversal of these two—the head and the post—is in predictable accordance with the Draupadī cult's sacrificial logic, which imputes actual sacrifice to the cult's periphery, where it is overseen by Muttāl Rāvuttan, yet retains the symbolism of sacrifice at its center, where it is overseen by Pōttu Rāja and multivocally represented by the head in his hand. For there the head-holding Pōttu Rāja can stand facing Draupadī with a symbol of both the ultimate sin of Brahmanicide and of the devotee's own self-offering (remember, Pōttu Rāja is a Brahman too) to the goddess.

Finally, however, it is the goddess, in our case Draupadī herself, who must explain these themes. As I put it earlier somewhat metaphorically, it is the violent implications of her mythology that become the nirmālya of Muttāl Rāvuttan. Indeed, she stops his sacrifice of his pregnant sister—and its implied aborticide—after she herself had ordered it, because "she is a woman like me": an evocation of the theme of the goddess as sacrificial victim (like Reṇukā or Satī), a reminder that Draupadī is herself treated as such a victim when the Kauravas drag her about by the hair,[31] and a further reminder of themes in her cult that relate the murder of her own five children in the night raid that ends the Mahābhārata war to themes of abortive death and regeneration. The mantravādi's boundary enthrallments are thus inverted images of Draupadī's own mistreatments: that is, of the violation of the goddess.[32] Similarly, at least in the Gingee myth, the head which Pōttu Rāja holds is the last of a hundred which Draupadī herself has severed; and should Pōttu Rāja drop it she would turn instantly from victor to victim. Thus in both cases, Draupadī is not only implicated in the violatory acts of her guardians, but in the sacrificial imagery of those acts. Furthermore, her own cultic and epic mythology has its own trangressive themes with their own sacrificial dimensions. Most centrally, she vows to wear her hair dishevelled (an image of Kālī) through her years of exile, and not to rebraid it until she can "oil" it with the sacrificial blood of her chief Kaurava tormentor. Here there is no question of her remaining pure while her guardians handle the sacrificial impurity on her behalf. Defiled, she will remain defiled until she can purify herself with the very blood of her defiler. Moreover, from being the victim, she has become the victor, an image in fact of Durgā. And as the goddess who uses ritual weapons to achieve this end, she is not only the recipient of offerings, but the executor of sacrificial killings. It would thus seem that what her two guardians finally guard, one at her frontier and the other at the entrance to her sanctum—the "womb house" which all must enter but none must violate—is the mystery at the heart of these alternating sacrificial images: the goddess herself as śakti, the "power" who surpasses all boundaries, participates in and endures all transgressions, even those which violate and victimize her, who yet remains pure, inviolate, and regenerative, and who defeats and yet releases—the inevitable bhakti note—all those who have trespassed against her.

NOTES

1. See my larger study *The Cult of Draupadī, I. Mythologies: From Gingee to Kurukṣetra* (Chicago: University of Chicago Press, 1988), to be followed by a second volume on Draupadī cult rituals. Certain material in this essay is treated more fully in these studies.

2. On this etymology, see Madeleine Biardeau in Biardeau and Charles Malamoud, *Le sacrifice dans l'Inde ancienne* (Paris: Presses Universitaires de France, 1976), 151; Hiltebeitel, *The Cult of Draupadī*, I, chapter 2, n. 8.

3. The name is derived from Urdu *rāut*, "horseman," which is itself derived from either Prakrit *rājadūta* or *rājaputra*. My thanks to Lee Weissman for tracking down this etymology.

4. Muttāl Rāvuttan has also been found as an attendant to Māriyamman, and apparently to Aiyanar (see Hiltebeitel, *The Cult of Draupadī*, I, chapter 6). At the temple of Kuṭṭi Āṇṭavar (a form of Murukan) at Tīrttānpāḷaiyam village (Chidambaram Taluk, South Arcot District) he is the leader of the three guardians (*kāval*) of the separate maṇḍapa of Jampuliṅkam (a form of Śiva). The other two are named Lāṭan and Canyāsi (Sanskrit Saṃnyāsi), and all three are represented by small rectangular stones set in separate concrete platforms. But his only consistent presence seems to be in the Draupadī cult.

5. Draupadī is of course not unique in having two or more guardian (kāval) or "attendant" (parivāra) deities. For Tamilnadu alone, see Biardeau's discussion in this volume of Kāttavarāyan and Karuppu in the cult of Māriyamman, and Eveline Meyer, *Ankāḷaparamēcuvari: A Goddess of Tamilnadu, her Myths and Cult* (Wiesbaden: Franz Steiner Verlag, 1986), 74-82 on the four guardians of Aṅkāḷamman. See further Stanley in this volume on Khaṇḍobā's demon- and minister-attendants. This article will not attempt to move from the particulars of the rapport between Draupadī's two guardians to generalizations about this wider phenomenon, other than to note that any generalizations would require considerable caution.

6. See Hiltebeitel, *The Cult of Draupadī*, I, chapter 6 and plate 9.

7. On Pōttu Rāja as sacrificial post in Andhra, see Madeleine Biardeau,

"L'arbre śamī et le buffle sacrificiel," in Biardeau, ed., *Autour de la déesse hindoue, Puruṣārtha* 5 (1981), 230-238; Henry Whitehead, *The Village Gods of South India* (Delhi: Sumit Publications, 1976), Plate IV, facing p. 39.

8. At Vīrāṇantal (Chengam Taluk, North Arcot District), Tailāpuram (Tindivanam Taluk, South Arcot District), and Kūttampākkam (Vaniyambadi Taluk, North Arcot). On the latter, see Madeleine Biardeau, *Histoire de poteaux: variations védiques autour de la Déesse* (Paris: Bulletin de l'École Française d'Extrême Orient, in press).

9. On Pōttu Rāja and the Seven Sisters, see Biardeau, "L'arbe śamī," 231; Wilbur Theodore Elmore, *Dravidian Gods in Modern Hinduism. A Study of Local and Village Deities of Southern India* (Lincoln: University of Nebraska, 1915), 18-30.

10. Kōtaṇṭarāma Upāttiyāyar, Rā. Vē., *Caṅkuvati Kaliyāṇam ennum Pōr Mannan Caṇṭai Nāṭakam* (Madras: Caṇmukānanta Puttakacālai, 1980 [earliest edition found 1955; author's dates unknown]).

11. Biardeau, *Histoire de poteaux*, in press, from a pāratiyār interviewed at Pondicherry.

12. Actually, the Kalahasti myth draws its structure not only from the Pōrmannan cycle. Its theme of stealing the astrological knowledge of how and when to begin the war is probably adapted from the Tamil epic and Draupadī cult mythology of Arjuna's son Aravān; see Hiltebeitel, *The Cult of Draupadī*, I, chapter 15.

13. Biardeau, *"L'arbre śamī,"* 238.

14. M. Arunachalam, *Peeps into Tamil Literature: Ballad Poetry* (Tiruchitrambalam: Gandhi Vidyalayam, 1976), 187-194.

15. See Biardeau's and Shulman's essays in this volume, and A. K. Ramanujan, "Two Realms of Kannada Folklore," in Ramanujan and Stuart Blackburn, eds., *Another Harmony: New Essays on the Folklore of India* (Berkeley: University of California Press, 1986), 46. It might be investigated whether Kāttavarāyan bears any greater traces of a connection with Kārtavīrya in Reṇukā-Māriyamman temple mythologies, where one might expect such traces, than he does in the ballad literature discussed by Shulman and Masilamani-Meyer in this volume, where his links are with the cult of Kāmākṣī.

16. Marie Louise Reiniche, *Les dieux et les hommes: Étude des cultes d'un village du Tirunelveli Inde du Sud* (Paris: Mouton, 1979), 205-207; Arunachalam, *Ballad Poetry*, 191-192.

17. Edgar Thurston and K. Rangachari, *Castes and Tribes of Southern India*, 7 vols. (Madras: Government Press, 1904), vol. 6, 25-28, describe traditions of a group of magician-mendicants among Vanniyars around Madras called Jātippiḷḷais (literally, "Children of the Caste"): their ancestor won them their title and prerogatives by saving the rest of the caste from an impasse by sacrificing his own girl-wife, pregnant for the first time, to the goddess Kāmākṣī so as to counteract the spells of a rival caste's magicians. Such mantravādi myths must be differ-

entiated from myths and rituals that portray the goddess Aṅkāḷamman sacrificing and disemboweling a pregnant queen; see Meyer, *Aṅkāḷaparamēcuvari*, 12-14, 185-87, and 214-17 on the myth and related rituals, and 226-28 and 233 on comparison with Cuṭalai Māṭan.

18. Thurston and Rangachari, *Castes and Tribes*, vol. 6, 122-26.

19. Reiniche, *Les dieux et les hommes*, 206-207.

20. This play was also published in chapbook form by the now defunct Śrī Vāṇi Vilāca Press of Cuddalore. I was never able to locate a copy.

21. Certain ramifications of the Hindu-Muslim problematic of the rapport between Pōttu Rāja and Muttāl Rāvuttan would seem to be paralleled in human terms in Maharashtra, where the Hindu outcaste Potrāj divides certain sacrificial functions with a Muslim *mullana* who is in charge of the killing of cocks, goats, and hens: Traude Vetschera, "The Potaraja and Their Goddess," *Asian Folklore Studies* 37 (1978), 131.

22. See Biardeau in this volume.

23. Gabriella Eichinger Ferro-Luzzi, "The Logic of South Indian Food Offerings," *Anthropos* 72 (1977), 548.

24. See, e.g., Arunachalam, *Ballad Poetry*, 190; Meyer, *Aṅkāḷaparamēcuvari*, 81-82; Shulman in this volume on the pūjā to Kāttavarāyan's sacrificial stake.

25. See Biardeau, *Histoire de poteaux*.

26. The affinities would actually seem to deepen with Khaṇḍobā's Andhra counterpart Mallanna: Consider the latter's Muslim beard (compare plate 37 with plates 28 and 29); his horse and tiger-dogs; his Muslim identities, one as Rautrāy (could this be *raut* as in rāvuttan plus *rāy* as in "king"?), who fights a Liṅgāyat Rākṣasa, another as Malkhan, who tricks the Śivabhaktas of Mecca into smoking gañja; see Sontheimer in this volume.

27. Sunjukta Gupta, "Viṣvaksena the Divine Protector," *Wiener Zeitschrift für die kunde Südasiens und Arkhiv für Indische Philologie* 20 (1976), 80-85; Erik Af Edholm, "Caṇḍa and the Sacrificial Remnants. A Contribution to Indian Gastrotheology," *Indologica Taurinensia* 12 (1984), 75-89 on Caṇḍa-Caṇḍēśvara Nāyanār in the Śaiva cultus; p. 89 on Caṇḍeśvarī/Nirmālyadhāriṇī in the Śākta cultus; pp. 90-91 on Viṣvaksena in the Vaiṣṇava cultus; Helène Brunner, "De la consommation du nirmālya de Śiva," *Journal Asiatique* 27 (1969), 229-31. Compare Stanley's discussion in this volume of Heggaḍe Pradhān and my comments on Caṇḍēśvara Nāyanār in this book's Introduction (at n. 7).

28. See Citrabhanu Sen, *A Dictionary of Vedic Rituals* (Delhi: Concept Publishing Co., 1978), 110-111 and Plans 3 and 5; Charles Malamoud, "Les chemins du couteau. Remarques sur les découpages dans le sacrifice védique," in Cristiano Grottanelli, ed., *Divisione delle carni: Dinamica sociale e organizzazione del cosmo, L'Uomo* 9 (1985), 32-36.

29. At only one temple (Mutikai Nallānkuppam, Chingleput Taluk, Chingleput District) have I seen him represented with a glass of liquor, and that in a

painting on the same wall as the little stone representing Muttāl Rāvuttan: seemingly a case of the latter's "bad influence" or of "guilt by association."

30. On this theme, see especially Jan Heesterman, "The Case of the Severed Head," *Wiener Zeitschrift für die Kunde Süd- und Ostasiens* 11 (1967), 22-43.

31. See Madeleine Biardeau, "Comptes rendus" of seminars on the *Mahābhārata, Annuaire de l'École Pratique des Hautes Études,* Ve section, vol. 88 (1979-80), 180.

32. See also Meyer's discussion of the goddess's ambivalence as sacrificier and victim in *Aṅkāḷaparamēcuvari,* especially p. 214 and citations in n. 17 above.

13

Violent and Fanatical Devotion Among the Nāyanārs: A Study in the *Periya Purāṇam* of Cēkkilār

D. Dennis Hudson

The stories of the sixty-three Tamil Śaiva saints, or Nāyanārs, appear in their complete form in the twelfth century Tamil hagiography entitled "The Purāṇa of the Sacred Saints" (*Tiruttoṇṭar Purāṇam*), better known as the "Purāṇa of the Great" or "The Great Purāṇa" (*Periya Purāṇam*). The author is Cēkkilār, a Vēḷāḷa from Toṇṭai country, who, later tradition says, was a minister in the Chola court of Kulōttuṅga II (1130-1150).[1] Kulōttuṅga II was a devotee of Śiva Naṭarāja at Chidambaram and continued the reconstruction of that cultic center of Tamil Śaivism begun by his predecessors. At the same time he was enchanted by the Jaina epic, *Jīvaka Cintāmaṇi*. To wean him away from it, we are told, his minister Cēkkilār composed the *Periya Purāṇam*.

The *Cintāmaṇi* is a courtly epic infused with the erotic flavor called *sṛṅgāra rasa*. The hero is Jīvaka, a Kṣatriya who combined heroics with erotics to marry a series of seven women and to gain a kingdom. In the end he realized the transiency of possessions, renounced the kingship, took refuge in the Jaina Tīrthaṅkaras, and after prolonged tapas attained Nirvāṇa.[2] In contrast, the *Periya Purāṇam* is a poetic work about the sixty-three saints whose devotion or bhakti is infused with the flavor of love called anpu. The Nāyanārs love Śiva and Śiva loves them and the stories tell how that love manifested itself in everyday life and how it led the saints to transcendent freedom or mokṣa.

In the *Cintāmaṇi* the driving force is Jīvaka who stands in the foreground exciting the audience with his heroic and erotic adventures.

In the *Periya Purāṇam* the driving force is Śiva who stands in the background, stirring up things to elicit responses from the Nāyanārs. In the *Cintāmaṇi*, one might say, the focus is on the hero as he wins women to be his wives, but in the *Periya Purāṇam* the focus is on the "women" as they become "wives" to the hero.

Cēkkilār's concern, it seems, was not to wean his king away from Jaina lore so much as to wean him away from erotics. He did this by using stories that had been current for centuries. Sundaramūrtti Nāyanār, probably in the seventh century, had listed sixty Nāyanārs in his "List of Devotees" (*Tiruttoṇṭattōkai*), but had recorded none of their stories. About two centuries later Nambiyāṇṭār Nambi added the names of Sundaramūrtti and his parents to the list in his "*Antāṭi* of Devotees" (*Tiruttoṇṭar Tiruvantāṭi*) and included a sketch of each saint's life.

By this time the Nāyanārs were appearing visually in the Śiva cult as patronized by Tamil kings. A sculpture of the saint Kaṇṇappar appeared on a Pallava temple in the ninth century[3] and at the same time sculptures of most, if not all, of the Nāyanār narratives appeared on a gateway and a wall of a Chola temple.[4] The Chola king Rājarāja I (995-1012) linked his own rule to the saints Sundaramūrtti and Cēramān Perumāḷ by depicting their visit to the temple at Chidambaram where he had been crowned when he painted his coronation in his own great temple in Tanjore.[5] A century later the Chola king Kulōttuṅga I (1070-1122) sculpted many of the Nāyanār stories on a new temple,[6] and four decades later the Chola king Rājarāja II (1146-1172) sculpted narratives of all the Nāyanārs on the exterior of the temple and hall he built in his new capital.[7] And in the meantime metal moveable images of the Nāyanārs were being cast and used in the rituals of these and other temples.

We see, therefore, that Cēkkilār wrote his long poem in the context of royal attentiveness to the Nāyanārs as models of bhakti. In contrast to other hagiographies—the Telugu "Basavanna Purāṇa" for example—his is an "establishment" text. It provides Śaiva kings with religious justification for their rule. By his time seventy-two Nāyanārs had been identified—the sixty listed by Sundaramūrtti, the three added by Nambiyāṇṭār Nambi, and nine others who appear individually in the stories of the sixty-three—and he gave each one individual attention, following the canons of Tamil courtly epics to create a poetic work that fits no specific genre of literature, a hagiography of four thousand two hundred and fifty-three verses that portrays the love the Nāyanārs had for Śiva in its most absolute sense.

Considering that its theme of absolute devotion to God is addressed to a warrior king, we can view the *Periya Purāṇam* as a Tamil Śaiva gloss on the central theme of the *Bhagavad Gītā*, that famous Sanskrit discourse on bhakti that Kṛṣṇa gave to the warrior Arjuna as his battle began. A tradition of Chidambaram, in fact, says that long ago Kṛṣṇa himself received initiation there into the service of Śiva.[8] The lives of the Nāyanārs, after all, do illustrate several aspects of bhakti that the *Bhagavad Gītā* leaves undeveloped. They portray, for example, the cultic context of bhakti, the meaning of bhakti as "participation" in the object of devotion, and the consequences of absolute devotion to the Lord for the ordinary householder.

One wonders, however, how the violent or fanatical acts that at least twenty-four of the Nāyanārs performed out of love for Śiva fit the *Bhagavad Gītā*'s notion of saintly devotion.[9] How, for example, is it saintly to give your wife away to an ascetic who asks for her and then to chop up your relatives and hers when they try to stop him from taking her out of town? How is it saintly to chop the heads off of everyone in your family, including servants and a nursing child, because during a famine they ate the food you had set apart for Śiva's temples? How is it saintly to kill your only son because a sādhu asks you to and then to cook him and sit down to eat him?

On reflection, though, these violent acts are not inconsistent with the *Bhagavad Gītā*. After all, the context of that text is a war and the pretext of that text is the anxiety Arjuna had about whether it is "criminal" to kill his own relatives and teachers for the sake of a kingdom, acts that he then went on to perform with many of the disastrous consequences he feared. During the battle Kṛṣṇa himself performed acts that transgressed the accepted law and order of battle in order to win.

But of course Kṛṣṇa ultimately stands outside of law and order, for as chapters 11 through 14 of the *Bhagavad Gītā* tell us, as the transcendent Vāsudeva he himself eats the body of the universe and its order, gestates it once again within himself, gives it birth, brings it to maturation, and then eats it again. From a human point of view these look like acts of murder and cannibalism and, since the universe is a transformed mode of God himself, self-slaughter. But God transcends the order of the universe and his actions cannot be judged in our moral categories.

A problem for his devotees arises, however, when the transcendent God enters into the universe, stirs its order up, and forces them to respond, often in ways that resemble his transcendent acts but in fact transgress the moral norms of society. The stories of the Nāyanārs tell us that Śiva does this to demonstrate the extraordinary and ideal nature of their love for him and to submerge himself in that love. At times their responses are so fanatical and violent that we do not know where to place them morally.

For example, there is the story of Kaṇṇappa Nāyanār. He was, Śiva tradition says, Arjuna reborn and his life is thus a commentary on the bhakti of the *Bhagavad Gītā*. The *Mahābhārata* tells us that on a mountain Arjuna had fought with a hunter over a pig, but the hunter was Śiva in disguise. Because he had scorned him as hunter, Śaivism tells us, Arjuna was himself reborn as a hunter. But this reborn Arjuna felt an extraordinary love for Śiva's liṅga on a mountain and offered him a pig, other animals, and then his eyes. In response, Śiva took him out of rebirth to stand at his right side. Kaṇṇappa Nāyanār was now forever yoked to Śiva by love in mokṣa, or as Tamil Śaivas say, in *sāyujyam*.[10]

Our intention here is to examine these acts of violent and fanatical devotion in the *Periya Purāṇam* to see how we can understand them in terms that are consistent with Tamil Hindu culture. We shall begin by looking at the *Purāṇa* in its cultic context and then consider what it tells us about anpu, about love of Śiva as participation in him and about Śiva's lovers as extensions of him. We shall end with the question of why some devotees kill themselves out of love for Śiva and some observations about the *Purāṇa* as an "establishment" text.

A. The Cultic Context of the *Periya Purāṇam*

One theme besides bhakti that unifies the stories of the Nāyanārs is the sanctity of the three cultic elements of Āgamic Śaivism: the liṅga, the guru, and the assembly of the "slaves of Śiva." The slaves are devotees who wear ashes (vibhūti) and beads (rudrākṣa) that are the emblems of Śiva, and they may be either householders or ascetics—and the ascetics may belong to any of six orders recognized by the liturgical texts that guide the rituals and thought, the Āgamas.[11]

All the Nāyanārs treat the liṅga, the guru, and the slaves as manifestations of Śiva himself and all of them attain sāyujyam because of undeviating service to one of them. Among those who perform violent acts, however, none does so out of devotion to a guru. Violent devotion derives from emotional attachment, not from insightful detachment.

"Attach your mind to Me," Krishna had told Arjuna, and Cēkkilār shows us how to do it.[12] Love for Śiva, he makes clear, is not a vague feeling towards a generalized object, but an orientation of the mind, body, and speech towards a concrete cultic element in a specific context. Love for Śiva, it seems, does not develop without attention to the details of cultic service, nor is it expressed except through such service and usually in the midst of one's daily householder life. Attention to the liṅga, for example, may mean a commitment to supply the oil for lamps in a specific temple, or to grind the sandalpaste for a specific liṅga, or to prevent the temple services from being disrupted or its articles from being polluted, or to throw back the first fish of each day's catch. Attention to a slave of Śiva always means bestowing the rites of hospitality that include washing his feet and giving him whatever he asks. The slave one serves need not even be genuine—it is enough to honor the emblems of Śiva that a man wears, even if he wears them under false pretenses.

The unusual—and paradigmatic—quality of the Nāyanārs' love for Śiva, and the reason for their fierce acts, is its absolute nature. When the Tamil word for this love, *aṉpu,* is used in the sense of wanting to perform acts of love for Śiva incessantly, it means the same thing as bhakti. And anpu itself is *iṉpam,* joy, or more accurately, I think, deep satisfaction.[13] A saint's commitment to a particular cultic element gives him life-fulfilling satisfaction (inpam) and takes precedent over every other duty and relationship he has. He carries it out consistently to a degree that can only be termed fanatical.

The Nāyanārs give no room at all to the normal and relative values of pleasure (*kāma*), prosperity (*artha*), and righteousness (dharma); nor do they aspire for transcendent freedom (mokṣa); all they desire is lovingly to serve Śiva in the concrete here and now. And when Śiva, in his graciousness, stirs up the limiting realities of time and space (saṃsāra), they sustain their absolute commitment and end up behaving like fanatics, madmen or criminals. Nothing will divert them from fulfilling their commitment to serve Śiva, not even when Śiva himself provides a way out. One might call this a form of "individualism," for the Nāyanār is prepared to break all normal social bonds. But the Nāyanār does not see himself as being "individualistic" for everything he does is motivated not out of self-interest but out of love for Śiva—out of "Śiva-interest," one might say.

The simplest and most extreme example of commitment to cult taking precedence over the relative values of family life is Kōṭpuli Nāyanār, "Saint Ferocious Tiger."[14] His service to Śiva was setting aside paddy to use in Śiva temples. When he went away to war he instructed each member of his household not to use the grain, but a famine came while he was gone and they ate the rice, planning to replace it later. He learned of it when he returned and so, setting a guard at the door of his house, he slaughtered everyone in the household—his father, mother, wife, brothers, sisters, and all other relatives, and also the servants. Only a baby boy was left and the guard asked to save him since he had not eaten the paddy. "Yes, but he nursed from a woman who had," said the Nāyanār, and chopped the baby's head off (see plate 40).[15]

The story of Iyarpakai Nāyanār, "Saint Hostile Nature," illustrates the kind of "individualism" based on Śiva-interest that this anpu may lead to.[16] In order to demonstrate that Hostile Nature joyfully would give the slaves of Śiva whatever they asked for, Śiva appeared at his door in the guise of a lecherous Brahman smeared in ashes. When he asked for the Nāyanār's wife, he happily complied, as did she. When the Brahman then asked him to protect him and the wife from attacks by their relatives and townspeople, the Nāyanār regretted only that he had not thought of that first and picked up his sword and shield. As they crossed the town, both his and her relatives gathered murmuring, "Even though Saint Hostile Nature, out of his craziness, gave her away, is it right that anyone should take her?" Then holding weapons they approached the three and angrily expressed their fears:

> Hey! Hostile Nature! What do you think you're doing? You don't give a damn about the way the townspeople will censure us or about the way our enemies will sneer and ridicule us. You talk as if you alone have the right to give away your wife to the Brahman. Only if we all agree can you give her to him.

Then they went for the Brahman, whereupon Hostile Nature flew into a rage and swinging his sword left and right chopped off their shoulders, legs, and heads until no one was left standing. Then he continued to walk with the Brahman and the wife until both were safe.

Love for Śiva can also create irreconcilable cultic commitments, as the story of Ēyarkōn Kalikkāma Nāyanār illustrates. "Saint Kalikkāma, King of the Ēyars," grew enormously angry when he heard that Saint Sundaramūrtti had sent Śiva as a messenger in the night to a woman he loved. It is one thing for Śiva to agree to act as a messenger for a slave, he figured, but quite another for a slave to order his master to do it—a grievous fault in service to the liṅga. Śiva learned of his anger and decided to stir things up by bringing Kalikkāma and the hated Sundaramūrtti together. He afflicted Kalikkāma with a painful disorder of bodily humors and then told him in a dream that only

40. Saint Ferocious tiger (Kōṭpuli Nāyanār) destroys his family and servants who during a famine had eaten paddy set aside for Śiva. A guard urges him to save a nursing infant. Photo by Dennis Hudson.

Sundaramūrtti could heal him. Kalikkāma said he would rather go on suffering than be healed by Sundaramūrtti. "Besides," he lovingly told Śiva, "who knows your greatness? You will give strength to those who are firm in serving you."

Śiva then told Sundaramūrtti to go and heal Kalikkāma, but when Kalikkāma heard that Sundaramūrtti was coming, he realized his dilemma: Either be faithful to the liṅga and remain aloof from the criminal devotee, or be faithful to the slave of Śiva and let himself be healed by him. He opted for the liṅga and picked up a knife and disembowled himself. When Sundaramūrtti arrived and saw what he had done, he was so impressed that he decided to walk the same path and he picked up the knife to rip open his own stomach when Śiva brought him to a halt.

Kalikkāma believed, of course, that even though Sundaramūrtti was a rogue, he did wear the emblems of Śiva and deserved his loving service. The story of Ēnātināta Nāyanār, "Saint Lord of the Generals," makes vividly clear the sacred quality of the ashes and the rudrākṣa beads independent of their wearer. His job was to train Chola rulers in swordsmanship. A rival for his post tried to defeat him in a battle but was routed in disgrace. Deciding that he could beat the Nāyanār only by deceit, the rival challenged him to a private duel. Saint Lord of the Generals appeared at the appointed place and waited. Soon his deceiving opponent appeared with his head hidden behind his shield. As he drew near and as the Nāyanār made his move to attack, the deceiver pulled his head out from behind the shield, revealing ash on his forehead. The Nāyanār thought to himself, "Alas, I'm finished. I never saw ash on his forehead before, but I see it now. What choice do I have? He's become a slave of Śiva and so I'll follow whatever course he chooses." He was about to throw aside his sword and shield when he thought, "No, he shouldn't bear the guilt of killing an unarmed man." So he stood there holding his sword as if he really were an opponent and the deceiver killed him.

B. Love as Participation in Śiva

Śiva's dharma, Arumuka Nāvalar tells us, consists of both mild (*manta*) and fierce (*tīvira*) acts.

> Among these, mild acts are the Path of Action that follows the way laid down for temple service (*caryā*) and ritual service (*kriyā*) in the Āgamas. Fierce acts are the Path of Bhakti that transgresses the way of the world,

> a path motivated by a flood of anpu for Śiva. This anpu, which arises without limits and ripens very quickly, occurs in a birth that itself is a result of having walked the Path of action for a long time and without missing a step.[17]

Excessive rather than restrained love is the ideal, Nāvalar suggests, and expresses itself in what we see as bizarre behaviour. These fierce acts of devotion reveal the quality of the devotee's love, and one can only stand awestruck, mouth gaping, when seeing them. The paradigm for this excessive anpu is the story of the young Untouchable hunter chief whose name was Tiṇṇanār, "The Robust," Arjuna reborn whom we have already met.[18]

The story touches on several topics but let us focus on four things it says about anpu. First, it tells us that when anpu ripens a transubstantiation of the devotee's nature occurs that dissolves his bonds to others in society. For example, when the barbaric hunter saw the Kāḷatti (or Kālahasti) mountain where Śiva the Lord of the Mountain dwells as a liṅga, an urgent desire to climb the mountain welled up within him. As soon as Tiṇṇanār spotted the liṅga Śiva gazed upon him and transformed his entire being into love for Śiva. As Nāvalar put it, "By the initiation [dīkṣā] of Śiva's gracious look, his individual nature [*pacuttuvam*] was removed and he received Śiva's nature [*civattuvam*]."[19] From now on his hunter identity was only the mode through which love for Śiva expressed itself, a love for God who was now part of himself.

Now he derived satisfaction in life solely from taking care of Śiva, that is, from attention to the cultic service of the liṅga named Kāḷattiyappa, Lord of the Kāḷatti Mountain. And because he remained a hunter, though of a transformed nature, he was subject to the normal feelings of joy and sorrow that follow inevitably from attachment to anyone in this world. While joy that Kāḷattiyappa had chosen him was overwhelming, he nevertheless worried that the Lord stood alone and hungry and was subject to the prowlings of wild animals. This fanatical infatuation led his fellow castemen to see him as subject to some sort of divine madness they could not exorcise and his parents to find him beyond their authority altogether. Śiva had pulled Tiṇṇanār completely out of the web of conventions that make up the communal life of hunters.[20]

Second, the story tells us that anpu need not include learning and ritual purity, only a singleminded commitment of one's total nature to Śiva, a commitment expressed in a specific cultic context and experienced by others as a psychotic infatuation. When Tiṇṇanār decided to clean his Lord up and to feed him, he did so in complete ignorance of the Āgamas and acted as an infatuated Untouchable hunter would. He brought to the liṅga pig's meat that he chewed in order to find the tastiest morsels, water that he carried in his mouth, and flowers that he stuck in his hair. He then performed pūjā in ways that the Āgamas rank as defiling. He brushed the liṅga off with the sandal on his foot, he bathed it by spitting water over it, he dropped the flowers from his head onto Śiva's, and he fed him the saliva-drenched pork. He did this for six days.

In the meantime, Kāḷattiyappa explained to a Brahman who served the liṅga while Tiṇṇanār was away hunting why he enjoyed Tiṇṇanār's abominable ritual, a lengthy explanation summed up by one example: "The water that he spits on us from his mouth, because it flows from the vessel made of love called his body, is more pure to us than even the Ganges and all auspicious tīrthas."[21] Anpu is the normal experience we have when our feeling, thinking, and speaking are unified in an attentiveness to another that we call infatuation, but infatuation for Śiva may carry one far beyond normal moral boundaries. For practical human purposes, Tiṇṇanār was mad, crazy, psychotic—out of touch with reality. Only the fact that the center of his fanatic attention was a liṅga made it tolerable to others, though nevertheless he remained useless to hunter society.

Third, the story tells us that not only was Tiṇṇanār "hooked" on Śiva, Śiva was himself "hooked" on Tiṇṇanār. Anpu, one might say, is a drug they shared in common. In order to show the Brahman what true bhakti is, Śiva created a situation that pushed Tiṇṇanār to express his love to the extreme, but Śiva himself could only take so much of it. A surfeit of anpu welled up within him and he brought the Nāyanār's extreme behaviour to a halt. The story is popular. Śiva made blood flow from his right eye. Tiṇṇanār tried everything he could to stop it, but only when he remembered the adage, "Put flesh on flesh," did he find the remedy. With an arrow he dug out his own eye and stuck it on the bleeding eye of the liṅga. Instantly the bleeding stopped. Like a madman Tiṇṇanār danced in a delirium of joy until Śiva made his left eye bleed and he immediately fell into an ocean of sorrow. Then he remembered his other eye. Delighted that he had the remedy so near at hand, he sat in front of the liṅga, put the sandal on his foot next to the bleeding eye to mark it, picked up an arrow, and put it to his remaining eye. But, Cēkkilār tells us,

> The Lord, a treasure of compassion, could not bear it. He opened the sacred mouth that had revealed the Vedas and Āgamas and graciously said, "Stop, darling of my eye. Stop, Kaṇṇappa. Stop stimulating my love, Kaṇṇappa," and reaching out from the liṅga, seized the hand holding the arrow.

The Lord then said, "Kaṇṇappa, you have pure bhakti. Come and stand at our right side" (see plate 41).[22]

The final point the story makes about anpu for Śiva is that it is connected with flesh and blood. In response to Śiva's bleeding eyes Tiṇṇanār gives his bleeding eyes and through their mingled blood Śiva reveals himself. Śiva's blood and the injury to his vision it implies evokes Tiṇṇanār's sacrifice of his vision which allows him finally to see truly. And Tiṇṇanār's own dismemberment of himself actually heals Śiva and provokes his response. Perhaps the old saying he follows, "flesh on flesh," means that to heal a god one must give one's own flesh and blood. But why would a god need healing? Perhaps because he has been injured physically through his icon, as is the case here, or because he has been injured through disparagement of his honor and status, as is the case in other stories. One would think the injurer would pay the price of healing, but the greatness of Tiṇṇanār's love is that though he had not injured the liṅga he joyfully paid the price to heal it with his own flesh and blood. When one gives one's own flesh and blood in love to heal God, God responds with love and one sees him—and to see him is to participate in him.

Kṛṣṇa told Arjuna, in the *Bhagavad Gītā,*

> Be it a leaf or flower or fruit or water that a zealous soul may offer Me with love's devotion, that do I accept, for it was love that made the offering . . . [T]hose who commune with Me in love's devotion abide in Me, and I in them.[23]

Sometime before the tenth century Tirumūla Nāyanār had made the same point about love in his *Tirumantiram:* "Those who say anpu and Śiva are two," he said, "do not understand. They do not know that anpu itself is the avatar of Śiva. But once they realize that anpu is indeed the avatar of Śiva, they themselves abide as Śiva in anpu."[24] Ārumuka Nāvalar repeated the point in the nineteenth century in his commentary on the story of Kaṇṇappa Nāyanār:

41. Tiṇṇaṉār, Saint Darling of My Eye (Kaṇṇappa Nāyaṉār), having healed Śiva's bleeding eye with one of his own, prepares to gouge out his remaining eye with an arrow, marking Śiva's second bleeding eye with his foot. A Brahman watches this Untouchable hunter as Śiva, overcome by his love, reaches out to restrain him. Photo by Dennis Hudson.

In the maturity of anpu that grows and ripens without interruption, Śiva is revealed. Anpu and Śiva, therefore, exist non-differently and not as two.[25]

The Nāyanār and Śiva share anpu in common and in that sharing there lies a mystery, the mystery of individual will and the divine will being two and yet not-two at the same time. Arjuna had been told of this mystery, too, but his love was not ripe enough to experience it. "In the region of the heart of all contingent beings dwells the Lord," Kṛṣṇa had told him, "twirling them hither and thither by his uncanny power like puppets mounted on a machine."[26] He who loves the Lord fully lets himself twirl with the twirling of the puppeteer, living in the fullest of satisfactions. Śaivas say that Arjuna experienced the climax of this love only when it ripened when he loved Śiva as Kaṇṇappa Nāyanār.

If this be the case, then love as participation accounts for the fierce, violent, and fanatic behaviour of the Nāyanārs. Their acts, it turns out, are not just their own; they are also the acts of Śiva and they reveal his nature to us—a nature that appears to us at times as mad.[27] The stories of the Nāyanārs, the Tamil scholar Mu. Arunācalam observes, are first of all stories of Śiva. It is the experience of being enslaved to Śiva, he says, that intoxicates the Nāyanārs and causes them to do all sorts of violent acts (*maṟam*). Bhakti makes them drunk and being drunk, he says, they are not responsible for what they do.[28] The responsibility, then, we might say, lies with the one who allowed them to get drunk, Śiva.

C. The Nāyanārs as Extensions of Śiva

By virtue of their love for Śiva, the Nāyanārs are extensions of Śiva. The emblems they wear—ash and rudrākṣa beads—are worn by Śiva and some Nāyanārs treat them as Śiva himself. The slaves of Śiva are to be regarded as Śiva in the same way the liṅga is—"moving" as opposed to "stationary" liṅgas. "Slavery" (āṭimai) is a metonym indicating that Śiva, like a medieval landowner, keeps slaves in the "field" of saṃsāra to do his work. These slaves, in fact, are miniature Śivas, human versions of the assembly of gaṇas that always surround the Lord,[29] though they are divinized humans usually, not incarnate divinities.[30] Insofar as the slaves act in accord with the master's will, the master is responsible for their actions. When slaves have anpu for their master, they know his will instinctively. Thus the actions that flow from this love, "criminal" as they may seem, belong both to the slaves and to the master.

Tamil Śaivism expresses this belief in the Nāyanārs as extensions of Śiva through the ritual of Māhēśvara Pūjā, a mode of worshipping one's guru (guru pūjā). On the anniversary of each saint's attainment of sāyujyam, devotees attend rituals in temples, and in their homes they worship and feed initiated slaves whom they call Māhēśvarar, "those who belong to the Great Lord Śiva," Maheśvara. The slave stands in for the Nāyanār who himself stands in for Śiva. In return the worshipers receive the grace of Śiva that flows through the Nāyanār by virtue of his anpu.[31]

The idea that various people are extensions of oneself is common among Tamils. Śiva, for example, is the Supreme Person whose full identity is expressed through a collection of other persons, each of whom looks like him and is yoked to him in sāyujyam by a shared love. The divine personality is collective. Valentine Daniel has recently analyzed the way Tamil villagers today view themselves as extended into other people, usually kin,[32] and the medieval *Periya Purāṇam* amply illustrates that same view. Without hesitation a Nāyanār will involve his wife and children in his fanatical commitment to the cult of Śiva as if they are modes of himself that he is giving to the Lord. His individuality, like Śiva's, is communal; his social self extends beyond his own bodily boundaries into the bodies of his kin.[33]

Now, such a close identification with a Nāyanār can prove beneficial to those family members who willingly enable him to fulfill his commitment to Śiva. They do not participate in Śiva as the Nāyanār does, but they do participate in the Nāyanār because they have anpu for him and that link suffices to pull them into mokṣa along with him. Thus the wife and son that Amarnīti Nāyanār gave away to a brahmacārin along with himself were granted sāyujyam, as was the wife of Saint Hostile Nature after she faithfully let herself be given to the lecherous Brahman, never doubting that her husband would defend him even to the point of butchering their kinsmen. Similarly, sāyujyam was given to the wife, son, and nurse in the household of Ciruttoṇṭar Nāyanār, "Saint Little Servant," after he and they had killed his son, cooked him, and sat down to eat him together with a slave of Śiva (see plate 42).[34] So also the wife of Arivāṭṭāya Nāyanār went to Śiva's realm with him because she enabled him to fulfill his commitment to feed Śiva ripe paddy, red greens, and young mangoes, despite increasing famine and their own hunger, and even though it was she who stumbled and caused him to spill his offerings into a crack in the parched ground

42. Saint Little Servant (Ciruttoṇṭar Nāyanār) and his wife joyfully prepare their only son to be cooked and served to the *sādhu* in the upper left; he sets aside his son's head as unsuitable for eating. Photo by Dennis Hudson.

—a failure he dealt with by trying to slit his own throat.

We all know, however, that it is not easy to live with a saint and the Nāyanārs amply illustrate that fact, too. One, for example, tried to sell his wife to buy oil for temple lamps; one chopped his wife's hand off because she hesitated to wash the feet of a slave of Śiva who used to be their servant; one, a Chola king, chopped his queen's nose off because he mistakenly thought she had smelled a flower that was for Śiva's pūjā (the poor woman had already lost her hand to another mistaken saint); and one divorced his wife instantly because she blew a spider off a Śiva liṅga. And reversing the hierarchy, one Nāyanār chopped his father's feet off because he kicked over a pot of Śiva's milk.

The basis for these violent acts of devotion, I think, is the communal notion of the self. In each case—except the killing and cooking of his son by Saint Little Servant—the Nāyanār was compensating for what he perceived as an injury to Śiva, an offense that he had committed through the action of someone who represented him. The story of Saint Hostile Nature makes this mode of thinking explicit. When relatives on both sides of his family tried to stop him from letting the lecherous Brahman take his wife away, their argument was not based on the individual happiness or suffering of the wife who had been given away, but on the effect his crazy act would have on the social position of the family. The Nāyanār embodied the collective identity of the family just as the family embodied his identity—which is why he so readily butchered them all. Whatever in "himself" stands in the way of serving Śiva will be lopped off. Once lopped off, the crime will not spread to the rest of the "body"; the bloody sacrifice, it seems, creates a shield of purity around it.

This explains the removal of hands and noses, and even divorce. But in those cases where the crime has drenched the gross material body (*stūla śarīra*), the entire body will have to be sacrificed in order to cleanse the subtle material body inside it (*sūkṣma śarīra*).[35] For example, the relatives whom Saint Hostile Nature slaughtered after he gave his wife to the lecherous Brahman were cleansed enough to go to heaven in their subtle bodily forms, as were the relatives and servants whom Saint Ferocious Tiger beheaded after they had eaten the paddy set aside for Śiva.

The most telling example, however, is the story of Vicāra Sarma, better known as Caṇḍēśvara Nāyanār. His Brahman father thought that Vicāra Sarma was wasting the milk intended for the fire sacrifices by playing priest and pouring it over a sand liṅgam. He was wrong, of course, for Vicāra Sarma was mentally performing the ritual service of Śiva according to the Āgamas, and when his father angrily kicked over the pot of milk set aside for the ritual bath, the boy immediately took a stick (which turned into a sword) and chopped his father's feet off. Then he resumed the mental rituals. Although his father had committed an enormously grievous injury to Śiva, the mutilation he received from his son while he was absorbed in worship cleansed the father of his sin and he went to Śiva's realm. And although in principle Vicāra Sarma had in one stroke murdered his father, a Brahman, and his guru—the worst of crimes—no crime stuck to him. The anpu that filled his mind at the time and the actions it propelled served, it seems, to dissolve them instantly. Śiva—who himself had once been guilty of Brahmanicide—adopted him as his son and gave him a share in all his offerings by appointing him to the prestigious realm of Caṇḍēśvara.[36]

D. Love and Self-Slaughter

The idea that the slaughter of a sin-drenched outer body purifies the inner body explains why a Nāyanār kills himself when he thinks he has in someway injured Śiva. Tirukkurripputoṇṭa Nāyanār, the "Saint who Served the Sacred Will," for example, was a washerman who washed the rags of Śiva's slaves. Śiva appeared to him in the guise of a skinny slave who wanted his rag washed and told the washerman that he would suffer from the cold if the rag was not washed and dried before sundown. Then as the man washed, Śiva made it rain so that the rag would not dry before nightfall. The Nāyanār was so full of grief for having made a slave suffer out of his desire to serve him that he tried to kill himself by bashing his head against the washing stone. The Nāyanār believed that the slave he had injured was actually Śiva, which he was, and he presumably thought that by bashing in his head his blood would heal the injury he had done to the Lord. In the process he would protect his inner body from the crime.

Then there is Kaliya Nāyanār, an oil-presser, who served Śiva by keeping lamps lit in his temple day and night. After awhile Śiva decided to show others the strength of this Nāyanār's absolute love and graciously wiped away all of his wealth. The Nāyanār continued to supply oil through various degrading means until one day it was time to light the lamps and he had none. Unable to give up the satisfaction of serving Śiva according to his commitment, he chose to kill himself in the act of service. He put wicks in the lamp bowls, arranged them carefully, took a knife, and in order to substitute his blood for the missing oil, cut his throat. His blood, he probably knew, would not burn, but the absolute love it expressed would be an honor for Śiva.

There is no suggestion in the stories that the Nāyanārs killed themselves for the sake of a better rebirth, but the love that motivated their act cleansed them nevertheless for Śiva took them all to sāyujyam, either just before or just after they did themselves in. When the saint turns the sword against himself out of love for Śiva, therefore, he purifies himself of his failure in the service of his lord and heals the injury his failure has caused him. Self-slaughter is the extreme version of lopping off the offending limb to keep the rest of the body pure, only in this case, of course, there is no limb leftover to be pure, only the *ātman* embodied in subtle matter and ready for the next birth.

Why did the Nāyanārs choose bloody ways to kill themselves? Most used a knife or a sword and one bashed his head on a rock. Only one chose the more seemly act of stepping into a fire. There were, after all, other ways to do it. They could have followed the Jainas in self-starvation, for example, or they could have performed a ritual drowning as did a Chalukyan king in 1068.[37]

They chose bloody deaths, I think, because of the ancient Tamil belief that in blood and death the sacred power that regenerates life reveals itself,[38] a sensibility that is also Vedic.[39] The stories express the belief that through blood spilled for sacred purposes, whether in human sacrifices or animal sacrifices or in warfare, Śiva can be seen by those who possess anpu. Cultic models for bloody sacrifices abounded in the medieval period. The Chola and other dynasties expanded their rule through bloody warfare that was itself viewed as a sacrificial ritual to regenerate the dynasty and kingdom. The self-sacrifice of humans for God and king was present in literature and art and, according to E. A. Gait, a male child was sacrificed every Friday night to Kālī at the great Chola temple in Tanjore.[40] Orders of sādhus like the Kāpālikas who used blood and flesh in their sādhanas were common and Śiva, whom they imitated, had been viewed by some as a sacrificer of animals to whom animals were sacrificed. Some of Śiva's liṅgas had once received animal sacrifices, though during the Pallava and Chola periods priests guided by the Śiva Āgamas took animal sacrifices out of the temples housing the liṅga[41]—just as the classical Vedic liturgists had removed the animal sacrifice from the precincts of the fire—and left them for subordinate powers on the boundaries.

But the tradition of blood sacrifice to Śiva has continued in the stories of the Nāyanārs, even though the Āgamas they exalt had abolished it in the service of the liṅga. Instead of sacrificing a buffalo or goat, however, the Nāyanār took the sword directly on his own neck, or in his own gut, spilling his blood to purify himself and to heal Śiva of the injury he had sustained through the devotee's failure. And the Nāyanārs likewise regenerated Śiva's rule by expanding his cult, making themselves and others victims of devout violence in the process. Saint Guard of the Family, Kulaccirai Nāyanār, for example, was a Pandyan prime minister devoted to Saint Tirujñānasambandar, the successful defender of Śiva against the Jainas. At his master's instruction Saint Guard of the Family impaled eight thousand Jainas because they had reviled Śiva and had defiled his monastery in Madurai (see plate 43).

The result is an "inner conflict of tradition," in J. C. Heesterman's terms.[47] A cult that has no blood and death in its ritual service of Śiva in the temple, in the caryā and kriyā prescribed by the Āgamas, has stories about paradigmatic devotees who serve it, protect it, and expand it through blood and death. The Āgamic temple, representing Śiva's world without death, is grounded in the Chola kingdom, representing the world of life and death. The stories tell us that saints who live as householders in the life and death world ruled by kings may attain Śiva's deathless world through an *excess* of love, a *drunkenness*, that Śiva intentionally creates to make them go berserk and commit acts of blood and death. In Nāvalar's terms, the Path of Action in the temple with its non-violent and bloodless caryā and kriyā please Śiva, but the Path of Bhakti in the household and kingdom with its blood and death delights him even more. This inner conflict of the Tamil Śaiva tradition is resolved only by Śiva when he generates in his devotees the experience of anpu.

It is, after all, not the act of blood and death that gives Śiva his satisfaction. It is the emotional intensity of anpu driven to the excess of blood and death that pleases him—the intensely deep and orgasmic feeling that emerges when, to paraphrase Valentine Daniel, pain passes into the anpu that is Śiva.[43] Blood and death in Tamil and Vedic thought are connected with seed and birth, so that the blood of the sacrifice and the uterine blood of conception go hand-in-hand.[44] This intense feeling of anpu for Śiva, therefore, is potentially present both in bloody sacrifice and in sexual union, a fact that calls to mind the statement of a Kāpālika sādhu—a member of that order of monks which specialized in lopping off pieces of themselves and the heads of others and in sexual union to attain purity, power, and mokṣa—who said, "The bliss which becomes manifest through sexual union is the (true) form of Bhairava. The attainment of that (bliss) at death is mokṣa."[45] But it is noteworthy that while the Nāyanārs find Śiva in

43. Saint Guard of the Family (Kulaccirai Nāyanār), Pandyan prime minister, impales eight thousand Jainas for having reviled Śiva and having defiled his monastery at Madurai. Photo by Dennis Hudson.

blood and death, no story portrays them finding him in sexual union; in that respect, at least, they are not tantric.

Now, one question insists on emerging from this discussion. If the Nāyanār is a mode of Śiva in our midst, would he not cause enormous injury to Śiva if he killed himself? Our final story is especially instructive in this matter. It is the story of Eripatta Nāyanār, "Saint Cutting Devotion," and Pukalccōla Nāyanār, the "Celebrated Chola Saint." The Saint of Cutting Devotion used his battle-ax to chop up anyone who disrupted the slaves of Śiva in their service. On the first day of Mahānavamī, a festival for God and king,[46] a devotee was taking his usual basket of flowers to the Ānilai Temple in the Koṅgu capital. The king's royal elephant, while rushing to its bath with its five grooms, seized the basket and scattered the flowers. The Saint of Cutting Devotion appeared on the scene, learned what had happened, took out after the elephant, chopped off its trunk, and chopped the five grooms to death. The Nāyanār had defended bloodily the kingdom of Śiva over against the encroachments of an earthly king represented by his elephant and grooms.

The significant twist in the story is that the king, too, is a Nāyanār; and because the elephant and the grooms—especially during the Mahānavamī festival—are extensions of himself as king, he feels that it is he who has injured Śiva.

As soon as the "Celebrated Chola Saint" heard that his elephant and its grooms had been slaughtered, he rushed to the spot with his army and found a single man standing there dressed in the garb of Śiva. He realized that the elephant must have done something wrong to bring the saint to such anger and when the saint told him that the elephant had scattered the flowers of Śiva and that the grooms had not stopped him and so he killed them all, the king grew anxious. Venerating the warrior-saint he said,

> It isn't enough to kill the elephant and the grooms for the grievous crime of harming the slaves of Śiva. You must kill me too. But your own auspicious sword is more than I, a great criminal, deserve. It's not right to use it. Please use my own sword to kill me with.

And he held it out to him. Saint Cutting Devotion was astonished at the king's great love and hesitated to take the sword until he realized that the king might kill himself with it. The king then venerated the warrior-saint and said, "If this Śiva bhakta kills me with the sword, my sin will be removed." But when Cutting Devotion heard that, he anxiously thought to himself,

> This celebrated Chola king hadn't the slightest sorrow when he learned why his royal elephant and its grooms died and he handed me his own sword and asked me to kill him—and I meant to give him trouble! The only thing to do is to kill myself first.

So Cutting Devotion proceeded to cut his own throat with the king's sword. Startled, the king quickly intervened, grabbed his arm and the sword, and stopped him (see plate 44).

I think we now have the answer as to why, if a Nāyanār is a mode of Śiva, he would kill himself. It is because a Nāyanār sees only other slaves of Śiva as Śiva, he does not see himself that way. The king believed he would be purified if Saint Cutting Devotion slew him for it would actually be Śiva's grace expressed as death. But Saint Cutting Devotion did not want the king to kill himself because he saw the king as Śiva. This is the mystery of sharing anpu with Śiva: Śiva always appears as the other person whom one loves, even in sāyujyam. He never appears to oneself *as* oneself. Only others can recognize oneself as Śiva. Even if a Nāyanār looked in a mirror he would see Śiva in the costume he wears and himself as the one who wears it. Thus these two Nāyanārs, each thinking himself the criminal and the other Śiva, prevented each other from committing bloody suicide. By killing themselves they meant to purify themselves of crimes against Śiva; by preventing the suicide of the other they meant to keep Śiva from harm.

The story ends suggestively. Śiva resurrects the elephant and the five grooms and they go on to the palace with the king. The scattered flowers return to the basket and the devotee continues on to the temple. Saint Cutting Devotion continues in his warrior-like service to Śiva and eventually becomes the chief of Śiva's assembly in Kailāsa. And the Celebrated Chola Saint finally does manage to kill himself. One day, when his soldiers brought back the heads of those they had killed while attacking a ruler who refused to send the king tribute, the king spotted one head with matted locks on its top. He recognized it as the head of a slave of Śiva and—on the basis that the soldiers were extended modes of himself—he realized immediately that he had only one option. After turning his kingdom over to his son, he put the head in a golden pot, put the pot on his head, circumambulated a blazing fire, and while uttering the Five-Syllable Mantra, stepped into the fire and emerged in Śiva's realm (see plate 45).

44. Saint Cutting Devotion (Eripatta Nāyanār) cuts the trunk of the royal elephant and dismembers a groom (at the left) and then tries to slit his own throat (at the right). He is restrained by the king, Saint Celebrated Chola. Photo by Dennis Hudson.

45. Saint Celebrated Chola (Pukalccōla Nāyanār) sits as ruler and sees a basket of heads brought from battle (background); then, while royal officials watch, he carries on his head the head of a Śiva devotee found in the basket and prepares to immolate himself in a fire (foreground). Photo by Dennis Hudson.

It is significant that the king performed a mode of self-immolation prescribed for a wife, especially a warrior's wife, when her husband has died away from home.[47] Holding a piece of his clothing or his body, she is to burn herself on a pyre. In this case the husband's corpse is represented by the bhakta's head in the golden pot and the wife is the king. Does this mean that we are to regard the anpu of the Nāyanārs as a version of pativrata, of absolute faithfulness to one's husband? If so, then the Nāyanārs, almost all of whom are male and householders, are masculine versions of a Tamil belief about women: Their loving faithfulness to their master gives them a sacred power that can be destructive or salvific. They are faithful to Śiva in the same way their own wives are faithful to them. Śiva, in turn, treats them in the same way they treat their own wives—as an extension of himself, as an instrument of his will, as a slave to do his bidding, as a means for achieving paroxysms of pleasure, and as a companion in sharing anpu.

E. Conclusion

This brings us back to our beginning. When Cēkkilār composed the *Periya Purāṇam* to wean the Chola king away from the *Jīvaka Cintāmaṇi*, he changed the flavor of erotic love, sṛṅgāra rasa, into the flavor of devotional love, anpu rasa. He drew upon an old tradition of Śaiva ecstasy, one that had developed, I suspect, from the intense flood of feeling generated deep in the psyche by the cult of blood and death as it had been filtered through Vedic and Āgamic myths and practices. From the point of view of the Āgamas, the crucial element that defined this blood-begotten ecstasy as divine rather than as demonic (or as secular psychosis) was its focus on the liṅga, or on the guru, or on the slaves of Śiva. From the point of view of those in whom this ecstasy was begotten, it was the Śiva of the Āgamas who revealed himself in it.

Cēkkilār also showed his king, Kulōttuṅga II, that instead of looking forward to the end of his rule as the time for a full participation in the religious life, as Jīvaka did in the *Cintāmaṇi*, his daily life in the midst of kingship would be sacred as long as the service of Śiva's cult remained at its center. He provided the king with seventy-two concrete illustrations of what Kṛṣṇa had taught Arjuna in the *Bhagavad Gītā*.

He illustrated one other belief as well. The idea that Śiva's anpu transubstantiates the lover, as it did in the case of Kaṇṇappa Nāyanār, explains the sense in which the king was himself Śiva. The ancient idea of the king as god had continued among the medieval Cholas. By the seventh century it had emerged in iconography, for the Pallava king Mahēndravarmā I, in his cave-temple in Trichy, had sculpted his own portrait as the face of Śiva receiving the Ganges. His Pallava heirs, in their Sōmaskanda panels, portrayed themselves as Śiva and their crown prince as Skanda.[48] And the Cholas built temples whose liṅga bore a title that referred simultaneously to Śiva and to the king—Rājarājēśvara, for example, or Rājēndracōlīśvara, or Gaṅgaikoṇḍacōlīśvara.[49]

The implication of this idea is that Śiva dwells immanently in the mind and person of the king.[50] Cēkkilār explains that this is because of anpu—an anpu that the king may consciously cultivate and/or that may be present in him by virtue of an initiation (dīkṣā). The king is an extension of Śiva in the same way the Nāyanārs are and thus his acts are, like theirs, the acts of Śiva in this world. The king who is the slave of Śiva is Śiva to the world; all of his acts are the turning of himself with the puppet wheel Śiva turns, even when those acts are violent and fanatical.

What fanatical acts did Kulōttuṅga II perform out of devotion to Śiva? The worshipers of Viṣṇu from the Chola region remember two. While renovating the Chidambaram temple, he removed the icon of Viṣṇu who reclined there and threw it in the sea.[51] He also drew the blood of a devotee of Viṣṇu. Seeking to make the Vaiṣṇavas in Śrī Raṅgam, the cultic rival to Chidambaram, acknowledge Śiva as supreme, he summoned the famous scholar and devotee of Viṣṇu, Rāmānuja, to his court.[52] When a surrogate for Rāmānuja arrived, Kulōttuṅga insisted that he proclaim in writing that Śiva is the Supreme Lord. But the scholarly sādhu cunningly maintained his faithfulness to Viṣṇu by writing a pun on the word "Śiva" to make Viṣṇu the Lord of Śiva. Thinking perhaps of Kaṇṇappa Nāyanār who had sacrificed his eyes to heal Śiva, Kulōttuṅga had the sādhu's eyes taken out, his attempt probably to purify the sādhu of his "blindness" and to heal the injured Lord he deeply loved.

NOTES

1. The fullest discussion of Cēkkilār, on which the following is based, is given by Mu. Araṇācalam, *Tamil Ilakkiya Varalāru: Panniranṭām Nūrrāṇṭu*, 2 vols. (Tiruccirrampalam-Māyūram: Kanti Vittiyālayam, 1973), vol. 1, 103-337. The dates for kings and temples, however, follow Michael W. Meister, ed., M. A. Dhaky coordinator, *Encyclopaedia of Indian Temple Architecture: South India: Lower Drāviḍadēsa* (200 B.C.-A.D. 1324), Texts and Plates in 2 vols. (New Delhi:

American Institute of Indian Studies; Philadelphia: University of Pennsylvania, 1983), where discussion of Kulōttuṅga II is given in vol. I, 291 [cited henceforth as *Encyclopaedia*]. Traditional information about Cēkkilār comes from the *Cēkkilār Cuvāmikaḷ Purāṇam* written in one hundred and three verses by Umāpati Śivācārya in the beginning of the fourteenth century. Cēkkilār's given name was Arunmōli Tēvar, but he is remembered by the name of his Vēḷāḷa lineage, Cēkkilār.

2. The story is summarized by Appaswami Chakravarti, *Jaina Literature in Tamil*, Jñānapīṭha Mūrtidēvī Granthamālā: English Series 3, First Revised Edition (New Delhi: Bhāratīya Jñānapīṭha Publication, 1974; first ed. 1941), 63-83. The number sixty-three assigned to the Nāyanārs is symbolic, for there are actually seventy-two, and one of that number consists of three thousand Brahmans known simply as "Those who live in Tillai," another name for Chidambaram. If one adds Śiva as the sixty-forth Nāyanār, one has a symbol of totality analogous to the sixty-four heroes whom the Jainas celebrate in their own "Great Purāṇa," the *Mahāpurāṇa* or *Śrī Purāṇa*.

Puṣpadanta in 959-965 composed a *Mahāpurāṇa* in Apabhraṃśa verse on the lives of the sixty-three Jaina heroes. Jīnasēnācārya and Guṇabhadra composed the Sanskrit *Mahāpurāṇa* or *Triśastilakṣaṇa-Mahāpurāṇa* about the end of the ninth century (consisting of the *Ādipurāṇa* and the *Uttarapurāṇa*). Cāmuṇḍarāya composed the Kannada version of the *Mahāpurāṇa* in 977. See Krishna Kanta Handiqui, *Yaśastilaka and Indian Culture: Or, Somadeva's Yaśastilaka and Aspects of Jainism and Indian Thought and Culture in the Tenth Century* (Sholapur: Jaina Saṃskṛti Saṃrakshaka Sangha, 1949), 3; Chakravarti, *Jaina Literature*, 63-64, n. 2; and S. Vaiyāpura Pillai in *Śrī Purāṇam*, K. V. Venkatarājūlu Reddiyār ed., Madras University Tamil Department Publication, No. 14, 2nd ed. (Madras: University of Madras, 1946), xi.

3. Michael Lockwood, *Mamallapuram and the Pallavas* (Madras: The Christian Literature Society, 1982), 95-96.

4. In Tiruppaṇṭāl. See K. Veḷḷaivāraṇan, *Pannirutirumurai Varalāru: Iraṇṭām Pakuti*, Part II (8-12 Tirumuraikaḷ) (Annamalaip Palkalaikkalakam, 1980), Appendix 2. The *Encyclopaedia* places this temple before 1000 but gives almost no information about it.

5. He may have included illustrations of more Nāyanārs, but the fresco paintings are destroyed. See *Encyclopaedia* I, 238.

6. The Amṛtaghaṭēśvara temple in Melaikkaṭampūr, built before 1113. See *Encyclopaedia*, 296-97.

7. The Rājarājēśvara temple, known as Airāvatēśvara temple, in Dārāsuram. See *Encyclopaedia*, 299-304. *Veḷḷaivāraṇan, Pannirutirumurai Varalāru*, II, Appendix 1, discusses these sculptures, with photos.

8. Ārumuka Nāvalar, *Tiruttoṇṭar Periyapurāṇam: Itu karrōrum marrōrumākiya yāvarukkum eḷitilē payanpatumporuṭṭu, Nallūr Ārumukanāvalaravarkaḷ kattiya rūpamākac ceytu* (Cennapaṭṭaṇam: Citamparam Caivappirakācavittiyācālait Tarumapari-

pālakar, 1933 [15th printing], p. 2 of text [henceforth cited as *Tiruttoṇṭar Periya-purāṇam*].

9. The twenty-four Nāyanārs who represent this fierce, violent, and fanatical devotion are listed here according to the type of act they performed:

Injury or death ot oneself out of service to Śiva's slaves: Ēnātināta, Meypporuḷ, and Pukalccōla were faithful to the ashes and beads that Śiva's slaves wear; Tirukkurripputoṇṭa was faithful to the slaves' needs. *Injury or death to oneself* out of service to the liṅga: Kaṇampulla, Kaliya, Mūrtti, Kaṇṇappar, Ēyarkōn Kalikkāma, and Sundaramūrtti.

Injury to oneself and one's kin out of service to the slaves of Śiva: Amarnīti, Mānakkañcāra, and Kalikkāma. *Injury to oneself and one's kin* out of service to the liṅga: Atipatta, Tirunīlanakka, Arivāṭṭāya, Ceruttuṇai, Kalarciṅka, and Caṇḍēśvarar.

Killing one's kin out of service to the slave of Śiva: Ciruttoṇṭar, Iyarpakai, and Kōṭpuli.

Injury or killing non-kin out of service to the slaves of Śiva: Catti; out of service to the liṅga: Eripatta.

10. See Ārumuka Nāvalar, *Periyapurāṇam enru valaṅkukira Tiruttoṇṭarpurāṇam, Cēkkilārnāyanār aruḷcceytatu: Ikatu Yālppāṇattu Nallūr Ārumukanāvalaravarkaḷāl Kāraik-kalammaiyār Purāṇamvaraiyil paricōtittu, ovvorupurāṇattukkum irutiyil avarkaḷāl elutup-paṭṭa cūcanttōṭu* (Cennapaṭṭaṇam: Mērpaṭiyūr Catācivappiḷḷai, 1884), citing this Śaiva tradition on p. 130 [henceforth cited as *Tirruttoṇṭarpurāṇam*]. The story of Śiva as the hunter occurs in *Mahābhārata* 3.39-42; see J. A. B. van Buitenen, tr., *The Mahābhārata*, vol. 2 (Chicago: University of Chicago Press, 1975), 298-305.

11. These six orders of sādhus are: the Śaiva Siddhāntin, Pāśupata, Vāma, Bhairava, Māhāvrata, and Kālāmukha. See Vedajñāna, *Śaivāgamaparibhāṣā-mañjarī: Le Florilège de la Doctrine Śivaïte*, Critical Edition, trans. and notes by Bruno Dagens, Publications de l'Institute Français d'Indologie, No. 60 (Pondicherry: Institut Français d'Indologie, 1979), 68-69, n. 20. See also M. Winslow, *Winslow's A Comprehensive Tamil and English Dictionary* (1862; New Delhi: Asian Educational Services, 1981), 404: "*camayam: utcamayam.*"

12. *Bhagavad Gītā* VII.1; R. C. Zaehner, tr., *The Bhagavad Gītā: With a Commentary Based on the Original Sources* (London: Oxford University Press, 1969).

13. See Ārumuka Nāvalar, *Tiruttoṇṭarpurāṇam*, pp. 128 and 132. The *Bhāgavata Purāṇa* III.25.32-34 provides a similar discussion of this kind of bhakti: Swami Tapasyananda, tr., *Srimad Bhagavata: The Holy Book of God*, 4 vols. (Madras: Sri Ramakrishna Math, 1980-1982), 258-59.

14. All the Nāyanār stories discussed here are based on their Tamil prose rendering by Ārumuka Nāvalar, *Tiruttoṇṭar Periyapurāṇam*, with reference to the original poem by Cēkkilār Cuvāmikaḷ, *Tiruttoṇṭarkaḷ Carittiramennum Periya-purāṇam Vacanakāviyam: Tiruvuruvap paṭaṅkaḷuṭan* (Madras: B. Irattina Nāyakar and Sons, 1967).

15. The six illustrations for this article, representing a type of art commonly

found in Tamil Hindu books of the nineteenth and early twentieth centuries, are reproduced from *Periyapurāṇam Vācanakāviyam* [The *Periya Purāṇam* in Prose], published in Madras in 1967 by B. Ratna Nayakar Sons. The artist is not identified. The text of this version of the purāṇa is largely that of Ārumuka Nāvalar and the illustrations, like his text, may date from the later half of the nineteenth century. A valuable introduction to the style of art which, among other things, portrays several centers of interest simultaneously, is Judith Mara Gutman, *Through Indian Eyes: 19th and 20th Century Photography from India* (New York: Oxford University Press; International Center of Photography, 1982).

16. Cf. David Dean Shulman, *Tamil Temple Myths: Sacrifice and Divine Marriage in the South Indian Śaiva Tradition* (Princeton: Princeton University Press, 1980), 158-59, discussing the story of Saint Hostile Nature as an allegory for the soul.

17. Ārumuka Nāvalar, *Tiruttoṇṭarpurāṇam*, p. 4.

18. Emmons E. White, *The Wisdom of the Tamil People* (New Delhi: Munshiram Manoharlal, 1975), 58-70, gives his translation of this story from the *Periya Purāṇam* as "The Holy Hunter."

19. Ārumuka Nāvalar, *Tiruttoṇṭarpurāṇam*, p. 130.

20. Glenn E. Yocum, *Hymns to the Dancing Śiva: A Study of Maṇikkavācakar's Tiruvācakam* (Columbia, Missouri: South Asia Books, 1982), 180-94, discusses this same madness and possession with reference to Maṇikkavācakar.

21. The explanation in Nāvalar's prose retelling reads: "His entire nature is nothing less than the nature of love for us. All of his knowledge is knowledge of us. All of his deeds are done for our pleasure. The sandal on his foot that he uses to remove the flowers you place on our head gives us much more joy than even the foot of our son Subrahmaṇya. The water that he spits on us from his mouth, because it flows from the vessel made of love called his body, is purer to us than even the Ganges and all auspicious tīrthas. The flowers that he brings tucked in his hair to adorn us, because they fall on us in the way his true love blossoms and falls, are in no way equalled by the flowers that Brahmā, Viṣṇu, and the other gods adorn us with. The meat that he prepares for us, because he melts it with love wondering if it is cooked tenderly and because he chews and tastes it with gentle feelings, is much sweeter to us than the oblations offered to us by those who perform the Vedic sacrifices. The words he speaks to us while standing in our presence, because they emerge with a pure love that knows no one else but us, are much more delicious to us than all the Vedas and hymns of praise that munis sing to us in exaltation."

22. Nāvalar's rendering of *Periya Purāṇam* 10.183.

23. *Bhagavad Gītā* IX.26-34. Zaehner's translation.

24. Tirumūla Nāyanār, *Tirumantiram* 257; see *Tirumantiram: Mūvāyiram*, 2 vols., P. Irāmanāta Piḷḷai elutiya viḷḷakkamum; A. Citamparanār elutiya kurippum (Madras: Tirunelvēli, Tenintiya Caivacittānta Nūrpatippuk Kalakam, Limited, 1979, 1980).

25. Ārumuka Nāvalar, *Tiruttoṇṭarpurāṇam*, p. 129.

26. *Bhagavad Gītā* XVIII.62. Zaehner's translation.

27. For a discussion of this mad behaviour, see Yocum, *Hymns to the Dancing Śiva*, 144-49.

28. Aruṇācalam, *Tamil Ilakkiya Varalāru*, 227-28.

29. The ninth century Pallava sculpture of Kaṇṇappa Nāyanār, in fact, places him among Śiva's gaṇas. See Lockwood, *Mamallapuram and the Pallavas*, 95-96.

30. Sundaramūrtti Nāyanār, for example, was a reborn resident of Kailāsa. In this respect the Nāyanārs differ from the Śrī Vaiṣṇava Ālvārs, all of whom are believed to be avatars of aspects of Viṣṇu.

31. Ārumuka Nāvalar describes this as "Guru Pūjā" in *Tiruttoṇṭar Periya-purāṇam*, 22-24. Aruṇācalam discusses it as "Māhēśvara Pūjā" in *Tamil Ilakkiya Varalāru*, 328-39, where he also describes the popular celebration of "Saint Little Servant," Ciruttoṇṭar Nāyanār.

32. E. Valentine Daniel, *Fluid Signs: Being a Person the Tamil Way* (Berkeley: University of California Press, 1984).

33. The *Śiva Purāṇa* provides an instructive illustration of the notion of the extended self in the story of Satī, Śiva's wife. She has to respond to her father's verbal abuse of her husband, an enormous injury to him, she thinks. So she decides to kill herself, she says, because her body has become drenched with sin by hearing these terrible words, just as her father has by speaking them. She could purify both of them if she cut off his tongue, she notes, but she is not strong enough and he, after all, is her father. So she cleanses herself of his crime (which is now hers by absorption through the ears) by setting her polluted body on fire through Yoga, turning it to ash. About twenty thousand of her attendants follow her by cutting off their own limbs, heads, or faces. Her father she leaves to be "purified" by Śiva himself. See *Śiva Purāṇa: Rudra-saṃhitā* 29.38-41; 30.20-21, in J. L. Shastri, ed., The *Śiva Purāṇa*, tr. A. Board of Scholars, 4 vols., Ancient Indian Tradition and Mythology Series (Delhi: Motilal Banarsidass, 1969-1970), vol. 1, 412, 416.

There are two explanations for this behaviour of Satī and her attendants, I think. One is that all of them had heard her father's reviling words and thus were drenched with his crime, but not being able to cut out his tongue, they cleansed themselves through self-slaughter. The story itself makes this explanation obvious. The other less obvious one is that Satī viewed herself as both an extension of her father and of her husband, while her attendants viewed themselves as extensions of her. Her father's words had injured Śiva, though he did not actually hear them, because Śiva was represented by her; but since she also represented her father, his verbal injury of Śiva was also hers. Extended into two different males, she represented both. She could cleanse both herself and her father by cutting out his tongue, but she was both weak and his daughter and it was out of the question. Her alternative was to burn up her outer body drenched with the sin to purify her inner body, unlinking herself from her father while reaffirming her link with her husband. Her attendants, who shared in her pollution, cleansed themselves by hacking themselves to death, thereby reaffirming their link to her, and through her to her husband.

34. George L. Hart, III, "The Little Devotee: Cēkkilār's Story of Ciruttoṇṭar," in M. Nagatomi, B. K. Matilal, J. M. Masson, and E. Dimock, eds., *Sanskrit and Indian Studies* (New York: Reidel Publishing Company, 1979), 217-36, translates and discusses this popular story. Asim Roy discusses a Muslim parallel to it in *The Islamic Syncretistic Tradition in Bengal* (Princeton: Princeton University Press, 1983), 245-48.

35. Valentine Daniel discusses the Tamil perception of these distinctions in the "body" in *Fluid Signs*, 278-87.

36. The story is of Śiva as Bhairava who chopped off Brahmā's fifth head and had to perform the Kāpālika sādhana as penance. See *Śiva Purāṇa: Śatarudrasaṃhitā* 8 in Shastri, ed., *The Śiva Purāṇa*, vol. 3, 1097-1110. See also E. Visuvalingam and Lorenzen in this volume.

37. Sōmēśvara I performed *paramayoga* due to an incurable disease. See *Encyclopaedia* I, 226.

38. See George L. Hart, III, "The Nature of Tamil Devotion," in Madhav M. Deshpande and Peter Edwin Hook, eds., *Aryan and Non-Aryan in India*, Michigan Papers on South and Southeast Asia, No. 14 (Ann Arbor: Center for South and Southeast Asian Studies, The University of Michigan, 1979), 11-33; and Shulman, *Tamil Temple Myths*, chapter 3.

39. J. C. Heesterman, "The Case of the Severed Head," *The Inner Conflict of Tradition* (Chicago: University of Chicago Press, 1985), 45-58.

40. In the description of Indra's festival in the *Cilappatikāram*, warriors sacrifice their heads in the temple and hunter-warriors offer theirs to Durgā. See Ilaṅgo Āḍigaḷ, *Shilappadikaram (The Ankle Bracelet)*, tr. Alain Danielou (New York: New Directions Publishing Corporation, 1965), 19-20, 83. E. A. Gait mentions human sacrifices in Tanjore: "Human Sacrifice (Indian)," *Encyclopaedia of Religion and Ethics*, ed. James Hastings (New York: Charles Scribner's Sons, 1908-1927), vol. 4 (1914), 850a.

41. Archaeological excavations of the liṅgam at Guḍimallam (a shrine near the Kāḷahasti mountain where Kaṇṇappa Nāyanār sacrificed animals and his own eyes to the liṅgam) reveals bones around the liṅgam, offered to Śiva who is portrayed on the liṅgam as an animal sacrificer in the Vedic tradition. See I. K. Sarma, "New Light from Gudimallam Excavation," *Ananthacharya Indological Research Institute Series*, No. 11, Proceedings of the Seminar on "Symbolism in Temple Art and Architecture" held in February, 1981, ed. K. K. A. Venkatachari (Bombay: Ananthacharya Indological Research Institute, 1982), 31-50.

42. Or, an "irredeemable contradiction" as he names it on p. 58 of Heesterman, *Inner Conflict*.

43. Daniel analyzes a contemporary experience of this in *Fluid Signs*, 268-70. Animal slaughter and eros is also brought out in the story of Kṛṣṇa slaying seven bulls to win Pinnai as his bride. A thirteenth century commentator on the phrase from an Ālvār poem that says of Kṛṣṇa, "He seized seven bulls," observes:

> He expects in the next moment to grasp her and therefore, just as if he is embracing her already, he joins himself to the bulls. Because killing them is the means by which he obtains her, he is joined to their horns (*kompu*) just as if he were united with this girl slim as a twig (*kompu*), and he enjoys it.

Slightly revised translation from Dennis Hudson, "Pinnai, Krishna's Cowherd Wife," in John Stratton Hawley and Donna Marie Wulff, eds., *The Divine Consort: Rādhā and the Goddesses of India*, Berkeley Religious Studies Series (Berkeley: Graduate Theological Union, 1982), 251.

44. See Shulman, *Tamil Temple Myths*, 93-109.

45. Quoted by David N. Lorenzen, *The Kāpālikas and Kālāmukhas: Two Lost Śaivite Sects* (Berkeley: University of California Press, 1972), 91.

46. See Burton Stein, "Mahānavamī: Medieval and Modern Kingly Ritual in South India," in Bardwell L. Smith, ed., *Essays on Gupta Culture* (Delhi: Motilal Banarsidass, 1983), 67-92.

47. See Edward Thompson, *Suttee: A Historical and Philosophical Enquiry into the Hindu Rite of Widow-Burning* (Boston and New York: Houghton Mifflin and Company, 1928).

48. Lockwood, *Mamallapuram and the Pallavas*, 62-73; and Frederick M. Asher, "Historical and Political Allegory in Gupta Art," in Smith, ed., *Essays on Gupta Culture*, 53-66.

49. Lockwood discusses the intended ambiguity of these titles in *Mamallapuram and the Pallavas*, 84-85. Rājarāja I built the Rājarājēśvara *vimāna* of the Bṛhadēśvara complex in Tanjore in 1003-1010. Rājēndra I (1012-1044) built the Rājēndracōlīśvara or Gangaikoṇḍacōlīśvara temple in Gangaikoṇḍacōlapuram. See *Encyclopaedia* I, 225, 234.

50. This is the way Lockwood interprets Mahendravarma's phrase, "bore on his head God immanent." See his *Mamallapuram and the Pallavas*, p. 66.

51. Rāmānuja later retrieved it, tradition says, and installed it in the temple at Tirupati until a Vijayanagara king returned it to Chidambaram. See *Encyclopaedia*, 291.

52. T. N. Subramanian plausibly identifies the "Kulōttuṅga" of Śrī Vaiṣṇava tradition with Kulōttuṅga II. See John Braisted Carman, *The Theology of Ramanuja: An Essay in Interreligious Understanding* (New Haven and London: Yale University Press, 1974), 44-45.

14

From Robber Baron to Royal Servant of God? Gaining a Divine Body in South India[1]

Joanne Punzo Waghorne

In 1882, His Highness Rāja Rāmacandra Toṇṭaimān of Pudukkottai, the only remaining princely state in Tamilnadu, took the title "Brihadambal Das," the servant of the goddess Brihadambal.[2] With the open prodding of his Tanjore-born wife and a silent but sure nod from his Brahman dewan, the rāja took the last step in the long process by which this openly Kaḷḷar caste royal family attempted to secure an honorable place among Hindu rājas who reigned in India. In the nineteenth century the title of "servant" of God increasingly carried status among human kings just as surely as it made a demon into a divine devotee in the world of the gods. The once low caste rājas of Puri, although now without a domain, were greatly respected with their title of "servant" of Jagannāth.[3] Within the century, the rājas of Travancore, also Śūdra, at best, in origin, had taken a similar title in relationship to their tutelary deity.[4] Like the tamed and devoted demon servants who had a place at the feet of God in many nearby temples, rājas of questionable caste origins, and even more questionable pasts, found both legitimation and a sure share of divinity as the first among the servants of their God.

Rāja Rāmacandra's action was almost predictable as a logical extension of the kind of orthodoxy that the bhakti movement defined for South India after the tenth century. As Madeleine Biardeau has shown, bhakti provided the means of moving local deities with a taste for meat and a liking for blood into a new definition of Hindu orthodoxy.[5]

The relationship between God and the outsider/sinner was set. The demon was made to realize his dependency on God and to acknowledge with gratitude his place at the Lord's feet as a devotee-servant. The demon lost his own wayward, but once independent power, for a share of God's own divinity. A similar process operated to integrate rājas of low caste origin, and therefore often of scandalous habits, into an acceptable orthodoxy. During the turmoil of the seventeenth and eighteenth centuries, the old chieftains of the outlying regions of India rose to become rājas through their military support of various contenders for paramount power in the more settled regions. The British used the fluid situation and followed an ad hoc policy to maintain the hill kingdoms as buffer states and to annex the settled agricultural belts to their domain. As a result, few of the remaining ruling rājas of the nineteenth century could truly claim Kṣatriya status. These hill lords with their odd social, political, and religious habits pleased neither the Brahmans nor the respectable gentry of the established agricultural areas. They sought legitimation as they moved into more established regions or as they turned their own hill country—willingly or because of pressure from the now paramount British—from a confederacy of clans into a royal domain. By the late eighteenth century, the royal houses of Tanjore, Nagpur, Mysore, Travancore, Hyderabad and others in South India were now descended from Śivāji's hearty Maratha freebooters, Muslim soldiers of fortune, or the older Tamil pāḷaiyakkārs—Polegars as the British called them—who had long ruled the Tamil backlands as chieftains of the cattle-raising/cattle-rustling castes.[6] The founding legends of such royal houses frequently cast the family patriarch as a gem-in-the-rough who came to royalty through power which in later generations was sanctified in devotion to the state deity.[7] Mark Wilks in his 1817 collection of the founding legends of Mysore, for example, described generations of the family as powerful robber barons. He makes special mention of "Canterava Narsa Raj" who established the worship of a state deity and established the royal celebration of Dasarā. Wilks offered the typical terse comment of an eighteenth-century rationalist on this would-be pious prince: "He is of course the idol of his Brahman historians, whose system of ethics is not disturbed by any troublesome reflections on the simple transfer of property, by which the fruits of industry are transformed into pious plunder."[8]

This was the historical antecedent inherent in Rāja Rāmacandra's quest for legitimacy. The Toṇṭaimān were classic pāḷaiyakkārs whose family's roots were in the free-wheeling days when plunder made wealth, and wealth made magnanimity, and magnanimity made friends of much needed troops, of the Brahmans, and of the gods. But as a young ruler, Rāja Rāmacandra had not been a paragon of either the coming Victorian virtures, or the old give-and-take of the Kaḷḷar clansmen. He had perhaps over-patronized the Brahmans by employing them in his library and accounts office in great numbers, and by paying for elaborate rituals. In short he *paid* in the manner of the eighteenth century but did not pay heed as the coming age of ethics would demand. With an old pāḷaiyakkār's taste for jewels and little sense of economy, and with a budget stretched too thin between old retainers and his desire for royal splendor in an expanded arena of the British Raj, he almost lost his throne first to a rebellion of his own Kaḷḷar militia and later to a threatened take-over by a British administration anxious to keep good order with or without him.[9] Old and seemingly chastened, he sought new status and expiation as his Divine Lady's devotee.

But this new effort of the Pudukkottai rāja to secure a place among the new all-India orthodox was not a resounding success. Perhaps the Toṇṭaimān family's shady past as members of the supposed robber caste of Kaḷḷars[10] was too recent to have slid out of common memory. Descriptions of Pudukkottai just ten years previous to the rāja's reformation as a servant of God portrayed a domain with robbers lurking on roads overgrown with thorns "grown in enormous bushes sheltering venomous reptiles."[11] The British, therefore, quickly concluded that this rāja was making a pretentious bid for aggrandizement of his power and objected that he was overstepping his bounds by imitating the practices of the greater court of Travancore. Much quiet politics was needed to secure the government's permission to take the title.[12] The general public outside of Pudukkottai likely remained similarly unimpressed. Today among the more orthodox outside of the Pudukkottai district, the rājas of Pudukkottai remain "products of the British" and not Hindu kings of unquestioned distinction. Perhaps the rājas of Pudukkottai hesitated too long to take up their role as devoted servants to be taken seriously in this exalted yet humble position of sharing in the divinity of an overarching and superior God.

In spite of Rāmacandra's dubious success in the title role of the servant of God, the Toṇṭaimāns did not fail to gain a serious religious role within their own kingdom.[13] The process of securing religious legitimation began in earnest during the long reign of Vijaya Raghunātha Rāya Toṇṭaimān, 1730-1769. The rāja had emerged from a succession dispute with the question of his legitimacy to settle with a more than ready sword. While the rival to the throne had been installed in the temple of Kudumiyamalai, as was the family tradition, a hasty ceremony for Vijaya was performed in front of the image of Brihadambal in the Tirugōkarṇam temple. Thus did the great goddess enter into a serious relationship with the Toṇṭaimāns. But unlike his nineteenth century progeny, Vijaya Raghunātha did not propose to become the goddess's "servant."[14] This earlier rāja may well have had something much more radical in mind for his position in the world of divine powers.

The eighteenth century was not the nineteenth. In spite of all the talk of reform, the religious movements of nineteenth century India operated on the larger imperial logic that a return to "origins," Sanskrit scripture in the case of India and Biblical text in England, was the best means of "reforming" contemporary popular practices. The nineteenth century in both India and Britain sought the legitimation of holy texts and long-dead holy men. But in the previous century, few dared to define a Brahmanical orthodoxy as the route to divine or human power when a Muslim Nawab of Arcot reigned as the tutelary overlord of the Carnatic and when the actual power supporting the throne was the British East India Trading Company made up of post-enlightenment rational pragmatists whose adherence to orthodox Christianity was rarely even nominal. The eighteenth century was the era of men like George Patterson who was employed as a councilor by the Nawab of the Carnatic. In his diary of an official journey through South India in 1774, Patterson freely portrayed one missionary as a buffoon while a century later this person was virtually canonized as a heroic preacher of the faith.[15] But then the eighteenth century was not a time for the prudent to espouse the staid ancientness of orthodoxy. It was a time for the nonorthodox to move freely in and out of power.

Borders, both social and political, were fluid in the eighteenth century in South India. Hindu rājas proudly wore the badges of honor given by Muslim, British, French, and indigenous rulers. This was a time when freebooter Muslims, Hindus, and tribals became kings, when daring "shopkeepers" were made British lords, and when the commandment to know one's place was not taken too seriously either theologically or politically. Brahmans took employment with petty rājas whom they carefully treated as kings with that seeming disregard for logic that annoyed Mark Wilks and others like him.[16] But the eighteenth century British too had begun to purchase the legitimacy that adhered to the Brahmans by employing them as clerks and later granting them many important offices in the Presidency. Yet while the Brahmans continued to find a place in the new early British order, they did not command the ideological, theological, or political order of the day. Gone was the careful bowing to Brahmanical tradition that marked the previous centuries in places like Tanjore, whose earlier complex struggles to attain orthodoxy are the focus of David Shulman's recent book on kingship in South India. Such times as the eighteenth century, as Shulman also suggests,[17] may have allowed the ancient indigenous Tamil culture(s) free play to offer its own rules on the acquisition of power as a modus operandi for the other outsiders who had come to its door. And, not yet apparent in the eighteenth century were the forces that would bring a new kind of orthodoxy back to both India and Britain, and which would send Rāmacandra Toṇṭaimān scurrying for a place among the "servants" of God, when a century earlier his great ancestor, as we will see, took nothing less than a place among the gods.

In many respects, the British and their dependent Hindu rājas of the nineteenth century had much in common with the period that preceded the freewheeling times of Vijaya Raghunātha Toṇṭaimān. Myths with timeless messages, texts claiming eternal relevance, concern with a carefully formulated overarching order were the stuff that satisfied the needs of an imperial claim to universal power. But when times are locally made and locally defined as in South India after the demise of both the Vijayanagar, the late Chola dynasties, and even of nominal Moghul rule, kings may take another road to securing legitimacy both theologically and politically. Rāmacandra Toṇṭaimān's claim to the title of a divine devotee is predictable for his day, but the more interesting issues rest with the earlier Toṇṭaimān. The world of Vijaya Raghunātha Toṇṭaimān was filled with the kind of events, and even the kind of myths, that indeed altered and illuminated his times and perhaps any time in South India when universality gives way to particularity and to an earthy and unabashed grab at power—divine or human. It is then that the divine and the human meet in ways that scandalize the theology of more ordered times.

The reign of Vijaya Raghunātha fortunately has left two "myths" that each tell the story of the Toṇṭaimān family's rise to power and of Vijaya Raghunātha's own hard road to the expiations of his past sins. The events in the first narrative cycle center on Vijaya Raghunātha's conversion as the devotee, not of the goddess, but of a naked ascetic, Sadāśiva Brahma. These events are carefully dated to 1738 but the tale remained oral until the twentieth century version took pamphlet and history book form.[18] The second narrative put into elegant courtly verse as the *Toṇḍaman Vaṃśāvaḷi* near the end of Rāya Vijaya's reign, relates the genealogy and the history of the Toṇṭaimāns including the grand tale of the first of these Kaḷḷar chieftains to secure the status of independent rule. Neither of the two narratives is "myth" in any classical sense. The line between "myth" and "history," as would be expected, is especially thin in the origin stories of the royal lines of these hinterland districts. Here, as Nicholas Dirks points out in his analysis of Pudukkottai's family history as told in *vaṃśāvaḷi* form, "Anthropologists must realize both that myths have histories and that they are histories."[19] Important also is the Tamil classification of its own "popular" literature. The ballads of the hinterland rājas, like the rājas of Pudukkottai, are classified most often as *varalāru*, which is used to this day as the word "history" in text books. Interestingly, the tales of gods seem to be lumped into those of kings with no literary distinction made, for example, between tales of the love between young women and God or between lovely maidens and the king.[20] In this sense, the stories of gods are presented as "histories" just like the tales of men. Here is an interesting reversal between myth and history. It seems that while gods fit into the world's history, humans do not fit themselves into myth. The medium in which these Pudukkottai traditions originate fits the nature of the special kind of divine-human relationships which the tales helped to create and to advocate.

A. The Sadāśiva Legend: King, Brahman, Ascetic, God and Goddess

The narrative of Vijaya Raghunātha's first meeting with his future guru, Sadāśiva Brahma, is part of the folklore and history of Pudukkottai. The story is central to kingship there because it relates the origins, not of the kingdom itself, but of the beginning of the religious "blessing" of the state which insured its fertility and growth. Like the stories of the demon who submits to God, this narrative emphasizes the rāja's state of sin and the expiation of that sin by the good graces of the Brahman ascetic. The story has many oral and written variants, but the version told by S. Radhakrishna Aiyar in *A General History of Pudukkottai* is the most accessible and widely known.

Once the ascetic Sadāśiva Brahma, after renouncing worldly life, could not renounce his love of talking. The strong advice of his guru led Sadāśiva into a lifelong vow of silence. He is said to have wandered naked and utterly silent through the forests of South India. Ramakrishna Aiyar continues the story as follows in his stylized nineteenth century prose.

> In 1738 or just before, Vijaya Raghunātha Raya Tondaiman had the good fortune to receive spiritual instruction from Sadasiva Brahma. It is not definitely known where the meeting took place between the ruler and the Yogi. Some say that the Tondaiman met him in the forests near Sivagnanapuram, a little to the south-east of the Pudukkottai town where the ruler often lived. . . . The Tondaiman must, immediately on seeing the Yogi, have known him to be a great sage, and made obeisance to him requesting spiritual instruction. The sage thereupon wrote on the sand by his side the Dakshinamurti Mantram, i.e., the prayer to Shiva in his form as the *south-faced* preceptor of the Rishis, and also a direction that the Tondaiman should have as his spiritual Guru Mahabashyam Gopalakrishna Sastriar, a class-mate of the Yogi in his boy-hood.
>
> Gopalakrishna Sastriar was sent for, was made the Palace Guru. . . . The Tondaiman was required by the Guru, for the expiation of his past sins and for the security of the future welfare and prosperity of the State, to institute the worship of Dakshinamurti in the Palace and to arrange for the annual conduct of the *Navarātri* or Dassara festival, when Lakshmi, Durga and Sarasvati were to be worshiped and a large number of Brahmans were to be fed and given doles of rice and money, etc., and for the distribution of *Svayampakam* (rice and other articles required for a Hindu meal) to a number of Brahmins every day and to all girls that might apply therefore on Friday. . . .
>
> Sadasiva Brahma, after the incident referred to above, again wandered where he liked and ultimately sank into eternal repose at Nerur near Karur. A few days before he closed his earthly career, he . . . asked the inhabitants of Nerur to have a pit ready for his Samadhi, in which was to be buried a *bana lingam* (a white stone representing the essence of Shiva). . . . A temple was built by the Tondaiman over his tomb, which was endowed with two villages in the Tirumayyam Taluk by the Tondaiman.[21]

All of these charities and festivals were maintained until 1945 when the celebration of Dasarā was cut back in the name of both reform and economy. Many people in Pudukkottai blame this rash action for the loss of the state's sovereignty just three years later.

Certainly on first reading this narrative seems to fit neatly into the pattern of many classical Hindu myths which center on the relationship between the key characters of king, Brahman, and ascetic, the subject of much recent discussion initiated by Louis Dumont and followed up by Veena Das, J. C. Heesterman, and T. N. Madan.[22] There is a clear interdependence established between the ruler and the

Brahmans through the mediation of an ascetic. In good classical form, the Brahmans relieve the king of his evil by accepting his food as an expiation for sin. In oral versions of the story, the king's sins are related to his self-polluting but necessary acts of killing, especially during the civil wars in which Vijaya Raghunātha had emerged as a rāja of importance through his support of the East India Company and its candidate for succession to the rule of the Carnatic.[23] The rāja himself had won his own power through a year of interfamilial war in Pudukkottai. Much like the lingering myth of the evil King Vena which Wendy O'Flaherty traced from the Veda to the late Purāṇas and David Shulman found again in Tamilnadu,[24] this story on the surface tells of the purification of a fierce warrior-king now settling into righteous rule.

In this story, however, the importance of the roles of the purifying God who grants salvation and the righteous Brahman are eclipsed by the yogi who actually established a series of analogous relationships between king, Brahman, and ascetic, and the gods whose roles are shared, swapped, and even duplicated among both human and divine participants. Sadāśiva Brahma as yogi is also Brahman *and* god *and* king. His asceticism is hardly quiescent. He is a power-house of energy—the kind of creative energy that Frédérique Marglin has classified among those forms of divine "power" in India to which each person "has access by actions in this life"[25] and not by right of caste birth.

Thus here the naked ascetic, because of his vow of silence, cannot verbally articulate his position. Instead he must, like the star of a silent movie, act with all the more energy in the key parts of this drama. Like a *king*, Sadāśiva Brahma wields power through action. There is a Tamil version of the story that has Sadāśiva worshiping the goddess at Tirugōkarṇam with flowers and a gift of golden beads.[26] Here in another role reversal Sadāśiva acts as if he were the king, because the care, dressing, and feeding of the goddess was a royal duty for this state temple. But he also maintains his role as a Brahman. His caste friend substitutes for his presence as the rāja's Brahman teacher in the palace while he remains in the forest as a perfect ascetic. This single actor plays the roles of "Brahman, King, and Sanyasi" which Veena Das has defined as the key to the conceptual order of Hinduism.[27]

But Sadāśiva Brahma is not alone in his capacity to wear many garbs of power. Even the form of Lord Śiva as preceptor to the gods is the perfect analogue to Sadāśiva's own position as Brahman, ascetic, and king. Śiva's own asceticism is confirmed by his position as guru to the gods and by his separation from female divinity within the sacred geography of the capital city of Pudukkottai. In his small temple placed inside the palace, Śiva is not accompanied by his great consort. The goddess Brihadambal, the great Śakti, lives in a temple several miles away in Tirugōkarṇam. Although this great temple was once dedicated to Śiva, he is now overshadowed by the image of the goddess.[28] His presence in this state temple is in the aniconic form of the liṅga. The rāja was thus brought into separate types of relationships with Śiva and Śakti. His relationship with the goddess is established, as ordered by Sadāśiva, through Dasarā which by this time was an orthodox ritual within South India. It is also possible to say, à la Shulman, that Śiva is also brought into a safe relationship with his otherwise overpowering wife. However, as the occupant of the temple that Sadāśiva had established for him, Śiva sits as the lord's Lord within the palace grounds right under the Durbar Hall where the king officially sat in state. But again the entire reaffirmation of king-ascetic-Brahman roles for the god is affected through the ironically more important human guru—the stage manager and script writer for this royal play.

Notice that the emphasis on the ascetic is not the only audacious "mixing" of roles. By the logic of the myth, the king also plays the dual role of ascetic, and god—the king's position as a Brahman is not apparent in this myth but can be inferred in descriptions of the structure of the royal court.[29] In the Tamil temple myths, Śiva tames and then cares for his aggressive and dangerous bride.[30] Here, however, Śiva is made to sit alone in the king's palace while the king now fills in for both the ascetic and the absent God. A modern Tamil biography of Sadāśiva has Rāja Vijaya Raghunātha as a serious ascetic even before his meeting with Sadāśiva. "Although of royal lineage, he preferred solitude and prayer in the forests of Tiruvaranulam."[31] The children of the state were instructed in their history text that the rāja "built himself a lonely home in the Sivagnana-puram jungle ["the city of the knowledge of Shiva"] to the south of town, where he spent days and nights in prayer and study."[32] During Dasarā the Toṇṭaimān rājas always maintained a fast and were supposed to live secluded during the ten days of the festival. Thus the king took on the yogi's role as well as casting himself as the meditative Śiva. A miniature painting from the Śaivite court of the Rāja of Mundi in the Punjab hills could so easily be the rāja of Pudukkottai in a striking example of the Hindu hill lord as the ascetic god-king ornamented with royal turban, tiger skins, and Śiva's third eye on his forehead.[33] A British account of a Dasarā in another state relates that the "Maharaja is supposed by many of his subjects to have reached, temporarily, a state of semi-divinity as a result of his austerities."[34] But unlike Sadāśiva Brahma, and even unlike the God, the king can act as the goddess's "husband" because he is not sworn to permanent celibacy nor to permanent fasting. This was made apparent during the Dasarā processions when the image of Brihadambal was accompanied by the rāja of Pudukkottai, who was also carried in a palanquin. The god is conspicuously absent from the festivities as his divine image simply stays at home in the palace while the king goes out with his wife!

The action of the tale, then, is shared between two human figures, the king and the ascetic. And, both finally share a particularly interesting end as images in a temple. The point is obvious for Sadāśiva whose remains form the foundation for a temple which traditionally would have included his image, yet the same metamorphosis happened to the king. Witnesses to the Dasarā ceremony attest that the king was carried during the Dasarā procession in exactly the same manner as was the image of the goddess. He stood absolutely still, covered with garlands, his hands folded. Here the rāja's pose is much like that of the saints in the many temple processions who have become themselves images for worship.[35] The sight of the king gave darśan just as does the sight of any divine image. Thus both the rāja and his spiritual teacher have not simply become divine, they have become divine images!

Thus all the characters in this myth live out their earthly life as *icons*. Śiva lives in a new icon body within the palace. Śakti will be worshiped carefully in many icons during Dasarā. Sadāśiva Brahma is housed in his own temple, and the king will take up his role as icon during the very festivals that his Brahman guru instituted. The more orthodox bhakti motifs in the myth have been themselves englobed by the almost alchemic formula that embodied god eventually equals icon. But Pudukkottai did not invent this formula nor the theological embarrassment to orthodox Hinduism that went with it. Pious texts from Madurai and nearby Tanjore collected at the turn of the eighteenth century provide examples of the king's close affinity to the divine image in the temple. In the Mackenzie collection in London, texts collected and translated into English by Brahman clerks for the East India Company do not fail to mention the still famous story of the king of Madurai who perfected himself in all of the Brahmanical sciences culminating in the mastery of dance so that he could imitate his divine lord, Śiva. But when the king could no longer stand on one foot like the divine icon, the embodied god reversed his own position so that his royal devotee could use the other foot.[36] Here the king's attempt to make his own body into an image of the divine image-body is sanctioned by god's grace. In yet another story collected from Tanjore in 1804, Rāja Rājendra Chola becomes irate when one of the uncouth kings from Andhra actually reveals a third eye.

> One day Rajendra seeing his figure in a painting fell into a sudden rage exclaiming as he pointed with his finger "Wretch! do you flatter yourself that you have three eyes equal to the God of my adoration." Having said this, he darted his finger at one of the eyes of the picture and at the same time the third eye was broken: from that day he [the Andhra king] became subject to Rajendra.[37]

This story was in Marathi and was translated by "A Maratta Brahmin" from Tanjore. These Brahmans had come with Śivāji's forces into Tanjore less than a century earlier. The royal house of Tanjore at this time was not Chola, but obviously intended to claim that status by out-orthodoxing those Andhra kings who had kept their hinterland ways. This sermon was, ironically, condemned as it admitted the close relationship between icon and king. It is an icon of the Andhra king that Rājendra held in his hands and that was as much a form of the errant king's body as the divine icon was of the god's. Paintings of the rājas of the Punjab hills from the daring eighteenth century still proudly portrayed the king with the third eye of Śiva. The theological tug-of-war between the supremacy of the king as icon and the embodied god seems a struggle with some push, much pull, but with no clear wins for either side. Yet no matter how rough the play, no one let go of this bond that connected king to God.

There exists within this legend yet another set of paradoxes for orthodox Hinduism, even for orthodox bhakti. It is not the king's unscathed righteousness that wins him divine status but rather his sins. In this sense, the categories of bhakti are present. God does care for the sinner more than the righteous, for sin gives God the opportunity to exhibit his divine grace. Yet in Pudukkottai the process has some vital variations. The Dasarā festival is a grand expiation of the king's "sins," and yet at the same time this festival ensures the kingdom's prosperity. Expiation for royal "sins" results not in the simple forgiveness that would be expected for sins of disobedience, nor in a purifying of the rāja, nor in the intervention of God and the flow of divine grace. Certainly the rāja must set up the worship of both Śiva and his consort, but the energy from the expiation is not presented as a direct gift of the gods. The rāja, with his luxurious dress in close relationship with his direct opposite, the naked ascetic, creates the kingdom's fertility which flows from naked ascetic to the splendidly dressed royal "sinner," and from king to the kingdom at large. The rāja's sins appear almost material in nature—a kind of base ingredient necessary to very substantive blessings. The process of transmutations and transformations, then, dominates the issue of the king's "evil" in Pudukkottai. When viewed in the context of the myth of the legitimation of kingship, the story of Sadāśiva Brahma and the rāja, the transformation process becomes a process in which both human-body and god-body come to take the *same* form as icons. The catalyst is "sin."

B. The *Toṇṭaimāṉ Varalāṟu:* Tigers, Panthers, Elephants, and Kings

In Pudukkottai no one is the least surprised if questioned about the historical origins of the Toṇṭaimān's rise to royal status. The question makes perfect sense here in an area where families could rise to royal power and fall back into commonness within a matter of decades. Royalty has a beginning and an end here, and stories of the rise and fall of just about everybody were the stuff that made folk legends in these arid regions of Tamilnadu. While the origin of the kingdom's prosperity and of the expiation of the king's sins adopted an overt Brahmanical and Sanskritic idiom for its covert purposes, the type of continually forming "history" of the actual rise of the Toṇṭaimāns to royal power openly reflects both the content and the idiom of Tamil folk culture.

Stories explaining the end of Toṇṭaimān power in 1948 are just beginning to take shape, but a complete cycle of origin legends exists in text from as early as the eighteenth century and orally into the present. The basic scenario has remained stable with varied delicacy and tone added in the different tellings. A person close to the royal family told the tale with great flourish.

> The Toṇṭaimāns were elephant trainers in the armies of the Vijayanagar empire who came south from Andhra Pradesh and settled in this region in a place which they called Ambukkōvil, "the palace of compassion." They were chieftains at that time and began to gain a good reputation for wisely settling disputes. One day the king of the Vijayanagar empire was traveling through the Ambukkōvil area on a pilgrimage to the Rameś-varam Temple when one of his elephants turned wild and began to ravage the countryside. The king sent drummers to warn the people to get out of the way. When the drummers came to Ambukkōvil, the Toṇṭaimān

> asked how could a king be so weak as not to be able to tame his own elephants and keep them under control? The Toṇṭaimān went straightaway to complain to the king who told the Toṇṭaimān that if he could tame the elephant, he would be granted honors and a title. But, if he could not, he would be executed. The Toṇṭaimān located the elephant and tricked it into flinging its tusks into a sand bank while he cleverly leaped on its back. The Toṇṭaimān rode the elephant, now quite tame, back to the king. For this act, he was granted the title of "rāya" (Tamil: *rāja*), a large tract of land and the following honors: the right to have torch lights carried before him in the day; to wear a special sword; to have a lion flag as his standard, and to have an umbrella carried over him as he walked.

While telling the legend, Mr. Sadasivam dwelt with great relish on the battle between the Toṇṭaimān and the elephant which was, for him, the central act of the story.

The old Telugu poems *Toṇḍaimān Palegaru Kaifiyatu*[38] and the *Toṇḍamān Vaṃśāvaḷi* by Court Poet Nudurupati Venkanna[39] are still extant and give poetic versions of this story with considerable detail and flourish.[40] Radhakrishna Aiyar in his *General History of the Pudukkottai State* fortunately summarized the old Tamil versions of the legend, the full text of which is now lost.[41] These older ballads on the origin of the Toṇṭaimān rule expand the story to include a long genealogy of the family. The capture of the Vijayanagar rāja's own elephant is inevitably mentioned. These poems also give an exacting and bewildering list of over twenty pirutu[42] —usually transcribed from the Tamil and Telugu into English as "Biruthus"—which were bestowed upon the first Toṇṭaimān Rāya for his valor. The Biruthus were badges of honor that took the form of titles, of clothing, of emblems carried before the rāja, or persons who formed part of the rāja's entourage. The *Toṇḍamān Vaṃśāvaḷi* lists the first Biruthus as: a copper image of the Gandabherunda (a mythical bird that preys on elephants), five-colored flags, umbrellas, a horse with bells, a Bheri (a high pitched trumpet carried on an elephant), a horn made from white conch shell, flags with the emblems of a lion, fish, and Garuḍa (an eagle), special musical instruments, incense, a vessel containing special scents, good horses, a finely decorated knife, a large drum, a palanquin painted with a lion's head emblem, the right to burn silver torches in the daytime, an elephant with a drum on its back, two white fans (*cāmaram*), bards, and a troop of dancing girls in addition to titles of honor. All of these assorted items were meant to be taken along when the new rāja went in procession. In addition to these the poems casually mention that the new rāja was also given a tract of land.

Undaunted with this long enumeration of emblems, the ballads relate the rest of the story of the Toṇṭaimāns' rise to power as if this were a long game of Biruthus monopoly. The first Rāya Toṇṭaimān was childless, but after praying in a temple in his village, Śiva appeared to him in a dream and promised two sons who would be like precious pearls. These boys soon grew up and began to collect Biruthus on their own. The rāja of Tanjore heard of the fame and beauty of these two young men and invited them to come to stay at his court. One version has the rāja asking them to take service as warriors but another hints that their good company alone was desired. The boys' chief exploit was to capture a tiger and a panther, for which they were awarded another set of Biruthus: a necklace with a coin bearing Rāma's image, a sword called the Rāmabhanda, more umbrellas, long coats with gold lace, jewelry, a herd of elephants. When the Tanjore rāja tried to force them to abjure their devotion to Śiva for Viṣṇu, the brothers returned home. Sometime later the Setupati (the title of the rājas of Ramnad) needed their services to catch some bigger game than elephants and tigers. He called them to help quell a rebellion of local chieftains. By "using kind words only" the elder brother talked the rebellious Tevars back into submission. Not to be outdone, his younger brother Namana returned to the more usual acts of bravery and killed one of the Setupati's own elephants which had gone wild. Again the brothers returned home laden with more Biruthus, another tract of land, and the elder brother received the title from which he took his name, Raghunātha. As one final round of play, the two brothers took service at the court of the rāja of Madurai and tamed an entire rebellion of local chieftains to the south—this time by more bloody means. The Pandyan rāja granted Raghunātha the right to use all of his own royal titles. The longest and most classical of the Telegu poems continues the narration of war deeds in a staggering list of conquests from aid rendered to the Trichinopoly royal family to victory over the kings of Kerala and wars with former allies in Tanjore. By the time Raghunātha Rāya and his brother Namana completed his round of "services," the rāya was himself ruler of most of the territory called Pudukkottai. It is at this point that the *Toṇḍaman Vaṃśāvaḷi* says that Rāya Toṇṭaimān worshiped the goddess Brihadambal at the Tirugōkarṇam temple and built Pudukkottai, "a new fort," as the capital of what was now his kingdom. The tale ends as the Toṇṭaimāns entered history as the independent rulers of the new district of Pudukkottai in the year 1689.

This story of the Toṇṭaimāns was no doubt considered a truly epic tale. The *Toṇḍaman Vaṃśāvaḷi* adopts a grand tone for recitation at the court of a great monarch and even the oral retelling was no less serious. Yet some of the most prominent figures expected in any epic are not here, and much of what is here seems almost trivial. Foremost in this cast of missing characters are the gods who pour their blessings on the struggling hero. The *Toṇḍaman Vaṃśāvaḷi* traces the Toṇṭaimāṉ line back fourteen generations to one of Indra's earthly love affairs. The divine seed was long hybridized before the heroic deeds of Raghunātha Rāya. Indra himself never appears on the scene. Śiva does intervene as usual in the process of fertility but again his presence hardly pervades the story. And most surprisingly, the great goddess Brihadambal, the present tutelary deity of the Toṇṭaimāṉ, enters the picture only after the kingdom was won. Here other sources confirm that Raghunātha Rāya indeed was the first Toṇṭaimāṉ to "pray to" the great goddess, but he was not the first of his line to be installed in front of the goddess's dais. Interestingly, evidence is clear that the goddess who viewed Rāya Raghunātha's *paṭṭāpiṣēkam*, his coronation, was not Brihadambal of Tirugōkarṇam but the Divine Lady who resided in the nearby temple of Kudumiyamalai.[43] Present opinion in Pudukkottai and older sources holds that this first coronation was done "in imitation" of the practices of the former rulers of the area and was not indigenous to the Kaḷḷar chieftains. It took centuries for the lady of Tirugōkarṇam to absorb the religious attention of the Toṇṭaimāṉs. For, the final admission that she indeed was vital to their rule came when Rāmacandra Toṇṭaimāṉ took the title Brihadambal Das. Up to that point, the Toṇṭaimāṉs maintained good relationships with gods of their kingdom but the ultimate source of their power did not arise directly from such deities.

The audience for the epic tale of the Toṇṭaimāṉ's royal origins must have been expected to take seriously what the narration in fact makes surprisingly clear. The Toṇṭaimāṉs' rise to power was initiated by several bouts with two elephants, one tiger, and one panther gone wild, for which the family received an odd assortment of what may seem figuratively, and also even literally, white elephants. But such stories are common to this region. The rājas of nearby Ramnad told similar tales of their origin.[44] In these tales are those same acts of creative violence that in Sanskritized Tamil myth cause great concern about the proper means of absolution from such pollution and sin. But here in the *Toṇḍaman Vaṃśāvaḷi* as in other such tales, violence occurs with absolutely no apology. The Toṇṭaimāṉs kill or tame both animals and men and are much rewarded for their actions in the form of

Biruthus. These very tangible honors became part of the king's public dress—part of his public *body.*

In the *Toṇḍaman Vaṃśāvaḷi* the Toṇṭaimān both made themselves, and are made, into kings as they seem to incorporate the power of each of their victims into their own body. The process resembles the process by which persons become village deities after a violent death. Stuart Blackburn suggests that the violence of murder or fateful accident or brutality releases a power that accrues to the victim whose shade becomes a spiritual body of considerable power.[45] The king here is not victim but rather is the doer, the actor who can grasp the power of his victims for his own use. Notice, however, that the would-be rāja cannot directly transform his creative violence into Biruthus. The Biruthus are always "given" by a higher lord who in publicly confirming the Toṇṭaimān's acts as heroic effects the change whereby the power residue in the act of taming men or beasts becomes a tangible part of the rāja's new body. In this sense the rāja both makes himself and is made a king. But neither Brahman nor ascetic nor oddly even gods effect the transmutation of his body from that of a Kaḷḷar chieftain to a royal lord. This process of body-building remains a human drama set in an unabashed warriors' world.[46]

The king's body in this tale of tamed elephants and footloose clansmen, however, is no less divine than the icon-king that Sadāśiva Brahma brought forth. For those Biruthus which the Toṇṭaimān collected remained in daily use in the palace. The Biruthus are both things and persons that minister to the body of the king. Some are actual clothes which he wears to glorify his body, others such as the bards and the dancing girls "feed" his body through song and dance to keep his passionate nature—his own *royal* nature—alive.[47] The care, dressing, and feeding of the king closely parallels the same attentions that are said to maintain the life of the divine icon of the goddess in her own holy *kōyil,* temple/palace. Thus the function of the Biruthus follows the same theo-logic as the ritual process of the fruitful expiation of the rāja's sins in the Sadāśiva Brahma legends. The rāja's body is again transformed from simple flesh to an icon body—like the icon body of god.

C. Conclusion: The "Devotee" as God-keeper and as God

Something unorthodox lingers in these two "myths" from Pudukkottai. The traditional relationship between the outsider/sinner and the gracious deity is eclipsed by another theological formula. The moral lesson taught to the Chola king by the myths of kingship collected around 1800 by Colin Mackenzie, and others recently cited by David Shulman,[48] seem to center always on the issue of the king's overstepping his humanity in a bid for unlawful divine status equal to gods. The Pudukkottai rājas apparently never learned this Brahmanical lesson and ironically managed to outlast those more noble kings who did.

But the issue of the relationship between the king as icon and the king as "devotee" cannot end here with the simple theory that here is yet another example of the conflict between popular and Brahmanical traditions. The meaning of "devotee" was itself absorbed into the iconic culture of Pudukkottai and given new meaning. Rāmacandra Toṇṭaimān's bid for the position had a different meaning within Pudukkottai than it did outside of the state. The rāja, as the fountainhead of the kingdom's wealth, was the ultimate provider not only for his human subjects but of the gods of the kingdom as well. It was the rāja who provided the food, dress, and the entertainers for his Divine Lady. It was also the rāja who could provide for the installation of new deities, and for the building of new temples to house them. This function he shared with any wealthy human, but even when others paid, the king was still seen as the ultimate source of the "honors," the tangible services and "clothing" that were provided for each divine icon. In this sense, he "served" the gods. But what a service! Their very bodies were in his care, their life as icons depended on his ability to give and his willingness to serve just as the kingdom's life equally depended on the gods' contented presence within the realm.[49] The hidden tension between the Brahmanical and the popular in India rests in a complex and very ancient theological issue over who, and what, and how the divine body of God is related to the divinity in the body of humankind. The royal myths from Pudukkottai can therefore be used to argue what texts like those from the late Chola period only hint but never in their Brahmanical fear admit: that the king's body is a divine icon and that the king as a human has also become the keeper of the God's own divine body. It is this awe-full theological dilemma that has always created the discomfort in Brahmanical theology over the power of the king and the power of God. In this Brahmanical sense, the king is the sinner —the demon who, by definition, always seeks to take the place of the gods, to eat their food during the sacrifice, and to occupy their throne. Like the demons, the king never was satisfied with the place the Brahmans assigned to him. The Pudukkottai rājas played their role as "sinners" well—always overstepping the bounds of social and theological decency to take power when there was power waiting to be taken. Ironically, the Toṇṭaimāns seemed to continually provide the Brahmans and the moral-minded Victorian overlords with those necessary examples of sin that the righteous need to survive. Yet within Pudukkottai, the gods never went hungry nor did the people ever suffer the loss of a god in their own human flesh. The Victorian British are long gone. The Brahmans have lost their hegemony in administrative and even theological power in Tamilnadu. His Highness Rājagopāla Toṇṭaimān, the "former" rāja of Pudukkottai, is alive, and few in Pudukkottai would not stop to catch a glimpse of him when his car drives along the well-worn road from Trichinopoly to the city which his ancestors built among the rocks and the thorns of the Tamil hinterlands.

NOTES

1. This article is written in the context of a larger work, "The King's New Clothes: Toward a Recovery of Religious Things," which is in manuscript form. Many of the subjects mentioned here are treated in detail in the manuscript.

2. The title was taken in English and spelled in this form of anglicized Tamil Grantha. When written in Tamil the title appeared as *Pirukatampāḷ*.

3. For a detailed account of this relationship between God and king see Frédérique Apffel Marglin, *Wives of the God-King: The Rituals of the Devadasis of Puri* (Delhi: Oxford University Press, 1985).

4. See Samuel Mateer, *Native Life in Travancore* (London: W. H. Allen & Co., 1883).

5. Madeleine Biardeau, "L'arbre *śamī* et le buffle sacrificiel." *Puruṣārtha* 5 (1981), 234-238. For a detailed discussion of Biardeau's thesis as presented in her many other works, see Alf Hiltebeitel, "Toward a Coherent Study of Hinduism," *Religious Studies Review* 9(1983), 206-211.

6. Recent works on the hinterland rājas in both northern and southern India include Richard Fox, *Kin, Clan, Raja and Rule: State-Hinterland Relations in Preindustrial India* (Berkeley: University of California Press, 1971); Burton Stein, "Integration of the Agrarian System in South India" in *Land Control and Social Structure in Indian History*, edited by Robert Frykenberg (Madison: University of Wisconsin Press, 1969); David Shulman, "On South Indian Bandits and Kings." *The Indian Economic and Social History Review* 17(1980), 283-306; Nicholas Dirks, "The Pasts of a Pāḷaiyakārar: The Ethnohistory of a South Indian Little King," *Journal of Asian Studies* 41 (1982), 655-686.

7. Examples of such epic tales are numerous. Families of hill lords who became emperors continue to include their past as outsiders in the founding

legends of their house. Readily accessible examples can be found in J. Duncan M. Derrett, *The Hoysalas: A Medieval Indian Royal Family* (Oxford: Oxford University Press, 1957), 1-37; B. A. Saletore, *Social and Political Life in the Vijayanagar Empire* (Madras: B. G. Paul & Co., 1934), 23-36. The early British residents to the princely states often collected these family histories as genealogies. For example, see the British resident to Nagpur, H. T. Colebrook's "Memoir of the Origin and Descent of the Present Bonslaah Family Now on the Musmud of Berar" in the "Correspondence of H. T. Colebrooke, October 13, 1838" in the Wellesley Papers/ADD 13589, European Manuscripts, The British Library).

8. Mark Wilks, *Historical Sketches of the South of India.* 1810-1817 (2nd ed. Madras: Higgenbotham & Co., 1869), 33.

9. The rāja's plight is sensitively analysed by Nicholas B. Dirks, "Little Kingdoms of South India: Political Authority and Social Relations in the Southern Tamil Countryside" (Manuscript, 1983), 445ff.

10. Stuart Blackburn has recently argued against the usual classification of the Kaḷḷars as a criminal tribe. See "The Kaḷḷars: A Tamil 'Criminal Tribe' Reconsidered." *South Asia* 1(1978), 38-51.

11. This description was given in the memoirs of the Brahman Dewan appointed by the rāja under pressure from the British. See A. Sashiah Sastri, "Resumé of My Sixteen Years of Administration of the Pudukkottai State," in the "Collected Letters of A. Sashiah Sastriar." Manuscripts kindly lent by Tiru A. R. Seshia Sastri of Kumbakonam.

12. See "The Biruthus of the Tondaimans," manuscript in the Palace Records housed at the Residency, Pudukkottai, p. 7.

13. The Toṇṭaimāns were the subject of many poems composed for them within Pudukkottai. Their status, both assumed and acknowledged, as rulers becomes apparent in these. A late example is R. Ulakanāṭu Piḷḷai, *Iyalicaippāmālai* (Plain Songs for Ordinary People, Songs in Praise of H. H. Marthanda Bairava Tondaiman) (Pudukkottai: Pudukkottai Kamala Press, 1937).

14. The early Toṇṭaimāns did write devotional music to the goddess but the extant verses address her as "merciful mother." There is a texture of intimacy here that is not always implied in the later devotee-servant relationship. These songs were sung in concert by the former head court musician of Pudukkottai at the American Counsulate in Madras for opening of "Mahamaya: Batiks by Dick Waghorne" in 1979. Tape is available.

15. This was the later famous Christian F. Swartz. George Patterson, "The Diary of George Patterson, 1772-1773," in the European Manuscripts/E379 of the Indian Office Library, London, volumns 8-9.

16. See S. R. Lushington, "The Origin of the Polegars." Letter dated August 18, 1799 in the Wellesley Papers/ADD 13,657, European Manuscripts, The British Library. Lushington disparages the Brahmans whose presence at courts, he supposed, inflated the Polegars' false sense of independence.

17. David Shulman, *The King and the Clown in South Indian Myth and Poetry* (Princeton: Princeton University Press, 1985).

18. Two examples still available in Pudukkottai libraries are *Catāciva Piramentira Carittiram* (The Story of Sadāśiva Brahma) (Pudukkottai: Neroor Sadāśiva Bramendra Sabha, 1950); and N. Thiagarajan, *A Child's History of Pudukkottai: The Place and Its People* (Pudukkottai: Sri Brihadambal State Press, 1932). The latter was a school text book and retold the story of Sadāśiva as an important event in the state's history.

19. Dirks, "Pasts of a Pāḷaiyakārar," 659.

20. There is a wealth of information on this genre of epic/folk literature which uses the same forms to praise both gods and kings in the U. V. Swaminatha Iyer library in Madras. See *Descriptive Catalogue of Tamil Manuscripts* in the Dr. U. V. Swaminatha Iyer Library, Tiruvanmiyur, Madras. The use of common poetic forms to praise both gods and kings, of course, is nothing new to Tamilnadu and can be found in Sangam literature, as Geroge Hart has clearly shown in *The Poems of Ancient Tamil: Their Milieu and Their Sanskrit Counterparts* (Berkeley: University of California Press, 1975).

21. S. Radhakrishna Aiyar, *A General History of Pudukkottai* (Pudukkottai: Sri Brihadambal State Press, 1917), 176-178.

22. See J. C. Heesterman, *The Inner Conflict of Tradition: Essays in Indian Ritual, Kingship, and Society* (Chicago: The University of Chicago Press, 1985); Veena Das, *Structure and Cognition: Aspects of Hindu Caste and Ritual* (New Delhi: Oxford University Press, 1977); T. N. Madan, ed., *Ways of Life: King, Householder, Renouncer —Essays in Honour of Louis Dumont* (New Delhi: Vikas Publishing House, 1982).

23. People in Pudukkottai frequently relate the story of the Toṇṭaimān's capture of the famed rebel Kattabomman and their turning him over to the British. This act is increasingly seen as a great sin since Kattabomman is now regarded as an early freedom fighter. Interestingly, it was Vijaya Raghunātha Rāya's father who captured the "rebel," but that sin is now visited on the son. The nature of the Toṇṭaimān's "sins" seem to vary according to the teller. More Brahmanical versions of his sinful acts put the story in a common myth frame and stress the rāja's accidental wounding of Sadāśiva and disturbance of his meditation. But everyone agrees that he indeed did "sin."

24. See Wendy O'Flaherty, *The Origins of Evil in Hindu Mythology* (Berkeley: University of California Press, 1976), 321ff; Shulman, *King and Clown*, 75ff.

25. "Power, Purity and Pollution: Aspects of the Caste System Reconsidered," *Contributions to Indian Sociology* (NS) 2(1977), 267.

26. "The Legend of Bakaulavaneswari (Brihadambal)," collected and translated from the Tamil by Rajkumari Rema Deva, personal correspondence dated September 13, 1980.

27. Veena Das, *Structure and Cognition*, 18-56.

28. "The Legend of Bakaulavaneswari."

29. This becomes clear in an analysis of the relationship between the rājas and the Rājgurus. The royal priest is treated with the respect due to a rāja, not a priest. He appears to stand in the rāja's stead in the world of the Brahmans.

30. This is a major thesis in David Shulman's *Tamil Temple Myths: Sacrifice and Divine Marriage in the South Indian Saiva Tradition* (Princeton: Princeton University Press, 1980).

31. *Catāciva Piramentira Carittiram.* This section was translated by Rajkumari Rema Devi.

32. Thiagarajan, *A Child's History,* 23.

33. Vishakha N. Desai, ed., *Life at Court: Art for India's Rulers,* a catalogue of the exhibit organized by the Museum of Fine Arts, Boston and sponsored by the Festival of India, 1985-86. See the plate of "Raja Sidh of Mandi in the Assumed Form of Shiva," Mundi, Punjab Hills, about 1725-1730.

34. William Barton, *The Princes of India with a Chapter on Nepal* (London: Nibet and Co., 1934), 146.

35. In the spring festival of the Kāpalīśvara Temple in Mylapore, Madras, images of both gods and saints are carried in procession as they come to the annual wedding celebration of the Lord and Lady of the temple. See the cover photo for *Gods of Flesh/Gods of Stone* edited by Joanne Waghorne and Norman Cutler (Chambersburg: Anima Press, 1985).

36. "The Madoora Poorannum, 24th Chapter, Translated from the Tamil Language by Cheenevassiah in 1807," in Mackenzie Collections, General Section, "The Hindoo Collection—Memoirs and Pieces of the Ancient History of the South, the Chola, Chera, and Pandyas Mundalums. Collected and translated for Major Mackenzie or communicated by his friends and correspondents, 1810," European Manuscripts, India Office Library, p. 102.

37. "Ancient History of the Chola Rajahs: This Ancient Story written in the Maratta Language is now Translated into English by the Hindoo, Venket-Row a Maratta Brahmin, & Native of Tanjore in the Year 1804," in the Mackenzie Collection, p. 139.

38. Telugu Manuscripts/D2620, Oriental Manuscripts Library, Madras.

39. Telugu Manuscripts/295, Oriental Manuscripts Library, Madras.

40. Similar to the Telugu versions but with a genealogy is the *Tondamanpalegarubiradavuli.* Telugu Manuscripts/D2621, Oriental Manuscripts Library, Madras.

41. *Raya Tondaiman Anuragamalai* and the *Tondaiman Irattaimanimalai,* mentioned on pp. 119-120. See also Sayimadha Siva Brindadevi, *Pudukkottai Simaiyum Puttuyirperrakalai Kalum* ("Pudukkottai and the Revitalized Arts") in *The Souvenir Volume of the Tamil Isai Sangam,* 1978, 53.

42. For another interpretation of the Biruthus, see Nicholas Dirks, "The Structure and Meaning of Political Relations in a South Indian Little Kingdom," Humanities Working Paper 14 (Pasadena: California Institute of Technology,

1978). The term is originally Sanskrit, here a Telugu-Sanskrit form as "Biruthu" but *pirutu* in Tamil. The word appeared in English as Biruthu well into the twentieth century.

43. From an interview with K. A. Panchapagesa Dikshitar who read verses from a palm leaf manuscript used in the last coronation ceremony held in Kudumiyamalai in 1730, the *Sikagirida Charitam* by Gotra Swamidikshitar and Siva Rama Dikshitar, Tamil Grantha on palmleaf. Manuscript in the keeping of Sri K. A. Panchapagesa Dikshitar, Pudukkottai.

44. See Pamela G. Price, "Raja-dharma in 19th century South India: land, litgation and largess in Ramnad Zamindari." *Contributions to Indian Sociology* N.S. 132(1979), 209.

45. "Death and Deification: Folk Cults in Hinduism." *History of Religions* 24(1985), 255-274.

46. For the full import of this term in South Asia see Heesterman, *Inner Conflict*, 99ff.

47. See Adrian Mayer, "Perceptions of Princely Rule: Perspectives from a Biography," in T. N. Madan, *Ways of Life.*

48. In summarizing the cycle of royal myths from the Chola period, Shulman suggests that one of the major lessons meant for the king in these tales is that "the essential relationship of the king and god is now an analogical one that is always in danger of being taken too literally." *The King and the Clown*, 405.

49. The interdependent relationship between gods and the human community is complex. See my "From Geertz's Ethnography to an Ethnotheology?" in *Anthropology and the Study of Religion*, Frank E. Reynolds and Robert L. Moore, eds. (Chicago: Center for the Scientific Study of Religion, 1984).

15

The Transgressive Sacrality of the Dīkṣita: Sacrifice, Criminality and *Bhakti* in the Hindu Tradition[1]

Sunthar Visuvalingam

A. Divine Purity and Demoniac Power: A Semiotic Definition of Transgressive Sacrality[2]

"If for other-worldly exploits, this world
shows no reverence, what alas! are we to say to that?
But with this fellow's boisterous laughter here,
who would not roar with laughter holding both his sides?"[3]

The clownish Pāśupata, an inextricable fusion of ascetic renunciation and symbolic violation, immediately offers us the ideal semiotic definition of transgressive sacrality, for his divine purity exaggerates the interdictory regimen of the classical Brahman sacrificer only as a preparation for the demoniac power of the outcaste criminal Kāpālika. He is the focal point of tension that holds together the perspectives, by mediating between the values, of the impure pre-classical and the pure classical dīkṣita, the orthodox sannyāsin and the heterodox monk,

---

Dedicated to my generous American patron and *alter ego*, the late Professor HARVEY PAUL ALPER, who could not wait to present his contribution on "Transgression, Revolution and Universalization: the Future of Hindu Civilization" to our panel on *Transgressive Sacrality and the Other.*

the Śaiva bhakta and the Vedic ritualist, the Brahman Vidūṣaka and the tribal shaman. A proper hermeneutic of the Pāśupata spiritual praxis, intent on restoring its unity as an integral discipline contributing to a single goal, can therefore provide the indispensable conceptual framework for a dialectical understanding of the complex relations between the mutually interfering categories of the pure and the impure, the sacred and the profane, orthodoxy and heterodoxy, sacrifice and bhakti, external ritual and internal yoga, Vedism and Śaivism, Brahmanical law and tantric transgression.

Unlike the alert studied reserve and chaste self-control of the orthodox vegetarian Brahman with his ritual safeguards against the impurity of death, the Pāśupata was obliged to worship Rudra with loud laughter, songs, dance, and meaningless sounds (*Pāśupata-Sūtra* I.8) and practice an unorthodox Yoga (I.1) of pretending to be asleep when awake (III.12: *krāṭhana* "snoring"), limping as if his feet were deformed (III.14: *manṭana*), performing lewd gestures in the proximity of women (III.15: *śṛṅgāraṇa*), improper actions (e.g., blurring the distinction between the pure and the impure; III.16) and nonsensical speech (full of repetition and contradiction; III.17), but whose sacred character and intent is so artfully disguised before the profane public (IV.1-5) as to invite abuse and even assault (III.1-7, 18, IV.14) for his apparent idiocy and madness (IV.6, 8). Yet in its classical Lākula form it was particularly meant for (loin-clothed or even naked, I.10-11) Brahmans compelled to avoid (at least in the initial stages) the sight of (impurities like) urine and excrement (I.12) and all contact with women and low castes (I.13)—even accidental pollution required meticulous purification (I.14-17)—and who assiduously cultivated mental purity (I.18) culminating in yogic detachment and conquest of the senses, and the universal friendliness (maitra) that accompanies constant union with the Lord (V.1-7, 11).

Even while reinforcing his interdictory sacrality by providing the (unconscious) safety-valve for the repressed primal energies that he seeks to master, the symbolic transgressions of the Brahman(ized) ascetic form a system that finds concrete fulfillment in the ritual praxis of the impure Kāpālika as the supreme Mahāpāśupata.[4] The "contradiction" between the "paranoid" avoidance of impurity in the first or "marked" (*vyakta*) stage and living in the cemetery infested with Cāṇḍālas, dogs, vultures, Kāpālikas, etc., in the fifth and last stage, where "the accomplished Yogin is not [any longer] tainted by [his] actions or sins" (PS V.20), imposes a dialectical reading of the Pāśupata aphorisms, against the "apologetic" interpretation of the commentary which is necessarily obliged to camouflage its transgressive finality in a manner suitable to the interdictory requirements of the novice at the first stage or even would-be candidates from the ranks of orthodox Brahmanism. Whereas the Brahman (formerly) worshiped the gods in an auspicious right-handed and the manes in an inauspicious left-handed manner, the ambidextrous bhakta now adored the intrinsically ambivalent Rudra in both these modes as containing both gods and manes in his demoniac divinity (PS II.7-11). Whereas the left-over offering to the terrible divinity is dangerously unfit for normal use, the abnormal Śaiva adept should wear only the garland already worn by the terrible Rudra (I.5), as all that was inauspicious in normal worship became auspicious (II.7) for the symbolic transgressor. The lewd bearer of the phallic liṅga (I.6) should ultimately revert to animal behaviour like that of a cow or deer (V.18), best understood in the light of the transgressive sexuality of the deer-skinned dīkṣita finding full expression in the ritual incest of sacrifices like the *Gosava.* The royal Indra who first practiced the Pāśupata vow among the demoniac Asuras (IV.10) in order to defeat them through their own magic (IV.12: *māyā*) is but the mythical projection of the Brahmanical sacrificer.

Although (initially) committed to non-violence and other traditional restraints (yama/niyama), the wielder of the club relished meat (buffalo, boar, etc.) and, although not to be killed by others, acquired the (magical) power to injure and kill others, in order to become chief of the (warrior-)hosts (*mahāgaṇapati*) of the great God (I.31-2, 37). It is legitimate to pose the question whether the ascetic does not owe his manifold suprahuman powers as much to his (symbolic) transgressions as to his severe austerities (I.20-37). The rule of bathing thrice daily with ashes, lying on a bed of ashes and rebathing with ashes in the case of (accidental) defilement (I.2-4), which commentaries beginning with Kauṇḍinya prescribe as "purification" potent enough to absolve from even Brahmanicidal transgressions (ad I.9), served in reality only to reinscribe the ghostly initiate (III.11 pretavaccaret) into the impure universe of death before he culminated (the last stage of) his yoga confined to the cremation ground where he constantly meditated upon and awaited union with Rudra (V.30-4). The impurity of death affirms itself as the cornerstone of the purified Pāśupata asceticism already in the founding myth, reported in the *Vāyu* (ch. 23) and *Liṅga* (ch. 24) Purāṇas, of Rudra entering a dead body thrown into the cremation ground at Kāyāvatāra or Kāyāvarohaṇa in order to incarnate himself as the brahmacārin Lakulin. In the Kāpālika, the aggressive club is replaced by the murderous skull-topped khaṭvāṅga, and the (Mahā-)

Pāśupata's becoming "Dharma incarnate" (V.31) by residing in the cremation ground (V.30) again reveals that underworldly foundation of the socio-religious order governed by royal Death as Yama-Dharmarāja.

The (feigning of) epileptic fits (III.13) and psychopathological states, combined with the recommended exclusive meditation on the "quivering" (vipra) sound-syllable Omkāra (V.24-8) and the archaic terminology of the aphorisms where the (raudra) bráhman still refers to compressed liturgical formulas (I.15, 39, II.21-7, III.20-6, IV.21-4, V.21-2, 41-7), not only suggest the ritual systematization of the original identity of the vision of the Ṛgvedic seer (ṛṣi) and the ecstatic trance of the shaman but also the cultivation of a transgressive technique of "divine madness" regulated by the interdictory controls that also define classical Brahmanism.[5] Concealment of his "purified" ritual(ized) speech (IV.3: *gūḍhapavitravāṇīḥ*) and behaviour (IV.2: *gūḍhavrataḥ*) by the erudite Mahābrāhmaṇa, who thereby seeks to transform his knowledge into consummate penance (III.19, IV.1), suggests that much of his incoherent rambling was only the comic disguise assumed by the enigmatic bráhman, whose "purest" essence was Omkāra (V.27: *vāgviśuddhaḥ*). The deformed (Mahā-)Gaṇapati, "Lord of the *Pramathas*," who presides over the comic sentiment (*hāsya*) in the Sanskrit drama, is himself born from Omkāra's bi-unity (mithuna). Issuing thunderously from the sacrificial stake in the form of the cosmic liṅga, Omkāra's mysterious laughter, while affirming the supremacy of Rudra, is indistinguishable from the violent laughter (*aṭṭahāsa*) of the Great God (*Mahādeva*) himself.[6]

All these essentially *comic* figures of symbolic violation like Pāśupata, Gaṇeśa and Vidūṣaka have for their sacred syllable the inarticulate (anirukta) Omkāra because, like the *vacarme* of explosive laughter, it signifies chaotic indifferentiation in the acoustic/linguistic code. In a traditional culture sharing a depreciative, repressive attitude to profane laughter, the Pāśupata's "sacred" laughter in imitation of the aṭṭahāsa of his elect divinity Rudra can only further signify transgression.[7] The recoding of these Pāśupata notations into the nonsensical poetic humor (*kāvyhāsya*) of the laughing Vidūṣaka is only the profane spectacle of that archaic shamanic inspiration dramatically objectivizing itself through the *kavi*'s aesthetic creation[8] under this inscrutably familiar guise of folly that psychoanalysis must appropriate at its own risk. The contrarying Varuṇa-Vidūṣaka who "deforms" (vidūṣ- = virūp-) the well-structured propositions of the hero-Indra in the ritual preliminaries (*pūrvaraṅga*) to the Sanskrit drama is none other than the transgressive Vedic Gandharva who, bearing onomatopoeic names like "Hāhā" or "Hūhū," still conserved the comic dimension of the stammering pre-classical dīkṣita.[9] Torn apart, in the post-axial differentiation of classical Hinduism, between the anti-social Pāśupata transgressions of the unorthodox Brahman renunciate and the domesticated "non-Vedic" stage-figure of the privileged Mahābrāhmaṇa Vidūṣaka, primitive clowning recognizes its lost organic unity in the spectacular performance of the Pueblo Koyemshi, where the highest specialists of the sacred publicly violate fundamental taboos before the half-terrified half-amused spectators of the tribe, whose entire religion would seem to be founded on the observance of these very interdictions, which the clowns indeed help maintain by their ridiculous negative example.[10]

Hence, transgression acquires a sacred dimension only when it is subordinated to a suprahuman aim, either explicitly or through its inscription in a symbolic context which, by paradoxically juxtaposing and especially infusing them with the values of the interdictory sacred, charges even the crudest profanities with a transcendent significance. As the social organization becomes more differentiated, the process of reinscription may well be translated into mythico-ritual "sectarian" confrontations between renunciatory ascetic orders and frankly transgressive religious currents, or between the hierarchized gods and perspectives of pure sacerdotal and impure even "marginal" castes. By reserving, as ordained by Prometheus in the Hesiodic founding-myth, the aromatized fumes of the burnt bones for the gods and the cooked animal for human consumption, on the one hand, and by inscribing, within the sacrificial procedure itself, the culinary progression from a "savage" roasting of the victim's unsalted vital organs consumed on the spot to the "civilized" boiling of its seasoned flesh fit for delayed consumption on the other hand, the Greek citizen sought to maintain his political life at a reasoned mid-distance mediating between the beastly and the divine. By inverting this culinary sequence, the central Orphic initiatic myth of the ritual murder of the child-Dionysos by the Titans, cast in the image of primordial mankind, who first boil his members before roasting them, reveals and condemns the animal-sacrifice that sustains the Greek city-state to be no more than a reversion to primitive cannibalism, shunned with horror by the pure vegetarian spirituality of the Orphics who rejected this institutionalized violence. Yet, not only did Dionysos, whose pure, purified pole was adored by the Orphics themselves as the benign incarnation of the paradisaical Golden Age, receive blood sacrifices and even raw flesh from the *polis*, but his transgressive essence took possession of his frenzied devotees to sanctify even their omophagy and anthropophagy. By presenting itself as that critical point where the interdictory masculine spirituality of Orphic asceticism reaches its zenith only to plunge into the abysmal depths of dionysiac transgression, the savage dismemberment of the sun-worshipping apollonian Orpheus at the impure female hands of the furious Bacchae, could just as well be read, in the light of the profound complicity between the delphic Apollo and the victimized Dionysos, as the tacit sacralization of the unmitigated crime of cannibalism that nourishes the roots of Greek humanity.[11]

Brahmanicide likewise sacralizes the demoniac Bhairava, even while debasing and excommunicating him, only because the mytheme of decapitation, reinforced by the precise ritualization of its symbolic notations, allows him to participate in the interdictory sacrality of his victim Brahmā. If the terrible Mahāvrata of the criminal Kāpālika corresponds so exactly to the punishment prescribed by the Brahmanical law books of the sacrificial dharma, this is only because this juridical order was itself determined by the equation of the Soma-dīkṣita to the ritual murderer of the sacrificial animal. The continuity is attested even in the sixth century A.D. in South India in the person of Kapāliśarman of the Taittirīya-caraṇa who performed Soma sacrifices, which has rightly been linked to the *Somasiddhānta* of another 11th C. Brahman Kāpālika, Somi-bhaṭṭaraka.[12] The Kutsa-gotra to which Kapāliśarman belonged was a clan of despicable, degraded Brahmans from whose ranks the Soma seller impersonating the Vedic Gandharva could be drawn, a role otherwise often played by a Śūdra who was subsequently abused and beaten. This ambivalent Soma seller is one of the models of the likewise manhandled Mahābrāhmaṇa-Vidūṣaka who, as Māḍhavya, is himself assimilated to the sacrificial animal, whose ritual identity with the Soma-dīkṣita projected as the Brahman Kāpālika is retained in the persistent belief in Nepal that the best human victims are the semi-Untouchable Kusles, descendants of the Kāpālikas and often custodians of the Newar cult of Bhairava. The deradicalization, attributed to Macchanda/Matsyendranāth, of the clan-structured (kula) Kāpālika praxis of the cremation ground, reformed by the abandoning of sect-distinctive signs which permitted its domesticated generalization as the Kaula secret societies attracting converts from the ranks of Brahmanical orthodoxy and penetrating deeply into the royal courts and the "patrician intelligentsia," could therefore just as well be understood as a Tantric reworking, around the *Bhairavāgamas*, of the preclassical sacrificial ideology which was thereby rendered accessible to especially householders from all levels of the caste society. For the Trika Brahman, schooled in all the classical "philosophies" and thoroughly imbued with "Āryan" culture, it is not the impurity of the Untouchable in itself, but rather its radical exploitation in the violation of interiorized norms of purity that is the source of the Kaula's sacred power.[13] Likewise the founding discourse of the Mahābrāhmaṇa-Vidūṣaka, in whom the pre-classical Vedic dīkṣita has assimilated the tantric notations of the Kaula adept, continued to be enacted at the transgressive centre of the nevertheless Brahmanical stage.

The semiotics of transgressive sacrality finds its ideal symbolic operator in the multidimensional category of the pure/impure, which resists all attempts by anthropologists to reduce it to the purely sociological opposition that, in Indian civilization, rules the separation of the Brahman and the Untouchable, even while embracing their conflicting functions within the hierarchical norm(s) of the caste society. Far from being a simple first principle that would have proliferated into a bewildering variety of substances and situations so as to regulate human conduct in its entirety, the apparently "mixed" category of the impure, the point of articulation of conceptual levels that we would now distinguish as physical, physiological, psychic, juridical, moral or metaphysical, and not only social, appears rather as the complex terminal concept precipitated by an invisible semiology generating the diverse taboos of which it is the object. In other words, impurity is not the independent objective property generally presupposed by interdictory sacrality but itself on the contrary the hypostatized effect projected by the operation of a network of taboos held together by a mythico-ritual symbolic system which needs to be adequately deciphered in order to understand why certain objects, actions, and persons are impure in certain contexts.[14] The quasi-Untouchability of the Mahābrāhmaṇa as funerary priest defies any functionalist or structuralist sociology that defines (the supreme status of) the Brahman in terms of his ritual purity alone, instead of deriving the inscrutable symbolism of death invested in this (in principle) Vedic Brahman in a dialectical manner from the impure sacrality of the Brahman(ized) initiate (dīkṣita) during his embryonic regression in the pre-classical sacrifice.[15] For the symbolic universe of the Vedic yajña, itself the social dramatization of an inner lived experience of transgressive sacrality, is the formal paradigm whereby the strict observance of ritually prescribed injunctions (*vidhi*) and interdictions (*niṣedha*) paradoxically culminates in the sacralization of the forbidden impure so as to consecrate even the criminal Brahmanicide of the Kāpālika Mahābrāhmaṇa.

It is this enigmatically structured universe of mythico-ritual correspondences and its mana-like sacred power released by their assimilation and mastery as evidenced in the riddle-like hymnology of the Ṛgvedic poet (kavi), that constitutes the original meaning of the term *bráhman*, which later appears in a primarily liturgical form as ritualized enigma contests (*brahmodya*) whose key was hidden in the officiating brahmán priest who silently supervised the mysterious workings of the sacrifice.[16] Makarius has sought to demonstrate that mana as power is unleashed through transgression, and resolving the enigma is symbolically equated by Lévi-Strauss with committing incest, such as is bequeathed by Prajāpati in the form of the black antelope skin to the (royal) dīkṣita before it came to characterize the transgressive fifth head of the Purāṇic Brahmā.[17] Although apparently suffering from exaggerated timidity, constant allusions, often teasingly by his royal patron himself, are made to the formidable (magical) powers of the mock-heroic Vidūṣaka, who brandishes the crooked (kuṭilaka) weapon of Brahmā in phallic gestures of displaced aggressivity ultimately aimed at the protectress of the heroine, the mythical Sarasvatī, incestuous daughter of Brahmā(-Prajāpati). If this "caricature of the purohita," though always a Brahman and indeed protected by Omkāra the quintessence of bráhman, is regularly depicted profaning the cherished values of Brahmanism and even (symbolically) violating its sacralizing interdictions, so as to earn the mocking label of "Brahman par excellence" (*Mahābrāhmaṇa*), this is no doubt because the semiotics of transgression reveals this enigmatic buffoon, who revels in abrupt irrelevant nonsensical pretentious remarks dismissed as puerile jokes, to be the delightful bearer of the primordial bráhman.[18]

B. The Royal Murder of the Brahman(ized) Dīkṣita: The Inner Conflict of Man

"Vice is the profound truth and heart of Man."

—*Bataille*

Archaic religion was universally centered on a deliberate, carefully delimited although often violent transgression which, in the founding mechanism of the sacrifice, even assumed the form of ritual(ized) murder. Having posed the problem as to whether the instincts that seek and find expression in these sacralized transgressions could possibly be eradicated in the course of human progress or "if it is a question on the contrary of a sovereign and irreducible part of man, *but which would hide itself from his consciousness?* If in a word it is a question of his heart . . . ?" (loc. cit.), Bataille himself is inclined to the latter view that, to use Indian terminology, the organized *sát* aspect of life is founded on the original but suppressed chaos *ásat* which, as the ultimate truth of man's humanity, must be given conscious but circumscribed expression within this very order itself.[19]

The pre-classical Vedic dīkṣā charged the royal sacrificer of the world-conquering Horse Sacrifice (*Aśvamedha*) with the impurity of death which he discharged during his final purificatory bath (avabhṛtha) onto a deformed (Ātreya) Brahman (jumbaka) representing the evil aspect of Varuṇa(*-pāparūpa*), after which the scapegoat emerged from the mouth-deep water bearing the sins of not only the Brahmanized dīkṣita but of the entire community from which he was permanently expelled.[20] This Brahman jumbaka, charged with the impurity of the village outcastes (*apagrāmāḥ*), is the very personification of Death and Brahmanicide. By his simultaneous emergence from the pool in order to allow other evildoers to bathe away their sins, the Vedic dīkṣita is himself assimilated to a Brahmanicide, for which reason alone even the later law books recommend a real Brahman-slayer to purify himself by performing the royal Aśvamedha.[21] "The purifications that the sacrificer had to undergo after the sacrifice moreover resembled the expiation of the criminal," and the sacrificial mechanisms revolving around the identification of the Soma-dīkṣita, the victim and the divinity, ultimately offered the yajamāna the means of sacrificing himself to the divinity, but through the mediation of the victim with whom he was symbolically identified.[22] The sacrificer was not only anointed at the same time as the sacrificial stake (yūpa) but actually took for some time the victim's place on the post which, although traversing the three cosmic levels, was measured to the dimensions of the sacrificer.

But the Brahman jumbaka immersed in the amniotic waters personified bhrūṇahatyā, which means not only Brahmanicide but also *foeticide.* For the bhrūṇa is ambiguously both a Śrotriya initiated into the secrets of the Veda *and* an embryo before its sex can be determined, a linguistic precipitate of the sacrificial ideology that clearly reveals the embryogonic foundation of Vedic religion.[23] That Brahmanism overrides the caste hierarchy, understood in the narrow sociological sense, is clear from the killing of even a Kṣatriya or Vaiśya who has studied the Veda or has been initiated for the Soma sacrifice being equated with Brahmanicide. The transgressive character of the embryonic regression resulting in the androgynous fusion of the male dīkṣita and the maternal womb (-psyche) is also suggested by the extension of the Brahmanicide punishments to one who has killed a pregnant or menstruating wife of a twice-born performing a Soma sacrifice.[24] It is through his transgressive sacrality, symbolized by his Brahmanicide, that the dīkṣita regresses into the embryonic realm of Varuṇa to regain the rejuvenating potentialities of the hidden Agni-Soma. Conversely, the embryogonic exploitation of real Brahmanicide is reinforced by the prescription of the law books that the *brahmahan* or Brahman-slayer should expiate himself by retracing the motherly Sarasvatī river upstream back to its hidden source. There, at the centre of the Vedic universe, towered the world-tree Plakṣa Prāsravana, on reaching which the dīkṣitas completing the Sārasvata sattras had to likewise undergo the avabhṛtha bath.[25]

Whereas the sexualized embryonic regression is generally relived in the form of a maternal incest, the violent death undergone by the androgynized dīkṣita in his own womb is also experienced as an infanticide and/or matricide, the whole complex of ideas being symbolically projected in highly condensed mythico-ritual scenarios to which the closest parallel are the rhetorical figures of the enigmatic dream.[26] The brahmán-priest, who embodies this inner embryonic state in the outer sacrificial drama, comes to be himself identified with the mother, and the yajamāna's "traumatic" rebirth as a Brahman from the womb of bráhman is assimilated to a matricidal Brahmanicide, the equation of mother and Brahman being especially codified in the cultural institution of the inviolability of the sacred cow. Vīrabhadra, who decapitated the sacrificer Dakṣa-Prajāpati, not only assumes a "universal" (viśvarūpa) form to behead the "demoniac" king Vallāḷarājan in the Aṅkāḷamman cycle of myths but is himself identified with the child-Śiva (Iruḷappan) dismembered in the (surrogate) womb of the queen by his mother, the goddess herself. Indeed, in his Andhra cult centering on the termite mound, that is still celebrated in Rajahmundry also during the dīkṣā-like obscurity of Mahāśivarātri, there is likewise a nightly funerary procession where the marchers impersonating this Bhairava-like deity are possessed rather by real children who have died an early and untimely death.[27]

The pastoral Gollas themselves traditionally unite their "bandit-king" Mallanna with his companion and equal, the purohita-like "Sanganna, the son of Brahmans of the Viśvāmitra Gotra," and even identify the two through the simultaneity of their births. Khaṇḍobā bore the transgressive sword, donated by the Brahman general of Malhārgad fort, of the purohita's son Aśvatthāman, to be offered, in the form of five lambs, the voluntary sacrifice of the "five heroes" (pañcavīra) made to Mailāra, no different from the five children demanded by Mhaskobā. Mallanna regains his kingdom by marrying a Brahman girl Ratnāngī in order to consummate his embryogonic worship of the termite mound, where this outcaste seventh son discovered Pārvatī's golden nose-ring which, identified with the pastoral wealth of sheep, is simultaneously the Soma in the form of boiled milk and the Agni stolen from the (Brahma-) rāksasa/ī of confused sex, whose skull is transformed into a bowl for gruel. The definition, in the Deccan folk cult, of true bhakti as the feeding of Mārtaṇḍa-Bhairava in the form of a Brahman, readily transformed like the pastoral Vāghyā into a vicious dog his theriomorph, reflects the "Brahmanization" of tribal shamanism through identifying Mallanna's naked canine brother, the yūpa-like single-footed (ekapāda) Bhairava found in the primordial mound, with the Vedic solar (superfluous) eighth (= 7 + 1) son still-born (mṛta + aṇḍa) for progeny and death from the womb of Aditi the universal Mother.[28]

The Ātreyas, like the Vāsiṣṭhas, were highly prized for the office of purohita, whose image becomes caricaturably fused with that of the scapegoat jumbaka in the deformed Brahman Vidūṣaka who, through his transgressive traits, is as it were his own Brahmanicide. One of the functions of the purohita, devalued in the eyes of the orthodox Śrotriya Brahmans, consisted in taking over the impurity of his essentially Untouchable royal patron, whose universalization through the dīkṣā is expressed through the mytheme of Indra's decapitation of his demoniac purohita Viśvarūpa.[29] Whereas Bhairava is Indra-like in his Brahmanicide, and the Vidūṣaka Kapiñjala derives his name from Viśvarūpa's decapitated Soma-drinking head, transformed into a partridge (*kapiñjala*), the names of Tantric texts like *Triśirobhairava*, apparently coined on the image of the gluttonous three-headed Viśvarūpa, not only indicate the identity of sacrificer and victim but also suggest that these "non-Vedic" doctrines were formulated in those esoteric circles where Brahman, king and Untouchable could come together in the not merely symbolic figure of the royal Mahābrāhmaṇa.[30] Sacred, as opposed to profane, laughter should rather be interpreted as the manifestation of death-in-life; and the profane laughter that was expected to greet and echo the Vidūṣaka's own "exaggerated" laughter (atihāsya) unconsciously participates in the paradoxical dialectic of the "sardonic" laughter, obligatorily indulged in by the victim and/or by the sacrificers on his behalf.[31]

C. Incestuous Marriage and Embryogonic Death in the Folk-Cult of Kāttavarāyan

Having now discussed the embryogonic and androgynous dimension of the dīkṣā-ideology, we may see how it is expressed through the story of Kāttavarāyan.[32] Left undeveloped in the Brahmanicide Bhairava probably because of his being cast in the direct image of Kāpālika ritual praxis, the trickster possibilities of the transgressor (Makarius; see n. 17) are on the contrary highlighted in the Tamil Kāttavarāyan who, despite the characteristic malicious pranks, still remains even etymologically a guardian-figure (kāval) like our classic kṣetrapāla. The whole "tragedy" of this Untouchable outcaste revolves specifically around his consuming "Brahmanicidal" passion for the pure Brahman virgin Āriyamālai, "daughter of a thousand vaidika Brahmans," which culminates rather in his fatal union with an impaling stake. The "lawful irregularities" in the narrative logic, resisting any psychologizing or sociologizing reductionism, are easily resolved by posing the following two sets of sacrificial equations partly organizing and repeatedly interfering with the normal or "romanesque" development of the plot: Āriyamālai = stake (kalu) = his mother Kāmāṭchi [Kāmākṣī] = Kālī = the (youngest of the) Seven Maidens; and Kāttavarāyan = (child-)Śiva = (Brahman-)king.

His mother's constant admonishment that the stake for which he is predestined was born and grows with the forbidden Brahman girl suggests that even when he does not end up happily married to her, as in the *Nāṭakam*, his final impalement should itself be understood as a divine marriage. It is because his mother's boon of embracing Āriyamālai is fulfilled by the fatal marriage with the stake that strangely enough the *Katai* mentions the latter's abduction only in passing and Kāttavarāyan, having sacrificed himself on the stake for her sake alone, is paradoxically willing to finally renounce her. Although married to her with all the gods as witnesses in the *Ammānai*, where his finally revealed Brahman birth renders him more than a welcome bridegroom in the hearts of the king and the vaidika Brahmans, he therefore still insists on consummating his passion on the stake. Kāttavarāyan's apparently divergent main aims, Āriyamālai in the *Katai* and apotheosis on the stake in the *Ammānai*, are in fact indissolubly merged at the symbolic level.

The incestuous desire for Kāmāṭchi, devoted to intense asceticism since her separation from Śiva's left side, has been translated into the equally transgressive union with the Brahman virgin who, though more a pattini than his own mother, manifests an ambivalent attitude to her Untouchable lover, by both lamenting the social stigma and also reciprocating his passion. His attachment to Kāmāṭchi is such that he feels obliged to repeatedly beg her permission and seek her blessings even after having kidnapped Āriyamālai without his mother's permission. Although the ascetic mother, cast in the mould of the sacred interdictions, opposes the union only to helplessly give in to his wishes at the end, she sets him various invariably successful tasks as "diversions" which could serve only to inflame his passion. That Kāmāṭchi's opposition to the transgressive union of her beloved outcaste son with the, for him, "Untouchable" Brahman Āriyamālai cannot be taken seriously at face value is confirmed by the fact that she herself instigates the trickster to not only make the thousand vaidika Brahmans lose their purity in a general way, but especially by bringing a thousand Paraiya men to sleep with the Brahman wives and transporting the thousand Brahmans likewise to the beds of the Paraiya women, and then impersonating their revered guru, the Kāśī-kurukkaḷ, to implicate them in a comically transgressive homa ritual, which reminds one of the use of repugnant materials in the often incestuous Tantric *Kula-Yāga* (E. Visuvalingam, n. 114; in this volume). Far from constituting the two opposed poles of the double-bind between which the indecisive hero oscillates, the resolution of the sexual triad at the heart of the tale is realized in the symbolic identity of the bride-mother.

The symbolic identity of the fatal bride and despairing mother implies and also confirms the latter's equation with the stake, for Kāmāṭchi has a vested interest in Kāttavarāyan's impalement, which is the precondition for her heavenly reunion with Śiva as his left side. The symbolic mediator between the benign mother and his embryonic death at the bridal-stake is Vallatu Māṅkāḷiyamman, a form of Kālī, to whom Kāmāṭchi sends him in recognition of her superior power, and who attacks, swallows, and brings him forth again as a fondling in her arms. It is she who instructs him how to fashion a properly decorated stake from the fatal tree which she had been tending with such maternal care and she who finally grants him permission to abduct the forbidden Āriyamālai even while warning him of its fruition on the stake. Kāttavarāyan threatens to decapitate himself with Kālī's magic sword or to throw himself on a sword unless Kāmāṭchi grants him the boon of abducting Āriyamālai. The mutual aggressivity of mother and son is already seen in their very first earthly encounter when the "hungry" child-hero displaces his deadly blow to the wretched bird perched on the banyan tree under which Kāmāṭchi was performing her penance; the mother-goddess reduces her new-found son to ashes with her third eye before resuscitating him as an infant in her arms.[33]

The embryogonic dimension, evident in Kālī, is expressed more specifically through Kāttavarāyan's foster-mothers, the Seven Maidens who, like Kāmāṭchi herself, have been performing extreme austerities for twelve years before he obliges them to recognize him as the long-awaited one (Murukan and/or Śiva) from Kailāsa. Their maternal equivalence with Āriyamālai is hinted at through even such trivial sequences as Kāttavarāyan disguising himself, like Śiva, as an old man selling bangles successively to Kāmāṭchi, the Seven Maidens, and, finally, to his beloved, before he succeeds in fastening the marriage-cord (tālī) around the neck of the sleeping Brahman virgin. In the *Katai*, it is they who take the infant from the decrepit Kāmāṭchi's arms to teach him various magical powers, especially that of changing his form at will, before returning him at the age of five to his "true" mother. Reborn on earth in different castes and localities in the *Ammānai* as a result of Śiva's curse for intruding into Pārvatī's flower garden, the youngest, who is also the first to recognize him, and actually falls in love with and even embraces him, completes the list of terrestrial incarnations to be married, along with Karuppalaki and Ukantalaki, to Kāttavarāyan. She serves as the symbolic mediator between his ascetic mother and the virgin Āriyamālai, with whom she is explicitly identified and whose real divine identity is known to Kāttavarāyan from the very beginning. Whereas his entire tragic destiny is originally attributed to his stealing her clothes while she bathed with her six virgin companions in his mother's flower garden (Pūṅkāvanam is a name of the goddess herself) turned penance-grove, which he was created to guard, here it is Kāmāṭchi herself who instigates him to destroy their tapas on earth. Fleeing them in the embryonic disguises of a tortoise, ant, ear-ring, and mouse after having seduced especially the youngest maiden, he promises to guard their clothes while they bathe in the ocean of milk but, repeating his "original sin," steals their saris, and is finally saved from their wrath only by his "true" mother who transforms him again into a baby and petrifies them into the seven stones still worshipped as village-goddesses.

All these embryogonic notations colored with maternal aggressivity converge at Kāttavarāyan's incestuous union with the virgin impaling stake and are most poignantly summed up by the *Ēcal*'s declaration that "he dies like a child in a crib." The "criminal" character of the (transposed) dīkṣita is suggested by the corresponding punishment for real criminals by hanging them in a basket or box for several days on top of a long pole. The kalu is a symbol for rebirth, for the victim still swirls around it holding a child to guarantee it healthy longevity; and the regenerative power of the dīkṣā is exploited by bringing sick people on a bier (like dead bodies) to be revived by the goddess. The substitution of his human sacrifice by an immortal lime impaled on a spike (śūla) beside the kalumaram, surrounded by men dressed as Kālī, is rendered possible by its representing the seed(-state) to which Kāttavarāyan had already reverted at his first birth when he was unwittingly swallowed by a Brahman-girl as a sacred lime, still distributed by the priests to women seeking pregnancy. The embryogonic dimension of the final impalement is already prefigured, through the accumulation of womb-symbols, in the *Ammānai*-episode where, "at Kāmāṭchi's place" which is "beyond many forests, in the middle of a flower garden, Kāttavarāyan does tapas by standing on a copper needle which is on top of a copper pot, which in turn is on top of a 60 foot pole (kampam)." The transgressive reversal implied in the pot on the skambha is explicated by the demonic Brahman who tests the would-be victim by claiming to have done the same tapas "standing on his head," and it is in this very context that he threatens to decapitate himself with Kālī's magic sword. Elsewhere standing on the Vaiṣṇava head of Vairiceṭṭi, the Untouchable Kāttavarāyan, like the Ceṭṭi ruthlessly sacrificed to become the "Master of the impalement stake," suffers to attain immortality at Kāmāṭchi's feet through the ritual dramatization of the fatally incestuous embryonic regression, which is the precondition to the dīkṣita's ascent up the suṣumnā, itself projected as the kalu, axis-mundi of the Tamil folk cult.

Hence the Vedic image of the inverted tree at the Māriyamman festival,[34] where the pūcāri crushes the ram's head in the hole with the base of the spinal kampam, whereas the pot-womb is placed on the triple fork at its head, corresponding to the fusion of the three motherly nāḍīs represented by the central ambā and the lateral diminutive ambikā and ambālikā during the fatal union of the royal Aśvamedha horse with the queen-mother (mahiṣī). The incestuous dimension of this initiatic death is revealed in the invocation of all the "mothers" (ammai) during the parallel marriage, reflecting that between the post and the pot, of a male buffalo with Vīrakālī in the form of a "dead" mare, a union mediated by a Brahman adept himself incarnating the goddess to "feed" the sacrificial buffalo. The real victim is, however, the priest entering into trance while being drenched along with the uprooted kampam in the amniotic waters poured by devotees, who having earlier carried fire-pots instead on their heads, thereby indirectly participate in this rejuvenating Agni-Soma embryogony. Whereas the "matricide" is translated into his killing Campaṅkitāci and especially the impure washerwoman bride-to-be Vaṇṇāravalli, the sexual dimension of the fatal union, already hinted at by Kāttavarāyan's being fed by most of the Seven Maidens, is especially expressed in the *Ammānai* by Nallataṅkāḷ climbing the stake to quench the dying hero's thirst with buttermilk. At the bottom of the stake, having secret devices installed by seven carpenters on Kāttavarāyan's instructions, Āriyamālai dies with the rest of the "virgins" to be taken by the Brahman Untouchable to the feet of his mother who divinizes him.

The impure evil aspect of the Brahman(ized) pre-classical dīkṣita, intolerable from the point of view of the purified classical sacrifice, is retained in Kāttavarāyan's split identity determined by his double birth, first as a Brahman and then adopted by a Paraiya outcaste woman. The underlying dīkṣā embryogony reveals itself especially in the otherwise unnecessary second sequence where the Brahman mother is replaced at the shrine of the impure Kālī by the womb-belly of the deer, whose skin charged with Vedic incest symbolism is worn by the embryonic dīkṣita. Gaṇeśa, at the Oṭṭapiḷḷaiyār shrine where the first birth sequence unfolds, is himself a Mahābrāhmaṇa born of his mother's impurities, and the initiatic Death confers the host of demoniac servants of Yama himself. Substituted by Toṭṭiyattu-Cinnan when bound by the king within the Piḷḷaiyār shrine, the black powers of this transgressive snake-charmer find superlative expression in his Keralite *alter ego*, whom he decapitates in the *Ammānai*. Kāttavarāyan's gift of knowing his former births is only a transposition of the *jātavidyā* of the Vedic dīkṣita, whose state of undifferentiated "universalization" (*viśvarūpatā*) is likewise translated into the Untouchable magician's protean capacity to change his form at will. Already embodying in himself the extrememost poles of the caste hierarchy, the pañcavarṇar encompasses the entire social order by assuming a whole range of social roles and by uniting, like the king, with the multiple caste earthly representatives of the Seven Maidens. The initial image of Kāttavarāyan as a fish trapped in Āriyamālai's hair, which suggests the subsequent unfolding of the plot, reveals its true significance when we compare her remarkable coiffure (kūntal) with the fishing net of the Cempaṭavar fishermen identified with the infanticide Aṅkāḷamman.[35] Not only is Kāttavarāyan the earthly son of the head fisherman, but Kāmāṭchi actually tries to dissuade him from marrying the stake by pleading: "Why should you writhe and die on the fisherman's hook?" Apart from its aesthetic and romanesque charm, this image again identifies Kāttavarāyan from the beginning as the fishy dīkṣita enmeshed in the hair-net womb of the virgin mother-goddess.

Śiva's wholly unjustifiable curse on his son to "die as a Brahman Untouchable fisherman on the stake," for only doing his duty in guarding his mother (and her flower-garden) is explicable as yet another "lawful irregularity" generated by the symbolic identity of father and son, within the underlying dīkṣā ideology implicit in Pārvatī's locking up an ant in the womb-like obscurity of the (usually golden) casket for which her divine consort exiles her to the terrestrial garden and creates Kāttavarāyan in the first place. If Śiva condemns his "Untouchable" son to death for erotically prolonging the nudity of the seventh Maiden as punishment for having violated his mother's sanctity, and if Pārvatī herself is condemned to separation as an earthly demoness merely on account of maternal compassion for her innocent child, this would be because it is his own mother(-substitute) that the son has thereby symbolically violated. And if Kāttavarāyan's self-sacrifice at the stake is the necessary precondition for the celestial reunion of his divine parents, would this not be simply because it is only through his initiatic death in the womb of the wife-mother that the husband-son is able to reunite with her to form the primordial androgyne? By placing the onus of the interdictory sacred on the victimized wife-mother and on the "Brahmanical" Śiva, the pure husband-pole of the split-yajamāna, and investing the transgressive sacred in the impure son-pole, the story of the dīkṣita-trickster is rendered all the more palatable, even if not wholly digestible, to the exoteric consumer, including the perplexed Indologist for whom the myth seems unable to make up its mind on more points than one.

Already at the centre of events in the *Ēcal*, the king is very favorably disposed towards the Untouchable in the *Ammānai*, even appointing him chief watchman over his kingdom. Apart from directly disguising himself as the king, the reversal of roles in the *Katai*, when the criminal tricks the latter into being locked in the same iron box in which the king had shackled and imprisoned him, also suggests the symbolic identity of the two antagonists. Just before his impalement, Kāttavarāyan "the guardian-king," assuming the form of Murukan, in fact reveals himself to Āriyappūrājan as "the king who took Āriyamālai" and is publicly accorded royal worship at the foot of and along with the stake. Even the heavy chains in which (the impersonator of) Kāttavarāyan used to be bound in the cult remind one of the images of the royal Indra bound and put in a cage at the base of the Kathmandu Indradhvaja, and both are probably derived from the Vedic paradigm of the (royal) dīkṣita being bound in Varuṇa's noose before he substitutes for himsef with the victim on the sacrificial yūpa. The "heroic feat" (pavādā) performed during Dasarā by the Kuruba Vaggayyas and Māḍigas, who pierce their legs to pass a long rope through the wound, is itself reminiscent of the royal cowherd Āryaka chained by his foot to the sacrificial post in the Sanskrit drama *Mṛcchakaṭikā*, "The Little Clay Cart." As Shulman rightly observes (in this volume), "the king's role as sacrificial patron, yajamāna, is relevant to this portrait, though here the patron is also quite literally the victim of the rite," and "kingship here appears tied to a self-sacrificial ritual act."

Like that of the king Arjuna-Kārttavīrya, the arrogance in the *Katai* of the literally out-caste Kāttavarāyan, who embraces the entire caste hierarchy to reveal his royal identity at the fatal stake and receive the first pūjā in the sanctum of the Trimūrti, expresses the same universalization of the dīkṣā. Inherited from the Brahmanicide Indra his Vedic father, the scandalous boasting of the royal Arjuna, after abusively "murdering" the Brahmanized Yudhiṣṭhira, is equated to an expiatory ritual "suicide," because the universalization of egoism (*pūrṇāhambhāva* or *pūrṇāhamtā*) is paradoxically also the death of the sclerosed constricted ego. The overweening ahaṃkāra of the demon-devotee, mercifully slain by the god of bhakti, is ultimately no more than the negative image of the divine omniscience and omnipotence of the God himself.[36]

The striking coincidence in the names of the king and the Brahman Āriyamālai, coupled with our knowledge that it is he who initiates the ritual mechanisms for her birth to his temple priest, subsequently bestows wealth on her, and inexplicably appoints Civapputaiyān, Kāttavarāyan's father, to guard her within 21 fortresses, confirms this Brahmanical aspect of the king. It also reflects the purification of the classical yajamāna into a (temporary) Brahman, and is matched by the hidden (impure) Brahmanhood of Śiva's son himself, whose birth initiates the whole sacrificial sequence. For the sake of the Untouchable royal goddess his mother, the criminal son's humiliating transgressions are thus especially directed against the Untouchable watchman father, representing the Brahmanical authority of the king, the temple priest and Śiva. Yet this Tamil Oedipus Rex, who vows from the beginning to "ruin the Brahman's family" by seducing doe-eyed women, for he is himself the "whore-monger" Murugan, nevertheless assumes his favorite disguise of a decrepit old man, who cannot stand the smell of females, to reveal his interdictory dimension as his own ascetic father Śiva. In the single nuclear family, reduplicated *ad infinitum* throughout this folkloric empire of the Hindu socio-religious hierarchy, the divine father dies in the form of the Untouchable son to celebrate his royal marriage with the mysterious Annamuttu, the beloved dreamlike image of the Brahman Āriyamālai-Annattuḷaciyammāḷ, the virgin-mother.

Already evidenced in the ritually more "authentic" *Ammānai* and the *Ēcal*, the comically exagerated humiliation of the orthodox (not only) Brahmans in the *Katai*, which accentuates Kāttavarāyan's trickster aspect and lends itself readily even to modern exploitation for political purposes, does not suffice to define him as a champion of lower caste resentment against Brahmanical hegemony. For not only does the hero accept his guilt and eagerly embrace his punishment, which is imitated by his unresentful devotees, but the proposed "mission" is ultimately compromised by the revelation of his Brahman birth even in the *Katai*, devoted chiefly to the entertaining diffusion of the sacrificial paradigm to the lowest levels of the caste hierarchy. His tricking of the 1000 Brahmans and their wives, beginning with Āriyamālai's father, into getting stuck to the tail of a donkey, symbol of the Untouchable, could just as well betray their, like his own, Vedic status as Mahābrāhmaṇas. Chorused by a lachrymose pulampal, it is clearly his death at the sacrificial stake, in other words his incestuous union with the virgin-mother, that is ultimately responsible for the Untouchable Brahman dīkṣita's divinization in a tragic scenario that forces even the Brahmanical Śiva to beg at his feet. Similarly, the annual marriage of Kāla-Bhairava with the Lāṭ or Mahāśmaśāna-Stambha in Kāśī, which marks the beginning of the period of death rituals, has been shown, through a systematic comparison with the simultaneous emergence of the mother-goddess in the form of the Kumārī during the Indra-Jātrā, and the decapitation of Kāśī-Bhairava at the Bisket pole-festival in Nepal, to be a criminal execution with embryonic implications.[37] Just as Bhairava's punishment for Brahmanicide in fact corresponds to the "supreme penance" (Mahāvrata) exalted by the Kāpālikas, so too does this criminal pañcavarṇar personify the transgressive sacrality of the Untouchable Vedic dīkṣita who, by dying at the yūpa, regresses into the virgin-womb of his wife-mother for a renewed lease of life on earth. It is for this reason, no doubt, that this Tamil folktale still prefers to situate Kāmāṭchi's flower garden, where Kāttavarāyan first appeared, on the banks of the Gaṅgā near Kāśī, embryogonic centre of the Hindu universe.

D. Criminal Gods and Demon Devotees: Sacrifice, Bhakti and Terror

Flectere si nequeo superos, Acheronta movebo[38]

Otherwise inadmissible in a religion based exclusively on the love of God, the valorized mythical figures of the criminal god, the projection of the murderous sacrificer as identified with his transcendent divinity, and of the demon devotee, the extrapolation of the same transgressive dīkṣita as incarnated in the evil victim, are still indissolubly bound together in the "Christian" figure of the (son of) God who sacrifices himself for our sins.[39] The transformation of the demon-devotee Bhairavanātha, through his fatal violation of the virgin womb of the mother-goddess, into the criminal-god Bhairava, a transgressive itinerary that nevertheless provides the exemplary model for the popular pilgrimage instituted by the devout Śrīdhara at Vaiṣṇodevī, reveals the essential identity of murderer and victim even within the context of a purified bhakti.[40] Likewise, the "confusion" of Maṇi and Malla and the conflation of their respective dying boons in the composite figure of Maṇimal, with Maṇi sometimes reduced to the horse of Malla, would have been possible only if the two were perceived as constituting a single demoniac essence. Khaṇḍobā's acceptance of Maṇi's white horse as his own vehicle and his accordance of public worship to the reformed demon within his temple precincts, coupled with his assumption, as "destroyer of Malla" or Malhārī/Mallāri, of the name of the unreformed demon, suggests a similar identification of the god and his demoniac victim. If Khaṇḍobā provides goats as naivedya to satisfy the still unreformed Malla's desire for human sacrifices and accepts that the demon's decapitated human head be placed under the threshold of the temple to be trodden by his devotees and himself, this could then be interpreted as a symbolic subterfuge divulging that it is Khaṇḍobā himself who ultimately demands human sacrifice of his devotees as exemplified by the now goat-headed Malla.[41] The Untouchable Mātaṅga, sacrificed for the foundation of Khaṇḍobā's temple-fortress at his capital Jejuri and divinized into its guardian officer Yesvant Rāo, is himself the Śiva he thereby establishes there and is able to cure bone fractures, like the medicine man Rudra, only through the regenerative power of his fatal dīkṣā. Likewise, it is he himself whom the "demoniac" (Bētāla) Cevvi Reddi had to murder in the form of the Untouchable Rēca in order to gain a treasure (and, finally, a kingdom), for he changed the gotra name into Rēcerla in commemoration of his faithful servant's voluntary sacrifice. The indirect identification of even the purified vegetarian god with the carnivorous demon devotee completes the triangular dialectics of *self-sacrifice* whereby the purified devotee continues to offer himself in the form of the evil egoistic victim to himself as the transcendent god of bhakti, so that he may secure abundance in his worldly life. The confluence of sacrificial paradigms and shamanizing practices in folk religion is most vividly underlined in their repeated encounter in the cult of the pastoral Khaṇḍobā assimilated to the Brahmanical Mārtaṇḍa-Bhairava: though himself denied direct vision of the god he worships so regularly in the temple, it is the Brahman who confirms the bhakti of the tribal by revealing that the mysterious and overpowering divine presence the latter had experienced in the solitude of the forest is indeed the god Khaṇḍobā.[42]

Between the extreme poles of the popular "shamanizing" level of Tamil folk religion, where the deity, who possesses his devotees, is injured or killed in a bloody sacrificial scenario, and the Brahmanical purity of the royal temple, where the transcendent undying god, worshiped according to the strict rules of the Āgamas, is ritually extricated from all violence, we are faced with the fanatical anpu of 24 Nāyanārs who kill or injure themselves and/or their kin, as extensions of themselves, for the *love* of the manifestations of Śiva in his slaves or liṅga.[43] Although in the bhakti context based on a dualistic metaphysics, the Nāyanār's suicide appears to be vindicated in terms of his recognition of the Lord (only) in the Other and not in his own debased self, it is nevertheless through this very self-sacrifice that he attains union (sāyujyam) with Śiva, who has in reality already taken possession of him through anpu. Moreover, the hagiographies themselves seem to provide symbolic equations that continue to identify the eager victim and his demanding god. His human bondage (*paśutva*) replaced by divine autonomy (*śivatva*) through the dīkṣā of Śiva's gracious look, the hunter Tiṇṇanār feels immediately impelled to defiling worship of the liṅga, and his self-sacrifice is equated with the deity's own self-mutilation. This Kaṇṇappa is after all an incarnation of Arjuna, mortally crushed in the *Mahābhārata* by the tribal Kirāta-Śiva, with whom he is identified in the context of a symbolic dīkṣā.[44] Whereas Ēnātināta allows himself to be killed by his treacherous rival wearing Śiva's sacred ash on his forehead, Pukalccōla Nāyanār, by bearing the decapitated head of a Śaiva devotee in the golden pot on his own head during his self-immolation in the sacrificial fire, is, as it were, identifying himself with his own victim. Pukalccōla had, after all, already offered himself as victim to his own sword at the hands of Eripatta Nāyanār, dressed in the garb of Śiva, only to be faced with the disconcerting prospect of his executioner using it to cut his own throat instead. The Nāyanār's devout horror at killing Śiva in the form of his slaves has become the bhakti pretext for his own divinization through selfless suicide, the ritual model for which is ironically provided by the original self-sacrifice of the god himself.

Other scenarios seem to extrapolate tantricizing transgressive values onto a public setting where the underlying ritual patterns are now justifiable only in terms of a shocking but exemplary anpu. Thus Ciruttoṇṭar's sacrifice to the Bhairava-ascetic of his own cooked son, left untasted by the bhakti religion, has still all the flavour of Kāpālika cannibalism. Vicāra Śarma's reward for his Bhairava-like Brahmanicide of his own father is to receive, as Caṇḍeśvara, the dangerous nirmālya from the temple offerings to Śiva, whose problematic status is explicitly compared to the ambivalence of the transgressive Soma-dīkṣita.[45] By slaughtering his next-of-kin to defend the privilege of the lecherous ash-smeared Brahman to cohabit with his own wife, Iyarpakai Nāyanār's "immoral" anpu only preserves the obscure ritual traditions amply depicted on Śaiva temple walls elsewhere. The fundamental, and no doubt revealing, question that must be posed to the hagiography of Tamil bhakti, even independently of these selected episodes, is why the Nāyanār is able to recognize his Lord's omnipresence *only* in (those who bear) his overt ritual insignia. And more important for our problematic than the retention of the violent elements, common to both archaic Tamil culture and the Vedic blood sacrifice, is that such impetuously transgressive outbursts of divine possession are understood not in opposition to the restrained socialized bhakti of the temples but rather, as emphasized by Ārumuka Nāvalar, as the ripening, into an irresistible overflow of anpu, of prior scrupulous performance of Āgamic ritual service (caryā/kriyā). The same god who insists that his bhakta purify himself before entering his sacred presence within the temple also chides his exemplary devotee for being unable to immediately recognize Him when He assumes the profane impurity of the Untouchable.

Although Hindu bhakti does encompass and even re-interprets the sacrificial values of the still central Brahmanism which would have receded into the background, the crucial question is whether this transformation spells the subversion, surpassment or at least suspension of the archaic Vedic ideology, or rather achieves the generalization and triumph, at least on the symbolic level, of its constituting dialectics of transgressive sacrality.[46] If bhakti is no more than love of God (Īśvara) clarified by true knowledge (jñāna) of his relationship with the soul (aṇu) and aesthetically reinforced by the variegated props of ritual activity (kriyā), why should it nevertheless stubbornly maintain the tension and even opposition between its pure and impure poles instead of eliminating them altogether? Why are, on the one hand, concerns with ritual purity so central to the nuclear temples of Brahmanical pilgrimage, as exemplified by Kāśī-Viśvanātha, that Untouchables are barred from participating fully in a supposedly universalistic devotional religion? On the other hand, why are supposedly reformed (kāval) "demon devotees" like Kāttavarāyan, who as Murukan is the all-in-all of Tamil bhakti, not allowed to surrender once and for all to the high caste pure divinity but instead obliged to regularly reassert their ritual identity as "criminal gods" in order to re-enact the archaic sacrificial scenario even without the manifest patronage of the Brahmans? And, in between, why should even the purified Śaiva Siddhānta venerate such transgresive Rudraic examples of bhakti which its apologists have to uneasily rationalize in terms of a paradoxically fanatical anpu?

These questions must necessarily be resolved in the light of our understanding of the strategies and mechanisms through which Brahmanism succeeded in imposing itself on not only Tamil but Indian culture as a whole. The decisive consideration which derives from our analysis of the folk cults above is that bhakti, far from pitting the impure "indigenous" pole of Tamil religion against its pure "Brahmanized" pole, continues on the contrary to hold them firmly together within the single all-embracing symbolic universe of the pre-classical sacrifice. The bloody obstetrics that the impure Cempaṭavar have so scrupulously preserved in the cremation ground restores the vital primitive base to the Vedic dīkṣā-ideology whose profound social significance is revealed in the annual coronation by the Brahmans of the royal divinity in the garbhagṛha of the Aṇṇāmalaiyār temple.[47] And eager to give away the whole kingdom with his throne, the "mad" Kerala king Ceramān Perumāl, who understood the sacrificial language (*kalarir̲r̲' arivār̲*) of all creation so well that he falls from his elephant prostrate at the lowly feet of the protesting ash-white washerman, is but the inseparable *alter ego* (*kalantav unarvāl*) of the Ādiśaiva poet-saint Cuntarar, the princely Brahman on his celestial white elephant eager to reunite with Śiva like an errant calf with its mother.[48]

The real conflict is therefore not between an ill-understood Brahmanical sacrifice mysteriously imposed from above on a royal bhakti surging spontaneously from some conveniently undefined "folk" religion,[49] but rather between a desacralized profane world, opaque to all symbolic meaning, and its uncompromising rejection in favor of an other-worldly salvation as propounded especially by the heterodox renunciation of the Jainas and Buddhists. Whereas the Jaina epic, *Jīvaka Cintāmaṇi*, offered Kulōttuṅga II a life of transient heroic and erotic adventures to be finally abandoned in quest of Nirvāṇa, Cēkkilār converted his southern patron to the Śaiva mode of sanctifying his royal duties in life—and in death—through imitating the exemplary devotion of the Nāyanārs. The *Mṛcchakaṭikā*'s exaggeration of the renunciatory dimension of the Brahmanized yajamāna in the ambivalent figure of the chaste self-controlled Śākya mendicant,[50] accurately delineates the inner tensions of Buddhism in its Indian milieu. If the symbolic exchanges condensed in the iconic Biruthus could so easily legitimize the rise of a thieving Kaḷḷar caste into a Toṇṭaimān dynasty of worshipers of the "Great Mother" Bṛhadambāl, this is no doubt because the central narrative of the "taming of the wild elephant," where the cloak of death is also the embryonic sheath of rebirth, was sufficient, like the vajra-wielding Indra's Vṛtrahatyā, to sacralize the sum total of their profane sins into a transgressive royal obstetrics.[51]

By asserting its own uniqueness as a mode of spiritual experience in the post-axial crisis of an Indianizing Āryan tradition faced with the challenge of indigenous tribal and Dravidian culture from without and renunciatory ideals from within, Hindu bhakti seems to have not only served as the vehicle of sacrificial values but also to have generalized them quite independently of the material reality of the Vedic sacrifice whose complicated technicalities were monopolized by the Brahmans. More than being merely a diluted substitute of the Śrauta sacrifice for non-Brahmans in an increasingly commercialized society menaced by secularization, the emotionalism of bhakti in its own paradoxical way revivifies the purified abstract symbolism of the classical ritual by restoring that archaic transgressive dimension of the sacred, divulged only in cryptic suppressed fashion in its Āgamic nuclear temples, but preserved so faithfully in tantricized folk religion especially by the otherwise excluded lowest castes. But the paradox of bhakti, whose sociological function is definable as the unceasing yet never wholly successful effort to sacralize life-in-the-world by infusing it with the transcendence of the absolute, is that it tolerates the violation of sacralizing interdictions, if at all, only through the "remissive" attitude[52] of a cruelly merciful (karuṇā/kṛpā) God, who thereby effectively disguises the disquietening *mysterium tremendum et fascinans* of his own sinister essence.[53] The shocking excesses of a still exemplary bhakti (re-)assume their full transgressive significance only when perceived through the intersecting theistic worlds of a binding public ritualism modelled on the purified Mīmāṃsā and of an underground flagrantly Tantricizing antinomianism held together, especially in the nuclear temple of pilgrimage, by the shared sacralizing symbolic universe of Hindu mythology.[54] The classical reform which (all but) eliminated the impure violent dimension from the agonistic Vedic sacrifice and exaggerated the pure pole to the point of transforming even the transgressive dīkṣā into a preliminary purification of the individualized yajamāna into a temporary Brahman,[55] has been compensated for by the reworking of the original transgressive ideology and much of the accompanying symbolism into the tantric systems developing through the influx of vast amounts of pre-Vedic, Dravidian[56] and even aboriginal elements. This consistent strategy, whereby the Brahmanical tradition succeeded in assimilating (not only) the Indian universe without surrendering the continuity of Hindu identity with its roots in the Vedic revelation, has been possible only because the primordial sacrifice (ādiyāga) is itself largely the formal codification and ritual dramatization of an inner lived "shamanizing" experience of transgressive sacrality so central to the religious life of so-called "primitive" societies, and systematically conserved in the preclassical dīkṣita.[57] Transgression is able to dialectically surpass its (profane) opposition to (desacralized) interdiction and present itself as the fulfillment of the latter, only when both poles reveal their complementary nature within a common symbol of transcendence that defines the sacred.[58]

Regeneratively turned upon itself through the symbolic, where not explicit, identification of devotee, divinity, and victim within the hierarchic and regional tensions of a classical Hinduism transfigured by the pacific ideals (ahiṃsā) of Indian renunciation, the primordial violence of man has been, in the cohesive homogeneity of an expansionist Islam submissive to a wholly transcendent divine will, rather directed outwards through the disciplined warrior-band whose proselytizing zeal is revealed in an unmatchable readiness to kill and be killed.[59] The martyred (śahīd) Muslim warrior (ghāzī) has thereby admirably lent himself to assimilation into the Hindu folk cult of the deified dead beside not only the heroic Bir (Pir) Babas, but also the samādhis of ascetics, the privileged Brahms and the widowed Satīs, so much so that even the invading Muslim slaughterer Ghazi Miya's Bahraich tomb, replicated in other North Indian centers, is worshiped by both Muslim and Hindu pilgrims, especially the Doms of Banaras[60] specializing in the "human sacrifice" of the death ritual. "Imprinted with blood-red sandal paste all over the victimized body of the ascetic Brahman hero, the extended hand" (*Mṛcchakaṭikā*, X.5), so characteristic of the Satī, carried in Muharram processions or topping (with five finger-pegs) the primordial earthen mounds of household shrines from the Punjab to Bengal, easily represented the Shiite quintet of Muhammad, Fatimah, Ali, Hasan, and Husain and/or the Vedic "five tribes" (pañcajanāḥ = the Pāṇḍavas married to Pāñcālī) to the Indo-Islamic Panchpiriyas. Worshiped by not only Liṅgāyats and Jains, but also Muslims, the "tribal" Khaṇḍobā, called Mallu or Ajmat Khān (or Rautrāy), has a Muslim wife and kotvāl and appears as a Pathān on horseback. After corrupting their traditions, Mallana alias Malkhān even converts the Muslim "Śiva bhaktas" of Mecca, by replenishing a dried well with water and producing golden turmeric powder beside it at the end of twelve years through the matricidal slaughter of a black cow, and finally escapes by jumping with the "gold" needed for his marriage into mother Gaṅgā, whose outstreched hand is cut off by his Muslim pursuers (for the Pīrla Paṇḍuga festival?). The symbolic projection of the transgressive dīkṣā embryogony onto the hostile presence of the carnivorous Muslim neighbour, thereby assimilated to a Hindu king or even North Indian Brahman, is also recognizable, within the popular bhakti context, in Muttāl Rāvuttan's abortive sacrifice of his own pregnant sister to the vegetarian Tamil Draupadī whom she so resembled, at the suggestion of the dark Kālī-like goddess herself, in order to be relegated to the place corresponding to the "pacified" butcher śāmitṛ in the Vedic sacrifice.[61]

The splitting of the ever imminent Jewish messiah into a martyred ben-Joseph and a triumphant ben-David itself reflects the identity of executioner and victim in the archaic sacrifice to be reinstituted in the temple of Jerusalem at the end of the exile. After being dipped in the blood of the sacrificial bird, which was then used in the purification of the leper (*Leviticus* 14:7), the other bird was set free as if still bearing the guilt of the murder. Their roles differentiated by lot only on Kippur, i.e. on the actual day of collective expiation (*Leviticus* 16), the two goats, one killed "for the Lord" and the other banished into the desert as "scapegoat" for the demon Azazel (*'ez* + *azal* = "goat who escaped"), likewise suggest the sacrificial identity of victim and murderer. For both goats were consecrated with a replica of the golden crown worn by the high priest. The "crimson tongue" of thread binding together the cedar-wood and the hyssop (*Mishnah*, Parah 3:11), the highest and lowest limits of the vegetable kingdom, which was dipped into the blood of the sacrificed bird (14:6), was also tied between the horns of both the slaughtered goat and the scapegoat (*Mishnah*), whose death by being thrown over a cliff had the purificatory effect of immediately whitening a similar red thread hung in the porch of the temple (late apocryphal tradition). A brush of hyssop was used for daubing the lintels of the doors of the Israelites with blood from the sacrificed lamb during the tenth plague in Egypt (*Exodus* 12:22); and the same implement was also cast by the officiating priest into the midst of the burning red cow, whose ashes served to purify (*Numbers* 19:6) and with whom the Sabbataians later identified the secret of the messiah himself.[62] Esoteric commentaries not only attribute to the banished Cain the authentic sacrifice, denied to his innocent brother, with whom he is sometimes identified, but even elevate this archetype of the "sacred executioner" to the rank of the archangel Metatron. And the only significant reference to (sacred) laughter in the Bible is in the meaning (*yishaq* "he will laugh") of Isaac, to be sacrificed to the merciful God of Abraham, a privilege that is claimed instead for the likewise "laughing" (Gen. XXI:9 *mesahheq*) Ismaël by the Islamic version of the founding myth, to be historically realized in the Shiite figure of the martyred Ali.[63]

In the shrunken incarceral world of *homo oeconomicus*,[64] increasingly menaced by the "reactionary" puritanism of divine fundamentalist fury on the one hand and the "revolutionary" permissiveness of demoniac anarchist egalitarianism on the other, and where the universal God of bhakti is posthumously impeached for violations of the rights of man even while human justice stands exposed as the naked instrument of legalized violence, what immortal amnesty can India's "criminal gods" offer to the fast-multiplying race of disinherited terrorists, these intransigent "demon devotees" who are the modern exemplars of the primordial sacrifice in their readiness to gamble away their own lives, and those of others, for a sacred cause that is not even their own? Can we still hear the wrathful prophetic judgment of the omniscient wholly Other[65] imperiously trying to make itself heard through the verbose humanist rhetoric of the bourgeois ventriloquist Narcissus, heroically monologuing with the dumb royal Clown in his gilded Oriental mirror,[66] to be richly rewarded for the hilarious mercenary labor by a multinational Mammonic tribe of enterprising moneylenders just grasping at homeless Abel's Fool-sceptre?[67] "Jewish history is familiar to us for its dualities: *two* groups of people who came together to form the nation, *two* kingdoms into which this nation fell apart, *two* gods' names in the documentary sources of the Bible. To these we add two fresh ones: the foundation of *two* religions—the first repressed by the second but nevertheless later emerging victoriously behind it, and *two* religious founders, who are both called by the name of Moses and whose personalities we have to distinguish from each other."[68] Through the inner conflict of Indian tradition, the profane duplicity of Orientalist discourse is forced to rediscover its own inescapable unconscious inheritance, violently repressed in the founding monotheistic opposition of the one universal imperialist God to his colonized satanic Other, of man's dialectical essence still enshrined in primitive dualism.[69]

NOTES

1. This article will appear in a longer and modified version, with full sections on "The Perverse Humour of the Infantile Vidūṣaka: Psychoanalysis, Criminal Law and Sacrificial *Dharma*" (discussing at length the Sanskrit drama, *Mṛcchakaṭikā*) and "The Infanticide Aṅkāḷamman: The Termite-Mound of the Untouchable Cempaṭavars and the Royal Obstetrics in the Cremation Ground," in Sunthar and Elizabeth-Chalier Visuvalingam, *Transgressive Sacrality in the Hindu Tradition* (= TSHT), TS Series vol. 1 (Cambridge: Rudra Press).

2. For an elementary introduction to the subject, see my "Transgressive Sacrality in the Hindu Tradition: As a basis of interreligious dialogue, the ethical problem it poses, and its symbolic communication through the buffoon of the Sanskrit drama," originally presented to the Assembly of the World's Religions, 15-21 November 1985 (New York), before serving as the prospectus for the pilot conference on this problematic within the 15th Annual Conference on South Asia, University of Wisconsin, 8 November 1986 (Madison). It is appearing in TSHT (see n. 1) and also in Serbo-Croat in *Kulture Istoka*, 5, No. 17 (Belgrade: July-September, 1988). I am indebted to Alf Hiltebeitel not only for having presided but also for reviewing the proceedings of his own "Criminal gods and Demon Devotees" conference within what I regard to be the more fundamental, global, and immediate problem of transgressive sacrality.

3. Abhinavagupta, citing his relative Vāmanagupta, on the semblance of humor and of sorrow in *Abhinavabhāratī*.

4. For the continuity between Pāśupata and Kāpālika praxis, see E. Visuvalingam's section D in this volume (esp. nn. 16 and 60-62).

5. See M. Eliade, *Shamanism: Archaic Techniques of Ecstasy* (New Jersey: Princeton University Press, 1964), xi, 15, 20, 23-32, 365n.

6. S. Kramrisch, *The Presence of Śiva* (Delhi: Oxford University Press, 1981), 159; see n. 22 of E. Visuvalingam's rendering of "The Origin-Myth of Bhairava" in this volume.

7. For the distinction between "sacred" and the repressed "profane" laughter in Amerindian religion, see Lévi-Strauss, "Suppressed Laughter," in *The Raw and the Cooked*, Introduction to a Science of Mythology: vol. 1 (1970; Penguin, 1986), 109, 120-132, which also provides evidence, overlooked by Lévi-Strauss himself, of not only comic behaviour but also tickling serving as symbolic substitutes for transgression in mythology. Otherwise devalorized, (sacred) laughter is nevertheles credited, in myth 45, with the origin of language itself (p. 123, cf. p. 132).

8. L. Renou, *Religions of Ancient India* (London: Univ. of London Athlone Press, 1953), 10, 18; also *L'Inde Fondamentale*, ed. C. Malamoud (Paris: Hermann, 1978), 11-80.

9. See G. Dumézil, *Mitra-Varuṇa*, 2nd ed. (Paris: Gallimard, 1948), and especially my treatment of the Gāndharva musical symbolism in the Vidūṣaka Maitreya and the criminal Śakāra in the *Mṛcchakaṭikā* (see n. 1).

10. See L. Makarius, "Ritual Clowns and Symbolic Behaviour," *Diogenes* no. 69 (Spring 1970).

11. See M. Detienne, "Dionysos orphique et le bouilli rôti," in *Dionysos mis à Mort* (Paris: Gallimard, 1977), 163-217; also W. Burkert, *Homo Necans: The Anthropology of Ancient Greek Sacrificial Ritual and Myth* (Berkeley: Univ. of California Press, 1983), pp. 89, n. 29; pp. 105, 119, 122-5, 177-8. Cf. J. C. Heesterman's keynote paper on "The Vedic origin of Vegetarianism," delivered to the 15th South Asia Conference (see n. 1) along with his contribution there to the Transgressive Sacrality seminar on "The Notion of Anthropophagy in Vedic Ritual" centered on the consumption of the dionysiac dīkṣita reduced (nowadays) to a he-goat.

12. See D. Lorenzen and especially E. Visuvalingam's section B, both in this volume.

13. See A. Sanderson, "Purity and Power among the Brahmans of Kashmir" in M. Carrithers *et al.* eds., *The Category of the Person: Anthropology, Philosophy, History* (Cambridge: Cambridge Univ. Press, 1986), 190-216; and "Maṇḍala and Āgamic Identity in the *Trika* of Kashmir," *Mantras et Diagrammes Rituels dans l'Hindouisme* (Paris: CNRS, 1986) 169-214.

14. This is also the gist of J.-P. Vernant's treatment of "The Pure and the Impure," in *Myth and Society in Ancient Greece* (Sussex: Harvester Press, and New Jersey: Humanities Press, 1980), 110-29.

15. See J. Parry, "Ghosts, Greed and Sin: The Occupational Identity of the Benares Funeral Priests," in *Man* (NS) 15 (1980), 88-111; "Sacrificial death and the necrophagous ascetic," in M. Bloch and J. P. Parry eds., *Death and the Regeneration of Life* (Cambridge: Cambridge Univ. Press, 1982), and esp. E. Visuvalingam's section F in this volume.

16. See J. Gonda, *Notes on Brahman* (Utrecht: J. L. Beyers, 1950), 16-18, 57-61; and especially L. Renou (and L. Silburn), "Sur la notion *bráhman*," in *L'Inde*, 83-116 (see n. 8).

17. See L. Makarius, *Le Sacré et la Violation des Interdits* (Paris: Payot, 1974), 311; C. Lévi-Strauss, *Anthropologie Structurale*, vol. 2 (Paris: Plon, 1973), 32-34, and *Le Regard Eloigné* (Paris: Plon, 1983), 301-18; with the criticisms of Makarius, *Structuralisme ou Ethnologie: Pour une critique radicale de l'anthropologie de Lévi-Strauss* (Paris: Anthropos, 1973), 16-19. See esp. E. Visuvalingam, n. 4 above.

18. See my Ph.D. thesis on "Abhinavagupta's Bisociative Conception of Humour: Its Resonances in Indian Aesthetics, Transgressive Sacrality and Contemporary Indology" (Banaras: Hindu University, 1983).

19. G. Bataille, *L'Erotisme* (Paris: Editions de Minuit, 1957), 204, subtitle of his chapter on "Sade et l'Homme Normal." See *Ṛgveda* X.129.4, discussed in F. B. J. Kuiper, *Ancient Indian Cosmogony*, ed. J. Irwin (Delhi: Vikas, 1983), 131, in terms of (peri- or) pre-natal psycho-analysis.

20. See the pioneering work of F. B. J. Kuiper, *Varuṇa and Vidūṣaka: On the Origin of the Sanskrit Drama* (Amsterdam: North Holland Publishing Co., 1979), 213-22, to whom I owe my initiation into the embryogonic foundations of Vedic religion. Also G. Dumézil, *Flamen-Brahman* (Paris: Geuthner, 1935), 28-9, seeking to substantiate his argument that the purohita was originally the sacrificial substitute for the king as victim.

21. P. V. Kane, *History of Dharmaśāstra*, 2nd ed., Govt. Oriental Series (Poona: Bhandarkar Oriental Research Institute), II (1974), p. 1236; IV (1973), pp. 91-2. For the impurity of the dīkṣita bound in Varuṇa's noose (*mekhalā*), see J. C. Heesterman, "Vrātya and Sacrifice," *Indo-Iranian Journal* VI (1962), 11-15.

22. H. Hubert and M. Mauss, "Essai sur la Nature et la Fonction du Sacrifice" (1899) reproduced in *Marcel Mauss: Oeuvres, 1. les fonctions sociales du sacré* (Paris: Minuit, 1968), 234; cf. also pp. 225, n. 145; 230ff., 302-5. See E. Visuvalingam in this volume, Section B and n. 28.

23. Kane, II, p. 148, n. 334; p. 131, n. 290; III (1973), p. 612, n. 1161; IV, p. 11, n. 22, where the bhrūṇa, having performed the Soma sacrifices, is ranked even higher than the Śrotriya.

24. The duration of which was reckoned from the dīkṣaṇīya-iṣṭi until even the end of the avabhṛtha bath; Kane, I, pp. 13, 18, 29, 96; III, p. 527, n. 970. In *Śatapatha Brāhmaṇa* 1.4.5.13, Ātreyī is a menstruating woman identified with the goddess Vāc from whom Atri is elsewhere said to have originated, which brings us back a full circle to the eunuch-like Ātreya jumbaka. On the mythical level, see E. Visuvalingam, nn. 67, 76, 77, 87, in this volume.

25. Kane, IV, pp. 93, n. 218; 557-8. For the Iranian parallels to this sacrificial embryogony around the Sarasvatī as the terrestrial Milky Way, and the transposition of the Vedic astronomical coordinates onto the later Hindu sacred geography, see M. Witzel, "Sur le Chemin du Ciel," *Bulletin d'Études Indiennes* 2 (1984), 213-279. Another penance for Brahmanicide was the pilgrimage to see Rāma's bridge (*samudra-setu*) to Laṅkā (Kane IV, pp. 55, 94), for the Brahman Rāvaṇa had mastered the four Vedas. See E. Visuvalingam's section F in this volume.

26. Sigmund Freud's *Interpretation of Dreams* (1953; rpt. New York: Avon, 1965) is itself profoundly influenced and justified by the invocation of myth, folklore, proverbs, and jokes. See also T. Todorov, "La Rhétorique de Freud," in *Théories du Symbole* (Paris: Seuil, 1977), 285-321.

27. See Knipe's contribution to this volume, where the dead children are also represented by embryonic "ash-fruits" obtained from the snake-anthill temple and from potters. See E. Visuvalingam, nn. 39, 59, 83-4, 109, etc. in this volume, and the longer version of my article (see n. 1) for further examples.

28. *Ṛgveda* X.72; see Sontheimer in this volume, the source, unless otherwise specified, for all further references to this cult. So striking are the symbolic correspondences between the cult of Mārtaṇḍa-Bhairava and our paradigmatic Aśvamedha, that even the *Mṛcchakaṭikā*, if not for the classical purification of the (Untouchable) Brahman (Śūdraka) himself, could just as well be read as a manual of (not only Indian) tribal religion.

29. Heesterman, "Vrātya" (see n. 19) 20-33; and *Inner Conflict of Tradition: Essays in Indian Ritual, Kingship and Society* (Chicago and London: Chicago Univ. Press, 1985), 37-8, 42, 155 (Vidūṣaka).

30. See E. Visuvalingam's section I, and nn. 66 and 131, in this volume.

31. Vladimir Propp, "Ritual Laughter in Folklore: A Propos of the Tale of the Princess who would not Laugh, Nesmejana," *Theory and History of Folklore* (Manchester: Univ. of Minnesota, 1984), 124-46, equates the interdiction of laughter with death and obligatory ritual laughter with life, particularly rebirth. For Bataille's transgressive laughter as the mutual imbrication and equilibration of the pulsions of life and death, see D. Pérard, "Rire en majeur," in *L'Interdit et la Transgression*, ed. R. Dorey et al. (Paris: Dunod, 1983), 9-33. For "sardonic" laughter, see S. Reinach, "Le Rire Rituel," *Cultes, Mythes, Religions*, vol. IV (Paris: 1912), 109-29.

32. This (re-) interpretation of the Kāttavarāyan narrative is almost wholly based on the data provided by the contributions of Masilamani-Meyer and Shulman in this volume.

33. This mother-son hostility is also central to the Aṅkāḷamman cult and its myths; see Eveline Meyer, *Aṅkāḷaparamēcuvari: A Goddess of Tamilnadu, Her Myths and Cult*, Beitrage zur Südasienforschung, South Asian Institute, University of Heidelberg, 107 (Wiesbaden: Franz Steiner Verlag, 1986), *passim*, and n. 27 above.

34. See Biardeau in this volume.

35. See Meyer, *Aṅkāḷaparamēcuvari*, 34-5: Aṅkāḷamman made a net of all the divinities and a copper boat so that her father, their mythic ancestor Malaiyarācan (Parvatarājan) could kill the oppressive demons hiding as fish but, since the fish were jumping back into the sea, she was obliged to open her mouth as wide as the boat in order to swallow the fishes. The net, made with the rope of Yama's noose (= death) and whose top pulled together to trap the fishes

is Viṣṇu's cakra (= womb), is clearly equated with Aṅkāḷamman, whose "eyes" (*kaṇ*) form its interstices. Although the fish, like the dīkṣita charged with evil, are Asuras or Rākṣasas, their assimilation to the fish-tailed Mīnamaharṣi also caught in the net underlines by contrast the positive function and valorization of the dīkṣā.

36. Vallāḷarājan likewise undergoes his violent embryogonic death so that the Trimūrti, incorporating the sacrificial dialectic, may become his slaves. Contrast the treatment of "the Demon Devotee" by D. D. Shulman, *Tamil Temple Myths: Sacrifice and Divine Marriage in the South Indian Śaiva Tradition* (New Jersey: Princeton University Press, 1980), 317-21, 131-37. See E. Visuvalingam, nn. 68 and 132 in this volume.

37. See E. Visuvalingam's section G in this volume.

38. Virgil, *Aenid*, VII, 312; Freud's motto for his *Traumdeutung*.

39. The incestuous and even parricidal but royal Judas (or king of Syria called Jesus) who expiated by voluntarily substituting himself for Christ on the Cross, in certain Gnostic theories also adopted by Muslim commentators, completes this picture of "the king of kings" as a demon-devotee who dies to become a criminal god. Compare also the double (birth/marriage) incest sacralizing the medieval destiny of the legendary "Pope Gregory" after his (embryogonic?) expiation in a cave on an island in the middle of the ocean. See F. Delpech, "Fragments Hispaniques d'un Discours Incestueux," *Autour des Parentes en Espagne aux XVI et XVII scl. Histoire, Mythe, et Littérature*, A. Redindi, ed. (Paris: Sorbonne, 1987), 91-93, 85ff.

40. E. Visuvalingam, "Adepts of Bhairava in the Hindu Tradition" (in TSHT), also appearing in Serbo-Croat in *Kulture Istoka*, 5, No. 17 (see nn. 1 and 2). For more details see Erndl in this volume.

41. See Stanley and Sontheimer in this volume: also the latter's discussion in which the five sheep sacrificed to the anthill Mhaskobā or Khaṇḍobā are assimilated to voluntary human sacrifice, and representations of heads of rams and humans alternate under the sandals of Khaṇḍobā. The Vīraśaiva saints of the Liṅgāyats, who nevertheless often served as his temple priests and even established temples for him, were therefore not altogether wrong in rationalizing that it was Śiva, and not the demon (Śiva-)Mailāra, who actually killed Malla. Although (or rather because?) the Torah or Pentateuch formally forbids sacrifices to demons, Dr. Charles Mopsik (letter of 12/02/88) informs me that, during Kippur, the day of collective expiation, a goat is offered to the demoniac power which haunts the mountainous desert, Azazel, himself figured as a goat. See n. 62 below.

42. See G. D. Sontheimer, *Birobā, Mhaskobā und Khaṇḍobā: Ursprung, Geschichte und Umwelt von Pastoralen Gottheiten in Mahārāṣṭra* (Wiesbaden: Franz Steiner, 1976), 143-47, 246.

43. See Dennis Hudson in this volume.

44. See E. Visuvalingam's section E in this volume (esp. n. 68). Hudson cites archaeological excavations near Kaṇṇappa's Kālahasti mountain revealing bones around the Guḍimallam liṅgam, offered to Śiva "portrayed on the liṅgam as an animal sacrificer in the Vedic tradition."

45. See H. Brunner-Lachaux, "De la Consommation du *Nirmālya* de Śiva," *Journal Asiatique* (1970), 213-263.

46. Cf. A. Hiltebeitel, *The Ritual of Battle: Krishna in the Mahābhārata* (Ithaca and London: Cornell Univ. Press, 1976), 312. Gomes da Siva, *Pouvoir et Hierarchie* (Bruxelles: Université Libre de Bruxelles, in press) has been able to offer a highly successful interpretation of the cult of Jagannātha in the light of a positive utilization of Biardeau's unravelling of the deep-structures of the Hindu mythico-ritual universe, especially of the *Mahābhārata*, but in terms of a cyclic regenerative hierarchy founded on the nature/culture (other/self) opposition that does full justice to Dumézil's pioneering tri-functionalism even while conforming to an African model which makes no reference to bhakti. Although to a great extent these necessarily ambiguous structures admit both these and the transgressive perspectives, the crucial criteria for determining the fundamental model would lie in our interpretation of the various "irregular" but insistently recurring details within the bhakti scenario but which bear no direct relevance to or even subtly subvert it. See E. Visuvalingam, n. 30 above.

47. Both the Vallāḷarājan and the Brahmanicide myths discussed in Meyer, *Aṅkāḷaparamēcuvari* (pp. 12-14, 50-51, 126, 185-87, 197 for the former and pp. 36-37, 161, 164-65, 178, 274 for the latter) refer back, directly or indirectly, to a former royal cult, far removed from the impure violence of the cremation ground, at the great Śiva temple at the foot of the nearby Tiruvaṇṇāmalai, vestiges of which still persist in the ritual cycle. The Malayanūr version of the Vallāḷan myth identifies him with the historical Hoysala Ballāḷa III who built one of the nine *gopurams* of the Tiruvaṇṇāmalai temple in the first half of the fourteenth century. According to the *Vallāḷamakārājan Carittiram* of the *Aruṇācala-Purāṇa* (Meyer, p. 199; cf. Shulman, *King and the Clown*, 331-39), the younger queen of the childless but perfectly virtuous Vallāḷa had to substitute herself for a courtesan to embrace the Liṅgāyat-Śiva, who transformed himself into a child and promised, before disappearing, to perform Vallāḷan's funerary rites and succeed him as his own son. The annual reenthronement of Śiva in the absence of a real human king is explicable only in terms of the sacrificial death/rebirth of the single royal divinity on the model of Jagannātha at Puri, and suggests that the dīkṣā symbolism invested in the historical childless (Śiva-) Ballāḷa has been split so as to translate his rebirth from the womb of his own queen into the birth of the so ardently desired son-Śiva. See E. Visuvalingam section F (esp. n. 87) in this volume.

48. David Dean Shulman, *The King and the Clown in South Indian Myth and Poetry* (Princeton: Princeton University Press, 1985), pp. 246-256. For a comparative soteriology of dualistic Śaiva Siddhānta and non-dualistic Trika bhakti, see my

contribution on "Are *Tamil Temple Myths* really Tamil: Brahmanical Sacrifice, Tamil *Bhakti* and Hindu Transgressive Sacrality," to the VIth World Tamil Conference-Seminar, Kuala Lumpur, 15-19 November 1987, which is also appearing in the volume referred to in n. 1.

49. M. Biardeau, *L'Hindouisme: Anthropologie d'une Civilisation* (Paris: Flammarion, 1981), especially 93-101, is *indispensable* for a proper appreciation of the treatment of bhakti in this concluding paper. See A. Hiltebeitel, "Towards a Coherent Study of Hinduism," in *Religious Studies Review* vol. 9, no.3 (July 1983), 206-211.

50. For the continuity between the classical sacrifice and heterodox renunciation, see J. C. Heesterman, "Brahman: Ritual and Renouncer" (1964), *Inner Conflict* (see n. 29), 26-44.

51. See Waghorne in this volume, and F. B. J. Kuiper, "Cosmogony and Conception: A Query," in Kuiper, *Ancient Indian Cosmogony*, 90-137 (see n. 19). See my treatment of chapters 2 and 8 of the *Mṛcchakaṭikā* in the unabridged version of this essay (see n. 1).

52. By (conditionally) suspending the interdiction, "remission" only deprives the corresponding violation of its transgressive significance which necessarily presupposes the unconditional operation of the taboo. See P. Rieff, "Towards a theory of culture: with special reference to the psychoanalytic case," in T. J. Nossiter *et al.* eds., *Imagination and Precision in the Social Sciences: Essays in Memory of Peter Nettl* (New York: Humanities Press, 1972), 97-108; and "By what authority? Post-Freudian reflections on the repression of the repressive as modern culture," in J. P. Diggins & M. E. Kann eds., *The Problem of Authority in America* (Philadelphia: Temple Univ. Press, 1981), 225-55.

53. See Makarius, *Le Sacré* (see n. 17), 332-7, esp. p. 341 n. 21, on Rudolf Otto's *Das Heilige.*

54. See Biardeau, *L'Hindouisme* (see n. 49), 135-171 for the complex relations between bhakti, aesthetics and transgression.

55. See Heesterman, "Brahman" (see n. 50); "Vedic Sacrifice and Transcendence" (81-94); "Ritual, Revelation and the Axial Age" (95-107); in *Inner Conflict* (see n. 29); and "Vrātya" (see n. 21), 18-20.

56. See Shulman, *Tamil Temple Myths* and *The King and the Clown*; in the latter he "sees no great divide between North and South, and the parallels with the ancient, including even Vedic, patterns are often very striking" (p. 9).

57. Heesterman, "Vrātya" (see n. 21), p. 36, n. 103; and especially E. Visuvalingam's section H in this volume.

58. The essential contribution of Mircea Eliade's "phenomenology of religion" is the refusal of all attempts by the "human sciences" to reduce the Sacred to anthropology, psychoanalysis or even linguistics, these counter-sciences which have converged so admirably in the "archaeology of Man" reduced to his Other by Michel Foucault, *The Order of Things* (London: Tavistock;

New York: Pantheon, 1973).

59. See G. Bataille, *La Part Maudite* (Paris: Minuit, 1967), 127; and *Théories de Religion* (Paris: Gallimard, 1973), 78-80, 87-88, for the relation between sacrifice and war in general.

60. The "conflation" (e.g., Jogi Bir) of Brahman, ascetic, heroic, feminine (Satī) and even Muslim traditions in Coccari's contribution to this volume could be more readily seen as a diffraction at the popular level of the transgressive dīkṣā. See E. Visuvalingam's Section F in this volume.

61. See Coccari, Sontheimer, Hiltebeitel and E. Visuvalingam (n. 101 on Ghāzī Mīya) in this volume. For the projection of the transgressive dimension of Athenian sacrificial ideology onto her Other, the rival sister-city of Thebes, see P. Vidal-Naquet, "Oedipe entre deux cités: Essai sur l'*Oedipe à Colone,*" in J.-P. Vernant & P. V-Naquet, *Mythe et Tragédie* II (Paris: la Découverte, 1986), 175-211.

62. See Hyam Maccoby, *The Sacred Executioner: Human Sacrifice and the Legacy of Guilt* (Thames and Hudson, 1982), pp. 35-39, and *passim* for further examples of sacrificial ideology in the Old Testament. Also Gershom Scholem, *The Messianic Idea in Judaism* (New York, 1971), p. 198. For Azazel, cf. n. 41 above on the identity of Khaṇḍobā and the goat-headed Malla.

63. Further details on Cain and the scapegoat, missing in Maccoby, were also provided by Dr. Charles Mopsik, to whom I express my gratitude for our regular discussions during the Parisian summer of 1988. For Isaac, see Paul B. Fenton, "Le pénitent: Ismaël dans la tradition juive," in *Israel Face aux Nations: Figures Juives d'Autrui* (= *Pardès*, 7/1988) pp. 50, 56 n. 4. For sacred laughter, see n. 31 above.

64. See Michel Foucault, *Discipline and Punish* (New York: Pantheon, London: Allen Lane; 1977).

65. For the "unspeakable" criminal origins of Yahweh (p. 290: citing *Deuteronomy*, xiii, 15) and the systematic plagiarism of his Egyptian Revelation, see Freud, "Moses and Monotheism" in *The Origins of Religion*, The Pelican Freud Library, vol. 13 (rpt. Penguin, 1985), 239-386.

66. For the appropriateness of this ridiculous image, see Shulman, *The King and the Clown*, esp. p. 324, who, in his own amusing fashion, explores the transformative relations between this couple, the Untouchable Brahman criminal and the feminine presupposed in our present paper.

67. It is high time that Indologists learnt their lessons from the "terrorist" apropriation of the power of Foucault's discourse in Edward Saïd's *Orientalism* (London: Routledge & Kegan Paul, 1987). For the archetypal character of this image of man, see W. Willeford, *The Fool and his Sceptre: A Study in Clowns and Jesters and their Audience* (London: Edwin Arnold, 1969).

68. Freud, "Moses and Monotheism," 293. It is, however, not the atheistic founder of psychoanalysis but the "apostate" Jewish Messiah of transgressive

sacrality who, through his "conversion" to Islam, seems to have realized the real implications of this insight into his own historical unconscious. See G. Scholem, *The Messianic Idea in Judaism* (New York, 1971), 49-77; and especially his *Sabbatai Sévi: The Mystical Messiah* (N. Jersey: Princeton Univ. Press, 1973). See C. Mopsik, ed., *Transgressive Sacrality in the Jewish Tradition* (Cambridge, Mass.: Rudra Press, forthcoming).

69. See A. Bergaigne, *Vedic Religion* (1978; rpt. Delhi: Motilal Banarsidass); Lévi-Strauss *Les Structures Elémentaires de la Parenté* (Paris: Mouton, 1967); G. J. Held, *The Mahābhārata: An Ethnological Study* (London: Kegan Paul, Trench, Trubner & Co.; Amsterdam: Uitgeversmaatschappij; 1935); and Gomes da Silva, *Pouvoir et Hierarchie* (see n. 46). We may now look forward to W. D. O'Flaherty's structural analysis of "Jewish scholars and Indian Studies" in *Between Jerusalem and Benares.*

Selected Bibliography*

Adiceam, Marguerite E. 1965. "Les Images de Śiva dans l'Inde du Sud II—Bhairava," *Arts Asiatiques* 11, 2:23-44.

Anderson, Mary M. 1971. *The Festivals of Nepal.* London: Allen & Unwin. (Rich on Bhairava.)

Appadurai, Arjun. 1983. "The Puzzling Status of Brahman Temple Priests in Hindu India," *South Asian Anthropologist* 4:43-52.

Archer, W. G. 1947. *The Vertical Man.* London: George Allen & Unwin.

Arunachalam, M. 1976. *Peeps into Tamil Literature: Ballad Poetry.* Tiruchitrambalam: Gandhi Vidyalayam. (See especially discussion of "Ballads Glorifying Criminals").

Ayrookuzhiel, A. M. Abraham. 1983. *The Sacred in Popular Hinduism.* Madras: The Christian Literature Society. (See material on Poṭṭan, Guḷikan, and other Kerala deities.)

Babb, Lawrence. 1975. *The Divine Hierarchy: Popular Hinduism in Central India.* New York: Columbia University Press (See especially discussion of Thakur Dev, Bhairava, Hanumān).

Bang, B. C. 1973. "Current Concepts of the Smallpox Goddess in Parts of West Bengal," *Man in India* 53:79-104. (See discussion of Jvarāsura, Ghantakarna, Raktabati, and Olabibi; cf. Nicholas 1978).

Beck, Brenda E. F. 1975. *The Story of the Brothers: An Oral Epic from the Coimbatore District of Tamilnadu,* Collected in 1965 and translated in 1975. Mimeographed and privately circulated by the author. (See the figure of Cāmpukā.)

———. 1981. "The Goddess and the Demon. A Local South Indian Festival and its Wider Context," in Madeleine Biardeau, ed., *Autour de la déesse hindoue. Puruṣārtha* 5:83-136.

———. 1982. *The Three Twins. The Telling of a South Indian Folk Epic.* Bloomington: Indiana University Press (See discussion of Cāmpukā.)

Bhattacharya, France. 1981. "La déesse et le royaume selon le Kālaketu

* Lightly Annotated.

Upākhyāna du Caṇḍī Maṅgala," in Madeleine Biardeau, ed., *Autour de la déesse hindoue. Puruṣārtha* 5:17-54.

Biardeau, Madeleine. 1967-68. "Brâhmaṇes combattantes dans un mythe de sud de l'Inde," *Adyar Library Bulletin, Dr. V. Raghavan Felicitation Volume* 31-32:519—30. (See discussion of Akkinivīran.)

———. 1981a. "L'arbre *śamī* et le buffle sacrificiel," in Biardeau, ed., *Autour de la déesse hindoue. Puruṣārtha* 5:215-244. (An integrative overview, in short compass, of matters relating "demon devotees" to transformations of the Vedic sacrificial stake.)

———. 1981b. *L'Hinduisme: Anthropologie d'une civilisation.* Paris: Flammarion. (See section on "La Déesse").

———. 1984. "The Śamī Tree and the Sacrificial Buffalo," Richard Nice trans. in collaboration with the author, *Contributions to Indian Sociology* (n.s.) 18, 1 (1984):1-23 (English version of Biardeau 1981a).

———. In press. *Histoire de poteaux: variations védiques autour de la Déesse.* Paris: Bulletin de l'École Française d'Extrême Orient. (Full exploration of subject of Biardeau 1981a.)

———, and Charles Malamoud. 1976. *Le sacrifice dans l'Inde ancienne.* Paris: Presses Universitaires de France. (See Biardeau's discussion of "āgamic sacrifice and blood sacrifice," especially concerning Khaṇḍobā, Pōttu Rāja, and Akkinivīran, Chapter 3-D.)

Blackburn, Stuart H. 1978. "The Folk Hero and Class Interest in Tamil Heroic Ballads," *Asian Folklore Studies* 37, 1:131-149.

———. 1981. "Oral Performance: Narrative and Ritual in a Tamil Folk Tradition," *Journal of American Folklore* 94:207-227. (See discussions of the Tamil category "cut-up spirits," and of Cuṭalai Māṭan and Pula Māṭan.)

———. 1985. "Death and Deification: Folk Cults in Hinduism," *History of Religions* 24:255-74. (On "violent deaths" and "small gods": a valuable overview.)

———. 1986. "Performance Markers in an Indian Story-Type." In Blackburn and A. K. Ramanujan, eds., *Another Harmony. New Essays on the Folklore of India.* Berkeley: University of California Press, pp. 167-194. (See material on the two Palavēcam brothers.)

Brubaker, Richard Lee. 1978. "The Ambivalent Mistress: A Study of South Indian Village Goddesses and their Religious Meaning." Ph.D. Dissertation, University of Chicago.

Burkert, Geoffrey. 1987. "Family Deity Temples and Spatial Variance among Udayars of Northern Tamil Nadu." In V. Sudarsen, G. Prakash Reddy, and M. Suryanarayana, eds., *Religion and Society in South India. A Volume in Honor of Prof. N. Subba Reddy.* Delhi: B. R. Publications.

pp. 3-20.

Chidanandamurti, M. 1982. "Two Māsti Temples in Karnataka." In G. D. Sontheimer and S. Settar, *Memorial Stones* [for full reference see Sontheimer 1982]. Pp. 117-131. (See account of Māstyamma temple at Koṇḍadahaḷḷi, where the suttee-goddess is attended by stones for both her husband, beheaded by their lecherous outcaste servant, and the servant himself who was in turn beheaded by her.)

Claus, Peter J. 1973. "Possession, Protection, and Punishment as Attributes of the Deities in a South Indian Village," *Man in India* 53, 3:231-42.

———. 1978. "Oral Traditions, Royal Cults and Materials for a Reconsideration of the Caste System in South India," *Journal of Indian Folkloristics* 1, 1:1-25.

Coccari, Diane M. 1984. "The Bir Babas of Banaras: An Analysis of a Folk Deity in North Indian Hinduism," Ph.D. Dissertation, University of Wisconsin, Madison.

Courtright, Paul B. 1985. *Gaṇeśa. Lord of Obstacles, Lord of Beginnings.* New York: Oxford University Press. (Note Gaṇeśa's demonic affinities and guardian functions.)

Crooke, William. 1968 (1896). *The Popular Religion and Folklore of Northern India,* 2 vols. Delhi: Munshiram Manoharlal. (Relevant material throughout.)

Deppert, Joachim. 1977. *Rudras Geburt: Systematische Untersuchungen zum Inzest in der Mythologie der Brāhmaṇas.* Beitrage zur Sudasien-Forschung, South Asian Institute, University of Heidelberg, vol. 28. Wiesbaden: Franz Steiner Verlag. (See discussion of Brahmanicide myths.)

Dimock, Edward C., Jr., and A. K. Ramanujan. 1964. "The Goddess of Snakes and Medieval Bengali Literature," Pt. 2. *History of Religions* 3:300-322. (See discussions of Candō.)

———. 1982. "A Theology of the Repulsive: The Myth of the Goddess Sītalā." In John Stratton Hawley and Donna Marie Wulff, eds., *The Divine Consort. Rādhā and the Goddesses of India.* Berkeley: Berkeley Religious Studies Series. (See material on Jvarāsura.)

Dumont, Louis. 1957. *Une sous-caste de l'Inde du sud: organisation sociale et religion des Pramalai Kallar.* Paris and The Hague: Mouton. (See especially discussion of Karuppanaswāmi.)

———. 1959. "A Structural Definition of a Folk Deity of Tamil Nad: Aiyanar, the Lord," *Contributions to Indian Sociology* 3:75-87.

Eck, Diana L. 1982. *Banaras. City of Light.* Princeton: Princeton University Press. (See especially on Bhairava.)

Edholm, Erik Af, "Caṇḍa and the Sacrificial Remnants. A Contribution to Indian Gastrotheology," *Indologica Taurinensia* 12 (1984), 75-91.

Elmore, Wilbur Theodore. 1915. *Dravidian Gods in Modern Hinduism. A Study of the Local and Village Deities of Southern India.* Lincoln, Neb., University of Nebraska. (Valuable throughout, but see especially material on Potu Razu (Pōta Rāju), Katama Razu (Kāṭamarāju), and vīrulu or "heroes.")

Eschmann, Anncharlott, Hermann Kulke and Gaya Charan Tripathi, eds. 1978. *The Cult of Jagannath and the Regional Tradition of Orissa.* South Asia Institute, New Delhi Branch, Heidelberg University. New Delhi: Manohar. (See especially discussions of Khambheśvarī the "lady of the post" and Narasiṃha).

Fischer, Eberhard and Haku Shah. 1973. *Vetra ne Khambha—Memorials for the Dead.* Ahmedabad: Gujarat Vidyapith.

Galey, Jean-Claude. 1986. "Totalité et hierarchie dans les sanctuaires royaux du Tehri-Garhwal (Himalaya indien)." In Galey, ed., *L'Espace du Temple II: Les Sanctuaires dans le Royaume, Puruṣārtha* 10:55-96. (See especially discussion of Mahasu and Narasiṃha).

Gopinatha Rao, T. A. 1971. *Elements of Hindu Iconography.* 2nd. ed. 2 Vols. (Parts 1 and 2 of each bound separately). Varanasi: Indological Book House. (Valuable on Kṣetrapālas, Bhairava, Vīrabhadra.)

Greeven, Richard. 1892. *The Heroes Five.* Allahabad: Pioneer Press.

Guha, K. 1960. "Bhairon: A Śaivite Deity in Transition," *Folklore* (Calcutta) 1:207-22. (Valuable material on ten Delhi Bhairava temples.)

Gupta, Sanjukta. 1976. "Viṣvaksena the Divine Protector," *Wiener Zeitschrift für die Kunde Südasiens und Archiv für Indische Philologie* 20:75-89.

Harper, Edward B. 1959. "A Hindu Village Pantheon," *Journal of Anthropological Research (Southwestern Journal of Anthropology)* 15:227-34.

Heesterman, J. C. 1962. "Vrātya and Sacrifice," *Indo-Iranian Journal* 6:1-37.

———. 1985. *The Inner Conflict of Tradition: Essayus in Indian Ritual, Kingship, and Society.* Chicago: University of Chicago Press.

Hiltebeitel, Alf. 1982. "Sexuality and Sacrifice: Convergent Subcurrents in the Firewalking Cult of Draupadī." In Fred W. Clothey, ed., *Images of Man: Religion and Historical Process in South Asia.* Madras: New Era Publications.

———. 1985. "On the Handling of the Meat, and Related Matters, in Two South Indian Buffalo Sacrifices." In Christiano Grottanelli, ed., *Divisione della Carni: Dinamica Sociale e Organizzazione del Cosmo. L'Uomo* 9:171-99.

———. 1988. *The Cult of Draupadī, I. Mythologies: From Gingee to Kurukṣetra.* Chicago: University of Chicago Press.

Inglis, Stephen. 1985. "Possession and Pottery. Serving the Divine in a South Indian Community." In Joanne Punzo Waghorne and Norman Cutler, eds., *Gods of Flesh, Gods of Stone*. Chambersburg, Pa.: Anima.

Jayakar, Pupul. 1980. *The Earthen Drum. An Introduction to the Ritual Arts of India*. New Delhi: National Museum.

Junghare, Indira Y. 1975. "Songs of the Goddess Shītalā: Religion-Cultural and Linguistic Features," *Man in India* 55:298-316. (On Shītalā in Nagpur District, Maharashtra, see discussion of her hungry, white horse-riding, drum playing and ganja smoking brother Bhiwsan.)

Kapferer, Bruce. 1983. *A Celebration of Demons. Exorcism and the Aesthetics of Healing in Sri Lanka*. Bloomington: Indiana University Press. (Indispensible on demons and the limits of their illusions.)

Kramrisch, Stella. 1981. *The Presence of Śiva*. Princeton: Princeton University Press. (See discussion of Bhairava.)

Kurup, K. K. N. 1973. *The Cult of Teyyam and Hero Worship*. Calcutta: Indian Publications.

———. 1977. *Aryan and Dravidian Elements in Malabar Folklore*. Trivandrum: Kerala Historical Society. (Brief discussion of "Śaiva Gods" and "Hero-Worship.")

Lorenzen, David N. 1972. *The Kāpālikas and Kālāmukhas. Two Lost Śaivite Sects*. Berkeley: University of California Press.

Meyer, Eveline (Masilamani-Meyer). 1981. "The Greatness of Aṅkāḷaparamēsvari, Told Through the Story of How Paramaicivam Plucked the Head of Pirammā in the Play Called *The Destruction of Turuvācar*," *South Asian Digest of Regional Writing* 10:38-47.

———. 1986. *Aṅkāḷaparamēcuvari—A Goddess of Tamilnadu, Her Myths and Cult*. Wiesbaden: Franz Steiner Verlag. (See especially discussion of Vīrabhadra, Pāvāṭairāyan, and the skull of Brahmā.)

Moffatt, Michael. 1979. *An Untouchable Community in Southern India. Structure and Consensus*. Princeton: Princeton University Press. (See discussion of Kudiraikaran, Periyandavar, Munadiyan, and the marriages of the goddess and the Vettiyan.)

Mookerjee, Priya. 1987. *Pathway Icons. The Wayside Art of India*. London: Thames and Hudson.

Murty, M. L. K. 1982. "Memorial Stones in Andhra Pradesh." In G. D. Sontheimer and S. Settar, eds., *Memorial Stones* [for full reference see Sontheimer 1982], 209-218. (See discussion of cattle raid memorial stones, the Palnad hero cult, head-offerings, and worship of Mahiṣāsuramardinī, Kālī, Bhairava, and Vīrabhadra.)

———, and Günther D. Sontheimer. 1980. "Prehistoric Background to Pastoralism in the Southern Deccan in the Light of Oral Traditions and Cults of Some Pastoral Communities," *Anthropos* 75:163-184.

Narayana Rao, Velcheru. 1986. "Epics and Ideologies: Six Telugu Folk Epics." In Stuart H. Blackburn and A. K. Ramanujan, eds., *Another Harmony. New Essays on the Folklore of India.* Berkeley: University of California Press. Pp. 131-166.

Nicholas, Ralph. 1978. "Sītalā and the Art of Printing: The Transmission and Propogation of the Myth of the Goddess of Smallpox in Rural West Bengal." In Mahadev L. Apte, ed., *Mass Culture, Language and Arts in India.* Bombay: Popular Prakashan. 152-180. (See discussion of Sītalā's servants Jvarāsur, Raktabali, and the Muslim cholera goddess Olabibi.)

———, and Aditi Nath Sarkar. 1976. "The Fever Demon and the Census Commissioner: Sītalā Mythology in Eighteenth and Nineteenth Century Bengal." In Marvin Davis, ed., *Bengal: Studies in Literature, Society, and History,* Asian Studies Center Occasional Papers, South Asia Series, No. 27. East Lansing: Michigan State University. Pp. 3-68. (Further discussion and texts concerning Jvarāsur.)

Nirmala Devi, R., ed., and V. Murugan, trans. 1987. *The Wandering Voice. Three Ballads from Palm Leaf Manuscripts.* Folklore of Tamilnadu Series, No. 1. Thiruvanmiyur, Madras: 1987. (See especially the stories of Cinnattampi and Kurukkulañci).

Obeyesekere, Gananath. 1984. *The Cult of the Goddess Pattini.* Chicago: University of Chicago Press. (See especially discussion of Gini Kurumbara, the various Baṇḍāras, Mahasōna, the Devol Deviyo, and Vibhīṣaṇa.)

O'Flaherty, Wendy Doniger. 1973. *Asceticism and Eroticism in the Mythology of Śiva.* London: Oxford University Press. (See discussion of Brahmanicide myths.)

———. 1976. *The Origins of Evil in Hindu Mythology.* Berkeley: University of California Press. (See discussion of "good demon" and Brahmanicide myths.)

———. 1980. *Women, Androgynes, and Other Mythical Beasts.* Chicago: University of Chicago Press. (See discussion of demon devotees.)

Oppert, Gustav. 1893. *The Original Inhabitants of Bharatavarṣa or India.* Westminster: Archibald Constable & Co.; Leipzig: Otto Harrassowitz. (See the section of chapter eighteen "On the Grāmadēvatās.")

Östör, Akos. 1980. *The Play of the Gods: Locality, Ideology, Structure, and Time in the Festivals of a Bengali Town.* Chicago: University of Chicago Press. (See especially discussion of Bhairab and his "sign," the pāṭā.)

Parry, Jonathan. 1980. "Ghosts, Greed and Sin: The Occupational

Identity of the Benares Funeral Priests," *Man* (n.s.) 15:88-111.

Prabhu, K. Sanjiva. 1977. *Special Study Report on Bhuta Cult in South Kanara District. Census of India 1971, Mysore,* Series 14. Delhi: Controller of Publications. (Rich materials on a "demon"-rich district.)

Ramanujan, A. K. 1986. "Two Realm of Kannada Folklore." In Stuart Blackburn and Ramanujan, eds., *Another Harmony. New Essays on the Folklore of India.* Berkeley: University of California Press.

Reiniche, Marie Louise. 1975. "Les 'demons' et leur culte dans un village du Tiruneveli," *Puruṣārtha* 2:173-203.

———. 1979. *Les dieux et les hommes: Étude des cultes d'un village du Tirunelveli Inde du Sud.* "Cahiers de l'homme Ethnologie-Geographie-Linguistique," NS 18. Paris: Mouton. (See various Māṭans and Karuppans.)

———. "Worship of Kāḷiyamman in some Tamil Villages: The Sacrifice of the warrior-weavers." In V. Sudarsen, G. Prakash Reddy, and M. Suryanarayana, eds., *Religion and Society in South India. A Volume in Honor of Professor N. Subba Reddy.* Delhi: B. R. Publications. Pp. 89-103.

Richards, F. J. 1914-15. "Notes on Muni Worship and on Weights and Measures," *Quarterly Journal of the Mythic Society* 5:53-55.

Roghair, Gene H. 1982. *The Epic of Palnāḍu. A Study and Translation of Palnāṭi Vīrula Katha, a Telugu Oral Tradition from Andhra Pradesh, India.* Oxford: Clarendon Press. (See material on Pōta Rāju and Bhairava.)

Sarkar, Benoy Kumar. 1972. *The Folk Element in Hindu Culture.* New Delhi: Munshiram Manoharlal.

Sarkar, Rebati Mohan. 1986. *Regional Cults and Rural Traditions: An Interacting Pattern of Divinity and Humanity in Rural Bengal.* New Delhi: Inter-India Publications. (Rich material on the varied cult of the "tutelary"/ "village" deity Dharmaraja at different villages, one still practicing hook swinging; related discussion of Bhairava, Mahadana, Brahmadaitya, and goddesses.)

Settar, S. 1982. "Memorial Stones in South India." In G. D. Sontheimer and S. Settar, *Memorial Stones* [for full reference see Sontheimer 1982]. Pp. 183-197.

Shastri, H. Krishna. 1974. (1916). *South Indian Images of Gods and Goddesses.* Varanasi: Bharatiya Publishing House.

Shulman, David. 1980. *Tamil Temple Myths: Sacrifice and Divine Marriage in South Indian Śaiva Tradition.* Princeton: Princeton University Press.

———. 1980. "The Green Goddess of Tirumullaivāyil," *East and West* 30:117-131.

———. 1985. *The King and the Clown in South Indian Myth and Poetry.* Princeton: Princeton University Press. (See especially Chapter VII: "Bandits and Other Tragic Heroes," with its section 4 on Maturaivīran.)

———. 1986. "Battle as Metaphor in Tamil Folk and Classical Traditions." In Stuart H. Blackburn and A. K. Ramanujan, *Another Harmony. New Essays on the Folklore of India.* Berkeley: University of California Press. Pp. 105-130.

Smith, W. L. 1980. *The One-Eyed Goddess. A Study of the Manasā Mangal.* Acta Universitatis Stockholmiensis 12. Stockholm: Almqvist & Wiksell International. (See discussion of Caṇḍō.)

Sontheimer, Günther-Dietz. 1974. "Some Notes on Birobā, the Dhangar God of Maharashtra." In D. D. Kosambi Commemoration Committee, ed., *Science and Human Progress.* Bombay: Popular Prakashan. Pp. 167-175.

———. 1976. *Birobā, Mhaskobā und Khaṇḍobā. Ursprung, Geschichte und Unwelt von pastoralen Gottheiten in Mahārāṣṭra.* "Schriftenreihe des Südasien-Institut der Universität Heidelberg," 21. Wiesbaden: Franz Steiner Verlag.

———. 1979. "Some Incidents in the History of the God Khaṇḍobā." In Marc Gaborieau and Alice Thorner, eds., *Asie du Sud. Traditions et changements.* Colloques Internationaux du Centre National de Récherche Scientifique, No. 582. Paris: CNRS. Pp. 111-117.

———. 1982. "Hero and Satī-Stones in Maharashtra." In Sontheimer and S. Settar, eds., *Memorial Stones. A Study of their Origin, Significance, and Variety.* South Asian Series, no. 11. Dharwad: Institute of Indian Art History, Karnatak University; Heidelberg: South Asia Institute. Pp. 261-281. (See discussion of hero stones from cattle herder communities linked with worship of Bhairava, Khaṇḍobā, Mhasobā-Mahiṣāsura, and Bīrobā-Vīrabhadra; also discussion of hero-stone iconographies of self-beheading.)

———. 1984a. "Dasarā at Devaragudda. Ritual and Play in the Cult of Mailār/Khaṇḍobā," *South Asian Digest of Regional Writing* 10:1-28.

———. 1984b. "The Mallari/Khaṇḍobā Myth as Relfected in Folk Art and Ritual," *Anthropos* 79:155-70.

———. 1987. "Rudra and Khaṇḍobā: Continuity in Folk Religion." In N. K. Wagle, ed., *Religion and Society in Maharashtra.* Toronto: University of Toronto Press. Pp. 1-31.

———. In press. "Folk Hero, King and God: Some Themes According to the Folk and Textual Traditions of the Khaṇḍobā Cult."

Srinivas, M. N. 1965. (1st ed. 1952). *Religion and Society among the Coorgs of South India.* Bombay: Asia Publishing House. (See especially discussion of Kētrappa or Kṣetrapāla.)

Stanley, John M. 1977. "Special Time, Special Power: The Fluidity of Power in a Popular Hindu Festival," *JAS* 37:27-43.

———. 1978. "Turner, Jacobson, Eknath, Tukaram and Khaṇḍobā: An Examination of the Relationship Between Ritual Symbolism and Poetic Metaphor in a Popular Hindu Cult." Paper presented at American Academy of Religion Conference, New Orleans.

———. 1984. "The Dassara Divination Ritual at Mangsuli." Paper presented at Association of Asian Studies annual meeting, Washington, D.C.

———. 1987. "Nishkama and Sakama, Bhakti: Pandharpur and Jejuri." In N. K. Wagle, ed., *Religion and Society in Maharashtra*. Toronto: University of Toronto Press. Pp. 51-67.

Stietencron, H. von. 1969. "Bhairava," *Zeitschrift der Deutschen Morgenländichen Gesellschaft*, Supplement I, Vorträge, Part 3:863-71.

Subba Rao, Tangirala V. 1972. "The Ballad Cycle of Śakti in Āndhra." In *Proceedings of the All-India Oriental Conference*, 26. Session, Vikram University.

Suntharalingam, V. (a.k.a. S. Visuvalingam). 1983. "Abhinavagupta's Conception of Humour: Its Resonances in Sanskrit Drama, Poetry, Hindu Mythology and Spiritual Practice." Ph.D. Dissertation. Banaras: Banaras Hindu University. (See especially discussion of Bhairava, and throughout of the Vidūṣaka in Sanskrit drama.)

Tanaka, Masakazu. 1987. *Sacrifice for Power: Hindu Temple Rituals and Village Festivals in a Fishing Village, Sri Lanka*. Senri: National Museum of Ethnology. (See discussions of Kāṭan, Māṭan, and Bhairava, and treatment of kāvaṭis.)

Tapper, Bruce Elliot. 1987. *Rivalry and Tribute. Society and Ritual in a Telugu Village in South India*. Delhi: Hindustan Publishing Corporation. (See material on Poturaju.)

Tarabout, Gilles. 1986. *Sacrifier et donner à voir en pays Malabar. Les fêtes de temple au Kerala (Inde du Sud)*. Paris: École Française d'Extrême Orient. (Indispensible material on Darikan, Garudan, Mahābali, Ghantakarnnan-Vīrabhadra, Tampuran.)

Thurston, Edgar. 1906. *Ethnographic Notes in Southern India*. Madras: Government Press. (See material on Vīrabhadra in cult of Aṅkāḷamman.)

———. 1975 (1st ed. 1909). *Castes and Tribes of Southern India*. 7 vols. Delhi: Cosmo Publications. (Material throughout on the kuladevatās of various castes, and related rites.)

Vetschera, Traude. 1976. "Laxmiai—A Mother Goddess of the Deccan," *Anthropos* 71:457-465.

———. "The Potaraja and their Goddess," *Asian Folklore Studies* 37:105-53. (Both Vetschera articles treat the Maharashtrian Potrāj, human form of Pōta Rāju.)

Vidal, Denis. 1986. "Le puits et le sanctuaire. Organisation cultuelle et souveraineté dans une ancienne principauté de l'Himalaya occidental." In Jean-Claude Galey, ed., *L'Espace du Temple II. Les Sanctuaires dans le royaume, Puruṣārtha* 10:31-54 (see discussion of Lankṛā Bīr).

Visuvalingam, Elizabeth-Chalier. In press. "Bhairava: Kotwâl of Vârâṇasī." To appear in V. P. Verma, *Vārāṇasī Through the Ages.* Proceedings of a Seminar during the Fifth Session of the Bhāratīya Itihās Sankalan. Banaras: Banaras Hindu University.

Wadley, Susan. 1980. "Sitala: The Cool One," *Asian Folklore Studies* 39:33-62.

Waterfield, William and George Grierson. 1923. *The Lay of Alha: A Saga of Rajput Chivalry as Sung by Minstrels in Northern India.* London: Oxford University Press. (See the guardian roles of the Banāphars.)

Whitehead, Henry. 1921. *The Village Gods of South India.* Calcutta: Association Press. (Relevant material throughout.)

Williams, Joanna Gottfried. 1984. "Śiva and Jagannātha: Iconography and Ambiguity." In Michael W. Meister, ed., *Discourses on Śiva.* Philadelphia: University of Pennsylvania Press. Pp. 298-311. (See discussion of Ekapāda-Bhairava).

Yang, Anand A., ed. 1985. *Crime and Criminality in British India.* Association for Asian Studies Monographs, No. 42. Tucson: University of Arizona Press. (Discussions of "criminal" tribes, castes, and rituals as defined through colonialist culture contact.)

Ziegenbalg, Bartholomaeus. 1984. (1st ed. 1869; completed in German 1713). *Genealogy of the South Indian Gods: A Manual of the Mythology and Religion of the People of South India, Including a Description of Popular Hinduism.* W. Germann, ed., G. J. Metzger, trans. New Delhi: Unity Book Service. (See Part III on "Grāmadevatās, Tutelar Deities, and Demons.")

Zvelebil, Kamil V., trans. 1987. *Two Tamil Folktales: The Story of King Matanakāma; The Story of Peacock Rāvaṇa.* Delhi: Motilal Banarsidass; Paris: Unesco. (See the complementary guardian roles of Hanumān and Maccakarpan in the second story.)

Contributors

Madeleine Biardeau is Professor at the École des Hautes Études, 5th Section, Sorbonne, Paris. She has recently published two volumes of extracts from the *Mahābhārata*, translated into French with a running commentary. Forthcoming is her *Histoire de poteaux: variations védiques autour de la Déesse.* She is now working on the *Mahābhārata* and the *Rāmāyaṇa* from a comparative standpoint.

Elizabeth-Chalier Visuvalingam received a (double) Ph.D. in Ethnology and Comparative Sociology from the University of Nanterre, Paris-X (1981), and in Sanskrit and Indian Religion from Banaras Hindu University (1983), with her work on "The Significance of Unmatta-Bhairava in the Hindu Tradition." She is currently preparing a French "thèse d'état" on "The Cult of Bhairava in North India and Nepal" as a member of two research groups (E.R. 249 and 299) attached to the National Center for Scientific Research.

Diane M. Coccari completed her dissertation on "The Bir Babas of Banaras: An Analysis of a Folk Deity in North Indian Hinduism" (1986), and has written several related articles. She is currently teaching language and religion as a Faculty Assistant at the University of Wisconsin in Madison.

Kathleen M. Erndl is Assistant Professor of Religious Studies at Lewis and Clark College and has taught at the University of Wisconsin and DePauw University. She is the author of several articles on the goddess cult of northwest India.

Alf Hiltebeitel is Professor of Religion at the George Washington University, Washington, D.C. His publications include *The Ritual of Battle: Krishna in the Mahābhārata* (1976) and *The Cult of Draupadī*, I. *Mythologies: From Gingee to Kurukṣetra* (1988), the first volume of a three-part study.

D. Dennis Hudson is Professor in the Department of Religion and Biblical Studies, Smith College, Northampton, Massachusetts. Confining his research and writing to the Tamil regions of India and Śri Laṅkā he has published articles on Indian Christians, *Śaiva* and *Vaiṣṇava* temple festivals, Vaiṣṇava theology and tradition, and Indian responses to the West. His current work includes studies in Vaiṣṇava temples, Hindu lives of the saints, poems of the saints in their cultic contexts, and Hindu responses to Christian missions.

David M. Knipe is Professor of South Asian Studies at the University of Wisconsin in Madison, and also Chair of Religious Studies. He is the author of *In the Image of Fire* (1975) and several articles on myths, rituals, and traditional medicine. A book on Hinduism is forthcoming.

David N. Lorenzen is Professor and Research Scholar in the Center of Asian and African Studies of El Colegio de Mexico and chief editor of *Estudios de Asia y Africa.* He has written a book on *The Kāpālikas and Kālāmukhas* (1972), articles on Śaivism and on the Kabir Panth, and several Spanish translations of Sanskrit works including Kṛṣṇamiśra's *Prabodhacandrodaya* (1984). He is currently working on a book on the Kabir Panth and a translation of Anantadās' sixteenth century Hindi text, the *Kabīr paracāī.*

Eveline Masilamani-Meyer completed her Ph.D. at Heidelberg University with a study of the goddess Aṅkāḷamman, now published as *Aṅkāḷaparamēcuvari—A Goddess of Tamilnadu, Her Myths and Cult* (1986). She is now working on a study and translation of the *Kāttavarāyan Katai* and on guardian deities of Tamilnadu.

Velcheru Narayana Rao is Associate Professor of South Asian Studies at the University of Wisconsin, Madison. He is a published poet in Telugu, the author of several articles on Telugu literature, and of a forthcoming translation of the life of the Lingayat reformer Basava. Most recently he has been working on Telugu folk epics and riddles.

David Dean Shulman is Professor of Indian Studies and Comparative Religion at the Hebrew University, Jerusalem. He is the author of *Tamil Temple Myths* (1980), *The King and the Clown in South Indian Myth and Poetry* (1985), and of various studies on aspects of Sanskrit, Tamil, and Telugu literature and culture.

Günther D. Sontheimer is Professor at the South Asia Institute of the University of Heidelberg and teaches South Asian Religions, traditional law (*dharmaśāstra*) and Marathi language and literature.

His publications include *The Hindu Joint Family: Its Evolution as a Legal Institution* (1977), *Birobā, Mhaskobā und Khaṇḍobā* (Wiesbaden, 1976), and *Memorial Stones* (ed. with S. Settar, Dharwad/New Delhi, 1982).

John M. Stanley is the Ellen Sabin Professor of Comparative Religions and Ethics at Lawrence University in Appleton, Wisconsin. His publications on popular religions in Maharashtra include articles and chapters on pilgrimages, festivals, spirit possession and exorcism, and myth and ritual patterns.

Sunthar Visuvalingam received his Ph.D. in Sanskrit and (Indian) Philosophy from the Banaras Hindu University (1983) with his work on "Abhinavagupta's Conception of Humour: Its Resonances in Sanskrit Drama, Poetry, Hindu Mythology and Spiritual Praxis." He is currently preparing a French "thèse d'état" on "The Semiotics of the Vidūṣaka: The Ideology of Transgression in Brahmanical India," and also editing three volumes on Aesthetics, Philosophy, and Religion in a series on *Abhinavagupta and the Synthesis of Indian Culture.*

Joanne Punzo Waghorne has taught, researched, and published on religion in modern India for the last ten years. Her work includes a book on C. Rajagopalachari, *Images of Dharma,* an anthology edited with Norman Cutler, *Gods of Flesh/Gods of Stone,* articles on methodology in the history of religions, and a recently completed manuscript on sacral kingship in the former princely state of Pudukkottai. Following a year of new research in Madras in 1986-87, she joined the Department of Religious Studies, University of North Carolina, Chapel Hill.

Index